Understanding Israel/Palestine

Teaching Race and Ethnicity

VOLUME 8

Series Editor

Patricia Leavy (*USA*)

International Editorial Board

Theodorea Regina Berry (*Mercer University, USA*)
Owen Crankshaw (*University of Cape Town, South Africa*)
Payi Linda Ford (*Charles Darwin University, Australia*)
Patricia Hill Collins (*University of Maryland, USA*)
Virinder Kalra (*University of Manchester, UK*)
Marvin Lynn (*Indiana University, USA*)
Nuria Rosich (*Barcelona University (Emerita), Spain*)
Beverley Anne Yamamoto (*Osaka University, Japan*)

Scope

The *Teaching Race and Ethnicity series* publishes monographs, anthologies and reference books that deal centrally with race and/or ethnicity. The books are intended to be used in undergraduate and graduate classes across the disciplines. The series aims to promote social justice with an emphasis on multicultural, indigenous, intersectionality and critical race perspectives.

Please consult www.patricialeavy.com for submission requirements (click the book series tab).

Understanding Israel/Palestine

Race, Nation, and Human Rights in the Conflict

Second Edition

By

Eve Spangler

BRILL

SENSE

LEIDEN | BOSTON

All chapters in this book have undergone peer review.

Library of Congress Cataloging-in-Publication Data

Names: Spangler, Eve, 1946-, author.
Title: Understanding Israel/Palestine : race, nation, and human rights in the conflict / by Eve Spangler.
Description: Second edition. | Boston : Brill Sense, [2019] | Series: Teaching race and ethnicity | Includes bibliographical references and index.
Identifiers: LCCN 2019007922 (print) | LCCN 2019013550 (ebook) | ISBN 9789004394148 (ebook) | ISBN 9789004394124 (pbk. : alk. paper) | ISBN 9789004394131 (hardback : alk. paper)
Subjects: LCSH: Arab-Israeli conflict. | Jewish-Arab relations. | Palestine--History.
Classification: LCC DS119.7 (ebook) | LCC DS119.7 .S6465 2019 (print) | DDC 956.94--dc23
LC record available at https://lccn.loc.gov/2019007922

ISSN 2542-9264
ISBN 978-90-04-39412-4 (paperback)
ISBN 978-90-04-39413-1 (hardback)
ISBN 978-90-04-39414-8 (e-book)

ADVANCE PRAISE FOR
UNDERSTANDING ISRAEL/PALESTINE

"This is not only an unflinchingly clear-eyed assessment of how Israel has gone so terribly wrong in persecuting another people, the Palestinians, in its efforts to secure for Jews a place of safety from European anti-semitism. Eve Spangler's book also does that much rarer thing: it answers the more troubling question of *why* Jews and Palestinians are locked in a seemingly interminable struggle over a small patch of land.

This book places Zionism squarely in its historical and ideological context, showing how Israel's founders were driven to repeat the follies and outrages committed by earlier, similar settler colonial movements. Israel's leaders exploited the very racism that had forced Jews to flee Europe to galvanise western support – financial, diplomatic and military – for their own racist ethno-national project against the region's native Palestinian population.

As Spangler so clearly sets out, the western narrative of a 'good Israel' inside its recognised borders and a 'bad Israel' in the occupied territories only serves to confuse and mislead. The Zionist 'dream' could be realised only at a terrible cost, including to the 'victors'. Israel has turned its Jews into oppressors, created a self-ghettoising state, and failed to deliver on the promise of a safe haven.

In the post-Oslo era, when the old paradigms are obsolete, this is an important book that all interested observers of the Israeli-Palestinian conflict urgently need to read."
– Jonathan Cook, journalist and author of *Disappearing Palestine*

"Eve Spangler is a veteran teacher, and *Understanding Israel/Palestine* is a model of her profession: it does what it says it will do, and takes some of the thorniest issues facing humanity and makes them understandable and clear.

The book is written, as Spangler states clearly, for 'students, parishioners, neighbors, voters or dinner guests' – in short, anyone who recognizes the importance of the Israel Palestine conflict but does not know much about it. It is illuminated by dozens of personal vignettes, often involving an individual shedding conceptual confusions, about the west and Islam, about anti-Semitism and Jewish commitment to Zionism, that make this difficult path more visible.

Like other stellar primers, this one is not aimed at merely conveying information but in moving the reader to action. Spangler was called to the subject herself from other intellectual pursuits because she is Jewish; and her moral will be a hard one for many to swallow but it is a truthful one. There are two equally valuable human groups in equal numbers in this land, she says; but in profoundly unequal relationship to one another. So her story comes down to a simple question, of the denial of human rights.

That injustice will only change when more people in our country are engaged and conversant. Spangler has taken up that challenge with energy and seriousness, and *Understanding Israel/Palestine* is a marvelous gate that many will pass through."
– **Philip Weiss, Co-Editor of *Mondoweiss***

"Professor Spangler, sociologist and daughter of Holocaust survivors, has written an engaging, well researched, and provocative primer on Israel/ Palestine. Her intellectual foundation lies in a belief in human rights for all, but her quest for historical and political understanding takes us on a brave and intimate journey into the consequences of Jewish privilege and Jewish victimhood, the agendas of imperial superpowers, and the Palestinian struggle for self-determination.

With sensitivity and candor, she challenges much of the dominant paradigm, examining the 'complexities' of history, Islamophobia, as well as the price of political Zionism; the consequences of building a system of total subordination of Palestinians through settlement building, expulsions, pacification, and containment with the goal of creating an exclusively Jewish state. She finds the parallels between the Back to Africa movement and Zionism 'startlingly strong' and makes it painfully obvious that the US civil rights movement has indeed done far more for African-Americans than the existence of Liberia. There are important lessons to be learned.

Professor Spangler challenges the reader with humor and an abundance of historical material and analysis to examine every sacred myth from indigeniety, race, Jewish existential fears, failures of Palestinian resistance movements, and the roles of hallowed organizations such as the Jewish National Fund, Jewish Agency, and Zionist Organization that began their work in the 1890s.

Ultimately, she makes the case for the inherent dangers of establishing what is essentially a militarized Jewish ghetto in historic Palestine, based on systematic ethnic cleansing and sociocide, at a time in history when

de-colonization, democracy, tolerance, and universal human rights are the basic standards for a civilized and sustainable world."
– Alice Rothchild, MD, author of *Broken Promises, Broken Dreams: Stories of Jewish and Palestinian Trauma and Resilience, On the Brink: Israel and Palestine on the Eve of the 2014 Gaza Invasion*, and producer and director of documentary film, *Voices across the Divide*

"Just as one thought that all the primers that could be written about the Palestine-Israel conflict have already been published, Dr. Spangler proves us wrong with this sharp, poignant, well-documented dossier. Much more than merely a primer for newcomers to the issue, this factually-grounded overview buries tired slogans and provides readers with all the most-needed facts to grasp the conflict and get involved. Above all, knowing this comes from a researcher who understands that the current state of affairs are being propagated 'in her name' gives hope that she can light the way for others in the Jewish community to reclaim their history and sense of social justice and contribute to realizing human rights, freedom and independence for all, including all Palestinians."
– Sam Bahour, co-editor of *Homeland: Oral Histories of Palestine and Palestinians* and business development consultant and activist based in Palestine

"Of the tens – or is it hundreds? – of books about the Israeli-Palestinian conflict that have seen the light of day in the past few years, this one is exceptional! It recounts a historical tale; it provides theoretical underpinnings; it does comparative work; it examines all the details and aspects of ongoing debates; and it brings all to life with real-life stories. Eve Spangler melds all of these together with spectacular sensibility and incomparable personal integrity. She is not afraid to take risks and to tell her readers the unpleasant, sometimes devastating, truths about the history of Zionism and the intractable, current situation in Israel-Palestine. She doesn't hesitate to take the side of the weak against the strong and the victim against the victimizer. And she is not shy about offering an explanation and a resolution for it all through the construct of human rights. Still, the wonder of this book is its insistence on hope – not a naïve, idealistic hope, but one accompanied by a tool-box for concrete action that might right the wrongs of this tragic tale."
– Anat Biletzki, Professor Emeritus of Philosophy, Tel Aviv University and Albert Schweitzer Professor of Philosophy, Quinnipiac University; Chairperson of B'Tselem, 2001–2006

"Oriented firmly around a human rights perspective, this book will be an extraordinary introduction to the Israeli-Palestinian conflict for many, as well as a good resource for those with some background in the conflict. This volume is both extremely well researched and admirably grounded, as much of it draws upon Spangler's experiences taking student study groups to the occupied Palestinian territory of the West Bank and to Israel. Both the analytical sections and the narrative sections are eloquently delivered. Spangler masterfully brings many voices into the text, including those of prominent Palestinians and Israelis, Palestinians whose everyday experiences of conflict are rarely recognized, and Americans who encounter this issue from multiple perspectives and experiential backgrounds. As she does this, she maintains and strengthens the moral and intellectual center of the book. While she gives a strong historical background to the conflict, she also treats important contemporary issues, including the importance of the boycott movement, the analogy with apartheid, and resistance to the wall. I expect this book will do a lot of good in the world."

– Amahl Bishara, Associate Professor of Anthropology, Tufts University, author of *Back Stories: U.S. News Production and Palestinian Politics*, director of documentary film *Degrees of Incarceration*

"Eve Spangler has produced an impressive resource for anyone interested in understanding the historical underpinnings and contemporary reality of Israel-Palestine. With encyclopedic knowledge, careful precision, and meticulous documentation, Spangler chronicles what has been at stake for Israeli, Palestinian, and international central actors in the region. While being attuned to critical political and sociological details that have animated the conflict for more than six decades, she also delineates compelling and accessible conceptual frameworks through which to analyze this complex terrain. For beginners and experts alike, this book is a rich and important read."

– Sa'ed Adel Atshan, Assistant Professor of Peace Studies, Swarthmore College

To Dean Albertson, for everything, forever

CONTENTS

Part 2: A Brief History of the Conflict: Another Look

Part 3: Moving Forward

PREFACE

Every story has a beginning. My interest in Israel/Palestine began on an evening in October 2003, in my faculty office at Boston College, where I had just finished grading a set of papers. As I prepared to leave, a colleague, newly arrived just the month before, stopped by my office. "You must come to the talk I'm hosting," she said. "It's the first talk I've organized, and I'm so worried that there will be no audience." My heart sank. I had been looking forward to an evening curled up with a glass of wine and my book club novel. "What talk is that?" I asked. "It's FFIPP," she replied, "The Faculty for Israeli-Palestinian Peace." They send teams of speakers, a Palestinian academic paired with an Israeli academic, to inform university audiences about the state of the longest running conflict in the Middle East. Reluctantly, I agreed to attend the talk.

The Palestinian professor spoke first. Saleh Abdel Jawad is a historian at Birzeit University whose work focuses on the villages lost by Palestine in the 1948 war.[1] He was then Harvard University's inaugural "Scholar at Risk"; the first professor to take up a one-year appointment reserved for distinguished academics around the world who were in danger not only because of the generally miserable political situations in their respective countries, but, more specifically, because of the work they did in speaking truth to power. Abdel Jawad's talk outlined the history of the *Nakba*, the catastrophic expulsion that Palestinians experienced as part of the creation of the state of Israel. I had previously known nothing about the *Nakba* and was shocked by what I heard. Nevertheless, I thought to myself, "Well, that's the Palestinian point of view, let's hear what the Israeli professor has to say."

Yoav Peled, a political scientist from Tel Aviv University, came to the lectern. I later discovered that he is the son of a famous and distinguished Israeli family. His father, Matti Peled, is one of the architects of the Israeli military victory of 1967, who later came to repudiate the fruits of that war: the on-going control of conquered territory by Israeli settlers and the military, universally known as the Occupation. His sister, Nurit Peled-Elhanan, is a professor of education. She has shown how Israeli textbooks normalize the Occupation and immunize Israeli students against criticisms based on international human rights standards.[2] His brother, Miko Peled, is the author of a best-selling book, *The General's Son*, which also unmasks the crimes of Occupation.[3] Yoav Peled is also the uncle of Smadar Peled-Elhanan, killed by a Palestinian suicide bomber at a shopping mall during the popular uprising against the Israeli Occupation known as the Second *Intifada*.[4] Peled opened his speech by pointing to Abdel Jawad and saying "What he says is an understatement, the truth is really much worse."[5]

I was riveted and, despite their later intense disagreement about the term "sociocide," I realized that both speakers were painting a bleak and entirely consistent picture of ethnic cleansing and endless war.

After the talk, my colleague again appeared at my side. "They are our guests," she said, "you must help me entertain them at dinner." My book club novel receded further into the distance. We adjourned to a Thai restaurant and talked late into the evening. At one point I remember Abdel Jawad saying to me "you really don't know anything about the Middle East, do you?" which, alas, was an entirely correct observation.

But a hook had been planted; my curiosity was piqued. As with so many beginnings, this one, upon closer examination, was revealed to have antecedents – small seeds and tendrils of interest that remained curled in the shade of other, more pressing concerns and commitments.

My earliest memory of any conversation about the Middle East dates back to 1956 and the Suez Crisis in which England, France, and Israel invaded Egypt.[6] I was then the ten-year-old child of two Holocaust survivors who taught themselves English, mainly from American newspapers. Every evening at precisely 6 p.m., we sat down to dinner in Brooklyn and listened to the international news on WQXR, a deep, masculine voice announcing in plummy tones that this was "the radio station of the *New York Times*." That newspaper was an object of near veneration in our home. After the broadcast, dinner was spent discussing the news. Without yet having the words to describe myself as skeptical about Zionism, I do remember asking my father, "If everyone hates the Jews as much Auntie Sylvia says they do, why would you want to put all the Jews in one place?" I do not remember my father's answer; only that Israel was rarely a topic of conversation at our dinner table. In general, both of my parents preferred left-leaning politics to religion as a spur to social justice.

A second memory surfaces from 1967. In June of that year I was a newly minted college graduate, about to embark on a PhD program in anthropology. I had become a child of "the sixties," involved since high school in the civil rights movement, and recently immersed in the peace movement critical of the Vietnam War. I spent a lot of time in Greenwich Village. Over coffee at Rienzi's Coffee House, a classmate told me about attending the big, Vietnam-focused peace demonstration at the United Nations Plaza. He was disconcerted by how many of his Jewish friends ran back and forth between the peace rally at the UN Plaza and the Israeli victory parade on 5th Avenue, celebrating Israel's victory in the Six Day War that brought all of historic Palestine under its control. Something about that seemed perverse and wrong. Over time, I encountered this contradiction again and again: the American left is disproportionately Jewish and progressive on many issues, but not on questions of Israel and Palestine.

Many other issues and projects came to fill my life before those early, tentative observations were prompted to resurface. I immersed myself in the women's movement and the green movement. I switched from anthropology to sociology, earned a doctorate, found a faculty position, and achieved tenure. Throughout that time, I thought of my work as belonging to "public sociology"[7] – a place where scholarship and social justice meet. I investigated class inequalities in higher education,[8] gender discrimination in the work place,[9] and the subordination of professionals in the context of organizational restructuring.[10] I spent ten years, with others, on issues of worker health and safety, especially in the post-Soviet world of Central and Eastern Europe.[11]

I was aware of many injustices in the world and knew that I could not effectively address all of them. Without looking too closely, I recognized that Israel's treatment of the Palestinians was a massive violation of human rights. At the same time, however, I knew that if I pursued this particular injustice, my family (though not my immediate family) would be unhappy. And indeed, to this day, when I criticize Zionism as a Jew, I am often asked: "Why do you focus on this conflict? Aren't there more important struggles, more poignant, or massive, or immediate injustices?" My reply is that while the struggle for a just peace between Israelis and Palestinians is not the most urgent problem in the world, it is the one being perpetrated most directly in my name and allegedly on my behalf. It calls to me. It is an issue in which everything about my life – my family's Holocaust heritage, my citizenship in a country siding with an occupier, even my tenure and safety to speak out – require that I pay attention.

When I began to pay attention, I recognized that the Israeli-Palestinian conflict is a profound struggle for human rights. There are some 12 million people who live in Israel/Palestine, "between the [Jordan] River and the [Mediterranean] Sea," as people in the area often say. Each one of them is of equal human value. And each must struggle against vicious stereotypes that have harmed their group's life chances: Jews are not the killers of Christ, the bringers of the Black Death, the secret bankers in control of the world. And, similarly, Palestinians are not murderous terrorists intent on the destruction of Jews. The 12 million people of Palestine and Israel are simply human beings, the vast majority of whom are just trying to live their lives as best they can. Each and every one of them is entitled to be treated fairly in accord with human rights standards.

The Israelis and the Palestinians even belong to communities that are approximately equal in numbers: some 6 million Jewish Israelis[12] and roughly as many Palestinians in Israel and the Occupied Territories of the West Bank (including East Jerusalem) and the Gaza Strip.[13]

And yet, paradoxically, these equally valuable human beings in their relatively equal numbers are grouped in two profoundly unequal communities: an occupier and an occupied. The occupier, Israel, enjoys a modern, Western standard of living, is heavily armed and protected diplomatically, economically, and militarily by the last remaining superpower in the world, the United States. The occupied, the Palestinians, are a stateless people, a sizable percentage of whom live as refugees.[14] Their leadership is divided, and periodically subject to arrest and even assassination. Their allies pay lip service to their needs more often than they provide real aid. Despite their long tradition of literacy[15] and entrepreneurship,[16] Palestinians live constricted lives, uncertain of their ability either to remain in their homes or to rebuild their lives elsewhere.

Confronting that paradox – human beings of equal human worth grouped into such unequal communities – is where this book began three years ago and where it still draws its inspiration.

Alas, since the first edition of the book was published, a great deal has changed, mostly for the worse. On the ground in Palestine and in Israel, both regimes are losing their political legitimacy, and their respective populations are considering new goals that are, paradoxically, increasingly antithetical and increasingly convergent at the same time. In America, the Trump administration has deepened the asymmetry in the conflict, and discarded even the pretense of observing international law as a framework for its resolution. In the region, ISIS' rise and fall and the power struggle between Iran and Saudi Arabia have become the new foci of attention, leaving Israel more room to expand the Occupation under the cover of global indifference. Even the scholarship addressed to Israel/Palestine continues to shift into new paradigms.

In Palestine, there is political disarray. The Palestinian Authority, long past the expiration of its last elected term of office, governs by executive order. Whether one believes that the PA was ever meant to be an embryonic state or whether one considers it to have been a subcontractor to the Israeli

Occupation from its inception, its behavior today lacks political legitimacy. It enjoys pallid support within the West Bank because it employs more than 150,000 of some two and one half million people directly, and thus supports their families and the various professionals and businesses who serve them, acting as the largest and most important economic entity in Palestine.[17] Before last summer, when the PA openly supported the cutback of power services in Gaza,[18] it perhaps enjoyed pallid support there as well, because it was not Hamas, and not tarnished by Hamas' failure to improve the lives and livelihood of the nearly 2 million Palestinians besieged in Gaza. Nevertheless, leading intellectuals now refer to the Palestinian Authority as the Vichy government.[19] The failures of the Palestinian Authority include the inability, despite significant concessions in Hamas' new charter,[20] to create a coalition that would establish a united Palestinian leadership and the inability to engage in succession planning even as the 83 year-old President Abbas' health appears to be deteriorating.[21]

In Israel, there is also political disarray. The sitting Prime Minister, Benjamin Netanyahu, faces possible indictment on any of five corruption scandals being investigated by the police. This makes him vulnerable to the destabilizing demands of his right wing coalition partners, many of whom advocate annexing most of the West Bank, especially Area C (explained further in Chapter 8) that has been largely cleansed of Palestinians. The Trump administration's policy further pushes the Israeli political system toward over-reaching.[22]

Contradictory regional and global forces also buffet the Israeli political system. On the one hand, the surrounding Sunni states, particularly Saudi Arabia, are ever more overtly uninterested in the plight of the Palestinians.[23] Yet, at the same time, the population ratios between Israeli Jews and Palestinians, once evenly balanced, are now tipping decisively toward a Palestinian majority.[24] Similarly, Israel is moving ever more assertively to be a leading source of arms sales and security consulting in the international market.[25] At the same time, however, a growing Boycott, Sanctions, Divestment movement attempts to undermine Israel's hold on this economic niche.[26]

The counter-move to BDS has been the attempt to label every critic of Israel as a "new anti-Semite." This effort is credible only to people whose attitude is "Israel, right or wrong." Beyond that narrow group, as Israeli historian Neve Gordon explains, the attempt at silencing fails. "The logic of the 'new anti-Semitism' can be formulated as a syllogism: (i) anti-Semitism is hatred of Jews; (ii) to be Jewish is to be Zionist; (iii) therefore anti-Zionism is anti-Semitic. The error has to do with the second proposition. The claims that Zionism is identical to Jewishness, or that a seamless equation can be made between the State of Israel and the Jewish people, are false. Many Jews are not Zionists."[27] As Gordon points out, not all Jews are Zionists, and, further, not all Zionists are Jews. In fact, in the United States, Christian Zionists far outnumber Jewish ones. Paradoxically, some Christian Zionists are also anti-Semitic. This phenomenon is particularly relevant to the American political scene at present.[28]

In the United States, too, there is political disarray. The election of Trump has meant the ascension of an administration marked by inconsistency, and profound disregard of international law. This administration, like its Israeli counterpart, is mired in allegations and investigations into wrongdoing that are spreading to engulf more and more members of the Executive Branch. Trump's decision to move the U.S. Embassy to Jerusalem definitively discredits America's already dubious claim to being an "honest broker," and his ambassador's support for settlements embodies the entire administration's disregard for international law. Finally, as Judith Butler has pointed out, Trump's tacit endorsement of white supremacist groups and their rhetoric points to the confluence of two unlikely political impulses: an anti-Semitic white nationalist program and simultaneous unlimited support for Israel, presumably because the Israeli state represents the "white guys" in the Middle East.[29] Politics does, indeed, make for strange bedfellows.

The turmoil in the wider Middle East adds to the difficulty of imagining a reasonably settled future for Palestinians and Israelis. The nation state model imposed by European powers – through the League of Nations mandate system and through secret agreements among individual European countries – appears to be crumbling. Iraq and Syria lie in ruins. Kurdish nationalism raises the possibility of re-drawing international boundaries. There are intensified struggles among Iran, Turkey, and Saudi Arabia to become the dominant regional power, and these, too, work against a just or balanced Israeli/Palestinian agreement. And, finally, climate change is an emerging threat that adds a growing swell of climate refugees to the many political refugees already suffering inadequate care in Lebanon and Jordan.[30]

The scholarship on the Israeli-Palestinian conflict has also changed significantly since the first edition of this book was written.

The earliest generation of historians parroted the Israeli government's line that the 1967 Six Day War, in which Israel conquered the entirety of historic Palestine, was a necessary war of self-defense, even though Israelis struck the first military blows. Gradually, as archives opened some thirty years after the war, a movement referred to as the New Historians began to produce a very different version of the events surrounding the Occupation. In 2005, Tom Segev's *1967* detailed the extent to which the war of that year arose not out of an inevitability, but through a series of miscalculations.[31] A year later, Gershon Gorenberg's *The Accidental Empire*, caste the settlement movement as an opportunistic achievement following swiftly on the military victory of 1967 and soon thereafter supported by the Israeli state.[32]

More recently however, the ground has shifted again. In 2006, Norman Finkelstein made the point that the Israelis could have chosen simply to defeat the Jordanian and Egyptian armies without also occupying the West Bank and the Gaza Strip.[33] And finally, in a series of groundbreaking books culminating in the 2017 publication of *The Biggest Prison on Earth*, Ilan Pappe shows that Israel had made comprehensive plans for organizing the Occupation from 1956 to 1963.[34] The war of 1967, therefore, was no more than an opportunity to put a long-planned program into effect, the government and the settlement movement acting in conscious support of one another.

In part because of such incremental shifts in the understanding of 1967, the framework that is emerging for understanding the Occupation and, indeed, Zionism itself is that of settler colonialism. Chapter 9 explores the most common frames for understanding the Occupation (Israeli self-defense, genocide, apartheid, and settler colonialism). Suffice it here to say that the settler colonial frame, first advocated by French historian Maxime Rodinson,[35] and later affirmed by the work of Israeli historian Gershon Shafir,[36] has the great advantage of creating a unified story from the beginnings of Zionism in the 19th century to the present day, instead of treating the half-century Occupation as something qualitatively different from all that had gone before.[37] Though the scholarship itself dates back decades, it is only now, with the cumulative weight of the New Historians' arguments (especially that of Pappe), that the settler colonial framework is taking its rightful place in the understanding of the whole history of Palestine and Israel.

With all that has changed, some things remain the same in both editions of this book.

First, I remain convinced that, Americans should not aspire to dictate a solution to the Israeli-Palestinian conflict. At the same time, however, they should employ the standard of human rights in assessing any proposal to do so, and in evaluating the behavior of all the parties to the conflict. As I discuss in Chapter 3, human rights doctrine is not a magic wand that contains all the solutions, but it is, I will argue, the only metric that aspires to universalism and that avoids the powerful undertow in American conversations about

Palestine and Israel, that always puts Israeli needs, real or imagined, ahead of Palestinian rights.

Second, I am even more convinced than before that the Black American experience remains the best point of reference for Americans who wish to understand the Palestinian/Israeli conflict. In the first edition, I used this comparison mainly for historic reasons, focusing on the strategies that oppressed populations can employ in pursuit of their rights. For the future, the comparison turns more on the repressive ways that Israelis police Palestinian communities and that Americans, not coincidentally, police Black communities.

Third, I will continue to argue that the situation now existing between Israel and Palestine is tragic, but not incomprehensible. The framework I used in Chapters 5 through 8 in the first edition remains in place. I understand this conflict as arising out of the interaction of three parties: Zionists, Palestinians, and great powers. Each of these behaves according to a logic that is self-interested and consistent and therefore not incomprehensible. The history has not changed. Zionism remains the project of building an ethno-religiously exclusively Jewish state in Palestine. Palestinians, continue to want normal lives, whether through national liberation or by securing civil rights in a single state. Either resolution poses a serious challenge to Zionist ambitions to Jewish exclusivity in the whole of the land. Great powers continue to care only how the area serves their national agendas.

Fourth, and finally, I maintain that the future is uncertain but not hopeless. Despite the image of the conflict in the American media,[38] there is a great deal of activity, beneath the surface of a seemingly immovable Occupation, in which Palestinians and Israelis are working together on projects that I call "thinking about the day after:" the day after the Palestinian Authority collapses, the day after an even more right wing Israeli government decides to annex the West Bank, the day after the U.N. reaffirms the refugees' right of return, the day after younger, more diverse American voters signal an openness to the Palestinian voice[39] – in short, the day after the current impasse shifts in any one of a myriad of unpredictable ways.

My purpose, in re-writing this book, continues to be to make available a reasonably concise and even-handed account of the conflict for those who know it is important and who want to understand it without becoming experts in Middle East history and political theory.

NOTES

[1] Saleh Abdel Jawad. Zionist Massacres: the Creation of the Palestinian Refugee Problem in the 1948 War, in Eyal Benvenisti, Chaim Gans, C. & Sari Hanafi (eds.). (2007). *Israel*

and the Palestinian Refugees (Heidelberg and New York: Springer), 59–127; and Saleh Abdel Jawad. The Arab and Palestinian Narratives of the 1948 War, in Robert I. Rotberg (ed.). (2006). *Israeli and Palestinian Narratives of Conflict: History's Double Helix* (Bloomington: Indiana University Press), 72–144.

[2] Nurit Peled–Elhanan. (2012). *Palestine in Israeli School Books: Ideology and Propaganda in Education.* London: I.B.Tauris.

[3] Miko Peled. (2013). *The General's Son.* Charlottesville: Just World Books.

[4] Nurit-Peled Elhanan. (2007, January 9). "Let Our Children Live," *Counterpunch*, retrieved from http://www.counterpunch.org/2007/01/29/let-our-children-live/

[5] Yoav Peled and Nadim Rouhana. (2007). Transitional Justice and the Right of Return of the Palestinian Refugees, in Benvenisti, Gans, and Hanafi (eds.), *op. cit.*, 141–157.

[6] For a concise summary of the conflicting Cold War moves and countermoves by all the parties, see: "Suez crisis" McLean, I. and McMillan, A. (eds.) (2003). *The Concise Oxford Dictionary of Politics*, Oxford University Press.

[7] Michael Burawoy. (2004). Presidential Address to the American Sociological Association: For Public Sociology, *American Sociological Review*, 70: 4–28.

[8] Eve Spangler. Small Winnings: Blue Collar Students in College and at Work, in Michael Lewis (ed.) (1981). *Research in Social Problems and Public Policy.* Vol. I (Greenwich, Connecticut: JAI Press), 15–41.

[9] Eve Spangler. (1992). Sexual Harassment: Labor Relations by Other Means? in *New Solutions*, 3(1):23030 and reprinted in Charles Levenstein (ed.). (2009) *At the Point of Production: The Social Analysis of Occupational and Environmental Health.* (New York: Baywood Publishing), 167–178.

[10] Eve Spangler. (1986). *Lawyers for Hire: Salaried Professionals at Work.* New Haven, Connecticut: Yale University Press. Eve Spangler and Richard Campbell. The Curious History of the Toxics Use Reduction Planner, in Helena Z. Lopata (ed.) (2000). *Current Research on Occupations and Professions: Unusual Occupations, Vol. 11* (Greenwich, Connecticut: JAI Press), 75–94.

[11] Eve Spangler. (1993). "Occupational Medicine and the State: Lessons from Hungary" with Charles Levenstein, Zuzanna Fuzesi, & Lazlo Tishtian in *New Solutions* 4(1): 52–57.

[12] The Israeli Census Bureau, states that as of 2012, there were 6 million Israeli Jews, who constituted some 75% of the population. Retrieved from http://embassies.gov.il/zagreb/Pages/Population-of-Israel-on-the-eve-of-2013---8-Million.aspx

[13] Estimates of the Palestinian population are more complicated. The CIA World Fact Book acknowledges some *2.7 million Palestinians in the West Bank* and another *1.8 million in Gaza*, retrieved from https://www.cia.gov/library/publications/the-world-factbook/geos/we.html; https://www.cia.gov/library/publications/the-world-factbook/geos/gz.html. Additionally, the Israeli state recognizes *1.6 million Palestinians inside Israel*, retrieved from http://embassies.gov.il/zagreb/Pages/Population-of-Israel-on-the-eve-of-2013---8-Million.aspx. This brings the total number of Palestinians to 6.1 million – or almost perfect parity with Israeli Jews. However this seeming parity is complicated by the question of Palestinian refugees. See note 14, below.

[14] Under international law, Palestinian refugees and their descendants have an unconditional right to return to the places from which they were displaced. The agency charged with their care (the United Nations Relief and Works Agency, known as UNRWA) recognizes that for various social and political reasons Palestinian refugees are undercounted. That said, as of December 2012, UNRWA recorded nearly 5 million Palestinian refugees, more than

3 million of whom were living outside the territory controlled by Israel, retrieved from http://www.unrwa.org/etemplate.php?id=253.

[15] Statistics on college enrollment can be retrieved from http://stats.uis.unesco.org/unesco/TableViewer/tableView.aspx?ReportId=16.8. Statistics on college completion retrieved from http://stats.uis.unesco.org/unesco/TableViewer/tableView.aspx?ReportId=169. This data is reported in raw numbers. To arrive at percentages of enrollment and completion, population base data retrieved from http://data.uis.unesco.org/. Personal calculations of percentages enrolled show that Palestinians have the highest rate of tertiary enrollment (i.e. college attendance) in the Arab world.

[16] Alexander Scholch. (1993). *Palestine in Transformation, 1856–1882* Washington D.C.: Institute for Palestine Studies.

[17] *The Guardian* staff. (2011, November 28). Israeli sanctions mean Palestinian Authority cannot pay employees' wages, *The Guardian*, retrieved from https://www.theguardian.com/world/2011/nov/28/israel-sanctions-palestinian-authority-wages

[18] *Al Jazeera* staff. (2017). Palestinian Authority to Stop funding Gaza electricity, *Al Jazeera News*, retrieved from https://www.aljazeera.com/news/2017/04/palestinian-authority-stop-funding-gaza-electricity-170427105910755.html

[19] Mazin Qumsiyeh. (2018, February 25). *Human Rights Newsletter* (blog), retrieved from http://lists.qumsiyeh.org/listinfo/humanrights

[20] Khaled Hroub. (2017, Spring). A Newer Hamas? The Revised Charter, *Journal of Palestine Studies*, 46(4):100–111.

[21] Amos Harel. (2018, March 7). Mahmoud Abbas' Health Deteriorates and Israel Prepares for a Bloody Succession Fight, *Ha'aretz*, retrieved from https://www.haaretz.com/israel-news/.premium-health-of-palestinian-leader-mahmoud-abbas-82-deteriorates-in-recent-1.5883942

[22] Jonathan Cook. (2018, March 19). US Smooths Israel's Path to Annexing the West Bank, *Mondoweiss*, retrieved from http://mondoweiss.net/2018/03/smooths-israels-annexing/

[23] Amos Harel. (2018, March 6). Israel Finds New Regional Allies: Greece and the Sunni States, *Ha'aretz*, retrieved from https://www.haaretz.com/israel-news/israeli-finds-new-regional-allies-greece-and-the-sunni-states-1.5866886
Yaniv Kubovich. (2018, March 21). Who's Hiding Israeli Airforce Participation in Major Exercise with UAE and US? *Ha'aretz*, retrieved from https://www.haaretz.com/israel-news/who-s-hiding-iaf-participation-in-major-exercise-with-uae-1.5919421

[24] *Ha'aretz*. (2017, May 1). This is How Israel Inflates its Jewish Majority. *Ha'aretz*, retrieved from https://www.haaretz.com/opinion/editorial/this-is-how-israel-inflates-its-jewish-majority-1.5466549

[25] Jeff Halper. (2015). *War Against the People*, London: Pluto Press; Adi Kuntsman and Rebecca Stein. (2015) *Digital Militarism: Israel's Occupation in the Social Media Age*, Stanford, CA: Stanford University Press; Yotam Feldman. (2013). *The Lab* Israel: Gum Films; Naomi Klein. (2007, June 5). Gaza: Not Just a Prison, A Laboratory, *The Nation*, retrieved from https://www.commondreams.org/views/2007/06/15/gaza-not-just-prison-laboratory
Eitay Mack, U.S. Embassy Celebrations: A who's who of the Israeli arms trade, *+972*, retrieved from https://972mag.com/u-s-embassy-opening-a-whos-who-of-the-israeli-arms-trade/135681/

[26] See for example, Jewish Voice For Peace Deadly Exchange: Ending US-Israel Police Partnerships, Reclaiming Safety campaign within its BDS efforts. Retrieved from deadlyexchange.org

27 Neve Gordon. (2018, January 4). The 'New' Anti-Semitism, *London Review of Books*, 40(1):18ff, retrieved from https://www.lrb.co.uk/v40/n01/neve-gordon/the-new-anti-semitism

28 Matthew Haag. (2018, May 14). Pastor Who Said Jews Are Going to Hell Led Prayer at Jerusalem Embassy Opening, *New York Times*, retrieved from https://www.nytimes.com/2018/05/14/world/middleeast/robert-jeffress-embassy-jerusalem-us.html

29 Judith Butler. (2017, April 1). Address to the Biennial Jewish Voice for Peace National Members Meeting, retrieved from https://www.facebook.com/JewishVoiceforPeace/videos/vb.186525784991/10156505121949992/?type=2&theater. Azriel Bermant (2018, July 4) Israel's Long History of Cooperation with Ruthless, anti-Semitic Dictators, *Ha'aretz*, retrieved from https://www.haaretz.com/israel-news/.premium-not-just-orban-israel-has-long-cooperated-with-anti-semitic-dictators-1.6243037

30 Eyal Weizman and Fazal Sheikh. (2015). *The Conflict Shoreline, Colonialism as Climate Change in the Negev Desert*. Gottingen, Germany: Steidl Verlag.

31 Tom Segev. (2005). *1967: Israel, The War, and The Year That Transformed the Middle East*, New York: Henry Holt.

32 Gershom Gorenberg. (2006). *The Accidental Empire, Israel and the Birth of the Settlements, 1967–1977*. New York: Henry Holt.

33 Finkelstein quoted in Ilan Pappe. (2017). *The Biggest Prison on Earth: A History of the Occupied Territories*. (London: One World Publications), p. 42.

34 Pappe, *op. cit.*, p. xiv.

35 Maxime Rodinson. (1973). *Israel A Colonial Settler State?* New York: Pathfinder Press.

36 Gershon Shafir. (1996). *Land, Labor and the Origins of the Israeli-Palestinian Conflict, 1882–1914*, updated edition, Berkeley: University of California Press.

37 Rashid I. Khalidi (2017, Autumn). The Hundred Years' War on Palestine, *Journal of Palestine Studies*, 47(1): 6–17.

38 Sut Jhally and Bathsheba Ratzkoff. (2004). *Peace, Propaganda, and the Promised Land*. Media Education Foundation. Loretta Alper, et. al. (2016). *The Occupation of the American Mind: Israel's Public Relations War in the United States*. Massachusetts: Media Education Foundation.

39 Nicole Goodkind. (2018, June 28). Alexandria Ocasio-Cortez is Democrats' new rising star. Will the DSA's support for an Israel Boycott slow her down? *Newsweek*, retrieved from http://www.newsweek.com/alexandria-ocasio-cortez-israel-palestine-bds-socialists-999888

ACKNOWLEDGMENTS

Since this book has been incubating for 10 years, I am indebted to more people than I can name. I am so grateful for the many kinds of support I have received: intellectual, political, social, and emotional. The people acknowledged here are only the tip of the iceberg.

Starting from the end and working backwards, I am indebted beyond measure to my wonderful editor and friend Patricia Leavy (aka The Energizer Bunny), whose invitation made this book possible. I have also benefitted from extraordinary editing by Peter Lehman whose painstaking, challenging line-by-line edits, accompanied by the best substantive questions, have made this a much better book. Kaitlin Astrella understands the difference between "a woman without her man is nothing" and "a woman: with her, man is nothing." Thank you Kaitlin. Sa'ed Adel Atshan spent endless time and effort, balancing praise and challenge in exactly the right proportions. He is a friend, a colleague, and a comrade. Others have read the manuscript in whole or in part with equal care and insight – in alphabetical order, my thanks to Sam Bahour, Anat and Alex Biletzki, Amahl Bishara, Jim Bowley, Elizabeth Burki, Diana Buttu, Jonathan Cook, Irene Gendzier, Maheen Haider, Nicole and John Harrington, Kat Lancaster, Dana Sajdi, Elizabeth Sherman, Anne Wagner, and Sarah Woodside. The usual disclaimers are in order: the genius is theirs; the mistakes are mine.

In Boston, I am blessed to be a member of the Palestinian and the Jewish activist communities, both of which have been supportive of this work. For all the conversations, hospitality, and wisdom I thank Thomas Abowd, Sa'ed Adel Atshan, Nidal Al Azraq, Paul Beran, Amahl Bishara, Martin Federman, Munir and Naila Jermanus, Dan Klein, Jeff Klein, Karen Klein, Howard Lenow, Steven, Barbara and Shaina Low, Hilary Rantisi, Alice Rothchild, Sara Roy, and Hannah Schwarzschild.

In the academic community I am immeasurably grateful to the two women who have been such supportive Chairs while this book is being written: Sarah Babb and Zine Magubane, I can't thank you enough. The Boston College administration has also been uniformly supportive, from the Provost, David Quigley and the Associate Provosts Don Hafner and Pat DeLeeuw, Associate Dean of the Graduate School Candace Hetzner, Dean Greg Kalscheur, SJ, to the people in Student Affairs, in the Chaplaincy, at the Volunteer and Service Learning Center, and the Montserrat Coalition: Karl Bell, Paul Chebator,

ACKNOWLEDGMENTS

Kate Daly, Paula Dias, Maria DiChiappari, Burt Howell, Daniel Leahy, Yvonne McBarnett, Marina Pastrana, Daniel Ponsetto, Akua Sarr, Mer Zovko. I am indebted to for the support and advice of my colleagues in the Middle Eastern and Islamic Civilization program, in International Studies, and in African and African Diaspora Studies: Kathleen Bailey, Ali Banuazizi, David Deese, David DiPasquale, Peter Krause, and Cynthia Young.

I benefitted from the hard work, commitment, and insight of my wonderful research assistants and tech assistants: Kaitlin Astrella, Annelise Hagar, William Hubschman, Hannah Kazal, Kyla Longman, Anna Mascagni and Erin Zoellick.

A very special thank you also to all the faculty who have allowed me to try out some of my ideas in their classes or who have provided opportunities for thinking, speaking, writing, and intellectual companionship: Pam Berger, Fr. James Bernauer, SJ, Charlie Derber, Elizabeth Goizueta, Fr. Raymond Helmick, SJ, John Michalczyck, and Matt Mulane.

This work would not have been possible without the habits of reflection, the conversations about serving the world, that are hosted at Boston College by the much missed Fr. Joe Appleyard, SJ, Burt Howell, and the Intersections Project within the Division of Mission and Ministry, and by James Weiss in the Capstone program.

Nor would the work have been possible without the wonderful and loving companionship of the people who trusted themselves to my judgment and came with me and my students to Israel and Palestine: Karl Bell, Scott Easton, Kimberly Kay Hoang, Deborah Levenson-Estrada, John McDargh (aka Mr. Sherman), Fr. Gustavo Morello, SJ, Erik Owen, Adam Saltsman, David Scanlan, and Sarah Woodside.

I also want to extend very special gratitude to friends and family who profoundly disagree with me and who kept talking and listening anyway. You are my heroes, Shoshanna Bravmann, Carol Haspel, Jeff Haspel.

In Palestine, I am deeply indebted to the wisdom, patience, and friendship of Laila Atshan, Sam Bahour, Diana Buttu and Tom Dallal, Daoud Nasser, Nader Said and Renad Qbbaj, Samer, Noora and Nala Said, Sami Abou Shehadeh and all the wonderful people at the Siraj Center: George Rishmawi, Michel Awad, Iliana Awad, Rania Awad.

In (or from) Israel, I am equally indebted to my friends Eitan Alimi, Anat and Alex Biletzki, Michelle Gawerc, Sarit Larry, Oded Na'aman, and Ilan Pappe. Sami Abou Shehadeh and Diana Buttu are both Palestinian and Israeli; in a sane world they would be numbered among the most valued and honored people of their society.

Most of important of all, there are the almost 200 students who have taken this journey with me, in class, on the ground in Israel/Palestine, in political activism on campus: you are my *raison d'être*. Watching you becoming the writers, teachers, thinkers, doctors, lawyers, actors, social workers, senate staffers, soldiers, state department staffers, business leaders, peace activists, yoga instructors, gadflies, and nomads you are in the process of becoming makes me optimistic about the future. Knowing you is one of the great gifts of my life.

My special thanks to trip alumnus Emil Tsao for the photographs found on my Amazon author page and on the cover of this second edition.

My family has listened to me talking about bits and pieces of this project for a decade. To Connie and John, Sarah and Blake, Mark and Diane, Julia and Jill, and to my goddaughters Petra and Jennifer: thank you … just for being you.

And to Dean Albertson: you gave me the life-long gift of seeing you stand up for your beliefs with dignity and courage. Everything I do is built on the platform of the things I learned from you.

PART 1

INTRODUCTION

CHAPTER 1

INTRODUCTION

Tell Our Story

[T]he ... task is not so much to be balanced as to give balance, particularly in situations of disproportionate power relationships.
Michael Leunig, Cartoonist[1]

If you are neutral in situations of injustice, you have chosen the side of the oppressor. If an elephant has its foot on the tail of a mouse and you say that you are neutral, the mouse will not appreciate your neutrality.
Archbishop Desmond Tutu[2]

Richard's Story

More than a decade ago, when I first became engrossed with the issues of Israel/Palestine, I began reading voraciously on the subject. And immediately thereafter, my friends came to be at the receiving end of many book reviews masquerading as conversation. "Did you know?" I would begin; or "I was just reading that" … and then I would go on for quite some time.

At one point, my good friend Richard broke into the recitation. "Stop!" he cried. "You're getting way ahead of me." And then he proceeded to tell me this story from his own experience.

When he was a student in junior high school, his social studies teacher assigned each member of the class an area of the world to study. Richard was assigned the Middle East. Over a period of some weeks, each student was to read everything he or she could find about their assigned area, as though they were a reporter assigned to that "beat." At the end of the assignment, each student was to submit a newspaper-article-cum-review-of-the-region and, together, the class would publish a world newspaper for the rest of the school.

© KONINKLIJKE BRILL NV, LEIDEN, 2019 | DOI:10.1163/9789004394148_001

Unfortunately, Richard did not know exactly where the Middle East was. But he was the kind of ambitious and self-motivated student teachers love. So, without asking for clarification, Richard got out a map of the United States, looked carefully at the Eastern seaboard, and dutifully became very attentive to all news coming from Maryland and Virginia (this was in the days before the internet and Wikipedia). Luckily his father read all his papers before Richard turned them in to his teachers, and thus he was spared the humiliation of having anyone else know that he had confused the Middle East and the Mid-Atlantic states!

But his advice to me, in that long-ago conversation rings true today: "Start small; start with the most basic information."

This book is written for readers who know that the Israeli-Palestinian conflict is important, but who do not know much about it. It offers a point of entry into the conversation. It is written for those who want to learn more, for those who want to be active in the search for a just peace, for those who are fearful about the complexity of the issues, for those who suspect that the mainstream media provide only a one-sided understanding, and for those who remember that, in foreign affairs, good intentions sometimes produce catastrophic results.[3] This book provides a framework that allows readers to sort out many of the claims and counterclaims they hear and to act thoughtfully, whether as students, parishioners, neighbors, voters, or dinner guests. Within these pages, I will try to provide a concise and easily understood history of the situation in ways that point to actions we might take in the future to bring this seemingly intractable conflict to a just resolution. Throughout the book I will argue that human rights provide the basis for a just resolution and that, surprisingly, no one has ever used human rights as the standard to which both Israelis and Palestinians should be held at more than a rhetorical level.[4]

Since 2008 I have taught a fall semester seminar on human rights in the Israeli-Palestinian conflict. The course has two unusual requirements: in addition to the class itself, students are required to participate in a study trip to Palestine/Israel over the winter break and, upon their return, to create a project to increase American interest in finding a just resolution to the Israeli-Palestinian conflict. While planning the first trip, I went to great lengths to ensure that students would be exposed to a wide variety of human rights groups in both Palestine and Israel whose work is centered on the conflict: those who focus on land rights,[5] water rights,[6] prisoners' rights,[7] women's, children's and gay rights,[8] refugee rights,[9] students' rights,[10] rights of the Palestinian citizens of Israel in the Negev and elsewhere,[11] and rights to cultural survival.[12] I assumed that each student would be impressed by at least one of the many projects we visited, and would want to raise money for them in the United States. But, in fact, our hosts never asked us for money.

Instead, they begged, over and over again, "Just tell our story. Please tell our story. If Americans knew what is going on here, their politics would change. Americans could play an important and useful role in promoting a just peace. Please tell them our story."

Every year since that first trip we hear exactly the same plea: to transmit Palestinian voices and to tell their story. So we come home, determined to tell their story, only to find that this is easier said than done. Typically, we encounter four obstacles standing in the way.

The first is Islamophobia. Arabs, Palestinians among them, are depicted in the American imagination as shadowy and ominous figures: ill shaven and gun toting – always a threat to our safety.[13] It is not hard for the average American to be exposed to Islamophobia; indeed, it would be hard to avoid it. Both "realistic" and avowedly fictitious accounts of events in the Middle East are filled with simplistic stereotypes. They ignore the fact that there are large Christian Arab communities, especially in Palestine, that most Muslims are not Arab, that differences of nationality and class are important in the Arab world, as they are elsewhere, that much of recent Arab history is shaped by imperial and Cold War politics.

The documentary, *Reel Bad Arabs,* captures the enactment of Islamophobia in that powerful medium of American popular culture, the action movie, showing how pervasive and xenophobic the stereotypes are.[14] Nor are the stereotypes offset by any counter-knowledge of the role of Arabs in American history, for example that Arab-Americans fought against slavery in the Civil War or stood with Caesar Chavez's United Farm Workers or, in the person of Ralph Nader, agitated for consumer and environmental safety.[15]

Alas, serious news coverage of Palestine is hardly better. Illegal Israeli settlements are described as "neighborhoods," and spokespersons from one side predominate.[16] The former Jerusalem bureau chief of the *New York Times* had a son serving in the Israeli military, and his successor published articles on rock-throwing as part of the "culture" of Palestinian children without specifying that the rock throwers are aiming at the military vehicles, the visible symbol of the Occupation that suffocates their communities.[17]

Second, in the case of Israel/Palestine, violence is typically presented *ahistorically,* as though there are two equal parties who, inexplicably, refuse to "just use their words." Coverage like this makes it impossible for an American audience to recognize the struggle as one between an occupying force and an occupied population engaged in a grassroots liberation struggle.[18] The popular Israeli television series *Fauda* exemplifies this problem. The show focuses on the on-going duels between a company of Israeli undercover agents, often Arab Jews who can pass as Palestinians (*Mustarivim*), and various Palestinian villains (Hamas in the first season and ISIS in the second). In Israel *Fauda* is considered to manifest a liberal bias because it divides screen time about equally between Israeli Jewish characters and Palestinian ones who actually speak Arabic. However, the show could just as well be *Romeo and Juliet* or *West Side Story* in that it provides no context at all that explains why the parties are fighting each other. It does not recognize the possibility of any legitimate Palestinian objection to Occupation; indeed, it does not even notice that there is an Occupation.

Third, even for people too generous or too smart to be taken in by Islamophobia, *complexity is a challenge*. "No, no," we are told repeatedly, often accompanied by dismissive hand motions, the Israeli-Palestinian conflict is "just too complicated." "Haven't they always hated each other?" we are asked. "Wouldn't we have to understand hundreds of years of a very complicated history to be informed about this conflict?"

Perhaps some of this professed bewilderment is a mask for prejudice and distaste, genteelly expressed. But genuine humility is also at work, and appropriately so. We have seen American intervention produce unintended and disastrous results in many places around the world and in much of recent history. So asking Americans to attend to this particular Middle Eastern conflict with a view to, yet again, changing the course of events for the better in far-off places is, indeed, a task to be approached with caution and humility.

A fourth difficulty is that people cannot learn even a fairly straightforward history one fact at a time. *We all need a framework that organizes our questions* about the unknown (For a discussion of frameworks, see Chapter 3). Yet the choice of frameworks is itself highly controversial, since every point of view is, simultaneously, also a point of blindness. This difficulty reinforces some people's belief that the Palestinian-Israeli conflict is just too complex to be understood.

This book is grounded in the belief that the best framework for studying the Israeli-Palestinian conflict is human rights, which provides the standard by which Israeli and Palestinian actions, and all possible resolutions of the conflict between them, should be evaluated. I chose the human rights standards because I believe it is essential to start from the assumption that all human beings are of equal value. I can see no other starting point for the conversation. Human rights doctrine also has a practical aspect. In a conflict situation, applying human rights criteria points the way to acceptable solutions and to the standards they must embody. The alternative *realpolitik* point of view has been spectacularly unsuccessful in providing any solution, let alone a sustainable one. Finally, human rights allow us to compare the Palestinian-Israeli conflict to other difficult conflicts such as the anti-Apartheid struggle in South Africa or the search for peace in Northern Ireland or the resolution of competitive land claims in countries like New Zealand or Canada that are dominated by colonial settler populations. This comparative perspective broadens our frame of reference and invites more people into the conversation. It makes the Israeli-Palestinian conflict less of a "boutique" issue and allows it to be seen, instead, as another example of anti-colonial, national liberation, or civil rights struggles.

This book is essentially a call to action. More people are needed in the conversation. The hope for a just peace in Israel/Palestine cannot rest solely on the shoulders of those with highly specialized Middle Eastern expertise (at a minimum, Arabic and Hebrew). If the experts were able to resolve the issue, they would have done so by now. Clearly the conversation will also benefit from the knowledge of those who understand the work of grassroots social movements, the impact of non-governmental organizations (NGOs), the role of truth and reconciliation commissions, the actions of transnational market forces, etc. In short, the human rights perspective is able to welcome the efforts of all those who wish to contribute to the creation of a just peace.

For all these reasons, human rights advocacy forms the backbone of this book. Many NGOs funded by U.S. and European sources wave the banner of human rights. But, too often, they miss the most essential point: that the Occupation is elephant in the room. Until it is dismantled, most other efforts are more or less beside the point.[19] The failure of human rights programs to address this crucial issue must end.

Most readers, I suspect, will be favorably inclined toward human rights as the place to start. But the challenge is that, if human rights standards are applied rigorously, we face uncomfortable insights and demands. The Israel that Americans think they know ("the only democracy in the Middle East," a place of vibrant capitalism based on advanced military and medical technology, a safe haven for Holocaust survivors,[20] a place where a frontier mentality of nation-building still prevails,[21] a tourist destination of Mediterranean beaches, ancient holy sites, and modern plumbing) has a darker underside in its brutal colonization of the Palestinians. Likewise, recognizing the Palestinian right to self-determination challenges the popular and ahistoric depiction of Palestinians as senselessly violent and devious. In Western discourse, this right has been ignored, sidelined, and silenced in favor of a chorus of denunciations of the sometimes-violent means, inconsistent with human rights, which Palestinians use to achieve their ends.

Perhaps the greatest challenge to adopting a human rights framework is that it does not lend itself to simple, formulaic bromides like "the truth is probably half way between the two contending sides." Instead, the human rights standard demands that we take sides. It requires us to recognize that the truth is not to be found half way between Martin Luther King and the Ku Klux Klan. The latter is just wrong. Neither is the truth half way between the slave trader and his captive, the polluter and the defenseless earth or sea, the sweatshop owner and the child worker.

In the case of Israel/Palestine, the human rights perspective reveals at least two paradoxes. There are two equally valuable communities of the same size but vastly disparate power, making it very difficult for the weaker side (the Palestinians) to insist on human rights. And while this book advocates for the application of human rights to the conflict, the very same standards also remind us that we should not be in the business of telling other people what to do.

Nevertheless, those who serve the vision of Zionism as it is currently embodied by the Israeli state stand indicted by human rights standards. This is not Zionism as it *might have been* had the early Zionists followed the advice of Martin Buber, Albert Einstein, or Hannah Arendt – namely to seek a Jewish *homeland* rather than a Jewish *state*. Nor is it Zionism *as it could yet become*: one voice in an egalitarian and multi-ethnic society. Alas, application of the human rights standards to the current situation in Palestine/Israel will show that the "actually existing" Zionism *requires* human rights violations to achieve its goals. The Occupation is a trap for all who enter it: it invites Israelis to abuse power in order to maintain their position, and it invites Palestinians to resort to any means necessary to liberate themselves. Human rights doctrine demands that we recognize this unpalatable truth.

You are entitled to your opinion. But you are not entitled to your own facts.

Daniel Patrick Moynihan[22]

BACKGROUND INFORMATION

Before we go too much further into the details of this book, the reader will want a brief synopsis of the situation. (The second part of the book provides the historic detail underlying this summary.) The basics are as follows.

Israel/Palestine is a small space, only slightly larger than the state of New Jersey (or the country of Wales).[23] When Zionism began, the population of Palestine was mostly Muslim but also contained substantial Christian communities. Palestinians were, in fact, the first Christians, living in Nazareth, Bethlehem, Jerusalem and all the places central to the Christian narrative. There was also a Palestinian Jewish community – that is, a community whose members practiced Judaism as a religion, whose culture and language was Arabic, and who lived peacefully in Palestine.

The cultural diversity of Palestine at the beginning of Zionism is no coincidence. Historic Palestine is situated at a crucial crossroads; it forms the land bridge between Africa and Asia, and between Asia and Europe. Nearly all the ancient civilizations have been part of its history, genetics, and culture.[24]

In the mid- to late-1800s, a minority of European Jews, who referred to themselves as Zionists, concluded that they would never be safe from anti-Semitism in Christian Europe. They began talking and writing, planning and fund raising, to establish a Jewish homeland elsewhere. Argentina and Uganda were considered as possible sites. But Zionist ambitions soon came to focus on Palestine, the Promised Land of the Jews, the Holy Land of the Christians, and part of the Islamic *waqf*, vouchsafed to Muslims by their god. Clearly, such competing claims presaged trouble.

European Zionist Jews began actually to emigrate to Palestine by the 1890s, long before the Holocaust itself, but already subject to the kind of systematic anti-Semitism that would later give rise to the Holocaust. By the 1920s it was clear to the older inhabitants of Palestine that the Zionists meant to build a state of their own rather than simply joining the communities already in place. It was also clear from the behavior of the militias formed by the Zionists that they were prepared to create this exclusively Jewish state by force of arms if necessary.

World War II and the Holocaust gave impetus to the Zionist movement. In 1947, the newly formed United Nations voted in General Assembly Resolution 181 (a non-binding resolution) to partition historic Palestine in order to create one Jewish and one Arab state there. They did so over the objections of both the Palestinians and the Zionist and non-Zionist Jews actually inhabiting the land. Since the Jewish state was expected to absorb Jewish refugees uprooted by the Second World War, Israel was allocated 55 percent of the land although the Jewish population of Palestine constituted only about a third of the people living there.

The creation of the state of Israel triggered intense and bitter violence between the Palestinians and the new state, and between the new state and its Arab neighbors. Beginning at the time of the U.N. vote to partition Palestine, the Jewish militias, later merged into the Israeli Defense Forces (IDF), expelled as many Palestinians as they could, not only from the land that the U.N. had apportioned for Israel, but also from land assigned to the Palestinian state. Then, on the very day that Israel was created, neighboring Arab countries invaded. In the end, however, the Arab armies did not succeed in holding even the 44 percent of the land that U.N. had designated as Palestine.

By 1949, the war, which Palestinians call the *Nakba* (the Catastrophe) and Israelis call the War of Independence, was officially over, although expulsions of Palestinians continued. Israel now held 78 percent of the land. Jordan controlled the West Bank and Egypt controlled Gaza. Both areas had been earmarked for Palestine. The Palestinians controlled nothing.

The boundary defined by the armistice lines of 1949 became the new *de facto* boundary of Israel. It was drawn on maps of the time in green ink and so it became known as the Green Line. It is, even today, the point of reference for international discussion of the still unrealized and ever elusive "two-state" solution that the U.N. called for back in 1947. But note the violation of human rights standards: using the Green Line as the international boundary means ratifying a change of national boundaries through acts of war. This resolution would be inadmissible under international law anywhere else in the world, but it is universally endorsed in the case of Palestine and Israel.

The *Nakba* or War of Independence took a catastrophic toll on everyone. The new State of Israel lost 1 percent of its population. By the most conservative estimates, more than 50 percent of Palestinians were expelled from their homes[25]; and most of their towns and villages and virtually all of their cities within reach of the Israeli army were destroyed.[26]

The Palestinian people were reduced to dependent status. In the West Bank they were subject to Jordanian rule, in Gaza, Egyptian rule. Many more were crowded into refugee camps, in the West Bank and Gaza, and also in the surrounding countries: Lebanon, Syria, Jordan, and Egypt. Even in the new Israeli state very few Palestinians remained in their own homes; many of them were internally displaced, that is, still in areas under Israeli control, but not where they had always lived.

Fast forward to 1967. In the Six Day War of that year, Israel wrested the West Bank from Jordan and Gaza from Egypt. It now controlled all of historic Palestine and all of the Palestinians who lived there. Once again, Palestinians had no control over their own land, society, or government.

At present, there are roughly thirteen million people in Israel and the Occupied Palestinian Territories, all living under one form or another of Israeli control. The Palestinian and Israeli Jewish communities are nearly evenly divided between roughly 6.6 million Muslim and Christian Palestinians and 6.2 million Jewish Israelis.[27]

- Among the 6.2 million Jews, more than 12%, some 764,000 persons, live as illegal settlers in areas allocated to Palestine (or to Syria in the Occupied Golan Heights). The rest live west of the Green Line, i.e. in Israel proper if a two-state solution continues to be the frame of reference.[28]
- Among the Palestinians, 32 percent (2.1 million) live in Israel as Israeli citizens but not as Israeli nationals (the distinction will be discussed in Chapter 6). The rest are divided between the West Bank (2.75 million) and Gaza (1.8 million).[29]
- The intermixing of Palestinian citizens of Israel with the Jewish population and the illegal Jewish settlers with the Palestinian community make it impossible to create any two state division of the territory that doesn't leave huge numbers of people on the "wrong" side of whatever line is proposed.
- In the Gaza Strip and West Bank, 2.1 million Palestinians are refugees. They remain in refugee camps even within Palestinian areas for a variety of reasons: they cannot get permission to acquire land or build homes outside the camps, they do not have the resources to do so, or they fear surrendering their right of return to land that is now inside Israel.[30] For purposes of this book, unless otherwise specified, when I speak of refugees I will be focusing on those Palestinians who live under Israeli control, within Israel or in the Occupied Territories.
- An additional three million Palestinians are living as refugees in camps in neighboring countries, Lebanon, Jordan, Egypt and Syria. They include those who actually fled during the *Nakba* and their direct descendants. Under international law, they have the right to return to the places from which they were expelled. All of the proposed peace agreements have compromised this right into an inferior right to return only to the territory of an eventual, ever shrinking Palestinian state. Once again, the failure to insist on human rights law complicates the situation and leaves the Palestinian refugees in a perpetual limbo.[31]

- Within the West Bank, the most populous Palestinian area, the land has been divided (following provisions of the Oslo Accords signed in 1993 and 1995) into three areas: Areas A, B, and C. Area C is 61 percent of the West Bank and most Palestinians have been driven out of it; only 4 percent of the 2.75 million Palestinian West Bankers remain there. Instead, 96 percent of West Bank Palestinians are crowded into Area A (the major Palestinian cities) and Area B (villages immediately surrounding the cities).[32] Areas A and B together are discrete chunks of land, leaving the Palestinian population of the West Bank simultaneously herded into crowded cities and scattered across the landscape in non-contiguous clumps. In short, Palestinians in the West Bank live in areas that look more like Indian reservations or Bantustans than like the nucleus of an emerging state.
- Looking at these numbers, it may be difficult to understand why Israel continues to think of itself as small and defenseless. However, globally, there are 13 million Jews (43% of them in Israel and 40% in the United States)[33] and 1.6 billion Muslims, 317 million of them in the Middle East and North Africa.[34] These numbers explain why Israel continues to talk about being surrounded by enemies.

All of these numbers add up to is this: both the Israeli and Palestinian communities number in the millions. The Israeli community is expanding the areas in which it lives, pushing the Palestinian community into smaller and smaller non-contiguous spaces. Palestinians continue to resist, and are winning increasing sympathy for their resistance, even in Europe and America, even in Jewish communities. The "universally agreed upon" two-state solution would create two micro-states (imagine subdividing New Jersey into two sovereign nations) each with a huge number of "the other" living within its borders. This is the same problem that bedeviled early European nationalisms that called for ethnically pure nation states. Europe responded to this challenge, eventually, by developing a sense of nationalism that allows for ethnic and cultural diversity. Human rights standards requires the same of Israelis and Palestinians, whatever form the state(s) may take.

Hope is being able to see that there is light despite all of the darkness.
Desmond Tutu[35]

REASONS TO HOPE

Despite the difficulties revealed in the foregoing summary, there is room for hope. The Palestinian and Jewish Israeli communities are of roughly equal size, and both populations are highly educated and entrepreneurial.[36] Virtually all versions of development theory would predict from these facts that Israelis and Palestinians, whether together or apart, could be among the most successful examples of post-colonial national development following World War II. This insight allows us to ask new questions: instead of assuming eternal enmity between Jewish Israelis and Palestinians, we can ask, instead, how did politics manage to fritter away all that potential for development, to snatch defeat from the jaws of victory? Flipping the question in this way allows us to look for correctible errors instead of assuming that there is nothing to be done.

Indeed, I will argue that studying the Israeli/Palestinian conflict begins with three pieces of very good news. First, the conflict between Palestinians and Zionists, though acute, is neither ancient nor eternal. It is simply not true that Jews and Muslims have "always hated each other." Second, while millions of individual human beings have been caught up in the conflict, there are really only three major parties to the conflict: Zionists (who, for purposes of this work are mostly Jewish), colonial superpowers, and Palestinians. These three actors have acted from the beginning of Zionism to the present from consistent, coherent, and understandable motives. The Zionists want to "Judaize" the land; the superpowers want to exploit something in the region (e.g. access to intelligence, control over the regional balance of power, military bases, or shipping routes); and the Palestinians want control over their own lives and society in the face of Zionist and superpower agendas – their behaviors have been largely reactive to the initiatives of others. The limited cast of characters and the constancy of their purposes allow us to understand the situation, while the relative newness of the Palestinian-Israeli conflict allows hope for a resolution.

A Recent Conflict

The struggle between Zionists and Palestinians dates back only to the 1880s, a little more than a century and a quarter. While that is more than long enough for so much suffering, in the span of human history, a conflict that is barely 125 years old cannot be regarded as eternal. In fact, the tension between Jews and Muslims dates only to the advent of Zionism. Before Zionism, Jews were generally safer in the Muslim societies than in the Christian world. If they were not fully equal to their Muslim neighbors, at least they were not ghettoized into economically, socially, and politically constricted lives, as they often were in Christian Europe.

Between Jews and Arabs there are common sacred texts, and hence no doctrinal necessity for hatred. The Old Testament was written long before the development of Islam and therefore cannot make any reference to it. And the Qur'an explicitly recognizes Jewish and Christian texts and prophets as worthy of respect.[37]

Of course, it is also true that both the Old Testament and the Qur'an are ancient and complex documents. Those wishing to smite their neighbors can find textual support for doing so,[38] as can those who wish to love their neighbors. But, in the end, it is far more the practical circumstances of the communities of believers than the requirements of creed that dictate whether these communities will emphasize neighborliness or hostility.[39] Put differently, context can trump creed when it comes to choosing between the more aggressive and the more conciliatory strands within religious texts.

So what were the practical circumstances that lent themselves to a more welcoming attitude toward Jews in the Muslim Middle East and more virulent anti-Semitism in Christian Europe for centuries before the advent of Zionism? Princeton historian Mark Cohen provides the most measured comparison of Muslim-Jewish and Christian-Jewish relations in the pre-modern era.[40] He argues that the Muslim world is geographically, historically, and socially multicultural. In this context, Jews were only one of many ethnic minorities. And, for ideological reasons, Jews were the preferred minority in Islamic societies, since they were also monotheists, "people of the book." In the Christian world, by contrast, Jews were the single most significant minority and were hated for a variety of ideological and practical reasons. Ideologically, they were deemed to be the killers of Christ, and the bringers of the Black Death. Practically, they were excluded from many occupations and then despised as moneylenders. They were excluded from political life and then viewed with suspicion as "rootless cosmopolitans."[41]

One need not romanticize a lost "golden age" of Jewish-Muslim amity[42] to argue quite realistically that any sensible Jew, during the long Middle Ages, would have been wise to choose life in Beirut rather than Bialystok, had such a choice been available. Nor need one be foolishly optimistic about reviving Muslim-Jewish tolerance to argue that Muslim-Jewish enmity is neither ancient nor inevitable.

Moreover, the possibility for peaceful coexistence did not end with the Middle Ages. Today, inside the West Bank city of Nablus, an ancient community of Samaritans, who claim to practice the earliest version of Israelite worship, continue to live among their Palestinian neighbors in safety and acceptance despite the depredations of the Occupation and despite the obvious favors (Israeli passports and drivers' licenses) they enjoy from the occupier.[43] By contrast, indigenous Palestinians inside Israel live beleaguered lives (for reasons that will be discussed more fully in Chapter 6).

Clearly, this history points to deep divisions. At the same time, there is room for hope. The core of the current conflict is not senseless, atavistic xenophobia. Rather, intransigence is limited to those on both sides who will accept only an ethno-religiously exclusive enclave in the area that is now Palestine/Israel. Any person who is willing to live in a religiously and ethnically diverse modern democracy, in a country that is a state of all its citizens, is a possible advocate for a just peace.

Put differently, the conflict is not between two groups, each born into a religious identity they can do little to change. Rather, the conflict is between two ideological camps, both of which could choose to become less intransigent and more pluralistic. The real barrier to co-existence, thus, is not religious doctrine but political struggle: on the Israeli side, to maintain control over all of Palestine, and, on the Palestinian side, to achieve national liberation or the vindication of their civil rights. This struggle is very real and inflamed, but, at the same time, no less capable of resolution than were the equally entrenched conflicts of Northern Ireland or Apartheid South Africa.

Three Actors

While millions of individuals have been caught up in this conflict, there are really only three major collective actors whose interactions produce the present impasse: Zionists, imperial superpowers who pursue their own agendas in the region, and Palestinians.[44]

In the case of the Israeli-Palestinian conflict, Zionism, as a social movement, changes everything (as we shall explore further in Chapters 4 and 10). Although the United States today includes many Christian Zionist groups, unless otherwise specified, Zionism in this book refers to Jews who, beginning in the late nineteenth century, chose to leave Europe in order to build an exclusively Jewish state away from Christian anti-Semitism.

The imperial powers, the second party of the Palestinian-Israeli conflict, include a changing cast of characters. Almost every empire of the ancient world has left its mark, making the Middle East the heir to the greatest possible cultural diversity. Groups that dominated the terrain that comprises the present territory of Israel/Palestine include, in chronological order, the Pharaonic Egyptians 3,000 years before the Christian era, the Hittites (one of the Canaanite nations), the Israelites, co-existing with the Philistines, the Assyrians,[45] the Babylonians, the Persians, the Greeks, the Romans, the Byzantine empire, the Sassanids, the Caliphate, the Seljuks, the Crusaders, Saladin's forces, the Mongols, the Ottoman empire, and the British Empire.[46] The Romanov, Hohenzollern, and Hapsburg empires, though never governing the land of Israel/Palestine, also influenced events there through policies that made Jews under their dominion more or less likely to emigrate.

It is worth noting that even the most aggressive and expansionist versions of Jewish history acknowledge the multi-cultural character of this place, positing that the Canaanites preceded the Israelites and that the Philistines were co-inhabitants of the area with them in Old Testament times. Indeed, the very name "Philistine" is clearly connected to *Filastin,* the Arabic word for Palestine.

For purposes of understanding the present conflict, the two most significant superpowers in the recent past were the Ottoman Empire, which ruled the area for four centuries, ending in 1918, and the British Empire, which was charged, under League of Nations auspices, with a mandate to prepare the area for national self-governance. British Mandatory Palestine lasted 30 years, from 1918 to 1948.

In recent times, the United States is the most important foreign power operating in the area. It operates without the formal machinery of colonial domination and control, but nevertheless exercises its influence through foreign aid, through political maneuvering at the U.N. and in other international forums, and by acting as Israel's chief source of arms.

In some cases, the interests of British and American colonialism have converged with those of Zionism, to the disadvantage of the Palestinians. As early as 1907, the – Campbell-Bannerman Report concluded:

There are people [the Arabs] who control spacious territories teeming with manifest and hidden resources. They dominate the intersections of world routes. Their lands were the cradles of human civilizations and religions. These people have one faith, one language, one history and the same aspirations. No natural barriers can isolate these people from one another ... if, per chance, this nation were to be unified into one state, it would then take the fate of the world into its hands and would separate Europe from the rest of the world. Taking these considerations seriously, *a foreign body should be planted in the heart of this nation to prevent the convergence of its wings in such a way that it could exhaust its powers in never-ending wars.* It could also serve as a springboard for the West to gain its coveted objects (emphasis mine).[47]

The master strategy suggested by Campbell-Bannerman tilted the playing field heavily against Palestinian aspirations; it meant that the Palestinians, who have lived, especially in the coastal cities, for many centuries had very little chance of realizing their national aims.

Here it becomes crucial to acknowledge that, in the present climate, every historical statement, indeed every scholarly statement, literally from archaeology to zoology, is contested between Zionists and Palestinians. The struggle is largely about competing claims of who got here first: who can legitimately claim indigeneity in the land between the river and the sea. Zionists claim not only that they are the direct descendants of the "original" inhabitants of the land, expelled some two thousand or more years ago by the Romans, but also that they have maintained a sense of common "nationhood" across centuries and continents of Diaspora. The present Zionist project is thereby framed as the return to the land that is originally, rightfully, unquestionably, theirs.[48]

Nearly every one of these assertions has been vigorously contested, not only by those concerned with justice for Palestinians, but by Jews themselves. *Some* present-day Jews are undoubtedly the descendants of the Hebrews of biblical text. But, just as undoubtedly, others are the descendants of mixed marriages or the descendants of people who converted to Judaism and had no history in the Middle East.[49] Still others emphasize the degree to which Jews, whether assimilated or marginalized, took on the identities of their host communities, leaving the ceremonial mantra "Next year in Jerusalem" a slender thread from which to hang claims of timeless communalism.

Those who make the claims for Jewish indigeneity usually also deny Palestinian claims to being the descendants of ancient inhabitants of the land. Given the history that is widely known, of waves of conquerors succeeding each other, one after another,[50] it is almost certainly correct to argue that the original Canaanite population is now highly intermixed with others. "Arabization," for example, occurred following the creation of Islam in the 7th century A.D. Islam soon spread beyond the Arabian Peninsula, partly through conquest and partly through trade and the diffusion of the Arabic language. No credible source, however, argues that Arabization entirely displaced the indigenous population, or that Palestinians today are related exclusively to Arab migrants of the 8th century and not at all to the older Canaanite communities.

Common sense would suggest that the indigenous population of what is now Israel/Palestine is a polyglot group, including, among others, Canaanite and Israelite elements in its heritage. The competitive arguments

17

for indigeneity, the mutual insistence on an "either-or" heritage, fail to be persuasive. Given the human capacity to "love the one you're with," every human group has a "both-and" ethnic heritage revealing the full range of human experience: marrying within ones' ethnic group, intermarriage with other groups, migration, and conversion.

In the last decade and a half, Israel has sought to enlist genetic research in pressing its claims of Jewish indigeneity. The primary results of these efforts have been to unmask an exceptionally crude political control over science. In 2000, there was a flurry of interest in mutations on the Y (male) chromosome, but when these genetic studies indicated that about two thirds of European Jews and the same proportion of Palestinians shared three male ancestors some 8,000 years ago, the results were soon revised and reinterpreted.[51] Results were quickly revised again a year later, when research into mitochondrial DNA, inherited only through the mother, revealed that Jewish women in nine kosher communities appeared to have no foremothers of Middle Eastern origin, suggesting an ancient precedent for intermarriage and/or conversion.[52]

Conventional history writing did not fare much better than scientific research. Early on, in the context of arguing for Palestine rather than Uganda or Argentina as the site of the Zionist project, Ber Borochov argued that Jews were racially related to Palestinians.[53] In a book entitled *The Land of Israel, Past and Present*,[54] David Ben Gurion, Israel's first Prime Minister, and his co-author Yitzhak Ben Zvi followed Borochov's lead, arguing that Palestinians were descended from Jewish ancestors and so could readily be incorporated into the Zionist project.[55] Ben Gurion and Ben Zvi used linguistic evidence, citing the prevalence of Hebrew and Aramaic vocabulary in the rural Palestinian dialects as a basis for their claims.[56] It was only after the intense conflicts of 1929 that Zionist writers abandoned this possible fraternity with Palestinians in favor of a more oppositional stance.

I do not cite this history simply to make Zionist historians and geneticists look silly or venal. Any sophisticated reader will recognize that much of what once passed for historical writing is simply mythological (think of George Washington and the cherry tree). The Israeli sociologist Tom Segev, for example, says of the Israeli "new historians" who emerged in the 1980s, "It would be more precise to call them the 'first historians.' Because during Israel's early years there was no historiography; there was mythology, there was ideology. There was a lot of indoctrination."[57] His comments are assuredly equally true of every national history. Saleh Abdel Jawad, for example, is eloquent about the difficulties of writing Palestinian history, citing among other sources of frustration for Arab historians the lack of respect for archives, political interference with scholarship, and the conservative view of sources that seeks to exclude oral history from the evidentiary record.[58]

In any case, I will argue that, from a human rights perspective, the whole issue of indigeneity is somewhat beside the point. Certainly it cannot be used to justify ethnic cleansing or an ethos of expulsion. The simple fact is that, today, there are roughly equal numbers of Jews and Palestinians living between the river and the sea, and all of them have human rights, as do the nearly 3 million refugees outside the area who, under international human rights standards, have an inalienable right of return.[59] If, ironically, genetic testing establishes that at least some Israelis and Palestinians are also cousins, more similar to each other than either is to Europeans, then that is all the more reason for them to find a just and lasting resolution of their differences.[60]

Consistency of Purpose

Finally, the third reason to hope that understanding the conflict is possible is that each of these institutional actors – the Zionists, the superpowers and the Palestinians – has acted with a constancy of purpose that permits us to understand their behavior. As events unfold and circumstances change, their intentions are expressed in a variety of ways, producing the complicated narratives we see in both scholarly and popular sources. Yet the intentions themselves remain constant. Thus, we can understand any given moment of the Israeli-Palestinian conflict by asking how the Zionist intention to Judaize the land, superpower interests, and the Palestinian will to self-determination are being expressed.

Zionist immigrants to Palestine began by purchasing land that was for sale for reasons to be discussed in Chapter 5. As Zionist settlements grew stronger, they resorted to more aggressive means of raiding and warfare, culminating in the mass expulsions of Palestinians that marked the creation of the state of Israel.[61] Since its creation, Israelis have continued on the path of military conquest, especially during the Six Day War in 1967, which brought all of historic Palestine under their control. Since then, military might has been augmented by legal and bureaucratic measures. Today, the Palestinian population is controlled both by an occupying army and by an army of bureaucrats who give or, more often, withhold permits that allow Palestinians to go to school, go to the doctor, marry and live with their spouse, deepen wells, build houses, move goods, access bank accounts, etc.

19

Apparently the details of bureaucratic domination were worked out even in advance of the actual military victory of 1967 and were deployed shortly thereafter.[62] Even today, in the face of declining international legitimacy, the Israeli government proudly announces plans to further "Judaize" broad swathes of land in the Negev and the Galilee, continuing the process of ethnic cleansing, variously called "the transfer,"[63] or "taking all of the land with none of the [Palestinian] people" or, simply, "maximum geography, minimum demography."[64]

Similarly, external superpowers have always exhibited a self-interested if not actively exploitive stance toward their Palestinian dominion. The Turks, for example, encouraged land registration mostly to expand their tax revenues, and to conscript Palestinian youngsters into the most dangerous positions in their army.[65] The British promised all things to all people – a Jewish state in Palestine to the Zionists, an Arab state to the Arabs – all the while planning to make Palestine into a colony for themselves. Americans wanted a forward listening post in the midst of the Cold War; they wanted to contain radical change; and they wanted a place to develop and test weapons.[66] They also wanted to appease a powerful domestic political constituency.[67] None of the great powers, despite lofty rhetoric, have ever been motivated by doing good in Israel/Palestine.

In the face of superpower exploitation and Zionist ambition, the Palestinians have tried to participate in the wave of national liberation that brought all the other former colonies in the world to a place of self-determination after World War II. At various times, Palestinians have tried petitioning, using economic weapons such as a general strike, engaging in armed struggle, looking to Pan-Arab secular nationalism for a solution, going it alone with a leadership in exile, going it alone with a leadership in the community, reconsidering economic tools like boycotts, sanctions and divestment (BDS), and, most recently, flirting with political Islam. None of their efforts have so far won them the right to self-determination. Their leaders are criticized for a lack of solidarity and a lack of organizational skills; in the words of Israeli diplomat Abba Eban "the Palestinians never miss a chance to miss a chance."[68] The stricture is much less valid for Palestinian civil society leaders than it is for their politicians. Moreover, ordinary Palestinians have shown extraordinary resilience, perseverance, and steadfastness, which they call *sumud*, in pursuit of their dreams. The oft-quoted (and possibly apocryphal) Israeli prediction that the old generation of Palestinians will die and the young will forget their ties to the land has, so far, proved to be a bad bet.[69]

The wisdom of an old Jew of Galicia: When someone is honestly 55 percent right, that's very good and there's no use wrangling. And if someone is 60 percent right, it's wonderful, it's great luck, and let him thank God. But what's to be said about 75 percent right? Wise people say this is suspicious. Well, and what about 100 percent right? Whoever says he's 100 percent right is a fanatic, a thug, and the worst kind of rascal.

Bret Stephens[70]

METHODOLOGICAL CONSIDERATIONS

Readers of all non-fiction must rely on the author to marshal facts and to tell a story that is an honest representation of the situation. The question of trust becomes particularly acute when the facts are startling, and the story radically different from the one the reader has heard before.

Fortunately, in the Israeli, Euro-American, and Palestinian academic communities there is now substantial agreement about the facts of expulsion and ethnic cleansing that accompanied the establishment of the Israeli state. Observers differ in their responses to these facts: some excuse and the other denounce the events of the past. But the historiography of the conflict is no longer a contest about facts themselves.[71]

Nevertheless, much of this material is contentious, so I have made every effort to clearly distinguish stories that represent an extremist or minority view among either Israelis or Palestinians from those that represent official and/or "everyday" views.[72] Let me offer a protracted example from each side.

On the Israeli side, the behavior by ultra-Zionist, ultra-Nationalist settlers near Hebron, shown in the YouTube entitled "We Killed Jesus, We're Proud of it,"[73] clearly represents an extremist voice, a group of settlers most Israelis, including even many other settlers, would find abhorrent. The group depicted in this YouTube might justly be thought of as an Israeli equivalent to the Ku Klux Klan or some other hate group.

The situation becomes more complicated when obnoxious and extreme statements made by individuals are clearly tolerated by the government. Consider this recent instance: Two weeks ago outside a courtroom in the mixed Jewish-Palestinian town of Lod, some 20 young Jews danced and chanted in celebration of the grisly 2015 fire-bombing murder of an 18-month-old Palestinian baby, Ali Dawabshe, killed in his bed in the West Bank village of Duma. Ali's parents were also killed in the attack, and his four-year-old brother Ahmed was critically burned. The celebrants, wearing the outsize skullcaps and long forelocks favored by militant "price-tag" settlers, surrounded Ali and Ahmed's grandfather Hussein Dawabshe as he left the court where the three Jewish murder suspects were on trial. "Where is Ali? Dead! Burned! There is no Ali!" they jeered at the grandfather, who has raised the four-year-old Ahmed and seen him through the grueling healing process since the attack. "Ali is on fire! Ali is on the grill!" "Police officers and the ministers who were present at the court chose not to intervene," Ynet reported at the time, "letting the demonstration of hatred and racism continue."[74]

At least in this Israeli case, the government employees who stood by were not high level national officials, as is President Trump when he comments that the white supremacist, Nazi-saluting demonstrators in Charlottesville, Virginia included some "fine people."[75] Neverthless, the Israeli case also includes high ranking officials who articulate an intensely hateful view of all the Arabs around them. For example, a former Israeli Counsel General (to New York) says about the Syrian conflict: "This is a playoff situation in which you need both teams to lose ... let them both bleed, hemorrhage to death: that's the strategic thinking here [i.e. in Israel].[76]

Similarly, it is ordinary, everyday Israelis who, after a February, 2012 school bus crash in which nine Palestinian school children were burned to death, posted messages to Facebook and Twitter with comments like "Relax, these are Palestinian children" and "I hope every day there is a bus like this." Their comments were featured on the Prime Minister's web page.[77]

On the Palestinian side, perhaps the most famous troublesome statements are found in the old Hamas charter, endorsed by the ruling party in Gaza until very recently. The old charter includes the following language[78]: "Israel will rise and will remain erect until Islam eliminates it as it had eliminated its predecessors" (Preamble); "The Islamic Resistance Movement is a distinct Palestinian Movement which owes its loyalty to Allah, derives from Islam its way of life and strives to raise the banner of Allah over every inch of Palestine. Only under the shadow of Islam could the members of all regions coexist in safety and security for their lives, properties and rights. In the absence of Islam, conflict arises, oppression reigns, corruption is rampant and struggles and wars prevail" (Article 6); "The Islamic Resistance Movement believes that the land of Palestine has been an Islamic *Waqf* throughout the generations and until the Day of Resurrection, no one can renounce it or part of it, or abandon it or part of it" (Article 11); And, as a follow-on, "Renouncing any part of Palestine means renouncing part of the religion" (Article 13).

This language is, at best, a call for the whole of Palestine to be brought under Muslim control. Safeguards for Christians, Jews and secular people are mentioned in passing but never specified. The possibility of a genuinely egalitarian multi-religious, multi-ethnic society is discounted entirely, as is international human rights law.

In May of 2017 Hamas issued what amounted to a revised charter. Advocates of Palestinian unity – i.e. reconciliation between the Islamist Hamas and the secular Palestine Liberation Organization – can take comfort from the fact that the tone and some of the language seems to position Hamas in a less religious and more nationalistic frame. Political analysts see the new charter as a response to contextual pressure, an attempt to satisfy many audiences at once: internal ones like the secular Palestinian Authority and the Islamist Islamic Jihad, regional ones like Iran and Turkey, and international ones, especially Israel and the United States who have succeeded in keeping Hamas out of all international negotiations and using its existence as a pretext for undermining the Palestinian Authority's position as a negotiating partner.[79] However, none of these changes, pragmatic or ideological, signal a principled commitment to human rights for everyone between the river and the sea.

Nor is Hamas the source of all the problematic language from the Palestinian side. Palestinian leaders even inside Israel have sounded an ominous note: "We will push the Zionists into the sea or they will push us into the desert," said the Jaffa Muslim-Christian Council, shortly after World War I.[80] And, following closely upon the defeat of combined Arab forces and the beginning of the Occupation of the West Bank (including East Jerusalem) and the Gaza Strip by Israelis in June, 1967 the 4th Arab League Summit, held in Khartoum in August, 1967 issued the famous Three No's of Khartoum – "no peace with Israeli, no recognition of Israel, no negotiations with Israel."[81] Both of these statements have been grievously twisted and misunderstood, as we shall see in Chapter 7. Suffice it here to note that both come from mainstream and even official bodies, not from marginal groups whose words could be easily dismissed.

In addition to identifying extremist or atypical comments as such, I will be careful to use damaging quotes, quotes that discredit the speaker, only to the degree that they are of continuing relevance to the conflict today. Thus, for example, Herzl's rather racist contention that Jewish settlement in Palestine would constitute "a rampart of Europe against Asia, an outpost of civilization as opposed to barbarism"[82] would be a mere historical curiosity, were it not for the fact that it echoes the eerily prescient remarks of Campbell-Bannerman on the necessity of implanting a foreign body in the heart of the

[Arab] nation as well as those of the recently retired former Israeli Prime Minister, later Defense Minister, Ehud Barak, who describes Israel as "a villa in the jungle."[83] Similarly, a Palestinian Authority Minister is quoted as saying: "The Palestinian people accepted the Oslo agreements as a first step and not as a permanent settlement, based on the premise that war and struggle in the land is more efficient than a struggle from a distant land" [i.e. Tunisia].[84] This statement was made at the height of the first Intifada, but it perfectly captures Israelis' ongoing fears that, when Palestinian leaders are not "speaking English," they still have Israel's destruction in mind.

To protect the privacy of the people whose stories I tell I have changed the names and, when it does not violate the essence of the story, sometimes also the gender of the protagonist. All of the people whose stories are told here have agreed to my use of their experiences. Because this book is addressed primarily to an American audience, 12 of the 25 stories recount the experiences of Americans trying to understand the conflict; seven focus on Palestinian lives and six on Israeli lives.

Lastly, since Israel has never told the world exactly where its national boundaries lie, there is a problem of how to refer to the place that is the subject of this book. Is Israel the place that is defined by the Mediterranean on the west and the armistice line of the 1947–1949 war, the Green Line, in the East? The Green Line is the eastern boundary of the "universally agreed upon" two-state solution, at least as a point of departure for some as-yet-to-be-negotiated land swaps. If the term "Israel" were used to denote this land, then the land to the east of the Green line, up to the Jordan River, would be the State of Palestine (including Gaza). The United Nations General Assembly has recognized Palestine as an observer (i.e. non-voting) state. But, given the reality of Israeli settlement expansion into Palestinian territory and the imagined land-swaps to come, the Palestinian-Israeli boundary is unknown at present.

What *is* known is this: Israel has controlled the entire area of historic Palestine since 1967, governing the Occupied Territories by military law and Israel inside the Green Line (but excluding Gaza) by civil law. This combined entity can be referred to in several ways: as "Israel and Palestine," as "Israel and the Occupied Territories," as "historic Palestine," as "Mandate Palestine" or as "British Palestine" (the latter two terms referring to the League of Nations Palestine Mandate that allowed Great Britain to govern this land from 1918 to 1948).

Israeli hard-liners will object to this vocabulary. They do not concede that there is an Israeli occupation, on the grounds that Palestine was never an independent state and therefore its territory is "disputed" rather than occupied. Further, these same people will argue that because Great Britain severed what is now Jordan from the original "Palestinian mandate" of 1918, Jordan should rightly continue to be considered part of Mandatory Palestine. The thinly veiled implication is this: were Jordan to be considered part of Mandatory Palestine, it could become the home of Palestinians, with the result that all the land from the Jordan River to the Mediterranean Sea could be turned into an exclusively Jewish Israel. This hoped-for arrangement is sometimes referred to as the "Transjordan option." Some Israeli governments have made attempts to argue for the Transjordan option, but the entire hard-line position – that there is no Occupation, that Israel's rightful eastern and western boundaries are the Jordan River and the Mediterranean Sea, respectively, and that Jordan is the proper home of the Palestinians – has been rejected by virtually the whole world and is not in play as a political option at the present time.[85]

Despite the fact that the Transjordan option has been universally rejected, it draws some of its strength from observations that *are* correct. First, national boundaries are neither eternal nor immutable, as witness the on-going debate at the core of this book about the boundaries of Israel and Palestine. Second, Jordan's sense of national identity is, indeed, a recent and somewhat arbitrary construction.[86] Third, given the recent collapse of the peace talks and the increasingly open discussion of the possibility that Palestine and Israel might wind up being one state, the Zionists most desperately committed to ethno-religious exclusivity need to imagine a place to which Palestinians could be "transferred" with a fig leaf of legitimacy. The Transjordan option is their hedge against the one-state solution, which would require Israel to become multi-cultural and multi-national. To the degree that discussions of the one-state solution will be heard with greater frequency in the future, we can expect to also hear more of the counter-discourse, the "Transjordan option."

For purposes of this book, I will use the terms "historic Palestine," "Mandate Palestine," "Israel/Palestine" and "Israel and the Occupied Territories" to mean the same thing: the land from the river to the sea.

PLAN OF THE BOOK

In the book that follows, I begin in the present, depicting things that politically minded tourists can easily see if they choose to travel in the area. My account of the contemporary facts on the ground and the logic that governs them (Chapter 2) is drawn from more than a decade of my own annual observations of the unfolding reality of the conflict, as well as eleven years of academic fact-finding trips to the region. I begin with contemporary realities because only in the murder mystery does the reader really want to wait until the very end to find out what happened. I hope that beginning in the highly contentious present will arouse the readers' interest in the history that brought us to the current impasse.

Having described present conditions, I use Chapter 3 to offer some basic concepts – human rights, theories of race, and nation – that will be useful for understanding this conflict as well as many others. Chapter 4 provides a fuller analysis of the logic of Zionism, a doctrine that is at the heart of the present troubles. To make Zionism more understandable to western audiences, I explore the parallels between Zionism and the civil rights struggle in America.

The second part of the book is a brief history, divided into periods defined in the work of historian Mark Tessler[87]:

- from the beginnings of Zionism in the late 19th century to the founding of the state of Israel and the associated expulsion of the Palestinians (the *Nakba)* in 1947–1949 (Chapter 5);
- from the early days of the Israeli state to its 1967 conquest of the entirety of historic Palestine (Chapter 6);
- from the beginning of the Occupation to the emergence of the first wave of massive, organized resistance, the *Intifada* of 1987 (Chapter 7); and
- from the first *Intifada* through the wilderness of the interminable, fruitless and, I argue, disingenuous "peace processes" to the present time (Chapter 8).

At the end of the history section, in the third part of the book, I turn to a discussion of the primary frameworks that historians, journalists, and activists use for summing up this history (Chapter 9): Israeli self-defense, genocide, apartheid, and settler colonialism: ethnic cleansing/sociocide. In Chapter 10, I revisit the question of Zionism, asking whether, when all the historic evidence is considered, it might be judged to be a successful or a failed political project.

In the final chapter of the book, I consider how Americans might want to respond to the current situation in Israel/Palestine; what tools of education, law, economics, volunteering, and popular resistance might change the course of events for the better. Put differently, the final part of the book considers what we might do once we have been told the stories and the facts, and can no longer unknow what we have come to know.

NOTES

[1] Michael Leunig. (2012, December 11). Just a Cartoonist with a Moral Duty to Speak. *The Sunday Morning Herald*, Melbourne, Australia, retrieved from https://blackwar.org/art/

[2] https://www.traffickinginstitute.org/incontext-archbishop-desmond-tutu/

[3] Mahmood Mamdani. (2004). Good Muslim, Bad Muslim. New York: Pantheon Books.

[4] Isabel Kershner. (2008, December 16). UN human rights investigator expelled by Israel, *The New York Times*, retrieved from http://www.nytimes.com/2008/12/16/world/middleeast/16mideast.html?_r=0. When the human rights standard is suppressed or ignored, the analysis inevitably places self-defined Israeli "security" concerns far ahead of the human rights of Palestinian individuals and their communities.

[5] Adalah retrieved from http://adalah.org/eng

[6] 1for3 retrieved from http://1for3.org/

[7] Addameer retrieved from http://www.addameer.org/

[8] Al-Qaws retrieved from http://www.alqaws.org/?id=500

[9] Badil retrieved from http://www.badil.org/

[10] Right to Education retrieved from http://electronicintifada.net/people/birzeit-university-right-education-campaign/

[11] Al Bustan retrieved from https://buildpalestine.com/campaign/help-build-al-bustan-community-center/

[12] Riwaq retrieved from http://www.riwaq.org/home. Alice Rothchild. (2010, January 5). Beautiful Resistance in Bethlehem's Aida Refugee Camp, *Mondoweiss*, retrieved http://mondoweiss.net/2010/01/beautiful-resistance-in-bethlehems-aida-refugee-camp

[13] Edward Said. (1979). *Orientalism*. New York: Vintage Books. Sut Jhally (2009). *Reel Bad Arabs*. Media Education Foundation retrieved from http://www.mediaed.org/cgi-bin/commerce.cgi?preadd=action&key=412

[14] Jhally *op. cit.*

[15] Alison Kysia. (2014, April 21). A People's History of Muslims in the United States *If We Knew Our History*, Zinn Educational Project, retrieved from http://www.juancole.com/2014/04/peoples-history-muslims.html?utm_source=dlvr.it&utm_medium=twitter

[16] Sut Jhally and Bathsheba Ratzkoff. (2008). *Peace, Propaganda and the Promised Land*. Media Education Foundation, retrieved from http://www.mediaed.org/cgi-bin/commerce.cgi?preadd=action&key=117

[17] Jodi Rudoren. (2013, August 4). In a West Bank Culture of Conflict, Boys Wield the Weapon at Hand, *New York Times*, retrieved from http://www.nytimes.com/2013/08/05/world/middleeast/rocks-in-hand-a-boy-fights-for-his-west-bank-village.html?r=0

[18] Jhally and Ratzkoff, *op. cit.*

[19] Lori Allen. (2013). *The Rise and Fall of Human Rights: Cynicism and Politics in Occupied Palestine*. Stanford: Stanford University Press.

[20] In fact, because Israel taxes German and Austrian reparations payments to Holocaust survivors (which the United States declined to do), *Ha'aretz* reports that more than a quarter of Israel's population of Holocaust survivors live in poverty. Yarden Skop. (2014, April 24). 50,000 Holocaust survivors in Israel live in poverty, *Ha'aretz*, retrieved from http://www.haaretz.com/news/national/.premium-1.586970

[21] "Zionism has often been described as a pioneering mentality. Given that Zionism, the desire to live in an exclusively Jewish state, was developed at a time when no such state existed, the insistence on understanding Zionism as pioneering is probably correct, at least

for the first generation of Israelis. Now, however, many Israelis have living grandparents who went to the same schools and served in the same army regiments and, thus, the pioneering analogy is less apt." Tom Segev. (2001). *Elvis in Jerusalem: Post-Zionism and the Americanization of Israel* (New York: Holt and Company), p. 14. Some analysts argue that Israeli society has entered a "post-Zionist" (i.e. routinized, no longer pioneering) phase. See Ephraim Nimni (ed.). (2003). *The Challenge of Post-Zionism: Alternatives to Israeli Fundamentalist Politics* London: Zed Books. And now that Israel faces renewed and ever more acute challenges to its legitimacy, its Prime Minister, Benyamin Netanyahu, has jokingly referred to the arrival of a post-post-Zionist era. See Segev, *op. cit.*, p. 8, and Horit Herman Peled and Yoav Peled. (2011). "Post-post-Zionism: Confronting the Death of the Two-State Solution," *New Left Review*, 67: 97–118.

[22] http://www.ezquotes.com/author/10512-Daniel_Patrick_Moynihan

[23] Israel is about 8,000 square miles in size, the Occupied Palestinian Territories, about 2,324 square miles. New Jersey is 8, 721 square miles in size. Retrieved from http://www.cartercenter.org/countries/israel_and_the_palestinian_territories.html

[24] Maps of War, "The Imperial History of the Middle East," retrieved from http://mapsofwar.com/ind/imperial-history.html

[25] I have used most of the information in this footnote in Eve Spangler. (2013). No Exit: Palestinian Film in the Shadow of the Nakba, in John Michalczyk and Raymond G. Helmick, SJ (eds.) *Through a Lens Darkly: Films of Genocide, Ethnic Cleansing and Atrocities* (New York: Peter Lang), p. 211.

Statistics about the *Nakba* are difficult to pin down. The count of the original Palestinian population is distorted by the fact that many people tried to stay away from official censuses, fearing their association with taxation and conscription. The chaos of the war also made population estimates more difficult. And finally the toll of the *Nakba* has been a matter of political controversy, giving one set of scholars motives for exaggerating the count and others a stake in minimizing it.

Nevertheless, there is considerable consistency between the most careful Palestinian and Israeli scholarship. Their findings, in turn, are also consistent with UN sources. Rashid Khalidi (1997) puts the expulsions of the Nakba a 50% of the Palestinian population in *Palestinian Identity: The Construction of Modern National Consciousness* (New York: Columbia University Press), 21. Ilan Pappe. (2006). *The Ethnic Cleansing of Palestine* (London: One World Publications), p. 9, concurs, but notes that expulsions did not end in 1949. Instead they continued, albeit in less intense form, until 1956 and resumed in 1967. In 1950, at the end of the Nakba but amidst on-going "transfer," the Israeli Central Bureau of Statistics put the Arab population of Israel/Palestine 1,172,100. Retrieved from http://israelipalestinian.procon.org/view.resource.php?resourceID=000636#chart10).

In the same year, 1950, the United Nations Relief Works Agency (UNRWA), whose mandate is to serve Palestinian refugees, lists over 750,000 refugees on its rolls, while acknowledging that their figures undercount the true number of refugees, retrieved from http://www.unrwa.org/palestine-refugees. By 1952, UNRWA's count wast 914,000 refugees. This would include a more exact count as well as births within the refugee community, retrieved from https://www.unrwa.org/what-we-do/eligibility-registration

Although the Israeli and UN numbers do not align perfectly (not all refugees were inside Israel/Palestine and not all Palestinians in that territory were refugees) these figures nevertheless suggest that as many as three quarters of all Palestinians could have been refugees by 1950. Certainly these official figures support the claim that 50% is a conservative estimate of the number of Palestinian refugees.

[26] I have used most of the information in this footnote in Spangler, *op. cit.* p. 212. The same problems that plague the measurement of refugees also beset estimates of the number of destroyed villages. Here the principle sources in English are Walid Khalidi (ed.) (1992). *All that Remains: The Palestinian Villages Occupied and Depopulated by Israeli in 1948* (Washington, D.C.: Institute for Palestine Studies), Salman Abu Sitta. (2000). *The Palestinian Nakba 1948* (London: The Palestine Return Centre) and Benny Morris. (2004). *The Birth of the Palestinian Refugee Problem Revisited* (Cambridge, England: Cambridge University Press). These scholars have much of their bibliography in common, but use different metrics and methodologies – disagreeing, for example, on how they count the displacement of Bedouin communities that lacked permanent structures, neighborhoods (villages) within cities, and adjacent villages that had merged. Walid Khalidi and his contributing authors actually visited the sites of the destroyed villages. Despite differences, however, a reasonably consistent picture of catastrophic removal emerges from all three sources: Benny Morris lists 369 totally destroyed, partially destroyed, and depopulated villages, Walid Khalidi 418, and Abu Sitta 531. For a summary of the methodological choices made by these three authors, see Walid Khalidi, *op. cit.*, Appendix IV, 585–586.

[27] https://www.cia.gov/library/publications/the-world-factbook/geos/is.html. For the West Bank and Gazan populations see, respectively: *CIA World Factbook,* retrieved from https://www.cia.gov/library/publications/the-world-factbook/geos/we.html; https://www.cia.gov/library/publications/the-world-factbook/geos/gz.html

[28] Data about population size is always a politically sensitive and contested topic in Palestine and Israel. The number of settlers is particularly controversial. Arutz Sheva, a settler source, acknowledges 389, 250 Jewish settlers in the West Bank and another 375,000 in East Jerusalem, whose "annexation" is universally recognized as illegal, totaling some 764,000 illegal settlers. These numbers date from 2014, and the same source claims that by now the number of settlers has risen to 800,000. *Arutz Sheva,* retrieved from http://www.israelnationalnews.com/Articles/Article.aspx/18210#.VpK885scTIU.
The population growth rate in the settlements, though declining, is still approximately twice as high as that in Jerusalem, see Jacob Magid, "Settler growth rate declines for sixth straight year," *The Times of Israel,* January 21, 2018, retrieved from https://www.timesofisrael.com/settler-growth-rate-declines-for-sixth-straight-year/

[29] *CIA World Factbook,* retrieved from https://www.cia.gov/library/publications/the-world-factbook/geos/we.html; https://www.cia.gov/library/publications/the-world-factbook/geos/gz.html

[30] *Ibid.*

[31] United Nations Relief and Work Agency for Palestine Refugees in the Near East (UNRWA) now reports Gaza and West Bank population data separately. For Gaza see https://www.unrwa.org/where-we-work/gaza-strip, and for the West Bank see https://www.unrwa.org/where-we-work/west-bank

[32] http://www.cartercenter.org/countries/israel_and_the_palestinian_territories.html

[33] Jewish Virtual Library, retrieved from http://www.jewishvirtuallibrary.org/jsource/Judaism/jewpop.html

[34] Pew Research Center, retrieved from http://www.pewforum.org/global-religious-landscape-muslim.aspx

[35] https://www.brainyquote.com/topics/hope

[36] http://uis.unesco.org/en/country/ps?theme=education-and-literacy

[37] The degree to which Islam recognizes its Jewish and Christian antecedents is also reflected in popular child-naming practices. There are many Moussa's in the Palestinian

community and many Aisa's as well. These names are translations of Moses and Jesus, respectively.

38 "Why Can't I Own a Canadian?" (2002), retrieved from http://www.humanistsofutah.org/archivalsample/archive-2001-2010/2002-2/

39 Max Weber, The Social Psychology of the World Religions, in Hans Gerth and C. Wright Mills (eds.). (1958). *From Max Weber* (New York: Oxford University Press), 267–301.

40 Mark R. Cohen, (1994) *Under Crescent and Cross: The Jews in the Middle Ages.* Princeton: Princeton University Press.

41 Norman M. Naimark (1997). *The Russians in Germany: A History of the Soviet Zone of Occupation, 1945–1949.* (Cambridge, MA.: Harvard University Press), p. 37.

42 Cohen, *op. cit.,* chapter 1 "Myths and Countermyths," is also masterful in tracing changes in Jewish accounts of Jewish-Muslim relations; emphasizing hostility between the two groups only after the development of the Zionist project and especially after the 1968 occupation, creating a retrospective narrative of eternal enmity that "justifies" Israeli state policies. His conclusion, quoting Iraqi Jewish historian Heskel Haddad (p. 14), is: "Although there were trying times for Jews in Muslim lands, many historians consider their lot superior to those of Jews in European countries … [I]nstances of persecution did occur: Jews were killed and robbed with greater frequency than their Moslem neighbors. Nevertheless, anti-Jewish pogroms were less common in Moslem countries than in Christian lands. The mass burnings at the stake which took place in many sections of Europe were not known to have occurred in the Moslem world. Whereas Jews in Europe were expelled many times form their homes, only one similar instance is recorded in Moslem history."

43 A recent Ha'aretz article notes that young people in the tiny West Bank community of Samaritans prefer the Israeli experience less from fear of the Muslim neighbors and more from the lure of Israeli economic growth. Davide Lerner and Esrz Whitehouse. (2018, May 10). "Not Muslim, Not Jewish: Ancient Community in the West Bank feels Increasingly Israeli," *Ha'aretz,* retrieved from https://www.haaretz.com/israel-news/.premium.MAGAZINE-for-ancient-samaritan-community-a-new-test-of-loyalty-1.6075509

44 For purposes of this book I am using the terms "collective actor" and "parties" interchangeably. In either case, I am referring to the behavior that individuals engage in with others, and in service to a sense of purpose that binds them together and that transcends each member's own purely private agendas. Collective actors or parties can take many forms – corporations, unions, non-government organizations, faith communities, social movements. Some are formally structured to take maximum advantage of the legal, the socio-cultural, and economic environment in which they operate. Others are organizationally fluid and ephemeral. But all, from the most informal to the most structured, are self-consciously dedicated to a common purpose and can be expected to act, with great variations in competence, to achieve those goals.

45 Recent critical scholarship suggests that, in this long and tumultuous history, the Israelite Kingdom was of relatively minor significance. Keith W. Whitelam. (1996). *The Invention of Ancient Israel: The Silencing of Palestinian History.* New York: Routledge. Yael Zerubavel. (1995). *Recovered Roots: Collective Memory and the Making of Israeli National Tradition.* Chicago: University of Chicago Press. Edward Said. (2000). Invention, Memory, Place. *Critical Inquiry* 26(2):175–192.

46 For a compelling visual presentation of this history see the website Maps of War, *The Imperial History of the Middle East,* retrieved from http://www.mapsofwar.com/ind/imperial-history.html

[47] The Campbell-Bannerman Report. (1907) full text retrieved from https://archive.org/stream/imperialconferen02jebbuoft/imperialconferen02jebbuoft_djvu.txt.
Dr. Mohsen Saleh makes the point that even if, as some allege, the Campbell-Bannerman Report cannot be taken at face value, many other sources affirm the same point. Mohsen Saleh. (2017, December 12). Is the Campbell-Bannerman document real or fake? Al Zaytouna Centre for Studies and Consultations, retrieved from https://eng.alzaytouna.net/2017/09/28/political-analysis-campbell-bannerman-document-real-fake/

[48] Shlomo Sand. (2009). *The Invention of the Jewish People* (New York: Verso) provides a thorough and skeptical evaluation of these claims. For a similar historical review focused only on Jerusalem, see Gary Leupp. (2014, November 26). A Brief History of Jerusalem: Eternal, Undivided Jewish Capital? *Counterpunch,* retrieved from http://www.counterpunch.org/2014/11/26/a-brief-history-of-jerusalem/

[49] Sand, *ibid.*

[50] "Maps of War," *op. cit.*

[51] Sand, *op. cit.*, pp. 275–276.

[52] Sand, *op. cit.*, p. 277.

[53] Sand, *op. cit.*, p. 184.

[54] Adam Keller. (2014, February 14). "From Canaan to Spain," *Crazy Country,* retrieved from http://adam-keller2.blogspot.com/2014/02/from-canaan-to-spain.html/

[55] Sand, *op. cit.*, p. 262.

[56] Keller, *op. cit.*

[57] Tom Segev, *op. cit.*, p. 5.

[58] Saleh Abdel Jawad, The Arab and Palestinian Narratives of the 1948 War, in Robert I. Rotberg (ed.). (2006). *Israeli and Palestinian Narratives of Conflict: History's Double Helix* (Bloomington: Indian University Press), 72–114. See also, Amira Hass. (2014). A Nightmare Question highlights the importance of Oral History, *Ha'aretz*, retrieved from http://www.haaretz.com/news/national/.premium-1.620414

[59] Refugee statistics are nearly always confusing to those not immersed in the subject. Of the 4.9 million Palestinians registered with the United Nations as refugees, roughly three million live outside the area of Israel/Palestine in refugee camps around the Middle East, while another 2.0 million refugees live as people internally displaced somewhere within the lands of Israel/Palestine. About 90% of Gaza's population, for example, are refugees from the Negev.

[60] Sand, *op. cit.*, pp. 272–280.

[61] Anita Shapira, a left of center Zionist historian reluctantly concludes that, by 1947, even the left-most Zionists had committed to the use of force for securing Palestinian lands. Anita Shapira. (1992). *Land and Power: The Zionist Resort to Force, 2881–1948.* Stanford: Stanford University Press.

[62] Ilan Pappe (2017). *The Biggest Prison on Earth: A History of the Occupied Territories.* London: One World Publishers.

[63] Nur Masalha. (1992) *The Expulsion of the Palestinians: The Concept of "Transfer" in Zionist Political Thought.* Washington, D.C.: The Institute for Palestine Studies.

[64] Eve Spangler (2010, June 14). Attacking Humanitarian Aid. *Counterpunch,* retrieved from http://www.counterpunch.org/2010/06/14/attacking-humanitarian-aid/ and Mazen Qumsiyeh. (2011). *Popular Resistance in Palestine: A History of Hope and Empowerment* (London: Pluto Press), p. 16.

[65] Baruch Kimmerling and Joel Migdal (2003). *The Palestinian People, A History.* (Cambridge, MA: Harvard University Press), Chapter 1.

66 Jeff Halper (2010) The Global Pacification Industry – an Interview, retrieved from https://www.youtube.com/watch?v=SVa0QbH8YcA. Naomi Klein (2007). *The Shock Doctrine*. (New York: Henry Holt and Company), chapter 21. Yotam Feldman (2014) "The Lab," retrieved from http://www.aljazeera.com/programmes/witness/2014/05/lab-20145475423526313.html
Stephen Zunes. (2002, May 1). Why the US Supports Israel. *Foreign Policy in Focus,* retrieved from http://www.fpif.org/articles/why_the_us_supports_israel

67 John J. Mearsheimer and Stephen M. Walt. (2007). *The Israel Lobby and U.S. Foreign Policy.* New York: Farrar, Straus and Giroux. Joseph Massad. (2006). Blaming the Lobby, *Al Ahram Weekly*, retrieved from https://electronicintifada.net/content/blaming-lobby/5910

68 Carlos Stenger. (2012). Israel Missed Its Chance – Again, *The Daily Beast*, retrieved from http://www.americantaskforce.org/daily_news_article/2012/11/27/israel_missed_its_chance%E2%80%94again

69 Asa Winstanley. (2013) The old will die and the young will forget – did Ben Gurion say it? *Electronic Intifada*, retrieved from http://electronicintifada.net/blogs/asa-winstanley/old-will-die-and-young-will-forget-did-ben-gurion-say-it

70 Bret Stephens. (2017, April 29). The Climate of Complete Certainty, *New York Times*, retrieved from https://www.nytimes.com/2017/04/28/opinion/climate-of-complete-certainty.html

71 There is substantial agreement on the basic facts of the Nakba among Palestinian scholars like Saleh Abdel Jawad, Salman Abu Sitta, Ghada Karmi, Rashid Khalidi, and Walid Khalidi and those of Israeli "new" historians (and their American co-authors) including Benny Morris, Tom Segev, Baruch Kimmerling, Joel Migdal, Avi Shlaim, Eugene Rogan, and Ilan Pappe all of whose works have been cited in this chapter.

72 The distinction between extremist, unrepresentative comments and mainstream, representative ones can be a moving target in an unstable political environment. Nevertheless, using common sense criteria does allow us to recognize that some comments, if made in everyday conversation, would pass muster, while others would elicit protests and disclaimers from the audience.

73 http://www.youtube.com/watch?v=M539PgDjbas

74 Bradley Burston. (2018, June 26). Zionism's Terrorist Heritage, *Ha'aretz*, retrieved from https://www.haaretz.com/opinion/.premium-zionism-s-terrorist-heritage-1.6217633

75 https://www.cnn.com/2017/08/15/politics/trump-charlottesville-delay/index.html

76 Alon Pinkas. (2013, September 6). Israel Backs Limited Strike against Syria, retrieved from http://www.nytimes.com/2013/09/06/world/middleeast/israel-backs-limited-strike-against-syria.html?pagewanted=all&_r=0/

77 Gideon Levy. (2012, February 19). Enemies, A Hate Story, *Ha'aretz,* retrieved from http://www.haaretz.com/print-edition/opinion/enemies-a-hate-story-1.413424

78 Hamas Charter. (1988), retrieved from http://www.hamascharter.com

79 Khaled Hroub. (2017, Summer). A Newer Hamas? The Revised Charter, *Journal of Palestine Studies*, XLVI(4):100–111.

80 Benny Morris. (1999). *Righteous Victims.* (New York: Knopf), p. 99.

81 The League of Arab States. (1967). The Khartoum Declaration, retrieved from http://www.jewishvirtuallibrary.org/the-khartoum-resolutions

82 Theodor Herzl, *The Jewish State* in the section Palestine or Argentina? Retrieved from http://www.jewishvirtuallibrary.org/jsource/Zionism/herzl2b.html

83 Ehud Barak famously referred to Israel as "a villa in the jungle" and reiterated this position on a number of occasions. For a relatively sympathetic assessment, see Larry Derfner.

(2012, November 26). Ehud Barak to Step Down: On his De-evolution and Israel's, *+972*, retrieved from http://972mag.com/ehud-baraks-de-evolution-and-israels/60889/. He re-echoes this sentiment in a 2011 address to the United Nations: "Israel is clearly an island of stability," Barak said. "An outpost of the free world values in a tough neighborhood, where there is no mercy for the weak, no second opportunity for those who cannot defend themselves." Speech reported in *Ha'aretz*, March 23, 2011, retrieved from http://www.haaretz.com/news/diplomacy-defense/barak-israel-facing-regional-earthquake-and-diplomatic-tsunami-1.351285

[84] This statement is attributed to Palestinian Authority Minister of Supplies, Abdel Aziz Shahian, allegedly in a May 30, 2000 article in *Al Ayyam*, a West Bank daily. However the original document cannot be found on the internet. Nevertheless, the echo chamber of the internet produces multiple undocumented uses of the quote, the best of which can be found from http://www.wildolive.co.uk/quotes.htm

[85] In the article cited here, conservative Israeli politicians admit that the "Transjordan option" is nonsense. Noam Sheizaf. (2014, May 12). What is the Israeli Right's one-state vision? *+972*, retrieved from http://972mag.com/what-is-the-israeli-rights-one-state-vision/90755/

[86] Joseph Massad. (2001). *Colonial Effects: The Making of National Identity in Jordan* (New York: Columbia University Press), also emphasizes the socially constructed character of Jordanian national identity.

[87] Mark Tessler (2009). *A History of the Israeli-Palestinian Conflict*. Indiana University Press.

IN ISRAEL AND PALESTINE

What You See Is What We Bought

Once you know some things, you can't unknow them. It's a burden that can never be given away.

Alice Hoffman[1]

Paul's Story

Recently an old friend, now a technology consultant, came to advise a client in the Boston area. He stayed at my house and, over dinner, asked me what I was working on these days. Paul knows very little about the Middle East, so when I began explaining my work he responded with the usual "Oh it's too complicated." But when I pointed out that Israel demands three things that were incompatible – control over all the land of Israel/Palestine, to be a Jewish state, and to be a democracy – Paul's face lit up. "Oh, I get it," he said, drawing on his own experience as a consultant. "Sooner or later, every good technology consultant needs to remind clients: "Fast, Cheap, Reliable. Pick any two."

And that, indeed, is exactly the right way to grasp the Israeli position. Land, democracy, Jewish dominance. Pick any two.

Some of the possible combinations are less problematic than others. Were Israelis to choose land and genuine democracy, they could create a single multi-cultural state hospitable to both Palestinians and Israelis. Were they to choose Jewish identity and democracy, pursued only in the areas where Jews are a supermajority, they could create the two-state solution that the world calls for. But the combination of land and Jewishness (with democratic rights monopolized by the dominant group) is particularly lethal, creating the kind of incident we encountered on a recent trip. An Israeli soldier stands guard over streets in the Palestinian

© KONINKLIJKE BRILL NV, LEIDEN, 2019 | DOI:10.1163/9789004394148_002

> city of Hebron where only illegal settlers may walk or drive, Palestinian residents of the city being forbidden their own streets. He barks at us "Who is your guide?" and we reply that he is a Palestinian peace activist, forbidden to accompany us into this part of town. "Peace activist?" snorts the soldier. "Oh yeah, they all say that, but this – pointing to his automatic rifle – is the only peace there will be."

Every year for the last thirteen years I have visited Palestine/Israel, eleven times leading a group of students who had spent a semester studying the conflict. While my students are better informed than most Americans even before the trip begins, seeing Israel/Palestine in person creates the most vivid and compelling form of knowledge. We spend about half our time in Israel and half in Palestine, visiting human rights groups, religious landmarks, sites of human rights violations, and communities that embody "normal life" on both sides.

The Occupation comes to life when we see checkpoints, settlements, settler-only roads, and the ubiquitous presence of armed Israeli settlers and soldiers. It also comes to life when we see Palestinian resistance and efficacy; when we meet community leaders who brag about their kids' education, show us grants they are writing to fund summer circus camps, walk us through high-tech gleaming skyscrapers in Ramallah, and welcome us to tea in their tents in the desert.

We spend time with the little known Palestinian communities inside Israel in the Negev and the Galilee. They are precariously poised between the citizenship rights they enjoy (e.g. to vote, to attend segregated public schools, to use the health care system) and the "national" rights they are denied as "non-Jews" (e.g. to buy land, to unify their families), living lives marked by discrimination, marginalization, and oppression.[2] Their sense of ethnicity does not permit them to forget either their claims to a Palestinian identity or their ties to Palestinian land. In Ayn Hod, the families displaced from Ein Hod look down on their former homes (now an Israeli artists' colony) and teach their children the names of the Palestinian families who once owned each building. In the Negev, some Palestinians, the Bedouin, still follow a pastoral way of life. One of them, Mariam Abu Rogaig,[3] created a cosmetics company using traditional Bedouin formulas and operating from a complex of tents. She, too, must balance her popularity with Israeli customers against her anger at the water restrictions that burden her community and her business.

Israeli activists who work with Palestinians to ensure their rights broaden our understanding of the conflict. Some of them have paid a considerable price in career advancement and social acceptance for joining the anti-Occupation Israeli left. Some have even put their lives on the line for their political beliefs.[4] Israeli politicians and soldiers can be seen in any television news broadcast about the "peace process," while Israeli dissidents, working in NGO's like *Zochrot* (Remembrance)[5] and *Who Profits?*[6] are almost unknown in America. The more mainstream Israeli settlers and soldiers express varying opinions about their relationships to Palestinians, some arguing for repression, some for accommodation.

We come away learning that, contrary to media images, victimhood and rage are not the sum and substance of either Palestinian or Israeli identity. We see people on both sides of the conflict choosing to make a difference, choosing to devote all or part of their lives to the struggle for justice. We also see people on both sides living ordinary lives, taking pride in their children's accomplishments, dancing at weddings, arguing with the in-laws. All of this would be virtually impossible to learn from American mainstream media. Palestinians are never depicted as warm and hospitable, highly educated[7] and immensely imaginative about living the largest possible lives under the most constricting of circumstances. Israel is rarely depicted as containing a vital Palestinian community and even a Jewish activist community willing to challenge the legitimacy of Zionism in its current ultra-nationalistic form.

Most vividly, the trip allows us to see how Israel uses two major strategies to rid itself of Palestinians or to achieve their total subordination. The first is physical violence, not limited to the early years of state formation, but ongoing today. The second is bureaucratic violence, operating under the color of law that makes life unreasonably burdensome for Palestinians, imposing on them an inferior set of rights and an inferior quality of life. Two stories illustrate the use and misuse of violence and bureaucratic domination.

Anwar's Story

For many years, Anwar was the bus driver for my students' trip through Israel and Palestine. On most days, Anwar was a cheerful presence, greeting students by name, occasionally buying them ice cream, and always willing to answer their questions about where we were going and what we would see. But one day Anwar appeared to be deeply unhappy. We were on our way to a site I had seen many times, so I sent the students off with other faculty members and sat with Anwar. I asked if something was indeed wrong.

After some hesitation he told me that his nephew had been killed the week before and that just yesterday his family had received an official notice that there was to be no further police investigation into his death. Of course I asked how his nephew had died, imagining a teenage boy in a road accident, but my imagination was way off the mark.

In fact, Anwar's nephew, in his last year of high school, had just received notice that he was admitted to his first choice college for the following academic year. The boy was ecstatic, jumping up and down on his bed, and shouting his happiness to the world. Suddenly all his closest friends showed up, dressed in their "Sunday best." Anwar's nephew asked how they knew he had such great news to share, and how they organized a party so quickly. His friends just laughed, reminding him that they were invited to a wedding that night and they had only come to pick him up. They urged him to be quick about changing into his "wedding" suit and to come along.

Then a group of laughing, jostling teenagers proceeded to walk a mile or so along a dirt road connecting them to the next village, picking their way around the settlement that was growing near the road. Unbeknownst to the boys or anyone at the wedding, the settlers called the army, reporting a group of suspiciously well-dressed young Palestinian males in the vicinity. To oblige them, the highest-ranking Israeli soldier responding to their call declared the road a closed military zone. No signs were posted and no one was informed of this decision but nevertheless a closed military zone had now been created.

When the boys returned from the wedding walking along the same road they had used just hours before, they suddenly found themselves surrounded by an Israeli Army patrol shouting at them, demanding to know why they were in a closed military zone, demanding their IDs. All the other boys produced their papers. Anwar's nephew realized that his ID was in the pocket of his blue jeans on his bed at home. The other boys backed him up – explaining that he lived in their village and that he'd dressed in a hurry and forgot to transfer his papers from one pair of pants to another.

But the soldiers viewed the boys as potential terrorists: young men, well dressed (as suicide bombers sometimes were), one of them without papers, in a closed military zone. One soldier walked around behind Anwar's nephew and smashed his gun butt into the back of the boy's knees. He fell to the ground, the soldier leaned in, put his gun to the boy's head and fired, killing him instantly. A week later the official investigation was closed without a finding of wrongdoing on the soldier's part.

I have twice told this story to audiences that included a number of self-identified Israeli dissidents. Uniformly this story infuriates them. Interestingly none challenge the veracity of the account. Instead they argue that such egregious behavior is atypical and, in fact, a violation of the Israeli army's code of conduct. They may well be right in both these assertions, but that is not the point.

Rather, this story perfectly illustrates how violence is used by the Occupation: the incident is a horrible injustice, and Anwar's nephew is not the only victim. Everyone in his village and in surrounding villages now knows this story. It spread through the school, the Mosque, the Church, the market. Fear and powerlessness were reinforced; Palestinians were reminded that they live under military law and have no rights. The violence, however devastating to the boy's family and community, is as much a message as an act of policing run amok.

Munir's Story

On the second student trip, we met Munir in a village near Bethlehem, a five-minute bus ride to Manger Square and the Church of the Nativity. Recently, the Israelis re-zoned the village from Bethlehem into Jerusalem.

Now … watch closely … having made the village a part of Jerusalem with the stroke of a pen, the Israelis refused to issue blue Jerusalem ID cards to any of the residents, thereby making them illegal in their own homes since Palestinians need residency permits to live in Jerusalem. So one day, shortly before our arrival, Munir was arrested for trespass while sitting in the living room of the home built by his grandfather, in which he, his father, and his children were born. After his arrest, his home was put under demolition orders. The first time we met Munir, he had just returned from detention and was engaged in contesting the demolition order. On our next trip, Munir and his family were gone, but the house still stood. On the trip after that, the house had been demolished and Munir and his family were living abroad. Today the separation Wall fills the site of Munir's home, an Israeli McMansion showing over the top. Everything that happened to Munir's family was done under the cover of law.

During that same trip, one student made a film, focused on our Palestinian hosts. She asked respondents unexpected questions while the camera was recording. She asked Munir what peace would mean for him. "Peace?" he responded in a puzzled way. The film rolls as Munir shrugs and grimaces, looking for inspiration. Then you see his delight has he gropes for and finds his answer. "Peace," he says, nodding now with growing enthusiasm, "yes, peace would be the day I turn on the radio and I don't hear a report of anyone I know having been killed." Unsatisfied with that answer he tries again: "Peace would be getting on a bus and not seeing any soldiers carrying guns."

If you consider Anwar's story together with Munir's, you will understand that violence and bureaucratic domination work in tandem rather than separately. While bureaucratic domination is much more common than physical violence in the West Bank (the opposite is true in Gaza), it always trails in its wake the possibility of violence, hence Munir's summons to detention. When violence and bureaucracy work together, they produce the following strategies for ordering Israel's relations to the Palestinians living under Occupation: *settlement building* appropriates the land, *expulsions* remove Palestinians from the land, *suppression* renders the remaining Palestinians mute, and *containment* creates conditions of life that make it more likely that Palestinians will leave their land voluntarily. By these means Israel seeks to achieve its dream of an exclusively Jewish state.

SETTLEMENT BUILDING

Settlements are the most visible way that Israel is conquering Palestine. Israeli settlements expropriate Palestinian land[8] and divide Palestinian cities and villages from one another. Settlements are situated to command strategic hilltops and/or aquifers. They are connected to one another and to Israel inside the Green Line by a network of "Jewish only" roads that further divide Palestinian land into disconnected slivers. Settlers are a major source of violence and vigilantism against Palestinians, attacking individuals,[9] such as the Dawabsheh family mentioned before, uprooting olive and fruit orchards,[10] vandalizing mosques,[11] slaughtering livestock,[12] disposing of settlement waste on Palestinian lands.[13] Settler violence is simultaneously disclaimed and tolerated by the Israeli government. Settlements embody the central logic of the Occupation, which is designed to take all the land while making life so miserable and difficult for Palestinians that they will voluntarily leave.[14]

We see settlements everywhere we go in Palestine. It is literally impossible to drive through the West Bank for 10 minutes on any road without seeing a settlement. During our last trip we visited the settlement of Efrat. Students were surprised by how much it feels like a small suburban town and, in fact, the representative who met with us insisted that it is a town and denies that it is a settlement. When asked whether Efrat is a member of the Yesha (Settlement) Council, he just rolls his eyes. He tells us that he was a "sixties person" in Chicago years ago, when he realized that "he was fighting for everyone's rights but his own." So, he tells us, he claimed his right as a Jew to come to Israel and move into a settlement. He insists that the land of Efrat, which he claims to have walked decades ago as an exchange student, was unoccupied. But he refuses to answer the question: then who built the extensive terracing we see everywhere? He insists that Efrat is on the friendliest of terms with the surrounding Palestinian villages and that their leaders have been to Efrat to share meals. Since he described his past political activity in the U.S. as being an "ally" to various causes, we ask him what he does now to protect his Palestinian friends – whether he is part of any group trying to rein in settler violence against Palestinians. He responds that he's now too old for politics. On the morning of our visit, we had seen a photo of a young Palestinian boy, probably 8 or 9 years old, blindfolded and surrounded by Israeli soldiers in Hebron. When one of my students asked, in exasperation, whether our host thought that terrorizing children was acceptable behavior his reply was "Absolutely yes. Next question."

On the 2014 trip, I had a student hospitalized for emergency surgery. As it happened, that night the surgical recovery room was empty except for my student. Her anesthesiologist, a soft-spoken and conscientious young man, was an American doctor who had recently made *aliyah* to Israel (i.e. exercised his right as a Jewish person to move to Israel and instantly become a citizen with full rights). He seemed a little homesick. Perhaps for that reason, he spent a long time chatting with me and with the patient's roommate while monitoring his patient's recovery. Over the course of the conversation, we discovered that he, too, lived in a settlement and he discovered that we were touring Israel and Palestine on a human rights trip.

Without waiting to be asked, he began reciting the common settler talking points: why couldn't the Palestinians go to Jordan and leave Israel for the Jews? Didn't we know that the settlers took state land, not Palestinian land? Did we not know that *B'Tselem* (an Israeli human rights monitoring group) "staged" incidents designed to make settlers look bad? That no Israeli soldier would ever use his big machine gun against civilians, the guns were all just for show. His points were easily refuted. Jordan is a separate country whose king has been absolutely clear: he is not volunteering his country to be turned into a proxy version of Palestine. The Israeli state has the power to define any land it wants, especially privately owned Palestinian land, as "state land." A number of Israeli prime ministers have acknowledged the validity of *B'Tselem*'s findings. For a while the conversation felt a little bit like a skeet-shooting match: he lobbed his talking points into the air and one of us, the patient's roommate or I, shot them down.

The next morning, I felt very bad about that conversation and wished I had recognized sooner what his words were really showing me. Unlike the Efrat spokesperson, this was a very nice young man who one day discovered in himself the desire to live in Israel. Clearly he never paused to wonder that he could immediately accomplish his goal, while Palestinians born in Israel could not bring family members who lived 10 miles away, on the other side of a border, to rejoin their family. He never asked who lived on the land his settlement now occupied or how the settlement got that land – and nothing he encountered prompted him to do so. He was either deliberately instructed, or, being a very bright person, plucked out of the conversations around him all the settler justifications for their project. As long as he voiced those thoughts only to people who agreed with him, they sounded plausible. It was only in talking to us that he found that his taken-for-granted assumptions called into question.

I wish I had been less intent on debating and more sensitive to the essence of his claims, namely, that his life choices were ethically defensible. Had we focused more on where he was ethically right (in seeking a moral basis for his behavior, for example by insisting that he did not live on stolen land) than where he was factually wrong (in pretty much every statement he made) we might have been more successful in challenging his version of Zionism. The point-by-point rebuttals we offered him led only to frustration for all of us in the conversation.

Overall, settlement building expands the Jewish state at the expense of any possible Palestinian one. It reduces Palestinian areas to islands of land surrounded by checkpoints and barriers, stripped of water, contiguity, and economic viability. It exposes Palestinian villages to settler violence and harassment. Settlement building thus contributes directly and ferociously to the constriction of Palestinian life.

Moreover, settlement expansion is premised on thrusting Jewish settlers into territory denied them by international law, territory where they are hated by their Palestinian neighbors. The dangers that the Israeli government allows settlers to face on behalf of the state's expansionist policies give the lie to the claim that Israel is all about Jewish safety.

EXPULSION

Palestinian individuals deemed to have "no right" to live where they live are simply forced out, often without much warning. In Lifta, outside of Jerusalem, which we visit with a guide who experienced the expulsion as a child in 1948, we see a ghost town of empty stone homes, mosque, and granary. Israeli hippies are doing drugs by the spring-fed pool, and ultra-Orthodox settlers dog our footsteps, making rude noises. Graffiti saying "fuck the Arabs" deface the ancient stone interiors of the houses. In Lajun, we visit the "remains" of a Palestinian village that is completely obliterated but for a few cornerstones of old Palestinian homes. A kibbutz has taken over their land but does not use it, choosing instead to plant scraggly pine trees that cover the remains of the village and to use the village cemetery as a garbage dump.

Expulsion today is usually more bureaucratic and less physical. It is aided by another bureaucratic sleight of hand. A Palestinian citizen of Israel who marries a West Bank Palestinian cannot live with his/her spouse in Israel and may also be refused permission to live in the West Bank, which remains under military rule. In the case of such a dual refusal, the newly married couple has to seek refugee status outside the country.[15] The Israeli Supreme Court, in a 2012 ruling, said that to permit the Palestinian spouses of Israel's Palestinian citizens to live with them in Israel would be to "commit national suicide."[16] The prohibition on family unification for Palestinians thus leads to the expulsion of citizens and non-citizens alike. Adalah, a civil rights organization for Palestinian citizens of Israel, notes that, "no other state in the world denies the right to conduct a family life on the basis of national or ethnic belonging."[17]

In East Jerusalem, Palestinians need a Jerusalem residency permit to remain in their home. The permit creates Palestinians as legal residents, not citizens, despite the fact that Israel has illegally annexed East Jerusalem. Residency permits can be revoked if Israel decides that Jerusalem is not the center of life for a particular individual – for example, one who has gone abroad to study, one who is married to a Palestinian from the West Bank or Gaza, or who has fallen afoul of the Israeli bureaucracy in any of a variety of ways. B'Tselem, a leading Israeli human rights organization, documents the expulsion of 14,500 Palestinian residents of Jerusalem since the beginning of the Occupation.[18]

Notice here that many of these expulsions are enacted without bloodshed, and by recourse to legal tools of dubious morality. Shooting is not the only form of violence. Imagine, instead, the network of informants, the incentives to spy on neighbors, the distrust sown between teachers and students, employers and employees, and among family members in order to achieve the expulsion of 14,500 Jerusalemites in the last fifty years.

SUPPRESSION

 The balance between bureaucratic ploys and overt violence, prevalent in the West Bank, is reversed in Gaza. An alumnus of the trip who has returned numerous times to teach English as a second language in Nablus and in the town of Al Aqaba in the Jordan Valley, has written that "peace to Netanyahu means the pacification of the Palestinian people, not a Palestinian state as an equal partner in peace." [19]

The 2008–2009 "Operation Cast Lead" massacre in Gaza (which we witnessed from the relative safety of the West Bank during the first trip) represents one face of pacification. Operation Cast Lead involved the killing of at least 1,389 Palestinians in three weeks, the majority of them civilians, many of whom were taking refuge in places like schools and hospitals that should have been spared from the bombing.[20] In an outright violation of international humanitarian law Cast Lead embodied a deliberate policy of disproportionate response designed to punish civilian populations for acts of resistance to occupation committed by militants (another violation of international law).[21] This behavior was repeated in the summer of 2014 in Operation Protective Edge, which proved to be even more lethal than Operation Cast Lead. During July and August of 2014, Israeli Defense Forces killed some 2,200 Palestinians in Gaza[22] and wounded an additional 11,000.[23] The corresponding numbers of Israeli fatalities and wounded were 72 and 750 respectively.[24] As I re-write this chapter for the second edition, Israeli snipers shooting Palestinian protestors in the March of Return, have killed 135 Palestinians (including 17 women and children, and numerous journalists and paramedics) and injured 14, 605. No Israelis have been killed; five have been injured.[25]

"Disproportionate response" also has taken on new life in the form of vigilante violence by settlers all over the West Bank. "Price tag" attacks, discussed above, began as retaliations for specific acts of resistance by Palestinians as their name suggests. But these attacks also fit into the growing pattern of violence by which settlers harass and intimidate the Palestinian villagers and farmers around them, for example releasing wild boars on Palestinian farmland just as the crops ripen. Because Palestinians are forbidden to have guns, they are helpless to protect their crops from the marauding animals.[26] The U.S. State Department, which classifies "price tag" attacks as terrorism, reports that there were 399 such attacks in 2013 and that they went almost entirely uninvestigated and unpunished within the Israeli criminal justice system.[27]

"Price tag" attacks on mosques and churches are also occurring *inside* Israel – i.e. against Palestinian citizens of the country, as are settler attacks on Jews they deem insufficiently orthodox. For example, the Israeli blog *972 Magazine* posted an Israeli fundamentalist's justification for spitting on an 8-year-old Israeli Jewish girl who is insufficiently Orthodox.[28] Eventually the child's family decided that life in Beit Shemesh, where this incident occurred, had been made unbearable and they moved out.[29]

It seems that if you become sufficiently callous and determined to expel or pacify "the other" you will, soon enough, also expel and pacify the "other" within, anyone who has failed to support your plans with enough fervor. A current example comes from Facebook. In response to a *New York Times* ad in which Holocaust survivors and their descendants criticize an Israeli massacre in Gaza (Operation Protective Edge), some Israelis posted with comments like: "Go back to Auschwitz" and "Those are collaborators with the Nazis."[30] Labeling people who disagree with them as "collaborators" had a particularly eerie parallel during the week when Hamas publicly executed 18 Palestinian "collaborators" in Gaza.[31]

CONTAINMENT

Containment – or encirclement and constriction – is the predominant pattern of Israeli conduct in the West Bank and East Jerusalelm at the moment. The Israeli separation wall or barrier is the clearest visible form of containment. It is planned to be 709 kilometers long, or twice the length of the actual Green Line border between Israel and a possible Palestinian state. It's extended length means that it zigzags into Palestinian land, annexing farmland and aquifers as it goes. Eighty-five percent of the Israeli separation barrier deviates from the Green Line and intrudes into Palestinian property.[32]

Illegal settlements are also planted to surround Palestinian regions, cities, villages, neighborhoods, even streets, and individual homes. This strategic pattern of settlement placement means that Palestinian areas are cut off from transportation routes and from each other. The illegal settlements systematically squeeze Palestinian society until people leave or accept drastically truncated and beleaguered lives.

We saw the pattern of containment everywhere, from whole valleys, to cities, villages, neighborhoods, and even individual homes.

In Whole Valleys

Daoud Nasser is a Palestinian Christian who owns a beautiful piece of land on a cave-laced hillside near Bethlehem. His family is lucky: they possess land records from the Ottoman, English, and Jordanian periods that give them title to this land. Thus, settlers have not been able to take Daoud's land via the courts. Nevertheless, he has had to spend about $150,000 protecting his rights in more than 17 years of litigation that, as I write, is still ongoing. Now, his land is surrounded by five settlements and the road to his property is closed off in two places, so that all goods have to be carried in a mile to his home. While settlers have, thus far, not been successful in taking the land, they have they vandalized the fruit orchards belonging to the Nasser family just before the harvest. Settlers have also gotten the military administration to issue demolition orders against most of the buildings on the property and to refuse permission to build new ones. To stay on the land, Daoud and his family would therefore have to live in the caves that dot the hillsides they own.

Daoud, an engineer by training, has decided to turn his land into a peace camp. Since he cannot get permission to build on his own property, he has wired the many caves on his hillside for the electricity his generators produce.

One cave serves as a conference room, another as a dormitory, a third as a kitchen, and so on. The motto of his peace camp, *Tent of Nations,* is inscribed on one of the stones that settlers have positioned to block access to his land. "We refuse to be enemies," he writes.[33]

In Cities

On all our trips, we do a "gentrification" walk through the city of Jaffa. Our guide, Sami Abou Shehadeh, is a historian by training and, until recently, a member of the city council.[34] Before the *Nakba*, Jaffa was the cultural center of the Palestinian community, housing its major newspapers, theaters, and intellectual life. From its clock tower square, Palestinians could take busses or trains to Beirut, Damascus and Cairo. In 1946, city engineers were designing a stadium and dormitories to host the Arab Olympics. Two years later, during the *Nakba*, Jaffa's Palestinian population was reduced from about 120,000 to 4,000, with the refugees losing not only their homes, but their social networks as well. Even those Palestinians who remained in Jaffa were relocated into just one neighborhood. And then, they were forced to share their refugee apartments with newly arriving Jewish immigrants: in a three bedroom apartment, for example, one bedroom would be allocated to the forcibly relocated Palestinians, another to a newly arrived Bulgarian Jewish family, and the third to a newly arrived Romanian Jewish family. Some Palestinian families thus lived in the same apartment with those who bragged of joining the Israeli Defense Forces and killing Palestinians. This policy was known as "co-existence." In a final blow, Palestinians remaining in Jaffa were forbidden to make contact with those who had been expelled: to inquire about the fate of a cousin, or a neighbor, or a friend; to ask whether they had been killed or had made it safely to a refugee camp in Lebanon was deemed to be "collaboration with enemy states" and heavily punished.

Near the oceanfront, we stop to look at a traditional Palestinian home with odd scaffolding along the back. It seems this home once had a back porch, which slowly rotted in the sea air. The owners applied for a permit to rebuild the porch and were denied. They rebuilt it anyway and, promptly, the Israelis demolished the new porch. This happened several times. Finally, the family devised creative new scaffolding on wheels, which they use as a porch. Whenever Israeli inspectors appear, they wheel the "porch" away from the house and return it after the inspectors have left.

Jaffa has slowly rebuilt itself, albeit with many of the drug and crime problems associated with hopelessness, especially in the Ajami neighborhood.

The film *Ajami,* produced with non-professional actors and an improvised script, reflects this reality. Jaffa now faces another round of expropriations and demolitions in service to Israel's "greenwashing" – the process of creating a strip of parks along the oceanfront that extends the Tel Aviv board walk southward by demolishing Palestinian homes and planting over the debris.[35]

In the city of Hebron, in the West Bank, the usual pattern of ringing a Palestinian community with life-constricting settlements is augmented by a series of mini-settlements strung through the center of town, especially its once-thriving market, causing it to be divided into two areas, one for illegal Israeli settlers, usually ultra-Orthodox and militant, and one for Palestinians. The ultra-zealous settlers in and around Hebron produce the most intense violence in the Occupied Territories.

On the fourth trip, we arrived in Hebron on a Saturday, not realizing that this was the day that many Palestinians barricade their homes against the violence of the Jewish settlers who use the Sabbath to assault and terrorize their Palestinian neighbors. The city was eerily silent. The only signs of life were bunches of young Palestinian boys carrying pails to a nearby mosque soup kitchen and roving bands of heavily armed settlers. There were Israeli soldiers on every rooftop, but they are forbidden to lay a hand on settlers, no matter how murderous their violence; indeed, their sole role is to protect the settlers, which they do by confining Palestinians to progressively smaller areas of the city.

In other years we have walked through the Palestinian market in Hebron when it was open. It sports a heavy metal mesh screen overhead, designed to keep out the bricks and chairs that settlers throw down into the market from the rooftops to render it so unsafe as to lose all its customers. Since the wire mesh successfully keeps the heavier objects from crashing into the market, settlers have taken to filling plastic bags with human excrement and throwing them on the screen so that the bags will tear and drip excrement onto passing shoppers. On the fifth trip, one such bag struck me.

But shocking as this is, the most poignant moment in Hebron always comes during the walk downhill from the Ibrahimi Mosque, where Baruch Goldstein, an American born settler, gunned down 29 Muslims while they knelt at prayer.[36] We arrive at the bottom of a hill, passing a checkpoint where, inevitably, we see Palestinian men being detained and questioned, and turn right onto a street where we encounter a waist-high cement barrier, dividing the street into a narrow strip where Palestinians are permitted to walk and a broad swathe where Israeli settlers can walk and drive their cars. I have seen this sight many times, and at that moment on the trip, I always make a point of watching not the scene on the street, but the faces of my African American and Hispanic students as they see this visual representation of Occupation.[37] One such student turned to me and said "This is just like my grandmother's description of growing up in the South, when she had to step off the sidewalk so that passing white pedestrians did not have to share space with a black woman."

On the fifth trip, a young Palestinian boy, certainly no more than five years old, had inserted himself into our group, trying to sell us beaded bracelets for $1 each. Our group, being large and amorphous, walked down the Israeli side of the street, the little boy caught up in our midst. As we exited from the divided road into a street where Palestinians are entirely forbidden and all the shops are shuttered, the child was left exposed on the "wrong" side of the barrier. One of our girls looked back over her shoulder and saw two soldiers emerge from a side street and converge on the little boy, who bolted into a doorway where he cowered, his hands protecting his head. My student called out to the group. Without a word, all the students stopped, turned, and walked back to the intersection, where they stood quietly, staring at the Israeli soldiers, their cameras raised. The soldiers, keeping the little boy pinned in the doorway, twice checked that we were still there. Finally, they motioned the child away and he ran off down the street unharmed.

On another trip, as we left through the Shuhadeh Street checkpoint, one of the soldiers (in perfect American English) said to me "I hope you don't think I'm a war criminal." Soldiers like this, who come to doubt the rightness of what they see, have formed a group called Breaking the Silence, in which they appeal to their Israeli neighbors to witness what the Occupation actually does in practice. The key founders of Breaking the Silence are all veterans who served the Occupation in Hebron.

In Villages

Nowhere is the Israeli policy of encirclement and constriction more plainly in view than in the village of Nabi Saleh, where an Israeli settlement has cut the villagers off from their spring. Every Friday, the Palestinian villagers hold protests, with internationals and Israelis of conscience also in attendance. Since every Palestinian village has a spring, the Nabi Saleh protests have a tremendous potential to galvanize the entire West Bank.[38] Hence the Israelis have decided, according to the Palestinian inhabitants of the village, that "the virus of Nabi Saleh will be killed in Nabi Saleh." We are invited to visit the home of Bilal and Manal Tamimi, cousins of Mostafa Tamimi, who was killed during the weekly Friday protests in December, 2011.[39] We have met

Ahed Tamimi each year beginning when she was only 9 years old. When we stand on the ridge overlooking the spring and the expropriated orchards, Israeli soldiers immediately appear and take up defensive positions, clearly indicating that we are not to approach.

In Neighborhoods

Containment is also on display in the neighborhood of Sheikh Jerrah in East Jerusalem.[40] We have been visiting Palestinian families there every year. In the first year, we saw Um Kammal in a tent on a vacant lot, where she and her family lived after settlers invaded her home in the middle of the night and threw the family out on the street. Her grandchildren played on a bulldozer parked near her tent. That very bulldozer would be used to demolish the tent 12 times in a row.

Um Kammal is long gone, so for three years after her removal we've visited other Sheikh Jerrah families. The most photographed family lives under plastic tarps in the courtyard of the house from which they were evicted. Five years ago, the settlers who took over the house added attack dogs to their arsenal. I was very proud of my students. They were clearly uneasy that the attack dogs would be loosed on us (settlers opened the window letting the dogs strain at the bars). But, as they said later, during our daily reflections: "we realized that Palestinians live like this all the time so we felt we had to stand there and experience this for a few minutes." Today no Palestinian families remain in Sheikh Jerrah.

Around Individual Homes

Hani and Monera Amer live in what I call the "house in a box."[41] Their home is entirely surrounded by the Israeli separation barrier (a wall on one side and barbed wire fences around the other 3 sides). They are cut off from their village and are the victims of stone-throwing and house invasions from the settlers who live less than 10 yards away. On our third trip, I asked Hani Amer whether his children were scared walking to school, which is located in the village from which the wall has separated them. He replied "No, they're scared when they come home, because we have been invaded by settlers." The first few years we visited the Amer home there were only a few small settler houses nearby. By the fourth year, the horizon was filled with the shell of massive multi-story apartments going up as the settlement, kilometers deep into the West Bank, expands.

CREATIVITY AND RESILIENCE

Yakoub's Story

Two years ago, I spent my two night home stay of the class trip with the family of a carpenter in Bethlehem. My host's name was Yakoub. He was a member of the Palestinian Christian community and a carpenter by trade. In order to pursue his craft he had a veritable portfolio of identity documents that he showed me. He carried a basic ID issued by the Palestinian Authority. Then, in addition, because he ran his own business, he had applied for and received both a businessman's card issued by the Israelis and a security card with biometric ID, also issued by the Israelis. Finally he had papers from the Greek Orthodox Church for which he did the bulk of his work. With this entire complement of documents he went to the main check point between Bethlehem and Jerusalem every day to go to work. Even with all those IDs, he was allowed into Jerusalem only so long as he was working on Church property – i.e. in churches or in schools or hospitals affiliated with them. Over time he came to know a many of the soldiers who were stationed at that checkpoint, although their turnover was high.

One day Yakoub came to the checkpoint, only to be confronted with a new young 18 year old wearing the usual automatic weapon. He submitted his papers and placed his hand in the fingerprint reader. "No, refused" said the soldier and waved him off. Yakoub protested – he had seen the green light flash on the biometric machine. "Refused" the soldier insisted, so Yakoub picked up his tool kit and turned to leave. "Wait a minute. Come back. Try again," the soldier said. This routine – "No, refused. Wait. Try again." – was repeated five times in all. The last time the soldier looked Yakoub in the eye. "How do you feel," he asked, "when I make you go away and come back? Do you feel humiliated?" Yakoub took a deep breath, because he was, in fact, very angry. But instead of showing his true feelings, he beamed a huge smile at the soldier and replied "Oh no. I'm fine with this. I'm getting to walk around. You're the one stuck behind the desk." Palestinians refer to this quality as *sumud,* or steadfastness, and Yakoub has more than his share of it.

Ronit's Story

One of our best speakers each year is a woman only a little older than my students. Ronit is an Israeli refusenik who now works for a prominent American-based peace agency. Her official talk for my students is about the way Israeli society and culture are militarized.

Playgrounds for very young children are built with nets across the sandbox so that the little ones have to crawl through on elbows and knees. When they make it across, they are congratulated for being good soldiers. Elementary schools have the names of alumni killed in Israel's many wars, raids, and police actions etched on the walls and only the very best pupils get to read their names at the weekly assembly.

The cycle of holidays – Chanukah, Holocaust Remembrance Day, Fallen Soldier's Day, Independence Day – all tell the same story which Ronit describes this way: "Someone was trying to kill us (the Maccabees, the Tsar, Hitler, the Arabs) but we beat them miraculously. Let's eat."

Powerful though her talk is, my students tend to be most curious about the personal choices Ronit made in refusing to be inducted into the Israeli army as a conscientious objector, especially since her parents served in the military and her beloved brother is a career soldier. Ronit talks about the time she served in jail and how she was finally discharged as unfit for service on psychiatric grounds. Both of these facts will disqualify her from many mainstream corporate jobs that rely on army brigades as referral networks. Luckily Ronit has no interest in such jobs and is very happy and productive working for a peace NGO.

But inevitably one of my students will bring up her choices in our daily reflections. "What should we learn from Ronit's example?" they ask. "Does this mean we have to be prepared to go to jail and damage our careers to do the right thing?" What is the price of conviction and integrity? Each of them will have to find answers for themselves. Ronit has made the question come alive.

Happily, our trip also reminds us that oppression and injustice never go unopposed. After we have seen valleys, cities, towns, neighborhoods, even single homes being choked by the Occupation, one of our most pressing questions becomes: how can there be so little rage in the face of such injustice? The question, of course, betrays some of our American privilege – the expectation that our society and state will treat us fairly. There is, naturally, some rage (in our case, the occasional tirade against American support for Israel) and, more commonly, despair among Palestinians. But there is also, surprisingly, endless imaginative resistance and efficacy. People who spoke to us said it over and over again: "we can't wait for a political solution," "we can't sit around bemoaning our fate," "we have to build for the future now."

It helps, of course, that Palestinians have a 95% literacy rate and the highest percent of PhDs per capita in the Arab world.[42] We heard and saw Palestinian efficacy at every turn and in every field: political, economic, cultural, medical.

The Palestinian community is host to economic enterprises from small craft shops where glass blowing or embroidery are made and sold, to mid-size businesses like the last kuffiyeh (Palestinian scarf) factory in Palestine, located in Hebron, and the Taybeh Beer Brewery whose productivity can hardly keep pace with the market, to large-scale businesses such as PalTel, housed in a glass-clad skyscraper that would be equally at home in New York, Dubai, or Hong Kong. On a sector-wide basis, the Palestine Fair Trade Association[43] helps farmers to get organic and fair trade certification and to find international market niches.

Despite the most difficult life circumstances, Palestinians are also highly politically engaged around all the issues that are critical to their collective future. They have effective NGOs[44] focused on land rights (Adalah),[45] prisoners' rights (Addameer),[46] and many other rights. Israeli Jews who work in solidarity with them have created allied organizations that bring Israelis and internationals to weekly protests (Anarchists Against the Wall)[47], and that document Israeli violence. B'Tselem,[48] an Israeli NGO, provides the gold standard for reporting on human rights violations in the Occupied Territories. More grassroots forms of resistance also abound, as in the Friday weekly protests at villages like Bili'in or Nili'in whose land is being appropriated by the separation wall or in Nabi Saleh, whose people's claim on their traditional village spring has been suppressed in favor of Israeli settlers. Five years ago, we met with Stanford graduate Fadi Quran who was pioneering a new generation of "Freedom Rides" in which Palestinians insisted on boarding "settler only" busses in the West Bank.[49]

Cultural survival projects also flourish. Riwaq[50] is active in architectural preservation and has done much to restore the old city of Birzeit. The Darwish Museum,[51] shaped like the leaves of an open book, commemorates the greatest national poet. There is a thriving film industry that produces landmark, academy award nominated documentaries like *Five Broken Cameras*, and fiction films like *Paradise Now* and *Omar*. At the Birzeit University art gallery we see a show on Palestinian poster art. Palestinian rappers such as Iron Sheik, hip-hop groups such as DAM, and spoken word artists such as Rafif Ziadeh, Suheir Hammad, and Remi Kanazi achieve international acclaim.

Political resistance even permeates the health care system and children's services. At the YMCA in Bethlehem, we hear Dr. Nader Abu Amsha tell the story of his project. Beginning with the need to treat *Intifada*-injured youth, he, his mentors, and his co-workers have produced sophisticated interdisciplinary counseling efforts that are now being copied in troubled areas around the world.[52]

Many of the projects we visit combine elements of economic, political, and cultural resistance. Thus, for example, we visit a business in the Negev where Mariam Abu Rogaig, the first Bedouin woman to complete a college degree in chemistry outside the country, has founded a cosmetic business based on her grandmother's herbal remedies. Rogaig's company, Desert Daughter,[53] is set in a flourishing tent complex that includes a restaurant established by neighboring women who cater to the tour groups that come to shop there. Desert Daughter also showcases other local craftswomen, promoting women's micro-economic development by finding commercial markets for traditional crafts. Rogaig is fully aware of her political setting, noting the water poverty to which she, an Israeli citizen, is subjected while pointing us to the nearby lushly watered Israel town, part of the campaign to "Judaize" the Negev. She is fierce in holding her political representatives responsible for helping with this problem.

The Bedouin town of Wadi al Na'am, situated between a petrochemical plant and a power generating station, is an unrecognized village, with no electricity, water, or clinic. It is to be demolished to allow for the "Judaization of the Negev." Many women in the village have had multiple miscarriages; childhood asthma and cancer are common in the village.

In the Dheisheh refugee camp, our host, Abu Rabieh, discusses his endlessly inventive programs and grants. Next to his house is a computer laboratory for which he secured the funding. Seven years ago his newest project involved applying for EU money for a summer circus camp for kids. Six years ago, he showed me the photos of kids walking on stilts, riding unicycles, and juggling. The year after that, he was writing grants to develop roof gardens – I have no doubt we'll be seeing them in the near future. All of his projects combine an emphasis on education and economic development.

In the nearby Aida refugee camp, we visit the Lajee Center[54] where Palestinian children are taught media skills in order to document Israeli violence in the camp. The same camp also contains the Al Ruwwad Children's Dance Theater[55] whose young dance companies tour Europe and the United States. Aida also houses ecological projects focused on water safety,[56] which is part of a growing Palestinian concern with environmental issues.

Environmentalism is a part of Palestinian business development, for example, in the hands of Khaled al Sabawi, a young Canadian-Palestinian geothermal engineer who is pioneering green building construction.[57] Environmentalism is also part of emerging Palestine scholarship, focused, for example, on such topics as sewage and waste management,[58] rural electrification,[59] and land use planning.[60] The trend to add environmental concerns to political concerns is especially important in light of the silence in human rights doctrines about environmental sustainability.

Since half the trip is spent in Israel, we meet not only Palestinian citizens of Israel but also Jewish Israelis who hold a broad range of political opinions. One of our opening meetings takes place at OCHA (the United Nations Office for the Coordination of Humanitarian Affairs), where Israeli staff members walk a knife edge: representing the U.N.'s position on monitoring illegal settlement expansion while also arguing that Israel has legitimate security concerns, especially vis-à-vis Gaza. In Tel Aviv, we meet with Zochrot (Remembrance), an Israeli NGO dedicated to telling the story of the Nakba in Israeli schools – we see a set of notebooks and lesson plans they share with teachers throughout the land. They lead tours to destroyed villages like Lifta, near Jerusalem, and petition the government to create more complete and balanced signs at national parks, especially those that are built over the ruins of Palestinian villages.

In the Zochrot offices we are also introduced to a group of Israeli women who do research on Israeli corporations that do business in the settlements. Who Profits?, their NGO, also provides research on the Israeli-American arms trade.

CONCLUSION

What we see today stands at the endpoint of much that has gone before, none more definitive than the decision, made by Zionists in the early years of their settlement in (then British Mandatory) Palestine to aspire to a Jewish *state* rather than a Jewish *homeland* – against the advice of Jews like Martin Buber, Albert Einstein, Hannah Arendt, and Judah Magnes.[61] The "statist" option posed a dilemma for Zionists because its aspirations – to incorporate all the land from the river to sea into a state that is both Jewish and democratic – are incompatible. Absent the complete ethnic cleansing of all or nearly all Palestinians, Israelis can pick any two of those demands, but they cannot have all three simultaneously, as Paul recognized so quickly in the story that opens this chapter.

If Israelis chose to be both democratic and Jewish, they would be required to pull back to the area where Jews are a supermajority. This is the internationally recognized and approved "two-state solution." It calls for Israel to be Jewish, democratic, and *small*. For Zionists, the two-state solution would mean giving up the dream to control all the *land*. The Israeli government has done everything within its power with fifty years of strategic, state-supported settlement building precisely to destroy this option.

Thus, as a practical matter, implementing the two-state solution would now entail giving back land that has been under Israeli control since 1967 and changing the lives of many of the 764,000 settlers now living in the Occupied Territories.[62] It would mean finding Israeli politicians who would have the courage to implement this solution over the objection of a highly mobilized settler community and numerous right wing political parties. The prospect of including land swaps around the Green Line to minimize the number of settlers to be uprooted has not made this prospect more appealing to the Israeli polity.

Second, Jews could live freely and legitimately throughout all the land and be part of a democratic society – but only to the degree that Israel is willing to be a state of *all* of its people, rather than a state only for Jews. People who make a case for the one-state solution (or, as a variant, a single bi-national state) argue for this option: a larger, stronger country, and one in which Jews, Muslims, Christians, Samaritans, Druze, and Baha'i live as equals.

For Zionists, the one-state solution means giving up the dream of an exclusively *Jewish* state. In addition, the one-state solution would also empower precisely those people, the Palestinians, whose dangerousness has been greatly exaggerated by Israeli politicians.[63] The one democratic state possibility is so repugnant to the Netanyahu government that it is has passed a "Jewish nation-state" bill, added to Israel's Basic Laws (the Israeli equivalent of a constitution). This bill explicitly rejects the idea that Israel needs to be a state of all its people, and lays the legal foundation for requiring the Israeli Supreme Court to rule against equal justice for Palestinian citizens of Israel.[64] The cynicism of this legislation reaches breathtaking proportions when it is combined with the rising call from the Israeli right to annex all or most of the West Bank, thus increasing the number of people whose needs the Supreme Court would be required to ignore.

The single democratic state option would not be easy for Palestinians either. To endorse it would mean accepting that what is now a national liberation struggle would become a civil rights struggle for equal rights within a state that is shared with others. While this idea is finding some acceptance among younger Palestinians, virtually none of the leaders in the Occupied Territories are able to contemplate a civil rights struggling superseding the national liberation struggle.

Third, Israel can be institutionally, bureaucratically Jewish and yet have all the land. The problem with this scenario is that half the people who live on that land are not Jews. So, for Zionists, this means giving up on all but the shallowest façade of *democracy*. It seems as if this option is, increasingly, spoken out loud. In the words of Sheldon Adelson, one of Israel's wealthiest American backers, "I don't think the Bible says anything about democracy ... God didn't say anything about democracy ... God talked about all the good things in life. He didn't talk about Israel remaining as a democratic state ... Israel isn't going to be a democratic state – so what?"[65]

Foregoing democracy means suppressing not only the non-Jews who constitute half the population but also all those, inside and outside Israel, who object to the suppression, even – or perhaps especially – when the critics are themselves Jewish. This is the reality that Israel is choosing daily. You can name it in a number of ways: apartheid, Indian reservations, settler colonialism, ethnic cleansing, or sociocide (for a comparison of these models, see Chapter 9). Whatever you call it, it rests on a program of denying the human and civil rights of the non-Jews under Zionist control and silencing critics of the regime.

In making this choice, Israel is beginning to diverge from its once monolithic American support. While Israel's internal politics favor Jewishness over democracy,[66] a recent poll shows that Americans, by a better than 2 to 1 margin, favor democracy over Jewishness should the two-state solution fail.[67] The American Jewish community is likewise shifting.[68] Some campus Hillel organizations refuse the orders of the national office and declare themselves as "Open Hillels" – i.e. ones in which concerns for Palestinian rights can be discussed and debated.[69] Every week brings another report of Jews who turn on other Jews, as when Israeli settlers vandalize the jeep of the Israel Defense Forces that protect their settlement,[70] and Jewish groups in New York battle each other over who may participate in an Israel Day parade.[71]

In the closing years of the Obama administration, then Secretary of State, John Kerry, was castigated for using the word "apartheid" to describe the reality that the Israeli occupation of Palestine has created. The criticism of Kerry was unjust, insofar as he was saying no more than Israeli leaders themselves have said. Ehud Barak, who is both a former Prime Minister and a former Defense Minister of Israel has said, "As long as in this territory west of the Jordan River there is only one political entity called Israel it is going to be either non-Jewish, or non-democratic. If this bloc of millions of Palestinians cannot vote, that will be an apartheid state."[72] And similarly, Ehud Olmert, another former Prime Minister admits: "If the day comes when the two-state solution collapses, and we face a South African-style struggle for equal voting rights ... then, as soon as that happens, the State of Israel is finished ... The Jewish organizations, which were our power base in America, will be the first to come out against us, because they will say they cannot support a state that does not support democracy and equal voting rights for all its residents."[73]

The sheer impossibility of reconciling land, democracy, and Jewishness did not become an irreconcilable dilemma until 1967, when Israel managed to take control of all the land from the river to the sea. The easy victory of the Six Day War came at a political if not a military cost. Taking land meant taking the people living on the land. This is when Israel changed from being a state with a 15–20 per cent Palestinian ethnic minority and a Jewish super majority, to being a state plus an Occupation ruling over a population that is, in total, 50+ percent Palestinian. In 1967, unlike 1947, the possibility of wholesale ethnic cleansing by expulsion was no longer on the menu. And so, everything Israel has done vis-à-vis the Palestinians since 1967 is designed to address this challenge; to get Palestinians to leave or, at the very least, to be completely pacified, to accept being confined to small, separated enclaves without social or political rights and without economic viability.

In so doing, the Israelis do not perceive themselves as evil. Like all other human beings, Israelis, even those living in the settlements (all of which are illegal) believe that their actions are morally grounded. We turn next (in Chapters 3, 4 and 10) to some of the ideas that inform their efforts to find an ethical basis for their actions.

Our trips were punctuated by our being witness to places of extreme violence – on the first day in Sheikh Jerrah, on the last in Nabi Saleh and, at the mid-point in Hebron. But, woven throughout were also the threads of hope, resilience, and vibrancy – mostly on the part of Palestinians, but also on the part of a few Israelis who stand ready to take up the project that Avraham Burg, an Israeli intellectual and political leader, has called "universal humanism,"[74] i.e. building a future that is based on equity and justice between themselves and the Palestinians. The first tentative steps have already been taken: Israelis who act in solidarity with Palestinians, Palestinians who leave the indigenous Jewish Samaritan community above Nablus unmolested even in the most contentious moments of their struggle with Israel.[75]

Yet so much remains to be done.

NOTES

1 AliceHoffman. (2007). *Incantation.* Boston: Little, Brown.
2 Sharon Shpurer. (2013, July 30). The Israeli bank that opens its doors to everyone – except Arabs, *Ha'aretz*, retrieved from http://www.haaretz.com/business/.premium-1.538667
3 http://nocamels.com/2013/01/desert-daughter-a-bedouin-womans-success-story/
4 Al Jazeera (2015, October 23). Rabbi attacked by alleged Jewish settler in West Bank, retrieved from https://www.youtube.com/watch?v=FpecFERU9wQ
5 http://zochrot.org/en
6 http://www.whoprofits.org/
7 Statistics on college enrollment, completion and population data base can be retrieved from http://stats.uis.unesco.org
8 http://www.arij.org/
9 YouTube (2015, October 23) Rabbi attacked by alleged Jewish settler in the West Bank, retrieved from https://www.youtube.com/watch?v=FpecFERU9wQ
10 Jacob Magid. (2018, April 29). Olive Trees cut down in second attack on Palestinian village in as many days, *The Times of Israel*, retrieved from https://www.timesofisrael.com/olive-trees-cut-down-in-second-attack-on-palestinian-village-in-as-many-days/
11 These actions are opposed even by Abe Foxman, former chair of the pro-Israel Anti-Defamation League. Abraham Foxman. (2014, May 18). Israel Cannot Wait Any Longer to Crush Price Tag Attacks, *Ha'aretz*, retrieved from https://www.haaretz.com/opinion/.premium-crush-price-tag-attacks-1.5248670
12 Amira Hass. (2013, December 26). Israel: Palestinian Farmers to Blame for Settler Attacks on their Land, *Ha'aretz*, retrieved from https://www.haaretz.com/.premium-price-tag-victims-to-blame-israel-says-1.5304165
13 Jaclynn Ashly. (2017, September 18). Drowning in the Waste of Israeli Settlers, *Al Jazeera*, retrieved from https://www.aljazeera.com/indepth/features/2017/09/drowning-waste-israeli-settlers-170916120027885.html
14 Saleh Abdel Jawad. (1998). War by Other Means, *Al Ahram Weekly*, retrieved from http://weekly.ahram.org.eg/archive/1998/1948/359_salh.htm
15 Tomer Zarchin, Jack Khoury, Jonathan Lis. (2012, January 12). Supreme Court upholds ban on Palestinians living with Israeli spouses, *Ha'aretz*, retrieved from http://www.haaretz.com/print-edition/news/supreme-court-upholds-ban-on-palestinians-living-with-israeli-spouses-1.406812

[16] Ha'aretz editorial. (2012, January 13). Supreme Court thrusts Israel down the slope of Apartheid, *Ha'aretz*, retrieved from http://www.haaretz.com/print-edition/opinion/supreme-court-thrusts-israel-down-the-slope-of-apartheid-1.407056

[17] Ben White. (2012). Palestinians in Israel: Segregation, *Discrimination and Democracy* (London: Pluto Press) p. 13.

[18] B'Tselem, (2017, November 11). East Jerusalem, retrieved from https://www.btselem.org/jerusalem

[19] Matt De Miao. (2011, November 23). Peace is a Poisoned Word, *Cognitive Liberty*, retrieved from http://cognitiveliberty.net/2011/peace-is-a-poisoned-word/

[20] http://www.btselem.org/gaza_strip/castlead_operation

[21] Uri Avnery. (2009), January 19). The Boss Has Gone Mad in *Counterpunch*, retrieved from http://www.counterpunch.org/2009/01/19/the-boss-has-gone-mad/
Jeff Halper. (2014, August 18). Globalizing Gaza, *Counterpunch*, retrieved from http://www.counterpunch.org/2014/08/18/globalizing-gaza/print

[22] United Nations Office for the Coordination of Humanitarian Affairs (OCHA). (August, 2014). Humanitarian Bulletin Monthly Report June – August, 2014, retrieved from http://www.ochaopt.org/content/monthly-humanitarian-bulletin-june-august=2014

[23] International Middle East Media Center, Ministry of Health. (August 27, 2014). 2,145 Palestinians, including 578 Children, killed by Israel's Aggression, August 27, 2014, retrieved from http://www.imemc.org/article/68969

[24] Ben Hartman. (2014, August 28). 50 Days of Israel's Gaza operation Protective Edge – by the numbers, *Jerusalem Post*, retrieved from http://www.jpost.com/Operation-Protective-Edge/50-days-of-Israels-Gaza-operation-Protective-Edge-by-the-numbers-372574

[25] United Nations Office for the Coordination of Humanitarian Affairs (UNOCHA). (2018, June 13). "Humanitarian Snapshot: casualties in the context of demonstrations and hostilities in Gaza; 30 March–12 June, 2018," retrieved from https://www.ochaopt.org/content/humanitarian-snapshot-casualties-context-demonstrations-and-hostilities-gaza-30-march-12 2018

[26] Israeli settlers release wild boars on Palestinian farmland to destroy crops, *Mondoweiss*, April 23, 2014, retrieved from http://mondoweiss.net/2014/04/israeli-settlers-palestinian.html

[27] Ha'aretz Staff. (2014, April 30). U.S. report: "Price tag" attacks spread into Israel, go unpunished, *Ha'aretz*, retrieved from http://www.haaretz.com/news/diplomacy-defense/1.588285

[28] http://972mag.com/watch-ultra-orthodox-spit-on-immodest-8-year-old-girl-in-bet-shemesh/31268/

[29] http://www.haaretz.com/blogs/routine-emergencies/.premium-1.538039

[30] Ami Kaufman. (2014, August 25). Israelis on Facebook wish death for Holocaust survivors against Protective Edge, *+972 Magazine*, retrieved from http://972mag.com/nstt_feeditem/israelis-on-facebook-wish-death-for-holocaust-survivors-against-protective-edge/

[31] Shabtai Gold. (2014, August 22). Hamas executes 18 'collaborators in Gaza, *Ha'aretz*, retrieved from http://www.haaretz.com/news/middle-east/1.611989

[32] http://www.btselem.org/separation_barrier

[33] http://www.tentofnations.org/

[34] All of information on Jaffa comes from Sami Abou Shehadeh, lecture, January 5, 2015.

[35] http://electronicintifada.net/content/jaffa-eminence-ethnic-cleansing/8088

[36] You can see their style, more recently, here: "We killed Jesus, we're proud of it," retrieved from http://www.youtube.com/watch?v=M539PgDjbas

37 B'Tselem How to Build a Fence in Hebron, retrieved from https://www.youtube.com/ watch?v=qC4EEPVRBsE

38 Ben Ehrenreich. (2013, March 15). Is this where the Third Intifada Will Start? *New York Times*, retrieved from http://www.nytimes.com/2013/03/17/magazine/is-this-where-the-third-intifada-will-start.html?pagewanted=all&_r=0

39 Ibid.

40 Al Jazeera, English. (2013, July 6). Al-Kurd Family Home Takeover (Sheikh Jerrah). [Video File], retrieved from http://www.youtube.com/watch?feature=endscreen&NR=1& v=wlQf41CJjjc

41 www.youtube.com/watch?v=c5uBA3F1Ghw

42 Palestinian education statistics, see note #2 above.

43 http://www.palestinefairtrade.org/

44 There are those who argue that NGOs are not an indigenous organizational form; that, rather, they are a problematic response to the demands of international donors. See, for example, Rema Hammami. (1995). NGOs: The Professionalization of Politics, Race and Class 37: 51–63, and Islah Jad. (2004). The NGOisation of Arab Women's Movements, retrieved from http://www.google.com/search?hl=en&q=Islah+Jad+%2B+Ngoization& btnG=Google+Search. I cannot resolve the debates and hesitations about NGO's here; suffice it to say that Palestinians are adept at building them, and at least some of them, the ones I cite, are doing work that is well-received in the Palestinian community.

45 http://adalah.org/eng/

46 http://www.addameer.org/

47 http://www.awalls.org/

48 http://www.btselem.org/

49 http://electronicintifada.net/blog/linah-alsaafin/palestinians-clarify-goal-freedom-rides-challenge-segregated-israeli-buses. This at a time when Israel is simultaneously engaged in "pink-washing" (claiming that Israel is distinctively gay-friendly) while expecting their own Orthodox Jewish women to ride at the back of the bus (for a closer look at the kind of people who want women to sit at the back of the bus, see: http://www.youtube.com/ watch?v=DejnrvU4z9w)

50 http://www.riwaq.org/

51 http://mahmouddarwish.ps/

52 http://www.ej-ymca.org/

53 See endnote #4, above.

54 http://www.lajee.org/

55 Alice Rothchild. (2010, January 5). Beautiful Resistance in Bethlehem's Aida Refugee Camp, *Mondoweiss*, retrieved from http://mondoweiss.net/2010/01/beautiful-resistance-in-bethlehems-aida-refugee-camp

56 http://1for3.org/

57 Khaled Al Sabawi Keeping Israel Cool, TedxRamallah, retrieved from http://www.youtube.com/watch?v=9fD2bMavK8Y

58 Sophia Stamatopoulos-Robbins. (2014, February 28). Infrastructure and Materiality in Palestine Studies, paper delivered at the New Directions in Palestinian Studies Symposium, Brown University.

59 Omar Jabary Salamanca. (2014, February 28). Hooked on Electricity: the charged political economy of electrification in the Palestinian West Bank, paper delivered at the New Directions in Palestinian Studies Symposium, Brown University.

[60] Kareem Rabie. (2014, March 1). Housing: the Production of the State, and the Day After, paper delivered at the New Directions in Palestinian Studies Symposium, Brown University.

[61] Anita Shapira (1999) *Land and Power: The Zionist Resort to Force, 1881–1948*. Stanford: Stanford University Press.

[62] Arutz Sheva, a settler source, acknowledges 389, 250 Jewish settlers in the West Bank and another 375,000 in East Jerusalem, whose "annexation" is universally recognized as illegal, totaling some 764,000 illegal settlers. These numbersdate from 2014, and the same source claims that by now the number of settlers has risen to 800,000. Arutz Sheva, retrieved from http://www.israelnationalnews.com/Articles/Article.aspx/18210#.VpK885scTIU. The population growthrate in the settlements, though declining, is still approximately twice as high as that in Jerusalem, see Jacob Magid. 92018, January 21).Settler growth rate declines for sixth straight year, *The Times of Israel*, retrieved from https://www.timesofisrael.com/settler-growth-rate-declines-for-sixth-straight-year/

[63] See, for example, *Defamation*, an Israeli film produced and directed by Yoav Shamir, retrieved from http://www.imdb.com/title/tt1377278/

[64] Jonathan Cook. (2017, May 11). Israel's Jewish Nation-State bill 'declaration of war,' retrieved from https://www.jonathan-cook.net/2017-05-11/israels-jewish-nation-state-bill-declaration-of-war/

[65] Yossi Sarid. (2014,November12). Adelson, Netanyahu a dour kingdom of priests and holiness, *Ha'aretz*, retrieved from http://www.haaretz.com/opinion/.premium-1.627582

[66] Roni Schocken. (2013, August 27). Jewish and Then Democratic, in *Ha'aretz*, retrieved from http://www.haaretz.com/opinion/.premium-1.543070. See also Catrina Stewart. (2012, October 23). The new Israeli apartheid: Poll reveals widespread Jewish support for policy of discrimination against Arab Minority, *The Independent*, retrieved from http://www.independent.co.uk/news/world/middle-east/the-new-israeli-apartheid-poll-reveals-widespread-jewish-support-for-policy-of-discrimination-8223548.html

[67] Philip Weiss. (2014, March 3). Poll: If two states collapse, American overwhelmingly favor 'democracy, *Mondweiss*, retrieved from http://mondoweiss.net/2014/03/collapse-americans-democracy.html

[68] Peter Beinart. (2010, May 12). The failure of the American Jewish establishment, *The New York Review of Books*, retrieved from http://www.nybooks.com/articles/archives/2010/jun/24/failure-american-jewish-establishment-exchange/

[69] Philip Weiss. (2014, April 5). No thanks for Zionist 'chaperones' – Wesleyan declares itself an Open Hillel, *Mondoweiss*, retrieved from http://mondoweiss.net/2014/04/chaperones-wesleyan-declares.html

[70] Gili Cohen. (2014, April 6). Senior IDF commander's jeep vandalized in West Bank settlement, *Ha'aretz*, retrieved from http://www.haaretz.com/.premimum-vandals-slash-jeep-tires-of-idf-commander-1.5244175

[71] Debra Nussbaum Cohen. (2014, April 6). Who has the right to Celebrate Israel? Ha'aretz, retrieved from http://www.haaretz.com/jewish-world/jewish/.premium-who-has-the-right-to-celebrate-israel-1.5244129

[72] John Cassidy. (2014, April 29). John Kerry and the A-Word: Three Takeaways, *The New Yorker*, retrieved from http://www.newyorker.com/online/blogs/johncassidy/2014/04/john-kerry-and-the-a-word-three-takeaways.html

[73] Ibid.

[74] Avraham Burg. (2011, April 1). When the Walls Come Tumbling Down, *Ha'aretz*, retrieved from http://www.haaretz.com/weekend/magazine/when-the-walls-come-tumbling-down-1.353501

[75] The Samaritans of Nablus describe themselves as Hebrews. They argue that the ancient Hebrew kingdoms of Judea and Samaria gave rise to the Jews and the Samaritans respectively. Samaritans worship in synagogues, follow their understanding of the Torah, and employ the religious rituals of the Orthodox Jewish community. The Israeli state regards them as Jewish and provides them with Israeli passports and license plates. The Palestinians regard the Samaritans as an indigenous community and live at peace with them.

BASIC CONCEPTS

Human Rights, Race, and Nation

If radicals wish to change their world, they [cannot do so] by political means alone ... For the old society is not held together merely by force and violence ... [T]he old society maintains itself also through theories ... It will be impossible to ... build a humane new one without beginning, here and now, the construction of new social theories ... The important issue is not [only] the determination of the facts, but the ordering of them.

Alvin Gouldner[1]

INTRODUCTION

We cannot learn the world one fact at a time. There are simply too many facts. And to make matters worse, many of those "too many" facts are also incomplete, ambiguous, and contested. Thus, people who want to achieve a comprehensive insight into the world need to organize their knowledge into frameworks (sometimes called paradigms by the scientific community).[2]

Frameworks define significant questions, appropriate data sources, and the shape of satisfactory answers. Perhaps the best known example comes from Thomas Kuhn who describes the transformation of astronomy from Ptolemy's earth-centered model to Copernicus' sun-centered one.[3] The success of the new model depended less on the discovery of new facts and more on its superior power to make sense of what was already known. Power also played a significant role: the proponents of the new model, especially Galileo, risked charges of heresy for undermining the Church's assertion that the earth was the center of creation. We all see the world through framework-colored glasses.

Recognition of the relationship between facts and frameworks does not, of course, mean that anything goes. Fake news is not ok. Kuhn's work gives us no license to invent convenient facts – to invent, for example, a "promised land" that has miraculously been emptied of all its people without anyone

© KONINKLIJKE BRILL NV, LEIDEN, 2019 | DOI:10.1163/9789004394148_003

ever noticing, just in time for the arrival of Zionists. Nor would Kuhn allow us to ignore inconvenient facts – to ignore, for example, that the divided and backward looking Palestinian leadership contributes greatly to the sufferings of its own people. Indeed, the great German sociologist Max Weber argues that science's highest value is precisely to inculcate in us respect for inconvenient facts.[4] Nevertheless, it remains true that facts and frameworks are inextricably linked and derive their salience from each other.

There are certainly many inconvenient facts and multiple frameworks available for understanding the Israeli-Palestinian conflict. In this chapter, I provide a brief introduction to three ideas or frameworks that are particularly useful in this matter. They are:

- a human rights framework,
- a race framework,
- a nationalism framework.

For each I provide a brief historic overview, analyze strengths and weaknesses in applying these ideas to the present conflict, and discuss the way that these ideas, whether right or wrong, used or misused, continue to be in play, shaping both perceptions and actions.

I begin with the human rights framework because I think it is understandable for most readers, because it situates this unique conflict in a broader, comparative perspective, and because it provides the basis on which to become politically engaged with efforts to find a just resolution to the conflict.

Nevertheless, a caveat is in order. Using a human rights standard provides a strong point of entry into the study of the most persistent conflict in the Middle East. By itself, however, it is not sufficient. It is useful only when coupled with some knowledge of the history, politics, economics, and even theology of the contending parties. For this reason, I begin by laying out basic concepts in the first part of this book, but spend the bulk of my effort on creating a succinct historical account of the conflict in the second part. Together, the value commitment to a human rights perspective and a systematic knowledge of history can provide a basis for a just resolution to the conflict.

HUMAN RIGHTS: BEYOND FAMILY AND TRIBE

To deny people their human rights is to challenge their very humanity.

Nelson Mandela[5]

Within a system which denies the existence of basic human rights, fear tends to be the order of the day. Fear of imprisonment, fear of torture, fear of death, fear of losing friends, family ... A most insidious form of fear is that which masquerades as common sense or even wisdom, condemning as foolish, reckless, insignificant or futile the small, daily acts of courage which help to preserve man's self-respect and inherent human dignity. ... Yet even under the most crushing state machinery courage rises up again and again, for fear is not the natural state of civilized man.

Aung San Suu Kyi, *Freedom from Fear*[6]

Adnan's Story

My friend Adnan spent some time, early in his career, working for the Negotiations Support Unit of the Palestinian Authority. He attended many rounds of talks that followed the signing of the Oslo Accords. At one such session, during the Taba negotiations, after a morning of contentious, acrimonious wrangling between the PA and the Israeli delegation, Adnan found himself alone with a member of the Israeli team as everyone filed out to lunch. Finding himself thus able to have a private conversation, he turned to his Israeli interlocutor and asked her: "On what possible basis of international law could you even think of making the land claims you are making?" His Israeli counterpart looked startled, glanced around the room to see that it was otherwise empty, and replied "What international law? In this room, there's only you and me, and I have all the guns."

For those who do not want to live in a world organized by the whims or even the deeply felt values of the schoolyard bully, human rights doctrine provides a basis for conflict resolution. The current international understanding of human rights is expressed in two key documents: the Universal Declaration of Human Rights (UDHR)[7] of the United Nations and the Geneva Conventions on the Rules of War.[8]

The context of the present human rights framework and these landmark documents is clearly the Second World War and particularly the Holocaust, which were fresh in the minds of the international authors,[9] as was the failure of the League of Nations to establish a system of international relations

67

that prevented world war. In addition, the drafters needed to engineer consent from countries on the two sides of the Cold War, the non-aligned nations, representatives of large, powerful, wealthy countries and small, poor, exploited ones, and countries with diverse and more or less deeply entrenched religious traditions.

Notice that both documents include social and economic rights, such as the right to health care and education, that go beyond the better-known legal rights of freedom from tyranny.

When I teach this material, I ask students to form an opinion: are the documents that emerge from this process persuasive in our contemporary context? Are they too ambitious? Not ambitious enough? Outdated or of timeless value?

Americans generally have been taught, through the Bill of Rights (the first 10 amendments to our Constitution), to value political rights such those of free speech, assembly, and worship. Americans are less familiar with and often more skeptical about the social and economic rights also included in the UDHR; the right to education, health care, work, and, in general, the means to participate as a full member of one's national community. Although students generally endorse the idea that every person should have the opportunity to become his or her best self, they do not always conclude that this aspiration requires access to good education or health care as a matter of *rights*.

I also ask students whether they feel that the documents have missed anything that should have been included or should now be added. Though students generally find human rights doctrine appealing, they also are quick to spot some obvious weaknesses. For example, they notice that, despite the generous provision of social and economic rights, there is no mention of the need to protect the natural environment within which human life flourishes.

The enforcement mechanisms for vindicating human rights seem underdeveloped and feeble in the documents as originally written. The lack of enforcement mechanisms undermines the standard of jurisprudence established by Justice William Blackstone that "it is a settled and invariable principle in the law ... that every right, when withheld, must have a remedy and every injury its proper redress."[10] Human rights standards without enforcement mechanisms are toothless, as the Palestinian-Israeli conflict so painfully reveals.

The two most important bodies intended to provide the remedies and redress that Blackstone calls for are the International Court of Justice and the International Criminal Court. The International Court of Justice, founded as the United Nations' judicial arm, adjudicates disputes only between nations and has thus been especially weak for the question of Palestinian rights in particular and the rights of minorities within states, refugees, and stateless people in general. So long as the Palestinian people had no nation-state, the ICJ was closed to them. The U.N.'s recent recognition of Palestine as an observer-state (albeit one that exists only on paper) opens the door to the ICJ for the first time. However, when Palestine does try to appeal to the ICJ, Israel and the United States inflict financial penalties on them.

The International Criminal Court, created only in 2002, has a serious but limited mandate. Unlike the ICJ it can hear cases brought by individuals and NGOs, but only those that raise the issues of crimes against humanity like apartheid or genocide. When such charges are made, the ICC can seek advisory opinions, and the Palestinians are now asking the U.N.'s Committee on the Elimination of Racial Discrimination (CERD) to find that the Israeli Occupation is guilty of racial discrimination and that its conduct constitutes both a war crime and a crime against humanity.[11] It remains to be seen whether this legal strategy will work. But even if it eventually does, the very convoluted path that is required points to the hardships wrought by a legal regime built to inhibit violence between countries but not within them.

A second concern about the human rights system is that politics and power imbalances have distorted the use of even its weak enforcement mechanisms. Radical scholars like Mahmood Mamdani, raise the question of whether human rights are, in fact, a last ditch attempt by the great powers to dictate the terms of international relations long after the last colonial flag has been lowered and the last colonial governor withdrawn.[12] Could it be that human rights doctrine is, in fact, neocolonialism dressed up in a tuxedo? It is sometimes not quite clear whether those leftists who are suspicious of human rights doctrine truly oppose the doctrine *per se*, or object only to its misuse in great power politics. Nevertheless, their caveats underscore the lesson: human rights doctrine does not operate automatically apart from the purposes of those who invoke it.[13]

Certainly it is easy to find instances where human rights standards are applied selectively by western countries. For example, since its inception in 2002, the caseload of the International Criminal Court has been almost exclusively focused on African cases and African individuals.[14] Even more suspect, the newly developed doctrine of Responsibility to Protect (sometimes call R2P) does seem to invite military intervention by western powers in third-world countries without clear and agreed-upon standards, guidelines, implementation protocols, or time limits, and most critically without the consent of the people intended to benefit from such interventions.[15]

There are three major U.N. resolutions that are meant to produce justice for both Palestinians and Israelis. They are: Resolution 181, dating from November, 1947, calling for the simultaneous co-creation of a Jewish and a Palestinian state[16]; Resolution 194, one year later, affirming the right of all Palestinian refugees to return to their homes[17]; and Resolution 242 of 1967, reaffirming the provisions of the Geneva Conventions that prohibit changes in national boundaries through acts of war.[18] None have ever been enforced.

In recent years, the Israeli government has tried to use the recognition that human rights doctrine is historically rooted to argue for changes that favor its own practices. They argue that the Geneva Conventions (1949) – the "humanitarian law" that, despite its Kafkaesque name, seeks to limit the harm done by war[19] – do not adequately address questions of asymmetric warfare waged between state and non-state actors. While they are correct to argue that asymmetric war is becoming more common, Israeli spokespersons overlook the most salient way that new developments change the need for human rights safeguards: as the carnage spills out from once well-defined battlefields to communities, schools, and hospitals, the need for the protection of civilians grows stronger rather than weaker.

Ironically, in seeking to change the rules of war – mostly in the directions of blurring the line between combatants and non-combatants, weakening the protections for noncombatants, allowing for use of human shields and collective punishment in the supposedly under-regulated area of asymmetrical warfare – Israel is, in fact, conceding the legitimacy of the very rules it is trying to change.

Nothing is more revealing of Israeli intentions or their will to ignore the demands of international human rights standards while paying lip service to them than their use of illegal settlements to inadmissibly change national boundaries and acquire territory by force of war.

The Fourth Geneva Convention, Article 49, paragraph 6 states unambiguously:

> The occupying power shall not deport or transfer parts of its own civilian population into the land it occupies.[20]

Though part of a larger body of text (Article 49), this is a stand-alone paragraph, that appears without any modification, or any indication in the preceding or following text that Article 6 is to be modified or nuanced in any way. The prohibition is absolute: the occupying power may staff its own occupation, but it may not transfer civilians under any pretext into the occupied territories. Period.

There is a matching provision in Article 49, paragraph 1, which also prohibits the expulsion of the civilian population of the occupied territories. The passage reads:

> Individual or mass forcible transfers, as well as deportations of protected persons from occupied territory to the territory of the Occupying Power or to that of any other country, occupied or not, are prohibited, regardless of their motive.[21]

The intent of this language is consistent with the overarching principle that states may not change their boundaries, may not acquire land, through acts of war. In short, occupations may occur in times of war, but their military necessity cannot be used as a lever with which to change the size and shape of countries, to change population ratios, or to promote willing or unwilling resettlement of civilian populations in either direction.

The provisions specified under these rules have been almost universally reaffirmed: by the United Nations General Assembly, the United Nations Security Council, the International Committee of the Red Cross, and the International Court of Justice.

In the face of such massive consensus, the Israeli state ignores these standards and continues to make counterclaims:

They argue that East Jerusalem is annexed rather than occupied. Such annexation is, of course, equally illegal under international law.

Israel denies that, in building settlements, it is "deporting" its own civilians. This argument is disingenuous: Article 49(6) is not meant only to inhibit the forced deportation of criminals or minority groups within an occupying society to the territories it occupies. Rather, it is meant to exclude ALL population transfers, including voluntary or state-incentivized ones.

The Israeli state absolutely incentivizes settlers to move to the Occupied Territories. It supplies water and electricity to the settlements[22]; it has built a network of roads linking the settlements to the parts of Israel within the Green Line[23]; it provides military and Border Police protection to settlers and settlements while failing to protect Palestinian communities under its control from vandalism, theft, and hate crimes[24]; it heavily subsidizes infrastructure development and home ownership by settlers in the settlements[25]; it maps settlement boundaries and encourages incursions into neighboring private lands.[26] The fact that individual settlers choose to accept these incentives does not lessen the Israeli state's responsibility for providing them.

Thus far, all my examples of human rights violations have focused on Israeli misconduct. Palestinians have also committed human rights violations, though their legal position is the opposite of Israel's. As the occupying power, the Geneva Conventions oblige Israel to provide a high standard of care for the civilians under its control; a standard which the Israelis have violated in systematic ways (i.e. not merely in the "fog of war") and for political purposes.

Palestinians, as the occupied population, are entitled to fight for their freedom, including by military means. What they are not allowed to do, however, is to deliberately or recklessly target civilians on the Israeli side. The argument that, because Israel has a seemingly universal draft, none of its citizens can be considered to be civilians is specious. Thus, the recourse of some Palestinian militias to suicide bombings and rocket fire from Gaza also constitutes a grievous human rights violation because it fails to distinguish between combatants and civilians.[27] The intra-Palestinian practice of murdering suspected collaborators without due process is also a gross human rights violation.[28]

The balance of terror between Israel and the Palestinians, as reported by *B'Tselem* (the leading human rights organization to have observers on the ground), stands at a ratio of approximately 10 Palestinian civilians killed for every Israeli civilian casualty.[29] Both sides can, thus, be accused of human rights violations. But the paradoxical context must always be kept in mind: while, per human rights doctrine, Palestinian and Israeli individuals are of equal value, they exist in two highly unequal communities: occupier and occupied. The importance of this contextual element cannot be ignored.

This brings us to the most serious and intractable challenge in human rights law. The fact is that human beings live in communities, and cannot thrive apart from them. Yet the human rights framework enshrines in law and morality a radical form of individualism. Each individual human being is seen as a rights-bearing subject, and the legitimacy of a community, whether familial or political, is evaluated by the degree to which that community serves its members. This is a worthwhile and popular standard, but it is also incomplete. If human beings truly cannot exist apart from larger groups (families, clans, neighbors, tribes and, in the modern world system, nation-states) then the human rights doctrine must become more complex. *If human life depends on viable communities, then those communities must also have rights to survival.* And if they do, then conflicts of interest between group needs and individual desires will necessarily arise.[30] Such a conflict, in turn, requires an extension of human rights doctrine to help us negotiate an appropriate balance between responsibilities and rights for individuals embedded in communities.

A recent example of debate focused on this very subject, the balance between individual and group rights, can be found in Susan Muller Okin's edited collection *Is Multiculturalism Bad for Women?*[31] In her opening essay, Okin argues that respect for traditional cultures requires acceptance of practices that are harmful to women. She cites, for example, the French government's acceptance of polygamous marriage in its immigration policies, despite the distress that polygamy creates for wives, especially in situations of crowded immigrant living.[32] Contributors to the volume, arguing from various shades of leftist politics, take her to task on a number of grounds: for implying that third-world cultures can be imagined as "stable, timeless, ancient, lacking in internal conflict, pre-modern[33];"for failing to recognize that traditional cultures include possibilities of reform and resistance[34]; for failing to recognize that gender relations are shaped by colonialism, neocolonialism and immigration[35]; and for failing to address issues of class as well as gender.[36] The point here is not to resolve the question of whether multiculturalism is bad for women, but to insist that human rights doctrine must address the issue of balance between individual and group rights and must, moreover, do so in a way that recognizes the power of historical and political forces to shape our understanding of the very idea of human rights.

Thus we end where we began. Human rights doctrine, as we know it today, arises in a particular time and place; it is a text with a context. In its official version, it seeks to provide a generous and humane grounding to the international order. It was incomplete even at its creation because its enforcement mechanisms were weak. Given weak enforcement mechanisms, superpowers can misuse human rights doctrines, reducing them to a dressed up, disguised version of neocolonialism. The classical statements of human rights (for example, the Universal Declaration), have to some degree, been overtaken by events that call for a reasonable extension of its core principles. The earth is today more fragile than it was known to be in the aftermath of WWII, and people are more interconnected by various forms of globalization. New practices and technologies of warfare present new challenges. Most importantly of all, human rights doctrine needs to recognize that people exist only in groups and must give us some direction in balancing the mutual rights and responsibilities of each to the other.

The two most common bases for grouping human beings are biology and politics. Biology recognizes the critical role of family in human survival. Politics recognizes that beyond the realm of family and clan, the earth is organized into politically defined communities – today largely nation-states. Each of these bases for grouping people also is relevant to the Palestinian-Israeli conflict.

RACE: ARABS AS THE EMERGING RACIAL "OTHER"

But race is the child of racism, not the father.

TaNehisi Coates[37]

I was born a Black woman/and now/I am become a Palestinian.

June Jordan[38]

Refugee camps that make you long for the projects ...Closed universities and open prisons ... Curfews and house demolitions.

Suheir Hamad[39]

What is racism? It is when 250 Lakota massacred at Wounded Knee are not regarded as the largest mass shooting in U.S. history.

Matt Sherman[40]

Yuri's Story[41]

At the time I met him, Yuri was a doctoral candidate at Harvard. He is an Israeli who, after serving in the army, became engaged with *Breaking the Silence*, a group of military veterans who use photographs to educate their fellow Israelis about the realities of the Occupation. They take no official position on whether the Occupation is right or wrong. They simply ask their elders to look at, to see, and to acknowledge, what is entailed in asking their sons and daughters to enact the occupation during their years of compulsory military service.

I have seen Yuri give a number of talks on behalf of *Breaking the Silence*. At one such talk, an audience member suggested that Yuri, like other soldiers manning the checkpoints, was a racist. Yuri sighed. Then he told this story.

While he was serving in the army, during the first *Intifada* he found himself assigned to checkpoint duty. He was determined to carry out his responsibilities in a kind and fair manner. He stuffed all the pockets of his uniform with candies for the children he would encounter. He was known in his circle of friends as a funny raconteur, and he rehearsed humorous anecdotes to lighten his interactions with Palestinians who would come before him.

Gradually, however, he realized that the Palestinians who stood before him at the checkpoint did not find him either charming or amusing. When he told funny stories they laughed in the most perfunctory manner. Over time, Yuri came to realize that, for the Palestinians standing before him, he was simply an 18 year old with a gun, who exercised power over them. By whim, he could decide who would get to their jobs and who would not pass and would miss a day's work. By whim, he could decide who would get to a clinic or a doctor's appointment and who would be turned back. By whim he could decide to humiliate a father in front of his children or to wave the family through. So, quite naturally, the Palestinians detested him.

And once he realized that he was hated, then, he said, "They all began to look alike to me."

The simple human fact is that people are born into families. Biological imperatives provide the first crucial basis of bonding with others. As children grow, their circle widens from the immediate family with whom they share clear ancestral links to a wider community. But even in this wider world where, today, many relationships are structured by state bureaucracies, people continue to use metaphors of kinship,[42] as when they address older family friends as Auntie or Uncle So-and-So.

People also use biological metaphors more broadly. For example, in the discussion of the recent massacre in Gaza, Operation Protective Edge, commentators from all ends of the political spectrum have depicted Gaza as a woman. Television pundit Bill Maher (in)famously tweeted "Dealing w/ Hamas is like dealing w/ a crazy woman who's trying to kill u – u can only hold her wrists so long before you slap her."[43] Yonatan Shapira, a well-known Israeli leftist, critical or Israel's behavior in Gaza, said "If I have to give one allegory for this whole thing … I would imagine it as gang rape."[44]

Both of these metaphorical uses of biology are a little strained. But perhaps the most problematic use of biology is our tendency to group our fellow humans into schemas of racial classification. Biologists define race as subpopulations of a single species that are *distinctive in appearance but not in genetic structure or in ability or talent* (emphasis mine).[45] Unfortunately, human beings seldom pay much attention to the biological definition of race.

75

For human beings the definition of *race is socially constructed*; it is not determined by biological facts. TaNehisi Coates, a chronicler of the African-American experience, is worth quoting at length about the social construction of race:

> But race is the child of racism, not the father. And the process of naming 'the people' has never been a matter of genealogy and physiognomy so much as one of hierarchy. Difference in hue and hair is old. But belief in the preeminence of hue and hair, the belief that these factors can correctly organize a society and that they signify deeper attributes which are indelible – this is the new idea at the heart of these new people who have been brought up hopelessly, tragically, to believe that they are white. These people are, like us, a modern invention. But unlike us, their new name has no real meaning divorced from the machinery of criminal power. The new people were something else before they were white – Catholic, Corsican, Welsh, Mennonite, Jewish – and if all our national hopes have any fulfillment, then they will have to be something else again.[46]

This particular practice, of naming the other in racial terms, was consolidated late in the 18th century, not coincidentally in the context of colonial settler projects.[47] Even a cursory glance at the history of racial "naming" reveals absurd contradictions. Eva Garroutte provides a stunning example from American Indian experience.[48] Some tribes, she reports, reject individuals who are universally agreed to be of entirely Indian ancestry because they cannot show at least two grandparents from the same tribe, a requirement for belonging in those particular tribes. At the same time, in other tribes, individuals who are universally recognized to have no Indian ancestry whatsoever can become full tribal members by marrying into the community. Such categorizations simultaneously make whites into Native Americans and prevent Native Americans from being recognized as such. Not surprisingly then, if you ask any class of sociology students in American to write a list of how many races co-exist in their country and then have them share their lists in discussions, you will find estimates that range from 2 to 11 different races.

Even when racial characterizations are intended to be benign – for example in medical practices that suggest screening for sickle cell anemia for black patients or Tay-Sachs disease for pregnant Jewish women – the doctors' stereotypical assumptions will cause them to miss the real incidence of the disease.[49]

Considerations of class, gender, and faith inflect and complicate the discussion of race. In the case of Islamophobia, for example, Pakistani immigrants who entered the United States shortly after the passage of the Immigration and Nationality Act of 1965 (which reopened the opportunity to immigrate to America to non-Europeans for the first time since the 1920s) were generally affluent and highly educated tech workers. They enjoyed a class advantage and were often treated as "honorary whites."[50] And similarly, gender matters in the process of racialization: Arab women, especially those who wear *hijab*, are often treated as people to be rescued by Americans, whereas Arab men are perceived as threatening others, potential terrorists.[51] Arab Christians are an unrecognized category in the eyes of most Americans, but they tend to identify themselves as white more often than Arab Muslims, even when their skin color is the same.[52]

For human beings, racial distinctions are seldom merely descriptive. Almost always, *racial distinctions are invidious*: they attribute greater virtues to one group than another. Native Americans were described as savages, even as European settlers were appropriating their lands.[53] Slave traders and slave owners claimed they were uplifting slaves by removing them from the backwardness of their native communities, even as slaves were being kidnapped, sold, and confined to a life of eternal labor without rights.[54] Similarly, Europeans have a long history of "orientalism" that allows them to mischaracterize and exploit Asian peoples.[55]

For human beings, *racial definitions are about power*. One racial group enjoys better life chances than others and this advantage is created in multiple ways. Racial privilege can be structural, encoded in law: for example, in the United States, the GI Bill of Rights subsidized home loans for former soldiers only in racially segregated communities.[56] It can be encoded in popular culture: for example, *Hidalgo*, a recent American movie, makes a strong case against racial purity and in favor of hybridity in its plot, which concerns an American cowboy (who is revealed to be of mixed racial ancestry) and an American hybrid pony who prove their superiority in a grueling endurance race over the "pure bred" Arab horses with whom they are competing. Nevertheless, even in a film ostensibly dedicated to hybridity, Arab men are depicted as threatening and devious individuals, daggers sticking out of their robes. Racial prejudice is also displayed in individual attitudes and behaviors, for example, taking the form of racial slurs, race-based perceptions of dangerousness (or beauty), evaluations of job performance or social acceptability.[57] Together these structural, cultural, attitudinal and behavioral forms of racism form a dense

77

cloud of everyday discomfort and disadvantage for some and unearned privilege for others.[58]

The content of all the varied forms of racism also reveals that *racial definitions are about history*; they reflect the tensions of a particular moment in time. Sociologists,[59] political commentators,[60] and historians[61] have all noted how the definitions of racial "others" change in relation to the challenges facing a particular community at a specific moment in time.

The present moment for American race relations is marked by the convergence of many factors, some economic and some political. In the economic realm, we have an economy held hostage to the "America first" mentality, the tariffs, trade wars, and repudiation of mutual obligations characteristic of the Trump administration. Deindustrialization and wage erosion,[62] inflationary pressures caused, in part, by Arab control over oil prices,[63] the emergence of the BRIC nations (Brazil, Russia, India and China) who challenge the ability and the right of America and Europe to set the terms of the global economy, and the rise of the WTO (the World Trade Organization) and other globalized forms of capital also challenge national sovereignty. In the political realm, we see the growth of political Islam, we hear pundits proclaiming a "clash of civilizations," and we suffer the attacks of 9/11, the depredations of ISIS (the Islamic State in Iraq and Syria) and the devastation of Yemen. This narrative is not mere reporting – a lot of dubious interpretation is involved in seeing the havoc in Yemen but not in Venezuela as the product of a clash of civilizations.

Many of these challenges together heighten our preoccupation with Islam and hence with Arabs – ignoring the fact that most Muslims are, in fact, not Arab, that many Arabs are Christian (including most of those who live in the United States), and that there are also Arab Jews. In popular discourse, Arab and Muslim are hopelessly conflated and both are deemed to be different from Americans in ways that are dangerous and that seem particularly noteworthy at the present moment.

It is no wonder, then, that anti-Arab, anti-Muslim prejudice is pervasive, as the following examples illustrate. All of the incidents listed below have occurred since I began writing this book.

- Many American universities teach Hebrew with textbooks imported from Israel. These textbooks routinely erase the Green Line that defines the internationally recognized boundary between Israel and Palestine – a practice that erases Palestine. Needless to say, no American university would dare teach Arabic from textbooks that erase Israel.

- In a recent incident at a university dining hall, a young Palestinian woman, wearing *hijab*, was verbally assaulted and pelted with food thrown from a nearby table of loud, probably drunken, young white men. When other minority students who witnessed the incident lodged a complaint, disciplinary authorities dismissed their concern. The incident was labeled a "food fight" in a spirit of "boys will be boys." Had Arab or African American students pelted a white woman with food, it is very hard to imagine that any university administration would have failed to recognize the assaultive character of this behavior.

- A graduate student, having found his seat on a plane returning to Boston, was speaking Arabic on his cell phone. The passenger sitting next to him called the stewardess and asked to be moved because she couldn't sit next to "a terrorist." The stewardess complied. One cannot imagine the stewardess complying with a request based on an expressed desire "not to sit next to a Jew."

- A university art museum refuses to let an Emirati prince visit the campus to see a prestigious exhibit of Islamic art because he would bring armed bodyguards and "we do not have guns on campus." A week later the Israeli Consul General, surrounded by armed bodyguards, is a guest speaker on the same campus.

- Israeli politicians routinely and unapologetically describe plans to Judaize the Negev or the Galilee or some other area under their control. When Palestinians[64] voice their objections to such plans, the world stands silent. It is hard to imagine a comparable silence were an American politician to announce plans to Aryanize Harlem or Watts, or to Christianize Brooklyn.

- Teach for America accepts free propaganda trips to Israel on behalf of its student volunteers, lending credence to an attempt by Israel to Zionize young American schoolteachers. No one tries to insure that the same set of young American teachers gets to personally experience any part of the Arab world.[65]

- Back in 1984, Jessie Jackson's references to New York as "Hymietown" very nearly ended his political career, at least at the national level – a well-deserved penalty. But in 2013, when Israeli Minister Naftali Bennet said of Arabs "when you catch terrorists, you simply have to kill them," and, upon being told by the head of the Israeli National Security Council that this is illegal, replied "I've killed lots of Arabs in my life – and there is no problem with that," the silence is deafening.[66]

- An October 2012 Israeli poll of Israeli Jews revealed that one third of them believed that Israel's Palestinian citizens should be denied the right to vote. Almost half supported stripping Palestinians born in Israel of their citizenship, and more than half thought the Israeli state should treat Israeli Jews better than it treats Palestinian citizens of Israel.[67] Only left wing Israelis (a tiny minority) objected. I leave it to the reader's imagination to picture the outcry had polls revealed that the citizens of any European country harbored such ideas about their own Jewish citizens.

- By now, Israel has ensured that everyone interested in the conflict knows that Hamas' charter contains objectionable language calling for the elimination of Israel (see Chapter 1). Few, however, recognize that the charter of the Likud Party denies Palestinian history in the land, Palestinian claims to civil rights, and even the possibility of a Palestinian state.[68] Fewer still object.

- The Simon Wiesenthal Center decides to construct a Museum of Tolerance in Jerusalem. Part of the construction involves disturbing the Mamilla Cemetery, an Arab burial ground.[69] This action evokes passionate objections from Arab groups and also from architects, from the U.N. Human Rights Commission, and even from the Central Conference of American Rabbis.[70] The construction continues. Imagine an Arab group deciding to build a Museum of Tolerance partially on the land of the Jewish Cemetery in Prague. Unthinkable.

- At Yale, a chaplain who wrote that Israeli conduct, specifically Operation Protective Edge, was fueling anti-Semitism finds himself denounced as an anti-Semite and resigns his position.[71] The argument of his accusers is that the only person responsible for anti-Semitism is the anti-Semite him- or herself, and that Israeli behavior is irrelevant. All well and good, so long as criticism of Israel and anti-Semitism are not conflated. But note, that no one has been criticized for saying that the behavior of ISIS feeds Islamophobia. Why is the same logic not applicable?

Perhaps these multiple, subtle and not-so-subtle examples of anti-Arab racism and Islamophobia can best be summarized by saying that, in America, Arab is the new black. This phenomenon began as far back as 1990, when then President George H. W. Bush tried to define Saddam Hussein as "the new Hitler"[72] only a year after the collapse of the Soviet Union and the end of the Cold War. His efforts proved to be singularly unconvincing. However, after Americans went to war, first in Iraq, and then in Afghanistan, and then again in Iraq, after 9/11, defining a shadowy and threatening Islamic figure as the new "them" found more traction with the public.

This generally tumultuous situation provided Israel with a significant opportunity to advance its own interests. It encouraged Americans and

Europeans to identify Arabs as enemies and the Israeli state, as it has always wanted to be seen since Herzl's day, as the "rampart of Europe against Asia, an outpost of civilization as opposed to barbarism."[73] Immediately after 9/11, Ariel Sharon, then the Prime Minister of Israel, made much of the common Israeli and American interest in defeating Arab terror.[74]

Sharon's advocacy fell on fertile ground, as Islamophobia is common not only in the United States but also in Western Europe. In a recent article entitled "Eurozionism and its Discontents" Gabriel Pitersberg, following the Israeli poet and cultural critic Yitzak La'or, argues that a new, highly orchestrated form of admiration for Jews serves many purposes in Europe: it reduces the Holocaust to Auschwitz, thereby focusing on German behavior and ignoring the extent of complicity by other European powers, especially Italy and Vichy France. It reduces the Second World War to the Holocaust, thereby deflecting attention from Allied atrocities. It reduces the history of the twentieth century to the Second World War, thereby erasing the murderous impact of European colonialism.[75] All of this allows Europe to see itself as a place of liberality, tolerance, and inclusion, even as the old anti-Semitism, once directed at Jews, finds new forms in despising Arabs.

Americans, in general, agree with the European view of the Middle East. But in America additional factors are at work in promoting anti-Arab racism. Recently, the very success of the civil rights movement introduces yet another element to the story of race as a filter for perceiving the Middle East. In a recent *American Quarterly* article, Cynthia Young describes the Bush Administration's persistent attempts (think Condoleeza Rice and Colin Powell) to align the history of the civil rights movement with the war on terror.[76] For that ploy to work, black men are promoted, in fiction and in fact, as the ideal new patriots, uncritically eager to spread American influence, by force of arms if necessary, against political Islam.[77] Young traces the use of black actors and black characters in popular media – actor Dennis Haysbert in the role of President David Palmer in the long-running television show *24,* actor Jamie Foxx in *The Kingdom* – to depict the new superpatriot. And since this superpatriot is African-American, why, then, America cannot be accused of racism when its new heroes go to war against people of color in the Middle East. Young quotes rapper Talib Kweli's succinct statement of the position "Niggas ain't become American till 9/11."[78]

I began this section by acknowledging that biology plays a crucial role in structuring human beings' ties to one another. Nevertheless, I argue that the particular application of biology that groups human subjects into separate races is harmful in political affairs. Such groupings never honor the scientific definition of race: differences in appearance unrelated to differences in ability. Race as a social category virtually always carries a message of invidious and inaccurate distinctions among peoples. In the case of Palestinians, the world's decades-long indifference to their claims has now ceded to an ethnoracialization of the conflict that makes Israelis "the white guys" and the Palestinians a swarthy and suspect other. This phenomenon exists in plain view, shouted from the floor of the Israeli Knesset (unicameral legislature) in utterances like that of the right-wing member who asserts: "The whole Jewish race is (sic) the greatest human capital, and the smartest and the most understanding."[79]

But even if we disqualify the use of racial groupings as the basis for human community, we nevertheless need to ask on what basis individual human beings can be grouped into viable collectivities in the contemporary world. Clearly, today's globe is organized into a system of nation states, and so we need to understand how the theories and practice of nationalism shape the Palestinian conflict.

NATION AND NATIONALISM: THE RIGHT TO HAVE RIGHTS

Nationalism is not the awakening of nations to self-consciousness: it invents nations where they do not exist.

Ernest Gellner[80]

The drawback of this formulation is that Gellner ... assimilates 'invention' to 'fabrication' and 'falsity' rather than to 'imagining' and 'creation.

Benedict Anderson[81]

A Nation ... is a group of person united by a common error about their ancestry and a common dislike of their neighbors.

Karl Deutsch[82]

Peter's Story

A friend of mine was born in a traditional working-class area of East London during WWII. Fortunately, his primary and secondary school teachers recognized his exceptional artistic talent, and he won a stipend to attend a prestigious music conservatory. After his graduation, he became a professor of music at a college in Quebec. When his children were born, the family wanted their children to be educated in English-language schools, despite the fact that they lived in a francophone province. It turned out that this was possible so long as the family could furnish a letter from the father's secondary school, attesting to the fact that English was the primary language of instruction there. So Peter sent away to his old secondary school and promptly received a letter in reply. The primary language of instruction, said the School Head, was Urdu.

Today the modern nation state is a familiar entity. Schoolchildren are given maps to memorize: France is here, in purple, and below it are Spain in orange and Portugal in green. Implicitly, if not explicitly, we are taught to think of the contemporary map of states as eternal and immutable, despite the fact that we are also taught about our own revolutionary war, despite the fact that we welcome new nations such as South Sudan (but not Palestine) to the community of nations.[83]

In general, people think of modern nation states as having three levels.[84] At the top is the central government whose apparatus defines the territory under its jurisdiction, represents the nation in international affairs, and is responsible for organizing internal affairs so as to insure security and commerce. At the bottom are individual citizens, for whom participation in this national entity is a matter of personal importance and value, i.e. saying "I am an American" or "I am a Frenchman/woman" is experienced as an authentic element of one's identity. Between the bottom and the top are a series of mediating institutions. They do the work of transforming a name on a map into the real, substantive sense of national identity that ordinary citizens evince.[85] Mediating institutions[86] may be public, private, or some hybrid form, and include organizations such as museums, archives, libraries, monuments, courts, media – all of which furnish specific content to fill the cup of national identity. The most important of these mediating institutions are the schools, where young people and immigrants are instructed in both the national realities and the national myths.[87] The historian Ernest Gellner writes: "Time was when the minimal political unit was determined by the preconditions of defence (sic) or economy: it is now determined by the preconditions of education."[88] Through such sources as the media and the schools, people

83

who will never meet face-to-face come to think of themselves as sharing an identity as citizens of the nation and neighbors to one another. This is why the sociologist Benedict Anderson calls nation states "imagined communities."[89]

Anderson's depiction stresses the cultural and communal aspects of national identity. However, nationhood also has a more coercive aspect since the state is, by definition, the organization that holds a monopoly on the legitimate use of violence in a given territory. Nations are all peremptory as well, since, for all practical purposes, there is no other way to have rights but to have them as a citizen of a state. States guarantee the right to have rights, in the words of Hannah Arendt.[90] Thus stateless people like the Palestinians have no instrument that guarantees any rights to them, no matter how inspiring the language of human rights discourse may be.

The foregoing means that ideas of nationhood are startlingly similar to ideas of race: socially constructed, often implying invidious distinctions among people, shaped by historical moments and power relationships.

The current nation-state system is a relatively recent human arrangement, dating back only as far as the 18th century.[91] Before that, in the thousands of years of human history since the emergence of political units larger tribes, the world's political space was configured in a number of patterns, both smaller and larger than the current system of nation states. On the smaller end, were such entities as city-states, principalities, duchies, or dukedoms, and their counterparts in other cultures. On the larger end were empires that spanned the globe. Those most relevant to the Israeli-Palestinian conflict are the Ottoman and English empires, but others – the Romanov, Hapsburg and Hohenzollern empires – also played indirect roles in the development of Zionist national aspirations.

The process of transforming an earlier political geography into the map that we recognize today was always and everywhere highly contentious (as are invidious racial classifications). Every possible challenge to the nationalist project embodied in the present map has been made at some point. Regional differences proved to be challenging for nationalist projects, as was the case with tensions between northern and southern Italy. Language and ethnic differences also led to contestation, as is the case of Dutch and French speakers in Belgium, French and English speakers in Canada. Secessionist movements continue to operate to this day, for example, in modern Spain, in the United Kingdom, and in Canada. Since World War II, a number of countries have been divided into new states recalling their older component parts, as in the separation of the Czech and Slovak Republics and the re-emergence of the Balkan republics from the former Yugoslavia.

Religious differences have been vastly troubling almost everywhere, and governmental responses have varied. Some countries, such as France, have opted for a determined laicism, eschewing not only an established state religion but even, in some cases, the brandishing of religious symbols in the public square.[92] Other nations have established state churches, e.g. Lutheranism in Denmark and Anglicanism in England. Still other nations have a *de facto* but not a *de jure* religious character; Catholicism in Italy is an example of such an arrangement. Still other countries have accepted that their citizens are permanently divided among different faith communities, as is the case with Catholics, Protestants, and others in Germany.

Nationalist projects have been further complicated by the fact that human beings are a nomadic species, so that, often, a nationalist project will find that its "own" people actually reside in some foreign jurisdiction while many of the people living within its borders retain possible political ties to other states. The resulting population transfers that characterized the early twentieth century – "Greek" Christians leaving Turkey and "Turkish" Muslims leaving Greece; Poles leaving Ukraine and Ukrainians leaving Poland, Greeks leaving Bulgaria and Bulgarians leaving Greece, German and Italian minority groups being rearranged by treaties between Hitler and Mussolini, Hindus being moved to India while Moslems were moved to East and West Pakistan, etc. – almost always ended in massive human rights violations. People were compelled to comply with nationalist programs that required their forced uprooting from the places they had long lived. Nationalism is thus about power, shaped by evolving historical forces, both ideological and pragmatic.

Given all these points of contestation, it is no wonder that, even today, both national borders and national identities are subjects of dispute. On-going historical developments – the end of the Cold War, new alliances among emerging economies, and the development of global forms of governance, especially by capitalist interests – all guarantee that there is no final and stable configuration of nation-states. Examples drawn from the Canada, the UK, Spain and Belgium show that uncertain national boundaries and identities are a universal human condition, not the remnants of third-world decolonization or under-development.

Today, the Middle East is a place where national identities are profoundly unsettled and fiercely contested. All the forces named above are at work: religious disputes between various branches of Islam and, in Israel, among various shades of Judaism and between religiosity and secularism, all roil the waters. Christian minorities fit uneasily into this mix and sometimes maintain "national" aspirations that set them apart from their fellow citizens.[93] Language divides as well as uniting people, since many of the colloquial forms of Arabic that span the Maghreb and the Levant are not mutually intelligible. In Israel, struggles between those who wanted to make German the national language and those who opted for Hebrew resulted in a compromise that forced Hebrew pronunciation away from its resemblance to Arabic and toward the Germanic.[94]

Some groups are struggling to find or form a state that embodies their national aspirations. The Palestinians and Kurds have a strong sense of national identity but remain stateless; they are nationals without a nation. In other instances, the reverse is true: the Emirates have clearly defined state institutions and are struggling to define the substance (other than geographic location) of their national identities; they are nations without nationalism. The components of a nation-state that form Anderson's imagined community rarely come together seamlessly.

In the section that follows, we will explore the history of the Palestinian-Israeli struggle for national identity in more detail and with a chronological arc to the narrative. Suffice it here to start with these observations:

- From the beginning, both the Palestinians who lived in the area and Zionists who emigrated into it aspired to control the entirety of historic Palestine.
- Each side would, of course, have preferred to have the whole of historic Palestine to itself without the presence of the inconvenient other.
- The "two-state solution," i.e. the division of historic Palestine into a Jewish and a Palestinian state, is a relatively recent concept. It originated in the British Peel Report of 1936 although the Balfour Declaration of 1917 already implied it. With ever-changing boundaries, it resurfaced in 1947 as the advisory United Nations General Assembly Resolution 181, again in the 1988 with the acceptance by the PLO of a two-state formula, and since 1993 as the unimplemented Oslo Accords.
- Palestinians and Zionists pursued their respective nationalist projects with vastly different resources. The Zionists mounted their project largely from the territory they wished to control, received international diplomatic support, and secured the world's current superpower to provide massive foreign aid, military support, and diplomatic immunity. The Palestinians mounted their national struggle largely from a series of ever more remote exiles (Jordan, Lebanon, Tunisia), with uncertain allies who provided great rhetorical but little financial support.

• At present, given the more than 75 years in which the "good idea" of the two-state solution has proven to be unrealizable, we see a resurgent discussion of the one-state option,[95] not only by advocates of Palestinian rights,[96] but also by the more candid branches of the Israeli right wing,[97] who admit that the Zionist plan, all along, was to take all the land and incorporate it into a single state. This admission is of paramount importance since it reveals that it is Israeli intransigence rather than any other force that maintains the turmoil.[98]

With the credibility of the two-state solution diminishing daily and interest in the one-state solution re-emerging, the question is: can all those who live between the river and sea, and those who have the right to return there, learn to live together in a single, multi-ethnic and democratic state?

The answer to that question begins with a look at their history, in the following part of the book.

NOTES

[1]   AlvinGouldner. (1970). *The Coming Crisis of Western Sociology* (New York: Basic Books) pp. 5, 484.

[2]   Thomas Kuhn. (1970). *The Structure of Scientific Revolutions*, Chicago: University of Chicago Press.

[3]   *Ibid.*

[4]   Max Weber, Science as a Vocation, in Hans Gerth and C. Wright Mills (eds.). (1958). *From Max Weber* (New York: Oxford University Press), p. 147.

[5]   Trish McHenry. (2011). Keeping Mandela's Legacy Alive, CNN, retrieved from http://www.cnn.com/2011/US/07/18/iyw.mandela.legacy/

[6]   Aung San Suu Kyi (1990). Freedom from Fear, retrieved from http://www.thirdworldtraveler.com/Burma/FreedomFromFearSpeech.html

[7]   United Nations Office of the High Commissioner for Human Rights. (1948). *The Universal Declaration of Human Rights*, retrieved from http://www.ohchr.org/EN/UDHR/Pages/Introduction.aspx

[8]   The Geneva Conventions and the Rules of War. (1949). Retrieved from https://www.icrc.org/en/war-and-law/treaties-customary-law/geneva-conventions

[9]   Mary Ann Glendon. (1998). Knowing the Universal Declaration of Human Rights, *Notre Dame Law Review*, 73(5): 1153–1176.

[10] Blackstone, quoted in Ali Abunimeh. (2014, March 14). Does Israel have the right to exist as a Jewish state? *Mondoweiss*, retrieved from https://mondoweiss.net/2014/03/abunimahs-justice-palestine/

[11] Zaha Hassan. (2018, June 17). Palestine Sets Precedent with Legal Complaint, Al Shabaka Policy Analysis, retrieved from https://al-shabaka.org/memos/palestine-sets-precedent-with-legal-complaint/

[12] Mahmood Mamdani. (2004). *Good Muslim, Bad Muslim*. New York: Pantheon Books.

[13] Lori Allen. (2013). *The Rise and Fall of Human Rights: Cynicism and Politics in Occupied Palestine*. Stanford: Stanford University Press.

Michael Ignatieff. (1999, Fall). The Stories we Tell: Television and Humanitarian Aid, *The Social Contract* 10(1):1–8.

Eva Illouz. (2004). From the Lisbon Disaster to Oprah Winfrey: Suffering as Identity in the Era of Globalization, in Ulrich Beck et. al. (eds.). *Global America? The Cultural Consequences of Globalization.* Liverpool: Liverpool University Press.

[14] Michael Kearney. (2014, August 20). What would happen if Palestine joined the International Criminal Court? *Electronic Intifada*, retrieved from http://electronicintifada.net/content/what-would-happen-if-palestine-joined-international-criminal-court/13783

[15] *Ibid.*

[16] https://unispal.un.org/DPA/DPR/unispal.nsf/0/7F0AF2BD897689B785256C330061D253

[17] https://unispal.un.org/DPA/DPR/unispal.nsf/0/C758572B78D1CD0085256BCF0077E51A

[18] https://unispal.un.org/DPA/DPR/unispal.nsf/0/7D35E1F729DF491C85256EE700686136

[19] For purposes of this book, I will not maintain a distinction between human rights and humanitarian law, referring to both as human rights law.

[20] This provision is reaffirmed in the International Criminal Court's Article 8(2)(b)(viii), 1998, which states, in part, "the transfer by the Occupying Power of parts of its own civilian population into the territory it occupies constitutes a war crime in international armed conflicts." Retrieved from http://www.icrc.org/customary-ihl/eng/docs/v2_rul_rule130

[21] https://ihl-databases.icrc.org/ihl/WebART/380-600056

[22] Ronen Shamir. (2013). *Current Flow: The Electrification of Palestine.* Stanford: Stanford University Press. For water data see: Not Enough Water in the West Bank? *Visualizing Palestine*, retrieved from http://visualizingpalestine.org/infographic/wb-water, and Thirst, *Visualizing Occupation*, retrieved from http://972mag.com/visualizing-occupation-distribution-of-water/49925/

[23] Human Rights Watch. (2010). "Israel/West Bank: Separate and Unequal," retrieved from http://www.hrw.org/news/2010/12/18/israelwest-bank-separate-and-unequal

[24] B'Tselem. (2014). "Settler Violence: Lack of Accountability," retrieved from http://www.btselem.org/topic/settler_violence

[25] David A. Wesley. (2009). *State Practices and Zionist Images: Shaping Economic Development in Arab Towns in Israel* (Oxford: Berghahn Books), p. 68. Ben White (2012). *Palestinians in Israel: Segregation, Discrimination and Democracy* (London: Pluto Books), pp. 67–68. Taxes/Decades of tax breaks for the settler population, *Ha'aretz*, September 25, 2003, retrieved from http://www.haaretz.com/print-edition/business/taxes-decades-of-tax-breaks-for-the-settler-population-1.101212 "National Priority Areas – Economic Efficiency Law, 2009" in *Adalah, op. cit.*, retrieved from http://adalah.org/en/law/review/506. Yoav Stern. (2007, March 28). Study: Arabs may be poorer, but Jews get more welfare funds, *Ha'aretz*, retrieved from http://www.haaretz.com/news/study-arabs-may-be-poorer-but-jews-get-more-welfare-funds-1.216881. Adva Center. (2014, September 9). Report: Settlements receive disproportionate state funding, *Ha'aretz*, retrieved from http://www.haaretz.com/business/.premium-1.614765

[26] United Nations Office for the Coordination of Humanitarian Affairs. (2018). Occupied Palestinian Territories: West Bank access restrictions, retrieved from https://www.ochaopt.org/content/west-bank-access-restrictions-october-2017 United Nations Office for the Coordination of Humanitarian Affairs. (2017). Fragmented Lives:

Humanitarian Overview," retrieved from https://www.ochaopt.org/content/fragmented-lives-humanitarian-overview-2016

[27] The Goldstone Report finds evidence for war crimes and crimes against humanities on both sides, while still being respectful of the different obligations of occupier and occupied. Adam Horowitz, Lizzie Ratner, Philip Weiss (eds.). (2011). *The Goldstone Report: The Legacy of the Landmark Investigation of the Gaza Conflict*. New York: Nation Books.

[28] Fares Akram and Jodi Rudoren. (2014, August 22). Executions in Gaza are a Warning to Spies, *New York Times*, retrieved from http://www.nytimes.com/2014/08/23/world/middleeast/israel-gaza.html?_r=0

Yizhak Be'er and Saleh Abdel Jawad. (1994). *Collaborators in the Occupied Territories: Human Rights Abuses and Violations*. Jerusalem: B'Tselem, retrieved from http://www.google.com/url?sa=t&rct=j&q=&esrc=s&source=web&cd=1&ved=0CB4QF jAA&url=http%3A%2F%2Fwww.btselem.org%2Fdownload%2F199401_collaboration_suspects_eng.rtf&ei=SXg8VOnQA9SvyA TK1IKQBw&usg=AFQjCNF4d4qcywLQ9K hx PMXDyndHMdvPDQ&sig2=MdroDnX799S8SBCkVXeKyg&bvm=bv.77161500,d. aWw

[29] *B'Tselem*. Statistics, retrieved from http://www.btselem.org/statistics/casualties_clarifications

[30] Historian Yakov Rabkin makes precisely this point with regard to Zionism, when he says "The main threat to Zionism is European liberalism, which offers Jews an individual choice but, according to many Zionists, denies them the opportunity to live a true national life."

See Philip Weiss (2017, June 27) "Yakov Rabkin's devastating critique of Zionism: it is opposed to Jewish tradition and liberalism," *Mondoweiss*, retrieved from https://mondoweiss.net/2017/06/devastating-tradition-liberalism/?utm_source=Mondoweiss+List

[31] Susan Mullar Okin. (ed.). (1999). *Is Multiculturalism Bad for Women?* Princeton: Princeton University Press.

[32] *Ibid.*

[33] Katha Pollitt Whose Culture? *Ibid.* pp. 27–31.

[34] Saskia Sasson, Culture Beyond Gender, *ibid.* pp. 76–79.

[35] Homi Bhabha, Liberalism's Sacred Cow, *ibid.* pp. 79–84.

[36] Pollitt, *op. cit.*

[37] TaNehesi Coates. (2015). *Between the World and Me*. New York: Spiegel and Grau. Retrieved from https://www.goodreads.com/quotes/8236915-but-race-is-the-child-of-racism-not-the-father

[38] June Jordan. (1989). *Moving Towards Home*. London, UK: Virago Press.

[39] Suhair Hamad. (2010). "Taxi" in *Born Palestinian, Born Black*. (New York: UpSet Press, Inc.), pp. 26–27.

[40] https://me.me/i/what-is-racism-its-when-250-lakota-massacred-at-wounded-18917310

[41] A similar version of this account can be found in Oded Na'aman. (2012, November 13). The Checkpoint: Terror, Power, and Cruelty, *The Boston Review*, retrieved from http://www.bostonreview.net/world/checkpoint-oded-naaman

[42] In the social sciences this practice of absorbing people who are not related by birth or marriage into the web of family connections and obligations was traditionally referred to as "fictive kinship." See Janet Carsten (ed.). (2000). *Cultures and Relatedness: New Approaches to the Study of Kinship*, Cambridge: Cambridge University Press, and David

M Schneider. (1984). *A Critique of the Study of Kinship*, Ann Arbor, Michigan: University of Michigan Press.

43 Heike Schotten. (2014, August 30). Suppose Gaza were a woman, *Ma'an News Agency*, retrieved from http://www.maannews.net/eng/ViewDetails.aspx?ID=723865

44 *Ibid.*

45 Ian Whitmarsh and David S. Jones (eds.). (2010). *What's the Use of Race? Modern Governance and the Biology of Difference*. Cambridge, MA: MIT Press.

46 Coates, *op. cit.*

47 Patrick Wolfe. (2006). Settler Colonialism and the Elimination of the Native, *Journal of Genocide Research*, 8(4):387.

48 Eva Garroutte. (2003). *Real Indians: Identity and Survival of Native America*. Berkeley, CA: University of California Press.

49 Moises Velasquez-Manoff. (2017, December 10). "Should Doctors Ignore Race? *Science*, after all, has revealed how arbitrary those categories are," *New York Times*, retrieved from https://www.nytimes.com/2017/12/08/opinion/sunday/should-medicine-discard-race.html

50 Saher Selod. (2014). Citizenship denied: The racialization of Muslim American men and women post-9/11. *Critical Sociology*, retrieved from http://crs.sagepub.com/content/early/2014/03/31/0896920513516022

51 Lila Abu-Lughod (2013). *Do Muslim Women Need Saving?* Cambridge, MA: Harvard University Press.

52 Saher Selod and David G. Embrick. (2013). "Racialization and Muslims: Situating the Muslim Experience in Race Scholarship," *Sociology Compass*, 7(8): 644–655.

53 In the *Declaration of Independence*, Thomas Jefferson enumerates as one of the complaints of the colonists against the crown, the fact that royal rule was not sufficiently hostile to "the merciless Indian Savages, whose known rule of warfare, is an undistinguished destruction of all ages, sexes and conditions." *The Declaration of Independence*, retrieved from http://www.archives.gov/exhibits/charters/declaration_transcript.html. Later commentators were more candid in acknowledging the economic interests that drove the animosity toward Indians: "The idea that a handful of wild, half-naked, thieving, plundering, murdering savages should be dignified with the sovereign attributes of nations, enter into solemn treaties, and claim a country 500 miles wide by 1,000 miles long as theirs in fee simple, because they hunted buffalo or antelope over it, might do for a beautiful reading of Hiawatha, but is unsuited to the intelligence and justice of this age, or the natural rights of mankind." New Mexico Supreme Court, United States v. Lucero, 1 NM S. Ct. 422, 1869.

54 Dorothy Hammond and Alta Jablow. (1992). *The Africa that Never Was*. New York: Waveland Press. Later republished as Dorothy Hammond and Alta Jablow. (2012). *The Myth of Africa*. New York: Library of Social Science.

55 Edward Said. (1979). *Orientalism*. New York: Vintage Press.

56 Thomas Shapiro and Melvin Oliver. (1995). *Black Wealth, White Wealth: A New Perspective on Racial Inequality*. London: Routledge.

57 Peggy McIntosh (1989) describes the myriad ways that white racial advantage is "normalized" in everyday life. White Privilege: Unpacking the Invisible Knapsack, retrieved from https://psychology.umbc.edu/files/2016/10/white-privilege-mcIntosh-1989.pdf

58 Philomena Essed. (1990). *Understanding Everyday Racism: Reports from Women of Two Cultures*. London: Hunter House.

[59] Kai Erikson. (1966). *The Wayward Puritans: A Study in the Sociology of Deviance* New York: Allyn and Bacon. Craig Reinerman and Harry G. Levine. The Crack Attack: Politics and Media in the Crack Scare in Craig Reinerman and Harry G. Levine (eds.) (1997). *Crack in America: Demon Drugs and Social Justice.* (Berkeley, CA: University of California Press), pp. 18 – 51. Michael Omi and Howard Winant. (1994). *Racial Formation in the United States from the 1960s to the 1990s.* New York: Routledge.

[60] Thurman Arnold. (1937). *The Folklore of Capitalism.* New Haven, CT: Yale University Press.

[61] Perry Miller. (1956). *Errand into the Wilderness.* New York: Bellknap Press.

[62] Barry Bluestone and Bennett Harrison. (1982). *The Deindustrialization of America: Plant Closings, Community Abandonment and the Dismantling of Basic Industry.* New York: Basic Books.
David Harvey. (2007). *A Brief History of Neoliberalism.* New York: Oxford University Press.

[63] OPEC used its control over much of the world's petroleum supply to penalize Western support for Israel in the 1973 Yom Kippur War (see Chapter 7).

[64] Alison Deger. (2014, March 21). Israel teens dressed as KKK and in 'black face' for mock lynching at school Purim party, *Mondweiss*, retrieved from http://mondoweiss.net/2014/03/israeli-dressed-lynching.html

[65] Max Blumenthal. (2013, August 20). How school privatization hawks Teach For America promote Israel, *The Electronic Intifada*, retrieved from http://electronicintifada.net/content/how-school-privatization-hawks-teach-america-promote-israel/12700

[66] Larry Derfner. (2013, August 12). Israel's Everyday Racism – and how American Jews Turn a Blind Eye to it, *The Jewish Daily Forward*, retrieved from http://forward.com/articles/182171/israels-everyday-racism-and-how-american-jews-tu/

[67] Catrina Stewart. (2012, October 23). The new Israeli apartheid: Poll reveals widespread Jewish support for policy of discrimination against Arab minority, *The Independent*, retrieved from http://www.independent.co.uk/news/world/middle-east/the-new-israeli-apartheid-poll-reveals-widespread-jewish-support-for-policy-of-discrimination -8223548.html

[68] Noam Sheizaf. (2014, August 16). Netanyahu is talking to Hamas: It's about time, *972 Magazine*, retrieved from http://972mag.com/netanyahu-is-talking-to-hamas-its-about-time/95570/

[69] Saree Makdisi. (2010, Spring). The Architecture of Erasure. *Critical Inquiry*: 519–559, retrieved from https://www.journals.uchicago.edu/doi/10.1086/653411

[70] The Center for Constitutional Rights. (n.d.) Mamilla Cemetery in Jerusalem, retrieved from http://ccrjustice.org/Mamilla

[71] http://time.com/3340634/yale-chaplain-bruce-shipman-israel-anti-semitism/

[72] George Herbert Walker Bush and Brent Scrowcroft. (1998). *A World Transformed* (New York: Knopf), p. 375.

[73] Theodor Herzl. *The Jewish State*, retrieved from http://historymuse.net/readings/HerzlTHEJEWISHSTATE.htm

[74] Israel Ministry of Foreign Affairs. (2001). PM Sharon Address the Knesset's Special Solidarity Session, 16, September, 2001, retrieved from http://mfa.gov.il/MFA/PressRoom/2001/Pages/PM%20Sharon%20Addresses%20the%20Knesset-s%20Special%20Solidari.aspx

[75] Gabriel Piterberg. (2013). "Eurozionism and its Discontents," *New Left Review* 84: 43–65.

[76] Cynthia Young. (2014)."Black Ops: Black Masculinity and the War on Terror" *American Quarterly*, 66, no. 1: March.

[77] *Ibid.*

[78] *Ibid.* p. 1: Talib Kweli Around My Way, full lyrics retrieved from http://rapgenius.com/Talib-kweli-around-my-way-lyrics

[79] Jonathan Ofir. (2018, June 16). Israeli lawmaker: Jewish race is the greatest human capital, the smartest, *Mondoweiss*, retrieved from http://mondoweiss.net/2018/06/lawmaker-greatest-smartest/

[80] Ernest Gellner. Nationalism and Modernisation, in John Hutchinson and Anthony D. Smith (eds.) (1994). *Nationalism* (New York: Oxford University Press), p. 62.

[81] Benedict Anderson. (1991). *Imagined Communities* (London: Verso Press), p. 6.

[82] Karl Deutsch. (1969). *Nationality and Its Alternatives.* New York: Knopf.

[83] Mamdani, *op. cit.*

[84] I expand here on the work of Anderson (*op. cit.*), Gellner (*op. cit.*), Hobsbawm. The Nation as Invented Tradition, in Hutchinson and Smith (*op. cit.*, pp. 76–82) and, more recently, Homi Bhabha, Narrating the Nation, in Hutchinson and Smith, *op. cit.*, pp. 306–311, all of whose work focus on the narrative strategies that schools, media, intellectuals, etc. use to construct an inevitably paradoxical – simultaneous modern and ancient – sense of nationality. Their work implies that all this narrative labor knits together ordinary citizens with each other and with a central state apparatus, hence my three-tiered structure of government, mediating institutions, and disaggregated citizenry.

[85] Alexis De Toqueville. (2002). *Democracy in America.* Chicago: University of Chicago Press.

[86] Peter Berger and Richard John Neuhaus (1996) make the point that such institutions are not merely intermediate, i.e. smaller than the central state but larger than individuals, but *mediating,* i.e. actively promoting attachments between top and bottom. *To Empower People: From State to Civil Society.* Washington, DC: American Enterprise Institute.

[87] Gellner (*op. cit.*) makes the point that the very newness of emerging nations makes them seek legitimacy by claiming to be ancient. Gellner writes: "The self-image of nationalism involves the stress o[n] folk, folklore, popular culture, etc. In fact, nationalism becomes important precisely when these things become artificial. Genuine peasants or tribesmen, however proficient at folk-dancing, do not generally make good nationalists" (p. 58).

[88] Ernest Gellner, *op. cit.*, p. 56.

[89] Anderson, *op. cit.*

[90] Arendt quoted in Leilah Farsakh. (2017, Autumn). The 'Right to Have Rights': Partition and Palestinian Self-Determination, *Journal of Palestine Studies*, 47(1): 62–63.

[91] There is, of course, a prehistory to nationalism, which Anderson roots in the invention of the printing press and the use of vernacular languages in Protestant liturgy after the Reformation. The combining of these two elements contributes to the formation of political communities in which peasants, workers, and gentry of one language community develop common bonds that differentiate them from potential class allies speaking a different vernacular. *Ibid.* pp. 36–46.

[92] This is one of the places where Mamdani's criticism of human rights doctrines, *op. cit.* – that they are often selectively applied and not universal at all – needs to be revisited. France, like other countries, has recently debated a ban on head scarves associated with Muslim communities, while the use of crucifixes and Stars of David has not been equally contested.

93 Franck Salameh. (2006) Vous êtes Arabe, puisque je vous le dis! [You're an Arab if I say so!"] *Middle Eastern Review of International Affairs*, 1: 52–57.

94 Ilker Ayturk. (2010). Revisiting the Language Factor in Zionism: The Hebrew Language Council form 1904 – 1914, *Bulletin of SOAS*, 73(1): 45–64.

95 Jodi Rudoren. (2014, March 9). A Divide Among Palestinians on a Two-State Solution, *New York Times*, retrieved from http://www.nytimes.com/2014/03/19/world/middleeast/a-divide-among-palestinians-on-a-two-state-solution.html

96 "The One State Declaration" *Electronic Intifada*, November 29, 2007, retrieved from http://electronicintifada.net/content/one-state-declaration/793
Ali Abunimeh. (2007). *One Country: A Bold Proposal to end the Israeli-Palestinian Impasse*. New York: Picador Press.
Virginia Tilley. (2010). *The One-State Solution: A Breakthrough for Peace in the Israeli-Palestinian Deadlock*. Ann Arbor, MI: University of Michigan Press.

97 Jonathan Boyko. (2010). Likud MK says he wants Jewish State … With the Palestinians, *News that Matters*, retrieved from http://ivarfjeld.com/2010/05/02/likud-mk-says-wants-jewish-state%E2%80%A6-with-the-palestinians/ Naftali Bennett. (2014, November 5). For Israel, Two-State is No Solution," *New York Times*, retrieved from http://www.nytimes.com/2014/11/06/opinion/naftali-bennett-for-israel-two-state-is-no-solution.html

98 One- and two-state solutions do not exhaust the menu of possible options. Parallel states, federations, confederations and "condominium agreements" have also been proposed as possible solutions. Like the two-state option, they have all faltered in the face of Israeli intransigence. Sam Bahour. (2014, November 5). Flavors of end – Jung und Naiv in Israel & Palestine," retrieved from https://www.youtube.com/watch?v=L8RAZuqildE

CHAPTER 4

ZIONISM

The Idea That Changed Everything

Zionism demands a publicly recognized and legally secured homeland in Palestine for the Jewish people. This platform is unchangeable.

Theodor Herzl[1]

... the Lord made a covenant with Abraham, saying, 'To your descendants I give this land, from the river of Egypt to the great river, the river Euphrates.

Genesis (15:18)

I can't help but feel that the Jews didn't really have the right to appropriate a territory only because 2000 years ago, people they consider their ancestors, were living there. History moves on and you can't really turn it back.

Isaac Asimov[2]

Yasmine's Story

My first trip with students to Palestine/Israel occurred over the winter break from 2008–2009, right in the middle of Operation Cast Lead. On the day we arrived there were 485 dead in Gaza and, by the day we left, the death toll topped 1,200. Every café and shop we passed ran an endless tape loop of *Al Jazeera* news, showing bombed out rubble, dead babies, and massive protests all over Europe and the Middle East. Tensions were high.

Purely by chance, our itinerary brought us to Jerusalem on a Friday. Early in the morning we watched Israeli police and soldiers of every sort massing along Suleiman Street, opposite the Damascus Gate to the Arab Quarter of the Old City. Nevertheless, the five Muslim students who were enrolled in my class approached me to ask whether we could change our schedule to allow them the once-in-a-lifetime experience of

© KONINKLIJKE BRILL NV, LEIDEN, 2018 | DOI:10.1163/9789004394148_004

saying the noon prayers at the *Al Aqsa* Mosque, inside the *Haram-al-Sharif*, inside the walls of the Old City.

I wanted to oblige my students and, of course, I also wanted to keep them safe. The challenge was this: demonstrations against the Gaza massacre were set to begin as soon as the noon prayers ended, and the Old City, and the *Haram* within it, are both walled enclosures that can be easily sealed off and tear-gassed.

I told the students that they could go to the prayers, provided that returned immediately afterwards to the rest of the group who would wait for them at the nearby Jerusalem Hotel.

True to their word, the four boys returned swiftly after the noon prayers. But Yasmine, the lone girl, did not return with them. The boys explained that they were asked to exit by a different door than the girls and they expected Yasmine to appear momentarily in their wake. Ten minutes passed... a very long ten minutes in which we anxiously scanned the crowd to catch sight of Yasmine. Finally she appeared, looking pale and a bit shaken.

"Yasmine," I asked urgently, "were you tear-gassed?" She shook her head no. "I just got lost," she explained. "The place feels like a labyrinth. So I went into an Israeli shop and asked the clerk to direct me back to the Arab Quarter, the Damascus Gate." Yasmine, you have to know, is a petite and beautiful young woman who looks generically Mediterranean: dark eyes, dark hair, and olive complexion. She reported this dialogue with the Israeli shopkeeper:

"Please can you tell me how to get back to the Arab Quarter?"

"Why would you want to go *there*?" spoken in rather surly tones.

"I'm a student with a class. My professor is there; the students are there. I have to rejoin my group.

"Huh, what are you anyway?"

"I'm an American," Yasmine replied. (I rather wish she'd thought to say "I'm a human being.")

"No, no. That's not what I meant. Are you Jewish?"

"No, I am Muslim."

Eye roll, head shake from the shopkeeper. "What a waste of a pretty girl," he muttered.

I cannot resist adding that, two years ago, Yasmine married a Jewish man who, like her, is involved in humanitarian relief work.

Zionism is the doctrine that changed everything by calling for an ethno-religiously exclusive state in Palestine for Jews. I begin this historic review of the Israeli-Palestinian conflict with Zionism, not to reaffirm the practice of starting every account from the Israeli point of view, nor with the usual ritual obeisance to Jewish victimhood before issues of Palestinian rights can be addressed. Rather, understanding of the conflict starts with Zionism because, absent Zionism, there would be no Palestinian-Israeli struggle as we know it today.

But for Zionism, the history of Palestine would be only one more example of a story common all over Asia and Africa: post-World War II decolonization, independence, a more or less successful attempt at nation building (given the high literacy rates and sizable middle class characteristic of Palestinian society, possibly a successful effort),[3] possibly a slide into neo-colonial dependency on foreign capital, a choice between one or the other side in the Cold War, or an attempt to join the non-aligned nations, a flirtation with some form of fundamentalism if efforts at economic development failed, or an aspiration to join the BRIC nations, the Asian tigers, or other blocs of strong emerging economies if economic development succeeded. That is the normal, albeit contingent, course of events in all the former colonies of Britain, France, Germany, Portugal and Italy, and might have been Palestine's history as well.

But Zionism changed that trajectory dramatically. It is a doctrine, a nationalist project, deeply rooted in the history and experiences of European Jews, who then constituted almost 90% of all Jews, worldwide.[4] The history of European Jewry, as nearly everyone knows, is steeped in bleakness and misery. In almost all places in Europe, Jews were ostracized, despised, marginalized, ghettoized. Sometimes anti-Semitism took murderous forms, such as pogroms, filled with rape and murder. Sometimes it took less lethal but nonetheless life constricting forms: exclusion from land-owning, well-connected schools, key occupations, or political office. Sometimes, though more rarely, anti-Semitism could take the form of a sly devil's bargain: surrender your *de facto* if not your *de jure* Jewish identity in order to be accepted as an emancipated modern member of the nation.[5] And, of course, in the end, there was the absolute horror of the Holocaust, the close encounter with intentional evil, and the deliberate attempt at total annihilation. Zionism emerged in Europe in the late 19th century, well before the Holocaust itself, but certainly not apart from the kind of anti-Semitism, vicious or insidious, that would soon give rise to this genocidal monstrosity.

Nevertheless, even in an oppressive and dangerous atmosphere, the Jewish community was also the home of immense intellectual achievements. The modern world is virtually inconceivable without the works of Spinoza, Marx, Freud, Einstein, Buber, Arendt and many others in all forms of artistic and scientific endeavor. There is, thus, an element of choice in the histories that reduce Jewish identity to one of victimhood. I am not, here, denying the *facts* of victimization nor am I denying that this victimization was, for European Jews, pervasive, brutal, and unjust. I am, however, suggesting that there is a gap between the facts of anyone's (or any group's) biography and their assertion of a particular identity that is inevitably a matter of selective attention, perception, and narration. This is another way of saying, as the epigram for Chapter 3 suggests, that facts often derive their importance from frameworks. The overarching and critical point here is that Israel aspires to be the only framer or narrator of Jewish identity and relentlessly insists on presenting Jews as eternal victims of a senseless, atavistic anti-Semitism.[6] In doing so Israel is over-reaching in at least two ways: in emphasizing victimization while minimizing efficacy, and in claiming to speak for the whole of Judaism, which no one has the right to do.

That said, I acknowledge that I, too, am framing the analysis of the Israeli-Palestinian conflict in a particular way: as rooted not in Jewishness or even Israeliness, not in religion or even in conflicts over land and water, but in the ambitions of Zionism as a political project to build an exclusively Jewish state. There are those who, like the activist Norman Finkelstein, advise us not to use the term Zionism at all. He insists that most people in America do not know what the term means: "Zionism, for most people, is a hairspray or cologne," he argues.[7] He accuses those who use the term of being more interested in showing off their radical credentials than in communicating with their neighbors. If we really wish to defend human rights, he argues, then we should discipline ourselves to describe and, of course, object only to specific rights violations committed by Israelis or Palestinians, while always remembering the power differential between them. Finkelstein believes we can get more attention, enlist more sympathy, by sticking to the basics that anyone at the next table at McDonalds can understand. His scorn for buzzwords and radical posturing is, alas, not entirely misplaced.[8]

However, I think that he is wrong on the question of naming Zionism as the problem. If we fail to do so, we are left with an endless list of wrongdoings but no name for the forces generating them. When someone is serious about understanding the troubles between Israel and the Palestinians, then Zionism is a word they need to learn, not in order to demonize it, but in order to understand why British historian Tony Judt would say of Zionism that it "has imported a characteristically late 19th-century separatist project into a world that has moved on."[9]

Perhaps the best way for Western audiences, particularly American ones, to understand the development of Zionism is by analogy. The experiences of African Americans in the United States provide an illuminating parallel. Like European Jews, African Americans suffered a bleak and miserable history in white society. They came to the Americas as slaves, and even after the end of slavery, they were subject to murderous violence, discrimination, exclusion, vilification, fear, and rejection. Sadly, anti-Black prejudice and discrimination were not only characteristic of the bad old days that ended with the triumphal election of an African American man to the U.S. presidency, nor were they ever a matter of purely private behavior. The U.S. government was and is deeply complicit in maintaining racial disadvantage. For example after World War II, the GI Bill of Rights was administered so as to entrench residential racial segregation.[10] Today, the Trump Administration's dismantling of affirmative action programs threatens to diminish diversity in higher education and employment. And, again, in a parallel to Jewish experience, the black community, suffering enormous indignities, nevertheless managed to support a vital artistic community in the Harlem Renaissance and thereafter, and to produce iconic political and moral leaders from the crucible of the civil rights movement.

The questions for both Zionism and the civil rights struggle were primarily political. What can an oppressed community do to challenge the pervasive, structural injustices it confronts? How could European Jews or African Americans respond effectively to their circumstances? A comprehensive, historically rich answer to these questions would be infinitely varied (for a discussion of the tools for social justice struggles, see Chapter 11). Nevertheless, the variety of anti-racist projects and responses can, in fact, be grouped into four major strategies for dealing with oppression and exclusion: *assimilation*, *reform*, *confrontation*, and *exit*.[11]

ASSIMILATION

The most common response to the experience of marginalization is probably an attempt at *assimilation*. For most people, the ordinary work of life – getting an education, finding a partner, raising children, holding a job, caring for the sick and the elderly – is quite sufficient. In popular parlance, people go along to get along. They do not seek out more challenges than life imposes on them; rather, they would simply like to be on good terms with their neighbors. At the very least they would like not to be the targets of virulent forms of discrimination. For this reason, many people are willing to convert to the religion of the politically dominant group in society; to adopt modes of dress that blend in and do not call attention to a despised ethnic identity; to learn the language and cultural habits of the host society; to share in the cultural production and consumer patterns of those around them. Perhaps their taste in food, music, or literature is distinctive, but such potentially noticeable cultural differences can be enjoyed in relative privacy and safety. The assimilationist strategy requires the despised minority to argue that its members are people much like all others and should be accepted as such.

There have been many notable expressions of this sentiment. Perhaps two of the best known reflect, not incidentally, Jewish and African American experience. Shylock's speech from the *Merchant of Venice*, though written by Shakespeare, provides an empathetic reflection of Jewish experience. In Act III, Scene 1 Shylock famously and passionately says "I am a Jew. Hath not a Jew eyes? Hath not a Jew hands, organs, dimensions, senses, affections, passion? Fed with the same food, hurt with the same weapons, subject to the same means, warmed and cooled by the same sun, as a Christian is? If you prick us, do we not bleed? If you tickle us, do we not laugh? If you poison us, do we not die?"[12]

And, in a similar manner, 50 years ago Martin Luther King delivered his famous "I have a dream" speech to a vast audience on the national Mall; a crowd determined to seek an end to racial discrimination. King begins: "Now is the time to lift our nation from the quicksands of racial injustice to the solid rock of brotherhood." "I have a dream," he continues, "that one day on the red hills of Georgia the sons of former slaves and the sons of former slave owners will be able to sit down together at a table of brotherhood ... I have a dream that my four children will one day live in a nation where they will not be judged by the color of their skin but by the content of their character."[13]

Both of these famous and eloquent statements make sense from an assimilationist perspective that argues that the perception of difference is an act of arbitrary discrimination. This view posits that, in reality, the alleged differences between Jews and Christians, or between blacks and whites, are insubstantial and have no real meaning in the face of their common humanity.

Assimilationist strategies can be strategically deployed, as they were in certain branches of the Civil Rights movement, or they can be lived as an everyday reality without much self-reflection. The choice of dress, disciplining of children, etiquette and use of language in public spaces, choice of occupation, consumer goods, even conspicuous patriotic participation all become arenas for enacting conformity to majority expectations; if they are ever to become comfortable, they must permeate everyday behavior in ways that come to look, feel, and sound natural. And, as with any human activity, assimilationist strategies can be carried out with varying degrees of skill, with greater or lesser dignity, with greater or lesser intelligence, playfulness, and creativity.

Sometimes, of course, attempts at assimilation are accompanied by a level of ironic self-awareness that points to a degree of ambivalence and resistance among those trying so hard to be accepted. German Jews who attempted to be "more German than the Kaiser" were sometimes called "Jaeckes" – the German word for "jacket" – to denote their desire to "pass" as ordinary Germans who, as the stereotype would have it, always dressed in sober and respectable suits. And, similarly, in the African American community, being called an "Oreo" (black on the outside, white on the inside) is no compliment.

REFORM

Assimilation, in short, can be weakened by internal ambivalence and resistance, by a lack of the political acumen needed to make it succeed, or by a failure to convince a more powerful group to recognize to the demands of justice. Political mobilization is thus the second, and probably the second commonest, response to exclusion. Groups that have been mistreated attempt to *reform* the system that generates the mistreatment. As with assimilation, political resistance and reform comes in many varieties: some violent, some non-violent; some more and some less strategically savvy and attuned to the discourses of the dominant community[14]; some addressed directly and exclusively to the state and some played out on a broader terrain of cultural politics.[15] Again the parallel between the African American community in the United States and the Jews of Europe is instructive.

From the beginning, the black community has used every available avenue to pursue goals of equality and justice. Slaves were active in sabotaging the system that held them in bondage, and they participated in generating, supporting, and sheltering run-aways.[16] Free blacks were also active in opposing slavery.[17] And, for the last 60 years, the civil rights movement has had multiple projects: some, like voter registration, directed explicitly to the state,[18] some focused on securing both public and private educational opportunities,[19] some focused on community economic development,[20] some focused on emerging concerns like environmental justice.[21] These projects have varied greatly in achieving their objectives and none have triumphed finally and unconditionally. Voter suppression continues to be an issue, especially in Southern states. On-going racial segregation of homes and neighborhoods makes school equality hard to achieve. Affirmative action programs in schools and places of employment have been undermined by a series of Supreme Court rulings and abandoned by the current president. There is an on-going debate about whether black capitalism is any more socially responsible than its white counterpart, given the wealth disparities that distinguish the two communities. Nevertheless, few Americans would argue that either the aspiration to racial equality or its pursuit by political means is illegitimate in principle.

Similarly, European Jews tried to reform the systems that marginalized them – and, as with African Americans, they met with varying degrees of success. The big difference between the African American and European Jewish experience was one of political context. While African Americans had a single nation-state to which their complaints were addressed, European Jews were citizens of many different nations at a moment in time when the politically geography of Europe was being dramatically re-arranged. Empires – Hapsburg, Hohenzollern, Ottoman – were disappearing. German city-states were being unified into a new nation. In the wake of decolonization, nationalisms of all sorts were emerging in the Balkans and elsewhere. Jews bent on reform therefore found themselves in a situation somewhat different from that of African Americans: while they shared common aspirations to reform the systems in which they lived, those systems were themselves highly varied and dictated, for Jews, a uniquely cosmopolitan and multinational reform effort. Against this backdrop, socialism emerged as the primary vehicle for political reform among Jews.

Socialism seemed to hold out many advantages. First, it was an inherently global analysis that allowed its proponents to address all the emerging and varied forms of national capitalisms at once. Second, socialism raised the banner of economic justice and this was naturally attractive to European Jews who were impoverished after centuries of discrimination and exclusion, stereotypes of omnipotent Jewish bankers notwithstanding. And, third, as the Palestinian scholar Joseph Massad points out, European Jews were probably attracted to socialism for cultural reasons as well.[22] For those who believed the socialist narrative of a struggle between the proletariat (the workers) and the bourgeoisie (the owners), socialism offered two further enticements. If you were working class and a devout socialist, you were allowed, at last, to play on history's winning team, for Marx is clear in predicting the eventual victory of the proletariat. And, because all that mattered was your identity as a worker contributing to the class struggle, your Jewishness was no longer a burden from which you had to distance yourself, no longer a condition requiring the good will of your neighbors, and certainly not an identity you needed to conceal or renounce. You were a proletarian; you were struggling for economic justice; your struggle would advance not only the best interests of your own community but also those of all mankind. Socialism became a well-nigh irresistible movement for European Jews.

CONFRONTATION

Of course, the civil rights movement proved to be a long and bloody struggle, still incomplete to this day. Similarly, socialism did not make Jews safe even where it was enshrined, let alone where it failed. For those who did not wish to assimilate and who could not or would not devote themselves to political struggles, *confrontation*, embracing the "otherness" imposed upon them by the mainstream, became an option. — identity politics

Embracing one's "otherness" can take many forms. Within the African American community today, there are traditions of black separatism, embodied in my youth by Black Muslims and the Nation of Islam. There are others, often Black conservatives, who argue that Black capitalism is a distinctive, community-based, and socially responsible form of capitalism.[23] The arts also provide an arena for the assertion of otherness: black rap and hip hop can embody such claims, although there are those who argue that this once radical art form has been not only commodified but reduced to a fantasy of violence and misogyny whose primary audience is young white men.[24]

Jews also have been known to embrace their otherness. Communities of Orthodox, ultra-Orthodox and Lubavitcher Jews try to be self-contained and create a critical mass of like-minded neighbors to support a distinctive way of life – kosher food stores, religious schools, temple congregations, buildings with "Sabbath elevators" programmed to stop on every floor so that no one need push any buttons on the Sabbath.[25] Their religious teaching, which prohibits all work including driving, requires participants to live within walking distance of their houses of worship. Permissible zones for life activities, called "*eruv*" (pl: *eruvin*) are marked out physically, sometimes with wires strung along telephone poles, to create an enlarged sense of home. Thus people who are forbidden to carry outside the home on the Sabbath can nevertheless carry children, medicines, and keys as they go from their domicile to their places of worship as long as they stay inside the *eruv*. Often members of such orthodox communities are identifiable by their dress: women wear hats, scarves or wigs; men also cover their heads and wear prayer shawls whose fringes dangle below their jackets. Even among Jews who participate in none of these practices, there can be a private set of in-jokes, consumer preferences for Jewish or Israeli products, artists, movies, etc. that signify a preference for a discrete and distinctive Jewish way of life in the midst of the wider society.

The most recent example of embracing otherness comes from Israel, where educated young Ashkenazi Jews (i.e. those of white European ancestry) are returning to Europe or migrating to the United States if they see no economic future for themselves in the land of their birth. Their motives are purely personal and, apparently, neither they nor the journalists who write about them make any connection between Israeli spending on the Occupation and the financial difficulties of Israeli domestic life.[26] Within Israel, Jews who immigrate, who "make aliyah" (the term means "to go up," "to rise") are "olim." Those who are "olim" are much admired while those who leave, the "yordim," are disparaged. But now, the young people who are leaving not only refuse to be shamed, they have appropriated the label "olim" and formed groups like "Olim Berlin" and "Olim Prague" on Facebook.[27] The U.S. is home to at least a million Israelis who are unlikely to return to the land of their birth except for occasional visits.[28] Immigrants who arrived with the fall of Communism are also leaving Israel, sometimes to return to Russia and sometimes to move to the U.S.[29] The Israeli government worries that more people are leaving than arriving.[30] In much the same way that rap music has appropriated the notorious "n" word,[31] young Jews leaving Israel are telling their elders that "going up" means leaving Israel to return to Europe. This constitutes a complete inversion of all the hopes and dreams of Zionism.

Predictably, most of these confrontational attempts to embrace and validate "otherness" are quite controversial. Societies create a sense of their own mainstream and a sense of "the other" in order to collectively define who and what they are at any given moment.[32] The Massachusetts Bay Colony of Puritan New England defined itself as going into the physical wilderness in order to cast a moral light onto the world; when the Pilgrims discovered that the physical wilderness around them had been tamed, they replaced it with the social and domestic wilderness of witchcraft accusations.[33] In the height of the Cold War, America stopped fearing Nazis and, instead, discovered the Red Scare and McCarthyism. Since the decline of the Cold War, political

Islam became the new "other," although not convincingly so until the attacks of 9/11. In general, "othering" is not a benign process; the distinction between mainstream and "other" is often an invidious one. Minority groups who flaunt their "otherness" court rejection and repression.

Multiculturalists are well aware of this difficulty, which is why so much of their work emphasizes innocuous differences. The multi-cultural fair in the school gym, where you can wander from booth to booth, sampling a little raga and a samosa here, some mariachi music and an empanada there, and, in the next aisle, some klezmer music and a knish, is supposed to lead you to the insight that "gee, we all wrap meat in dough, so we are all one."

This approach avoids confronting the more difficult, culturally charged differences focused on the role of women, the use of unorthodox medical practices, and the degree to which church and state should be separated. Thus, strategies that emphasize and embrace difference, whether by African Americans or Jews, are likely to be costly and imperfect solutions to the problems of having equal life chances and of being treated fairly by the neighbors.

Obviously, oppressed people also can go back and forth in their strategies, depending upon practical circumstances and, likewise, can intermingle these strategies – assimilation, reform, and confrontation – as the moment dictates. For example, President Obama used all of these strategies with talent and acumen: he was a *Harvard Law Review* editor (assimilation), a community organizer (reform), and signaled comfort with and loyalty to black culture in mild ways, for example, the fist-bump greeting to his wife at the nominating convention (confrontation light). Similarly, well-known, successful Jewish artists like Steven Spielberg and Barbara Streisand excel at their craft to such a degree that they win many prestigious awards (assimilation), are associated with a variety of social justice struggles (reform), and also emphasize their Jewish ethnicity in a variety of artistic and political projects (confrontation light).

EXIT

While assimilation, reform, and the affirmation of difference can co-exist in varying combinations, there is a fourth possibility for responding to prejudice and exclusion that stands alone. Members of a mistreated minority community can come to the conclusion that no combination of resistance, reform, and assimilation will work, and can choose to leave, to *exit* from a society they regard as hopelessly, irredeemably hostile.

Over the years, small numbers of African Americans have come to exactly that conclusion and have turned to ideas of Africa as an original homeland to which they could seek return. The back-to-Africa movement had several waves. In the early 1800s it drew support from free blacks, from reformist whites who tied hopes of emancipation to hopes of repatriation, and, notably from white racists who were uneasy about the presence of free blacks posing a challenge to the legitimacy of slavery.[34] A second back-to-Africa wave crested with the failure of Reconstruction and the emergence of the Ku Klux Klan.[35] A third wave, led by Marcus Garvey in the early twentieth century, was associated with the frustrations encountered by African Americans in the supposedly more liberal cities of the north.[36]

Relatively few African Americans actually emigrated, and those who did encountered substantial hardships in Sierra Leone and in Liberia, which were their principle destinations.[37] Despite support from the American Colonization Society, returning African Americans soon found that neither this support, nor their African ancestry and black skin, provided sufficient protection against disease, famine, or the hostility of indigenous tribes who saw no legitimacy for the returnees' land claims.[38]

Attempts at exit by African Americans and a return to Africa were marked by a number of features:

- The majority of African-Americans were never interested in emigrating or "returning" to a place with which they had no personal familiarity and only tenuous claims of heritage or rootedness.
- The Back to Africa movement rose and fell on the strength of its organizational acumen. The American Colonization Society raised enough financial and social support to sustain the Liberian effort for a brief time, but émigrés soon found that they needed to create a self-sustaining new society or abandon the effort.
- The sources of support for African American repatriation to Africa were, from a moral perspective, a very mixed bag. There were those who genuinely wished to leave, and whose human rights to free movement were vindicated by the return to Africa. Others, often liberal whites, believed that real justice required abducted slaves and their descendants to be returned to their point of origin. This sentiment was, however, tinged with racism since abolitionists and slave holders agreed that free blacks could not and should not become part of American society.[39] In short, much of the support for the return to Africa movement came from those

whose racism led them to encourage any political project that removed blacks from a white-dominated society.

- The choice of Liberia as the site that embodied slaves' lost heritage was largely opportunistic. The rhetoric of a glorious return was compromised by ignorance of the actual points of origin of African Americans. The United States had long held control over land in Liberia while the rest of West Africa was under British and French control. Hence it was easiest for American émigrés to go to Liberia,[40] even though most slaves came from Nigeria, Ghana and points north and west.
- The indigenous people of Liberia were not part of the "back to Africa" movement's plans. Hence when the colonizing settlers arrived, they rode roughshod over the rights of individuals and tribes who stood in the way of their national aspirations.[41] The tensions between colonizers and colonized persist to this day. American-descended elites are accused of corruption,[42] while the UN Office for the Coordination of Humanitarian Affairs (OCHA, also active in Palestine), monitors indigenous rights violations such as female genital mutilation.[43]
- While few African Americans today are part of an organized social movement to return to Africa, the Back to Africa movement nevertheless lives on in cultural practices of heritage tourism,[44] and affection for novels and films, like the enormously successful mini-series *Roots*, that present a romantic view the "African" point of origin of most African Americans.[45]

Though it needs to be acknowledged at the outset that Israel is vastly more economically successful than Liberia, the parallels between the Back to Africa movement and Zionism are startlingly strong.

- Zionism was a minority movement among European and American Jews; to this day, less than half of the world's Jews choose to live in Israel. As we have seen in the preceding section, even among those Jews who chose to move to Israel or were born there, many are leaving. Israeli sociologist Tom Segev, commenting on the Jewish mantra "next year in Jerusalem" writes: "Most Jews didn't actually try to return to the Land o Israel; it was a religious object of desire, often an abstract spiritual concept, not a geographical destination they would actually consider moving to."[46]
- In spite of being a minority movement, Zionism displayed exceptional organizational acumen. The Zionist Organization succeeded in convincing European powers to rearrange the world map to accommodate Jewish nationalist aspirations. The Jewish National Fund pioneered effective mass fund-raising techniques, and continues to accumulate wealth to this

day on behalf of the nation of the Jewish people (NB: not the nation of its citizens, 20% of whom are not Jewish). The Jewish Agency recruited and assisted settlers upon their arrival.

- Early Zionist leaders were very clear that much of their support derived from anti-Semitism. Herzl, the founding genius of Zionism, went to far as to write in his diary: "The anti-Semites will be our most loyal friends; the anti-Semitic countries will be our allies."[47] This pattern continues to the present where the majority of Zionists in the U.S. are Christian fundamentalists who support Israel only as part of the plan for the return of the Messiah. Both the U.S. and Israeli governments are on the friendliest of terms with anti-Semites. Netanyahu welcomes closer ties with the Hungarian prime minister who makes anti-Semitic remarks about Jewish philanthropist George Soros, and with his Polish counterpart who denies Polish collaboration with the Nazis during WWII.[48] Trump appoints anti-Semitic fundamentalist clergy to pronounce the opening and closing prayers for our embassy's relocation to Jerusalem.[49] He also insists that there were some very fine people among the neo-Nazis giving the fascist salute in Charlottesville, Virginia. Moreover, while anti-Semites were and are welcomed as supporters of Zionism many critics of Zionism were and are Jewish. The ultra-Orthodox Jews saw Zionism as a heresy, an attempt to force the hand of God to create the biblical Zion ahead of schedule.[50] Marxist Jews were skeptical of nationalist claims on any kind.

- The choice of Palestine as a homeland for the Jewish state was at least partly opportunistic. Herzl and other Zionists had long been lobbying England to designate land for a Jewish state at a time when some Zionist colonies had already been established in Argentina. The British, however, were more susceptible to the Biblical argument that directed them towards Palestine, especially since the establishment of a Jewish state there also accomplished the purposes first voiced in the Campbell-Bannerman Report (mentioned in Chapter 1) to establish "a foreign body ... planted in the heart of this nation [the Arabs] to prevent the convergence of its wings"[51] to the detriment of European interests.

- Neither the early Zionists, nor their European sponsors, nor contemporary Israeli Jews have any concern for the rights of the Palestinians who had been living in the land for centuries. Palestinians are simply a population whose presence hinders the realization of the Zionist dream of an ethno-religiously exclusive state. Even Jews of Arab origins, whose ancestors arrived after the establishment of the State of Israel, are viewed with suspicion.[52] The troubles that follow from this enmity are the subject of this book.

- Finally, while the majority of the world's Jews and the vast majority of the world's Christian Zionists have no plans to move to Israel, Israel nevertheless enjoys a very good press in the western world. Many Jewish Americans travel there for holidays, weddings, and bar mitzvahs. All young Jews between the ages of 16 and 26 are eligible for a free Birthright trip to Israel and many avail themselves of that opportunity. Israel is rightly admired for some of it s real achievements in science and technology, and wrongly for its successful self-promotion as the "only democracy in the Middle East, " a propaganda success whose not very deeply hidden subtext is "We're the only white guys in the Middle East."[53]

The comparison of African American and Jewish experiences is fruitful. It allows us to understand that, like the movement that produced a contemporary Liberia associated with child soldiers, slave labor, and political corruption, Zionism produced an Israel mired in Occupation, corruption, and the selective affirmation of the right of return for Jews while denying the same right to Palestinian refugees. In the next section of the book, I provide a concise history of all that leads up to the present unhappy state of affairs.

NOTES

[1] http://www.brainyquote.com/quotes/keywords/zionism.html#MtRltxmvCjtPP6vR.99
[2] Isaac Asimov. (1993). *Asimov Laughs Again* (New York: William Morrow) p. 92.
[3] Statistics on college enrollment, completion and population data base can be retrieved from http://stats.uis.unesco.org
[4] Walter Laqueur. (1972). *The History of Zionism.* New York: MJF Books.
[5] Ari Shavit. (2014). *My Promised Land: The Triumph and Tragedy of Israel.* New York: Scribe Publishers.
[6] See Yoav Shamir. (2010). *Defamation.* YouTube, minutes 3:00–8:00, retrieved from https://archive.org/details/Sefamation2010
[7] Tony Greenstein. (2017, September 8). Lessons from Finkelstein: A Response to Seth Anderson, *Mondoweiss*, retrieved from https://mondoweiss.net/2017/09/finkelstein-response-anderson/
[8] For a thorough and balanced discussion of criticism from both the right and the left, see Sa'ed Adel Atshan. (forthcoming). The *Empire of Critique.* Stanford University Press.
[9] Tony Judt. (2003, October 23). Israel: The Alternative, *New York Review of Books*, 23 October 2003, retrieved from http://www.nybooks.com/article/2003/10/23/israel-the-alternative/
[10] Thomas Shapiro and Melvin Oliver. (1995). *Black Wealth, White Wealth: A New Perspective on Racial Inequality.* New York: Routledge.

[11] Albert O. Hirshman. (1970). *Exit, Voice and Loyalty.* Cambridge, Massachusetts: Harvard University Press. In creating this typology, I have used a device that the German sociologist Max Weber called an "ideal type." For Weber "ideal types" were not categories that described either the morally desirable or the statistically average form of a phenomenon. Instead, ideal types are the logically pure form of a phenomenon, a kind of thought-experiment that does not directly describe the complexity of the empirical world, but which delineates its underlying logic. Ideal types are thus akin to the periodic table of the elements, naming all the component parts, which, when mixed together in varying combinations, form the complex reality around us. Similarly, real social situations are combinations of different ideal types; Weber classically describes three types of legitimate domination, and, in the list above, I have attempted to describe the ideal type of political responses an oppressed community can make to the host society oppressing them: they can assimilate and obviate the contentious difference, they can reform the system so that differences do not lead to disadvantage, they can flaunt their differences defiantly or they can chose to leave the field. See: Max Weber, Politics as a Vocation, in Hans Gerth and C. Wright Mills. (eds.). (1958). *From Max Weber* (New York: Oxford University Press), pp. 77–128.

[12] William Shakespeare. (2004). *Merchant of Venice* Act 3, Scene 1. England: Folger Shakespeare Library.

[13] The Reverend Doctor Martin Luther King, I have a Dream, Speech delivered at The Lincoln Memorial, Washington, D.C. August 28, 1963, retrieved from http://www.americanrhetoric.com/speeches/mlkihaveadream.htm

[14] For an example of an especially savvy political reform effort, the campaign for gay marriage rights in Massachusetts, see Jeff Langstraat. (2006). *New Boston Marriages: News Representations, Respectability and the Politics of Same Sex Marriages.* Boston College Doctorate in Sociology.

[15] Two immensely popular Hollywood movies demonstrate the enormous power of culture to shape political discussion. *Guess Who's Coming to Dinner?* models a path for white liberal parents to accept their daughter's interracial marriage, since her fiancé, played by Sidney Poitier, is presented as a cancer doctor with Nobel potential. Similarly, *Exodus*, both the best-selling novel and the box office hit, made the somewhat melodramatic but nonetheless impactful case for the Zionist interpretation of the Nakba/War of Independence.

[16] Eric Foner. (2015). *Gateway to Freedom: The Hidden History of the Underground Railroad.* New York: W.W. Norton and Co.
Eugene Genovese. (1976). *Roll Jordan, Roll: The World the Slaves Made.* New York: Vintage Press.

[17] Genovese, *Ibid.*

[18] The issue of voter suppression continues to the present day. Gregg Levine. (2014, October 14). 40,000 Unprocessed Voter registrations Go To Court, *Al Jazeera America*, retrieved from http://america.aljazeera.com/blog/scrutineer/2014/10/14/georgia-voter-registrationsgotocourt.html

[19] bell hooks. (1994) *Teaching to Transgress.* New York: Routledge.

[20] Gregory D. Squires. (1994). *Capital and Communities in Black and White: The Intersections of Race, Class and Uneven Development.* New York: State University of New York (SUNY) Press.

[21] Robert D. Bullard. (ed.). (2005). *The Quest for Environmental Justice: Human Rights and the Politics of Pollution.* New York: Counterpoint.

22 Joseph Massad. (2005). The Persistence of the Palestinian Question, *Cultural Critique*, 59: 1–23.

23 Jim Klingman. (2014, April 7). Blackonomics: Black Capitalism – Fulfillment or Failure? *Black Press USA*, retrieved from http://www.blackpresusa.com/blackonomics-black-capitalism-fulfillment-or-failure/

24 Tricia Rose, *Black Noise*, also documents how assertions of difference can quickly become tamed and commodified. She concludes that, currently, white boys have become a major audience for black rappers, disguising their enjoyment of misogynist lyrics under the façade of inter-racial coolness. Tricia Rose. (1994). *Black Noise: Rap Music and Black Culture in Contemporary America*. New York: Wesleyan.

25 A wonderful depiction can be found in Anna Deveare Smith. (1998). *Fires in the Mirror: Crown Heights, Brooklyn and Other Identities*. New York: Dramatists Play Service.

26 Jodi Rudoren. (2014, October 17). In Exodus form Israel to Berlin, Young Nation's Fissures Show, *New York Times*, retrieved from http://www.nytimes.com/2014/10/17/world/middleeast/in-exodus-from-israel-to-berlin-young-nations-fissures-show.html

27 Judy Maltz. (2017, October 6). Why Would and Israeli Grandchild of Holocaust Survivors Move to Germany? *Ha'aretz*, retrieved from https://www.haaretz.com/israel-news/.premium-why-do-israeli-grandkids-of-holocaust-survivors-move-to-germany-1.5455634

28 Yardena Schwartz. (2018, May 10). More Israelis are Moving to the U.S. – and Staying for Good, *Newsweek*, retrieved from http://www.newsweek.com/2018/05/18/israel-brain-drain-technology-startup-nation-religion-palestinians-economy-919477.html See also, Philip Weiss. (2017, August 24). As Many as 1 Million Israelis have left for the U.S., *Mondweiss*, retrieved from https://mondoweiss.net/2017/08/many-million-israelis/

29 Liza Rozovsky. (2017, April 16). Why Members of the 'Putin Aliyah' are Abandoning Israel, *Ha'aretz*, retrieved from https://www.haaretz.com/israel-news/members-of-the-putin-aliyah-are-abandoning-israel-1.5460939

30 Lior Dattel. (2017, August 15). More Israelis Left Israel than Moved Back in Six Year Period, *Ha'aretz*, retrieved from https://www.haaretz.com/israel-news/.premium-more-israelis-left-israel-than-moved-back-data-reveals-1.5442809

31 *Ibid.*

32 Edwin Schur. (1972). *Labeling Deviant Behavior: Its Social Implications.* New York: Joanna Cottler Books.

33 Kai Erikson. (1966). *The Wayward Puritans*: *A study in the Sociology of Deviance*. New York: Allyn and Bacon. Perry Miller. (1956). *Errand into the Wilderness*. New York: Bellknap Press.

34 Kenneth C. Barnes. (2004). *Journey of Hope: The Back-to-Africa Movement in Arkansas* Chapel Hill: University of North Carolina Press.
   David Jenkins. (1975). *Black Zion: The Return of Afro-Americans and West Indians to Africa* London: Wildwood House.

35 Barnes, *op. cit.*

36 Daniel M. Johnson and Rex R. Campbell. (1981). *Black Migration in America: A Social Demographic History* Durham, N.C.; Duke University Press.

37 Dr. Washington Hyde, The Tortuous Route of Black American History, in James T. Campbell. (ed.). (2006). *Middle Passage: African American Journeys to Africa, 1787–2005* New York: Penguin Press.

38 J. T. Campbell, *op. cit.*

39 http://www.blackpast.org/aah/american-colonization-society-1816-1964

[40] U.S. State Department, Bureau of African Affairs (2013, July 26). U.S. Relations with Liberia, *Fact Sheet*, retrieved from http://www.state.gov/r/pa/ei/bgn/6618.htm

[41] Lisapo ya Kama. (nd). Liberia: the Unsuccessful Return of African descendants, *African History/Histoire Africaine*, retrieved from http://en.lisapoyakama.org/liberia-the-unsuccessful-return-of-african-descendants/

[42] Human Rights Watch. (2012, July 25). Even a 'big man' must face justice: lessons from the trial of Charles Taylor, retrieved from https://www.hrw.org/report/2012/07/25/even-big-man-must-face-justice/lessons-trial-charles-taylor

[43] UN OCHA. (2015, December). *An Assessment of Human Rights Issues Emanating from Traditional Practices in Liberia*, retrieved from https://www.ohchr.org/Documents/Countries/LR/Harmful_traditional_practices18Dec.2015.pdf

[44] For a contemporary conference on the subject see: Roots/Heritage Tourism in Africa and the African Diaspora: Case Studies for a Comparative Approach, Florida International University, February 12–14, 2015, retrieved from http://africana.fiu.edu/tourism-init/2015-rootsheritage-tourism-conference/2015ht-conference-program-12-11-2014.pdf

[45] Dorothy Hammond and Alta Jablow. (1992). *The Africa that Never Was*. New York: Waveland Press. Also published as Dorothy Hammond and Alta Jablow (2012). *The Myth of Africa*. New York: Library of the Social Sciences.

[46] Tom Segev. (2001). *Elvis in Jerusalem*. New York: Holt, p. 12.

[47] *Ibid*, p. 21.

[48] Chemi Shalev. (2018, July 3). Menachem Begin would be ashamed of Netanyahu's Whitewash of Hungary's Anti-Semitism, Poland's Holocaust Revisionism, *Ha'aretz*, retrieved from https://www.haaretz.com/israel-news/.premium-hungary-pm-orban-s-upcoming-visit-a-blot-on-netanyahu-s-record-and-a-stain-on-israel-s-history-1.6223675

[49] Matthew Haag. (2018, May 14). Robert Jeffress, Pastor Who Said Jews are Going to Hell, Led Prayer at Jerusalem Embassy, *New York Times*, retrieved from https://www.nytimes.com/2018/05/14/world/middleeast/robert-jeffress-embassy-jerusalem-us.html

[50] Segev, *Elvis*, p. 18–19.

[51] The Campbell-Bannerman Report. (1907). Full text retrieved from https://archive.org/stream/imperialconferen02jebbuoft/imperialconferen02jebbuoft_djvu.txt

[52] Ella Shohat. (1999, Autumn). The Invention of the Mizrahim, *Journal for Palestine Studies*, 29(1): 5–20.

[53] Julie Peteet. (2016, Winter). Language Matters: Talking about Palestine, *Journal of Palestine Studies*, 45(2): 24–40.

PART 2

A BRIEF HISTORY OF THE CONFLICT: ANOTHER LOOK

STATE BUILDERS, SETTLERS, AND COLONIAL SUBJECTS

The Past Is Prologue

If you will it, it is no dream.

Theodor Herzl[1]

What confusion would ensue all the world over if this principle on which the Jews base their "legitimate" claim were carried out in other parts of the world! What migrations of nations must follow! The Spaniards in Spain would have to make room for the Arabs and Moors who conquered and ruled their country for over 700 years.

Palestine Arab Delegation [2]

You say my house has been enriched by the strangers who have entered it. But it is my house, and I did not invite the strangers in, or ask them to enrich it, and I do not care how poor or bare it is if only I am master in it.

Arab witness to the 1937 Royal Commission[3]

Eve's Story

I have twice had the opportunity to serve on a jury and both times, found the experience to be fascinating. The first time I served, the jury was presented with a civil case, a lawsuit between two sisters who were quarrelling over their inheritance, a small insurance agency founded by their late father. Much of the argument turned on what was or was not standard business practice, as one of the sisters had taken over the day-to-day management of the company and was accused by the other of inventing unorthodox bookkeeping practices in order to conceal the skimming of profits. Much to the surprise of the jury and, I suspect, even the lawyers for both sides, no settlement emerged and the case

© KONINKLIJKE BRILL NV, LEIDEN, 2019 | DOI:10.1163/9789004394148_005

actually came to us, the jury panel, for resolution. In his instructions to us, the judge told us that we were bound to consider the facts, but that we were also empowered to use what he called "reasonable inference." To be sure we understood, he provided the following example: A woman leaves her purse on a table next to the living room window and retires to bed. In the morning she discovers that a light snowfall has blanketed the lawn. She also discovers that in this snowfall are footprints approaching the house. The living room window has been smashed. The purse is gone. There are also footprints retreating from the house. Given this array of facts, the woman may draw a reasonable inference that the house has been robbed, even if she slept through the actual events and did not observe them directly.

In the following chapters, I provide a synoptic account of the history of Palestine and Israel in four periods[4]: from the beginnings of Zionism in the mid-to-late 19th century to the establishment of the Israeli state in 1948; from the establishment of the state to its Occupation of the entire land of historic Palestine in 1967; from the Occupation to the first major challenge against it, a popular Palestinian uprising called the *Intifada* which began in 1987; and from the *Intifada* through the unending, fruitless and deceptive "peace process" to the present day.

In composing this synopsis, I have tried to keep the focus tightly on those events that were both consequential in their own time and that are also relevant to the conflict as it is being waged today; to keep names and dates – the kind of information that makes students claim to "hate history" – to a minimum. Thus some hugely important events, e.g. the Second World War, are covered only as they intersect with the subject matter of this book; and even the wars that are directly relevant – the mass expulsions that Palestinians call the *Nakba* and Israelis call the War of Independence, the popular uprising known as the *Intifada*, etc. – are described only as the result of the wider social forces that produced them and were, in turn, shaped by them.[5] For this same reason – to keep the focus tightly on the conflict between Palestinians and Israelis – I will have very little to say about the regional history of the Middle East following World War II, except as it pertains to the status of Palestinian refugees, or the vagaries of Arab support for Palestine. And likewise, I will not focus on the tensions among different groups of Jewish Israelis, the Ashkenazi Jews of Western and Central Europe vs. Iberian Jews, Jews from

Arab lands, and black African Jews, except insofar as their mutual struggles shape Israeli policies toward Palestinians under their control.

Each epoch has been shaped by the interaction among Zionists, great powers, and Palestinians. In each epoch, Zionists have sought to Judaize the land, great powers have sought to exploit it, and Palestinians have sought to build and protect their own communities, their own lives, within it.

In each epoch the story is a tragic one. All three parties doggedly pursue fixed ends that they never achieve, even at great costs in human suffering and loss of life. Each epoch ends in a conflagration, after which all three parties continue to pursue the same fixed ends without better prospects of achieving them.

This chapter will focus on the pre-state period in the history of Zionism: on the struggles of Zionist settlers, later militias against Turkish and British colonial rulers and the Palestinian inhabitants of the land who, in turn, fought for their own independence.

ZIONISTS IN THE PRE-STATE PERIOD

Zionism began in the mid to late 19th century, as the desire to create a Jewish state safe from the ravages of Christian anti-Semitism. As with any social movement, it began through dispersed efforts and has taproots that go far back in European history, recalling the mass expulsions of Jews from England in the 13th century, from the Iberian lands in the 15th century, and tempered by occasional, tepid acceptance as the Reformation reshaped Christian-Jewish hostility into Catholic-Protestant hostility.

Ironically, it is not only traditional anti-Semitism but also Enlightenment rationalism that helped to nurture Zionism. When Jews were persecuted and ghettoized, they naturally longed for a safe space under their own control. But when they were emancipated and accepted as citizens within the political mainstream of European nationalism, they then came to fear assimilation. Israeli historian Shlomo Avineri points out that Zionism emerged not at the time of the most intense persecution of the Jews, but at the time that their position, especially in urban centers, was coming to be assured; i.e. at the very moment when assimilation rather than persecution posed the greatest threat.[6]

Zionism, then, poses itself as the answer to both these fears: against physical annihilation, it claims a land of its own, and against social annihilation it requires a land that is ethno-religiously exclusive.

Driven by the desire to found a national home out of the reach of Christendom, Zionist emigration to what was then Ottoman Palestine actually began in the late 19th century. Settlers came from Eastern Europe and financial support came from Western European Jewish philanthropists. Diverse Zionist groups managed to establish some colonies in Argentina but mostly in Palestine. Uganda also came under serious consideration as a possible site for Zionist colonization.

There was a bewildering array of specific socialist, religious, and pragmatic sponsors who established a number of small settlements here and there. But the real success of Zionism lay elsewhere. It was secured by the organizational genius of early Zionist leaders who created a number of effective international organizations – the (World) Zionist Organization, the Jewish National Fund, and the Jewish Agency – that, together, advanced the Zionist agenda both within European power circles and on the ground in Palestine.

Theodor Herzl, an Austrian journalist, was the creative force behind the convening of the first Zionist Congress in 1897. And it was the First Zionist Congress, in turn, which spawned the most effective organizations that served Zionism.

Originally planned to take place in Munich among the affluent and emancipated German Jewish community, the Congress had to be moved to Basel, Switzerland due to the objections of secular Jews to the Zionist project. There were two major achievements of the first Zionist Congress: the creation of a durable organization and the endorsing of the Basel Plan.

The Zionist Organization (as of 1960, the World Zionist Organization) was created to fulfill an explicitly political mandate: to coordinate the lobbying effort that would be required of western Jews to secure European agreement for the creation of a new state. The Zionist Organization had its own internal executive branch and fundraising capabilities, and relied on annual meetings (later bi-annual and then quadrennial) to set policy.

The second significant achievement of the first Zionist Congress was to endorse the Basel Plan, authored by Max Nordau, a close associate of Herzl's. The Basel Plan declared "the aim of Zionism is to create for the Jewish people a home in Palestine secured by law."[7]

At the end of the conference, Herzl wrote in his diary "Were I to sum up the Basel Congress in a word—which I shall guard against pronouncing publicly—it would be this: At Basel, I founded the Jewish State. If I said this out loud today, I would be answered by universal laughter. Perhaps in five years, certainly in fifty, everyone will know it."[8] Note the subtle shift in vocabulary. When selling the Zionist project to Christians, Nordau calls for a "homeland" but when Herzl writes candidly in his diary he admits that

Zionism's aim was always to create a state that was exclusively Jewish, even if this meant ruling over (or, preferably, expelling) an indigenous population.

Herzl himself then continued his lobbying work, addressing himself to Ottoman leaders who did not trust a potential Zionist community in Palestine to respect their authority. He sought to bring pressure on the Ottomans through Germany and Russia, and eventually turned his attention to the British who, before the First World War, actually wanted to promote the stability of the Ottoman Empire "to ensure the safety of their routes across Ottoman lands to India, the centerpiece of the British Empire."[9]

Herzl died in 1904. Chaim Weizman (later the first president of Israel) succeeded Herzl and took over his negotiations with the British. In 1917 the Zionist Organization secured its greatest triumph when the British issued the Balfour Declaration, declaring that "His Majesty's government view with favour the establishment in Palestine of a national home for the Jewish people, and will use their best endeavours to facilitate the achievement of this object, it being clearly understood that nothing shall be done which may prejudice the civil and religious rights of existing non-Jewish communities in Palestine, or the rights and political status enjoyed by Jews in any other country."[10]

The actual language of the declaration had been shaped by a senior British Cabinet official, Herbert Samuel, who was himself an ardent Zionist and would later become the first British governor of Mandate Palestine. He worked to ensure that the final draft identified Palestine as "*a*" home and not "*the*" home of the Jews, in order to prevent the Balfour Declaration from being used as a pretext for expelling Jews from other nations. Samuel also understood that, for the Balfour Declaration to be consistent with British intentions expressed elsewhere (in the Sykes-Picot agreement and the Hussein-McMahon correspondence, discussed below), his original memo could not preclude the possibility that the Jewish homeland envisioned in Balfour would become part of the British Empire, perhaps as a Protectorate.[11] Finally, the language of a "national homeland" was chosen in preference to naming a "Jewish state" because this, too, allowed the British to maintain some credibility in promoting multiple but mutually exclusive agreements.

British policy interests shaped not only the phrasing but also the timing of the Balfour Declaration, issued in November, 1917. At that point it was already clear to military planners that the Allies (Great Britain, France, Russia, and the United States) would win the First World War. In that context, the timing was driven by the hope of realizing multiple aims: to incentivize German Jews to rise up against the Kaiser, to impress Woodrow Wilson's Jewish advisors Louis Brandeis and Felix Frankfurter, and to attract the favorable attention of Russian Bolsheviks, many of whom were also Jewish.[12]

With the Balfour Declaration in hand, the work of the Zionist Organization continued. Other European countries were lobbied to recognize the legitimacy of the Zionist aspirations. And, most important, once the British gained control of Palestine within the League of Nations Mandate system (whereby colonies were to be prepared for national independence), they had to be constantly chivvied to move forward on their commitments to the Zionist project.

Predictably, the British were unreliable allies who, by 1922, were already trying to cut back on financial support, pleading the lack of popularity of the Zionist cause among the England's tax-paying public.[13] In 1930 and again in 1939, driven by strenuous Palestinian objections to Zionist project, the British tried to limit the number of Jews entering Palestine as settlers, despite the implied promises of the Balfour Declaration.[14]

British backtracking notwithstanding, the political work of Zionism was moving forward. The next crucially important task for the Zionist project became financial: securing independent resources to buy land for Zionist settlers and to assist them with the costs of immigration. In order to achieve this end, the Zionist Organization created another successful body, the Jewish National Fund at its fifth annual meeting in 1901. The original mandate of the Jewish National Fund (JNF), a non-profit organization, was to raise money among Diaspora Jews, primarily to buy land in Palestine for Jewish settlers and, by extension, to support the cost of resettlement for Zionists who wished to move to Palestine.

The first thing to note is that the JNF was wildly successful in fundraising. Most American Jews of a certain age will remember the "blue boxes" that were passed around at every Jewish *bris*, *bar mitzvah*, and wedding, to collect money for the JNF. The strength of this strategy meant that Zionism could benefit both from major philanthropic donations and could also tap into the immense value of small donations from many people of ordinary low- and middle-income status. The JNF is alone among the major Zionist organizations to use this strategy, which has both financial and political implications, to be discussed below.

The second thing to note is that the JNF defined its *raison d'être* – to support Jewish immigration to Palestine – in a distinctive way from the beginning: to serve the Jewish Nation or the Jewish People, rather than the State of Israel. For example, the resolution by which it was created at the fifth Zionist Congress reads: "the Fund shall be the property of the Jewish people as a whole."[15] Its charter reads, in part, "Since the first land purchase in Eretz Israel in the early 1900s for and on behalf of the Jewish People, JNF has served as the Jewish People's trustee of the land."[16]

In short, the JNF is structured so that its properties are for the use of Jewish people whether in Israel or elsewhere, but not necessarily for the citizens of Israel, 20% of whom are Palestinians. This charter is extremely significant in the present, because it is used to deny Israel's Palestinian citizens access to land in their own country, which they cannot use, lease, or buy, in the same way that their Jewish neighbors can, i.e. as a matter of right. The JNF argues that as a private, non-governmental agency, it is obliged to use the money raised from Jewish donors in ways that are consistent with the donors' wishes. These wishes are always assumed to preclude treating Palestinian citizens of Israel as the equals of their Jewish neighbors. As a practical matter, the argument that it is the donors who tie the hands of the JNF is simply disingenuous. The JNF excludes Palestinian not only from land it has purchased with donor funds, but also from the land that the state of Israel has placed in its care, much of which is the confiscated property of "present absentees" – i.e. internally displaced Palestinian citizens of Israel.[17]

Today, the Jewish National Fund continues to play a significant and active role in managing the land under its jurisdiction. It has the power to encourage the formation of new agricultural communities and townships, to engage in water management, and to manage wildlife resources on its parklands, etc.

The land regimen of the JNF has positive and negative aspects. Among its positive achievements are extensive tree plantings (afforestation), managing water resources through systems of dams and reservoirs, and the development of more than 1,000 parks.[18]

However, these positive achievements also have a dark political underside. The two most significant examples are these:

The planting of JNF pine forests has been used as an instrument of Palestinian displacement. Historically, pine trees were chosen by Zionist settlers to make the landscape look less alien, more European. But pine trees, it turns out, are not productive in the Palestinian environment. They consume disproportionate amounts of water; they displace productive trees like olive and fruit trees that anchor Palestinian agricultural communities; and the pine-barrens created in their shade diminish grazing land for Palestinian shepherds.[19] Moreover, the best known use of pine tree plantings is also the most objectionable: planting over the ruins of Palestinian villages, destroyed during the *Nakba,* so as to obliterate all physical traces of Israel's Palestinian heritage. This pattern can be seen in the well-known tourist site of

Canada Park and, on our trips (see Chapter 2), at Kibbutz Megido, formerly the Palestinian town of Lajun, where pine tree roots are breaking up the foundation stones of demolished Palestinian homes.

The second example concerns the use and misuse of the JNF land leasing policies. Since the JNF controls vast swathes of Israeli land, it is empowered to sell or lease some of its acreage to Israelis for purposes consistent with the JNF charter. This situation provides yet another window into the dilemmas of Zionism, its desire to be simultaneously Jewish and democratic amidst many non-Jews.

On the one hand, Israel does have laws that prohibit discrimination against citizens on the basis of religion or ethnicity. On the other, Zionism aspires to an ethno-religiously exclusively Jewish state. A widely used and "creative" way out of this seeming contradiction with regard to land, is for the non-discriminatory Israeli state to work hand-in-hand with the JNF, which is unapologetically discriminatory. In practice, this means that the Israel state gives or leases land to the JNF, even including land confiscated from Palestinians under various pretexts (see Chapter 6 for laws surrounding the creation of state lands). Once the property has been passed from the Israeli state to the JNF, the requirements of anti-discrimination laws fall away and the JNF can refuse Palestinian bids to buy or lease land.

In the last 10 years this rather cynical dodge has been challenged in the Israeli courts by *Adalah*, an organization focused on vindicating the land rights of Palestinian citizens of Israel.[20] Plaintiffs have argued for the right of Palestinian citizens of Israel to lease JNF land on the same terms that Jewish citizens enjoy. In reply, the JNF has been brutally honest. It declares: "The JNF is not the trustee of the general public in Israel. Its loyalty is given to the Jewish people in the Diaspora and in the state of Israel … The JNF, in relation to being an owner of land, is not a public body that works for the benefit of all citizens of the state. The loyalty of the JNF is given to the Jewish people and only to them is the JNF obligated. The JNF, as the owner of the JNF land, does not have a duty to practice equality towards all citizens of the state."[21]

Today Bedouin lands in the Negev are the principal sites where the Israel and the JNF are, jointly, pursuing a project of "Judaization." The particularly cruel twist here is that the JNF is acquiring land in the Negev from the Israeli state as "compensation" for leasing other JNF lands to Palestinians inside Israel to defuse the allegations of racism.[22]

Of course, the primary tool for Judaizing Palestine has always been the settler: Jews from other parts of the world who were willing to uproot themselves and to build new lives within the Zionist *Yishuv* (the pre-state Zionist community in Palestine) or, later, the Israeli state and, later still, within the Occupied Palestinian Territories. If the Zionist Organization was meant to create a space for this enterprise within the international world order and if the JNF was meant to raise money and secure land for it, then a third agency was required to recruit and assist settlers through the process of immigration.

The first wave of Zionist settlers came to Palestine during the Ottoman period. A branch of the Zionist Organization called the Palestine Office was founded in Jaffa in 1908.[23] It was designed to help these early Zionist arrivals in their dealings with Ottoman functionaries. Unlike the JNF, the Palestine Office confined itself to seeking finances from major philanthropic donations, which gave wealthy American donors an important role in the agency. By 1918, the Palestine Office was dealing with the British Mandate rather than the Ottoman Empire, and had been retitled as the Zionist Commission for Palestine. Its work focused on repatriating Palestinian Jews expelled by the Turks. In 1921 the same body was retitled the Palestine Zionist Executive and was designated to work with the British Mandate to make good on the promises of the Balfour declaration by bringing more Jewish settlers to Palestine. Finally, in 1929 it assumed the name it holds to this day, the Jewish Agency. It remains a legally separate entity but nonetheless works in concert with the Zionist Organization and with the JNF to bring Jewish settlers and land together.

In order to fulfill its mandate, the Jewish Agency has had to change with the times. For most of its existence, it has been focused on the logistics of resettlement: organizing reception centers, intensive language courses (the *Ulpan* plan), and finding housing and jobs for newly arriving immigrants. The Jewish Agency has also had to deal with periods of intense emergencies: the resettling of Holocaust survivors after the Second World War, managing the influx of Jews from Arab states following the *Nakba,* orchestrating services for the large number of Ethiopian Jews and Soviet and post-Soviet Jews in later years.

Much of this work was relatively straightforward humanitarian assistance to newly arrived immigrants. But some of the Jewish Agency's work had a more overtly political character. During the period of the British Mandate, the Jewish Agency was a leader in lobbying for expanded immigration quotas. Its services to Jewish settlers also included the creation of the *Haganah,* the largest of the many militias formed to capture land from the Palestinians.[24] Later, when the State of Israel came into being, these militias combined to create the Israeli Defense Force.

Between the end of the Second World War in 1945 and the establishment of the State of Israel in 1948 the Jewish Agency, again with other groups, was instrumental in organizing hundreds of attempts to run the British blockade to bring Holocaust survivors to Palestine.[25] In 2010, in an ironic counterpoint, Israel brutally suppressed similar attempts by international solidarity activists to break the blockade of Gaza, firing on the Turkish led Gaza flotilla in international waters.[26]

By the mid 1990's most Jews who had not moved to Israel were living in countries that offered high levels of safety and stability. Given that, with the exception of occasional crises such as the recent one in Ukraine,[27] the major streams of Jewish immigration to Israel were exhausted, the Jewish Agency once again shifted gears. Their most urgent programs now are to build support for Israel as a Jewish state in Jewish communities around the world. To this end, the Jewish Agency offers a variety of travel and service opportunities, from gap year immersion programs, to social service opportunities,[28] to the popular 10-day "Birthright" trips to Israel for young Jews in the Diaspora. By extension, the Jewish Agency is also working hard to coordinate with campus organizations such as Hillel to make sure that young Jews remain favorably disposed to Israel.

The foregoing makes clear that, from the beginning, Zionists showed real genius in organizational development. In one generation, they built the capacity to meet the political, financial, military, and social needs of the Zionist project. They were able to secure the recognition of a Jewish state in the international system, to fund some land purchases necessary to realizing their dream, to form militias that took more land, and to develop social agencies to manage immigration to the fledgling Jewish state.

THE GREAT POWERS IN THE PRE-STATE PERIOD

Yet none of these tasks were accomplished in a vacuum. Organizational genius or not, Zionist organizations were subject to conditions not of their own making. The circumstances that molded Zionist efforts and shaped their outcomes were formed by the desires of the great powers, first the Ottomans and then the British, and the resistance of the Palestinians to the Zionist project.

From the beginning of Zionism in the late 19th century until the end of World War I in 1918, the Ottoman Empire was the great power whose actions were the most consequential for the Zionist project. By the middle years of the 19th century, the Ottoman Empire was clearly in trouble, impoverished, overextended, and faced with managing both the territorial ambitions of its European neighbors and the nationalist aspirations of its internal minorities.

As a response to these pressures, the Ottoman center undertook a sweeping reform and modernization program, known as the *Tanzimat* reforms. These reforms sought to rationalize the administration of the empire in ways that would ensure the loyalty of restive ethnic and religious minorities, streamline the administration, and recoup revenues for the central political body that were otherwise lost to "corruption" – i.e. payments to local notables who had traditionally served as regional administrators within the Ottoman system. The *Tanzimat* reforms sought, among other objectives, to establish a coherent educational system, to remove restrictions on non-Muslim citizens of the Empire, and to rationalize land tenure and the systems of taxation and conscription rooted in land registries.[29]

These reform efforts, especially those based on systematizing and recording land ownership, produced unintended consequences. The *Tanzimat* land reforms were layered over a traditional local system that already recognized private, communal, and state land and that also included a way of keeping track of land that did not fall into any of these categories. The reforms systematized the peasants' right to buy state lands, which was a boon, but one with hidden costs. Lands could be bought, but only on the condition that the buyer also assumed obligations to pay taxes on the land and, by enrolling in a land registry, exposed himself and his male family members to possible conscription.[30]

The linking of land ownership to tax obligations and possible involuntary military service produced at least two responses from Ottoman citizens that effect the current situation.

First, more than a century ago, some people simply refused to register land, choosing instead to stay in place and operate under traditional and informal local Palestinian rules for land use. The result is that people whose ancestors made this choice are now without title documents and therefore completely helpless in the face of Zionist rules and procedures for land appropriation. Palestinian families may have lived on the site for generations, farmed it, built all the structures and planted all the orchards upon it. Their family's graves may lie within that land. But such activities do not constitute ownership according to current Israeli law.[31] Absent registry deeds going back to the Ottoman period, families whose great-grandparents opted for informal land tenure rules cannot now protect themselves from the claim that Israel appropriates only "empty" lands.

Second, while some families chose not to register their land, other families chose to dodge the tax and conscription requirements associated with the land registry by allowing their land to be registered in the name of local leaders who could afford to pay the taxes and who, on paper at least, thus became "large" landowners.[32] Clearly, this was an opportunity for all kinds of chicanery at the expense of local families, including the sale of land to the JNF by "absentee" landlords. Within the Ottoman Empire, the sale of land from one absentee landlord to another would probably have allowed local peasants farmers to remain in place, since a rural labor force was needed for the owner to make a profit on his investment. But once the JNF bought land, they immediately evicted Palestinian peasants in favor of Zionist settlers. This pattern of eviction may not have been anticipated in the earliest land sales, but soon came to be recognized as the reality of doing business with the JNF.

In sum, the *Tanzimat* laws were not designed to be intentionally destructive or dishonest. Yet they produced a host of unintended consequences even in their own time – not least because they impinged on a complex indigenous culture with regional and class divisions. After the 1967 Six Day War brought all of Ottoman Palestine under Israeli control, the JNF would again exploit Ottoman law in its quest to nationalize Palestinian land.

The British, who succeeded the Ottomans in controlling Palestine, illustrate most clearly the duplicity of the great powers. The behavior of Great Britain is a very different and darker story, which can be understood by studying the three major agreements by which Great Britain operated in Palestine. The first was the Sykes-Picot Agreement, the second the Hussein-McMahon correspondence, and the third the Balfour Declaration. All three are rooted in the 1907 Campbell-Bannerman Report quoted in Chapter 1, which shows the British were clear, at least among themselves, that their mutually contradictory and dishonest dealings with Turks, Arabs, Jews, and even their European neighbors, was driven by the political realist position that sought "to implant a foreign body ... in the heart of this [Arab] nation to prevent the convergence of its wings in such a way that it could exhaust its powers in never-ending wars."[33]

As early as 1915 the British government, during the First World War, began to speculate about the possible ways it might benefit from the acquisition of Ottoman lands should the Allies emerge victorious. In order to leave nothing to chance, the British government, represented by Sir Mark Sykes, began negotiating with the French government, represented by Francois Georges Picot, about possible divisions of Arab lands then still under Ottoman control.

The Russian Tsar's representatives were also privy to the conversation and stood to gain control of land in Armenia by participating in the Sykes-Picot agreement.

By May of 1916 the negotiations had concluded and a map for the provisional dismemberment of Ottoman Arab lands was complete. The pact thus concluded became known as the Sykes-Picot Agreement. Under its terms, France was awarded a northern arc of influence, stretching from what is now southeastern Turkey, through Lebanon, parts of Syria, and Northern Iraq, to the Iranian border. England would have control over the Mediterranean ports in Palestine (Haifa, Acre) as well as what is now Jordan, and Southern Iraq. The exact political form by which French and British territories would be organized–whether the lands became colonies, protectorates or something else – was left open.[34] On the whole, the terms of the Sykes-Picot agreement were highly satisfactory to the British for multiple strategic reasons: they maintained access to the Suez Canal in the southwest and to the Persian Gulf in the east and they had no common border with Russia since the lands ceded to France serves as a buffer zone.[35]

The agreement itself and the negotiations that produced it had been kept secret from the world. However, when the Bolshevik revolution succeeded in replacing the Tsar in 1917, France and England reneged on their pledges to Russia and the newly empowered Communist government, in turn, publicized the secret agreements. This publicity was extremely unwelcome to the British because it raised immediate questions about their honesty.

The problem was that the terms of the Sykes-Picot agreement seemed to contradict two other important agreements that the British had signed: negotiations with Arabs in the Ottoman Empire known collectively as the Hussein-McMahon correspondence of 1916, and negotiations with European Jews, expressed in the Balfour Declaration of 1917. Eventually the Balfour Declaration prevailed and a Jewish state was created. But for 30 years, between the end of World War I in 1918 and the Israeli declaration of independence in 1948, the Sykes-Picot agreement prevailed, ratified by the League of Nations "mandatory" system that assigned Arab lands to European tutelage en route to independence.

In 1916, at exactly the same moment that England and France were concluding their plans for carving up the Ottoman Empire, England also was negotiating with Arabs under Ottoman control, seeking to foment an Arab rebellion that would challenge the Ottoman Empire from within. The essence of the deal was simple: if the Arabs would attack the Ottoman Empire from the rear, then they would be given independence and national sovereignty over Arab lands should the Allies win the war. The principal Arab leader who conducted these negotiations was King Hussein bin Ali, the Sharif of Mecca. Sir Henry McMahon, the High Commissioner in Cairo, represented Great Britain.

McMahon was eager to make the deal but wily in being vague about the lands that would, were the Arab Revolt to succeed, become independent Arab state(s). Palestine was of particular interest to both sides, and here McMahon was especially evasive. He insisted that land west of Homs, Hama, Aleppo, and Damascus (i.e. western Syria) was of mixed, not purely Arab population and therefore exempt from the land promised to Hussein. This left the door open for the British to argue that Palestine, a southwestern Syrian province, was not to be ceded to the Arabs, whereas Hussein could argue that only land to the west of Damascus has been cut out of the deal, leaving Palestine, south of Damascus, connected to the Arab areas that would become independent.[36] In dispatches home, McMahon was much clearer. He wrote: "What we have to arrive at now is to tempt the Arab peoples into the right path, detach them from the enemy and bring them over to our side. This on our part is at present largely a matter of words."[37]

In any case, the Arabs did uphold their end of the bargain and there was an Arab Revolt against the Ottoman Empire from 1916 to 1918, concentrated largely on pinning down Ottoman troops in the Hijaz, the western coast of the Arabian Peninsula.

But Anglo-Arab amity was seriously damaged when, first, the Russians publicized the terms of the Sykes-Picot Agreement, and, simultaneously, the British also announced the Balfour Declaration described above. In a 2002 interview with *The New Statesman*, Jack Straw, then the British Foreign Secretary, admitted: "A lot of the problems we are having to deal with now… are a consequence of our colonial past…The Balfour Declaration and the contradictory assurances which were being given to Palestine in private at the same time as they were being given to the Israelis – again, an interesting history for us, but not an entirely honourable one."[38] In 2017, Israeli journalist Gideon Levy said of Balfour even more succinctly: "There was never anything like it: an empire promising a land that it had not yet conquered to a people not living there, without asking the inhabitants. There's no other way to describe the unbelievable colonialist temerity that cries out from every letter in the Balfour Declaration, now marking its centenary."[39]

Contemplating the contradictory and incompatible promises made in the Sykes-Picot Agreement, the Hussein-McMahon correspondence, and the Balfour Declaration, one comes to understand why, according to one frequent visitor to the area, the only joke that Israelis and Palestinians find equally amusing is this: "Why does the sun never set on the British Empire? Because even God cannot trust them in the dark."[40]

THE PALESTINIANS IN THE PRE-STATE PERIOD

In the face of Zionist determination to colonize the land with the blessings of the whole world, and in the face of the British will to control trade routes from the Mediterranean to the Indian Ocean, Palestinians struggled to maintain their own communities. From the very beginning Palestinian leaders recognized that Zionist settlers were a new phenomenon, quite unlike indigenous Jews who had lived in Palestine for centuries, using the mother tongue of the region, participating in its culture and social life, while maintaining an independent religious identity.

As early as 1899, Palestinian leaders had articulated the position they would, unsuccessfully, reiterate to Europeans and to the world diplomatic community for the next century and more. A leader of the Arab community in Jerusalem wrote to Theodor Herzl: "The world is big enough, there are other uninhabited lands in which millions of poor Jews could be settled...in the name of God, leave Palestine alone!"[41]

But of course, neither the Zionists nor the British did leave Palestine alone, and so the Palestinians deployed an array of tools against those who sought to displace them from their native land. The startling thing is the degree to which Palestinian actions in the present day rely on the same instruments and strategies as were used in the British period. For Palestinians the past truly is prologue.

Early in the British period, the advancement of new Jewish settlements caused Palestinians to articulate their sense of identity against that of the Zionists. The timing of this conversation leads many prominent historians to conclude that Palestinian nationalism is a reaction to Zionism,[42] despite the fact that Palestinians began developing their collective identity at least as far back as 1834, when they attempted to eject Egyptian troops who, briefly, wrested Palestine from Ottoman control.[43]

The real issue, however, is not to name a date for the emergence of Palestinian national identity, but to understand the continuous frustration Palestinians faced in connecting a cultural sense of identity to the apparatus of a state that could take its place within the world system of nation-states. Given the disconnect between identity and state formation, Palestinian nationalism went through a series of drafts, as it were: with aspirations to be an independent state,[44] to be part of a Pan Arab community, as envisioned by a Palestinian elite in the late Ottoman and early British periods,[45] to be a province within a Greater Syria, as peasants more commonly imagined.[46]

Both the aspiration to global pan-Arab unity and to union with Syria were frustrated by the fact that the Sykes-Picot agreement divided the land in question between French and British mandates, thus defeating any hope for unification. In the 1950s, the hope of pan-Arab unity resurfaced as a secular movement, Nasserism, and today it expresses itself as political Islam. In both the secular and religious cases, geographic divisions created long ago in Whitehall and in Paris continue to play a part in defeating regional initiatives.

In the face of Zionist ambitions and (as the Palestinians viewed it) British perfidy, Palestinians were deft at creating many different types of groups that were active in protecting Palestinian interests: village committees, leagues, multiple political parties and umbrella groups to lobby the British and to organize their own internal capacity for resistance. There was the Arab Higher Committee, local committees (confusingly known as national committees),[47] and also a complex series of organizations speaking jointly for Christian and Muslim Palestinians under the title of the Palestine Arab Congress.[48] There were multiple political parties rooted in a variety of class and regional constituencies.

These Palestinian lobbying efforts mirrored the efforts of the Zionist Organization, but they were notably less successful internally and externally. Internally, Palestinians were less able than their Zionist adversaries to conquer the divisive power of class (notables vs. peasants), region (urban vs. rural), and faith (Muslims vs. Christians) in order to present a united front.[49]

Externally, Europeans disdained their claims, most consequentially, by the British, from the beginning. In 1919, Lord Balfour wrote in a confidential memo: "Zionism, be it right or wrong, good or bad, is rooted in age-long traditions, in present needs, in future hopes, of far greater importance that the desires and prejudices of the 700,000 Arabs who now inhabit that ancient land."[50]

In the eyes of the British, Zionism was exempt from moral accountability; the age-long traditions, present needs, and future hopes of the Jews simply trumped mere desire and prejudice on the part of the Arabs. Palestinian spokespersons have never been able to overcome this formulation and are limited by it to the present day. Nor have Palestinian spokespersons ever found a way to simultaneously acknowledge the "special relationship" between Israel and first Great Britain and now the U.S., and still make an argument for the connection between their own national interests and those of western powers.[51]

Given that their political efforts did not produce results, Palestinians turned to economic means to make their claims. The recourse to economic struggle was rooted in the Ottoman period, when the Palestinians had no international patrons and no prospects of fund-raising of the sort the JNF did so successfully. Instead, Palestinian economic efforts, in the 1930s as they are today, were focused on boycotts and strikes designed to be part of a national liberation struggle.

In the years following WWI, influenza epidemics, crop failure, and famine caused enormous harm to the agricultural sectors of Palestine, Lebanon, and Syria. At the same time of economic crisis for Palestinians, Zionist agriculture flourished, in part by displacing Palestinian labor and giving jobs to Jewish immigrants, and in part by benefitting from the charitable donations garnered from Zionist and Christian philanthropists.[52]

By 1936, British and Zionist practices of displacing Palestinians through land purchases, the preferential hiring of Jewish labor in Zionist businesses, and the rising number of Zionist immigrants from Europe reached a flashpoint. Following a report of Jewish arms smuggling, Arab militias, first acting independently, then in unison, and later independently again, began attacking Jewish settlements. Very quickly, the demands of the Palestinian side came to include a call for a general strike, a refusal by labor to staff Jewish-owned workplaces, and a refusal by consumers to buy Jewish goods.[53]

The general strike lasted some 6 months (April – October of 1936) and was understood to be part of a larger Arab Rebellion that included armed attacks not only on Zionist settlements, but also on the British. Sustaining the strike, and the larger armed struggle in which it was embedded, took tremendous organizational acumen. Nevertheless, the success of the first part of the Arab Rebellion is unclear.

To this day, Palestinians disagree among themselves about the impact of the General Strike. On the one hand, it was a moment of solidarity in an otherwise highly factionalized Palestinian political history. On the other hand, it probably accelerated the Zionist commitment to replacing Palestinian labor with Jewish labor.[54] Certainly, whatever one thinks of the balance between ideological gains and economic costs, Palestinian recourse to economic measures on behalf of their community proved to be vastly less successful than Zionist fund raising efforts were in advancing the cause of Zionism.

As violence receded in 1937, Great Britain appointed the Peel Commission to visit Palestine to inquire into the causes of the unrest. The fact-finding mission officially recommended, for the first time, the partition of Palestine into a Jewish and an Arab state. In so doing, they were echoing Winston Churchill's 1921 White Paper that had already implied partition. Churchill said: "it is essential that [the Jewish community] should know that it is in Palestine as of right and not on sufferance."[55] But then he adds: "The terms of the Balfour Declaration…do not contemplate that Palestine as a whole should be converted into a Jewish National Home, but that such a home should be founded in Palestine."[56]

What Churchill had implied became official and explicit in the Peel Commission Report. Elements of the final report included a proposed map, giving northern Palestine, the fertile Galilee and the Mediterranean coast from the Lebanese border through all the port cities until well south of Jaffa to the Israelis, and the western hill country, Gaza, and the Negev to the Palestinian state.[57] Although, under this plan, the Palestinian state would have been 80% of British Palestine, the most fertile lands in the Galilee were allocated for the Jewish state. Even more problematically, the partition suggested by the Peel Commission also required the removal of some 250,000 Palestinians living on land allocated to the Jewish state. The Peel Commission report was thus, *de facto*, a transfer plan.[58]

The Palestinians, long before the creation of the Palestine Liberation Organization (PLO), rejected the Peel Commission report outright, refusing to agree to any partition of their homeland. The Zionists understood this refusal to mean "the only way to reach an agreement with the Arabs would have been to renounce the Zionist dream itself. …It wasn't a debate over where the border would run…but rather the fundamental and absolute refusal of the Arabs to acquiesce in the Zionist enterprise itself."[59]

As we shall see immediately below, by the time of the Peel Report, Palestinian understood that, indeed, the debate was not about borders because neither borders nor partition was the Zionist aim. From the beginning, Zionists strove for pacification rather than peace with Palestinians. Pacification would require Palestinians not only to accept military defeat, but also to acquiesce in the *right* of others to displace them. This was an unrealistic expectation in 1936 and remains at the heart of the contention today in the demand that the Palestinians recognize Israel, as it now defines itself, a Jewish state and not the state of its citizens.[60]

The Zionists were smart enough to appear favorably inclined to the Peel Commission Report and every subsequent partition plan, mostly because such plans provided an internationally recognized base from which they could continue to expand their control over territory. David Ben Gurion, later the first prime minister of Israel, was very clear on this point. The Israeli historian Avi Shlaim writes: "Ben Gurion professed himself to be an enthusiastic advocate of a Jewish state, even if it involved the partitioning of Palestine, because he worked on the assumption that this state would not be the end but only the beginning. A state would enable Jews to have unlimited immigration, to build a Jewish economy, and to organize a first-class army. 'I am certain,' he wrote [to his son, Amos], 'we will be able to settle in all the other parts of the country, whether through agreement and mutual understanding with our Arab neighbours or *in another way*...[He concludes]: 'Erect a Jewish State at once, even if it not in the whole of the land. The rest will come in the course of time. It *must* come (emphasis mine)."[61] Put differently: we will accept what we are given and then take the rest.

This created an irreducible clash: the Palestinians could see no legitimacy to carving up their homeland to accommodate other people's needs, and the Zionists felt entitled to exclusive control over all of historic Palestine. It is no surprise that armed struggle soon resumed.

The Arab Rebellion, which lasted until 1939 ended in the defeat of the Palestinian militias, but also brought small wins for Palestinian interests. The British, seeking to reestablish order (and reflecting on the repeated findings of their own commissions, that Arab fears of Zionism's territorial ambitions were well-founded) decided to offer some accommodation to Palestinians' objection to continued Jewish immigration and land purchases. Thus, Great Britain issued the White Paper of 1939, effectively shelving the Peel Commission proposal to partition Palestine, opting instead for a unified country with proportional representation of Jews and Palestinians in a government supervised by the British.

Further, the 1939 White paper proposed to limit Jewish immigration for five years and placed restrictions on land sales to Jews. These limitations, of course, only hardened the determination of the Zionists to find ways to run the British blockade and to take Palestinian land, if not through sales, then by force.

This determination led directly to the second significant result of the Palestinian defeat in the Arab Rebellion. As a condition of their surrender, the Palestinian forces were completely disarmed. The loss of the weapons thus left the Palestinian community defenseless in the face of growing Zionist military aggression, which was tolerated by the British who continued to pay lip service to the idea of a Palestinian state while, in actuality, preventing that scenario from ever being realized.[62]

THE SPIRAL INTO TRAGEDY

In 1939, of course, the British became engulfed in WWII. The combination of the military defeat of the Palestinian Rebellion and the official containment of Jewish immigration through the White Paper, appeared to establish a sufficient period of quiet to allow the British to focus their attentions on the war effort.

The war, and the growing knowledge of the Holocaust, however, had a different effect on the Zionists in Palestine, strengthening their determination to create an exclusively Jewish country. Zionist politicians differed among themselves on the degree to which they could collude with Nazism to harvest Jewish immigration to Palestine,[63] on the extent to which it was necessary to actively, militarily oppose the British, and on their obligations to set aside the development of the *Yishuv* and to join the war in Europe. What they always agreed on, however, was the desire to de-Arabize Palestine. The very logic of their aspirations seemed to dictate that end, buttressed by Zionist rhetoric that sought to make the goal of ethnic cleansing more legitimate and more necessary.

For example, in 1929, during one of the periods of sporadic but nonetheless intense violence, some 65–68 Orthodox Jews were killed by Palestinian mob action in Hebron. The Hebron killings were part of a colony-wide wave of violence triggered by Palestinian perceptions of Jewish provocations at the Wailing Wall in the Old City of Jerusalem. In fact, the Orthodox Jews murdered in Hebron were not Zionists. Like many other Orthodox and ultra-orthodox Jewish communities, they were theologically opposed to Zionism, holding that it was an impious attempt to force God's hand. Creating the Zion of Biblical prophecy before its time was, for them, a usurpation of the deity's creative powers. Nevertheless, the massacres occurred and Orthodox Jews were killed. This is indisputable. But it is also indisputable that popular accounts omit the fact that while nearly 70 Orthodox Jews were murdered, hundreds more were saved from the mob by their Palestinian neighbors.[64]

Anita Shapira, an Israeli historian, takes a psychological view of Zionist violence,[65] which, like Shavit's work, emphasizes conflict, contradiction, and ambivalence. Using socialist labor (i.e. the most left-leaning) variant of Zionism as her focus, she concludes that the commitment to violence was driven not only by practical concerns, e.g. controlling land and expelling Palestinians, but also by psychosocial forces. Specifically, she argues that new circumstances, i.e. nation building, called for new definitions of Jewish identity, emphasizing aggressive rather than passive qualities.[66] She writes:

"[T]he evolving national ethos contained undertones of admiration and longing for power. The Jews were presented as powerless and without a homeland – two essential characteristics that the national movement aspired to remedy.... Zionist psychology was molded by the conflicting parameters of a national liberation movement and a movement of European colonization in a Middle Eastern country."[67]

In the end, one can think of the history of Zionism as over-determined. There were the original problems to which it was a response, the twin threats of annihilation and assimilation in Europe. There was the fatal imbalance between Zionists and the indigenous Palestinians whereby Zionist organizing, fund-raising, and military preparedness far outstripped Palestinian efforts. There were traumatic events, the Second World War, the Holocaust and in its aftermath, the plight of Jewish survivors. There were psychological impulses among Jews to assert efficacy in the face of the brutal encounter with near extinction. In addition, given the reluctance of Western countries to absorb large numbers of Jewish refugees, there were barriers to considering any other pathway but Zionism for resolving Jewish problems.

And finally, there was the British announcement of its intentions to withdraw from the Palestinian Mandate. This led directly to the United Nations' decision to partition the country into a Jewish and a Palestinian state, over the objections of the Palestinians and the *Yishuv*, both of whom were interviewed and both of whom were ignored.[68]

U.N. General Assembly Resolution 181 called for the division of Mandate Palestine into a Jewish and a Palestinian state. Israel was to occupy 55% of the land, Palestine 44%, and the Jerusalem-Bethlehem corridor, the final 1% of the land, was to become an international zone, a *corpus separatum*. The two states were to have open borders and form an economic union. The map would look like a checkerboard, with both countries having to cross through each other's territory to access part of their own land. Neither country could come into existence in the absence of the other and the creation of both nation-states was left in the hands of the U.N.[69]

Palestinians rejected the partition of their homeland outright. The Zionists appeared to accept the partition, but only because it gave them a secure staging area for further expansion, as Ben Gurion had predicted.

Zionist behavior was always consistent with Ben Gurion's ambition to occupy all the land. Thus the passage of GA Resolution 181 unleashed the final Zionist push to take as much land as possible and to expel as many Palestinians as possible before the Partition Plan went into effect. Menachim Begin, later an Israeli Prime Minister, spoke candidly when he said:

"My greatest worry in those months [between the U.N. partition resolution of November, 1947 and the self-declaration of statehood by the Israelis, May 15, 1948] was that the Arabs might accept the United Nations plan. Then we would have had the ultimate tragedy, a Jewish state so small that it could not absorb all the Jews of the world."[70]

From this point forward, the mass expulsions that Palestinians call the *Nakba* (the Catastrophe) began.[71] What follows here is a cursory account that does not do justice to the terrible human costs of the war, but emphasizes instead those features that remain most germane for the conflict as it exists today.

The *Nakba* occurred in two waves: the first before the Partition Plan was put into effect, when the expulsions perpetrated by Jewish militias went virtually unopposed; and the second after the state of Israel came into existence, in the context of a war between Israel and its external neighbors as well as its internal Palestinian subjects.

In the first half of the *Nakba*, multiple Zionist militias, although competitive with one another on some issues, worked together toward the expulsion of Palestinians. For example, even well before the notorious *Deir Yassin* massacre in April, 1948, Sir Alan Cunningham, the last British governor of Mandate Palestine, said: "[T]he Haganah and the dissident groups are now working so closely together that the [Jewish] Agency's claim that they cannot control the dissidents is inadmissible."[72]

The militias did not act randomly or in "the fog of war."[73] Rather, they acted on strategic plans to de-Arabize Palestine by gaining control of key assets: fertile land, water, transportation routes, communication nodes, major Jewish cities and settlements, but also and critically, Palestinian cities and territories beyond the land allocated to Israel by the United Nations. Nor did they act in accordance with rules of war. Instead they used terror campaigns,[74] rape,[75] and collective punishment,[76] along with standard military techniques to depopulate the countryside and encourage flight.

One window into their intentions was Plan *Dalet* (Plan D). First drafts of this plan existed as far back as 1944.[77] Ostensibly independent militias began to act on Plan *Dalet* well before the British withdrew or the Partition Plan was put into effect. Plan *Dalet's* objectives included taking over land allocated to Palestine under the Partition Plan (for example the major Palestinian cities of Jaffa and Acre), protecting Jewish settlements also in territory allocated to Palestine, attacking civilian institutions in the Palestinian community, as well as the more conventional military objectives of securing such geographic points as convoy routes or strategic hilltops. The document of Plan *Dalet* itself is not an eloquent statement of strategy; it is, more nearly, a list of tactical goals and targets.[78] Nevertheless, the goals and targets, and the behavior to which they gave rise, and the expulsions that they accomplished all align. Together, they are systematic enough to support the inference that a master plan of ethnic cleansing was being enacted not only within the land allocated to Israel by the U.N., but well beyond it, and in such as way as to undermine the viability of an independent Palestinian state.[79]

By the time the British withdrew from Palestine and Israel unilaterally declared itself into existence on May 15, 1948, about half the *Nakba* had already been accomplished, creating some 370,000 Palestinian refugees and internally displaced persons. The systematic destruction of Palestinian cities and villages was also well under way.

With the creation of the state of Israel, the one-sided expulsion of Palestinians by Zionists was reconfigured. On the day of its self-declared independence, six Arab armies – Lebanese, Egyptian, Jordanian, Syrian, Iraqi and combined Arab League forces – invaded Israel. Americans have heard this story many times: a Jewish David facing an Arab Goliath and miraculously prevailing. The reality is exactly the reverse of the common image.

The truth is that the individual Arab countries sent small contingents of troops and never put them under a single unified command. The most militarily effective troops, the Jordanian Army, and the Iraqi army acting under Jordanian command, sought only to hold the land (the West Bank) that Jordan hoped to control to the detriment of Palestinian national aspirations.[80] U.S. Secretary of State, George C. Marshall, had a clear view of Arab military capabilities. His assessment read: "Whole govt structure Iraq is endangered by political and economic disorders and Iraq Govt can not at this moment afford to send more than [the] handful of troops it has already dispatched. Egypt has suffered recently from strikes and disorders. Its army has insufficient equipment because of its refusal of Brit aid, and what it has is needed for police duty at home. Syria has neither arms nor army worthy of name and has not been able to organize one since French left three years ago. Lebanon has no real army while Saudi Arabia has small army which is barely sufficient to keep tribes in order. Jealousies between Saudi Arabia and Syrians on one hand and Hashemite govts of Transjordan and Iraq, prevent Arabs from making even best use of existing forces (sic)."[81]

Given the weakness of the Arab response, Jewish forces continued to advance, taking more land and expelling more Palestinians. By the time the contending parties reached an agreement to end the hostilities in January of 1949, the War of Independence among the Israelis was complete although expulsions of Palestinians continued.[82] The Palestinians were utterly defeated: some 750,000 of them had been expelled,[83] between 370 and 540 villages were destroyed and depopulated,[84] virtually all the Palestinian urban centers were demolished, and the cultural archives they contained had been expropriated.[85] The potential Palestinian state had been dismembered, some of its land under Israeli control (especially the fertile land in the Galilee), the West Bank under Jordanian control, and Gaza under Egyptian control. From that moment forward, the Palestinian struggle for justice had to be conducted from dispersed sites controlled by a variety of state and quasi-state entities (Jordan, Egypt, the United Nations refugee camps in Arab countries, the Palestinian Diaspora in Jordan, Lebanon, and Tunisia, local non-state actors in the West Bank and Gaza).

The state of Israel had grown from the 55% of Mandatory Palestine allotted to it by the United Nations to 78% up to the Green Line, the armistice line of 1949. This left about 22% of Palestine, *all of it under foreign control*, to become a possible Palestinian state.

Bear in mind that changing national boundaries by the acts of war is inadmissible under international law. This point is critical to understanding events that were to unfold from the basis of Green Line established in 1949, principally the interminable "peace process" in which Palestinians are exhorted to make "difficult compromises." Their response is that they were not consulted about the division of Palestine and, having been allotted 44% of the land, they then proved willing to settle for 22% of the land.[86] The division of that remaining 22% during the Oslo Process (see Chapter 8) into Areas A, B, and C with area C (61 percent of the 22 percent of historic Palestine that is the West Bank) being largely depopulated, now leaves about 11% of the land, a series of Palestinian islets isolated from one another, as a potential Palestinian state. Given changes in the map of Palestine from 1949 to 2018, it is not hard to see why the "peace process" has floundered.[87]

The war was tragic not only for the loss of life and for the fate that befell a displaced people, but also for its futility. None of the three parties to this on-going conflict achieved what they sought. The Zionists got the most from the war by securing a state that was, through ethnic cleansing, predominantly Jewish. But they lost one percent (some 6,000 young men and women) of their population. And they did not secure that state on terms that made them a normal part of the region in which they existed; they did not secure that state in ways that allowed them to honor the universalistic Enlightenment values they proclaimed; and they did not secure the consent or the withdrawal or the forgetting of their victims.

On the contrary, the Palestinians who were dispossessed or occupied continue to challenge the legitimacy of the Jewish state, with growing rather than declining efficacy at the present time. Great Britain, exhausted by the Second World War and the costs maintaining colonies in an era of decolonization, lost control over strategic land and lost standing in the international community. The Palestinians, of course, lost most of all, not only the right to live in their homeland but also, as a stateless people, the right to have their rights acknowledged by others.

None of the instruments all sides used gave anyone a definitive, stable, lasting victory. Neither internal political organizing nor the appeal to the world system, neither fundraising and nor boycotts, neither local nor regional self-definitions, neither idealized narratives of an edenic past (or future) nor jaded *realpolitik,* neither appeals to international law nor armed struggle worked to vindicate Palestinian rights or to secure Zionist dreams from continuous challenge.

Inevitably, these multiple losses fueled the next round of the conflict.

SUMMARY: THE PRE-STATE PERIOD

History of Israel-Palestine Conflict I
1870's – 1948:
From the Founding of Zionism to the Founding of Israel

Zionists	Great Powers	Palestine
WZO (1897)	Turks: *Tanzimat* Land Reforms	Petition
JNF (1901)	Great Britain (1918–1948) Sykes-Picot (1916)	Economics: General Strike 1936
	Balfour Declaration (1917) Hussein-McMahon (1917)	
JA (1929)	Partition Plan ('21, '37)	Armed Struggle: 1936–1939
Transfer Plan	U.N. Partition Plan ('47)	

NAKBA – WAR OF INDEPENDENCE
Expulsion of the Palestinians – Establishment of Israel

NOTES

[1] Theodor Herzl. (1902). *Altneuland* (*Old New Land*), New York: Create Space Independent Publishing Platform.

[2] "Palestine Arab Delegation, Observations on the High Commissioner's Interim Report on the Civil Administration of Palestine," quoted in Natasha Gill. (2013, June 19). The Original "No": Why the Arabs Rejected Zionism, and Why it Matters, in *Middle East Policy Council Commentary*, retrieved from http://www.mepc.org/articles-commentary/commentary/original-no-why-arabs-rejected-zionism-and-why-it-matters

[3] *Ibid.*

[4] For a similar periodization, see Mark Tessler. (1994). *The History of the Israeli-Palestinian Conflict*, Bloomington, Indiana: Indiana University Press.

[5] The details of the various periods of war are adequately described elsewhere. For the Nakba/War of Independence see: Nur Masalha. (1992). *Expulsion of the Palestinians: The Concept of "Transfer" in Zionist Political Thought, 1882–1948*, Washington, D.C.: Institute for Palestine Studies.
Saleh Abdel Jawad, The Arab and Palestinian Narratives of the 1948 War, in Robert Rotberg (ed.) (2006). *Israeli and Palestinian Narratives of Conflict: History's Double Helix* (Bloomington: Indiana University Press), pp 72–114, and Benny Morris. (2004). *The Birth of the Palestinian Refugee Problem Revisited*, Cambridge: Cambridge University Press.

[6] Shlomo Avinieri. (1981). *The Making of Modern Zionism: The Intellectual Origins of the Jewish State* (New York: Basic Books), pp. 5ff. The same point is made by S. Eisenstadt. (1992). *Jewish Civilization: The Jewish Historical Experience in Comparative Perspective*. New York: State University of New York Press. Avinieri's observations are echoed by Ari Shavit, who also argues that Israelis are plagued by the twin existential fears of annihilation and assimilation. Ari Shavit. (2013). *My Promised Land*, New York: Spiegel and Grau.

[7] Different translations of the Basel Plan are available, one calling for a Jewish home in Palestine, the other in Eretz Israel. For the former see: Tessler, *op. cit.*, p. 48.
For the latter, see, "Zionist Congress," *Jewish Virtual Library* retrieved from https://www.jewishvirtuallibrary.org/jsource/Zionism/First_Cong_&_Basel_Program.html

[8] Judy S. Bertelsen. (1976). *Nonstate Nations in International Politics: Comparative System Analysis* (New York: Praeger), p. 37.

[9] Charles Smith. (2013). *Palestine and the Arab Israeli Conflict: A History with Documents* (New York: St. Martin's Press, 8th edition), p. 15.

[10] M.E. Yapp. (1987). *The Making of the Modern Near East, 1792–1923* (London: Longman) p. 290.

[11] Viscount Herbert Samuel. (1946). *Grooves of Change*. New York: Bobbs Merrill.

[12] James Gelvin. (2005). *The Israel-Palestine Conflict: One Hundred Years of War* (London: Cambridge University Press), pp. 82–83.

[13] Colonial Office (CO) 733/18, Churchill to Samuel, Telegram, Private and Personal, 25 February 1922. In Sahar Huneidi. (2001). *A Broken Trust, Herbert Samuel, Zionism and the Palestinians* (London: I. B.Tauris), p. 57.

[14] http://www.jewishvirtuallibrary.org/jsource/Orgs/jafi.html

[15] http://www.jnf.org/menu-3/our-history

[16] The most comprehensive account of JNF purposes and policies can be found in Walter Lehn with Uri Davis. (1988). *The Jewish National Fund*. London: Kegan Paul International,

and at the Central Zionist Archives, Jerusalem. "Collections of the Jewish National Fund (KKKL1 – KKKL 17).

[17] Amiram Barkat. (2007, July 24). Ex-Minister Rubinstein: State Should Reclaim Land Given to the JNF, *Ha'aretz*, retrieved from http://www.haaretz.com/news/ex-minister-rubinstein-state-should-reclaim-land-given-to-jnf-1.226146

[18] http://www.jnf.org/

[19] Sara Kershnar, et. al. (2011). Greenwashing Apartheid: The Jewish National Fund's Environmental Cover-up, in *JNF: Colonizing Palestine since 1901*, JNF eBook (volume 4) p. 26, retrieved from http://stopthejnf.org/documents/JNFeBookVol4.pdf

[20] Supreme Court Petition: H.C. 9205/04, Adalah v. The Israel Lands Administration, the Minister of Finance and the Jewish National Fund and H.C. 9010/04, The Arab Center for Alternative Planning, et al. v. The Israel Lands Administration, et al.

[21] *Ibid.*

[22] Yuval Yoaz. (2005, January 28). JNF, treasury seek formula for continued Jews-only land sales, *Ha'aretz*, retrieved from http://www.haaretz.com/print-edition/news/jnf-treasury-seek-formula-for-continued-jews-only-land-sales-1.148521

[23] Walter Laqueur. (1972). *A History of Zionism* (London: Wiedenfeld and Nicholson), p. 153.

[24] Israel Pocket Library. (1973). *Zionism*. (Tel Aviv: Keter Books) p. 39.

[25] Mordechai Naor. (2002). *Zionism: The First 120 Years:1882–2002*. The Zionist Library.

[26] Eve Spangler. (2010). Attacking Humanitarian Aid, *Counterpunch*, retrieved from https://www.facebook.com/groups/272917749406507/?notif_t=group_activity

[27] Live from Ukraine: In Fast-Paced Operation, Jewish Agency Rescues Group of Immigrants from Donetsk, *Jewish Agency of Israel website*, retrieved from http://www.jewishagency.org/blog/1/tag/4666

[28] Project TEN: Global Tikkun Olam *Jewish Agency website*, retrieved from http://www.jewishagency.org/jewish-social-action/program/215

[29] Charles D. Smith, *op. cit.*, pp. 18–22.

[30] *Ibid.* p. 21.

[31] Similar problems exist throughout the world, even absent the distortions of Zionist ambitions. Cf. Hernan DeSoto. (2002) *The Mystery of Capital: Why Capitalism Triumphs in the West and Fails Everywhere Else*. New York: Basic Books.

[32] Smith, *op. cit.*, pp. 20–22.

[33] The Campbell-Bannerman Report. (1907) full text retrieved from https://archive.org/stream/imperialconferen02jebbuoft/imperialconferen02jebbuoft_djvu.txt

[34] Smith, *op. cit.*, pp. 60–63.

[35] *Ibid.*

[36] *Ibid.* pp 58–59.

[37] *Ibid.* p. 61.

[38] NS interview – Jack Straw in *The New Statesman* (2002, November 18), retrieved from https://www.newstatesman.com/node/1566411

[39] Gideon Levy. (2017, October 28). Balfour's Original Sin, *Ha'aretz*, retrieved from https://www.haaretz.com/opinion/.premium-british-colonialism-prepared-way-for-israeli-colonialism-1.5461035

[40] Private communication from President Leon Botstein, Bard College, April, 2004.

[41] Tom Segev. (2001). *Elvis in Jerusalem* (New York: Holt Books) p. 39.

[42] Gelvin, *op. cit.*, p. 93.

43   Baruch Kimmerling and Joel Migdal. (2003). The Revolt of 1834 and the Making of Modern Palestine, *The Palestinian People* (Harvard University Press), 1–37.

44   *Ibid.*

45   Gelvin, *op. cit.*, p. 95.

46   *Ibid.*

47   Tessler, *op. cit.*, pp. 185–268.

48   Rashid Khalidi. (2006). *The Iron Cage: the Story of the Palestinian Struggle for Statehood* (Boston: Beacon Press), p. 42.

49   *Ibid.* pp. 9–22.

50   *Ibid.* p. 36

51   Hussein Ibish. (2012, August 28). Bulldozing the Special Relationship, *Foreign Policy*, retrieved from http://www.foreignpolicy.com/articles/2012/08/28/bulldozing_the_special_relationship

52   Smith, *op. cit.*, p. 103.

53   *Ibid.* p. 134.

54   Gelvin, *op. cit.*, p. 111.

55   Gelvin, *op. cit.*, p. 90.

56   Smith, *op. cit.*, p. 153.

57   Smith, *op. cit.*, p. 137.

58   *Ibid.* p. 136.

59   Segev, *op. cit.*, p. 38.

60   Jonathan Lis. (2018, June 4). Knesset Council Bans Bill to Define Israel as a State for All Its Citizens, *Ha'aretz*, retrieved from https://www.haaretz.com/israel-news/.premium-knesset-council-bans-bill-to-define-israel-as-state-for-all-citizens-1.6145333

61   Avi Shlaim. (2001). *The Iron Wall, Israel and the Arab World* (New York: Norton) p. 21.

62   Khalidi, *op. cit.*, p. xxi.

63   Segev, *op. cit.*, p. 21, p. 30.

64   Tom Segev. (1999). *One Palestine, Complete* (Metropolitan Books) pp. 295–313.

65   Anita Shapira. (1992). *Land and Power: The Zionist Resort to Force, 1881–1948* Stanford: Stanford University Press.

66   In this assertion, her work parallels other historians who trace redefinitions of group identities to changing environmental demands Cf. Kai Erikson. (1966). *The Wayward Puritans: A study in the Sociology of Deviance*. New York: Allyn and Bacon. Perry Miller. (1956). *Errand into the Wilderness*. New York: Bellknap Press.

67   Shapira, *op. cit.*, pp. 354–355.

68   James Zogby. (2017, November 12). The danger of ignoring Arab opinion: 100 years since Balfour, *+972*, retrieved from https://972mag.com/the-danger-of-ignoring-arab-opinion-100-years-since-balfour/130658/

69   United Nations General Assembly Resolution 181, November 29, 1947, retrieved from http://avalon.law.yale.edu/20-century/res181.asp

70   Segev, *op. cit.*, pp. 34–35.

71   The starting date of the Nakba is a matter of contention, although all sources agree that it is sometime after the UN vote. For a more detailed discussion see: Abdel Jawad in Rotberg, *op. cit.*, pp. 80–83, and Michael Palumbo. (1987). *The Palestinian Catastrophe: the 1948 Expulsion of a People from their Homeland* (London: Faber and Faber), pp. 35–36.

72   Palumbo, *op. cit.*, p. 36.

[73] Benny Morris. (1988). *The Birth of the Palestinian Refugee Problem, 1947–1949.* First Edition. Cambridge, England: Cambridge University Press.

[74] Abdel Jawad in Rotberg, *op. cit.*

[75] Susan Slyomovic. The Rape of Qula, a Destroyed Palestinian Village, in Ahmed Sa'di and Lila Abu-Lughod (eds.). (2007). *Nakba: Palestine, 1948 and the Claims of Memory.* New York: Columbia University Press.

[76] Benny Morris. (2004). *The Birth of the Palestinian Refugee Problem Revisited.* (Cambridge, England: Cambridge University Press) pp.79–80.

[77] *Ibid.* p. 39.

[78] *Ibid.* pp. 34–46; and Nur Masalha, *op. cit.*, p. 176.

[79] From the first edition of his work to the revised second edition, Benny Morris, Israel's leading historian of the *Nakba*, concedes, over the span of his work, that the inference of a central plan is warranted. See Abdel Jawad in Rotberg, *op. cit.*, footnote 100, p. 112. Ilan Pappe makes the same argument in Ilan Pappe. (2006). *The Ethnic Cleansing of Palestine,* Oxford, England: One World Press.

[80] Pappe, *op. cit.,* pp. 127–131.

[81] George C. Marshall, May 13, 1948, The Secretary of State to Certain Diplomatic Offices, FRUS, 1948, V, part 2, pp.983–984. Quoted in Irene Gendzier, "Why the U.S. recognized Israel" in Israeli Occupation Archive, November, 2011 retrieved from http://www.israeli-occupation.org/2011-11-09/irene-gendzier-why-the-us-recognised-israel/

[82] Eugene L. Rogan and Avi Shlaim. (eds.) (2001). *The War for Palestine: Rewriting the History of 1948* Cambridge: Cambridge University Press.

[83] Eve Spangler, No Exit: Palestinian Film in the Shadow of the Nakba, in John Michalcyzk and Raymond Helmick, SJ. (eds.) (2013). *Through a Lens Darkly: Films of Genocide, Ethnic Cleansing, and Atrocities* (New York: Peter Lang), footnote 4, pp. 211–212.

[84] *Ibid.* footnote 5, p. 212.

[85] Abdel Jawad in Rotberg, *op. cit.*

[86] Arafat's Speech in the UN General Assembly, 1988 retrieved from http://www.mideastweb.org/arafat1988.htm

[87] Adam Entous. (2018, July 9). The Maps of Israeli Settlements that Shocked Barack Obama, *The New Yorker*, retrieved from https://www.newyorker.com/news/news-desk/the-map-of-israeli-settlements-that-shocked-barack-obama

ESTABLISHING THE STATE, PREPARING OCCUPATION

Things will come out in the end. The question is how to live with this.
Aryeh Yitzachi[1]

An Israeli Story

"On one of the first days of 1949 and on one of her first days in Israel, Mrs. Rivka Waxmann … went out shopping on Herzl Street in Haifa. [She] happened to notice a soldier emerge from a jeep and walk up to the ticket window of the Ora Movie Theater. Mrs. Waxmann froze on the spot, then shouting, "Haim?" The soldier turned toward her and for the next few seconds the two figures stared at one another in stunned disbelief. Then the woman stretched out her arms and flung herself at the young man. She was his mother. The last time Mrs. Waxmann had seen her son was eight years earlier … and until meeting him the street in Haifa she believed that Haim had perished in the Holocaust. The afternoon daily *Maariv,* then barely a year old, published the story on the same day; it has symbolic value."[2]

A Palestinian Story

Today, Elias is a highly respected dentist in Ramallah. He grew up in a prominent and politically active local family. On the first day of the brief but, for Palestinians, disastrous 1967 war, his father rushed off to the city center to volunteer for whatever tasks were needed. By the late afternoon, Ramallah was already flooded with refugees from the surrounding areas, all of whom needed a place to stay and food to eat. Elias' mother, realizing that her husband and older sons would not be

© KONINKLIJKE BRILL NV, LEIDEN, 2018 | DOI:10.1163/9789004394148_006

coming home for dinner, decided to send dinner to them. Six-year-old Elias was commissioned to bring a tray of cooked food to his father and brothers. Just as he was walking down the main road from his house to the nearby city center, Israeli fighter planes appeared overhead. They flew low over the main street, strafing people as they came. Around Elias people fell, some of them mortally wounded. Stunned by the assault and not knowing what else to do, Elias simply kept on walking toward the place where his father stood, watching in horror. Finally, Elias arrived before his dad. His hands were still extended, as if holding the tray, but the tray itself lay smashed behind him in the street, its food spilled and trampled.[3] This story has never been published until now; it has symbolic value.

The history of the early national period in Israel, like the one before it, is shaped by the interactions of three parties: the Israelis, the Palestinians, and ambitious outside powers, each with constant and self-interested motives. As in the previous period, the conflicts of interest that arose among them ended in a war whose results brought great losses to the Palestinians and to some of the great or aspiring-to-be great powers and only a Pyrrhic victory to Israelis.

THE ISRAELIS: CREATING A NATIONAL FRAMEWORK

In 1949, with the War of Independence over, the newly established Israeli state faced all the tasks of building a new society. These included establishing a basic legal framework, developing a nascent economy, securing the population it sought, positioning itself in a regional and global context, and, not least, dealing with the Palestinians, who were anathema to the new state.

On March 11 of that year, David Ben Gurion, the first prime minister of Israel and a famous diarist, wrote himself a "to do" list for the new government: "We must begin to formulate a number of laws: 1.Civil equality, freedom of religion; freedom of conscience, language, education and culture, equality for women; freedom of association and expression; universal suffrage. 2. General conscription law. 3. *Nationalization of water sources, natural resources, unused lands* [emphasis mine]. 4. Control of imports and prices. 5. Taxes – progressive, inheritance, increment. 6. Encouragement of childbirth. 7. General education. 8. Demobilization benefits. 9. Labor laws."[4]

Note that some of these laws – for universal suffrage, women's equality, progressive taxation– were much in keeping with the liberal, even Socialist, bent of many of the Ashkenazi founders of Israel. At the same time, however, Ben Gurion was moving quickly to monopolize all those strategic resources, particularly land and water, which would allow the Israeli state to flourish but would also undermine the development of the Palestinian community. His reference to "unused land"[5] (to be discussed below) is particularly ominous.

His focus was on establishing the legal and administrative framework for the new state but he also devoted attention to questions of economic development: "How many industrial plants will be needed, what types of industry will be developed, which lands shall we settle, how much money will be needed, what equipment will be required, what the import and the export (sic) ... We have to discuss with each local and municipal council what are its development plans ... What of the machinery in the factories (sic) is there a way of renewing or developing it? ... A road to be constructed from Beersheba to the south, via the Dead Sea. There is a plan to pump up the water of the Dead Sea and transport it .... Workers' committees should be created to support the state, on the basis of the governments plan for occupational training, improvement of the standard of living, improvement of production, labor laws."[6]

The new state also needed to prepare for a rapidly expanding population. There were, after the 6,000 Israeli casualties in the War of Independence, some 594,000 Jews already in place.[7] But Europe was teeming with refugees from World War II, and Ben Gurion aspired to have all of the Jews among them sent to Israel. In addition, Israel wanted the Jews from neighboring Arab countries, especially the affluent ones, to immigrate. Ben Gurion thought that Israel should be preparing to welcome some 800,000 additional Jews during the first four years. To do so, he estimated, would require the establishment of new settlements at the rate of about one every three days, or 100 per year.[8]

In fact, Ben Gurion's estimates proved to be fairly accurate. Some 700,000 additional Jews did immigrate to Israel in the first four years of its existence.[9] They were roughly equally divided between European Jews and Jews from Arab countries.[10]

Between the end of WWII and the creation of the Israeli state (1945–1948), immigration of Jewish Holocaust survivors from Europe was complicated by the fact that the British, still operating under the 1939 White Paper rules, interdicted refugee ships whenever they could. However, once Israel became an independent state and opened its doors to all European Jews including

Holocaust survivors living in refugee camps, the interdiction stopped. Since the United States had not yet lifted its restrictive immigration policies, many Holocaust survivors went to Israel.

There they faced a number of difficulties. Some – like the need to learn a new language or to overcome the dire poverty associated with an as-yet underdeveloped economy – were purely pragmatic. Others – rooted in culture clashes between Jews in charge of a state apparatus and those used to living as a minority within a hostile host society – were more complex. On the one hand, Zionism stood for the ingathering of all the Jews. On the other hand, however, Israel was faced with the practical tasks of building up a new society. For this purpose, the supposedly bookish, intellectual Jew of the European ghetto was not as useful as the imagined hardy *Sabra* (Jews born in Israel/Palestine). Zionism thus dreamt not only of a (re)new(ed) Jewish home, but also of new, more virile Jews to populate that home.

Tom Segev, one of the Israeli "new historians" writes: "The 'rejections of the exile' led the Zionist ... ideologues to devise an ideal 'new Jew' or 'new man' they sought to create in the land of Israel, at times through coercion. Aharon Appelfeld, a novelist, has written about a boy, an immigrant from Poland, whose classmates bullied and beat him up because he could not suntan as they did ... His pale skin seemed to bring the Exile and the Holocaust to them, so they beat him up ... Working the land was ... considered a moral obligation, a 'religion of labor.' ... An article in ... *Ha'aretz* stated of the graduates of the Ben-Shemen Agricultural School, 'They will bring pure and clean blood to our national labor, the labor of the land ... Living in Tel Aviv [on the other hand] would lead to 'hucksterism, assimilation, and apostasy,' not national revival ... Soft drink vendors were a popular and disparaged symbol for immigrants who preferred the convenience of city life to farming."[11]

Perhaps the most poignant way the conflict between the Jews of the ghetto and the "new Jews" manifested itself was Israel's decision to tax the reparations payments that Holocaust survivors received from the German and Austrian governments (such payments were tax exempt in the United States). This decision left fully one quarter of Israel's elderly Holocaust survivors living below the poverty line – a situation that remains true to this day.[12]

Clearly, the aspiration to create a "new man" defined by a hyper-masculine ethos of physical and military strength and by "clean and pure blood" (and a "new woman" defined by her fecundity) had echoes of fascist ideology and profoundly racist implications. Consider, for example, the iconic photo of an Israeli soldier gazing reverently at the Western Wall on the day that the Israeli army conquered East Jerusalem in 1967.[13] He is startlingly Aryan in appearance. Nor did the preference for blondes end in 1967. Recently social workers told an Israeli friend of mine who is waiting to adopt a baby, that her family could have a "defective" baby immediately, but would have to wait about a year for a "normal" baby or up to five years if they insisted on having a blond, blue-eyed child.[14] "Defective" children, this family was told, were dark-skinned.[15]

If all the expectations of becoming an exemplary "new Jew" sometimes made the life of European refugees more difficult, imagine how much more difficult it was for the dark-skinned Jews from Arab countries to become the "new Jew" desired by the state. They were caught in a double bind: deemed to be closer to the soil and more natural – nearly noble savages – and yet despised for their dark skin and lack of European culture.

At the time of Israel's founding, there were many Arab Jews, two thirds in Francophone North Africa (the Maghreb), far fewer in front line states around Israel: Lebanon, Syria, Jordan, and Egypt. A significant community of Arab Jews lived in Iraq, with smaller groups in Egypt and Yemen, and fewer still in Iran and Turkey.

Conventional Israeli narratives stress that all these Arab countries were hostile to Israel and, by extension, to their own Jewish citizens, propelling a wave of Jewish flight from Arab lands soon after the Jewish state (called the "Zionist entity" by hostile Arab neighbors) came into being. However, the facts of that expulsion are more complex than Zionist propaganda would have us believe.

The Iraqi Jews, an affluent and assimilated community, were the first large group following the *Nakba* to immigrate to Israel. Less affluent Libyan and Yemeni Jews soon followed. In the case of the Iraqi Jews, a number of reputable sources argue that Israeli dirty tricks, such as planting bombs in Jewish cafes in Baghdad, played a significant role in convincing them to uproot themselves[16] despite the fact that at least their leading intellectuals were highly assimilated to Arab culture.[17] Egyptian Jews came to Israel in large numbers only after the Suez crisis in 1956 and, Maghrebi Jews arrived later still, in the 1960s.[18] During the years of peak Jewish emigration from Arab countries, the Lebanese Jewish community actually grew in numbers, largely by being an alternative destination for Syrian Jews who wanted to leave Syria without going to Israel.[19]

For Arab Jews who came to Israel, the intersection of their "race" with their class and national origin worked to their disadvantage to create a deeply unequal experience of Israeli citizenship and nationality. There is no better illustration of this difficulty than the still on-going controversy over the missing babies of the Yemeni Jewish community – were they simply lost to their parents in the graceless interface between chaotic refugee camps and embryonic health care facilities, or were they deliberately kidnapped and sold into adoption rings working in Israel and elsewhere? The controversy remains unresolved to this day, with estimates of such missing (deceased? kidnapped?) children that range from less than 100[20] to more than 1,000.[21] What is clear is this: the official investigations into Mizrahi claims were less than rigorous, the investigators having been denied subpoena power,[22] and at least two "kidnapped" babies, now adults, have been reunited with their families through genetic testing.[23]

Estimates for the number of Palestinians displaced by the *Nakba* vary, as do estimates of Arab Jewish immigration to Israel. The Zionist narrative claims that the number of Jewish refugees from Arab lands exceeded the number of displaced Palestinians. They therefore argue that the expulsion of the Arab Jews cancels out the expulsion of the Palestinians. In this story, Palestinian losses in the *Nakba* also are smaller than the loss of Jewish property in Arab lands, and thus, not only return, but also compensation to Palestinians expelled in the *Nakba* is settled and closed.

To agree to this argument would be to institutionalize the standard that "two wrongs make a right." International law unambiguously rejects this interpretation, but it nevertheless re-surfaces from time to time in Israeli propaganda efforts. A more plausible argument would be to say that, just as Palestinian refugees have a right to return and a right to have their property restored, so too do Jews expelled from Arab countries. Those claims would have to be addressed to Arab states and have nothing to do with Palestinians.

In sum, a more accurate picture shows that Arab Jewish migration to Israel occurred over a period of decades and was fueled by many sources that included "push" forces like expulsion, but also "pull" forces like expected economic opportunities. It is not correct to say that the creation of the state of Israel, by itself, caused the mass expulsion of all or most Jews living in Arab states. It is true, however, that after five Israeli-Arab wars (1948, 1956, 1967, 1973, and 1982), a 51 year Occupation of Palestinian land, an unresolved refugee crisis, and Israel's relentless, noisy insistence that it speaks for all Jews, the Jewish communities remaining in Arab countries today are small and suspect.[24]

The Law of Return, passed in 1950,[25] is the mechanism that organizes Jewish immigration to Israel by creating an inalienable right for Jews anywhere in the world to move to Israel with the support of the state. The Law of Return is a critical part of the Basic Laws that Israel began to develop in the early 1950s. It formally makes the case that Israel is the state of the Jewish people, not all of whom are its citizens. As a corollary, then, Israel is not the state of its citizens, since some of its citizens are not Jewish.[26]

Israel's Basic Laws serve as a substitute for the constitution called for in Israel's Declaration of Independence, but still not in existence. The constitution remains unwritten, in part because Israel refuses to specify its boundaries and, in part, because the Orthodox community might object to some of the more modern and egalitarian provisions that would normally be part of a national constitution.[27]

Originally, the Basic Laws established a unique dual identity for people living in Israel: individuals were to be *citizens* of Israel and, in addition, the carriers of a separate "*national*" identity. "National identity," in turn, explicitly distinguished the Jewish "nation" from all others (a confused hodgepodge of some 130 ethnic and geographic "nations" such as the Circassian, Catalonian, French, and Arab nations).[28] All citizens enjoyed certain rights by virtue of their citizenship (e.g. to vote, to participate in the national health care system, to send their children to public schools that are, however, segregated so as to keep Jewish children apart from the rest). But other rights were reserved for Jewish *nationals,* making them the sole group in Israel entitled the right to family unification[29] and to lease or buy land through the Jewish National Fund. Palestinians born in Israel could be citizens, but even this was more nearly a concession than a right, as the recent attempts to strip Bedouins of the citizenship illustrate.[30]

Recently, mixed groups of secular Israelis, Arabs, and other non-Jewish "nationals" have petitioned the Supreme Court to recognize an Israeli nationality based on residency rather than on admission to Israel under the Law of Return (i.e. ethnicity). The Israeli Supreme Court continues to deny the possibility of an Israeli nationality that might be shared among Jewish and Palestinian citizens of the state.[31] The organized American Jewish community has endorsed this opinion.[32]

Over time, this dual system of modest citizenship rights coupled with more generous national rights reserved for Jews has attracted a lot of unfavorable publicity. In response, Israel has attempted to blur the line between citizenship and nationality. For example, Israeli identity cards no longer include a formal "national" designation (although the difference between Jews and Palestinians can sometimes be discerned from the father's name, still included on the identity card). Moreover, the JNF has recognized that it can make money by renting land to Palestinians, and now does so in some cases. But fundamental rights, such as the right to family unification, remain reserved for Jewish Israelis and Israel remains a state for the Jews and not for its citizens.

THE GREAT AND REGIONAL POWERS IN THE ERA
OF DECOLONIZATION

Israel's internal arrangements for its own people and for the Palestinians living within the nation were shaped not only by the ideological requirements of Zionism but also by the power struggles among the great powers of the world and the near great powers of the region.

In 1946, two years before Israel proclaimed its existence, Winston Churchill defined the great power struggle of the post-war world. In a speech at Westminster College in Fulton, Missouri, he said: "A shadow has fallen upon the scenes so lately lighted by the Allied victory ... From Stettin in the Baltic to Trieste in the Adriatic, an iron curtain has descended across the continent. Behind that line lie all the capitals of the ancient states of Central and Eastern Europe. ... [A]ll are subject in one form or another, not only to Soviet influence but to a very high and, in many cases, increasing measure of control from Moscow ... Athens alone ... is free to decide its future ... Turkey and Persia are both profoundly alarmed ... If now the Soviet Government tries, by separate action, to build up a pro-Communist Germany in their areas, this will ... give the defeated Germans the power of putting themselves up to auction between the Soviets and the Western Democracies."[33] From then on, the power struggles between the Western and Soviet blocks came to be understood as the Cold War.

Rhetoric on both sides cast this competition between the great powers in messianic terms: from the U.S. and British point of view, the struggle of democracy and freedom against tyranny and totalitarianism; from the Russian point of view, the struggle by the vanguard of the proletariat, those speaking for the interests of all humankind, against the "unconscionable freedom of free trade,"[34] world capitalists speaking only for the privileges of property. The reality was, of course, considerably less glorious than either side would have liked, with tyranny, corruption, imperialism, neo-colonialism, and exploitation, under different guises, on both sides.

The Middle East was an important site of struggle for great power competition. Both sides were well aware of the oil reserves in the area as well as the strategic location of the Middle East as the hinge between Europe and

Asia. Both sides sought to establish their own spheres of influence, puppet regimes, and military bases in the region.

European countries were also drawn into the conflict, not only as part of the Cold War, but also based on their own, unique agendas. The French, for example, supplied Israel with its first nuclear capabilities (the Dimona reactor), in part as a response to Arab support for the Algerian insurgency against France.[35] And Germany provided massive reparations payments not only to individual Jews but also, in the form of armaments, to the Israeli state.[36]

Israel was particularly adept at playing one side against the other well into the 1970s. During the War of Independence/*Nakba* Israel received crucial military aid, especially airplanes, from the Soviet bloc via a Czech arms deal.[37] Many of its new citizens came from areas of Europe in the Soviet bloc, and Russia counted on the ties between the new Israelis and their countries of origin to create public opinion favorable to Russian interests.

But the Russians did not have the field to themselves. The American president formulated the Truman Doctrine, a policy for containing Russian influence worldwide. Yet even with a clear objective, the Truman administration faced many hard choices in the Middle East. American interests were divided, with a real stake not only against Russia, but also with both Israel and the Arab world.

Would it be more effective to side with the Israelis or with the Arabs? Clearly, the good opinion of the other Arab states would have required America to support Palestinian ambitions that rejected Partition. But Truman had already endorsed the partition plan embodied in Resolution 181.

Truman had not done this lightly. While sympathetic to the plight of the Jews in the aftermath of the Holocaust, he was not enthusiastic about the creation of a Jewish state, principally because he was a strong believer in the separation of church and state.[38] For all of the period between 1945 and 1948, Truman waffled on the Palestine issue. His strongest preferences were for Great Britain to suspend their ban on Jewish immigration to Palestine and for Jews and Arabs to reach some consensus about their conjoined fate. A number of political formulas would have served to secure those ends, for example, an independent bi-national state or an English trusteeship over an undivided Palestine.[39]

Much of Truman's government was, in fact, opposed both to the Partition Plan and to the idea of the U.S. unilaterally siding with Israel. The State Department, the CIA, and the Joint Chiefs of Staff in the Pentagon all urged caution about America's course for a variety of reasons: judgment that long term American interests lay with the oil producing countries, that Israel was set on a reckless path of territorial enlargement that would drag America into further bloodshed, that the Israeli-American alliance violated America's stated advocacy of national self-determination.[40]

In the end, however, Truman abandoned his previous positions and raced to make America the first country to recognize Israel after it proclaimed itself into statehood. Most commentators on Truman's decision interpret this reversal as domestic politics, detailing how Truman caved in to Jewish lobbyists, first during the mid-term elections of 1946 and later during the presidential election of 1948.[41]

Certainly the Jewish vote, Jewish campaign contributions, and the heft of the Jewish lobby counted for a lot in explaining Truman's about-face. But other factors were also at work. In the end, although the State Department thought that American interest lay with access to Arab oil, they were favorably impressed by Israel's military performance in the War of Independence, optimistic about persuading Israel to join the Western alliance (and to defend western oil interests if necessary), and they saw in the fractured Palestinian leadership no partner for strategic alliances.

New research also shows that officials in the Truman administration were very careful to promote consultation among the Department of the Interior (particularly the Oil and Gas Division), the Jewish Agency, and American oil companies. Hence, Truman became convinced that recognition of Israel would not harm either national or private oil interests.[42] The President was able to shed his concerns in part because the Israelis hinted that there might be oil in the Negev, and partly because the Saudis had signaled that, despite their rhetorical support for Palestine, they would not disrupt oil flows as retaliation for Truman's recognition of Israel.[43]

Reassured, Truman saw to it that America was the first country to recognize Israel, minutes after its self-declared independence. Russia, however, was the second country to recognize Israel and thus Israel was able to benefit from both U.S. and Russian courtship for decades.

In addition to the great powers, the fate of Israel and the Palestinians was embedded in the politics of the local region. The countries surrounding Israel were all newly minted products of decolonization. Lebanon and Syria were five years old in 1948, having achieved independence from France in 1943. Jordan's independence from Britain should have occurred in 1946, but the treaty establishing Jordanian independence was so compromised in favor of British dominance that the United Nations rejected it and an acceptable alternative was not negotiated until 1948. Egypt was still bound to England in ways that compromised its military autonomy well into the 1950s. Iraq, nominally independent since the 1930s, was actually renegotiating its independence from England, trying to diminish English military presence within its borders.[44]

Thus all of the front line states around Israel were preoccupied with the same tasks that preoccupied Israel: establishing a governmental framework, developing an economy, and finding their place in an international system of nation-states. But they were faced with additional challenges as well. Their citizens were appalled at the magnitude of the Arab humiliation in 1948. Within the next three years, all of the Arab front-line states were subjected to political upheavals: the prime ministers of Egypt and Lebanon and the king of Jordan were assassinated and military coups overthrew the Syrian and Egyptian regimes.[45]

This situation created maximum turbulence and uncertainty. Taking a page from Campbell-Bannerman, the Israelis responded by trying to foster chaos and weakness in the internal affairs of their front line neighbors while securing alliances with Iran and Turkey, relatively powerful nations on the far borders of the states abutting Israel. These actions, in turn, created a counter-move of intensive militarization in the emergent Arab states, to the detriment of their own domestic needs and to the prospects for international peace.[46] Israel, in turn, also committed to a highly militarized nationalism, as Ronit's story in Chapter 2 illustrates.

Out of this difficult and volatile situation, and despite long-standing rivalries between Egypt, Syria, and Iraq for regional predominance, the new Arab countries were attracted to two political programs: pan-Arab solidarity that would promote regional cooperation whereby Arab states could stand up to Israel's military and economic strengths, and joining the ranks of the "non-aligned" nations in the Cold War, thus positioning themselves to benefit from the competition between the Western and Soviet blocs. Both of these agendas were embodied in the person of Gamal Abdel Nasser, Egypt's political leader after the 1952 overthrow of King Farouk.

Nasser's initial determination to keep Egypt in the non-aligned bloc was frustrated by events on the ground. Palestinians living under Jordanian control in the West Bank and under Egyptian control in the Gaza strip staged many incursions into Israel, some to be reunited with family members, others to smuggle contraband goods, still others to challenge Israeli control of their homeland. Israel staged reprisals into the Jordanian controlled West Bank and into Egyptian controlled Gaza.

Ariel Sharon led the Israeli massacre in Qibya in the West Bank in which village houses were dynamited and more than 50 Palestinians killed.[47] A similar Israeli raid into Gaza saw some 40 Egyptian soldiers killed.[48]

155

This raid left Nasser determined to secure better arms for Egypt. He approached the United States first and, like Ho Chi Minh in Vietnam, was rejected. He turned then to the Soviet Union, who offered unlimited arms on generous terms. The pattern was repeated when Nasser sought financial support for the Aswan Dam project. The American foreign policy establishment feared that Nasser was not sufficiently loyal to western interests, and Southern senators voiced fear over potential competition between their constituents and Egyptian cotton growers, should the dam be completed. The terms offered to Nasser for supporting the dam reflected this reluctance, so Nasser turned instead to the Soviet Union, signifying the growing ties between their two countries by recognizing Communist China.[49]

In July of 1956 the growing tensions between Egypt and the Western powers came to a head when Nasser nationalized the Suez Canal, a vital shipping route between the Mediterranean and the Red Sea. In response, Israel, England, and France invaded Egypt. The allies achieved military gains but were nevertheless obliged to abandon their incursion. Egypt ensured that the Canal would remain closed by scuttling ships and blocking it even in the face of potential military defeat. And the United States, which normally would have backed an Anglo-French-Israeli mission, unexpectedly objected. American displeasure with the invasion stemmed from the fact that, at the same time that Western powers were invading Egypt, the Soviet Union invaded Hungary. The United States, intent on shrinking the Soviet sphere of influence in Europe, could not defend the invasion of a small country by Western superpowers just as it was denouncing the Soviet invasion of Hungary. And so Nasser emerged triumphant from the Suez Canal crisis in spite of his military weakness.[50]

To solidify the gains he had achieved, Nasser sought and got a political union with Syria, in 1958, creating a new state, The United Arab Republic. The hope was for other Arab states to join the union, but, instead, the UAR proved to be a short-lived project, ended by 1961. The failure of the UAR highlighted intra-Arab rivalries, political instabilities, and a nearly complete inability of Arab nations, singly or in combination, to protect the interests of the now stateless Palestinians.

THE PALESTINIANS: DIVIDED AND ABANDONED

The years immediately following the creation of the state of Israel were years of defeat for the Palestinians. Their community and their homeland were divided: the West Bank under Jordanian control, the Gaza strip under

Egyptian control, two thirds of their population reduced to refugee status, many of them living in refugee camps either in the West Bank and Gaza or in the surrounding countries, Lebanon, Jordan, Syria, and Egypt.

Approximately 170,000 Palestinians remained in Israel.[51] They, too, were living under terrible conditions.

Palestinians remaining in Israel were further divided into two groups. Some had managed to remain in place and avoid the expulsion designed for them in the *Nakba*. Among those who remained in place, some simply lived in such remote and inaccessible areas that the *Nakba* had passed their communities by, leaving them out of the collective disaster. Other Palestinians had been expelled but managed to return. Still others were simply lucky that, in the midst of ethnic cleansing all around them, their village, street, or house had been spared.

In addition to Palestinians who managed to remain in place during the *Nakba*, there was a second set of Palestinians living under Israeli jurisdiction. This second group is known in Israel as "present absentees." In plain English, these are internally displaced persons, i.e. persons who were expelled from their homes and, even as they fled, managed to remain inside Israeli territory, though not in their original places of residence. "Any Palestinian Arab could be declared absentee if he had left his usual place of residence on or after November 29, 1947, the date of the United Nations partition resolution."[52]

The phenomenon of "present absentees" created an enormous opportunity for Israelis to de-Arabize the places under their control. Israelis quickly created a Custodian of Absentee Property who was empowered to "find" and "declare" absenteeism of persons or property. As soon as such "absenteeism" had been established, Palestinian property was appropriated by the Israeli state. This was consistent with Ben Gurion's plans, described earlier in this chapter, to nationalize "unused" land and water resources. "The Custodian's powers were such that he could take over Arab property in Israel on the strength of his own judgment by certifying in writing that any persons or body of persons, and that any property, were 'absentee.' The burden of proof that any property was not absentee fell upon its owner, but the Custodian could not be questioned concerning the source of information on the grounds of which he had declared a person or property [to be absentee] ... He could [also] take over all property which might be obtained *in the future* by an individual whom he certified to be absentee."(emphasis mine).[53]

In short, the legal regime created by the Custodian of Absentee Property's office meant that Israel had systematized its control over land and water, and established, to its advantage, the rules whereby competing claims could be adjudicated. In the end, using these mechanisms, the Israeli state appropriated 94% of the property "abandoned" by Palestinians and gave it to Jewish Israelis.[54]

Put simply: Israeli forces created a large number of Palestinian refugees and then, because the refugees were absent, expropriated their homes, lands, and other possessions.

The Palestinians who remained in Israel, either in their own homes or as "absentees," did not get to live what anyone would consider a normal life. Israel declared State of Emergency in 1948, aimed at controlling Palestinians. "Under a state of emergency, a government can—to protect the state and its people—employ exceptional measures that violate civil rights or introduce sovereign arbitrariness."[55]

Not only were Palestinian claims to their own property assaulted, they themselves were deemed by Ben Gurion and later administrations to be security risks to the state. They were therefore required to live under military law. This state of affairs – Israeli Jews governed by civil law and Palestinian citizens of Israel under military rule – persisted until 1966. The declared state of emergency persists to this day.[56] These arrangements explain why Palestinians often say that "For Jews, Israel is a democracy and for Palestinians, Israel is a Jewish state."

Military law meant, *de facto*, that Palestinians were stripped of all civil rights and were subject to military authority. They could be arrested on the whim of any soldier and held in administrative detention without charges or rights for 6 months at a time, renewable indefinitely. Administrative detention was a period of interrogation and the likeliest moment for torture to occur.

"Israel's use of administrative detention blatantly violates the restrictions of international law. Israel carries it out in a highly classified manner that denies detainees the possibility of mounting a proper defense. Moreover, the detention has no upper time limit,"[57] notes *B'Tselem*, a prize-winning Israeli human rights NGO. "Over the years, Israel has placed thousands of Palestinians in administrative detention for prolonged periods of time, without trying them, without informing them of the charges against them, and without allowing them or their counsel to examine the evidence. In this way, the military judicial system ignores the right to freedom and due process, the right of defendants to state their case, and the presumption of innocence, all of which are protections clearly enshrined in both Israeli and international law."[58]

In the relatively rare instances were Palestinians actually received a trial, the proceedings were conducted in Hebrew in front of a military judge who could rule that Palestinian defendants were not entitled, on security grounds, to see the evidence against them or to confront their accusers. Lisa Hajjar, a Berkeley sociologist, reports that in the present day Israeli military courts in the West Bank 97% of all cases are settled with plea bargains and that pleas bargains invariably require a guilty plea on the part of the defendant – military courts thus produce a "guilty" verdicts in at least 97% of the cases before them.[59]

Administrative detention was only the tip of the iceberg of disabilities imposed upon Palestinians by military rule. Under military rule, individuals could, without recourse, be banished and/or have their properties confiscated. Indeed, entire villages could be moved by military decree.[60]

Even for those individual Palestinians who avoided administrative detention or the loss of property, military rule imposed crushing constraints. Military rule virtually quarantined Israel's Palestinian citizens to their own town or village. If they wished to leave for any mundane purpose – a job interview, to visit a friend in the hospital, to attend a family wedding or funeral, to go to university or to a doctor's appointment – Palestinians inside Israel needed permission from the local military governor to accomplish their tasks. Military rule served to constrict Palestinian lives while leaving Israel's Jewish citizens free to pursue their private purposes without hindrance.[61]

Clearly, Israel's Palestinian citizens lived in a "through the looking glass" world in which they had no opportunity to secure their personal safety or property rights. Their disadvantages were not only personal and economic, but also political. The state of emergency (and, later, amendments to the Basic Laws that serve as Israel's quasi-constitution) also prohibit all Palestinian political organizing that does not acknowledge Israel as a state of the Jews.[62] Palestinians in Israel were thus shut out of both market and state mechanisms for securing individual or communal wellbeing.

Palestinian refugees, those who were driven out of Israel, lived at the whim of the host societies to which they fled. Some communities – especially the Jordanian and Syrian – were more generous, offering refugees the opportunities to leave refugee camps, to find work, to participate in education. Life in other countries was much worse. In Lebanon, the Christian community feared the addition of more Muslims to the political mix and therefore banned Palestinians from nearly all jobs and all political rights.[63] In Egypt, Palestinian tent camps were left to parch in the desert.[64]

Beyond the vagaries of the host society, Palestinian refugees were systemically plagued by what legal scholar Susan Akram calls the "protection gap" whereby Palestinian refugees fall through the cracks of the international, United Nations protocols for protecting refugees.[65] As the previous chapter has shown, Palestinian refugees were created during the 1947 to 1949 period, at a time when no universal protocols yet existed within the U.N. system for dealing with refugees.

In 1950, the U.N. responded to the Palestinian plight by creating two organizations, the U.N. Conciliation Commission on Palestine (UNCCP) and the U.N. Relief Works Agency (UNRWA). UNCCP was to advocate for Palestinians vis-à-vis Israel, emphasizing the right of return, then the preferred strategy for resolving refugee issues. UNRWA was more nearly a social work/humanitarian agency, designed to run the schools and clinics in Palestinian refugee camps, but not to do advocacy work.

Israeli intransigence blocked every attempt by UNCCP to achieve a Palestinian return to the lands from which they had been expelled. UNCCP exists today only as a repository for Palestinian land records that may become relevant to property claims in the future, but it no longer plays an active role in trying to establish Israeli-Palestinian conciliation. Therefore there is no agency within the UN that is responsible for advocacy on behalf of Palestinian rights.

In later years, the United Nations began to develop a more systematic regimen for dealing with refugees, codified in the Refugee Convention of 1951, reaffirmed in the 1967 Refugee Protocol and implemented by the United Nations High Commissioner for Refugees (UNHCR). The U.N.'s ideas about solutions for refugee problems have also become more diversified and more nuanced. Refugees were recognized to have both individual and collective rights. Repatriation remained the preferred choice for ending their refugee status, but repatriation was now supplemented by the possibility of support either for absorption into the host country where refugees had first taken shelter or resettlement in other, more distant lands. Both of the resettlement solutions included provisions for compensation to refugees for their lost property.

Unfortunately, Palestinians were excluded from this newer, more comprehensive and flexible system. The Palestinian case was deemed to be unique for a number of reasons. First, the U.N. held itself to be, in part, responsible for the *creation* of the Palestinian refugee problem by its insistence on the partition plan that neither side wanted. Second, the Arab states insisted that only repatriation could provide a solution, since they were not willing to tacitly ratify the expulsion of the Palestinians by accepting resettlement in near or distant destinations. Lastly, the Palestinians themselves insisted on their collective right as a people and evinced very little interest in individual solutions.

As a direct result of these factors, Palestinians never had access to the rights provided by the Refugee Convention or Protocol or to the services of the UNHCR. Instead they were left with the humanitarian work of UNRWA and, after a time, no advocacy at all from UNCCP, which was defunded when all the participants recognized that Israeli intransigence mooted any possibility of conciliation.[66]

In a final and ironic twist, the Netanyahu administration is now trying to destroy UNRWA despite the fact that UNRWA is a dramatically under-funded agency that does no advocacy work, whose mission is limited to running schools, clinics, and other social services. Israeli objections to UNRWA are that its very existence maintains Palestinian refugees as a special legal entity whose claims the Israeli government rejects. Instead, Netanyahu wants the Palestinian refugees (but not their descendants) referred to the U.N. High Commission for Refugees on the (possibly mistaken) assumption that the UNHCR is less insistent on repatriation and more open to relocation as a solution to the continued demands of Palestinian refugees.[67]

Thus the Palestinians in Israel and in the Diaspora found themselves in a bleak situation: massively traumatized, physically disbursed, impoverished and, for all practical purposes, without recourse to legal remedies for their suffering. So, against great odds, they turned instead to advocacy and resistance to pursue their quest for justice.

THE SPIRAL INTO TRAGEDY

In turning to advocacy and resistance, the Palestinians became part of turbulent inter-Arab politics and part of the Cold War era. After the dissolution of the United Arab Republic in 1961, Syria and Egypt resumed their rivalry, part of which was framed in terms of the Palestinians.[68] Each side claimed to be the more effective champion of the Palestinians, and each side expressed their support in ways that were congruent with their own national aspirations.

The Syrians were more militant and they supported an organization called *Fatah*. Palestinian refugees from Gaza founded *Fatah* in 1958, and it, like its Syrian hosts, advocated armed struggle against Israel. Fatah sponsored raids that were not meant to conquer or dislodge Israel but to provoke it. Fatah's plan was that, in the face of mounting Israeli aggression, the Arab states would finally unify and then, having superior numbers, they would be able to crush Israel.[69] This plan was strategic but misinformed and, in the long run, produced unintended results – the Israeli occupation of all of Palestine-exactly opposite to *Fatah*'s aspirations.

Nasser, like his Jordanian counterpart King Hussein, had suffered the sting of Israeli reprisals and was less eager than the Syrians to go to war with Israel. In 1964, at an Arab League summit in Cairo, he sponsored an alternative to *Fatah*, the Palestine Liberation Organization. The PLO, in turn, eschewed raids and settled for a policy of (mostly bombastic) advocacy for Palestinian interests.[70] From 1969 onward, after the Israelis occupied Palestine in its entirety, Fatah and the PLO merged, with Fatah leader Yasir Arafat at the helm. The organization then dedicated itself to advocating for Palestinian interests on its own, without waiting for the support of Arab allies. The PLO claimed *all* Palestinians as its constituency, those in Israel, those living under Occupation in the West Bank and Gaza, and those in the Diaspora, mainly in the refugee camps of the Middle East.

Soon enough, Arab-Israeli hostility, inter-Arab rivalries, and great power meddling led to the Six Day War (June 5–10, 1967), whose results create the platform of the current Palestinian-Israeli conflict.

Originally, the Six Day War was portrayed in western media as a defensive effort on Israel's part, despite the fact that Israel won the war by using a pre-emptive first strike against the Egyptian, Syrian, and Jordanian air forces. The "defensive war" narrative is supported by two facts: Syrian and Egyptian rhetoric calling for Israel's destruction,[71] and by Egyptian and Syrian troop movements, massing their armies on Israel's border in the period immediately preceding the war.

Recent analyses, based on newly available documents in Israeli archives, suggest an additional dimensions to the story. The fuse for hostilities seems to have been set by Israel's unilateral diversion of the Jordan River in 1964 and Syrian incursions from the Golan Heights that were a response to Israel's act.[72]

Egypt, though severed from a formal relationship with Syria by the dissolution of the United Arab Republic, nonetheless wished to act as the protective big brother. Nasser had been hammered every time he tried to use the strategic assets available to him, closing the Straits of Tiran and the Suez Canal, and wished to reassert his claim to being *the* Arab leader in the face of Syria's more radical behavior.

Jordan, in turn, was tied to Egypt in a mutual defense pact. This network of Pan-Arab connection created a situation similar to the one that existed in Europe prior to the First World War, where a series of mutual defense pacts drew countries not directly involved in the hostilities into the war in defense of allies.

Israeli responses to Syrian and Egyptian actions were also more complex than the "defensive war" narrative suggests. Some elements of the Israeli government saw Nasser's troop movements as threats designed to impress an Arab audience more than real preparations for war.[73] Some interpreted it as a message to Israel, designed to rein in their military responses to Syrian incursions.[74] Others in the military genuinely feared an Arab military threat.[75] In a variant of this position, a number of Israeli leaders thought that Egypt had limited military objectives, wanting only to take out Israel's nuclear facility at Dimona.[76]

The most far-sighted of the Israeli military leaders saw the Syrian and Egyptian troop movements as an opportunity, even an excuse, to take territory they had always wanted.[77] For them it was a war of choice, although there was tension between those who preferred the strategic military advantage of a first strike and those who did not want to incur the diplomatic costs such a move would entail.[78] The war of choice analysis is greatly strengthened by the fact that all the administrative plans for what is now the Occupation had already been prepared starting in 1963, and the events of 1967 served merely as an opportunity to put them into action, which happened within days of the Israeli military victor.[79]

Every major party to the conflict acted both dishonestly and stupidly. Perhaps the greatest dishonesty was that both the Arabs, in massing troops on Israel's border, and Israel, in selling their American patrons on the idea of a pre-emptive first strike, argued that their behavior was designed to produce a lasting peace rather than an ongoing state of hot or cold war.[80] To this assertion, one can only agree with the person who warned: "If you blow smoke, you have to understand that the other side will think a fire has been lit."[81]

The United Nations, under U Thant's leadership, made strategic mistakes in removing U.N. peacekeepers from Gaza.[82] The Russians invented scare stories about Israel's military ambitions against Syria and fed them to Nasser.[83] The United States could not see over its Cold War, Manichean assumptions, reviling Nasser for acknowledging the reality of Communist China and for allowing the Vietnamese Liberation Front to open an office in Cairo.[84]

In the end, America proved to be a crucial player because Israeli political and military decision-makers waited to secure American support (or at least tacit acceptance) for their military ambitions.[85] To secure American acquiescence, Israeli diplomats were careful to direct their lobbying to the CIA and the Pentagon and to avoid the considerably less hawkish State Department.[86] The best American intelligence estimates, conveyed to Israel, were that Nasser did not really intend war and that, in the event war did break out, the Israelis would win handily against this combined forces of Egypt, Syria, and Jordan.[87]

This latter estimate proved to be accurate. Once hostilities commenced with the pre-emptive Israeli strike mentioned above, the war was won in a matter of days. The map of the area changed dramatically with Israel now in control of all the land between the river and the sea, all of Mandate Palestine, exactly as Zionist ambitions had always demanded. [88]

For most Americans, the Six Day War seems like a self-contained event that occurred in a far off place. I hope this chapter has shown how deeply events in the Middle East were embedded in larger global conflicts. Russian, American, British and French actions were all critical to the conflict: Russia deliberately lying to Nasser about an (entirely fictional) Israeli military plan to invade Syria,[89] French anger at Egypt for supporting Algerian independence, American proclivities to side with England, France and Israel thwarted by the Soviet invasion of Hungary, the Johnson administration's insistence on viewing the Israel-Palestine conflict through the lens of Vietnam – all of these factors insured that when the great powers acted in this arena, they did so without any real regard for the peoples of the area and in ways that exacerbated the conflict.

For Palestinians, the Six Day War meant that the entirety of their country was now under the control of a state that was actively hostile to both their national aspirations and their communal well-being. This marked a significant deterioration from the conditions that prevailed between 1948 and 1967, when Palestinians lived under the control of people who were rhetorically committed although practically indifferent to their well-being.

For Israelis, the days and months after the war were a time of near-euphoric triumph. Looking back, the eternally despised, oppressed, dispossessed European Jews now stood at the helm of a country able to repel foreign enemies on three fronts simultaneously; able to take what it wanted, to control all the land it had always coveted.

But, of course, along with the land, Israel also had taken control of the very people it did not wish to deal with, the Palestinians. The dilemma – how to have all of the land with none of the Palestinians (or as few of them as possible) – has been the basis of the conflict ever since.

SUMMARY: ESTABLISHING THE STATE AND PREPARING THE OCCUPATION

History of Israel-Palestine Conflict II
1948 – 1967: From the establishment of the state to the conquest of all the land

Israel	Great Powers	Palestine
Custodian of Absentee Property	Decolonization	Resistance in Exile Jordan
Military Rule	COLD WAR	Pan Arab Nationalism
Citizenship vs. Nationality	Petro-politics	PLO founded (1963)

6-DAY WAR:
CONTROL OF ENTIRETY OF PALESTINE BY ISRAEL

NOTES

[1] G. Ehrlich. (1992, May 6). Not Only in Deir Yassin, *Ha'ir*, p. 22 quoted in Saleh Abdel Jawad, Zionist Massacres: the Creation of the Palestinian Refugee Problem in the 1948 War, in Eyal Benvenisti, Chaim Gans, Sari Hanafi. (eds.). (2007). *Israel and the Palestinian Refugees* (Heidelberg and New York: Springer), p. 59.

[2] Tom Segev. (1998). *1949: The First Israelis*, 2nd edition (New York, N.Y.: Henry Holt), p. ix.

[3] Personal communication from a Palestinian friend.

[4] Segev, *op. cit.*, p. xiv.

[5] *Ibid.* p. 68.

[6] *Ibid.* p. xiii.

[7] *Ibid.* p. xv.

[8] *Ibid.*

[9] James Gelvin (2007). *The Israeli-Palestinian Conflict: One Hundred Years of War*, 2nd edition (Cambridge: Cambridge University Press), pp. 167–168.

[10] *Ibid.*

[11] Tom Segev. (2002). *Elvis in Jerusalem: Post-Zionism and the Americanization of Israel* (New York: Henry Holt), pp. 25–26.

[12] Yarden Skop. (2014, April 24). 50,000 Holocaust survivors in Israel live in poverty, *Ha'aretz*, retrieved from http://www.haaretz.com/news/national/.premium-1.586970

[13] David Rubinger. (2008). *Israel Through My Lens: Sixty Years as a Photojournalist* (London: Abbeville Press) Book Cover.

[14] Personal communication from a former student.

[15] *Ibid.*

[16] Michael Palumbo. (1997). *The Palestinian Catastrophe: The 1948 Expulsion of a People from their Homeland* (London: Faber and Faber) pp. 198–201. See also Charles D. Smith. (2013). *Palestine and the Arab-Israeli Conflict: A History with Documents.* 8th edition (New York: St. Martin's Press), p. 222 and note 4, p. 250.

[17] Nissim Rejwan. (2004). *The Last Jews in Baghdad.* Austin, TX: University of Press.

[18] Yehouda Shenhav. (2006). *The Arab Jews: A post-colonial reading of nationalism, religion and ethnicity.* Stanford, CA: Stanford University Press.

[19] Kristen Schulze. (2009). *The Jews of Lebanon: Between Coexistence and Conflict* 2nd edition, Sussex, England: Sussex Academic Press, cited in "Beirut's hidden Jewish community," *Deutsche Welle*, November 15, 2011 retrieved from http://www.dw.de/beiruts-hidden-jewish-community/a-6654644

[20] Joel Greenberg. (1997, September 1). The Babies from Yemen: An Enduring Mystery, *New York Times*, retrieved from https://www.nytimes.com/1997/09/02/world/the-babies-from-yemen-an-enduring-mystery.html

[21] Shoshanna Madmoni-Gerber. (2009). *Israeli Media and the Framing of Internal Conflict.* London: Palgrave McMillan.

[22] Haokets. (2013, July 12). The Yemeni Baby Affair: What if this was your child? +*972*, retrieved from https://972mag.com/the-yemenite-baby-affair-what-if-this-was-your-child/75672/

[23] Haggai Matar. (2017, June 18). Israel's National Wound that cannot heal, +*972*, retrieved from https://972mag.com/israels-national-wound-that-cannot-heal/128211/

[24] Gelvin, *op. cit.*, p. 168.

[25] Smith, *op. cit.*, p. 222.

[26] This arrangement echoes early Zionist organizational practices, for example those of the Jewish National Fund, discussed in Chapter 5.

[27] Smith, *op. cit.,* p. 221.

[28] For an amusing story of how a lower level clerk invented a Catalan "nationality" within the Israeli state system, see Shlomo Sand. (2009). *The Invention of the Jewish People* (London, UK: Verso), pp. 3–5.

[29] *Ha'aretz* Editorial. (2012, January 13). Supreme Court thrusts Israel down the slope of Apartheid, *Ha'aretz*, retrieved from http://www.haaretz.com/print-edition/opinion/supreme-court-thrusts-israel-down-the-slope-of-apartheid-1.407056

[30] Jack Khoury. (2017, August 25). Israel Revokes Citizenship of Hundreds of Negev Bedouin, Leaving them Stateless, *Ha'aretz*, retrieved from https://www.haaretz.com/israel-news/.premium-israel-revokes-citizenship-of-hundreds-of-bedouin-1.5445620

Orly Noy (2017, September 15). Is Israel turning its Bedouin citizens into a stateless people? +*972*, retrieved from https://972mag.com/is-israel-turning-its-bedouin-citizens-into-a-stateless-people/129775/

[31] Revita Hovel. (2013, October 3). Supreme Court rejects citizens' request to change nationality from 'Jewish' to 'Israeli,' *Ha'aretz*, retrieved from http://www.haaretz.com/news/national/.premium-1.550241

See also Ofra Yeshua-Lyth. (2014, June 3). Discrimination is legal, there are no Israelis: Reading the Supreme Court's decisions on Israeli nationality, *Mondoweiss*, retrieved from http://mondoweiss.net/2014/06/discrimination-decisions-nationality.html

[32] Yedidia Z. Stern and Jay Ruderman. (2014, March 3). Op. Ed: Why Israeli is not a nationality *Jewish Telegraphic Agency (JTA) News and Opinion*, retrieved from http://www.jta.org/2014/03/03/news-opinion/israel-middle-east/op-ed-why-israeli-is-not-a-nationality

[33] Winston Churchill. (1946, March 5). The Sinews of Peace, address delivered at Westminster College, Fulton, Missouri, retrieved from http://history1900s.about.com/od/churchillwinston/a/Iron-Curtain.htm

[34] Karl Marx, "The Manifesto of the Communist Party," in Robert C. Tucker (ed.). 1978. *The Marxian Revolutionary Idea*, 2nd edition (New York: Norton) p. 475.

[35] Ghada Kharmi. (2007). *Married to Another Man: Israel's Dilemma in Palestine* (London: Pluto Press), p. 14.

[36] *Ibid.* p. 15.

[37] Smith, *op. cit.*, p. 196.

[38] John Judis. (2014). *Genesis: Truman, American Jews, and the Origins of the Arab/Israeli Conflict* (New York: Farrar, Strauss and Giroux), pp. 207–227.

[39] *Ibid.* pp. 301–306.

[40] *Ibid.* pp. 198–207.

[41] *Ibid.* pp. 311–316.

[42] Irene Gendzier. (2015). *Dying to Forget: Oil, Power, Palestine and the Origins of United States Foreign Policy in the Middle East.* New York: Columbia University Press.

[43] Irene Gendzier. (2011)."Why the U.S. Recognized Israel," *Israeli Occupation Archives*, retrieved from http://www.israeli-occupation.org/2011-11-09/irene-gendzier-why-the-us-recognised-israel/

[44] Eugene L. Rogan and Avi Shlaim. (2001). *The War for Palestine: Rewriting the History of 1948* (Cambridge: Cambridge University Press), p. 1.

[45] *Ibid.*

[46] Kharmi, *op. cit.,* pp. 20–23.

[47] Smith, *op. cit.*, p. 227.

[48] *Ibid.* pp. 235–236.

[49] *Ibid.* pp. 232–239.

[50] *Ibid.* pp. 239–248.

[51] *Ibid.* p. 223. Segev, *op. cit.*, puts the number at 160,000, p. 67.

[52] *Ibid.*

[53] *Ibid.* Smith is here quoting Don Peretz. (1958). *Israel and the Palestine Arabs* (Washington, D.C.) p. 151, See also, Yoav Mehozay. (2012). The Rule of Difference: How Emergency Powers Prevent Palestinian Assimilation in Israel, *Israel Studies Review*, 27 (2): p. 24.

[54] Gelvin, *op. cit.*, p. 166.

[55] Mehozay, *op. cit.*, p.18.

[56] *Ibid.*

[57] *B'Tselem* "Administrative Detention," January 1, 2011, retrieved from http://www.btselem.org/administrative_detention

[58] *Ibid.*

[59] Lisa Hajjar. (2005). *Courting Conflict: The Israeli Military Court System in the West Bank and Gaza* (Berkeley: University of California Press), p. 219.

[60] Smith, *op. cit.*, p. 223, quoting Peretz, *op. cit.*, pp. 44ff.

[61] Lecture by Mohamad Zeidan, at the Arab Human Rights Association, Nazareth, Israel, January 5, 2015.

[62] Mehozay, *op. cit.*, pp. 26–32.

[63] *Ibid.* p. 224.

[64] Edward Said. (2000). *Out of Place: A Memoir*. New York: Vintage.

[65] Susan Akram. (2011). Palestinian Refugees and their Legal Status, *Journal of Palestine Studies* (special issue on refugees), pp. 36–51.

[66] *Ibid.*

[67] Hanin Abu Salem. (2017, June 22). Why is Netanyahu trying to disband the UNRWA? *Al Jazeera*, retrieved from https://mail.google.com/mail/u/0/#label/localfolders%2Fpalestine%2FBOOK%2F2nd+edition+revisions%2F2Chap6/15cdfe18dc3bc0 4c

[68] Smith, *op. cit.*, pp. 270–274.

[69] *Ibid.* pp. 271–73.

[70] *Ibid.* pp. 270–271.

[71] *Ibid.* pp. 281–282.

[72] Gelvin, *op. cit.*, p. 173.

[73] Segev, *op. cit.*, pp. 226, 230.

[74] *Ibid.* p. 222.

[75] *Ibid.* p. 233.

[76] *Ibid.*, pp. 229, 233.

[77] *Ibid.*, p. 255.

[78] *Ibid.* p. 262.

[79] Ilan Pappe. (2017). *The Biggest Prison on Earth: A History of the Occupied Territories*. London: One World Press.
Guy Laron. (2017, June 6). Was Israel under Existential Thereat in June 1967? *Counterpunch*, retrieved from https://www.counterpunch.org/2017/06/06/was-israel-under-existential-threat-in-june-1967/

[80] Smith, *op. cit.* p. 286.

[81] Segev, *op. cit.* p. 229.

[82] *Ibid.* pp. 281–286.

[83] *Ibid.* p. 281.

[84] *Ibid.* p. 278.

[85] Segv, 1998, *op. cit.*, pp. 236–241.

[86] *Ibid.* pp. 283–284.

[87] *Ibid.* p. 266.

[88] It is important to note that here and elsewhere, when I talk about the entirety of Mandate Palestine, I mean Mandate Palestine as it existed after Jordan was severed from it.

[89] Gelvin, *op. cit.*, p. 173.

OCCUPATION AND RESISTANCE

The Zionist Dream Comes True, or Be Careful What You Ask For

You know, and we know, as practical men that the question of justice arises only between parties equal in strength, [for] the strong do what they can and the weak submit.

Thucydides[1]

Story

Facebook Post: "For all of us who do not remember, on September 29, 1967, about 3 months after the Six Day War, *Ha'aretz* published the following op-ed: 'Our right to defend ourselves from annihilation does not give us the right to oppress others. Foreign occupation results in foreign rule, foreign rule results in resistance, resistance results in suppression, suppression results in terrorism and counter-terrorism. Victims of terrorism are usually innocents. Holding on to the Territories will turn us into a nation of murderers and murder victims. Let us get out of the Occupied Territories now!'"[2]

The Waiting Room – Nader's poem[3]
As you patiently endure the icy cold room,
Your soul is constantly tested
Your consciousness is eternally roaming the void.
The looming soldiers with their boyish guns, Well-dressed for the freezing winter and my aching heart
They come ... They go ...
They pretend to see our absence ...
They gaze into the shadows of our inner debilitation ...

The world around you is belittled. Diminished to a vision of what it used to be
The air … you must find in the corners of your inner soul
The warmth … of your heart must suffice
You separate yourself from your surrounding
Find your own sun, your inner warmth so you won't freeze Now … you are your own world …
You are your air to breathe … without
All of me is inside of me

The Israeli military victory in the June, 1967 Six Day War created an entirely new geographic reality, with Israel in control of all the land of Mandate Palestine from the Jordan River to the Mediterranean Sea.

The Israeli military victory was an unmitigated disaster for the Palestinians, delivering them to a power bent on their expulsion or pacification.

For the Israelis, the victory was both a blessing and a curse. It was a blessing because it put under their control the land they had always claimed as rightfully theirs. But it was also a curse because, with that land came an additional 1,500,000 Palestinians,[4] (today 4,000,000),[5] none of whom would ever consent to the new political configuration.

This is the heart of the conflict whose essence has not changed since 1967. In the two-decade period covered in this chapter, Israelis, Palestinians, and outside forces each continue to pursue ends that thwart the others,' producing an on-going, deadly and oppressive stasis.

THE ISRAELIS: REALIZING THE DREAM, GENERATING RESISTANCE

In the years following 1967 Israel met many challenges. It developed a high tech economy focused on defense, security, and science. It grew a vigorous tourist industry. It managed its international presence in the face of continuous challenges to its legitimacy. Many of these developments are beyond the scope of the present work. Central to our concerns however, are Israel's ongoing relationships with the Palestinians under their control.

Palestinians under Israeli control were divided into three main groups: those who were citizens of Israel (though not Jewish nationals), those who lived in East Jerusalem and became "residents" but not citizens of Israel, and those who lived under military rule in the Occupied Palestinian Territories.

Palestinian citizens of Israel had long lived as though they were under military occupation; their fate governed by a perpetual State of Emergency and military law. But, just before the 1967 War, the Israeli government had ended the military rule of its own citizens (though not the State of Emergency) and integrated Palestinians into the civil law system, while imposing the well-tested military law on the inhabitants of the Occupied Palestinian Territories (OPT). Together, these moves (along with Israel's earlier, legally-enshrined decision to distinguish Israeli citizens who were Jewish nationals from those who held some other nationality associated with inferior rights) created four distinctive legal systems summarized below.

Israel's Four Legal System

Person	Citizenship	Nationality	Legal Rights
Israeli Jew	yes	Jewish	All
Pal. Israeli	yes	Non-Jew	Some
Pal. OPT	no	stateless	Isr. Military Law
Jerusalemite	no	resident	permit, revocable

Mohammad Zeidan, the director of the Arab Association for Human Rights, an Israeli NGO, analyzes the results of the most positive legal change, that of freeing Palestinian citizens of Israel from the burdens of military law. His conclusion is that Palestinian citizens of Israel, while less subject to arbitrary state decisions, nevertheless continue to suffer from pervasive discrimination that takes four forms:

First, there was and is direct legal discrimination: rights accorded to those who enter Israel under the Law of Return (i.e. as Jews) that are withheld from others.[6] The most important of these rights is the right to come to Israel at all. All Jews around the world are invited to do so without having to establish that their ancestors ever lived in the Middle East. In contrast, Palestinian refugees from 1948 and 1967 are forbidden to return to their homes. Not even the standard of "family unification" allows Palestinian citizens of Israel to live in their own country with a Palestinian spouse from elsewhere, either the Occupied Territories or the Diaspora.[7] Similar discrimination applies to other activities as well: for example no political party is legal if it does not accept

Israel as a Jewish state.[8] Imagine the outcry were the American government to bar political groups that do not accept America as a Christian state.

Second there is indirect discrimination. There are laws that, on their face, appear to be neutral, making no overt distinction between Israeli citizens who are also Jewish nationals and those who are not. However, while appearing to be race/ethnicity neutral, these same laws in fact create enormous advantages for Israeli citizens who are also of Jewish nationality. The most important example is probably the case of veteran's preference: there is a ferocious system of preference for Israeli army veterans not only among private employers but also in the government and the tax code. This may seem like a sensible arrangement for a country so deeply steeped in warfare. But it has the added dimension of disadvantaging Palestinian citizens of Israel who, with the exception of the Druze and a few Bedouins, are barred from serving in the Israeli armed forces.[9] Examples of veteran's preference include the Absorption of Discharged Soldiers Law (Amendment No. 7) that, much like the American G.I. Bill, creates tuition and housing support for veterans.[10]

Third, there is administrative latitude: places where resources are allocated by the executive branch of government and can be spent in ways that benefit Jewish communities and deprive Palestinian ones inside the country. Examples abound. The Israeli state has a system for designating certain land and the towns within it as National Priority Areas (NPA). A town so designated receives state funds in excess of those granted to other communities, and its citizens also receive higher levels of tax relief.[11] Almost always, the NPA designation is reserved for Jewish communities in the Negev or the Galilee, areas particularly targeted for "Judaization."[12] More recently such benefits have also been extended to the illegal settlements.[13] When this practice was successfully challenged as discriminatory before the Israeli Supreme Court, the Knesset passed a new law, the Economic Efficiency Law of 2009, which reaffirms the right of the state administrator to "exclusive discretion" in selecting towns for NPA designation.[14] Social service budgets can be equally discriminatory: "The government spends more in welfare on the Jewish sector that it does on Arab citizens, even though the Arab population has a higher rate of poverty ... According to official data ... the state spends an average of NIS 378 on each Jewish citizen and only NIS 246 on each Arab citizen – a discrepancy of 35 percent, although there are three times as many Arab families under the poverty line as Jewish families."[15] Overall, it is clear that Israeli state expenditures privilege not only Israel Jewish communities but also the illegal settlements.[16] Public sector employment also reflects anti-Arab prejudice. Although some 20% of Israel's citizens are Palestinian, less than 7% of state employees are drawn from this group and only 8 senior official are Palestinian.[17]

Fourth, there is cultural discrimination, both by private parties and by the Israeli state. The Law and Governance Article 18A decrees that Jewish religious holidays (along with Israeli Independence Day) are state holidays.[18] The Flag and Emblem Law (1949), the State Stamp Law (1949) and the Use of Hebrew Date Law (1998) all similarly validate Jewish cultural practices as the law of the land.[19]

All of these forms of discrimination worked simultaneously to ensure that Palestinian citizens of Israel, though eligible to vote, to serve in the Knesset, to participate in the health care system, and to send their children to public schools (segregated by "nationality") nevertheless remained second-class citizens.

Their position, however, was immeasurably better than that of the Palestinians in the Occupied Territories. There, the Israelis exported the military law they had previously used on their own Palestinian citizens.

This export of Occupation was by no means an *ad hoc* or hastily contrived affair after the military victory in the Six Day War. New research demonstrates that it was carefully planned well in advance.[20] As early as 1963, Israeli military lawyers, academics, and lawyers from the Ministry of the Interior began a series of meetings to plan the Occupation.[21] Their mission was to create a comprehensive framework for the judicial and administrative infrastructure of Occupation. The plan included provisions for the appointment of a Governor General, the division of the Occupied Territories into eight districts, the creation of 4 military courts, and many of the rules of operation for that apparatus. Appendices to the reports included Arabic translations of the relevant laws that would govern the life of the Occupied, memos establishing the compatibility of these laws with the Geneva Conventions (which, inconveniently from the Israeli point of view, barred judicially sanctioned executions of citizens in the Occupied Territories), lists of books to be banned (including Thomas Kuhn's *The Structure of Scientific Revolutions*, allegedly because it contained the word "revolution" in its title), and lists of candidates for judicial appointment who had been pre-vetted.[22] The American experience of governing occupied Germany after the Second World War was an important source for the committee designing the legal structure of the Occupation.[23]

This framework was implemented within days of the beginning of the Occupation, when each district commander received a box with the entire plan laid out, including directions for immediate implementation. In Gaza,

173

for example, the establishment of military rule was accomplished within 2 days of the end of the war, thanks to this advance planning.[24] In East Jerusalem, beginning on the evening of June 10, 1967, the last day of the Six Day War, Israel announced plans to demolish the Maghrebi neighborhood (or Moroccan Quarter) that bordered the Western Wall within the Old City of Jerusalem. Starting the following night, over 600 Muslim families were evicted to widen the plaza to its present Disneyesque dimensions.[25] The demolitions were carried out by civilian contractors in order to shield the Army from international criticism of the evictions. Demolitions began at 11 p.m. and were complete by dawn. The only surviving contractor was interviewed on the 50th anniversary of the demolitions. He described the situation in these words: "I was sky high. It was a pleasure." Children of the remaining contractors note that, after the demolitions were complete, the 15 contractors who carried out the work created an honorary society, The Order of the Kotel (Western Wall), to commemorate their deeds.[26]

The existence of a carefully laid out plan and its swift and thorough implementation support the claim that, for Israel, the 1967 war was a war of choice. Clearly, it afforded Israelis the opportunity to put the long-planned next steps for the colonization of Palestine into effect.

Within two weeks, East Jerusalem was annexed by Israel, which declared the city to be the eternal and indivisible capital of the Israel state.[27] This did not, however, mean that the Palestinian inhabitants of East Jerusalem were accorded citizenship – even though they now lived in Israel. Instead, they were deemed to be "residents" of the city, requiring Israeli permits to remain in their own homes. Moreover, the Israeli government kept enlarging the boundaries of the annexed entity of East Jerusalem: expanding it more than tenfold, from 6 square kilometers to 70 square kilometers.[28] This constituted a continued silent expropriation. As we saw in Chapter 2, the redrawing of Jerusalem's boundaries by Israeli fiat continues to the present day.

Every time the Jerusalem boundaries were redrawn, the Palestinians' rights to remain in their own homes was endangered in two ways. Amazingly, the Israeli government could and did simply refuse to issue residency permits to Palestinians newly annexed into Jerusalem. This was the case for our host in Al Walejeh who, without a residency permit, was found guilty of trespass for residing in the house his grandfather had built and in which his father, he, and his children had been born. The house has since been demolished and the Palestinian family has moved abroad.

In addition, the Israeli government could revoke any Palestinian's residency permit if it made a determination that Jerusalem was no longer the "center of life" for a particular resident.[29] Between 1967 and 2013, the Israeli government made this determination to the detriment of individual Palestinians 14,309 times, an average of 6 per week.[30]

But the legal maneuverings of Occupation were, in the end, probably less consequential, certainly more easily reversed, than the development of Israeli, Jewish-only settlements all over the West Bank. Israel's official position at the time of the 1967 war was that they were willing to swap "land for peace," i.e. to return the territories conquered in the Six Day War in return for recognition from their Arab neighbors.[31] But in establishing settlements, often referred to as "facts on the ground," Israel has done everything in its power to derail the "land for peace" formula and to foreclose the "universally agreed upon" two-state solution that would reserve 22% of historic Palestine for the Palestinian state. As early as November 1967 the US State Department recognized the import of "facts on the ground:" considering Israeli diplomat Abba Eban's promise of June 9, that "Israel is [not] seeking territorial aggrandizement" to be untrue and unreliable.[32] In short, Israel has been consciously and deliberately disingenuous about the peace process from its very beginnings in 1967.

Israel began settlement building, the redrawing of boundaries, and the application of military law, immediately after their 1967 victory. The Labor government, then in office, established the first settlements, mostly in potentially disputed areas: the Jordan Valley, the edges of the Sinai Peninsula, and in the Golan Heights.[33] Bernard Avishai, an Israeli professor of business, says of this early period of settlement building: "Settlements were made in the territories beyond the Green Line so effortlessly after 1967 because the Zionist institutions that built them and the laws that drove them ... had all been going full throttle within the Green Line before 1967. To focus merely on West Bank settlers was always to beg the question." [34]

Some ten years later, during the right wing Begin-Sharon administrations, settlement building accelerated both in numbers of residents and placement all across the West Bank. Using a disingenuous interpretation of Ottoman land laws, Ariel Sharon declared vast swathes of the West Bank as "*mawat*" or dead land – i.e. land not under cultivation – and reassigned it to illegal Israeli settlements.[35]

In 2012, *B'Tselem*, using Israeli government statistics, put the number of settlers at well over a half million,[36] the number of settlements at 125, the number of outposts at 100, and the number of settler "neighborhoods" (i.e. settlements within a city) at 12, clustered in Jerusalem and Hebron.[37] Today the number of settlers stands at 764,000.[38] The annual growth rate of settlements is more than two and one half times the growth rate of the Israeli population (6% and 1.8% respectively).[39] All of the settlers are heavily subsidized by the Israeli state that connects the settlements to the Israeli power and water grids, builds "settler only" roads to connect the settlements to the Israeli job market, subsidizes school fees for settler children, provides below-market interest rates for mortgages, and substantial tax abatements on income and health taxes to settler families.[40]

Thus, Israel constructed a complex web of physical structures, legal arrangements, and cultural practices that make it almost impossible for any future Israeli government to come into compliance with international standards of human rights or with the "universally agreed upon" two-state solution. The Israelis themselves recognize this to be so. In 2012 a "report from the Council for Peace and Security, a body composed of retired Israeli military and security experts, [admitted] 'The settlement project not only does not contribute to the overall security of the State of Israel, but it incurs significant security, political, economic, and social prices and risks.'[41] ... . It is, of course, not surprising that colonization inevitably leads to conflict with those it displaces. But the willingness to undertake colonization in spite of the risks it incurs indicates that—instead of enhancing Israeli security—colonization merely marks the boundaries of land Israel wishes to eventually annex."[42]

THE GREAT AND REGIONAL POWERS: SELLING OUT PALESTINE

The Israeli victory in the Six Day War confronted the world with the question whether, in the late 20th century and in the context of the United Nations system, any country could change its boundaries through acts of war. The United States and the Soviet Union, the two superpowers of the time, both agreed that, at least in this instance, the answer was "no." Both were facing setbacks, the United States in Vietnam and the Soviet Union in what was then Czechoslovakia. In this instance, the two superpowers chose to cooperate, and by November of 1967, using British diplomats to do so, they shepherded a mutually agreed upon Resolution 242 to a unanimous endorsement in the United Nations Security Council.

Resolution 242 affirmed "the inadmissibility of the acquisition of territory by war."[43] Its language called for "withdrawal of Israel [sic] armed forces from territories occupied in the recent conflict."[44] It also required "a just settlement for the refugee problem."[45] And finally, it demanded the "territorial inviolability and political independence of every state in the area."[46] But this language seems more unequivocal than it is.

Even as Resolution 242 made its way through the Security Council ratification process, everyone concerned knew that its language was weak, incomplete, and riddled with loopholes. Quite deliberately, the text of the resolution demanded an Israeli withdrawal from unspecified "territories." The drafters eschewed language that would have required Israel to return *the* territories it had conquered, and certainly language that could have read *all* territories conquered in the recent war. Western diplomats argued that, in the context of a negotiated settlement, minor adjustments to Israel's borders could be accomplished. Israel, however, took the language of Resolution 242 to mean something entirely different: namely, that if they returned *any* territory to *any* neighboring state, as it did a decade later in returning the Sinai to Egypt, they had discharged their obligations under 242.

Worse, the Palestinians are not mentioned by name at all.[47] U.N. Resolution 181, calling for the creation of an independent Palestinian state, is not reaffirmed in Resolution 242. The U.N.'s preference for inter-state solutions meant that the status of the as-yet-unformed Palestinian state was called into question, at least implicitly. Certainly King Hussein of Jordan anticipated that any Israeli withdrawal from the West Bank would lead to a return of the *status quo ante*, i.e. a return to his control over the West Bank.

The only oblique reference to Palestinians is the call for an otherwise unspecified "just settlement" of refugee problems. This reduced Palestinian claims for national liberation to the right to ask for and receive humanitarian aid.

Perhaps the Western powers considered Resolution 242, with its reaffirmation of the inadmissibility of changing national boundaries by acts of war, to be a diplomatic success. Perhaps they accepted it as the best compromise that could be contrived. The Arab states, however, did not agree.

In the face of an overwhelming and utterly humiliating military rout, the Arab states convened in Khartoum, Sudan and, in the fall of 1967, affirmed what became known as "the three no's of Khartoum: no recognition of Israel, no negotiations with Israel, no peace with Israel."[48] Israelis and the popular press, looking no further than the language of the resolutions, regarded the Khartoum document as intractably hostile, threatening, and belligerent.

In fact, however, the meeting in Khartoum signaled a redirection of Arab objections to Zionism.[49] The Khartoum Document does not seek to eliminate *Israel*; instead it seeks to "ensure the withdrawal of the aggressive Israeli forces from the Arab lands which have been occupied since … 5 *June*" (emphasis mine).[50] In short, in the very first sentence of this supposedly anti-Israeli declaration, the Arab states implicitly concede Israel's existence within its pre-war boundaries. Moreover, while the Arab states insisted on a face-saving distance from Israel, they accepted the possibility of a U.S. or Russian or U.N. mediated resolution to the conflict.

Like Resolution 242 however, the Khartoum process was more focused on objections to Israel's enlargement than it was on Palestinian rights. The Palestinians were, once again, expendable. Eventually, beginning in 1969 the Arabs countenanced a war of attrition against Israel,[51] using their own troops and allowing Palestinians to stage raids into Israel from safe spaces in the surrounding Arab countries. In 1973, the Arab countries would again go to war against Israel. And, at the same time, they also become more sophisticated about using economic weapons, petro-power, to advance their agenda.[52] But in so doing, they were acting also in response to forces the Palestinians themselves set in motion. It is to Palestinian initiatives that we turn next.

THE PALESTINIANS: GOING IT ALONE

By the time Israel had won the Six Day War, it was clear to Palestinians that they were essentially on their own in the pursuit of their national aspirations. The Palestinian Liberation Organization (PLO), founded under Nasser's tutelage in the hope of keeping the Palestinian cause forever within the orbit of Pan-Arab politics,[53] went its own way, merging with Fatah and accepting Yasser Arafat, the leader of Fatah, as its head.

Arafat's credibility was won in the Battle of *Karameh*, in Jordan, in 1968. Many Palestinian factions were situated in Jordan and staged raids into Israel. Israel, in turn, mounted reprisals. One such reprisal raid was directed at the Palestinian guerilla camps in *Karameh*. The historian James Gelvin describes what happened: "The outnumbered *fedayeen* [Palestinian guerillas], backed by Jordanian artillery, inflicted more than a hundred casualties on the invaders and forced the Israelis to withdraw. The Battle of *Karameh* achieved mythic status in Palestinian lore. Three hundred Palestinian irregulars repulsed an invading force three times their number, accomplishing what entire Arab armies had been unable to achieve. And as far as mythmaking is concerned, it did not hurt that *karameh* means 'honor' in Arabic."[54]

Arafat's victory, although it did nothing to change the balance of power between Palestinians and Israelis, did allow him to grow his army from three hundred fighters to fifteen thousand within a few weeks.[55] He brought with him to his leadership role a preoccupation with the Algerian revolution against the French. He accepted from the Algerian precedent not only the practical estimate that armed struggle would serve his purposes but also the moral belief, articulated in the Algerian context by Franz Fanon, that violence served to demystify the power of the colonizer and to create an urgent sense of common purpose among the combatants.[56]

Arafat's swift success in growing the PLO came at a price. To some extent, its strength was illusory. The PLO actually became a loosely organized coalition of many different guerilla groups who only sporadically obeyed a central command. There were, from the beginning, diverse factions alongside *Fatah*, including the Popular Front for the Liberation of Palestine (PFLP), the Arab National Movement (ANM), and the Democratic Front for the Liberation of Palestine (DFLP). These groups represented a broad array of ideological (nationalist and communist) and religious (Muslim and Christian) differences, although the Muslim factions were largely secular, not Islamist in their politics. Each of these groups, in turn, was not wholly independent, but relied on support from outside sources, Syria, Iraq, and Egypt, and therefore harbored divided loyalties between the PLO and their funders.[57]

Arafat was acutely aware of the debilitating power of intra-Palestinian rivalries in the Arab Revolt of 1936–1939, and sought to keep this unruly coalition together. The cost of doing so meant relinquishing any possibility of a single coherent strategy and a disciplined movement to fight for Palestinian rights. Quoting an associate of Arafat's, the historian Charles D. Smith summarizes the situation: "That is why the Central Committee of the Palestinian Resistance, instead of being a coordinating and decision-making body, turned out to be a sort of parliament where all the conflicts and intrigues of the Arab world were reflected ... [It was difficult if not impossible] to enforce even a minimum of discipline at the very heart of the movement."[58]

One thing the various groups within the PLO did agree on, however, was the necessity of armed struggle. Multiple factions hijacked El Al airplanes, using bases in Jordan and Lebanon to do so.[59] Egypt engaged in a "war of attrition" with Israel, which took the form of continuous air raids and air force duels, which escalated gradually when Russian pilots began flying some of the missions on Egypt's behalf.[60] Perhaps the two most (in)famous incidents occurred when one of the commando groups within the PLO took the Israeli wrestling team hostage at the 1972 Olympics in Munich,[61] and, much later, when another hijacked the Italian cruise ship *Achille Lauro* in 1985.[62] Israel responded to highjackings, kidnappings, and cross-border raids with air and sea raids, military incursions (into Lebanon), home demolitions, and selective assassinations.

Palestinian armed struggle never reached the level of posing a real military threat to Israel's existence, although it did impose a certain cost for the Occupation. It also succeeded in putting the question of Palestine on the international agenda, though experts are divided as to whether the commando tactics did more harm than good, since Palestinians, photographed in ski masks and waving guns in the air, generated a very bad press in western countries.[63]

Moreover, the Palestinians were actually waging a two-front struggle, one against Israel and the other, often, against the host countries in which the commando groups were living within the Palestinian refugee population. Over time, the PLO came to be the recognized political authority in Palestinian camps in both Jordan and Lebanon, to the displeasure of the respective central governments of those countries.

In Jordan, the conflict with the PLO commando groups hinged on King Hussein's correct perception that some of those groups would overthrow his monarchy if they could. Palestinian distrust of Hussein, in turn, was based on the also correct assumption that he would prefer control over the West Bank to Palestinian independence in even a small portion of the country they understood to be their own. Over time, the Palestinian commando groups undertook enough operations that embarrassed Hussein's government (for example, landing hijacked planes on air strips near his palace and then blowing them up)[64] to render them *persona non grata*. In the end, Hussein used bloody operations in "Black September" of 1970 to expel the PLO cadres to Lebanon. Palestinian sources estimate that as many as 30,000 Palestinians may have been killed as part of the Black September expulsion.[65]

In Lebanon, the regime's objections to the Palestinians echoed those of the Jordanians. But there were added considerations as well. Lebanon was engulfed in a sectarian civil war and the ruling Christian minority groups were hostile to any demographic shift that could add Muslims to the population. In June 1982 the Israeli army invaded Lebanon, ostensibly to uproot the PLO who were staging raids into Israel from the refugee camps in Southern Lebanon, but also to tip the balance of power toward their Christian allies. By September, the PLO had agreed to leave the Lebanese camps and, under the protection of a Multi-National Peace Keeping force, PLO fighters boarded ships bound for Tunis. Shortly thereafter, the Israeli army moved northward to surround West Beirut, which was a violation of the ceasefire then in force. They secured the perimeters of the *Sabra* and *Shatila* refugee camps that were the center of Palestinian life and organized the entry of Lebanese Christian militias into the camp. Between the evening of September 16th and the morning of September 19, 1982,[66] the Christian militias slaughtered everyone in their path, largely the women and children who remained after the men had departed. The killings continued through the night, lit by flares furnished by the Israeli army. A Dutch nurse on the scene at a nearby hospital described the camps as lit as brightly as "a sports stadium during a football game."[67] The Israeli tally of casualties put the number of Palestinians killed in *Sabra* and *Shatila* at 700, but the Red Cross listed 2,750 Palestinians slaughtered.[68] Even a later Israeli report about the massacres by the Kahan Commission concluded that Israeli generals on the scene, particularly Ariel Sharon, were indirectly responsible for the massacres.[69]

For the Palestinian national struggle, the cumulative weight of all the PLO decisions – to allow multiple factions to pull the movement in different and incompatible directions, to antagonize the governments of the host countries in which they were based, to conduct the struggle from ever more remote locations, first in Jordan, then in Lebanon, and finally, in Tunisia – meant that going it alone was the inevitable result of their own choices.

THE SPIRAL INTO TRAGEDY AND MULTIPLE WARS

The period between the beginning of the Occupation and the first Palestinian *Intifada* is particularly turbulent and includes three further wars.

In 1973, the Syrians and Egyptians, tired of what seemed like an eternal stalemate with Israel, decided to go to war once more to retake their own territories. This time there was no strutting, no preliminary and ambiguous massing of forces on the border, no inflamed rhetoric. Instead, there was a surprise attack beginning on Yom Kippur, October 6, 1973. Enjoying the advantage of surprise, both the Egyptian and Syrian armies, who were coordinating their efforts, made rapid headway: the Egyptians retaking the Sinai and Syria the Golan Heights.

The Nixon administration, reeling from the effects of the "Saturday Night Massacre" within the larger Watergate Scandal (the firing of Watergate special prosecutor Archibald Cox), rushed to re-arm the Israeli forces. The Russians, likewise, provided arms to Egypt. Confronted with the possibility of the great powers being drawn into another major war, the U.S. and the Soviet Union instead imposed a ceasefire by October 22, 1973, ending the war. All the warring parties had suffered heavy casualties and the countries and the boundaries stood much as they had been before the war, with Israel holding both the Sinai Peninsula and the Golan Heights, along with the West Bank, East Jerusalem, and Gaza.[70]

The 1973 Yom Kippur War nevertheless produced several consequential outcomes. Israel was now firmly and permanently in the American camp of the Cold War. America decided to commit to the Kissinger Doctrine, namely that "supplying Israel with enough weaponry to keep it stronger than the sum total of its enemies"[71] would insure stability in the region.

The Arabs, in turn, decided to exact a price for American support of Israel and thus OPEC, the largely Arab Organization of Petroleum Exporting Countries, delivered the first "oil shock" to Western economies. Oil prices in the West rose by 380% over a few months.[72]

The next Arab summit, in Rabat, Morocco in 1974, saw further shifts in the Arab position on the Palestinian conflict. The *Rabat Declaration*, issued by the conference, now moved to recognize the Palestinian Liberation Organization as "the sole legitimate representative of the Palestinian people."[73] This put an end to King Hussein's hopes of reclaiming the West Bank. The Rabat Declaration also recognized the right of the PLO to establish an "independent national authority" in anticipation of receiving or conquering unspecified areas.[74] One month later, the United Nations General Assembly seconded the Rabat Declaration by admitting the PLO as an "observer entity."[75]

The careful framing of the PLO as a "national authority" to govern an as-yet unspecified area created both opportunity and confusion. The opportunity lay in the multiple hints that Arafat threw out, via associates, that he was ready to concede Palestinian claims to the entirety of Palestine and accept a Palestinian state in the West Bank, East Jerusalem, and Gaza. In so doing, Arafat had West Bankers, desperate to end the Occupation and to secure the places in which they lived, on his side.

Representatives of the refugees, on the other hand, were understandably adamant in their opposition. For them, any redefinition of "right of return" that required them to ratify Israel's expulsion and accept a compromised "return" only to that land under the control of the Palestinian "national authority" was unacceptable. These divisions, reflected in the PLO, led to confusion as to whether the "national authority" was a state and whether the Palestinians intended it as a fixed solution or (imitating their Israeli occupiers) as a staging area for further conquest.[76]

Perhaps the factor of the most enduring significance is that even at Rabat, among Arab countries, the word "state" was never applied to the Palestinian entity that was to emerge. An authority, Palestinian or otherwise, is not a state. Think, for example, of the New York Transit Authority, or the Massachusetts Turnpike Authority. Neither is in any sense a state. Rather, both are administrative instruments that serve a state by performing a delimited set of practical tasks. Thus, the calling forth of a Palestinian Authority in Rabat was eerily prescient, anticipating what would emerge from the Camp David negotiations that led to the peace treaty between Israel and Egypt in 1979 and, later, to the language of the Oslo Agreements that led to the creation of a Palestinian Authority with limited powers, in a small number of non-contiguous Palestinian urban enclaves.

In the aftermath of the Yom Kippur War, the Israelis also hit upon the negotiating strategy that has allowed them to present themselves as a partner for peace while, *sotto voce*, defining peace as the complete pacification of the surrounding Arab states. To pull off this sleight of hand, Israel appeared to participate in peace negotiations but always insisted on terms that they knew would be unacceptable to their opposite numbers. Thus, Syria, in the aftermath of the war, was willing to recognize Resolution 242, but that was not enough for Israel. They intended to (and in fact did) also keep the Golan Heights. Similarly they imposed unacceptable terms on negotiations with King Hussein of Jordan and thus got to keep the West Bank.[77] And of course Israel continues to use this technique, raising the stakes, most recently by demanding that Palestinians not only recognize Israel (which Arafat did officially and unequivocally in 1988), but also recognize it as a *Jewish* state, thereby officially agreeing to the marginalization of Palestinian citizens of Israel.

Over the next few years, Israel discovered that Egypt was the country most likely to break ranks with Arab opposition to them. By 1977, Anwar Sadat, who had succeeded Nasser upon his death, was struggling to shore up his popularity in Egypt. The lure of securing the return of the Sinai from Israel tempted him into breaking with Arab opposition to Israel. In 1977 Sadat flew to Israel and, speaking from the Knesset podium, addressed the Israeli people directly, over the heads of their (and his own) politicians. In 1978 he entered into negotiations brokered by the Carter administration at Camp David, and in 1979 signed a peace treaty with Israel. The terms of the treaty included mutual recognition between Israel and Egypt with full normalization – i.e. the exchange of ambassadors, opening of trade relations, etc. – to follow. Israel returned the Sinai to Egypt and Egypt, in turn, pledged to keep the area demilitarized. Egypt stipulated that previously contested waterways, the Straights of Tiran, the Suez Canal, and the Gulf of Aqaba, were in fact international waters that would always be open to Israeli shipping.

Because Sadat had hoped to spearhead a comprehensive Arab-Israeli peace deal, he also tried insisting on a Palestinian state. This effort failed, but from the time of these negotiations, Israel stipulated that it would, someday, allow Palestinians in the Occupied Territories to exercise administrative control over some aspects of Palestinian life.[78] This language echoed the Rabat Declaration of 1974 in discussing a Palestinian authority but not a Palestinian state.

In return for "making peace" (albeit a cold peace) with Israel, Egypt, also received massive infusions of foreign aid, especially military aid, from the United States. Sadat and Menachem Begin, the former terrorist head of the Irgun (see Chapter 5), were the actual signers of the treaty and were rewarded with a joint Nobel Peace Prize in 1979.

The Arab world objected, however, and expelled Egypt from the Arab League in 1979.[79] Sadat's hope of achieving popularity in Egypt by securing the return of the Sinai failed to materialize. Instead, members of Islamic Jihad assassinated him in 1981.

Peace with Egypt was part of a long-term strategic vision in Israel. Their plan called for either the pacification or the disruption of Israel's front line Arab neighbors, along with strong ties to the Muslim states, Turkey and Iran, which flanked Israel's Arab neighbors on their far side. This strategy was part of the "iron wall" mentality first enunciated by one of the Zionist founders, Vladimir Jabotinsky. He correctly anticipated that the Arabs would never accept the Zionist project of state-building and ethnic "succession" and that, therefore, Zionists would have to live behind an eternal "iron wall" of military preparedness and domination.[80] This "iron wall" strategy has been partially successful and partially not.

Turkey was the first Muslim state to recognize Israel, as early as 1949 and, over the years, developed a robust trade relationship and even military coordination with Israel.[81] But Israel itself put this relationship at risk in 2010 by firing on a Turkish vessel and killing Turkish passengers aboard the *Mavi Marmara*, a ship participating in a flotilla trying to break the Israeli blockade on Gaza.

Iran, in turn, was part of the United Nations body that promulgated the partition plan. The country was the second Muslim state to recognize Israel and remained favorably disposed toward it as long as the Shah ruled. But the Islamic government that overthrew the Shah in 1979 was adamantly opposed to Israel as well as the United States and withdrew recognition.

The Shah's overthrow and the installation of an Islamic state in Iran also tempted Iraq, a long-standing rival, to invade Iran in 1980. For the next seven years, Iran and Iraq fought a deadly and mutually debilitating war that preoccupied Arab diplomats, to the detriment of Palestinian interests.

Thus, despite some setbacks, Israel's strategic plan for the pacification or subordination of front line states and an alliance with remoter Muslim states succeeded at least enough to allow Israel a free hand against the Palestinians. Egypt was pacified as of 1979 and remained so, even as the Mubarak regime (Sadat's successor) was replaced first by an Islamic regime and then by a renewed military dictatorship. Jordan soon would be pacified, signing a peace treaty in 1994. Syria seemed quiescent – today of course it is in ruins as is Iraq, and the Arab states' diplomatic focus is directed at many different issues, with Palestinian rights often ignored.

After the signing of the 1979 Camp David Accords, the Israelis, particularly Ariel Sharon (then a Defense Minister, later a Prime Minister), turned their attention to pacifying the West Bank and to expropriating as much land as possible. The first objective was to be accomplished through the creation of collaborationist "village leagues."[82] The second was to be accomplished by using Ottoman law to declare land that was never recorded in the Ottoman or Jordanian land registries as "state land" open to Israeli expropriation despite the fact that Palestinian communities had lived their continuously for hundreds of years.[83] The first effort was largely unsuccessful as the PLO denounced the village leagues and assassinated collaborators. The second effort was far more successful and continues to the present day.

Sharon, however, was unwilling to accept even the minimal amount of resistance the PLO was able to create from its Lebanese refugee camp bases. Nor was the Lebanese government particularly enthusiastic about its Palestinian refugee guests.

Lebanon was itself embroiled a long civil war from 1975 to 1990. During the course of this conflict, the PLO managed to wrest control over the Palestinian refugee camps in Lebanon from the government, thus antagonizing its hosts.

These forces – Lebanon's internal sectarian strife, Israel's "iron wall" defense philosophy, and the Palestinian struggle for its national rights – converged in an Israeli invasion of Lebanon, officially aimed at wiping out the PLO bases in that country. What followed were the expulsion of the PLO to Tunisia, the slaughter of innocents at *Sabra* and *Shatila* (mentioned above), and an Israeli occupation that dragged on and on in a Vietnam like quagmire that ended only in 2000.

Thus, by 1982 the West Bank and Gaza were stripped of their political leadership, isolated from international and even Arab support, and subject to ever-increasing land loss and settlement growth. Nevertheless, the West Bank had also enjoyed a period of relative prosperity in the preceding decade, created by its own development efforts and the relative ease with which Palestinians could secure work permits in Israel.[84]

The formula of political oppression, occupation, home demolitions, expulsions, and land expropriation coupled with some economic opportunity did not prove to be effective in pacifying the Palestinians.[85] In December of 1987 an incident that might otherwise have been but one more tragedy in a generally miserable Occupation – the death of four Palestinians workers hit by an Israeli military vehicle in the Jabalya Refugee Camp in Gaza – erupted into a series of riots and military clashes that became known as the First *Intifada*. Historian James Gelvin describes the circumstances this way:

> As in the case of World War I and the Great Revolt, a historical accident would have passed with little notice had the spark not fallen on dry tinder. The conditions of the occupation provided that dry tinder ... Over the course of twenty years, the Israelis had buried the Palestinian population beneath a mound of regulations ... from land use to employment to travel. The Israelis had expropriated land in the occupied territories for "military training," for "public needs," and even nature preserves. They had constructed settlements that dominated the countryside ... Israeli agricultural policies had so devastated Palestinian agriculture that less land was under cultivation in 1987 than in 1947.[86] Israeli labor policies discriminated against Palestinian workers and barred them from enjoying the social benefits and wages granted Israeli workers. Tightfisted Israeli public investment policies ... wreaked havoc on infrastructure. Adding to the volatility of the territories were severe overcrowding ... a population that was overwhelmingly young and resentful ... and a policy of repression known as the "iron fist," which included administrative detentions, house demolitions, deportations, and school closings.[87]

None of this guaranteed that an explosion would occur ... Popular uprisings are rare occurrences in history, and populations are just as likely to be cowed or dispirited by repression and impoverishment as they are to rebel.

The Palestinians, however, were not too dispirited to rebel. On the contrary, they were watching not only their own circumstances, but also political discourse within Israel, with great care and precision. They understood that there was a divide, which they sought to deepen, between an Israeli peace/left movement that would have agreed to a Palestinian state and the more ambitious and powerful right wing that would continue to expropriate land and water and encourage settlement building.[88] The rapid choice of non-violent resistance once the initial outbreak of riots in Gaza began, was determined in part by the awareness of younger Palestinian leaders in the West Bank of Israel's internal political debates. As a [Palestinian] grassroots activist told Israeli political scientist Eitan Alimi "We realized that if we use deadly weapons, we will fail ... this [non-violent, grass roots resistance] was our way to strengthen those groups inside Israel that rejected the occupation.' ... There was a clear understanding of how media images of youths with sling shots confronting tanks would play, not only among third parties in the international arena, but among Israeli citizens who didn't fancy David becoming Goliath."[89]

Most interpretations of the First *Intifada* depict it as a spontaneous grass roots revolt against the Occupation. Alimi's work suggests, however, that the *Intifada,* though not as meticulously planned as the 1967 Occupation, nevertheless benefitted from considerable organizational skill, political acumen, and preparedness on the part of the Palestinians. A network of local committees rooted in earlier attempts to mitigate the hardships of Occupation went into action, coordinating Palestinian efforts, deciding on a non-violent strategy, achieving more inter-factional coherence at the local level than the "official leaders" in Tunis were able to achieve, and inventing new techniques of resistance. Among their more creative initiatives were boycotts of Israeli goods, tax revolts against Israel, family food gardens that circumvented the economic closures Israel imposed, the mobilization of labor and women's groups, and developing a cross-class alliance between professional groups and working class and poor youth from the internal refugee camps.[90] The Canadian-Palestinian film, *The Wanted 18*, describes one such effort in the Christian town of Beit Sahour near Bethlehem. The townspeople, concerned with the threat that Israeli-imposed closures posed to their access to dairy products, bought 18 cows from a nearby Israeli kibbutz, with the intentions of starting a local dairy for the community. Promptly the Israelis declared the 18 cows to be a threat to Israeli national security and announced their intentions to confiscate the cows. The townspeople then proceeded to hide the cows by moving them every night, sometimes even into people's homes. Alas, the story did not end well for the cows since they could not be hidden indefinitely, but the story of the fugitive, national-security-threatening bovines shows that the Palestinian resistance movement has a creative and even a playful side.

All of this effort was dedicated to achieving a Palestinian state in the West Bank and Gaza. This meant that it occurred within the framework of a two-state solution that, at least tacitly, recognized the irreversible character of Israel's national existence.

Palestinian initiatives were met with brutal Israeli repression. By 1989, "626 Palestinians and 43 Israelis had been killed, 37,439 Arabs wounded and between 35,000 and 40,000 arrested."[91]

Together, the Occupation itself, the resistance to it in the form of the *Intifada*, and the brutal repression of it by the Israelis, confronted Arafat with challenges on all fronts: from local young leadership able to mobilize efforts he could not control from Tunis; from the Israeli military, and from competition from the more militant Islamist factions in Gaza. In a desperate attempt to reassert his leadership in the international arena, Arafat convened a meeting of the Palestine National Congress (PNC) in late 1988 and, through that mechanism, declared into existence a Palestinian state in the West Bank and Gaza (thereby affirming the two-state solution) while renouncing terrorism in all its forms. His attempts at complying with American formulas for resolving the conflict were rebuffed by the United States who denied him a visa to address the United Nations in New York.[92] Likewise, the Israeli prime minister twisted his proposals and counter-proposed a plan for Palestinian "autonomy" (i.e. *not* statehood or sovereignty) and administrative power over some unspecified aspects of "affairs of daily life."[93]

Given his difficult situation, especially the criticism from the more militant Islamist factions of the Palestinian resistance, Arafat turned more and more to Saddam Hussein's Iraq for support of Palestinian rights. Thus, when Iraq invaded Kuwait in 1990, Arafat was caught up in supporting his sole sponsor and ally, an act of loyalty which led to Kuwait's expulsion of thousands of Palestinians[94] and a decision by the Americans to exclude the PLO from later peace talks in Madrid.

Midway through the first *Intifada*, the Soviet Union imploded. This collapse proved to be a boon to Israel, bringing roughly one million additional white European immigrants to the country. The collapse of the Soviet Union also shifted the international balance of power definitively in favor of Israel's patron, the United States. The Palestinians were left with no credible international support, and as the *Intifada* dragged on, the Americans became the sole brokers of the Israeli-Palestinian "peace process." But the Americans would prove to be dishonest brokers,[95] acting as Israel's lawyer rather than as a neutral party.[96] Not surprisingly, the peace process brought neither peace nor resolution to anyone.

SUMMARY: OCCUPATION AND RESISTANCE

History of Israel-Palestine Conflict III

1967–1987: From the Occupation to the Resistance

Israel	Great Powers	Palestine
Military Rule	1973 – Kissinger Doctrine	Resistance from Exile: Lebanon, Tunisia, Local

Settlements

YOM KIPPUR WAR (1973)
FIRST INTIFADA (1987–1993)

NOTES

[1] Thucydides. (1954). The Athenian Representative to Melos, *The History of the Peloponnesian War* (New York: Penguin Classics) p. 267.

[2] Shimon Tzabar. (1967, September 29). Op. Ed. in *Ha'aretz*, quoted in his obituary, *Ha'aretz*, March 21, 2007, retrieved from http://www.haaretz.com/print-edition/news/shimon-tzabar-81-dies-in-london-1.216138

[3] Nader Said-Foqahaa (2012, January 2). The Waiting Room, poem remembering the Six Day War and its aftermath. Dr. Said is a professor of sociology at Birzeit University and the director of Al Awrad, a Palestinian polling and analysis organization.

[4] Ilan Pappe. (2012). Keynote Address to the *Harvard University One State Conference*, retrieved from http://electronicintifada.net/blogs/ali-abunimah/audio-ali-abunimah-and-ilan-pappe-keynote-speeches-harvard-one-state-conference

[5] *CIA World Factbook*, retrieved from https://www.cia.gov/library/publications/the-world-factbook/geos/we.html;https://www.cia.gov/library/publications/the-world-factbook/geos/gz.html

[6] The Citizenship Law of 1952 and the Entry into Israel Law of the same year are associated with the 1950 Law of Return. Together, they codify the superior rights of Jewish immigrants to Israel. See *Adalah*, the Legal Center for Arab Minority Rights in Israel, "Discriminatory Laws in Israel. Retrieved from https://www.adalah.org/en/content/vieew/7771

[7] "Ban on Family Unification – Citizenship and Entry into Israel Law," 2003, *ibid.*

[8] The Law of Political Parties 2002, *ibid.* For a recent account of how this law continues in effect see Carol Daniel Casbari. (2014, June 15). So long, and thanks for nothing, *Ha'aretz*, retrieved from http://www.haaretz.com/opinion/.premium-1.598872

[9] For a discussion of Palestinians serving in the Israeli Defense Forces see Rhoda Ann Kanaaneh. (2009). *Surrounded: Palestinian Soldiers in the Israeli Military*. Stanford: Stanford University Press.

[10] *Ibid.*

[11] David A. Wesley. (2009). *State Practices and Zionist Images: Shaping Economic Development in Arab Towns in Israel* (Oxford: Berghahn Books), p. 68.

[12] Ben White. (2012). *Palestinians in Israel: Segregation, Discrimination and Democracy* (London: Pluto Books), pp. 67–68.

[13] Taxes/Decades of tax breaks for the settler population, *Ha'aretz*, September 25, 2003, retrieved from http://www.haaretz.com/print-edition/business/taxes-decades-of-tax-breaks-for-the-settler-population-1.101212

[14] National Priority Areas – Economic Efficiency Law, 2009 in *Adalah, op. cit.*, retrieved from https://www.adalah.org/en/law/view/506

[15] Yoav Stern. (2007, March 28). Study: Arabs may be poorer, but Jews get more welfare funds, *Ha'aretz*, retrieved from http://www.haaretz.com/news/study-arabs-may-be-poorer-but-jews-get-more-welfare-funds-1.216881

[16] Adva Center. (2014, Sept. 9). Report: Settlements receive disproportionate state funding, *Ha'aretz*, retrieved from http://www.haaretz.com/business/.premium-1.614765

[17] Akiva Eldar. (2010, August 16). Citizens, but not equal, *Ha'aretz*, retrieved from http://www.haaretz.com/print-edition/opinion/citizens-but-not-equal-1.308265

[18] Adalah, *op. cit.*

[19] *Ibid.*

[20] This material is drawn from Pappe, *op. cit.*, and will be discussed more fully in Ilan Pappe. (2017). *The Biggest Prison on Earth: A History of the Occupied Territorie*s, London: One World Books.

[21] *Ibid.*

[22] *Ibid.*

[23] *Ibid.*

[24] *Ibid.*

[25] Thomas Philip Abowd. (2014). *Colonial Jerusalem: The Spatial Construction of Identity and Difference in a City of Myth, 1948–2012* (Syracuse: Syracuse University Press), chapter 4. See also, Saree Makdisi. (2010, spring). The Architecture of Erasure. *Critical Inquiry*: 519–559. Retrieved from https://www.journals.uchicgo.edu/doi/10.1086653411

[26] Nir Hasson. (2017, June 3). How a Small Group of Israelis Made the Western Wall Jewish Again, *Ha'aretz*, retrieved from https://www.haaretz.com/israel-news/.premium.MAGAZINE-how-israel-quietly-demolished-the-western-walls-muslim-neighborhood-1.5478700

[27] James L. Gelvin. (2007). *The Israel-Palestine Conflict: One Hundred Years of War* (2nd ed.) (Cambridge: Cambridge University Press), p. 182.

[28] *Ibid.* p. 183 and Abowd, *op. cit.*, pp. 88–89.

[29] Michael Omar-Man. (2014, May 28). Jerusalem by the Numbers: Poverty, Segregation and Discrimination, *+972*, retrieved from http://972mag.com/jerusalem-by-the-numbers-poverty-segregation-and-discrimination/91425/

[30] *Ibid.*

[31] Charles D. Smith. (2013). *Palestine and the Arab-Israeli Conflict: A History with Documents* (8th ed.) (New York: St. Martin's Press), p. 301.

[32] *Ibid.* p. 303.

[33] *Ibid.*

See also, Gershon Shafir. (2017). *A Half-Century of Occupation: Israel, Palestine, and the World's Most Intractable Conflict*. Berkeley: University of California Press.

[34] Bernard Avishai. (2005, January). Saving Israel from Itself: a secular future for the Jewish State, *Harper's*, 310(1856):37, retrieved from https://harpers.org/archive/2005/01/saving-israel-from-itself/

[35] For a vivid account of this process, see the interview with Alexander Ramati in Alexandrowicz, R. (Director). (2012). *The law in these parts* [Motion picture]. Israel: RO*CO Films International at minutes 36:000 – 46:00.

[36] B'Tselem, Settlements: Background, retrieved from http://www.btselem.org/settlements

[37] *Ibid.*

[38] Data about population size is always a politically sensitive and contested topic in Palestine and Israel. The number of settlers is particularly controversial. Arutz Sheva, a settler source, acknowledges 389, 250 Jewish settlers in the West Bank and another 375,000 in East Jerusalem, whose "annexation" is universally recognized as illegal, totaling some 764,000 illegal settlers. These numbers date from 2014, and the same source claims that by now the number of settlers has risen to 800,000. *Arutz Sheva*, retrieved from http://www.israelnationalnews.com/Articles/Article.aspx/18210#. VpK885scTIU. The population growth rate in the settlements, though declining, is still approximately twice as high as that in Jerusalem, see Jacob Magid. (2018, Januay 21). Settler growth rate declines for sixth straight year, *The Times of Israel*, retrieved from https://www.timesofisrael.com/settler-growth-rate-declines-for-sixth-straight-year/

[39] B'Tselem. *op cit.*, retrieved from http://www.btselem.org/settlements/statistics

[40] Gelvin, *op. cit.*, p. 191.

[41] Shafir, *op. cit.*, p. 98.

[42] Gershon Shafir (2017, May 31). Why has the Occupation lasted this long? *Mondoweiss*, retrieved from https://mondoweiss.net/2017/05/occupation-lasted-this/

[43] United Nations Security Council Resolution 242. (1967, November 22). Retrieved from http://unispal.un.org/DPA/DPR/7D35E1F729DF491C85256EE700686136

[44] *Ibid.* article 1 (i).

[45] *Ibid.* article 2(b).

[46] *Ibid.* article 2 (c).

[47] Gelvin, *op. cit.*, p. 176.

[48] Gelvin, *ibid.* p. 380, and Smith, *op. cit.*, pp. 304–305.

[49] *Ibid.*

[50] Smith, *op. cit.*, p. 304. For the exact language of the Khartoum Declaration, see: The Arab League. (1967). The Khartoum Declaration, retrieved from http://ww.thejewishvirtuallibrary.org/the-khartoum-resolutions

[51] Gelvin, *op. cit.*, p. 181.

[52] *Ibid.*

[53] *Ibid.* p. 191.

[54] *Ibid.* p. 199.

[55] *Ibid.*

[56] *Ibid.* p. 202.

[57] Smith, *op. cit.*, pp. 308–309.

[58] *Ibid.* p. 109.

[59] *Ibid.* p. 310.

[60] *Ibid.*, pp. 311–312.

[61] *Ibid.* p. 316.

[62] *Ibid.* p. 400.

[63] Gelvin, *op. cit.*, p. 202.

[64] Smith, *op. cit.*, p. 315.

[65] Gelvin, *op. cit.* p. 209.

[66] Smith, *op. cit.*, p. 373.

[67] Thomas Friedman. (1982, September 26). The Beirut Massacre: The Four Days, *New York Times*, retrieved from http://www.nytimes.com/1982/09/26/world/the-beirut-massacre-the-four-days.html

[68] Gelvin, *op. cit.*, p. 242.

[69] *Ibid.* p. 243, and Smith, *op. cit.*, p. 3374.

[70] For detailed accounts of the war see Smith, *op. cit.*, pp. 322–327 and Gelvin, *op. cit.*, pp. 180–182.

[71] Gelvin, *op. cit.*, p. 180.
   See also Jeremy Sharp. (20008, January 2). *U.S. Foreign Aid to Israel: Congressional Research Service Report to Congress*, Retrieved from http://www.dtic.mil/dtic/tr/fulltext/u2/a484671.pdf

[72] *Ibid.* p. 181.

[73] Smith, *op. cit.*, p. 327.

[74] *Ibid.*

[75] *Ibid.*

[76] *Ibid.* pp. 327–330. The confusion and ambiguous language is reflected in the Ten Point Program endorsed by the PLO in Cairo in June of 1974, a copy of which can be retrieved from http://www.jewishvirtuallibrary.org/jsource/Terrorism/PNCProgram1974.html. Article 2, typifies the confusion. It reads, in part: "The Palestine Liberation Organization will employ all means, and first and foremost armed struggle, to liberate Palestinian territory and to establish the independent combatant national authority for the people over every part of Palestinian territory that is liberated." Note that this language can be read to mean that the PLO does not seek *all* (emphasis added) the territory of historic Palestine, and will content itself with the Palestinian territory that can be "liberated" – i.e. The West Bank, East Jerusalem and Gaza.

[77] *Ibid.* p. 326.

[78] Hannan Ashrawi, talk at the John F. Kennedy School of Government, Harvard University, March, 2014.

[79] Gelvin, *op. cit.*, p. 214.

[80] *Ibid.* pp. 241–242.
   See also Avi Shlaim. (2001). *The Iron Wall: Israel and the Arab World*, New York: Norton.

[81] Zvi Bar'. (2009, October 18). Comment; How do Turkey and Israel measure each other's love? *Ha'aretz*, retrieved from http://www.haaretz.com/print-edition/opinion/comment-how-do-turkey-and-israel-measure-each-other-s-love-1.5928

[82] Gelvin, *op. cit.*, p. 242.

[83] *The Law in These Parts*, minutes 36:00–46:00.

[84] Smith, *op. cit.*, p. 401.

[85] *Ibid.* pp. 401–408.

[86] This sentence is problematic. In 1947 the Israeli state did not yet exist. Hence the fact that Palestinians, absent an Israeli state, had more land under cultivation than they did 40 years

later, when Israel had come to dominate all of Palestine, seems tautological. Probably this statement is a misprint and should say instead the Palestinians had more land under cultivation in 1967 (i.e. under Jordanian and Egyptian control) than they did in 1987 after 20 years of Israeli domination.

87   Gelvin, *op. cit.*, p. 215.

88   Eitan Alimi. (2007). *Israeli Politics and the First Palestinian Intifada*, London: Routledge.

89   *Ibid.* p. xi.

90   Mazen Qumsiyeh. (2007). *Popular Resistance in Palestine* (London: Pluto Press) pp. 168 – 177 and Smith, *op. cit.*, pp. 408–412.

91   Robert Hunter. (1993). *The Palestinian Uprising: A War by Other Means* (Berkeley: University of California Press,) quoted in Smith, *op. cit.*, p. 412.

92   Smith, *op. cit.* p. 414.

93   *Ibid.*

94   *Ibid.* p. 420.

95   Rashid Khalidi. (2014). *Brokers of Deceit: How the U.S. Has Undermined Peace in the Middle East.* Boston: Beacon Press. Josh Ruebner. (2013). *Shattered Hopes: Obama's Failure to Broker Israeli-Palestinian Peace.* London: Verso Book.

96   Aaron David Miller. (2008). *The Much Too Promised Land: America's Elusive Search for Arab-Israeli Peace.* New York: Bantam Books.

CHAPTER 8

THE ENDLESS, DECEPTIVE PEACE PROCESS

We cannot negotiate with people who say what's mine is mine and what's yours is negotiable.

John Fitzgerald Kennedy[1]

To plunder, to butcher, to steal: These they falsely name empire: they make a desolation and they call it peace.

Tacitus[2]

We win every battle, but we lose the war.

Ami Ayalon, former head of Israel's *Shin Bet*[3]

Eve's Story

The first time I visited Palestine my hosts, who were forbidden to enter Israel, called a yellow-plate taxi to take me directly from Ramallah to Ben Gurion Airport. We passed many checkpoints en route, the first of which was Qalandiya, where every car was stopped and searched. As we pulled into one of the lanes I remarked to the driver, a retired engineer who spoke impeccable Arabic, Hebrew, French, and English that the 18 year old IDF soldier motioning us to halt probably had more rights in Palestine than he did, although she was clearly a recent Ethiopian immigrant while he and his ancestors had been born in Palestine. When it was our car's turn to be searched, this young woman, communicating mostly in gestures, demanded that we open the trunk and both of my suitcases. When she finished inspecting them, she turned to me and with a clearly ironic grin said: "Have a nice day" in halting English. Tense though I was, this parody of American politeness surprised a chuckle out of me, and without thinking much about it, I said: "Oh my god, you are so ready for the streets of New York." I saw the shock of that remark go through her: she inhaled sharply and stood stock still, looking completely startled. Then, very gently, she laid her hand on my arm and, in the most plaintive voice imaginable, said: "Oh, do you really think I could?"

When I wrote the first draft of Chapter 5 in the first edition, I ended the introduction by saying I would cover four time periods each of which, "(except perhaps the most recent one), ends in a conflagration, after which all three parties continue to pursue the same fixed ends without better prospects of achieving them." Sadly, by the time the first draft of *this* chapter was written Israelis were perpetrating yet another massacre in Gaza, Operation Protective Edge, so the pattern of conflagration continues to hold. Now, as the final draft for the second edition is being written, we have just seen the high civilian casualties in Gaza inflicted by Israeli snipers, followed by an increase in rocket fire from Gaza, and increasing calls for harsh retaliation coming from the Israeli political sector. Those who do not learn anything from history appear truly doomed to repeat its mistakes.

THE ISRAELIS AND THE "PEACE PROCESS"

For the Israelis, the period from the first *Intifada* to the present can be characterized as one in which they played out the hand they dealt themselves in the context of a changing world.

By the time the first *Intifada* wound down, the Israelis were in possession of a strong state of their own, almost 45 years old. They also had exercised full control over all the West Bank, East Jerusalem, Gaza, and the Golan Heights for more than two decades. The Israelis' dream was and is to take all of this land with none (or as few as possible) of the Palestinians on it, and the Zionist project continues to see how close it can come to making that dream come true.

The first challenge in the post-*Intifada* period was posed by the fact that an entire generation of Israeli control of Palestinian land and Palestinian people (1967–1987) had not produced the pacification that the Israelis sought. Land expropriation via the Custodian of Absentee Property inside Israel, or settlement building/colonization inside the Occupied Territories, military rule, the legal codification of Jewish culture, language, education as the law of the land – none of these instruments, alone or together, had produced a Palestinian population docile and resigned to living on Israeli terms. The *Intifada,* from the Israeli point of view, clearly required additional new strategies of control.

Initially, of course, the physical confrontations that were part of the *Intifada,* the rock-throwing Palestinian children and the Israeli tanks that confronted them, elicited the most repressive tactics, the era of "break their bones"[4] Israeli conduct in the Occupied Territories. In choosing violent repression, the Israeli government followed a pattern described by the criminologist Isaac Balbus who studied American race riots: the first response of the state to civil unrest is highly repressive: tanks roll in the streets until order is restored.[5]

But, Balbus argues, after the initial period in which a militarily enforced order is re-established, the more strategic thinkers in the dominant group try to find ways to address the underlying problems that led to the disturbances in the first place. Their thinking may not be genuinely progressive, humane, or rights based, but there is, nevertheless, an attempt to address root causes in ways that are co-optive and manipulative rather than repressive. In American cities that suffered race riots in the 1960s and 1970s, the long term and more thoughtful responses created a series of welfare programs designed to address inner city poverty (albeit without disturbing white privilege) and to keep Black voters within the Democratic Party.[6]

And indeed, during the first 12-hour humanitarian cease-fire in Operation Protective Edge (2014), those strategic Israeli voices emerged: Israeli military analyst Nahum Barnea, quoted in the *Jewish Daily Forward* writes:

> Israel is looking for a formula to end this … Yes, there are more tunnels to destroy, but there's apparently no way to destroy them all, and in the meantime more names are being added to the ranks of the fallen and anxiety grows over the possibility of a game-changing disaster befalling Israel's soldiers or the civilian population of Israel … the government should strive for a basic change in the reality in Gaza, and perhaps … for a change in the reality of our relations with the Palestinians as a whole. The statements of Netanyahu during the course of this operation indicate that he's beginning to speak of Abu Mazen not just as a problem, but also as a solution. Israel's attempt to isolate the West Bank from Gaza, to divide and rule, has not succeeded. A vision is needed. Hope is needed.[7]

Similarly, Israeli writer Etgar Keret says:

> Twelve years, five operations against Hamas (four of them in Gaza), and still we have this same convoluted slogan ["let the I.D.F. win"]. Young men who were only first-graders during Operation Defensive Shield are now soldiers invading Gaza by land … What is this end they're striving toward? Even if each and every Hamas fighter is taken out, does anyone truly believe that the Palestinian people's aspiration for national independence will disappear with them? Before Hamas, we

fought against the P.L.O., and after Hamas, assuming, hopefully, that we're still around, we'll probably find ourselves fighting against another Palestinian organization. The Israeli military can win the battles, but peace and quiet for the citizens of Israel will only be achieved through political compromise.[8]

Note that for both of these authors, it is concern for Israeli wellbeing, not Palestinian rights that inform their opinions. The range of variation among Israeli politicians is defined by the distance between those who would be more "generous" to the Palestinians and those who would be less, or very much less so. No Israeli politician has ever dealt with Palestinians from the premise that Palestinians, too, have rights.

In the past, from the first *Intifada* to the present, genuinely "root-cause" solutions were foreclosed since Israelis were not willing to tolerate the emergence of a Palestinian state.[9] And, to be fair, they never claimed to be committed to creating a Palestinian state. The two-state solution was always the agenda of the great powers seeking to regulate the affairs of the Middle East, at least as far back as the Machiavellian Campbell-Bannerman report of 1907. Neither the Israelis nor the Palestinians were ever more than perfunctory in their endorsement of the idea of two states, though the Palestinians and the surrounding Arab states appear to have acceded to it out of military weakness as far back as 1967 (see discussion of Khartoum resolution, Chapter 7).

To date, the Israelis have met the challenge posed by the *Intifada* and the aspirations and resistance that fueled it with engagement in a "peace process" orchestrated by the United States, their chief ally. Participating in the "peace process" has allowed them to do as they wish – principally to expropriate more land and build more settlements – while appearing to be negotiating a political end to the conflict.[10]

Perhaps the best way to understand the meaning of Israel's behavior in the "peace process" is to note that the most rapid period of settlement expansion occurred *after* Israel signed the Oslo Accords, during the years in which an independent Palestinian state should have been allowed to emerge. In 1993, the year that the first Oslo Accord was signed, there were 281,800 settlers distributed mostly in illegally annexed East Jerusalem and the West Bank, with smaller communities in Gaza and the illegally annexed Golan Heights.[11] In 2018, settler numbers had swelled to 764,000 on Palestinian land and another 20,000 in the Golan Heights (claimed by Syria)[12]; by now the illegal West Bank settlements outweigh the East Jerusalem settlements, foreclosing land that could have become an independent Palestinian state. The use of the "peace process" to establish "facts on the ground" that undermine the very ends the "peace process" is supposed to secure unmasks Israel's real purpose, supported at every turn by unconditional American financial, diplomatic, and military support.

In pursuing the simultaneous expansion of Israeil settlements and the manipulation of the "peace process" Israel benefitted from a number of events in the larger world outside its control. Primary among these was the implosion of the Soviet Union in 1989. The Cold War had divided much of the world, certainly in the Middle East, into a battlefield for power, influence, and control between the Soviet Union and the United States. Once the Soviet Union collapsed, the dynamics in the Middle East changed to reflect the absence of a superpower patron on the Arab side. America had a much freer hand to pursue policies without opposition and this freedom was immediately put at the disposal of Israeli aims.

The implosion of the Soviet Union also brought a massive new wave of immigrants to Israel, Russian Jews and their families. Prior to the collapse of the Soviet Union, the United States classified the few Russian Jews who were permitted to leave as political refugees. With refugee status came the ability to go to the head of the immigration queue.[13] Once the Soviet Union was no more, the immigration status of Jews wishing to leave Russia changed as they lost their "political refugee" designation. They went, instead, to Israel, nearly 1 million arriving between 1989 and 2006.[14] Although at least one quarter of them were not deemed to be Jewish by the Orthodox authorities who determine Jewish identity (using the rule of matrilineal descent), they were nevertheless allowed to use the Law of Return, by claiming patrilineal descent or marriage to a Jew, for entry into Israel. They thus entered with a fuller set of rights and entitlements from the moment they stepped off the plane than was accorded to Palestinians born in Israel. Part of their entitlement was economic: they benefitted from a full resettlement package of housing and job assistance.

Their presence became significant for the Israeli-Palestinian conflict in a number of ways: they swelled the number of Israelis at a time when most other sources for recruiting Jews to the *aliyah* process had been exhausted; they were used to settle disputed land,[15] and, as new, often under-employed migrants, they were frequently used to displace Palestinian labor.[16]

In addition to the fall of the Soviet Union, other world events also favored Israeli interests during the period immediately following the first *Intifada*. For reasons unrelated to the Israel-Palestine conflict, Iraq invaded Kuwait in 1990 and faced universal displeasure from the Arab petro-states for doing so. However, Arafat, the head of the Palestine Liberation Organization, sided with Saddam Hussein, largely because Iraq was the only Arab country to provide financial support for the PLO. Iraqis were quickly driven out of Kuwait by American troops, but Israel and the United States chose to penalize Arafat for his support of Iraq by excluding him and, with him, the PLO, from the first round of post-*Intifada* peace talks that were to begin in Madrid in 1991. The "peace process" with its endless parade of talks – Madrid, Oslo, Wye River, The Clinton Parameters, Camp David, Taba, the Geneva Initiative, the Road Map, Annapolis, etc. – will be discussed in detail below. For here, suffice it to note that the United States actually co-hosted a peace conference in Madrid in 1991, designed to settle the Palestinian-Israeli conflict, while excluding the PLO, the sole legitimate representative of the Palestinian people, from the conversation!

To sum up: from the end of the first *Intifada* to the present day, Israel has developed two major tools, one directed at Gaza and one at the West Bank, for dealing with the Palestinians. Jerusalem is, for the Israelis, not on the list of topics to be negotiated. Against Gaza, the Israelis use recurring violence, sometimes aerial bombardment (Operation Pillar of Defense), sometimes aerial bombardment plus a ground invasion (Operation Cast Lead, Operation Protective Edge) to do what they themselves call "mowing the lawn"[17] – i.e. periodically using intense violence to curtail to acceptable levels Gaza's capacity for resisting the Occupation. Against the West Bank, Israel has used a "peace process" of negotiations that buy themselves time to gobble up the land while appearing to discuss its fate.

THE GREAT AND REGIONAL POWERS AND THE PEACE PROCESS

The 1987 *Intifada* convinced both the United States and countries in the Middle East aspiring to regional leadership that some solution to the Palestinian-Israel conflict needed to be found. Americans understood that much of the hostility they encountered in the Arab world resulted from their support of Israel, and sought to dampen that conflict.[20] Perhaps the successful transformation in the early 1990s of South Africa from the apartheid system, through a bloodless election, to a multiracial, one-man-one-vote democracy also encouraged the idea that the world's most intractable conflicts could be bloodlessly transformed under American tutelage.

The Arab countries lent rhetorical support to the demand for Palestinian rights, a cause genuinely popular with the "Arab street." But, at the same time, the Arab regimes were driven by other concerns. Iran, Iraq, Egypt, and Turkey were engaged in a perpetual power struggle among themselves for regional pre-eminence and this competition formed the filter through which they responded to the Palestinian-Israeli conflict. Moreover, all the Arab regimes in the region were authoritarian and all (except Iran, where the Shah had already been deposed by an Islamic clerical regime) had reason to fear popular Islamist insurgencies that often used the Palestinian plight as their rhetorical staring point. The brief successes of the "Arab Spring" in Tunisia and Egypt, the regime change in Libya, and the widespread unrest throughout the region including Yemen,[21] Bahrain,[22] Syria,[23] Algeria,[24] Iraq,[25] Jordan,[26] Kuwait,[27] Morocco,[28] Sudan,[29] Mauritania,[30] Oman,[31] Saudi Arabia,[32] Djibouti,[33] Lebanon,[34] Western Sahara[35] and Mali[36] only underscored this point.

In short, whatever the real needs of the Palestinians and the Israelis in the period after the *Intifada*, the need of neighboring countries and even distant superpowers was for peace and quiet. And so a "peace process" began, which will be discussed in detail below, in the section focused on the spiral of conflict.

THE PALESTINIANS AND THE PEACE PROCESS

The Palestinians have always been well aware that their needs are of little genuine concern to Arab regimes. In a video released during the July, 2014 bombing of Gaza,[37] one woman emerges from the rubble of her home shouting "May god punish the Jews,"[38] but four other Gazans, also bombed out of their homes, shout "May God punish the Arabs" to the cameraman running alongside.

If the first *Intifada* represented an attempt by Palestinians to go it alone, then it did not succeed either in securing justice for Palestinians or even in preventing further deterioration of their situation. Yet it continues to garner respect and even nostalgia within the Palestinian community, in part because of its real achievements within Palestinian society and in part for putting the issue of Palestine on the map of global conversations.

The first *Intifada* revealed the capacity of grassroots communities to mobilize quickly and imaginatively in times of crisis. Acts of resistance took multiple forms besides marching and demonstrating. In an age with no social media, communities across the West Bank and Gaza organized themselves to pass information through leaflets, and to use popular committees for a variety of purposes: to work around Israeli economic blockades, to secure food through community gardens, to provide medical care and social services, and to organize tax strikes against the occupation.[39] This work, because it was not militarized, also provided an opportunity for the maximum participation of women in the liberation struggle.[40]

Many Palestinians and Jews who are not blinded by Zionism see this process in the same way. A former Palestinian negotiator has described the peace process as "trying to divide the pizza while the other side is eating the pizza."[18] Henry Siegman, an Orthodox Jewish rabbi and former Director of the American Jewish Congress, says: "What is required of statesmen is not more peace conferences or clever adjustments to previous peace formulations but the moral and political courage to end their collaboration with the massive hoax the peace process has been turned into ... [F]urther peace conferences, no matter how well intentioned, make their participants accessories to one of the longest and cruelest deceptions in the annals of international diplomacy."[19]

Palestinians were also, again without social media, very savvy in their analyses of the Israeli political climate and strategies for "messaging" to Western observers.[41] These efforts involved effective cooperation between generations, among different classes, and across significant geographic divides between the West Bank and Gaza and between the Occupied Palestinian Territories and the PLO leadership exiled in Tunisia.

Observers claim that at least some of the timidity of the present West Bank leadership stems from their dependence on foreign support and remember the first *Intifada* as a golden age of communal self-reliance.

Yet the *Intifada* did have internal challenges, beyond the long-standing factional divisions of different political camps. Protesters had to overcome class divisions that made professionals slow to join the ranks of protests led by youths from refugee camps.[42] There was a generational divide between the exiled PLO leaders in Tunis and the younger leadership in the West Bank and Gaza, as well as the obvious geographic distance. None of these difficulties were trivial or easily surmounted.

And finally, of course, the *Intifada*, which one observer called "war by other means"[43] produced neither national liberation nor civil rights for Palestinians. Instead, the *Intifada* ushered in the "peace process" – a new and different site of struggle in which Palestinians proved to be far less adept at making their case.

The principal story within the "peace process" is the Oslo Accords. Without going into details, it is enough to say that the expectations raised by Oslo form the background to what follows: there were documents signed in 1993 and again in 1995 that, together, projected the possibility of a Palestinian state to be created by 1999. As events unfolded, with both sides paying lip service to the process while undermining it by their actions – settlement building on the Israeli side and armed struggle on the Palestinian side – it became increasingly clear to anyone interested in the fate of the area that the terms of the Accord would not be met. Rising hostility between the parties grew in the soil of this disappointment. Perhaps the only achievement of the Oslo Accords was to allow for the return of PLO leaders, especially Yasser Arafat, from Tunisia to Palestine. This brought the official PLO leadership back to the actual reality of their community and its struggle, though often at the expense of the younger male and female leadership that had come of age in their absence.

As the *Intifada* segued into the "peace process" and the "peace process" visibly faltered, both sides of the conflict, the Israelis and the Palestinians, became harsher and more entrenched in their opposition to one another.

In Israel, people were outraged and alarmed by the fact that a generation of Occupation had not succeeded in pacifying the Palestinians – and, even worse, that the *Intifada* had cast the Israelis as the oppressors, at least in some people's view. In 1994, one year after the signing of the first of the Oslo accords that was supposed to end the conflict, an American-born settler named Baruch Goldstein entered the Ibrahimi Mosque in Hebron and gunned down 29 Muslims as they knelt in prayer. In the riots that followed the massacre, the Israeli Defense Forces gunned down an additional 25 Palestinians.[44]

One year later, the cultural incitement to violence common in the settler community and among the politicians who supported them, especially Benjamin Netanyahu, led to the assassination of Prime Minister Yitzhak Rabin. During the *Nakba*, the 1947 displacement of Palestinians, Rabin had been second in command over Operation Dani, the ethnic cleansing of the Palestinian towns of Lydda and Ramle. Operation Dani generated fully 10% of all the refugees made homeless during the *Nakba*.[45] Rabin had also, less than five years earlier, ordered the "break their bones" policy by which Israeli soldiers responded to the first *Intifada*.[46] Yet he was not sufficiently harsh on Palestinians in the opinion of many Israelis, especially the settlers. In 1995, another Hebron settler, Yigal Amir, assassinated him at a peace rally in Tel Aviv.[47]

Israeli harshness was mirrored on the Palestinian side by the growing popularity of the Muslim Brotherhood and the even more militant Islamic Jihad. Hamas, the Palestinian branch of the Muslim Brotherhood, was founded in 1988[48] during the first *Intifada* and, as we have seen in previous chapters, was initially welcomed (some even claim funded) by the Israelis as a counterweight to the PLO.[49]

While doctrinal differences separated the various Palestinian groups, all – both secular and Islamist – resorted to suicide bombings at least sporadically, beginning in 1987, continuing during the Oslo negotiations, and peaking during the years of the Second (*Al Aqsa*) *Intifada* (2000–2005).[50] American analysts using Israeli data on suicide bombings reveal how deeply entrenched this tactic was in Palestinian resistance: "39.9 percent of the suicide attacks were carried out by Hamas; 25.7 percent by the Palestinian Islamic Jihad (PIJ); 26.4 percent by the Fatah; 5.4 percent by the Popular Front for the Liberation of Palestine (PFLP); and 2.7 percent by other organizations."[51]

The suicide attacks were an utter failure for Palestinians. They neither inflicted unbearable costs nor shifted Israeli resolve to pursue the Zionist project. And they rightly caused an enormous backlash against the Palestinian cause among Western governments and publics. They were abandoned for a variety of reasons: massive military retaliation,[52] improved Israeli intelligence,[53] and a Hamas-declared truce in 2004–2005.[54] Worst of all from the Palestinian point of view, suicide attacks furnished Israelis with an opportunity to deploy a new technique for acquiring Palestinian land: the Separation Barrier, built in the name of "national security."

In some places the Separation Barrier is twice the height of the Berlin Wall, at others, along most of its route, it consists of a 60 meter wide series of electronic and barbed wire fences protecting a military road at its center, flanked by a deep ditch on the Palestinian side.[55] Upon completion the Separation Barrier will run a projected 680–709 kilometers in length,[56] twice the length of the Green Line.[57] Only 15–20% of the Separation Barrier's route runs along that supposed Israeli-Palestinian border.[58] Consider those last two facts together: the Separation Barrier is twice as long as the "border" and over 80% of it zigzags deep into territory assigned to a potential Palestinian state. Whatever its security payoffs, this barrier is also a tool of land expropriation. It surrounds most of the larger settlements and industrial zones, effectively excising them from Palestine and joining them to Israel. If completed as planned, the Separation Barrier will, in the end, appropriate nearly 10% of the West Bank.[59]

The Palestinians have, of course, mounted legal challenges to the Separation Barrier's existence and, often, its route. In 2004, the International Court of Justice issued an advisory opinion about the Barrier, saying: "Israel cannot rely on a right of self-defense or on a state of necessity in order to preclude the wrongfulness of the construction of the wall." The

ICJ concluded: "the construction of the wall, and its associated regime, are contrary to international law."[60] In 2005 the Israeli High Court ordered the Separation Barrier's route around the settlement of Alfei Menashe changed to reduce hardship on the nearby Palestinian villages of Wadi Rasha and Ras a-Tire. In 2007 the High Court ruled that 700 dunams of land cut off by the Barrier were to be returned to the village of Bili'in from the settlement of Modi'in Illit. Bili'in nevertheless lost a further 1,500 dunams to the wall route, not returned by court order.[61] The Israelis have ignored the ICJ entirely and sometimes even defied the orders of their own High Court with regard to the Barrier.

All of the foregoing violence – the assassinations, the suicide bombings, the construction of the Separation Barrier – are intertwined with the coming of the second *(Al Aqsa) Intifada.* By 2000 it was clear to the whole world that the Palestinian state foreseen in the Oslo Accords was further from realization than ever. Israel had just withdrawn from their occupation of southern Lebanon and this withdrawal seemed to signal Israeli weakness. Tensions mounted in both Palestinian and Israeli communities, so that when Ariel Sharon, accompanied by a thousand heavily armed security personnel, shouldered his way into the *Haram al Sharif,* the site of the *Al Aqsa* and Dome of the Rock mosques in Jerusalem's Old City, the spark to ignite the tinder was set off. Whether Sharon meant to set off an armed revolt or only to embarrass his political rival (Ehud Barak) is not clear,[62] but in any case, another period of intense violence began.

Actually, the second *Intifada* began much as the first had, with Palestinians throwing rocks and burning tires. But almost immediately, the Israeli response increased the level of violence. Live fire was used against demonstrators, targeted assassinations were brought into play, whole cities and towns were placed under curfew, schools and banks were closed, Palestinian access to power, water, and food disrupted.[63] On the Palestinian side, suicide bombings spiked, two Israeli soldiers caught in Ramallah were lynched (see also Chapter 9), and Arafat's attempt to re-arm the Palestinians was unmasked when the Israelis intercepted the *Karine A,* an arms-bearing ship.[64]

Adding to the difficulty, there was regime change in both Israel and America early in the second *Intifada.* Ariel Sharon replaced the more moderate Ehud Barak (who had, nevertheless, endorsed a policy of separation between Israelis and Palestinians in his own election campaign, using the slogan "Us here, them there" reminiscent of Herzl's rhetoric, mentioned in Chapter 1). Similarly, George Bush, a more conservative president, replaced Bill Clinton in the White House.

And then, of course, there was September 11, 2001, the bombing of the World Trade Center in downtown New York by Al Qaeda operatives. The tragedy of 9/11 led directly to the American invasion of Iraq and to a period of intense Islamophobia in American politics that strengthened ties between President Bush and Ariel Sharon. In this context, there was no hope that the United States could function as an even-handed mediator in the Israeli-Palestinian conflict.

The *Al Aqsa Intifada* continued into 2005 and left an enormous harvest of mutual distrust and suspicion between Palestinians and Israelis in its wake, along with a weakened PLO government in Ramallah. The West Bank and Gaza has become increasingly distant from one another, the ties between them frayed by long years of Israeli-imposed closure and travel restrictions. Hamas was about the only party to benefit, emerging from the second *Intifada* with enhanced grassroots credibility, especially in Gaza, for the resistance it mounted against Israel.

Given the seeming intractability of the Gazan resistance to Occupation, Ariel Sharon decided, in 2005, to alter the character of the Occupation there. His actions in Gaza were directed not only at Gaza but were also part of his strategy vis-à-vis the West Bank, and even vis-à-vis the Israeli peace movement whose 2003 Geneva Initiative (discussed below) it was meant to counter.[65]

Despite his early and enthusiastic endorsement of the settler movement, under the Disengagement Plan, Sharon ordered 8,000 settlers withdrawn from Gaza in 2005.[66] The withdrawal was highly contested and the Israeli Defense Forces were called upon to drag the most tenacious settlers away.[67] The uprooting of the Israeli settlements in Gaza served two purposes:

First, the withdrawal allowed Sharon to reconfigure Israeli control over Gaza as a siege. By 2007, Gaza's borders were sealed. Israel retained control over land, sea and air routes into Gaza. Gazan agricultural products were cut off from the Israeli market and thereby from all world markets, while, at the same time, Israel created a short list of items that could be imported into Gaza – excluding building materials, anything that could be labeled "dual (i.e. domestic and military) use" and,[68] inexplicably, school books, pencils, and pasta.[69] With each successive round of aerial bombardment Gaza's infrastructure was further undermined: as I wrote this chapter for the first edition in 2014, Israel had bombed 2 hospitals, many schools, a number of United Nations facilities (all places where people bombed out of residential areas might reasonably have sought refuge), as well as Gaza's electric, water and sewage treatment plants. There has been almost no rebuilding since.

The siege of Gaza served not only to suppress the area that produced the most militant resistance to Occupation. Israel also used the Gaza "withdrawal" to trade for enhanced control over the West Bank. Ariel Sharon assured Israelis of that, noting that the Bush administration had agreed to this trade-off before the Disengagement Plan was publicly announced.[70] Sharon's close associate, Dov Weissglass, spoke even more candidly about the motives for the dismantling of the Gaza settlements: "the disengagement plan is ... the bottle of formaldehyde necessary so that there will not be a political process with the Palestinians."[71]

THE PEACE PROCESS AND THE SPIRAL INTO TRAGEDY

It may seem odd to link the "peace process" to the spiral of conflict, but in fact, the peace process has done more harm than good, in exactly the way that Dov Weissglass foresaw. It has come close to legitimizing permanent Palestinian statelessness with its associated inequality, resistance, repression, and the recurring bouts of violence that the cycle of repression and resistance give rise to.

The earliest chapter of the "peace process" was written in the Rabat Declaration of 1974, discussed in the last chapter. The Rabat Declaration, issuing from the Arab League summit the year after the Yom Kippur War, had the distinct value of representing Arab voices free from Russian and American pressure. The combined wisdom of the Arab states affirmed the PLO as the sole legitimate representative of the Palestinian people, definitively resolving the power struggle between Arafat and Jordan's King Hussein in Arafat's favor.[72]

But the Rabat Declaration also proved to be an early harbinger of troubles to come, stipulating that the PLO had the right to become a national authority administering any territory that might one day be liberated from the Israeli Occupation.[73] This language was unhelpful in at least two respects. It named the PLO as a national *authority*, stopping short of calling upon it to constitute a *state*. The distinction is more than verbal: a state enjoys sovereignty: it can organize its own domestic affairs and it can enter into international relations on behalf of its polity. An "authority," on the other hand, does not enjoy sovereignty; it is merely an administrative entity under the control of overseeing powers.

Moreover, the Rabat Declaration, like the Khartoum Declaration of 1967 implicitly endorses the two-state solution, looking forward to Palestinian authority only over the lands – the West Bank, East Jerusalem and the Gaza

Strip – that might possibly be liberated from an existing Israeli state. Given world opinion at that time (1974), endorsement of the two-state formula is not inherently wrong. It did, however, set up a dynamic which reached its height in the Oslo negotiations: that Israel entered negotiations already in possession of 78% of historic Palestine and the PLO would then be required to make "difficult compromises" to take possession of something less than the full 22% remaining.

The 1978 Camp David Accords, principally a peace agreement between Israel and Egypt, peeled Egypt away from Arab unity in opposition to Israel. The Accord followed the precedent established in the Rabat Declaration, calling for the establishment of a Palestinian Authority to have administrative power in the West Bank and the Gaza Strip, but with no recognition of the legitimacy of a Palestinian state.[74]

The region as a whole remained unsettled, in 1979 the Shah was overthrown in Iran, an Iran-Iraq war raged between 1980 and 1987, and by 1990 Iraq had invaded Kuwait and been repulsed. Arafat, a client of Saddam Hussein, was alone in endorsing the Iraqi invasion of Kuwait and for this he would later pay a price. The most important event for the Palestinian-Israeli conflict in these years was, of course, the first *Intifada*.

In 1991, when the first *Intifada* has been raging for four years, the United States and Russia (no longer the Soviet Union), along with Spain, tried once again to engineer a peace agreement between Israel and the Palestinians. The Madrid Conference of 1991 was Russia's last appearance as a participant in the peace process. After Madrid it played no role, leaving America as the arbiter of the process.

The Madrid Conference experimented with a multi-lateral approach to the peace process, inviting Jordan, Lebanon, and Syria as well as representatives from China, India, the U.N., and the European Union. The inclusion of front-line Middle East states made sense, since large numbers of Palestinian refugees lived in those countries, and thus Jordan, Lebanon and Syria would have been implicated had any resettlement plan emerged.

What made no sense at all was that the American sponsors of the Madrid conference were so insistent on keeping the PLO in the penalty box for supporting Saddam Hussein that they excluded the "sole legitimate representative of the Palestinian people" from negotiations over the fate of Palestine (although a number of distinguished Palestinians did join the Jordanian delegation).

The Madrid Conference was also the one moment in the "peace process" when the Americans enjoyed some real leverage over the Israelis. Secretary or State James Baker and President George H. W. Bush threatened to withhold loan guarantees for money the Israelis need to resettle the huge influx of Russian immigrants. Despite this leverage no progress was achieved on the core issues between Israel and the Palestinians. President George H.W. Bush, who had dared to tamper with the loan guarantees, became a target for AIPAC and lost his presidential re-election bid in 1992, the year after the Madrid Conference.

The Israelis gained immeasurably however, advancing their trade relations and diplomatic acceptance with China and India. They had engaged in direct talks with Syrians, Jordanians, and Lebanese. And in the wider Muslim world the Madrid Conference also bore fruit, weakening the Arab boycott of Israel by opening trade relations between Israel and Oman, Qatar, Tunisia, Morocco, and Mauritania.[75]

The Intifada continued, though in attenuated form. The Palestinian-Israeli conflict remained as intractable as ever. In 1993, the most interested parties, the Palestinians and the Israelis, began meeting privately in Oslo, once again trying to resolve the conflict between them. The U.S. came to play an active role in promoting the Oslo Accords.

In theory, the Oslo Accords were designed to initiate a five-year process in which a series of carefully-calibrated, mutually confidence-building steps would lead to the creation of a Palestinian state. In practice, the Oslo Accords allowed the Israelis to reap all the benefits and kudos associated with being party to a complicated "peace process" while doing nothing to conform to the agreement and everything to undermine it. Israel offered no resolution on any of the key issues dividing Palestinians and Israelis: no commitment to final borders (thereby leaving any possible Palestinian state in limbo), no commitment to sharing Jerusalem, no commitment to even symbolic recognition of Palestinian refugees' right of return, and no agreement on water. All of these issues were put off, awaiting the ever-receding "final status" negotiations.[76] Instead, the negotiations began from the assumption that, even with land swaps, Israel would get at least 78% of historic Palestine and that all the concessions on land would come from the Palestinian side.

In fact, under Oslo, the West Bank came to be divided, for the very first time, into three non-contiguous parts: Areas A, B, and C. Area A consisted of the major Palestinian cities: Ramallah, Bethlehem, Jenin, Jericho, Nablus, Qalqilya, Tulkarem, and 80% of Hebron, the only major Palestinian city (apart from East Jerusalem, which Israel considered to be annexed) that not only was ringed by illegal settlements but also had a series of illegal mini-settlements strung through the heart of the city.[77] The Area A cities were to be under full Palestinian control, civil and military, once the Palestinian Authority began operations, which it did in 1994 shortly after the signing of Oslo I. Around the Area A cities were a cluster of villages and these were to be called Area B. Area B villages were to be governed jointly by Palestinian civil authorities and Israeli military authorities. The remainder of the West Bank, some 60+% (of the 22% of historic Palestine) was Area C and it remained under full Israeli civil and military control. For the first time ever, Palestinian could no longer move freely about the West Bank.[78]

The Palestinian Authority was conceived as an administrative entity. It was by no means a state with sovereignty, contiguity, or viability. The best case script was the hope that, if the Palestinian Authority proved itself adept at suppressing Palestinians' militant resistance to Occupation, then the Area B villages might eventually become part of Area A, while the Area C villages would be upgraded to Area B status, and so forth, until much of the West Bank came under PA control. This, of course, never happened. Palestinian discontent could never be wholly suppressed, and Israel depopulated much of Area C in order to promote settlement building.[79] Netanyahu was caught on an open microphone, bragging that he had stopped the Oslo process with settlement building.[80] But even without Netanyahu's machinations, the very premise that a Palestinian state could evolve only if and when it met Israel's security needs, meant that the entire Oslo process was based on accommodating Israeli "needs" and not on enforcing human rights or international humanitarian law.[81]

The Oslo Accords served Israel in additional ways as well. International human rights standards require an occupying power to bear the cost of maintaining the civilians of the occupied population at a high standard of living. But with the birth of the Palestinian Authority, the Israelis had created an entity capable of receiving foreign aid and charitable contributions. The U.S. and the European Union provide substantial funding to the Palestinian Authority. This arrangement relieves the Israelis of much of the financial burden that belongs to an occupier. It makes the PA dependent on Western funding and reduces it to being a virtual subcontractor for the Occupation.[82]

And finally, the Oslo Accords fixed the amount of water that would flow to the Palestinian Authority. Any changes in water allotments would require further negotiations, which the Israelis have never granted even as Palestinian births caused their numbers to swell. Thus the Oslo Accords have created acute water shortages in the West Bank, although the area is not geologically water-deprived.[83]

No documents capture the failure of Oslo more vividly than the exchange of Letters of Mutual Recognition between the two parties. Arafat writes effusively to Rabin: "Dear Mr. Prime Minister, The signing of the Declaration of Principles marks a new era in the history of the Middle East. In firm conviction thereof, I would like to confirm the following PLO commitments: The PLO recognizes the right of the State of Israel to exist in peace and security. The PLO accepts United Nations Security Council Resolution 242 and 338. The PLO commits itself to the Middle East peace process and to a peaceful resolution of the conflict between the two sides and declares that all outstanding issues relating to permanent status will be resolved through negotiations." Arafat's letter includes several more commitments undertaken by the PLO.[84] In return, Rabin replies: "Mr. Chairman, In response to your letter of September 19, 1993, I wish to inform you that, in light of the PLO commitments included in your letter, the Government of Israel has decided to recognize the PLO as the representative of the Palestinian people and commence negotiations with the PLO within the Middle East peace process." The Palestinians recognized the state of Israel and its right to a peaceful existence while the Israelis recognized the PLO negotiating team as such.[85]

The theme of privileging Israel's security needs over the provisions of human rights doctrine continued with the Wye River memorandum. By 1998 it was clear to all concerned that the five-year plan provided by Oslo had been derailed and that the aim of creating a Palestinian state would not be realized. In an attempt to save the Oslo Accords, U.S. President Clinton convened a further meeting at the Wye River Plantation in Maryland in 1998. The principle issues addressed at Wye River were Arafat's ability to suppress anti-Israeli terrorism. Again Israeli security needs were deemed to be more important than Palestinian human rights. Arafat secured American, Scandinavian, and World Bank aid for training his security forces. The PLO agreed to change the language of its charter, removing calls for the end of the Zionist entity. Not much else was accomplished,[86] although it is worth noting that, at Wye River, Arafat was invited to the table *before* he agreed to change the PLO charter – a lesson that Netanyahu ignores when he insists that Palestinians need to make major concessions *in order to be invited* to a peace conference.

Two further meetings, the Camp David Summit of 2000 and the Taba Talks of 2001, also were convened to try to salvage the Oslo Accords, even though no Palestinian state was remotely in sight.

The Camp David summit was convened because both the American president Bill Clinton, and Israeli Prime Minister Ehud Barak needed substantial diplomatic victories on the Israel/Palestine issue to save their political legacy (Clinton) or their re-election chances (Barak). Arafat's participation was virtually a command performance: Clinton promised him that he would not be scapegoated in the likely event that the talks failed. Clinton then reneged on that promise. Barak and the Israeli team made verbal offers more generous than any previous Israeli offer, but, at best, their offers foresaw Israel staying in the Jordan Valley for 12 more years (thus foreclosing any Palestinian border with an Arab state) and annexing settlement blocks that effectively trisected Palestinian lands. Barak's offers were never put in writing and he rejected all of Arafat's attempts to clarify his intentions.

The major outcome of the Camp David talks was a publicity victory for Barak, who narrated the events as that of a "generous offer" on his part, rejected by an intransigent Palestinian leader.[87] Clinton, too, appeared statesmanlike, announcing the "Clinton Parameters" that involved two states, the border roughly approximating the Green Line modified with agreed-upon land swaps, a divided Jerusalem, and a truncated right to return for the refugees, directing them exclusively to the Palestinian state rather than the sites from which they had actually been expelled. Explicit in the Clinton Parameters is the normalization of the major settlement blocks and the abandonment of international law, which guaranteed Palestine the return of land conquered in war, and guaranteed refugees the right to return to their points of origin.[88]

As the Camp David talks had been designed to salvage Oslo, so the Taba negotiations a year later were designed to salvage something from the Camp David talks. But the Taba talks were overtaken by events: Barak's electoral loss to Sharon who was openly hostile to the terms being offered, as well as the beginnings of the Second *Intifada* and, soon thereafter, the events of 9/11.

Nevertheless, the very failures of the "peace process," the emergence of a second *Intifada*, the hardening political climate, and an American war in Iraq, all made the quest for a settlement of the Palestinian/Israeli conflict more urgent.

The Arab states, meeting at their annual summit, proposed the Arab League Peace Initiative in 2002. The Arab Plan set slightly more rigorous terms than the Clinton Parameters, requiring a more nearly complete return to the 1967 borders, and a more generous treatment for the refugees. But in return it offered Israel peace with all 22 Arab states, the exchange of ambassadors, an end to the Arab boycott of Israel, and the opening of full bilateral trade relations between Israel and all the 22 Arab Muslim states.[89] The Arab League has re-endorsed this peace plan on several occasions including the 2007 Arab League Summit. But, despite considerable international enthusiasm, Israel has always dismissed the plan out of hand, claiming that a Palestinian state is an existential threat to Israeli security.

In 2003, a similar fate – Israeli dismissal – befell the Geneva Initiative, a grass roots initiative undertaken by Israelis and Palestinians, many of them diplomats and veterans of the Camp David and Taba negotiations. The initiative specified a peace deal consistent with all the others, the Camp David negotiations, the Clinton Parameters, the Road Map (of the Quartet of the U.S. Russia, NATO and the EU), the Arab Peace Initiative, etc. It fell into the same well of Israeli refusal as all the others.

Since then, we have seen Palestinian elections in 2006 that would have brought Hamas into the government along with the PLO, a retaliatory Israeli siege on Gaza since 2007, repeated Israeli incursions and massacres in Gaza (Operation Cast Lead in 2008, Operation Pillar of Defense in 2012, Operation Protective Edge in 2014), and accelerated settlement building in Area C. The Annapolis talks of 2007 and the Kerry shuttle diplomacy broke no new ground. In 2013 Netanyahu gave a talk at Bar Ilan University in which he reluctantly acknowledged that there would someday have to be a Palestinian State,[90] but, immediately afterwards, his father rushed to reassure his shocked supporters that: "Of course he didn't mean it. He will attach conditions that will make it impossible."[91]

Ultimately, the "peace process" did not deliver to Israel what it wanted most, an absent or a pacified Palestinian population and uncontested control over the entirety to historic Palestine. Nevertheless, the "peace process" did confer substantial benefits on Israel. Thanks to the "peace process" Israel enjoys a rising tide of diplomatic normalization and enlarged trade relations in the region and the world.

For Palestine, the "peace process" delivered only betrayal. Oslo, in particular, was an unmitigated disaster. It did not preclude settlement building. It allowed the West Bank to be subdivided which, in turn, created for the first time a regimen in which Palestinians could not move freely even in their "own" land. It removed from Israel the financial and physical burdens of administering their Occupation, delegating these tasks to the Palestinian Authority that benefitted from U.S. and European financial support. It codified the abandonment of human rights and the substitution of "Israeli security" as the basis for resolving the conflict. It created gratuitous water shortages for Palestinians.

Today, the Palestinian struggle for freedom continues, as does a quest for effective tools to secure their ends. Likely, the old tools will continue to be used: occasional outbursts of violent resistance, continued advocacy for national liberation (in essence a two-state solution), or more innovative advocacy for civil rights within a single state (the one-state solution). Likely Palestinian resistance will, over time, become more media savvy and more global, since both of those developments are occurring everywhere in the world.

BEYOND THE PEACE PROCESS: MARSHALLING INTERNATIONAL SUPPORT FOR HUMAN RIGHTS

Israel's success on every front – colonizing more land, suppressing armed struggle, securing impunity and diplomatic cover for all it did – convinced the Palestinians of the need for new ideas and programs. And so they began to turn their attention to other strategies – economic, political, and cultural – in their quest for justice. The endless "peace process" interested almost no one on the Palestinian side.

Israeli diplomat Abba Eban is reputed to have said: "the Palestinians never miss a chance to miss a chance."[92] But certainly in the period following the second *Intifada*, this stricture does not hold. Edward Said, the leading voice of Palestinians in the West until his death in 2003, articulated the case for an innovative mass movement as against the case for armed struggle. He is worth quoting at length:

> For decades we have relied in our minds on ideas about guns and killing, ideas that ... have brought us plentiful martyrs but have had little real effect either on Zionism or on our own ideas about what to do next. [T]he fighting is done by a small brave number of people pitted against hopeless odds ... Yet a quick look at other movements – say, the Indian nationalist movement, the South African liberation movement, the American civil rights movement – tell us first of all that only a mass movement employing tactics and strategy that maximizes the popular element ever makes any difference ... The future, like the past, is built by human beings. They, and not some distant mediator or savior, provide the agency for change.[93]

Whether explicitly or implicitly, Palestinian civil society seems to have heard Said, forging both economic and political initiatives, addressing both Palestinians and internationals, in an attempt to end the Occupation.

In 2005, over 170 organizations from the length and breadth of Palestinian civil society joined together to ask the world to use non-violent economic instruments – boycotts, sanctions and divestments (BDS) – to impose economic costs on Israel for their continued Occupation of Palestinian lands and communities. The boycott call[94] was issued by organizations representing virtually every segment of Palestinian society: the West Bank, Gaza, East Jerusalem, and the Diaspora, every class level from unions to professional organizations, women's groups, rights groups, charitable and social service groups, rural and urban groups, student groups, religious and secular organizations were all represented. The call for an economic boycott was supplemented by an additional call for an academic and cultural boycott of Israeli institutions.[95]

At first the BDS call was useful principally as educational tool: in explaining why someone should consider boycotting or sanctioning or divesting from Israeli companies and local companies that benefitted from the Occupation, organizers were able to share a lot of information about the history of the Israeli-Palestinian struggle. Over time, however, the boycott campaigns gathered strength until they achieved some real economic bite. The BDS campaign is discussed in more detail in Chapter 11; suffice it here to say that, especially in Europe, the labeling and shunning of Israeli consumer goods, especially those manufactured in the Occupied Territories, and business divestments from partnerships with Israeli institutions, are moving forward with some success. The cultural and academic boycotts have also had notable achievements: in the context of Operation Protective Edge, such stars as Robert De Niro, Mark Ruffalo, Mandy Patinkin, Javier Bardem, Penelope Cruz, Rihanna, and many others have spoken out against Israel's murderous conduct in Gaza.

Sanctions, actions by governments against the state of Israel, have been slower to follow the path of boycotts and divestments, but even here, Operation Protective Edge has led to some successes as Brazilian, Chilean, Ecuadorian, Salvadorian, Peruvian, and Bolivian envoys have been recalled from Israel while Brazil, Argentina, Venezuela, Uruguay and Paraguay have suspended Free Trade Agreement talks indefinitely.[96] Even Great Britain, normally content to follow America's lead on matters concerning Israel and Palestine, has threatened to suspend arms sales to Israel should they renew the assaults associated with Operation Protective Edge.[97]

More recently still, it remains to be seen whether the Palestinians themselves, via the Palestinian Authority, muster the energy to make more use of the options open to them in their new standing as an "observer state" within the United Nations system and whether the International Criminal Court and the International Court of Justice will agree to hear cases Palestine might bring.[98]

Discussion of sanctions, i.e. actions undertaken by states, also calls attention to Palestinian political moves. Fatah-Hamas rivalry had caused the delay of many scheduled elections, but in the period immediately following the second *Intifada*, Palestinians did try to organize multiple levels of elections: for president, for local mayors, and finally, in 2006, for the Palestinian Legislative Council, a body that had accountability to an electorate broader than the Palestinian Authority, which is limited to performing administrative functions in the West Bank. The Bush administration enthusiastically supported the call for Palestinian elections and, despite Israeli attempts to obstruct campaigns, especially in East Jerusalem, multiple monitoring groups, from the American Jimmy Carter Center[99] to the European Union,[100] concluded that the January, 2006 elections that finally took place were conducted in a fair, free, and professional manner. Surprisingly – or at least contrary to what the best internal Palestinian polling organizations had predicted – Hamas won a majority of seats in the newly enlarged PLC. Israel and the United States objected vociferously, Israel detained several Hamas legislators and the United States helped train Fatah cadre in anticipation of expelling Hamas from Gaza. Hamas staged a bloody counter-coup and the new Legislature was never able to function. Today, the West Bank is ruled largely by executive orders emanating from the Palestinian Authority. Gaza lies in ruins.

But despite all the hardships, the Palestinian public, particularly Palestinian youth, have been more forward thinking than their politicians (a common occurrence world wide). During the Arab Spring of 2010 and 2011, which the Israelis feared and dreaded, Palestinian youth took to the streets demanding a unity government. Such a government was finally re-introduced in 2014 and disrupting it was probably the real motive for Operation Protective Edge, Israel's most recent massacre in Gaza.

Given the frustrations Palestinians faced in creating a unified resistance to Occupation, and given Israeli intransigence vis-à-vis Palestinian political aspirations, the Palestinians began experimenting with two further strategies to break the deadlock.

First, a number of Palestinian intellectuals raised the question of whether the entire Palestinian agenda needed reframing. Palestinians had been trying for over 40 years to wage a national liberation struggle. Their objective, a contiguous, viable and sovereign Palestine seemed less likely to be realized with every passing day, even the mini version of it that accorded only 22% of historic Palestine to the Palestinians. Hence, a small group of intellectuals, many associated with the BDS movement, proposed to abandon the two-state solution, to face the fact that, since 1967, there had been only one state in historic Palestine, namely Israel. Recognizing this fact would require Palestinians to redefine their struggle entirely, to forget about national liberation and, instead, to take up a civil rights struggle within the single state of Israel. Edward Said was the earliest to acknowledge the impossibility of the two-state solution and to broach the one-state option. He did so as early as 1999.[101] On the Jewish side, British historian Tony Judt was the first to take up the case for the one-state solution in 2003.[102] These early calls were adopted by some Palestinian leaders in a series of conferences in Madrid and London in 2007,[103] followed by Boston in 2009,[104] Toronto in 2009,[105] and Cambridge, Massachusetts in 2012.[106]

The argument of the One-State proponents is simple and straightforward: there has been only one state in historic Palestine – the Israeli state – since 1967. That state controls the fate of some 6 million Palestinians, three quarters of whom live under military law without rights. That same state denies the rights of Palestinian refugees. That same state has created a unified infrastructure of water and power grids and road systems throughout the land. That state admits to placing more 764,000 Jewish settlers (i.e. more than 10% of Israel's Jewish population) in the West Bank, within and between existing Palestinian communities.[107] The struggle, therefore, must be for civil rights within that single controlling state. Difficult as it is for Palestinians to abandon the struggle for national liberation, the struggle for civil rights within a unitary state actually accords more closely with what Israelis, without irony, refer to as the "facts on the ground." Sherlock Holmes' *bon mot* is applicable here: "when you have eliminated the impossible, whatever remains, however improbable, must be the truth."[108]

Ironically, the one-state solution is also closer to the original aspirations for an undivided land held by both Palestinians and Zionists. So much the better. The problem, of course, is that while both Jewish Israelis and Palestinians would prefer an undivided land, neither wants much to do with the other. Given a choice between co-existing equitably in a single state or separating into two viable states, the Israelis, to date, have stymied both solutions, imagining that their program of Occupation and pacification can continue indefinitely.[109] It remains to be seen whether anything, for example a decisive rebuff from the United Nations or a third *Intifada*, could change this calculus for Israel.

Given that, at present, Israel, the more powerful party, prefers the Occupation to either the one-state or the two-state solution,[110] Palestinians have been strategic in trying to raise the costs of the stalemate and to do so in a non-violent manner. To the best of their ability, they have internationalized the conflict, attempting to draw other peoples and other nations into a role that will change the balance of power.

One version of internationalization is focused on the United Nations. In 2012, over the objections of the United States and intense pressure from Israel, the Palestinian Authority applied to and received from the United Nations General Assembly an upgrade in their status from "observer entity" to being a non-member "observer state."[111] The vote was 138 in favor, 9 against (the U.S., Canada, Czech Republic, Israel, Marshall Islands, Nauru, Panama and Palau) and 41 abstentions.[112] The vote would mean little besides a momentary verbal victory, except that, as an observer state, Palestine now has access to other U.N. agencies. Palestine has already sought and been granted membership in UNESCO, causing the United States untold embarrassment when it lost voting rights at the agency for refusing to pay its dues in protest against the new Palestinian membership.[113] In the midst of Operation Protective Edge, the Palestinian Authority announced a decision to sign onto the Rome Statute of the International Criminal Court. If they follow through, such a move would clear the way for its membership in the ICC also.[114] The possibility of bringing charges against Israel for its conduct during the various Gaza incursions has the potential to add considerably to Israel's costs for "mowing the lawn."

The second attempt at internationalization originated with the international solidarity movement that supports Palestinian rights from abroad. Perhaps the most famous project of the internationals was the attempt to break the siege of Gaza by running the Israeli blockade of the Mediterranean coast of Gaza. The very first boats to attempt this were sponsored by the Free Gaza and International Solidarity Movements respectively and were allowed to reach Gaza in August 2008 with a cargo of 200 hearing aids for children and 5,000 balloons.[115] Subsequently, another Free Gaza ship, the *Dignity*, also completed four voyages successfully, bringing further medical supplies to Gaza.[116] In December 2008 Operation Cast Lead called a halt to the activities of the Free Gaza flotilla. Activities resumed in 2010, with a flotilla of six ships staffed by volunteers from 37 different countries headed to Gaza in May of that year. This time the Israeli navy interdicted the flotilla in international waters, killing 9 Turkish passengers, including one Turkish American, aboard the lead ship, the Turkish vessel *Mavi*

Marmara.[117] Another sailing was planned but never materialized, until indignation over Operation Protective Edge re-animated the project. On July 26, 2014 the owners of the *Mavi Marmara* announced their plans to seek permission for another flotilla,[118] this one to be escorted by ships from the Turkish navy.[119]

Undoubtedly other international attempts at solidarity, especially in the area of medical relief will be forthcoming in the near future. However, the main problem remains that the very process officially designed to resolve the Israeli-Palestinian problem, namely the "peace process" has failed utterly to do so and we have learned nothing from that failure.

The crucial question is whether anyone will ever make human rights the "terms of reference," the standards by which the Palestinian-Israeli conflict is resolved. So far, that is the one option that no one has ever tried.

SUMMARY: THE ENDLESS, DECEPTIVE PEACE PROCESS

History of Israel-Palestine Conflict: IV

1987–Present: The endless, useless "Peace Process"

Israel	Great Powers	Palestine
Military Rule	End of Cold War	Intifada
Settlements	Islamophobia	Political Islam
Peace Process		BDS

INVASION OF LEBANON (1982–2000)

SECOND INTIFADA (2000–2005)

OPERATION DEFENSIVE SHIELD (2002)

OPERATION CAST LEAD (2008–2009)

OPERATION PILLAR OF DEFENSE (2012)

OPERATION BROTHERS KEEPER/OPERATION PROTECTIVE EDGE (2014)

CHRONOLOGY: THE PEACE PROCESS

1964: Founding of the Palestine Liberation Organization (PLO) – Palestinians get to speak for themselves. PLO is an umbrella group of secular nationalist parties (Fateh, PFLP, DFLP, etc.). The PLO is recognized world-wide as "the sole legitimate representative of the Palestinian people." But, because it is an umbrella group, its politics are weak and incoherent. The role of Palestinian refugees in the diaspora is increasingly unclear.

1967: Khartoum Declaration: The Arab League de facto recognizes two-state solution, despite the reputation of the Khartoum Declaration as a rejectionist document

The actual language of the document reads:

The Arab Heads of State have agreed to unite their political efforts at the international and diplomatic level to eliminate the effects of the aggression and *to ensure the withdrawal of the aggressive Israeli forces from the Arab lands which have been occupied since the aggression of June 5.* This will be done within the framework of the main principles by which the Arab States abide, namely, no peace with Israel, no recognition of Israel, no negotiations with it, and insistence on the rights of the Palestinian people in their own country.

1974: Rabat Declaration: First call for a Palestinian "Authority" (NB: not a state, but an authority – i.e. an administrative but not a sovereign entity)

1978: Camp David: Israeli Egyptian Peace Treaty signed 1979, affirmation of Palestinian "authority" NOT "state."

1988: Arafat accepts Two-State solution in attempt to remain relevant during the Intifada

1991: Madrid Conference – multi-lateral but *EXCLUDES PALESTINIANS* (punishment for backing Saddam Hussein's invasion of Kuwait)

1993–1995: Oslo Accords
   Abandon human rights standards as criteria for dispute resolution;
   Creates Palestinian Authority which shifts financial burden of Occupation from Israel to U.S., the E.U. and other donors;
   Subdivides Palestinians: Gaza vs. West Bank, Areas A, B, C within the West Bank (Area C = 62% of West Bank);
   Limits Palestinian access to water: Fixes the quantity of water allocated to the West Bank despite population increases.

1994: Israeli-Jordanian peace treaty signed

1998: Wye River (Arafat agrees to change PLO Charter)
This is a significant precedent because Arafat removed offensive language from PLO charter only AFTER he was recognized as a negotiating partner – relevant to the treatment of Hamas today.

2000: Camp David – Barak's "generous offer"[120] – both Clinton and Barak are lame ducks

2001: Taba Negotiations

2002: Arab Peace Initiative (followed by Geneva Accords, etc.)

2007: Annapolis Conference

2012–2014: Kerry Initiatives.

2018: Trump Administration moves U.S. Embassy to Jerusalem in defiance of international law, "best peace deal" to be announced.

NOTES

[1] The White House. (1961, July 25). *The Berlin Crisis: Radio and Television Address to the American People,* retrieved from http://www.jfklibrary.org/Asset-Viewer/Archives/ JFKWHA-045.aspx

[2] Tacitus, quoted by Yosi Gurvitz. (2014, May 11). It's the Little Things about Occupation, *+972,* retrieved from http://972mag.com/its-the-little-things-about-occupation/90744/

[3] Interview with Ami Ayalon, former director of the Shin Beit (Israel's State Security Service) from 1996–2000, quoted in Dror Moreh (Director). (2012). *The Gatekeepers,* Israel: Cinephile at: 1:36:40–1:38:00.

[4] Mark Tessler. (1994). *A History of the Israeli-Palestinian Conflict* (Bloomington, Indiana University Press), p. 697. Alex Kane. (2010, November 4). The Real Yitzhak Rabin, *Mondoweiss,* retrieved from http://mondoweiss.net/2010/11/the-real-yitzhak-rabin.html

[5] Isaac Balbus. (1974). *The Dialectics of Legal Repression: Black Rebels before the American Criminal Courts.* New York: Russell Sage Foundation.

[6] Richard Cloward and Frances Fox Piven (1974). *Regulating the Poor: The Functions of Public Welfare.* London: Tavistock Publications.

[7] http://blogs.forward.com/jj-goldberg/202855/israels-latest-fib-gaza-tunnels-were-surprise/#.U9PmnChGIrA.facebook#ixzz38bZjJCjm

[8] Etgar Keret. (2014, July 25). Israel's other war, *The New Yorker,* retrieved from http://www.newyorker.com/books/page-turner/israels-other-war?src=mp

[9] David Horovitz. (2014, July 13). Netanyahu finally speaks his mind, *The Times of Israel,* retrieved from http://www.timesofisrael.com/netanyahu-finally-speaks-his-mind/

[10] Henry Siegman. (2008, April 17). Tough Love for Israel, *The Nation,* retrieved from https://www.thenation.com/doc/20080505/siegman

[11] Israeli Central Bureau of Statistics, "Statistical Abstract of Israel: Comprehensive Settlement Population, 1972–2010," quoted by the Foundation for Middle East Peace, retrieved from http://www.fmep.org/resource/comprehensive-settlement-population-1972–2006

[12] Data about population size is always a politically sensitive and contested topic in Palestine and Israel. The number of settlers is particularly controversial. Arutz Sheva, a settler source, acknowledges 389, 250 Jewish settlers in the West Bank and another 375,000 in East Jerusalem, whose "annexation" is universally recognized as illegal, totaling some764,000 illegal settlers. These numbers date from 2014, and the same source claims that by now the number of settlers hasrisen to 800,000. *Arutz Sheva*, retrieved from http://www.israelnationalnews.com/Articles/Article.aspx/18210#.VpK885scTIU. The population growth rate in the settlements, though declining, is still approximately twice as high as that in Jerusalem, see Jacob Magid. (2018, January 21). Settler growth rate declines for sixth straight year, *The Times of Israel*, January 21, 2018, retrieved from https://www.timesofisrael.com/settler-growth-rate-declines-for-sixth-straight-year/

[13] Mark Tolts. (2009, August). Post-Soviet Aliyah and Jewish Demographic Transformation, Paper presented at the 15th World Congress of Jewish Studies, Jerusalem, retrieved from https://bjpa.org/search-results/publication/11924

[14] *Ibid.*

[15] Charles D. Smith. (2013). *Palestine and the Arab-Israeli Conflict: A History with Documents* (New York: St. Martin's Press, 8th edition) p. 321.

[16] Scott Wilson. (2006, March 22). Russian Bloc in Israel looks to a strongman, *The Washington Post*, retrieved from http://www.washingtonpost.com/wp-dyn/content/article/2006/03/21/AR2006032101721.html
Rachel M. Friedberg. (2001). The Impact of Mass Migration on the Israeli Labor Market, *The Quarterly Journal of Economics* 116(4): 1373–1408.

[17] Yaakov Katz. (2012, March 10). Easy to Start, Hard to End, *Jerusalem Post*, retrieved from http://www.jpost.com/Defense/Analysis-Easy-to-start-hard-to-end

[18] Uri Avnery. (2010, April 9). Damage Control, *Gush Shalom*, retrieved from http://zope.gush-shalom.org/home/en/channels/avnery/1283599151/

[19] Siegman, *op. cit.*

[20] Ha'aretz. (2010, March 17). U.S. general: Israel-Palestinian Conflict foments anti-U.S. Sentiment, *Ha'aretz*, retrieved from http://www.haaretz.com/news/u-s-general-israel-palestinian-conflict-foments-anti-u-s-sentiment-1.264910

[21] Nada Bakri and David Goodman. (2011, January 27). Thousands in Yemen Protest Against the Government, *The New York Times*, retrieved from http://www.nytimes.com/2011/01/28/world/middleeast/28yemen.html

[22] Frederik Richter. (2011, February 14). Protester killed in Bahrain "Day of Rage," *Reuters*, retrieved from http://uk.reuters.com/article/2011/02/14/uk-bahrain-protests-idUKTRE71D1G520110214

[23] Susanne Koelbl. (2011, March 28). It Will Not Stop: Syrian Uprising Continues Despite Crackdown, *Der Spiegel*, retrieved from http://www.spiegel.de/international/world/it-will-not-stop-syrian-uprising-continues-despite-crackdown-a-753517.html

[24] Associated Press, Algerian Protest Draws Thousands, *CBS News*, February 12, 2011, retrieved from http://www.cbc.ca/news/world/algeria-protest-draws-thousands-1.1065078

[25] Stephanie McCrummen. (2011, February 25). Thirteen killed in Iraq's 'Day of Rage' Protests, *The Washington Post*, retrieved from http://www.washingtonpost.com/wp-dyn/content/article/2011/02/24/AR2011022403117.html

26   Al Jazeera. (2011, January 28). Thousands Protest in Jordan, *Al Jazeera*, retrieved from http://www.aljazeera.com/news/middleeast/2011/01/2011128125157509196.html

27   Kuwaiti Stateless Protest for Third Day (2011, February 20). *Middle East Online*, retrieved from http://www.middle-east-online.com/english/?id=44476

28   Morocco King on holiday as people consider revolt (2011, January 30). *Afrol News*, retrieved from http://afrol.com/articles/37175

29   Sudan Police Clash with Protestors (2011, January 30). *Al Jazeera*, retrieved from http://www.aljazeera.com/news/africa/2011/01/2011130131451294670.html

30   Mohamed Yahya Abdel Wedoud. (2011, February 26). "Facebook Generation" continues Mauritania protests. *CNN*, retrieved from http://www/cnn/com/2011/WORLD/africa/02/26/mauritania.protest/index.html

31   Sunil K. Vaidya. (2011, February 27). One dead, dozen injured as Oman protest turns ugly, *Gulf News*, retrieved from http://gulfnews.com/news/gulf/oman/one-dead-dozen-injured-as-oman-protest-turns-ugly-1.768789

32   Man dies after setting himself on fire in Saudi Arabia (2011, January 23). *BBC News*, January, retrieved from http://www.bbc.co.uk/news/world-middle-east-12260465

33   Katrina Manson. (2011, June 1). Pro-Democracy Protests reach Djibouti, *Financial Times*, retrieved from http://www.ft.com/cms/s/001f94f6-3d18-11e0-bbff-00144feabdc0,Authorised=false.html?_i_location=http%3A%2F%2Fwww.ft.com%2Fcms%2Fs%2F0%2F001f94f6-3d18-11e0-bbff-00144feabdc0.html%3Fsiteeditio n%3Duk&siteedition=uk&_i_referer=#axzz38hwLlWPN

34   Syria-Related clashes rage in Lebanon, leaving 13 dead (2012, June 3). *CNN*, retrieved from http://www.cnn.com/2012/06/03/world/meast/lebanon-syria-violence/index.html

35   New Clashes in Occupied Western Sahara (2011, February 27). *Afrol News*, retrieved from http://afrol.com/articles/37450

36   Mali Coup: Arab Spring Spreads of Africa (2012, March 26). *UPI*, retrieved from http://www.upi.com/Top_News/Special/2012/03/26/Mali-coup-Arab-Spring-spreads-to-Africa/UPI-33131332791728/?spt=hs&or=tn

37   Amjad Almalki and Ahmad Ashour. (2014, July 27). Shujayea: Massacre at Dawn, *Al Jazeera* website, retrieved from http://www.aljazeera.com/programmes/specialseries/2014/07/shujayea-massacre-at-dawn-201472621348901563.html

38   In the sub-titles that accompany this film, she is said to yell "May God punish Israel," but it is clear that she actually says the word "Yehud" –i.e. "Jew."

39   Mazen Qumsiyeh. (2011). *Popular Resistance in Palestine: A History of Hope and Empowerment*, London, Pluto Press, and F. Robert Hunter. (1993). *The Palestinian Uprising: A War By Other Means*. Los Angeles and Berkeley: University of California Press, Revised and Expanded edition, 1993.

40   Islah Jad. (2009). "The Demobilization of Women's Movements: the Case of Palestine," *AWID Analysis of Women's Movements*, 2009, retrieved from https://www.awid.org/sites/default/files/atoms/files/changing_their_world_-_demobilization_of_womens_movements_-_palestine.pdf

41   Eitan Alimi. (2007). *Israeli Politics and the First Palestinian Intifada: Political opportunities, framing processes and contentious politics*, London: Routledge.

42   Smith, *op. cit.*, pp. 408–412.

43   Hunter, *op. cit.*

44   Smith, *op. cit.*, p. 448.

[45] Rabin, then a Lieutenant Colonel, was second in command to Yigal Allon. Operation Dani is described in Benny Morris. (1986). Operation Dani and the Palestinian Exodus form Lydda and Ramle in 1948, *The Middle East Journal* 40(1): 82–109.

[46] Tessler, *op. cit.*, pp. 696–706.

[47] Smith *op. cit.*, p. 449.

[48] Smith *op. cit.*, p. 412.

[49] Rashid Khalid. (2006). *The Iron Cage: The Story of the Palestinian Struggle for Statehood* (Boston: Beacon Press), pp. xvii–xxv and footnotes13 & 19, p. 220.
See also Smith *op. cit.*, p. 407.
Andrew Higgins. (2009, January 24). How Israel Helped Spawn Hamas, *Wall Street Journal*, retrieved from http://www.reuters.com/article/2011/03/12/us-palestinians-israel-violence-idUSTRE72B0B920110312 http://online.wsj.com/news/articles/SB123275572295011847?mg=reno64-wsj&url=http%3A%2F%2Fonline.wsj.com%2Fart icle%2FSB123275572295011847.html

[50] Efraim Benmelecha and Claude Berrebi. (2007). Human Capital and the Productivity of Suicide Bombers, *Journal of Economic Perspectives* 21(3): 223–238. Retrieved from http://www.kellogg.northwestern.edu/faculty/benmelech/html/BenmelechPapers/Human_Capital_Suicide_Bombers.pdf

[51] *Ibid.*

[52] Moshe Arens. (2008, October 28). The fence, revisited: Do our politicians have the courage to admit they made a mistake by building the security barrier? *Ha'aretz*, retrieved from http://www.haaretz.com/print-edition/opinion/the-fence-revisited-1.256157

[53] Amos Harel. (2006, January 2). Palestinian truce main cause for reduced terror, *Ha'aretz*, retrieved from http://www.haaretz.com/print-edition/news/shin-bet-palestinian-truce-main-cause-for-reduced-terror-1.61607

[54] Ben White. (2014, January 10). Did Israeli Apartheid wall really stop suicide bombings? *Electronic Intifada*, retrieved from http://electronicintifada.net/blogs/ben-white/did-israeli-apartheid-wall-really-stop-suicide-bombings

[55] *B'Tselem*: The Israeli Information Center for Human Rights in the Occupied Territories. (2011, January 1). The Separation Barrier, retrieved from http://www.btselem.org/separation_barrier

[56] The 680 km length of the projected wall, when completed comes from the Israeli army. The 709 km projected length is from B'Tselem. *Ibid.*
Haggai Matar. (2012, April 9). The Wall, 10 years on: The Great Israeli Project, *972 Magazine*, retrieved from http://972mag.com/the-wall-10-years-on-the-great-israeli-project/40683/

[57] *B'Tselem. The Separation Barrier, loc. cit.*

[58] *Ibid.*

[59] *Ibid.*

[60] The International Court of Justice. (2004, July 9). Legal Consequences of the Construction of a Wall in the Occupied Palestinian Territory: Advisory Opinion, retrieved from http://www.icj-cij.org/files/case-related/131/131-20040709-ADV-01-00-EN.pdf

[61] *B'Tselem,* "The Separation Barrier," *loc. cit.*

[62] Smith, *op. cit.*, p. 498.

[63] *Ibid.* pp. 498–504.

[64] *Ibid.*

[65] Smith, *Ibid.* pp. 511–514.

[66] Jewish Settlers Receive Hundreds of Thousands in Compensation for Leaving Gaza While Palestinians Working for them get Nothing (2005, August 16). *Democracy Now*, retrieved from http://www.democracynow.org/2005/8/16/jewish_settlers_receive_hundreds_of_thousands

[67] *Ibid.*

[68] *Gisha* – Legal Center for Freedom of Movement. (2010, July 7). Unraveling the closure of Gaza, retrieved from http://gisha.org/UserFiles/File/publications/UnravelingTheClosureEng.pdf

[69] *Gisha* – Legal Center for Freedom of Movement. (2009, September 21). Teaching Gaza a lesson, retrieved from http://gisha.org/en-blog/2009/09/21/teaching-gaza-a-lesson/

[70] Smith, *op. cit.*, p. 512.

[71] *Ibid.* p. 513.

[72] Mark Tessler, *op. cit.*, p. 484.

[73] *Ibid.*

[74] Smith, *op. cit.*, p. 355.

[75] The Israeli Ministry of Foreign Affairs. (n.d.) *The Fruits of Peace*, retrieved from http://www.mfa.gov.il/mfa/foreignpolicy/peace/guide/pages/the%20fruits%20of%20peace.aspx

[76] Smith, *op. cit.*, pp. 438–442.

[77] Joel Beinin. (1999, March 26). The Demise of the Oslo Process, *The Middle East Report*, retrieved from http://web.archive.org/web/20000816222849/, http://www.merip.org/pins/pin1.html

[78] Smith, *op. cit.* p. 452.

[79] *Ibid.* pp. 438–442.

[80] Gideon Levy. (2010, July 15). Tricky Bibi, *Ha'aretz*, retrieved from http://www.haaretz.com/print-edition/opinion/tricky-bibi-1.302053

[81] Aaron David Miller (2005, May 23). Israel's Lawyer, *The Washington Post*, retrieved from http://www.washingtonpost.com/wp-dyn/content/article/2005/05/22/AR2005052200883.html

[82] Saleh Abdel Jawad, "Secret Weaknesses," *Media Monitors Network*, April 16, 2001, retrieved from http://www.mediamonitors.net/jawad2.html

[83] Personal communication from Diana Buttu.

[84] Gelvin, *op. cit.* p. 233.

[85] *Ibid.* p. 234.

[86] Smith, *op. cit.*, pp. 465–466.

[87] *Ibid.* pp. 487–496.

[88] Meeting with President Clinton, White House, 23/12/2000, *The Palestine Papers,* retrieved from http://transparency.aljazeera.net/files/48.PDF

[89] Text: The Beirut Declaration (2002, March 28). *BBC News*, retrieved from http://news.bbc.co.uk/2/hi/world/monitoring/media_reports/1899395.stm

[90] Full text of Netanyahu's speech at Bar-Ilan (2013, October 7). *The Times of Israel*, retrieved from http://www.timesofisrael.com/full-text-of-netanyahus-speech-at-bar-ilan/

[91] Henry Siegman. (2014, September 1). A Slaughter of Innocents, *Democracy Now* interview, retrieved from http://www.democracynow.org/2014/9/1/a_slaughter_of_innocents_henry_siegman

[92] Carlos Stegner. (2008, December 30). What victimology does not account for, *The Guardian*, retrieved from http://www.theguardian.com/commentisfree/2008/dec/30/gaza-hamas-palestinians-israel

[93] Edward Said. (2004). *From Oslo to Iraq and the Road Map: Essays* (New York: Pantheon) pp. 29–30, quoted in Gelvin, *op. cit.* p. 203.

[94] Palestinian Civil Society Call for BDS, retrieved from http://www.bdsmovement.net/call

[95] http://pacbi.org/einside.php?id=69

[96] Guillermo Galdos. (2014, July 31). Gaza war prompts Latin Americans to break ties with Israel, *Channel 4 News*, retrieved from http://www.channel4.com/news/gaza-strip-latin-america-israel-diplomatic-brazil-argentina

[97] UK government to block arms export to Israel if military action resumes (2014, August 12). *The Guardian*, retrieved from http://www.theguardian.com/politics/2014/aug/12/british-arms-exports-israel-gaza-block-suspension?CMP=EMCNEWEML6619I2

[98] Dr. Michael Kearney discusses the structural impediments to having the International Court of Justice and especially the International Criminal Court hear cases brought by Palestine against Israel. The norm, in these courts, is to focus allegations of misconduct by individuals and their procedures are not well adapted to evaluating the behavior or individuals in service to an entire system of oppression. (2014, August 20). What Would Happen if Palestine jointed the International Criminal Court, *Electronic Intifada*, retrieved from http://electronicintifada.net/content/what-would-happen-if-palestine-joined-international-criminal-court/13783

[99] Palestinian Elections: Trip Report by Former U.S. President Jimmy Carter, The Carter Center, January 30, 2006, retrieved from http://www.cartercenter.org/news/documents/doc2287.html

[100] EU Presidency Statement on Palestinian Legislative Council elections, EU delegation at the United Nations, January 26, 2006, retrieved from http://www.eu-un.europa.eu/articles/fr/article_5626_fr.htm

[101] Edward Said. (1999, January 10). The One State Solution, *New York Times*, retrieved from http://www.nytimes.com/1999/01/10/magazine/the-one-state-solution.html

[102] Tony Judt. (2003, October 23). Israel: the alternative, *New York Review of Books*, retrieved from http://www.nybooks.com/articles/archives/2003/oct/23/israel-the-alternative/

[103] The One State Declaration (2007, November 29). *Electronic Intifada*, retrieved from http://electronicintifada.net/content/one-state-declaration/793

[104] Waging Peace: Boston Conference on One-State Settlement Draws Large Crowd (2009, November) *Washington Report on Middle East Affairs*, retrieved from http://www.wrmea.org/wrmea-archives/220-washington-report-archives-2006-2010/july-2009/waging-peace-boston-conference-on-one-state-settlement-draws-large-crowd.html

[105] Israel/Palestine: Mapping Models of Statehood and Paths of Peace. (2009, June). York University, retrieved from http://www.yorku.ca/ipconf/speakers.html

[106] Harvard Kennedy School (2012, March) Israel/Palestine and the One State Solution, retrieved from http://www.onestateconference.com/

[107] Israeli Central Bureau of Statistics, Statistical Abstract of Israel: Comprehensive Settlement Population, 1972–2010, quoted by the Foundation for Middle East Peace, retrieved from http://www.fmep.org/resource/comprehensive-settlement-population-1972–2010

[108] Sir Arthur Conan Doyle. (2001) *The Sign of the Four* (London: Penguin Classics), p. 111.

[109] Noam Sheizaf. (2012, March 25). One or Two States? The Status Quo is Israel's Rational Choice, *+972 Magazine*, retrieved from http://972mag.com/one-or-two-states-the-status-quo-is-israels-rational-third-choice/39169/

For a similar argument about Palestinian attachment to the status quo, see Gadi Taub. (2017, October 19). The Israeli Peace Camps Algorithms, *Ha'aretz*, retrieved from https://www.haaretz.com/opinion/.premium-1.818260

[110] *Ibid.*

[111] General Assembly votes overwhelmingly to accord Palestine "non-Member Observer State" Status in United Nations, November 29, 2012, retrieved from http://www.un.org/News/Press/docs/2012/ga11317.doc.htm

[112] *Ibid.*

[113] US loses UNESCO voting rights after stopping funds over Palestine decision (2013, November 8). *The Guardian*, retrieved from http://www.theguardian.com/world/2013/nov/08/us-unesco-voting-funds-palestine-decision

[114] PA to sign Rome Statute of the ICC (2014, July 13), retrieved from *The Times of Israel*, http://www.timesofisrael.com/pa-to-sign-rome-statute-of-international-criminal-court/

[115] Activist boats reach Gaza Strip (2008, August 23). *BBC News*, retrieved from http://news.bbc.co.uk/2/hi/middle_east/7578880.stm

[116] Gaza activists boat docks (2009, October 28). JTA: *The Global Jewish News Source*, retrieved from http://www.jta.org/2008/10/28/news-opinion/gaza-activist-boat-docks

[117] Deaths as Israeli forces storm Gaza aid ships. (2010, May 31). *BBC News*, retrieved from http://www.bbc.co.uk/news/10195838

[118] Turkey to Send Another Freedom Flotilla to Gaza (2014, July 26). *Middle East Monitor*, retrieved from https://www.middleeastmonitor.com/news/europe/13059-turkey-to-send-another-freedom-flotilla-to-gaza

[119] Turkish Prime Minister Erdogan has pledged a Turkish naval escort to the Gaza Flotilla. A private translation of this statement in Turkish reads: "As of now it is doubtless that our first degree battleships will be charged with the protection of our own ships. This is the primary step. There are people there whom we are going to help. And from now own this humanitarian aid will not be interfered with by any foul play like the Mavi Marmara was."

[120] Eve Spangler. (2011, October 11). The "Generous" Offer. *Counterpunch*, retrieved from https://www.counterpunch.org/2011/10/11/the-story-of-the-generous-offer/ http://www.aljazeera.com.tr/haber/erdogan-savas-gemileri-koruyacak

PART 3

MOVING FORWARD

CHAPTER 9

FOUR FRAMES

Israeli Self-Defense, Genocide, Apartheid, Settler Colonialism: Ethnic Cleansing/Sociocide

Rashomon .... Its very name has entered the common parlance to symbolize general notions about the relativity of truth and the unreliability, the inevitable subjectivity of memory.

Stephen Prince[1]

As I said in Chapter 3, the world cannot be learned one fact at a time; facts only make sense within particular frameworks. In the preceding history chapters, I created a relatively streamlined three-part model for understanding the vexed history of Palestine/Israel. I argued that the conflict is best understood as the interactions among Zionists, great powers, and Palestinians, each with a constant purpose (for the Zionists to "Judaize" the land, for great powers to extract some advantage from their involvement, for Palestinians to have the freedom to build their own society), acting under ever-changing circumstances and with tragic results for all.

Thus we saw that the Zionists were organizational geniuses in getting their project under way before the creation of the state of Israel but, after its creation, were not able to or did not choose to achieve a definitive peace with the Palestinians. Similarly, we have seen great power interests continuing to play a role, even as their preferred benefits shift from acquiring colonies to securing other strategic opportunities – e.g. trade routes, air and naval bases, and opportunities to test new weapons[2] – which, in turn, generate renewed international contestation and resistance. And we have seen Palestinians steadfastly seeking self-determination, also by a variety of means none of which have proven satisfactory. Petitions, general strikes, armed struggle, solidarity with Pan-Arab aspirations, reliance on a leadership in exile, reliance on local leaders, founding and encouraging a global boycott movement, and consideration of a renewed, religiously grounded Pan Arabism in the form of political Islam – none of these approaches have yet accomplished Palestinian goals.

Although this framework proves useful to organize the historical narrative and understand its unfolding dynamics, it is descriptive, not analytic or evaluative. It does not give us a clear basis for action should we want to be involved in the struggle for justice in this conflict.

For example, Israelis would argue that the entire history is really one of Jewish self-defense, required by local and global anti-Semitism. This "Jewish self-defense model" not only makes sense of the on-going Israeli actions in their own eyes but also justifies and celebrates them. "Jewish self-defense" is, of course, not the only evaluative framework, though it is the one most often heard.

In this chapter, I will review four evaluative frameworks, all in use in our public discourse: Israeli self-defense, genocide, Apartheid, and settler colonialism, including ethnic cleansing/sociocide. Each one is challenging to discuss because each implies heroes, villains, and solutions, and each leads us to a different set of actions on behalf of justice.

Of course none of these evaluative frameworks are wholly true or wholly false. All of them provide some insight and all are open to legitimate criticism. Nevertheless, I will argue at the end of the chapter, that the settler colonialism/ethnic cleansing/sociocide framework is more useful than others for understanding the conflict and acting to bring it to a just resolution.

ISRAELI SELF-DEFENSE

[It is the] iron law of every colonizing movement, a law which knows of no exceptions, a law which existed in all times and under all circumstances. If you wish to colonize land in which people are already living, you must provide a garrison on your behalf ... Zionism is a colonizing adventure and therefore it stands or falls by the question of armed force.

Vladimir Ze'ev Jabotinsky[3]

[L]et us not ignore the truth among ourselves ... politically we are the aggressors and they defend themselves.

David Ben Gurion[4]

What cause have we to complain about their fierce hatred to us? For eight years now, they sit in their refugee camps in Gaza, and before their eyes we turn into our homestead the land and villages in which they and their forefathers have lived.

Moshe Dayan[5]

Kathleen's Story

At a New Year's Eve party in Bethlehem, one of my students suddenly fell ill, complaining of unendurable abdominal pain. Our tour guide achieved miracles in getting through the New Year's Eve crowd in Manger Square, and delivered us in record time to a Palestinian clinic. There, within 10 minutes, Kathleen had an ultrasound, a pelvic exam, and lab tests. The diagnosis was unambiguously clear: an ovarian cyst that should be removed immediately lest it cut off the blood supply to the ovary and thereby kill it. The Palestinian doctor recommended laparoscopic surgery and advised us to go to Hadassah Hospital in Jerusalem, some five miles away. He explained that going by ambulance would be too time-consuming, because we would have to wait for an Israeli ambulance to meet the Palestinian ambulance at the border checkpoint. We were told to take a yellow-plate taxi with a license plate that could enter Israel directly. As we sped off towards the border, I worried about delays, knowing that many Palestinians had died waiting at checkpoints. But we were in luck. Even though Israel claims that the Separation Wall (85% of which intrudes on Palestinian land) is absolutely necessary for its security, on this New Year's Eve, the checkpoint was wide open and completely unmanned. We sped through with barely a tap on the brakes. Kathleen, I am happy to report, had successful surgery on New Year's Day has recovered completely. The claims of "national security" seem overused, in Israel as in America.

In considering the validity of the Israeli self-defense framework, it is useful to distinguish between the challenges Israel faces in common with all other nations from those that are unique to the Israeli-Palestinian conflict. Virtually all nations face challenges at many levels: global, regional, bi-lateral, and domestic. Israel is not exempt from these difficulties.

At the global level, all nations face fallout from environmental degradation – whether it is rising sea levels that threaten their coastal cities or island enclaves, or the depletion of natural resources that constituted their niche in international trade, or the health effects of holes in the ozone layer, every nation bears some costs and consequences from changes in the environmental health of the planet. Moreover, every country has to contend with the emergence of global forms of governance such as the World Trade

233

Organization, that is neither democratically elected nor accountable to any public good, but which nevertheless has the power to gut environmental regulations and treaties, to impose austerity programs on weak countries, and to establish international trade regulations.

At the regional level, most countries face ongoing struggles fueled by the eternal jockeying for preeminence of neighboring states. In the case of Israel, Turkey, Egypt, Iran, and Saudi Arabia each aspires to become the regional star, whether to recoup past Ottoman or Pharaonic glory or to establish dominance for the first time. As is often the case, regional power struggles also fuel arms races, and this is especially true because Israel's (alleged) nuclear arsenal is particularly ominous for its neighbors.

At the bilateral level, all countries face challenges not only with their immediate front-line neighbors but with countries around the world that send or receive vital resources, provide critical markets, or are sources of immigrant labor. In Israel, these generic bilateral challenges cannot be wholly separated from the Occupation. For example, Israel's need for migrant labor arises largely from the their decision to exclude Palestinian workers from the Israeli labor market. The Boycott, Sanctions, Divestment (BDS) movement (discussed at greater length below) is shaping Israel's access to credit, markets, and supplies of workers. Nevertheless, even were the Palestinian-Israeli conflict to be happily resolved, Israel would still face its own version of the bilateral tensions that every nation encounters.

Similarly, at the domestic level, Israel's difficulties are partly generic and partly a product of Occupation. Virtually every country faces tensions rooted in class differences, ethnic enmities, gender politics, internal regional competition, and political differences rooted in the conflict between social safety net and neoliberal economic policies. Israel is no exception. But again, the costs of the Occupation permeate even routine domestic problems. For example, Israel's commitment to settlement construction is deeply implicated in their domestic housing shortage.[6]

And, as if all of these generic challenges were not enough, Israel also faces unique difficulties associated with the Occupation. In the first chapter I argued that, over time, historians of the Israeli-Palestinian conflict have come to agree more and more on a common set of facts – the reality of the *Nakba,* at least as an historic event. The disputes among them now are about the implications of those facts, for example whether we should understand current expulsions of Palestinians as a continuation of the *Nakba*.

Similarly, the issue raised by the "Israeli self-defense" framework is less about facts: Palestine does face colonization and dismemberment, and

Israel, in turn, does face real problems and costs associated with Palestinian resistance. The debate now is how to understand Israel's difficulties: whether as self-inflicted, chosen suffering in service to Zionist ambitions, or as the result of senseless, atavistic anti-Semitism on the part of Palestinians that requires Israel to conduct itself as a garrison state.

Almost always this argument gains its emotional credibility from an invocation of the Holocaust: the Jews of Europe were once faced with total annihilation and this becomes the filter through which all other challenges are perceived. Ephraim Sneh, a former government minister (and, as is so often the case with the older generation of Israelis, also a former military officer), expresses this stance in its purest form: during a *Ha'aretz* interview with Ari Shavit, he points to a photograph on his office wall:

> This is an Israeli F-15 flying above ... Auschwitz ... To me, this is it in a nutshell: If there's an F-15, there's no Auschwitz. If there's no F-15, there could be an Auschwitz ... My grandfather and grandmother were murdered by the Polish peasant with whom they were hiding. That taught me that we have no one to rely upon but ourselves ...
>
> And when I again see a connection between an extreme ideology and absolute military power, I say wait a minute, this reminds me of something. This is something that already wiped out a third of the Jewish people. And when I see a combination of zealous hatred of Israel with unlimited destructive capability, I say: Friends, this is another thing I'm familiar with. This is something that once killed six million Jews ...
>
> The mental chasm between us and the Iranians is much deeper than people are ready to grasp. We sanctify life, while Shi'ism sanctifies death ...
>
> [A] nuclear Iran will cause Israel to wither. On the domestic side, an Iranian nuclear bomb will lead to three things: *aliyah* to Israel will stop, investment in Israel will plummet and the brain drain from Israel will accelerate.[7]

This statement, with its mixture of Holocaust memory (used or misused), profound racism, and practical concerns perfectly captures much of the Israeli discourse. For those who want to see this discourse in action, Yoav Shamir's film, *Defamation*, captures a similar incident: on a school sponsored trip to a concentration camp, group leaders drag three young Israeli girls away from three elderly Polish men with whom they are exchanging names. The group leader warns the girls "They're trying to kill you."[8]

There are some, like the former Knesset speaker Avraham Burg, who challenge the highly manipulative use of Holocaust memory[9] that is common in Israel and among its Zionist supporters. But even if their point is granted, and the emotional quality of the rhetoric allowed to cool, most Israelis would still agree that they live, as they so often say, "in a very tough neighborhood."

Such assessments often ignore or downplay the ways in which Israel's own behavior contributes to its difficulties. In general, the earlier Zionists were more candid about the fact that they were the aggressors, as the epigrams from Jabotinksy, Ben Gurion, and Dayan indicate. But even if every Israeli faced and took responsibility for the aggression revealed in the epigrams, they could still argue that their country faces real enmity and threats. Whether or not that enmity is righteous, it is certainly dangerous.

And, as with generic challenges, the dangers exist at every level: global, regional, bi-lateral, domestic, and within the Occupied Palestinian Territories (OPT). The following list is more illustrative than exhaustive, but it provides many examples of the real world issues that ground what Ari Shavit describes as Israel's perpetual existential fear.[10]

At the global level, Israel has become a target for a growing boycott, sanctions, and divestment movement. Moreover, the increased success of the boycott movement is echoed in the workings of global governance entities like the European Union and the United Nations. In 2012 Palestine's status within the United Nations was up-graded from "observer entity" to "observer state" by an overwhelming majority of the General Assembly.[11] This upgrade provides Palestinians with opportunities to use United Nations adjudicatory and service bodies – The International Court of Justice, the International Labor Organization, UNESCO – to pursue their interests. Similarly, the European Union has taken note of the Palestinian plight – labeling of settlement products looms on the horizon. And, in a parallel move, the United Nations Human Rights Council, while stopping short of a call for a full boycott of settlement businesses, passed a resolution advising member states to notify their citizens of the potential legal, financial, and reputational risks of doing business in the Occupied Territories.[12]

If the global political and economic scene is growing more critical of Israel, the regional situation is much worse.

Over its 70 years of existence, Israel has been involved in at least five major military confrontations: the 1947–1949 War of Independence (known as the *Nakba* to Palestinians), the humiliating and short-lived 1956 invasion of Egypt over the Suez Canal, the 1967 war in which Israel took complete control over the entirety of Mandate Palestine, the 1973 Yom Kippur war that

Israel also won, but at a much higher cost than they were prepared to pay, and lastly the 1982 invasion and occupation of Southern Lebanon that ended only in 2000. In addition, there has been a brief "incursion" into Lebanon in 2006 in addition to four rounds of "operations" against the Palestinians: Operation Defensive Shield (2002), Operation Cast Lead (2008–2009), Operation Pillar of Defense (2012) and Operation Protective Edge (2014). All of these actions fuel a rising tide of popular criticism of Israeli militarism.

Moreover, Israel has chosen not only to reject but to ignore the Arab Peace Initiative of 2002 which offered full normalization of relationships with all Arab states in return for creating a Palestinian state, as international law requires, on the Green Line (with mutually accepted land swaps). Defenders of Israel argue that the Arab Peace Initiative, coming as it did on the heels of 9/11, is no more than a publicity stunt. If so, what better way to unmask the "stunt" than to accept its terms. Israel chose to hold on to, indeed to continually expand, its settlements in preference to the comprehensive regional peace it has always said it wanted.[13]

In addition to actual wars, hostility to Israel is omnipresent in virtually all countries in the region– it is a cheap way for corrupt Arab and Muslim leaders to deflect attention from local domestic difficulties and rally the country – but at the cost of increasing the likelihood of war. Finally, the Arab Spring, with its cascade of revolutions and political upheavals, the tragedy of the civil war in Syria, the perpetually teetering political compromises in Lebanon, and the inundation of Jordan with Palestinian, Iraqi and, now, Syrian refugees, further increases the uncertainties and instabilities of the entire region.

Israel's bi-lateral relations are hardly in better shape. The growing BDS movement is affecting bi-lateral relations outside the area. For example, Romania has recently announced that it will no longer supply construction workers to the settlements.[14] And even in the United States, generally the source of uncritical financial, military, and diplomatic support for Israel, at least one high-ranking general dared to suggest that Israel is a military liability rather than an asset.[15]

Domestically, the divide between Israeli Jews and Palestinian citizens of Israel erodes the credibility of Israel's claim to be "the only democracy in the Middle East." In Chapter 6 I described the ways in which Israeli law mandates direct and indirect discrimination against its own Palestinian citizens, as well as creating vast administrative latitude in the executive branch to enact such discrimination. Of late, such restrictions are escalating, making it harder for Palestinian political parties to gain seats in the *Knesset*, affirming the rights of communities to exclude Palestinian citizens of Israel from their ranks, and creating arbitrary distinctions between Israel's Christian Palestinian citizens and their Muslim Palestinian counterparts.[16] Nor are the Palestinian citizens of Israel the only targets for repression. Increasingly, those Israeli Jews who object to the Occupation also are also subject to legal and financial harassment,[17] job discrimination, and even incarceration.[18]

And, finally, of course, Israel faces on-going dangers in the Occupied Palestinian Territories. There is no nice or safe way to occupy more than 4 million people who do not wish to be occupied. Occupation inherently requires violence, capriciousness, and cruelty, at least threatened if not overt.[19] Violence, in turn, generates resistance, which is why national liberation struggles in the post WWII period have often been able to defeat the superior military forces of the colonial power.

Sometimes anti-colonial resistance takes admirable forms – in the case of Palestine, the pursuit of the U.N. option by the Palestinian Authority, the insistence on non-violence within the BDS movement, the immensely courageous demonstrations against the Wall in Budrus, Bili'in and Ni'ilin, in Nabi Saleh, against settler appropriation of the village spring, and in the Great March of Return against the on-going siege imposed on Gaza.

Other times, the resistance is expressed in less admirable ways with incitement to violence,[20] or actual violence. Most Israelis are aware of stories like the one about a family stabbed to death in their beds in the settlement of Itamar in the West Bank,[21] or the lynching of two Israeli reservists who strayed into Ramallah during the second Intifada.[22] Of course the perpetrators of these horrible crimes must be held individually accountable for the choices they made, but a complete version of the story should also place the violence in context – for example, in the weeks before the lynching, 100 Palestinians in Ramallah, probably a quarter of them children, had been killed by Israelis, and the two soldiers, wearing civilian clothes, were thought to be undercover agents.[23]

In some cases, the violence Israel faces in its quest to pacify the Occupied Territories is not only a reaction to its conduct, but actually of its own making. The *Wall Street Journal* reports that, for decades, the Israelis actually turned a blind eye to the development of Hamas, hoping to use it as a counterweight to the then popular secular PLO.[24] This is less perverse than it sounds: "the enemy of my enemy is my friend," is an old adage. Many countries, including the United States, fund a variety of unsavory individuals and militias as long as they claim to be the enemies of our enemies. In the case of the US, this led us into ties with Saddam Hussein, the mujahedeen in Afghanistan, Manuel

238

Noriega in Panama, and Somoza in Nicaragua. In the Israeli case, it appears that despite warnings, even from other Gazan imams, the Israelis let Hamas get entrenched before acknowledging the danger they represent.[25]

Similarly, the expanding settlements, especially the hilltop outposts of trailer camps, deliberately put Israeli settlers in harm's way, despite the speed with which the Israeli government provides military guards, power lines, and water to the outposts. The point here is that individuals, with the Israeli state standing behind them, are more than willing to take these risks. Yet the conversation about Israel's safety never reflects that fact.

Nor do we generally recognize that even when settlers are at risk, their Palestinian neighbors are vastly more at risk, both from settler violence and from the Israeli military.[26] A cursory glance at statistics compiled by B'Tselem tells the story: during "peace time" (i.e. from the end of Operation Cast Lead in January, 2009 to the beginning of Occupation Protective Edge in July, 2014), Israeli armed forces and civilians killed 562 Palestinians and Palestinians, in turn, killed 37 Israelis.[27] This is a 15:1 ratio of deaths between Palestinians and Israelis. During the most recent Israeli operation in Gaza, preliminary statistics compiled by B'Tselem indicate 2,168 Palestinians killed versus 72 Israelis killed, making the ratio of deaths 30+:1.[28]

The issue here is not to deny that Israel faces real difficulties – bear in mind, even self-inflicted difficulties are nonetheless real and painful. Rather, the issue is to ask how Israel understands these difficulties. The answer seems to be that Israel sees itself as a perpetual victim; perpetually entitled to sympathy, perpetually to be given a free pass for anything it does to Palestinians. This has never been a good choice and, over time, it becomes daily less credible.

Consider the story I heard from an Israeli graduate student at Harvard. Her research focused on Israeli-Palestinian tensions and, as with many graduate students, her dissertation was grounded in her own autobiography. Her parents were North African Jews who migrated to Israel sometime after 1948. In Israel, her family flourished, her father becoming a respected neurologist. The family acquired an oceanfront apartment in Northern Israel with two walls of windows facing the beach. My student and her sister spent many happy hours playing and building sand castles within their mother's line of sight. On a rainy day, the children were standing at the windows with their father when they saw a rubber dinghy, rowed by several people, pull up on the beach. The passengers jumped out, pulled ski masks down over their faces, lifted machine guns out of the boat, and proceeded up the beach. The horror seemed surreal to both girls and their father. But then, from the

239

other beach-facing windows they saw a heavily pregnant woman strolling along, about to turn into the path of the masked gunmen. Before the children even fully understood what was happening, their father had raced down the stairs, grabbed the pregnant woman, and, shielding her with his body, shoved her into a stairwell and out of harm's way. The father however, was gunned down and killed by the masked men on the beach. His daughters, seven and nine at the time, witnessed the whole tragic episode. Today one of them is dedicated to hatred and vengeance and the other is a member of the Israeli peace movement.

In the face of real tragedy and unspeakable harm, they have each made their choices.

GENOCIDE

It would be my greatest sadness to see Zionists (Jews) do to Palestinian Arabs much of what Nazis did to Jews.

Albert Einstein[29]

Everybody is somebody's Jew. And today the Palestinians are the Jews of the Israelis.

Primo Levi[30]

Now we too have behaved like the Nazis and my whole being is shaken.

Aharon Cizling[31]

Ulrich's Story

In June of 1938, my cousin Ulrich was walking in a Jewish neighborhood in Nazi-occupied Vienna with two friends. The young men were on their way to pick up three young ladies to go to a concert. Ulrich, always a natty dresser, was wearing a white suit, a polka dot bow tie, and a straw boater. Suddenly SS troops and vehicles appeared at both ends of the street. Pedestrians were ordered to stand against the wall. Their papers were checked, and every third man was ordered into the police vans at the end of the block. Ulrich was one of those men. Luckily his companions knew what had happened to him and rushed to tell his family. Ulrich was sent to Dachau concentration camp without being charged, tried, or convicted for any offense. Because his father knew what had happened to him, the Nazis received daily appeals asserting that Ulrich had been mistakenly arrested, had done nothing to resist the Nazi regime (which, in fact, was true), was a harmless lad, etc. etc.

Later that year, in November 1938 the Nazis staged the massive pogrom known as *Kristalnacht* (the night of broken glass) across the realm of the Third Reich. Allies remonstrated with Hitler, and, as a gesture of good will, Hitler, in turn, released a handful of Jews held in concentration camps. Ulrich was one of them, chosen, perhaps, because his file was so thick with letters of appeal and protest.

On the day of his release, Ulrich's name was announced over the Dachau loudspeaker. He was convinced that his walk to the commandant's office was the first step on the road to death. Imagine his surprise when he was not only told he was being released, but was handed back his white suit, his bow tie, straw hat, and exactly the number of coins that had been in his jacket pocket. The Nazis had starved and beaten him into a state of complete shock and disorientation, but they were able to account for every dime of his property and return it to him because their laws required such punctilious record keeping.

Some advocates of the Palestinian cause goes so far as to accuse Israelis of genocide in their treatment of Palestinians. Usually their examples focus on Gaza[32]: massacres like Operation Cast Lead (with some 1,400 Gazans and 13 Israelis dead, and the use of illegal white phosphorus)[33] and Operation Protective Edge (with its 2,165 Gazan and 72 Israeli dead, and the extensive bombing of schools, hospitals, and U.N. facilities)[34] make their case. Ronnie Kasrils, a veteran of the South African anti-Apartheid struggle, compares Cast Lead to other well-known massacres (Guernica, Lidice, the Warsaw Ghetto, Deir Yassin, Mai Lai, Sabra and Shatilla, Sharpeville) some of which occurred in the context of the Nazi genocide.[35] More recently, a U.N. Report warns that if the conditions of the Israeli Occupation continue, Gaza will be uninhabitable for humans by 2020.[36] Bishop Naim Ateek of the Palestinian Episcopalian NGO, Sabeel, modifies the genocide argument slightly, calling the Israeli treatment of Gaza a "slow genocide, "[37] while Israeli historian Ilan Pappe describes it as "incremental genocide."[38]

Sometimes, the comparison of Israel and Nazi Germany rests on images. For example, Israeli historian Benny Morris notes that just two years after the concentration camps were liberated, pre-state Jewish militias besieging the town of Beisan (Bet She'an) required some Arabs to don yellow armbands, and to mark Arab stores with yellow decals, targeting them for looting by paramilitary forces.[39] The notion that Jews, for whom the Nazi-ordained yellow Star of David is the symbol of evil, should require the people they conquer to wear yellow insignia is enough to turn one's stomach. But the comparison with genocide is nevertheless more sentimental than real. Supposing, instead of requiring yellow armbands and tags, the militias had identified Palestinian individuals and shops with green armbands and tags, green being the symbolic color of Islam. That would also be horrific, but green insignia would be unlikely to elicit the charge of genocide.

Another Israeli commentator modifies the genocide comparison further, making the charge of Nazism prospective rather than retrospective. Uri Misgav writes: "Of course, at this stage, they [the group he calls the Judeo-Nazis] are on the margins. But history has proven that the question is how the center responds to the margins ... Israel will never be the Germany of 1942, but there is a moral obligation to prevent it from becoming like the Germany of 1932."[40]

On the other hand, the simplest and most fundamental criticism of the genocide analogy is that it is wrong and, because it is so overblown, in fact quite disrespectful to all the victims of the Holocaust, Jews and non-Jews alike.

The historical record supports the argument that Zionism requires *absent* Palestinians. Killing them – wrongfully, recklessly, and disproportionately – is certainly one way of getting them to be absent. But there really is no support for the notion that Zionism requires *dead* Palestinians in the same way that Nazism required dead Jews, dead Roma, dead gays.

Hard as it is to see the shocking photos of bombed out schools and hospitals in Gaza, the truth is that Israel had the firepower to kill ten times, a hundred times, more Gazans than it actually did over the years. Had killing been Israel's *only* objective, many more Palestinian casualties could have been produced. The accusation of genocide seems like needless over-reaching.

It is also worth noting that the very definition of genocide is clumsy and difficult to apply, except in retrospect. The definition is embedded in the 1948 (i.e. post-Holocaust) *Convention on the Prevention and Punishment of Genocide*.[41] To make the determination of genocide requires both a mental, intentional element as well as a physical element of extreme violence. The mental element is described as the "intent to destroy in whole or in part a national, ethnical, racial or religious group as such."[42] The physical element has five components: killing members of the targeted group, causing them serious bodily and mental harm, deliberately inflicting upon the group conditions of life calculated to bring about its physical destruction in whole or in part, imposing measures to prevent births within the group or forcibly transferring children of the group to others. The acts alone are not enough. They must be committed as part of an overall plan or project intending genocide.

The problem in applying this definition is that even political leaders with genocidal intentions hardly ever announce their programs in clear terms; the "final solution" crafted by Hitler and his associates at the Wannsee Conference came as close as possible but still used elliptical terminology.[43] Instead of explicit pronouncements, a culture of violence comes to pervade armies and militias, such that people understand the intent of their leaders without the orders to kill being put into words.[44]

Absent a clearly announced program of genocide, we can only infer its existence when the forbidden acts rise to the level of frequency and lethality that clearly imply genocidal intent. And even then, it might be possible to offer counterarguments: for example, torture, starvation, and psychological warfare could be in service to some other objective, not genocide. Ethnic cleansing, for example, would use many of the same techniques yet it would still remain distinguishable from genocide in its core intention to expel rather than to kill its victims.

These examples are not idly chosen; all of them pertain to the Palestinian-Israeli conflict:

- In March of 2018, Israeli army snipers shot unarmed Gazan demonstrators in the back during the on-going Friday demonstrations called the Great March of Return. Early on, an army spokesperson posted the following statement on twitter: "Yesterday we saw 30,000 people; we arrived prepared with precise reinforcements. Nothing was carried out uncontrolled, everything was accurate and measured, and we know where every bullet landed."[45]
- The Israeli documentary *The Law In These Parts* establishes the widespread practice of torturing political prisoners, often with the complicity of military judges.[46] When Palestinian community leaders organize programs to teach their neighbors how to resist torture associated with interrogation, their efforts are suppressed.[47]
- Dov Weissglass, a close associate of Prime Minister Ariel Sharon, boasted of creating food shortages in Gaza. He summed up the Israeli position: "The idea is to put the Palestinians on a diet, but not to make them die of hunger … The hunger pangs are supposed to encourage the

Palestinians to force Hamas to change its attitude towards Israel or force Hamas out of government."[48] Martin Kramer, speaking at the prestigious Herzliya Conference in 2010 provides intellectual grounding for "putting Palestinians on a diet." He argues: "The biggest radicalizer is fertility that hovers at 6 or 7 [children per family], and masses of economically superfluous young men of fighting age, between 15 and 29 ... Israel's present sanctions on Gaza have a political aim—undermine the Hamas regime—but if they also break Gaza's runaway population growth— and there is some evidence that they have—that might begin to crack the culture of martyrdom which demands a constant supply of superfluous young men."[49] Starvation, in short, is an acceptable instrument of governmental "peace keeping" policy.

• Similarly, psychological warfare is also in use everywhere within the Occupation. For example, Israel has announced that medical permits to leave the Occupied Territories will be granted preferentially to families willing to inform on their neighbors[50]; Israeli troops break into homes in the middle of the night and photograph children[51]; they erect arbitrary "flying checkpoints" to "show presence" across the West Bank at times that disrupt school schedules and workdays.[52]

Are all these practices, then, evidence of genocide? Certainly the Israelis argue against such a conclusion. They claim that shooting unarmed demonstrators in the back, including clearly marked medical personnel and journalists, is necessary self-defense. The torture of prisoners, they tell you, occurred during the Second Intifada and was thus also self-defense. The imposition of a blockade is designed to dislodge Hamas, whom the Israelis regard as a terrorist entity, from the government of Gaza. The psychological warfare is designed to keep Palestinians from "trying anything,"[53] since absolute pacification is the standard that Israelis try to impose on Palestinians. Horrible? Yes. Violations of human rights? Assuredly so. But genocide? Probably not.

In fact, the place that Israel most closely parallels Nazi Germany is not in a program of mass executions, but in its painstaking efforts to mask its suppression of Palestinians in the cloak of legality. The Knesset goes out of its way to give the imprimatur of legality to all sorts of behavior that the world should object to: housing discrimination against Israel's Palestinian citizens, arbitrary distinctions between Christian and Muslim Palestinians, legal barriers to Palestinian family unification, land and home ownership, etc. *Adalah* (an NGO that works on behalf of Palestinian citizens of Israel) lists 50 discriminatory laws against Palestinian Israelis already enacted and another 29 that are in the process of enactment.[54] Meanwhile, in the Occupied Territories, a possible annexation of the West Bank has begun with seemingly trivial incremental regulations: Ariel University, illegally situated in a settlement, is brought under the jurisdiction of the Israel Ministry of Education and, silly though it may sound, the efforts of chicken farmers in the settlements is brought under the jurisdiction of the Israeli Egg and Poultry Board.[55] These efforts, tiny incremental steps, are designed to extend Israeli sovereignty, as a matter of law, to the Occupied Territories, thereby entwining the illegal physical possession with (il)legal normalization.[56]

Given the disparity between Israeli and Palestinian military power, the question arises: why go to the trouble to enact such discriminatory or annexationist laws? Why not just let might make right? Here, I think, we have one of the distinguishing features of the Israeli Occupation – where other dictators around the world rule by brute force, the Israelis invest a lot of time legalizing, routinizing, bureaucratizing their domination. In this they follow both Nazi and Communist (i.e. totalitarian) precedent.[57]

APARTHEID

Questioned about Mandela's remarks, Arafat said: "We are in the same trench, struggling against the same enemies, against apartheid, racism, colonialism and neo-colonialism.

Yasser Arafat[58]

The Jews took Israel from the Arabs after the Arabs had lived there for a thousand years. Israel, like South Africa, is an apartheid state.

Hendrik Verwoerd[59]

I have witnessed the racially segregated roads and housing in the Holy Land that reminded me so much of the conditions we experienced in South Africa under apartheid ... I have witnessed the systematic humiliation of Palestinian men, women and children by members of the Israeli security forces. Their humiliation is familiar to all black South Africans who were corralled and harassed and insulted and assaulted by the security forces of the apartheid government.

Desmond Tutu[60]

Shula Aloni's Story, retold by John Dugard

The major difference I see between South Africa's apartheid system and what prevails in the Occupied Palestinian Territory is that the South African apartheid regime was more honest ... In the case of Israel, it is concealed. There's a lovely story told by Shulamit Aloni, a former minister of education in Israel, of an occasion in which she confronted a member of the IDF who was arresting a Palestinian for driving on a settler road and for confiscating [his identification] card. She said to him, "But how is he to know that this is a road for the exclusive use of settlers? There is no notice to that effect." And he said, "Of course Palestinians know or they should know." He said, "What do you want us to do? Do you want us to put up signs saying Palestinians only, settlers only and then everyone will say that we are an apartheid state like South Africa?"[61]

The Slap Heard 'round the World

Minutes before an Israeli military judge signed off on Ahed Tamimi's plea deal [8 months in military prison], something unexpected happened inside Israel's Ofer Military Court. A Jewish Israeli activist [Yifat Doron] rose from the back benches, approached the military prosecutor, slapped him across the face, and yelled, "who are you to judge her?" ... She was quickly arrested ... The judge [of a civilian court in Jerusalem] ... ordered Doron released [after two nights in jail]. Adding to the absurdity exposed by Doron's slap is that it took place inside the West Bank, where Israeli military law reigns supreme. If a Palestinian had simultaneously slapped the prosecutor's other cheek at the exact same moment as Doron, he or she would have been arrested by the military and brought to military court, where bail is a rarity and pre-trail detention the norm.[62]

In 2006 former U.S. President Jimmy Carter published a book entitled *Palestine, Peace not Apartheid,*[63] and was met with a firestorm of criticism from America's highly organized Zionist lobby. His arguments were actually quite mild, his criticism confined to Israel's treatment of Palestinians living under Occupation. He gave Israel's treatment of its own Palestinian citizens a nod of approval.

Less than a decade later, Apartheid has become the most commonly used framework for describing Israeli-Palestinian relations. In part this is because of the prominent role played by a number of South Africans who established their credibility in the struggle against Apartheid in their own country. The most prominent among them was, of course, Nelson Mandela who famously said "We know too well our freedom is incomplete without the freedom of the Palestinians."[64] In this sentiment he was joined by Nobel Laureate, Archbishop Desmond Tutu, who describes life in the Occupied Territories as "worse than Apartheid."[65] Additional South African luminaries like John Dugard, the United Nations Special Rapporteur for Palestine, Ronnie Kasrils, a white, Jewish member of the African National Congress, and Tony Karon, a Jewish South African ex-pat journalist, amplify the voices making that comparison. The Russell Tribunal, a grassroots social justice effort dedicated to preventing "the crime of silence,"[66] held no fewer than five hearings on the Israeli mistreatment of Palestine and opted for the Apartheid analogy as well.[67]

Despite the enormous controversy resulting from Secretary of State John Kerry's use of the term Apartheid, Israeli political leaders and journalists[68] of all stripes use it themselves – at least to describe the situation as it would be after the two-state solution is not only dead but also acknowledged to be so. Former Prime Ministers Olmert and Barak have warned against the emergence of an Apartheid reality should the fig leaf of a reversible Occupation be stripped away,[69] and even right wing politician Naftali Bennett uses the term – albeit disingenuously.[70]

The heart of the definition of apartheid is embedded in the very origin of the word, which means apartness or separation. Apartheid as a political system implies the arbitrary division of a population into an advantaged and an unfairly suppressed or disadvantaged group (or groups) who are not allowed to have the same package of human rights that the more powerful group keeps for itself. The separation, in turn, rests on concepts of race, once again showing the South African context of the text.

The Convention on the Suppression and Punishment of the Crime of Apartheid[71] defines apartheid as "similar policies and practices of racial segregation and discrimination as practiced in southern Africa which have the purpose of establishing and maintaining domination by one racial group of persons over any other racial group of persons and systematically oppressing them."[72] Recognizing (as was discussed in Chapter 3) that race is socially rather than biologically defined, the Apartheid Convention relies, in turn on the Convention on the Elimination of Racial Discrimination,[73] which describes racism as "any distinction, exclusion, restriction or preference based on race, color, descent, or national or ethnic origin which has the purpose or effect of nullifying or impairing the recognition, enjoyment or exercise, on an equal footing, of human rights and fundamental freedoms in the political, economic, social, cultural or any other field of public life."[74] The Conventions thus establish an expansive definition of racism that includes discrimination resting on ethnicity, national origin or, by further extension, religion. Such an inclusive definition of racism opens the door to transferring the Apartheid argument from South Africa to Palestine/Israel.

Moreover, at a descriptive level, the similarities between the two cases are certainly striking. John Dugard, a former United Nations Special Rapporteur for Palestine, describes three features of Apartheid: the misleadingly named "grand Apartheid" that refers to spatial, territorial separation of populations, the equally misleadingly named "petty Apartheid" that amounts to racial discrimination in all phases of everyday life in which the superior and suppressed groups continue to interact, and the security laws and practices whereby grand and petty Apartheid are enforced.

In Israel, in the Occupied Territories, and in the refugee camps in the region, as in South Africa, populations are divided into separate geographic areas: Israel west of the Green line, Gaza and the West Bank (including East Jerusalem), which, in turn, is subdivided into Areas A, B, and C. The areas available to the oppressed group are small compared to their proportion in the overall population, and of inferior quality – perhaps not intrinsically but certainly by being systematically underserved with water, roads, schools, hospitals, and social services. Just as indigenous South Africans were "de-nationalized" from South Africa and assigned "citizenship" in sterile Bantustans, Palestinian citizens of Israel are now threatened with loss of citizenship.[75] Palestinians in Gaza are living in an open-air prison that is an on-going public health calamity. Palestinians in refugee camps inside the Occupied Territories are cut off from water and electricity whenever the military occupation decides to do so.[76] Palestinians in the remainder of the Occupied Territories are kept off the network of excellent "settler only" roads, are obliged to work around some 500 or more checkpoints.[77] They receive about one sixth the water consumed by nearby Israeli settlers[78] and suffer much higher illness rates than their Israeli occupiers.[79]

The security laws that govern Palestinian life under Israeli control also clearly support the charge of Apartheid or separateness. Palestinians in the

Occupied Territories are governed by Israeli military law, which allows for pre-trial, pre-charge administrative detention of six months, renewable endlessly.[80] When a trial actually occurs, military courts produce a 97% conviction rate for Palestinian defendants.[81] For example, when sixteen year old Ahed Tamimi slapped an Israeli soldier who entered her home in the village of Nabi Saleh after shooting her 15 year old cousin in the head, Israeli culture minister Miri Regev said "We must immediately order that a soldier under attack be able to return fire" and even liberal Israeli journalist Ben Caspit wrote "we should exact a price at some other opportunity, in the dark, without witnesses and cameras."[82] Eventually, Tamimi agreed to a plea deal of 8 months, including the three months of time she had already served before the trial, but only after she became an iconic figure of international protest. By way of comparison, Israeli army medic Elor Azaria, who was filmed shooting a disabled Palestinian prisoner in the head, received a 9-month sentence that was lightened by generous furloughs.

Even in Israel west of the Green Line, Palestinian citizens enjoy a distinctively inferior set of rights to their Jewish neighbors. Israeli Jews are both citizens and nationals and can therefore buy land and enjoy family unification, rights denied to Palestinian citizens of the country. In fact, in a recent Israeli Supreme Court ruling against family unification for Israel's Palestinian citizens, the justice reaffirming the denial said that allowing Palestinian family unification would be tantamount to committing national suicide.[83] His argument was not about terrorism; rather, it was a frank acknowledgement that Palestinians represents a "demographic threat" to Israel's desired Jewish-supermajority population. A Kadima member of the Knesset commented: "The High Court decision articulates the rationale of separation between the [two] peoples and the need to maintain a Jewish majority and the [Jewish] character of the state."[84] Given this kind of racialized language, Israelis cannot complain when their critics begin to talk about Apartheid.

All analogies are, however, imperfect. They stand or fall on the utility of the comparisons they suggest, not on the exact resemblance among the cases they yoke together. Thus, despite the descriptive similarities between South Africa and Israel, despite the clearly oppressive limitations inflicted on Palestinians in Israel, in the refugee camps and in the Occupied Territories, the Apartheid analogy does not work well in two important ways.

First, however descriptively compelling it is, *the Apartheid framework does not capture the core, the heart, of Israeli intentions toward the Palestinians.* In South Africa, only about 13% of the population was white, while all others were Black (with various tribal and regional identities) or mixed race, or of Indian descent. With a 13% white minority, there was no possibility of excluding black labor from the economy. Apartheid was designed to *control* black labor (think of the passbooks) rather than to exclude it. Israel, by contrast, has a very different set of circumstances: 50% of the population under Israeli political control is Jewish; Israel is affluent enough to attract foreign guest workers; and Israel has a strong historic preference for "Jewish labor" (and the corollary – avoidance of Arab workers) rooted in Zionist ambitions to create a "new Jew" in place of the old European version who was deemed to be weak and unmanly.[85] The suicide bombings of the Second *Intifada* and the building of the Israeli Separation Wall only strengthen the Israeli determination to exclude Palestinian labor as much as possible. The difference in these two national agendas – to control blacks in the case of apartheid-era South Africa and to expel Palestinians in the case of Israel – makes for a very different purpose at the heart of the tensions.

And second, the struggle for justice in Palestine will look dramatically different from the earlier struggle in South Africa for strategic and practical reasons. This is another point where the analogy with South Africa breaks down. In South Africa, the successful struggle against Apartheid had three major components: armed resistance, a worldwide boycott, sanctions and divestment movement and, finally, white outmigration from the country. Together the impact of these three forces served to convince both White and Black leaders that neither side could throw a knockout punch and that both sides needed a settlement in order to get on with their lives.

In the Palestine-Israel struggle, only one of these factors is relevant at the present moment. The growing boycott, divestment, sanctions movement (see also Chapters 8 and 11) is beginning to be more than educational; it is achieving some real economic bite. But the other two factors that shaped the South African struggle, armed resistance and emigration,[86] are less in evidence in Israel-Palestine, at least for the moment.

The Israeli suppression of armed struggle in the second *Intifada* taught at least one generation of leaders that the price Palestinians would pay for violent resistance was higher than they could afford. At some point, this lesson, which is the lived experience of an older generation, will fade into "received wisdom" for a younger one and be open to challenge. The patterns of escalating violence in Aida refugee camp in Bethlehem reflect the multiple dimensions of this situation. Most of the resistance to Occupation at the camp is cultural in character (with a community reading and media center, a dance troupe, and vibrant graffiti art).[87] At the same time, camp youth are making more and more attempts to breach the Separation Wall that surrounds their camp, and the Israeli Defense Forces, in return, regularly blanket the camp with tear gas, fire live ammunition at children, cut off the camp's water and electricity supply and use dogs to intimidate children.[88] Where this will end is anyone's guess. Seen from Aida camp, it may be that, while organized armed struggle is absent, spontaneous outbursts of rage will keep the situation tense. In terms of ending the Occupation, the question then is: does this on-going tension cost Israel enough in shekels or in public opinion, to become a motive for negotiating an end to Occupation? No one can say with certainty that the answer is likely to be "yes."

And lastly, there is a question of whether Jewish out-migration from Israel might escalate because of the costs of Occupation. Conservative estimates acknowledge that, at any given moment, some 750,000 Israelis live outside the country.[89] But many of those are studying or working abroad, or taking a "gap year" between their army service and a university education and may well return to Israel eventually. There is a tiny stream of conscientious objectors who are leaving Israel because they cannot stand to be complicit in the Occupation or in any of the other right-leaning social policies characteristic of the Israeli state. There is also a much broader stream of well over a million people (discussed in Chapter 4) who leave Israel for what they describe as economic reasons – high cost of housing, low salaries, uncertain career ladders – without recognizing that the Israel's domestic and military economies are profoundly entwined and operate to the advantage of the Occupation.[90] And there are surely an unknown number of people who chose not to come to Israel because of costs they may not even recognize as related to the Occupation.

But, whatever out-migration Israel might be facing, they are certainly devoting enormous effort and money to encourage an off-setting *aliyah*, for example, with the Birthright program, which guarantees every American Jew between the ages of 16 and 26 a free trip to Israel. Students on these trips are urged to "plant their seed in Israel" (and even those who do not, the Israelis hope, will go home as pro-Israel voters).[91] At the moment, the balance between emigration and immigration seems to be one that Israel can sustain. The number of Jews in Israel is not sinking toward a point of crisis for the Zionist project.

Thus we see that, on the one hand, there is a great deal of resemblance between the structures and daily practices of Occupation and South African apartheid. On the other, there are also critical points of difference: most

251

importantly that Apartheid wanted submissive, toiling Blacks while Israel wants Palestinians gone from their economy, their polity, their sight. The measures that lead to the overthrow of Apartheid are also much weaker in the Palestinian case. So, in the end, the charm of the Apartheid analogy comes down to this: conventions and protocols have already established Apartheid as a crime within the realm of international law. There is thus a practical reason why many of those who struggle against the Occupation invoke the Apartheid metaphor. If the Occupation is, indeed, a new version of Apartheid, then it is not only immoral but also illegal and subject to legal remedies and redress.

Yet if it is true that the Apartheid analogy misses the heart of the matter, the motive force driving Israel's treatment of the Palestinians, then we must find other avenues for vindicating Palestinian rights. Ethnic cleansing is also an internationally recognized crime and thus provides legal tools that Palestinian rights advocates can use.

SETTLER COLONIALISM: ETHNIC CLEANSING AND SOCIOCIDE

In our lovely country there exists an entire people who have held it for centuries and to whom it would never occur to leave ... The time has come to dispel the misconception among Zionists that land in Palestine lies uncultivated for lack of working hands or the laziness of the local residents. There are no deserted fields.

Yitzhak Epstein[92]

Neither Jewish ethics nor Jewish tradition can disqualify terrorism as a means of combat. We are very far from having any moral qualms as far as our national war goes. We have before us the command of the Torah, whose morality surpasses that of any other body of laws in the world: "Ye shall blot them out to the last man." ... But first and foremost, terrorism is for us a part of the political battle being conducted under the present circumstances, and it has a great part to play.

Yitzak Shamir[93]

Settler colonialism is inherently eliminatory but not invariably genocidal.

Patrick Wolfe[94]

A Three-Family Story

On the third class trip, as on the two before it, we visited a demolished Palestinian home. The demolished homes we see are not in the Occupied Territories, but in Israel west of the Green Line. Students are astonished to learn that not only are Palestinian homes routinely demolished in Area C of the West Bank and in East Jerusalem – i.e. in places where the borders between Zionist and Palestinian communities are being redrawn daily – but also in areas long under Israeli control in the heart of Israel.

On this day we are at a site near Um al Fahm, one of Israel's "mixed" cities – i.e. a city in which Jewish and Palestinian Israelis live in fairly close proximity. The Palestinian neighborhoods are very crowded, with extensions built on top of original homes, as high as the foundations will support. But today we are in a new area, a suburb with modern homes that have been the target of demolitions. The story is always the same: Palestinians seek permission to build homes, are denied, and build them anyway. In this particular neighborhood, inhabited by fairly affluent professional families, there had been much litigation and the Palestinian homeowners were promised that there would soon be an administrative decision in their favor that would allow their houses to stand.

But that promise turned out to be false. In the middle of the night, the Israeli army appeared in a flotilla of jeeps and tanks and surrounded a new three family home. Helicopters illuminated the scene. Troops kept neighbors from going to the aid of the three families living in the multistory building. The residents, three young families, were given 15 minutes to evacuate their homes, and then the building was bulldozed.

Two days later, our tour guide brought us to the site. We saw the mountain of rubble, the bulldozer tracks studded with the bright, gaily colored fragments of children's toys, a woman's turquoise scarf fluttering listlessly from a broken concrete pillar. The guide was explaining to us that the families not only lost their homes but also would be billed, by the Israeli government, for the cost of the demolition.

Just as our guide was concluding his talk a car raced up the road to the site and parked next to our tour bus. Two well-dressed men leapt out, carrying cases of bottled water, which they began handing us most insistently. They spoke only halting English, so we asked the

> guide to find out who they were and why they were bringing us water. It turns out they were the owners of the demolished building – one an accountant who had gotten a master's degree in Belgium and one an electrical engineer trained in Italy. They told us that neighbors had alerted them to the fact that a tour group was walking around the ruins of their home and so they rushed to perform their tasks as hosts. They said that they were shamed by the fact that they no longer had kitchens and therefore could not offer us the appropriate hospitality of a freshly brewed cup of tea.

Colonialism is an old story in human history. It involves a stronger power, be it a tribe, nation, or empire, which conquers a weaker one. The colonial power wants something more than a brief military victory. Instead it wants to maintain control indefinitely, for a variety of reasons. The conquered territory may contain some geo-strategic advantage: a militarily valuable mountain pass, access routes to some other place, fresh water ports, oases, scarce and coveted natural resources. The conquered territory may tempt by a supply of cheap labor, or a population of captive consumers.

Colonialism is always a violation of human rights. It cheats the conquered people of their right to self-determination and it ignores the rule that countries cannot expand their territory through acts of war.

Not all colonialisms, however, are settler colonialisms. Settler colonialism is a particularly malign version, because it entails more than conquest, domination, exploitation, and enforced powerlessness. Settler colonialism is a project bent on replacing one population (the conquered) with another. Sometimes the new population consists of respected citizens of the conquering power; at other times, its dissidents or miscreants (as with Australia's origins as a penal colony); or, as in the case of Zionism and the back to Africa movement, a minority group the hosst society would like to be rid of. In every case, the essence of settler colonialism is a transfer plan, replacing one population with another.

As we saw in chapter 2, the transfer can be enacted by overtly violent means, in which case, we can think of it as ethnic cleansing. Transfer can also be enacted by bureaucratic means, albeit always in the shadow of the possible use of force should bureaucratic ploys fail. In this more contemporary case, "sociocide," a term coined by Palestinian political scientist Saleh Abdel Jawad, is an apt description.

Even a cursory look at Jewish history allows us to understand how ethnic cleansing became a temptation for Zionism.

From its inception, Zionism was faced with impossible contradictions. Looking backwards, towards the past, Zionism wanted to create a safe haven for the European Jews who had suffered so badly at the hands of Christian anti-Semitism. Yet, at the same time, and probably not only for strategic reasons, Zionism saw itself as the embodiment of the values of the very society from which it sought escape. Herzl, Zionism's founding genius, presented his project as the creation of the ramparts of Europe in Asia, i.e. as a civilizing force. Central to that claim was the aspiration to found a democratic society. Having been subjected to the arbitrary whims of various tsars, Kaisers, and other European monarchs, the insistence on democracy, freedom, and self-determination was, again, more than mere window-dressing for Zionism– it was a requirement for having community control over one's future.

At the same time, Zionist leaders certainly knew that the project of creating a new society, a safe haven for Jews, would collide with the fact that the land they were given as "a room of their own" was already occupied by an indigenous Palestinian population. This fact created an insurmountable challenge to the desire for an exclusively Jewish space.

The challenge itself was universally recognized by the broadest spectrum of early Zionist leaders: Herzl, Zangwill, Jabotinsky, Weizman, Ben-Gurion and a host of less well known individuals like Arthur Ruppin (an early head of the Jewish Agency), Menachem Ussishkin (of the Jewish National Fund), and Max Nordau (with Herzl, a co-founder of the World Zionist Organization), men who spanned the spectrum, right wing "revisionist" nationalists and left wing socialists, all knew that the land they coveted was heavily populated by Palestinians.

From the beginning, then, Zionist leaders had to figure out a way that their emerging society could be both Jewish and democratic when so many of the people who would be part of this society were not Jews. The "hidden question" at the heart of Zionism was precisely this: what to do with the non-Jews under its control.[95] Given the centrality of that question, it is inevitable that the solution of ethnic cleansing would occur to the Zionist pioneers, whether they accepted or rejected it.

As with any monumentally difficult question, denial played a role, especially early on. The Basel Program adopted by the first Zionist Congress in 1897 made no mention of the Palestinians.[96] In his utopian novel about Zionism, *Old New Land (Altneuland)* Herzl portrays a single Arab family so consumed with admiration for Jewish thrift and industry that they

255

convert to Judaism.[97] And similarly, even David Ben Gurion (along with co-author Yitzhak Ben Zvi as mentioned in Chapter 1) once tried to portray the Palestinians as descendants of the Biblical Israelites who would happily convert to Judaism, reclaiming their ancestral roots, once they saw the superiority of Zionist society.[98]

Such fictions had a hard time surviving the clash with reality, and so a second and more racist variant quickly followed the first denial. Zionists acknowledged that, indeed, there was an indigenous population standing in the way of the Zionist dream, but this population was deemed so racially inferior as to be irrelevant. Chaim Weizmann, later the first president of Israel, accepted the British estimate of "some hundred thousands negroes [Kushim] and for these there is no value."[99] In this stance he is echoes Lord Balfour who said: "Zionism, be it right or wrong, good or bad, is rooted in age-long traditions, in present deeds, in future hopes, of far profounder import than the desires and prejudices of 700,000 Arabs who now inhabit that ancient land."[100] Zionists had traditions and hopes, Arabs only desires and prejudices that could be rightfully disregarded.

Herzl hoped to "spirit the penniless population across the border procuring employment for it in the transit countries, while denying it any employment in our own country."[101] This is, perhaps, the first statement that economic policy could be a tool of Zionist settlement. The policy of starving out the Palestinians, denying them employment in favor of Jewish labor, was to be supplemented quickly with the practice of buying the farmland out from under them via transactions with absentee landlords.[102]

Some Zionists recognized that this tactic was highly problematic. In a famous speech to the 1907 Zionist Congress, Yitzhak Epstein warned: "In the end, they will wake up and return to us in blows what we have looted from them with our gold!"[103] Yet even Epstein, who harbored hopes for peaceful co-existence, could not restrain his condescension toward Arabs. Coexistence would be rooted in Jewish superiority: "Our agronomists will advise them, teaching them the sciences of agriculture, husbandry and cross-breeding, and show them the scientific ways to fight cattle and poultry epidemics and pests of the field, vineyard and garden. They will be able to cheaply purchase medicines against disease and, when in need, will have access to the Jewish doctor."[104]

Other tools were also proposed, especially the hope that the British, the rulers of Mandate Palestine early in the history of Zionism, would expel the indigenous population to make way for the Jews. The idea of population transfers was then a common one, and, at least in the mind of colonial powers, was not thought to have particularly ominous undertones. Population transfers (as discussed in Chapter 3), were contemplated between Greeks and Turks, Greeks and Bulgarians, and elsewhere. In fact, the British Peel Plan of 1937 was not only the first official attempt to divide Mandate Palestine between Zionists and Palestinians; it was itself a transfer plan.

In the end, however, the British declined to transfer Palestinians out of Palestine to make way for incoming Zionist settlers. So competing Zionist and indigenous claims continued to be made. And, eventually, both Zionists and Palestinians would denounce the British precisely because of its population policies: the Zionist settlers railed against British-imposed restrictions on immigration and land purchases and the Palestinians bemoaned the degree to which the British opened Palestine to Zionists.

Eventually, economic means proved insufficient to displace the Palestinians, and violence escalated sharply, especially in 1921 and again in 1929 (as discussed in chapter 5). Under these circumstances, the Zionist settlers in pre-state Palestine became more and more committed to violent ethnic cleansing as the way to accomplish "transfer."[105] Military means reached a crescendo during the *Nakba* which saw more than half of all Palestinians "transferred" out of the areas that fell under first the *Yishuv*'s and then the Israeli state's control. Rolling expulsions continued during the 1950s and peaked again in 1967 with the Six Day War and the Occupation by Israel of all of Mandate Palestine.

But even with all that military expulsion, the Palestinian question remained then and remains today. The Occupation has proven to be something of a pyrrhic victory – with the additional land Israel conquered in 1967, they also took back control over many of the Palestinians they had expelled during the *Nakba*. For some 51 years now they have controlled all of Israel/Palestine, but half the people under their control are not Jewish, are being mistreated, and are earning more and more attention in the arena of public opinion.

All of the most repressive features of a military occupation remain intact today east of the Green Line. There are over 500 checkpoints that form impediments to movement.[106] More than four million Palestinians live without civil rights under Israeli military rule. Settlement construction continues to gobble up the land: 60+% of the West Bank, Area C, has been all but cleansed of Palestinians and is seeing an unprecedented rate of settlement growth. Some 764,000 settlers constitute an immutable "fact on the ground."[107] All of the infrastructure development in the West Bank is dedicated to sustaining the settlements.[108] There is simply very little physical or social space left for Palestinian society to flourish. In his most recent book, Ilan Pappe, one

257

of Israel's leading historians of the *Nakba,* refers to the Occupation as "the bureaucracy of evil."[109]

Saleh Abdel Jawad, a Palestinian historian, has coined the term "sociocide" for describing the experience of the Occupation as seen through Palestinian eyes. He argues that since rounding up people, herding them into cattle cars, and dumping them across the border has become politically unacceptable, Israel has sought and found other ways to compel Palestinians to quit their land so that Zionists can take it over. Sociocide "set[s] out to achieve four main aims: firstly, to destroy the Palestinian economy; secondly, to decimate Palestinian national spirit and identity; thirdly, to deprive Palestinians of their political and civil rights, and fourthly, to transform Palestinian daily life into an endless chain of hardship."[110] Put differently, the Occupation is not merely a burdensome net of indirect rule beneath which a resilient Palestinian society can flourish. Rather it is a carefully designed, multi-pronged, comprehensive plan to make life unbearable for Palestinians so that they will leave. Because of their routinized character, veiled by endless claims of Israeli national security, many sociocidal policies fly under the human rights radar and do not trigger concern.

Israeli Occupational practices create emotional and psychological tensions at the individual level, for example through the permitting process. Nearly anything a Palestinian living under Occupation might want to do requires a permit: widening the path between one's house and one's fields or one's well, sending children abroad to university, sending grandmother to a clinic in Israel, going to Jordan for a family wedding, building a second floor on the house or an extension on the back to accommodate a newly married child, rebuilding a balcony that has been eroded by time – all of these things require a permit. Permits are never given unless, according to rumors fomented by the Israelis, you are willing to inform on your neighbors (or workmates, or schoolmates).[111] So no one can trust anyone else, and this makes political mobilization and resistance very risky.

Palestinian economic life is also besieged. In an agricultural economy, 500 checkpoints create a high level of economic waste, not to mention a lot of rotting produce. Periodic raids on banks and allegations of secret payments to terrorist groups insure that the banking system cannot operate normally; hence credit and investment are impaired.[112] Palestinian consumers cannot import the goods they want. Instead they constitute a market of four million people for the Israeli exports that flood their stores. Palestinian goods cannot travel to market except via Israeli container ships to which access is by no means guaranteed.

At the political and civil level, Palestinians are subject to Israeli military law. Their governmental bodies cannot function in a way that is truly responsive to Palestinian society. Outsiders dictate the timing and substance of Palestinian elections. Duly elected officials are prevented from serving – for example, the Israelis promptly jailed all the legislators elected on the Hamas slate in 2006.[113] On the rare occasions when the Palestinian Authority tries to improve the visibility of the Palestinian plight in the public eye, especially when it goes to the United Nations, money is withheld and threats are issued against the PA. The Palestine Liberation Organization, the Palestinian National Council, and the Palestinian Legislative Council all await new elections.

And finally, Palestinian social and communal life is also deeply impaired. Schools and universities are closed, often at the most inconvenient times. Palestinian archival and film collections are confiscated and the artistic heritage of the nation is lost. Books and libraries are decimated.[114] Clinics, especially in Gaza, have great difficulty in stocking enough medicines. Curfews and checkpoints make it difficult to maintain a robust theater and music scene, except in Ramallah where the foreign press and NGO workers congregate.

The cumulative weight of all those aggressions constitutes, in the words of Abdel Jawad, a Palestinian sociocide. Abdel Jawad's term has spawned a host of cognates – "spaciocide" to describe the incredible disappearing Palestine,[115] "politicide" to describe the dismembering of the Palestinian political hopes.[116] Clearly his term, sociocide, is the most inclusive and it also has the immense moral advantage of allowing Palestinians to name their own experience, if they so choose. Perhaps it is correct to understand that the ethnic cleansing of Palestine is Zionism's aim and "sociocide" describes the complex set of policies by which this aim is accomplished without unmasking "the only democracy in the Middle East."

At book talks for the first edition, I have been asked whether I'm positing a conspiracy for the Israeli expulsion and subordination of the Palestinians. Most emphatically I am not. Conspiracies are not required in this case; the logic of the Zionist political project alone suffices. If your mission is to create an exclusively Jewish state in a particular territory then it follows logically that all the non-Jews living there will have to go, pushed out by whatever means are available at any given historical moment.

So if not a conspiracy, then what? I am arguing here that Zionism has a central logic that has persisted from its inception to the present day and that this logic is an example of settler colonialism. As the history section of this

259

book demonstrates, Zionism is a project to build a state, not a community. It is a project to build this state in a particular location, Mandate Palestine, for religious, historic, and pragmatic reasons. It is a project to build a state in Palestine exclusive to Jews. It is a project to build a state with white European Jews at its helm. Hence, this project cannot tolerate the presence of Palestinian Muslims and Christians in its polity, and therefore seeks to expel them as a first choice (to transfer them), or, perhaps, to impose their complete subordination as a distant second choice.

Zionist leaders have never wavered from this agenda. In the late 1890s Herzl described the task as projecting European power in Asia. This Eurocentric agenda, perhaps, accounts for the fact that Arab and African Jews were not invited to the party until later. In 1923, Jabotinsky bemoaned that fact that there were so many Palestinians in the densely populated land of the Jewish national home. Ben Gurion insisted that the pre-state Zionist community in Palestine accept partition only because it provided them a base from which to take control of the rest of the land they desired. Leading Israeli historians and journalists argued that the ethnic cleansing of 1948 was a necessary and therefore acceptable tool for building the Jewish state. Israeli's most famous generals, like Moshe Dayan, admitted that Israeli towns were built on expropriation. After the military victory of 1967, Israel's politically left Labor Party built more illegal settlements in the West Bank than right wing administrations. The current crop of political leaders have repeated, clearly and loudly, what many Israeli leaders have said before them: that they will never permit a Palestinian state to emerge anywhere between the river and the sea. At present, they are talking about turning the 50+ years of *de facto* Israeli control over the whole of Palestine into a *de jure* situation by annexing all or most of the West Bank. This move would, of course, be illegal under the dictates of international law.

Settlement building, accompanied by violence against Palestinians, unifies the histories of the pre-state Zionist community in Palestine with that of the early state and that of the later Occupation into one seamless whole. That seamless whole is a settler colonial project par excellence[117]: conquering, uprooting and displacing an existing population, partly through violent means and partly through bureaucratic ones, and, finally, resettlement with a new population who legitimize their project either by the claim of return from ancient times or by arguing their superiority in making the land productive. Both of these possible narratives, about the "Promised Land" or "Manifest Destiny" (as in the American lexicon) are intensely nationalistic and racist.

Even when understood as settler colonialism, Zionism remains an extraordinary political project. Unlike other settler colonial projects that have evolved over time, Zionism has retained its racist roots unapologetically[118] and has managed to block the redefinitions and modernizations of national identity that are the fate of most settler-colonial nationalisms. Unlike Australia's and New Zealand's efforts to take responsibility for the abuse of the Maoris and the Aborigines, or Canada's institutional Anglo-French binationalism, or even the dubious claims of successive U.S. governments to multiculturalism, Zionism remains a state shaped by and for white European Jews with only reluctant acceptance of Arab and African Jews and relentless antipathy toward Palestinians. It is a project that moves forward in times of international support, in times of international indifference, and even in the face of international censure. More recently we see that Israeli leaders will even countenance anti-Semitism as long as it supports Zionism.[119] Most revealingly, Israel's political leaders choose to carry on with this project even when sustained peace offers for full normalization with all Arab states are available to them.[120]

CONCLUSION

As I said at the beginning of this chapter, each of the four most common frameworks offers some insights and contains some difficulties. Perhaps the best metric for evaluating them is the policy they imply.

Given the injustices of the Occupation inflicted on Palestinians, Israelis face real hostility and resistance. Thus they would legitimately have to be concerned about their own safety even without filtering all perceptions of danger through Holocaust memory. But the policy implications of the Israeli self-defense framework are woefully underdeveloped. Israelis act on the belief that their interests are best served by increasing surveillance, repression, and expulsion. The alternative, of coming to some just and mutually agreed upon resolution with the Palestinians, has been used to date only as a pretext for more settlement building. Such behavior undermines the persuasiveness of the "Israeli self defense" claim.

Genocide, apartheid, and ethnic cleansing are all crimes against humanity recognized in international law. Each framework, therefore, offers a legal remedy for Palestinians to pursue. But political realism suggests that a legal possibility alone, without the pressure of widespread public support for its implementation, is a weak remedy.

Genocide accusations, in particular, are hampered both by the complicated evidentiary demands that must be satisfied within the legal framework, and by the common perception that genocide accusations are over-reaching and not credible.

Apartheid is certainly the most popular framework at present and it offers the added advantage, for an American audience, of reminding us of the parallels between the quest for Palestinian and for Black rights. Nevertheless, the parallels are as much misleading as illuminating, and obscure the fact that Zionism hopes to be rid of Palestinians in ways that a tiny white minority could never hope to be rid of all of the native population of South Africa.

Settler colonialism is an old term, newly applied to the situation in Israel/ Palestine. It has a number of advantages.

First, it is inherently comparative. It allows us to get out of the bubble of Holocaust-defined needs and rights, and to see the similarities between the Zionist colonization of Palestine and other colonizations – American, Canadian, Australian, New Zealand, Algerian.[121] This not only widens our perspective, it offers an array of resolutions that have been implemented with more or less success in other cases, including the admonitory one of the defeat of settler colonialism in Algeria. In the first chapter, I argued that "de-boutiquing" the Israeli/Palestinian conflict is one of my purposes, and the settler colonialism framework achieves this end.

Second, because the settler colonial framework names ethic cleansing as one of its tools, it does incorporate a basis for a legal action on behalf of Palestinian rights not, at present, available in the term "settler colonialism" itself. In adding "sociocide" to the analysis of the ways that militarized bureaucratic oppression works, it also allows Palestinians to name their own experience, a quality not otherwise present in the conversation.[122]

Most importantly, the settler colonial framework allows us to understand the conflict between Palestinians and Israelis as a seamless whole. Events in the pre-state period, the early state years, and in the Occupation are all products of the same forces in which Zionists seek to claim all of the land with none of the (Palestinian) people, using different methods as changing circumstances allow.

However, I must acknowledge that the settler colonial framework also poses challenges. Precisely because it suggests that the real problem is not the Occupation (1967) but Zionism itself (i.e. 1948 or even 1897, the date of the first Zionist Congress), it generates stiff resistance. The very concept of settler colonialism implies a remedy of "decolonizing" that, in turn, raises the specter of expelling some 750,000 illegal settlers as the *Nakba* once expelled 750,000 Palestinian villagers and city dwellers. Misused, deliberately misinterpreted, the settler colonial framework seems to support Israeli allegations that Palestinians will be satisfied only by pushing them into the sea.

A joint Palestinian-Israeli working group, The One Democratic State Campaign, offers a thoughtful rebuttal to this fear-mongering.[123] Their program meets the three requirements for credibility that South Africans deployed effectively in the struggle against Apartheid: they have shifted from being opposed to injustices to being in favor of a plan for a viable alternative, the beneficiaries of the plan include Palestinians and Jews, and the terms of the struggle are shifted from security to human rights.[124] But, at present, the One Democratic State Campaign still has an up-hill battle to get the hearing it deserves.

Indeed, the dilemma faced by this group, to acknowledge facts and to speak truthfully on the one hand, and to be politically effective on the other, is a challenge that permeates all efforts to vindicate Palestinian rights. Advocating for Palestinian rights, especially within the colonial settler framework, requires a willingness to go beyond "splitting the difference," to insist that the affirmation of human rights does not fall half-way between the ambitions of a colonizer and the losses of the colonized.

This brings us back full circle to the place where the historical narrative in this book began in Chapter 4. Zionism is the idea that changed everything. Perhaps now, at the end of the historic narrative, it is time to take another look at Zionism.

NOTES

[1] Stephen Prince. (2012, November 6).The Rashomon Effect, *Current*, retrieved from http://www.criterion.com/current/posts/195-the-rashomon-effect

[2] Shuki Sadeh. (2014, August 12). How Israel's arms manufacturers won the Gaza war, *Ha'aretz*, retrieved from http://www.haaretz.com/business/.premium-1.610032. Yotam Feldman. *The Lab* a documentary film retrieved from https://vimeo.com/65082874

[3] Jaobtinksy quoted in Annie Levin. (2002). The Hidden History of Zionism, *International Socialist Review*, 24, retrieved from http://www.isreview.org/issues/24/hidden_history.shtml

[4] Address at the Mapai Political Committee (1938, June 7) as quoted in Simha Flapan. *(1979). Zionism and the Palestinians.* New York: Barnes and Noble.

[5] Dayan, quoted in Ghada Karmi. (2007). *Married to Another Man: Israel's Dilemma in Palestine.* (London: Pluto Press), p. 3.

[6] "Larger Housing Protests set to take place in 10 Cities," *Jerusalem Post*, July 30, 2011, retrieved from http://www.jpost.com/National-News/Larger-housing-protests-set-to-take-place-in-10-cities

[7] Ari Shavit. (2012, August 23). Countdown: Former Minister Ephraim Sneh Fears Another Hiroshima, *Ha'aretz*, retrieved from http://www.haaretz.com/weekend/magazine/ari-shavit-s-countdown-former-minister-ephraim-sneh-fears-another-hiroshima-1.46028

[8] Yoav Shamir. (2010). *Defamation*. YouTube, minutes 3:00–8:00, retrieved from https://archive.org/details/Defamation-2010

[9] Avraham Burg. (2009). *The Holocaust is Over and We Must Rise from the Ashes*. London: Palgrave McMillan.

[10] Ari Shavit. (2013). *My Promised Land: The Triumph and Tragedy of Israel*. New York: Spiegel and Grau.

[11] http://www.un.org/News/Press/docs/2012/ga11317.doc.htm

[12] Annie Robbins. (2014, March 28). UN Human Rights council resolution warning companies to 'terminate business interests in the settlements' or face possible criminal liability gets watered down, *Mondoweiss*, retrieved from http://mondoweiss.net/2014/03/resolution-companies-settlements.html

[13] Eve Spangler. (2011, October 11). The Generous Offer, *Counterpunch*, retrieved from http://www.counterpunch.org/2011/10/11/the-story-of-the-generous-offer/

[14] http://www.bdsmovement.net/2014/2013-round-up-11579

[15] Ali Abunimah. (2012, November 11). When former CIA Chief David Petraeus Enraged the Israel Lobby, *Electronic Intifada*, retrieved from http://electronicintifada.net/blogs/ali-abunimah/when-former-cia-chief-david-petraeus-enraged-israel-lobby

[16] Ron Gerlitz. (2014, March 28). The correlation between Arab economic power and attacks by the Right, retrieved from +972 retrieved from http://972mag.com/the-correlation-between-arab-economic-power-and-attacks-by-the-right/89045/

[17] Palestinian Academic and Cultural Boycott of Israel (PACBI), "Israel's Anti-BDS law: Proving the Effectiveness of the Boycott," July 31, 2011, retrieved from http://www.pacbi.org/etemplate.php?id=1677

[18] Yulia Zemlinskaya (2010). "Between Militarism and Pacifism: Conscientious Objections and Draft Resistance in Israel," *Central European Journal of International and Security Studies*, retrieved from http://www.academia.edu/179941/Between_Militarism_and_Pacifism_Conscientious_Objection_and_Draft_Resistance_in_Israel

[19] Breaking the Silence. (2012). *Our Harsh Logic: Israeli Soldier's Testimonies from the Occupied Territories, 2000–2010*, New York: Holt.

[20] UNESCO cuts funding for Palestinian youth magazine over Hitler Praise, *The Telegraph*, December 23, 2011, retrieved from http://www.telegraph.co.uk/news/worldnews/middleeast/palestinianauthority/8975423/Unesco-cuts-funding-for-Palestinian-youth-magazine-over-Hitler-praise.html

[21] Rami Amichai (2011, March 12). Jewish Couple and three children killed in West Bank, *Reuters*, retrieved from http://www.reuters.com/article/2011/03/12/us-palestinians-israel-violence-idUSTRE72B0B920110312

[22] Martin Asser. (2000, October 13). Lynch mob's brutal attack, *BBC News Online*, retrieved from http://news.bbc.co.uk/2/hi/middle_east/969778.stm

[23] *Ibid.*

[24] Rashid Khalid (2006). *The Iron Cage: The Story of the Palestinian Struggle for Statehood* (Boston: Beacon Press), pp. xvii–xxv and footnotes 13 & 19, p. 220. See also: Charles D. Smith. (2013). *Palestine and the Arab-Israeli Conflict: A History with Documents* (Boston: St. Martins), p. 407. Andrew Higgins. (2009, January 24). How Israel

Helped Spawn Hamas, *Wall Street Journal*, retrieved from https://www.wsj.com/articles/ SB123275572295011847.html

[25] *Ibid.*

[26] *B'Tselem* – The Israeli Information Center for Human Rights in the Occupied Territories, "Statistics: Fatalities After Operation Cast Lead," retrieved from http://www.btselem.org/ statistics/fatalities/after-cast-lead/by-date-of-event

[27] *Ibid.*

[28] The figure of 2,168 Palestinian fatalities is conservative, since many Gazans died of injuries suffered during Operation Protective Edge after the hostilities had ended. Institute for Middle East Understanding (2014). 50 Days of Death and Destruction: Israel's 'Operation Protective Edge,' *IMEU Resources/Fact Sheets*, September 14, 2014, retrieved from http://imeu.org/article/50-days-of-death-destruction-israels-operation-protective-edge

[29] http://www.goodreads.com/quotes/tag/zionism

[30] Joan Acocella. (2002, June 17). "A Hard Case: The Life and Death of Primo Levi," *The New Yorker*, retrieved from http://www.newyorker.com/archive/2002/06/17/020617crbo_ books

[31] Aharon Cizling was a prominent early Zionist who contributed to the founding of the *Palmach* militia and the *Ahdut HaAvoda* party. He represented the Jewish Agency at the United Nations, and served as Minister of Agriculture under Ben-Gurion. He is quoted by Ronnie Kasrils. (2009, March 17). Who said nearly 50 years ago that Israel was an Apartheid State? *Media Monitors: Commentary*, retrieved from http://links.org.au/ node/960

[32] Richard Falk. (2007, July 7). Slouching toward a Palestinian Holocaust, *Countercurrents,* retrieved from http://www.countercurrents.org/falk070707.htm

[33] Adam Horowitz, et. al. (eds.) (2011). *The Goldstone Report: The Legacy of the Landmark Investigation of the Gaza Conflict*. New York: The Nation Books.

[34] International Middle East Media Center, retrieved from http://www.imemc.org/ article/68429

[35] Kasrils, *op. cit.*

[36] United Nations Relief Works Agency (UNRWA), *Gaza in 2020: A Livable Place?,* retrieved from http://www.unrwa.org/newsroom/press-releases/gaza-2020-liveable-place

[37] Naim Ateek. (2005, January 16). Suicide Bombing from a Palestinian Perspective, *PeacePalestine*, retrieved from http://peacepalestine.blogspot.com/2005/01/naim-ateek-suicide-bombing-from.html

[38] Ilan Pappe. (2014, July 13). Israel's incremental genocide in the Gaza ghetto, *Electronic Intifada*, retrieved from http://electronicintifada.net/content/israels-incremental-genocide-gaza-ghetto/13562

[39] Benny Morris. (2004). *The Birth of the Palestinian Refugee Problem Revisited* (New York: Cambridge University Press) p. 228.

[40] Uri Misgav. (2014, May 30). Not neo-Nazis, Judeo-Nazis, *Ha'aretz*, retrieved from http://www.haaretz.com/opinion/.premium-1.596157

[41] The United Nations, "The Convention on the Prevention and Punishment for the Crime of Genocide, 1948," retrieved from http://legal.un.org/avl/ha/cppcg/cppcg.html

[42] *Ibid.*, Article II, point 1.

[43] Mark Roseman (2002). *The Wannsee Conference and the 'Final Solution.'* New York: Metropolitan Books.

44 Saleh Abdel Jawad quoting Harvard historian John Womack, in Zionist Massacres: the Creation of the Palestinian Refugee Problem in the 1948 War, in Eyal Benvenisti, Chaim Gans and Sari Hanafi (eds.) (2007). *Israel and the Palestinian Refugees* (Heidelberg: Spring Verlag), p. 62, note 9.

45 Ali Abunimeh. (2018, March 31). Israel admits, then deletes, responsibility for Gaza killings, *Electronic Intifada*, retrieved from https://electronicintifada.net/blogs/ali-abunimah/israel-admits-then-deletes-responsibility-gaza-killings

46 Ra'anan Alexandrowicz, *The Law in These Parts.* 2011.

47 Personal communication from youth literacy coordinator, Lajee Community Center, Aida Refugee Camp, Bethlehem during student trip, December 30, 2013.

48 Coral Urquhart. (2006, April 15). Gaza on the brink of implosion as aid cut-off starts to bite *The Observer*, retrieved from http://www.theguardian.com/world/2006/apr/16/israel

49 Martin Kramer. (2010). Superfluous Young Men, address to the Herzliya Conference reproduced at *Sandbox* (Kramer's blog), retrieved from http://www.martinkramer.org/sandbox/2010/02/superfluous-young-men/

50 Daila Hatuqa. (2014, September 21). Israel in Grave Breach over Informants, *Al Jazeera*, retrieved from http://www.aljazeera.com/news/middleeast/2014/09/spying-palestinians-war-crime-20149215553352273.html

51 We Are Nabi Saleh, YouTube, retrieved from https://www.youtube.com/watch?v=DdyD8yZ68NA

52 Interview with Breaking the Silence spokesperson Oded Na'aman, in Christmas Break in Palestine, retrieved from http://vimeo.com/13478028

53 *Ibid.*

54 Adalah Legal Center for Arab Minority Rights in Israel, Discriminatory Laws in Israel, retrieved from http://adalah.org/eng/Israeli-Discriminatory-Law-Database

55 Carolina Landsman. (2018, August 18). How Israeli Right-wing Thinkers Envision the Annexation of the West Bank, *Ha'aretz*, retrieved from https://www.haaretz.com/israel-news/.premium.MAGAZINE-how-israeli-right-wing-thinkers-envision-the-west-bank-s-annexation-1.6387108

56 *Ibid.*

57 Amira Hass. (2014, May 29). A Lawyer for Every Labor, *Ha'aretz*, retrieved from http://www.haaretz.com/news/features/.premium-1.596134. This article is an analysis of how "legalization" is used as window-dressing to mask oppression.

58 Arafat quoted in Matthew Taylor. (2003, December 8). Israel apologists attempted to discredit Mandela with false Israel apartheid quote, *Mondoweiss*, retrieved from http://mondoweiss.net/2013/12/apologists-discredit-apartheid.html

59 Hendrik Vorwoerd, quoted in Chris McGreal. (2006, February 6). Wolds Apart, *The Guardian*, retrieved from http://www.theguardian.com/world/2006/feb/06/southafrica.israel

60 Brett Wilkins. (20214, March 10). Desmond Tutu urges boycott of 'Apartheid' Israel, *Digital Journal*, retrieved from http://digitaljournal.com/news/world/desmond-tutu-urges-boycott-of-apartheid-israel/article/375545]

61 John Dugard, Apartheid and Occupation under International Law, *Hisham B. Sharabi Memorial Lecture* of the Jerusalem Fund of the Palestine Center, retrieved from http://www.auphr.org/index.php/news/4227-sp-9067

62 Edo Konrad, An Israeli and a Palestinian slap a soldier. Guess who's still in prison? *+972* March 25, 2018, retrieved from https://972mag.com/an-israeli-and-a-palestinian-slap-a-soldier-guess-whos-still-in-prison/134017/

[63] Jimmy Carter. (2006). *Palestine Peace Not Apartheid*, New York: Simon and Shuster.

[64] Gideon Polya. (2013, December 8), Honor Anti-Apartheid Hero Nelson Mandela's Words: "Our Freedom Is Incomplete Without The Freedom Of The Palestinians *Countercurrents*, retrieved from http://www.countercurrents.org/polya081213.htm

[65] "Worse than Apartheid: the Movement to Boycott Israel, *Pulse*, February 27, 2009, retrieved from http://pulsemedia.org/2009/02/27/worse-than-apartheid-the-movement-to-boycott-israel/

[66] The Russell Tribunal on Palestine, retrieved from http://www.russelltribunalonpalestine.com/en/about-rtop

[67] *Ibid.*

[68] Aluf Benn. (2014, May 1). Netanyahu: Hero of the Binational State? *Ha'aretz*, retrieved from http://www.haaretz.com/opinion/.premium-1.588380

[69] John Cassidy. (2014, April 29). John Kerry and the A-Word: Three Takeaways, *The New Yorker*, retrieved from http://www.newyorker.com/online/blogs/johncassidy/2014/04/john-kerry-and-the-a-word-three-takeaways.html

[70] Bennett's use of the term Apartheid is disinguous because he is using it to argue for annexing Area C, largely depopulated, and according citizenship to the few remaining Palestinians therein, in order to pre-empt the Apartheid label. Arnon Degani. (2014, April 29). Guess Who Else Fears that Israel will be labeled an Apartheid state? *Mondoweiss*, retrieved from http://mondoweiss.net/2014/04/israel-become-apartheid.html

[71] United Nations General Assembly. (1973). *Convention on the Suppression and Punishment of the Crime of Apartheid*, retrieved from http://legal.un.org/avl/ha/cspca/cspca.html

[72] Karine MacAllister. (2008). Applicability of the Crime of Apartheid to Israel, *BDS and the Global Anti-Apartheid Movement*, Badil Resource Center, retrieved from http://www.badil.org/en/al-majdal/item/72-applicability-of-the-crime-of-apartheid-to-israel

[73] United Nations Office of the High Commissioner for Human Rights. (1965). *International Convention on the Elimination of All Forms of Racial Discrimination*. Retrieved from http://www.ohchr.org/EN/ProfessionalInterest/Pages/CERD.aspx

[74] *Ibid.*

[75] Barak Ravid. (2014, March 25). Israeli government doc: Population exchange legal under international law, *Ha'aretz*, retrieved from http://www.haaretz.com/news/diplomacy-defense/.premium-1.581784

[76] Christmas Break in Palestine minute 13:45, retrieved from http://vimeo.com/13478028

[77] B'Tselem – The Israeli Information Center for Human Rights in the Occupied Territories. (2014, March 11). Restrictions of Movement: Checkpoints, Physical Obstructions, and Forbidden Roads, retrieved from http://www.btselem.org/freedom_of_movement/checkpoints_and_forbidden_roads. NB: this site was last updated in March of 2014, i.e. prior to Operation Protective Edge. It therefore provides an extremely conservative estimate of the number of checkpoints and barriers.

[78] *B'Tselem* – The Israeli Information Center for Human Rights in the Occupied Territories. (2014, March 10). Water Crisis: Discriminatory Water Supply, retrieved from http://www.btselem.org/water/discrimination_in_water_supply.k

[79] Dani Filc. (2009) *Circles of Exclusion: The Politics of Health Care in Israel*. New York: Cornell University Press.

[80] B'Tselem – The Israeli Information Center for Human Rights in the Occupied Territories. (2014, December 4). Administrative Detention, retrieved from http://www.btselem.org/administrative_detention/statistics

[81] Lisa Hajjar. (2005) *Courting Conflict: The Israeli Military Court System in the West Bank and Gaza*. Berkeley: University of California Press.

[82] Edo Konrad, *op. cit.*, see note 60. Jonathan Ofir. (2017, December 23). We should "exact a price" from Ahed Tamimi "in the dark," Israeli journalist says, *Mondoweiss*, retrieved from http://mondoweiss.net/2017/12/should-israeli-journalist/

[83] Ben White. (2012, January 12). Israel's High Court upholds racist "Citizenship Law" to avoid "national suicide, *Electronic Intifada*, retrieved from http://electronicintifada.net/blogs/ben-white/israels-high-court-upholds-racist-citizenship-law-avoid-national-suicide

[84] *Ibid.*

[85] Tom Segev. (2001). *Elvis in Jerusalem.* (New York: Metropolitan Books) pp. 28 ff.

[86] Statistics on emigration are very difficult to compile. While official records may show people leaving the country, their possible return or lack thereof can only be known in hindsight, years later. Official statistics seems to count an absence of more than a year as evidence of emigration, but this clearly does not square with the length of graduate programs and fellowships. For a recent update see, Silvan Klingbail and Shanee Shiloh. (2012, December 5). Bye, the beloved country – why almost 40 percent of Israelis are thinking of emigrating, *Ha'aretz*, retrieved from http://www.haaretz.com/news/features/bye-the-beloved-country-why-almost-40-percent-of-israelis-are-thinking-of-emigrating.premium-1.484945. Interviewees in this article cite complex reasons for leaving. Among the most often named reasons are career/economic motives. But these economic motives are mixed in complex ways within intra-Israeli cultural concerns, and with hardships that the respondents themselves do not see as related to the costs of Occupation but which, in fact, do have such a relationship.

[87] Gideon Levy and Alex Levac. (2014, March 30). The most surreal place in the occupied territories, *Ha'aretz*, retrieved from http://www.haaretz.com/weekend/twilight-zone/.premium-1.582447

[88] Information from most of the major new sources gives convergent accounts. See, for example, Alex Shams. (2014, February 11). Camp on the front line of struggle against occupation, *Ma'an News Agency*, retrieved from http://www.maannews.net/eng/ViewDetails.aspx?ID=672795 and Adam Wolf. (2014, March 27). Repression and resistance in Bethlehem's Aida refugee camp, *Mondoweiss,* retrieved from http://mondoweiss.net/2014/03/repression-resistance-bethlehems.html

[89] Jodi Rudoren. (2014, October 17). In Exodus form Israel to Berlin, Young Nation's Fissures Show, *New York Times*, retrieved from http://www.nytimes.com/2014/10/17/world/middleeast/in-exodus-from-israel-to-berlin-young-nations-fissures-show.html

[90] Aron Heller. (2013, August 17). Israeli Settlements at Forefront of Palestinian Peace Talks, *Huffington Post*, retrieved from http://www.huffingtonpost.com/2013/08/17/israeli-settlements-peace-talks_n_3773187.html. For exact numbers, see also Chapter 4, endnotes 26–30.

[91] Leonard Saxe, et. al. *Evaluating Birthright Israel: Long Term Impact and Recent Findings,* The Cohen Center for Modern Jewish Studies, Brandeis University, retrieved from http://www.brandeis.edu/cmjs/pdfs/evaluatingbri.04.pdf

[92] Yitzhak Epstein, "The Hidden Question," quoted in Natasha Gill. (2013, June 19). The Original No; Why the Arabs rejected Zionism, and why it matters, *Middle East Policy Council Commentary*, retrieved from http://www.mepc.org/articles-commentary/commentary/original-no-why-arabs-rejected-zionism-and-why-it-matters/

[93] Shamir quoted in Gill, *op. cit.*

[94] Patrick Wolfe. (2006, December)."Settler Colonialism and the Elimination of the Native," *Journal of Genocide Research* 8(4): 387.

[95] Yitzhak Epstein "The Hidden Question," Lecture to the 7th Zionist Congress, Basel, Switzerland, 1905, retrieved from http://qumsiyeh.org/yitzhakepstein/

[96] Nur Masalha. (1992). *The Expulsion of the Palestinians: The Concept of "Transfer" in Zionist Political Thought, 1882–1948* (Washington, D.C.: The Institute for Palestine Studies), pp. 5–6.

[97] Theodor Herzl. (1902). *Old New Land (Altneuland)*, Currently available retrieved from Create Space Independent Publishing Platform, 2011.

[98] Shlomo Sand. (2009). *The Invention of the Jewish People* (New York, Verso) p. 262.

[99] Masalha, *op. cit.*, p. 6.

[100] Ghada Karmi, *op. cit.*, p. 4.

[101] Masalha, *op. cit.*, p. 9.

[102] see Epstein, *op. cit.*

[103] *Ibid.*

[104] *Ibid.*

[105] Anita Shapira (1999). *Land and Power: The Zionist Resort to Force, 1881–1948.* Stanford: Stanford University Press.

[106] B'Tselem – The Israeli Information Center for Human Rights in the Occupied Territories. (2014, March 11). *Restrictions of Movement: Checkpoints, Physical Obstructions, and Forbidden Roads*, retrieved from http://www.btselem.org/freedom_of_movement/ checkpoints_and_forbidden_roads. NB: this site was last updated in March of 2014, i.e. prior to Operation Protective Edge. It therefore provides an extremely conservative estimate the number of checkpoints and barriers.

[107] A Jewish source, Arutz Sheva, acknowledges 389, 250 Jewish settlers in the West Bank and another 375,000 in East Jerusalem, whose "annexation" is universally recognized as illegal. These numbers date from 2014, and the source claims that by now the number of settlers has risen to 800,000. *Arutz Sheva*, retrieved from http://www.israelnationalnews. com/Articles/Article.aspx/18210#.VpK885scTIU. The population growth rate in the settlements, though declining, is still approximately twice as high as that in Jerusalem, see Jacob Magid, "Settler growth rate declines for sixth straight year," *The Times of Israel*, January 21, 2018, retrieved from https://www.timesofisrael.com/settler-growth-rate-declines-for-sixth-straight-year/

[108] Sophia Stamatopoulou-Robbins, Infrastructure and Materiality in Palestine Studies, Omar Jabary Salamanca, "Hooked on Electricity: the charged political economy of electrification in the West Bank," and Kareem Rabie, "Housing, the Production of the State and the Day After," papers delivered at the 2014 *New Directions in Palestinian Studies Symposium* at Brown University, February 28–March 1, 2014.

[109] Ilan Pappe. (2017). *The Biggest Prison on Earth*, London: One World Books.

[110] Saleh Abdel Jawad. (1998). War by Other Means, *al-Ahram Weekly*, retrieved from http://www.mediamonitors.net/jawad3.html

[111] Yizhar Be'er and Saleh Abdel Jawad. (1994). *Collaborators in the Occupied Territories.* B'Tselem Report.

[112] Sam Bahour. (2014, May 24). Israel Declares War on Palestinian Banks, *Talking Points Memo*, retrieved from http://talkingpointsmemo.com/cafe/israel-declares-war-on-palestinian-banks

[113] Eric Schulenberg. (2012, January 24). Israel Arrests Hamas Lawmakers in Jerusalem, *The Jewish Press*, retrieved from http://www.jewishpress.com/news/israel/israel-arrests-hamas-lawmakers-in-jerusalem/2012/01/24/

[114] Al Abunimah. (2012, May 13). Watch The Great Book Robbery, Israel's 1948 Looting of Palestine's Cultural Heritage, *Electronic Intifada*, retrieved from http://electronicintifada.net/blogs/ali-abunimah/watch-great-book-robbery-israels-1948-looting-palestines-cultural-heritage

[115] Hanafi, S. (2009). Spacio-cide: colonial politics, invisibility and rezoning in Palestinian territory. *Contemporary Arab Affairs*, 2(1), 106–121. Retrieved from http://www.humanitarianibh.net/english/reportes/2009_Spacio-cide_CAA.pdf

[116] Baruch Kimmerling. (2006). *Politicide: The Real Legacy of Ariel Sharon*. London, UK: Verso Press.

[117] Sehana Tahan. (2017, November 28). How Israeli Leftists Trivialize the Palestinian Cause, *+972*, retrieved from https://972mag.com/how-israeli-leftists-trivialize-the-palestinian-cause/131031/. Recently, the settler colonial framework was adopted by the U.S. Presbyterian Church as part of its social justice mission in the Holy Land. See Rod Such. (2018, June 24). Ending Colonialism in Palestine, *Electronic Intifada*, retrieved from https://electronicintifada.net/content/ending-colonialism-palestine/24756. See also Linda Tabar and Chandni Desai. (2017). Decolonization is a global project: from Palestine to the Americas, *Decolonization: Indigeneity, Education & Society*, 6(1): i-ix. Tabar and Desai argue that settler colonial theory fits well with intersectionality theory by noting the way race, class, and gender co-define the fate of both colonizers and colonized. The also pursue the comparisons between Palestine and Native Americans, thus introducing a cross-national and comparative perspective.

[118] Jonathan Ofir. (2018, June 16). Jewish race is the greatest human capital, the smartest, *Mondoweiss*, retrieved from http://mondoweiss.net/2018/06/lawmaker-greatest-smartest/

[119] Matthew Haag. (2018, May 14). Robert Jeffress Pastor who Said Jews Are Going to Hell, Led Prayer at Jerusalem Embassy, *New York Times*, retrieved from https://www.nytimes.com/2018/05/14/world/middleeast/robert-jeffress-embassy-jerusalem-us.html. See also, Raphael Aren. (2017, July 20). Decrying "Betrayal" Hungary Jews say Netanyahu ignoring them, *The Times of Israel*, retrieved from https://www.timesofisrael.com/decrying-netanyahu-betrayal-hungary-jews-say-pm-ignoring-them/

[120] Nathan Thrall details Arab peace overtures that pre-date the 2002 comprehensive Arab Peace initiative. As early as 1948 Egypt offered the new Israeli state a peace deal in return for the Negev, and in 1973 Sadat suggested a peace deal that would return the Sinai to Egypt. In 1949 Syria offered not only a peace deal but also to absorb a large number of Palestinian refugees in return for half of the Sea of Galilee. Jordanians twice offered peace deals, supporting Egyptian and Syrian offers. Nathan Thrall. (2017). *The Only Language They Understand: Forcing Compromise in Israel and Palestine*. (New York: Holt), p. 97, footnote p. 264.

[121] See, for example, Linda Tabar and Chandni Desai. *Loc. cit.*

[122] Maha Ighbaria. (2018, June 8). I am a Palestinian Woman in Israel. You don't get to Define My Labels, *Ha'aretz*, retrieved from https://www.haaretz.com/opinion/i-am-a-palestinian-woman-in-israel-you-don-t-get-to-define-my-labels-1.6246707

[123] Jeff Halper. (2018, May 3).The One Democratic State Campaign' program for a multicultural democratic statein Palestine/Israel, *Mondoweiss*, retrieved from http://mondoweiss.net/2018/05/democratic-multicultural-palestine/?utm_

source=Mondoweiss+List&utm_campaign=f67fddf1a9-RSS_EMAIL_
CAMPAIGN&utm_medium=email&utm_term=0_b86bace129-f67fddf1a9-
332399817&mc_cid=f67fddf1a9&mc_eid=d3e0ecd0a6
See also Ahmed Abu Artena. (2018, August 17). One State: A View from Gaza, *Mondoweiss*, retrieved from https://mondoweiss.net/2018/08/state-view-from/

[124] Mahmood Mamdani. (2015, Autumn). "The South African Movement," *Journal of Palestine Studies*, 45(1):63.

CHAPTER 10

ZIONISM REVISITED

From 1967 back to 1948

[W]hen two opposite points of view are expressed with equal intensity, the truth does not necessarily lie exactly halfway between them. It is possible for one side to be simply wrong.

Richard Dawkins and Jeremy Coyne[1]

What incites protesters to throw stones is the sound of bullets, the Occupation's bulldozers as they destroy the land, the smell of tear gas and the smoke coming from burnt houses.

Bassem Tamimi[2]

In Chapter 4, I argued that Zionism was the doctrine that changed everything in the history of Palestine and Israel. The initial core idea of Zionism – to create a safe place for European Jews who had suffered centuries of persecution – was entirely understandable in the time and place where it originated. But we have now seen how it has actually played out: not its hopes, but its realities.

Early on, there were forks in the road.

Was Zionism to be established in Palestine or in Uganda, Argentina, or elsewhere? A combination of Zionist preference and British interests determined that it would be Palestine.

Was the Zionist project to be cultural or political? Was it to seek a homeland or to build a state? The decision was soon made to build a state, by violent means if necessary.[3]

It seems likely that many of the European Jews who arrived in Palestine as part of the Zionist project, especially early on, were more preoccupied with the terror they were leaving behind than with the community they were hoping to build. Consumed with the need to flee persecution, perhaps they gave too little thought to what they would find at their destination.

Even so, it seems lacking in common sense to suppose that the Holy Land of the Old Testament could possibly be what Zionist propaganda described it to be: "a land without people for a people without land."[4] Zionist leaders certainly

© KONINKLIJKE BRILL NV, LEIDEN, 2019 | DOI:10.1163/9789004394148_010

knew that the land was not empty. Israel Zangwill, for example, complained: "Palestine is already twice as thickly populated as the United States ... and not 25 per cent of them Jews."[5] In the rather poetic metaphor attributed to Zionist planners, the bride was very beautiful but already claimed by another.[6]

The juxtaposition of a deeply rooted indigenous population and the intense desire of the new arrivals to have exclusive dominion over the land made tragic consequences inevitable. The tragedy is not a product of the Jewish faith, or even of Jewish individuals *per se*. (In fact, Jewish people have no monopoly on Zionism; in the United States today, Christian Zionists far outnumber Jewish ones.[7])

Rather, it is Zionism itself – the will to exclusive possession of a place that was already inhabited by others – that caused the tragedy. Wherever and however Zionism has come to mean the right of Jews to displace the population already in place, a politics of ethnic cleansing inevitably followed. Henri Laurens, the French historian, describes ethnic cleansing as embedded in the gene code of Zionism,[8] and Israeli psychologist Benjamin Beit-Hallahmi calls it Zionism's "original sin."[9]

For this reason, a growing number of people have come to the conclusion that Zionism is morally untenable, even toxic.[10] This conclusion says nothing about Jews or even Israelis, and it is certainly not a justification for pushing any community into the sea. Rather, those criticizing Zionism recognize that for some 51 years now, by its own desire and choice, Israel has been the sole state controlling all the land between the river and the sea. Therefore it is time for a state so constituted to become a state of all the people under its control.[11] That is what a belief in democracy and human rights requires.

When Israeli spokespersons confront this position, they invariably assert that people who expect it to become "a state of all its people" are trying to "destroy Israel." This response is both extreme and absurd.

It is not a death warrant to demand that Israel be a modern, culturally diverse, and multi-ethnic democracy. The end of Apartheid did not destroy South Africa nor did it loose a bloodbath on whites. The end of slavery did not destroy the United States. The end of colonialism did not destroy Algeria or India or even, indeed, France or England. The call for an egalitarian democracy that respects human rights is thus not a death wish. It is exactly what it appears to be: a call for reform. Some Israelis do recognize the truth of this assertion. For example, prominent journalist Gideon Levy writes:

> An established country like Israel can return to its foundations and admit
> to its birth defects: Zionism was and is an ultranationalist movement,
> tainted by racism, cruel, discriminatory, oppressive and disinheriting.

Most important: *replaceable.* (italics mine). A moment before the usual wail goes up about the destruction of the State of Israel, something that should be obvious must be said: It's possible to have a just, thriving state that is not Zionist. Moreover, it is not possible to have a just state that continues to cling to Zionism.[12]

Whether or not one wishes to heed the call for rethinking Zionism and its relation to justice, hysterical fear mongering is never an appropriate response. People who reduce patriotism to cheerleading do their country a great disservice.

It is clear, however, that becoming a modern, culturally diverse, and multi-ethnic democracy would *change* Israel and there are those who insist that such changes—becoming inclusive and democratic—would destroy the Zionist dream of an ethnically exclusive community. This particular defense of Israel's identity contains a contradiction: at once deploring (and rightly so!) the state-sponsored violence of the Holocaust, while simultaneously demanding immense sentimentality about the state of Israel. Sentimentality about states and state-sponsored violence should not come easily to those who stand in the shadow of the Holocaust.

Over time, the public discourse about Israel is changing. In the years following revelations about the Holocaust (and given the immense popularity of Leon Uris' novel *Exodus*[13]) Israelis were seen as plucky underdogs, the good white guys building a gleaming modern democracy in a sea of swarthy Arabs. The expulsion of Palestinians was simply not a topic of discussion in American circles. After the Israeli military victory in 1967, the beginning of the Occupation and, even more critically, the immediate commencement of settlement building, a small voice of doubt began to surface. Criticisms were still spoken in a whisper, as the American Israeli Public Affairs Committee (AIPAC) was deemed to be the "third rail" in Washington politics. And criticism, however mild, was generally couched in terms of "saving Israel from itself."

Today the discourse is different, at least in part. There are many reasons for the shift. The Holocaust generation is dying out. Among their children and grandchildren and great grandchildren, the traditional Jewish concern for justice is open to reassignment – investing itself in environmentalism, human rights advocacy, and, sometimes, even criticism of Israel.[14] The Cold War has ended, strong third world economies are emerging, petro-politics have become a force to be reckoned with. The Arab world, though still enshrouded in Orientalist myths, has become more salient to Americans – whether they believe themselves to be engaged in a clash of civilizations, or whether they are concerned about oil prices, or whether they feel overwhelmed by the number of wars we have conducted in Muslim lands, Arabs are now on the American radar screen in complex ways. And then there is the behavior of Israel itself, for example, in Operation Protective Edge, which even the most accomplished spin-doctors cannot sell.

Early skepticism about Israel was voiced only as a cautious, diffident, and circumscribed criticism of 1967, that is, of the permanent Occupation, entrenched by 764,000 settlers who create "facts on the ground."[15] *What is emerging now is a criticism re-opening the question of 1948, that is, of Zionism itself as inherently colonial, racist, and untenable.*[16] Clearly this is a much more profound challenge than the common frame of a "good Israel" inside the Green Line and a "bad Israel" only in the West Bank, Gaza, and East Jerusalem. It is, nonetheless, the challenge that must faced.

There are at least four significant objections to Zionism:

- it requires harm to Palestinians wherever it establishes itself;
- it is inherently a project of Jewish self-ghettoization;
- it has failed to deliver on its own *raison d'être*: safety for Jews;
- and finally, Zionism blinds us to the real challenges of the future – the quest for a humane version of globalization and a viable response to global climate change.

ZIONISM AS COLONIZATION AND ETHNIC CLEANSING/SOCIOCIDE

It is impossible to evade it. Without the uprooting of the Palestinians, a Jewish state would not have arisen here … There are circumstances that justify ethnic cleansing. I know that this term is completely negative in the discourse of the 21st century, but when the choice is between ethnic cleansing and genocide—the annihilation of your people—I prefer ethnic cleansing.

Benny Morris[17]

Karen's Story

I was giving a lecture on the Israel/Palestine conflict to a Peace Studies course at a nearby university. Students who had selected this class were serious young men and women. In the conversation that followed, one of them, Karen, not necessarily a Zionist, but deeply respectful of all that she had learned about the suffering of Jews in the Holocaust, made a number of references to "the six million" [Jewish dead in the Holocaust]. It occurred to me to wonder how many students in that class associated the Holocaust with "the six million." A quick show of hands revealed that virtually all of them did.

But, in fact the Holocaust dead number upwards of 12 million,[18] and include many other targeted groups besides Jews: gay people, Roma peoples, Russian, Polish, and Yugoslavian prisoners of war, socialists, communists, people with mental or physical difficulties, often Catholics, and, of course, anyone who opposed the Nazi regime.

I asked people to do a thought experiment. Zionists claim that, because of the long history of European anti-Semitism, culminating in the Holocaust, they are owed not only a safe place, but an exclusive state of their own. Do we agree that they need a state to be safe? Show of hands please, did the class endorse that position? There was a great deal of hesitation but in the end, most of the students agreed.

But gay men and women, I argued, could make a similar claim. They have suffered a long history of discrimination, marginalization, and murderous rage at the hands of their neighbors, including also during the Holocaust. Tragically, we do not even have to go back 70 years in our own history. As recently as 1998, an American youngster, Matthew Shepherd, was tied to a fencepost and had his head smashed in with gun butts – all at the hands of two homophobes in Laramie, Wyoming. So gays could legitimately argue that they, too, need a safe space.

The history of the gay movement in America shows a valiant struggle to create this safety in all walks of life: in churches (ordination of gay clergy, performance of gay marriage), in workplaces (anti-discrimination rules, gay partner benefits), in medical settings (access to care giving decisions and visitation rights for gay partners) and, finally, state-by-state, in the recognition of gay families through marriage reform. Happily, Massachusetts is one such state, where gay marriage is legal and sanctified.

But supposing the gay movement now decided that these reforms were too slow, too piecemeal, and, even cumulatively, not enough to achieve safety for gay people. Supposing gay rights advocates in Massachusetts, having gained the beachhead of gay marriage, now decided they needed a state of their own. Supposing gays turned to their

> heterosexual neighbors and demanded: "Now don't take this personally, but you have to get out. We need a gay state of our own, and you'll just have to leave."
>
> How many students would assent to that proposition? Show of hands, please. There were no takers.

Note how easily Benny Morris, in the epigram above, invokes the Holocaust to legitimate a Zionist state building project that long precedes World War II. Nevertheless, as the leading researcher in Israeli military archives, he should be appreciated for his candor in admitting that Zionism pursues its dream of a Jewish state at the expense of the indigenous population. It is a disaster, a catastrophe, for Palestinians. And this disaster is ongoing, with violent settler encroachment on Palestinian land now the principal face of expropriation.[19] Much of the preceding history attests to the fact that the Zionist dream has been built on the ruins of Palestinian hope.

It is certainly true that all Zionists do not speak with one voice and never did. There were, among early Zionist settlers, those who dreamed of a state that would welcome Jews without expelling or suppressing Palestinians, who anticipated a safe multi-ethnic society. The leading voices of this position were Ahad Ha'am (Asher Ginsburg) and Judah Magnes (later the founder of Hebrew University) both of whom called for a cultural rather than a political version of Zionism.[20] Martin Buber advocated for a bi-national state[21] and cautioned that excessive nationalism could only produce "a tiny state of Jews, completely militarized and unsustainable.[22] They were augmented by Einstein, who was skeptical of all nationalisms,[23] and by Hannah Arendt, who specifically warned that the safety of a Jewish homeland must never be sacrificed to the "pseudo-sovereignty" of a Jewish state built on Arab suppression.[24]

There are, of course, those who claim that these "soft Zionists," who seemed to speak for coexistence rather than conquest, were only a front, a kind of Trojan horse concealing the real intentions of Zionism.[25] Alas, whatever their true intentions, the "soft" Zionists did not prevail.

Today's soft Zionists are people who want to acknowledge Palestinian suffering while yet insisting that there can be a legitimate Israel within the internationally proposed border defined by the Green Line, the armistice line of 1949. This position dismisses criticism of the *Nakba* (1947–1949), but is willing to criticize and deplore the Occupation begun in 1967.

The Israeli journalist and author Ari Shavit exemplifies the more aggressive version of this position. In his recent autobiographical bestseller, *My Promised Land*, he supplies an insightful cultural history of Israel as a place steeped in existential fear, fear both of annihilation and of assimilation.[26] Out of that fear, he suggests, came first the rejection of Palestinian nationalist claims and then the *Nakba*. He provides a candid, gruesome account of the Lydda massacre in July, 1948. He calls it Israel's quintessential black box, inside which the dirty work of ethnic cleansing is both accomplished and concealed. "He describes a PIAT anti-tank shell fired into a mosque from 6 meters, killing 70; soldiers spraying the wounded with automatic fire, walking into nearby houses and gunning down anyone they saw. But then he concludes that, absent such an atrocity, his own modern city could not have been created."[27] One *Ha'aretz* review of the book sums it up this way: "Zionism means never having to say you're sorry."[28]

There are also those who *are* willing to say they are sorry and yet remain Zionists. These are people who walk through Hebron, observe the concrete barriers that divide the street into Palestinian and Jewish paths, observe the besieged Palestinian markets and old Palestinian homes with their cage-like metal guards over every door and window, and are appalled. Many of them do more than pay lip service to this position: they put their jobs, their friendships, and sometimes even their lives on the line to register their disapproval. They stand in solidarity with Palestinians in front of bulldozers,[29] and risk tear gas and bullets at the various village demonstrations against the wall[30] and against settler violence during the olive harvest.[31] And yet many of these same people, who find Hebron or Nabi Saleh[32] so horrible, have no objection to Jaffa, where a community of 120,000 Palestinians was reduced to a wretched 4,000 people within a few months during the *Nakba*.[33]

This position makes a great deal of emotional sense – it situates Israel's oppression and human rights violations in the Occupied Territories (i.e. somewhere else, not rightly Israel) while preserving the image of a "good Israel" inside the 1949 borders.

Alas, this position does not make factual or logical sense. As horrible and unjust as today's Occupation is, it is considerably less bloody (even including massacres like Cast Lead and Protective Edge) than the *Nakba*. It seems willfully blind to object to suppression carried out largely with cumbersome rules and regulations and give a pass to expulsion carried out by force of arms. In some sense, Shavit's more abrasive position is also more honest in insisting on a "stark" choice: "either reject Zionism because of Lydda, or accept Zionism along with Lydda."[34]

Shavit, I suspect, meant this as a conversational trump card, a way of acknowledging the *Nakba* while forever silencing the demand that Israel take responsibility for it or that anything change because of it. As time goes on, however, more and more people who encounter that choice choose to reject Zionism.[35] Peter Beinart, an American Zionist who is nevertheless critical of Israel puts it this way: "For several decades, the Jewish establishment has asked American Jews to check their liberalism at Zionism's door, and now, to their horror, they are finding that many young Jews have checked their Zionism instead."[36]

ZIONISM AS SELF-GHETTOIZATION

I remember how it was in 1948 when Israel was being established and all my Jewish friends were ecstatic, I was not. I said: what are we doing? We are establishing ourselves in a ghetto.

Isaac Asimov[37]

There is a growing sense that Israel is becoming an isolated ghetto, which is exactly what the founding fathers and mothers hoped to leave behind them forever when they created the state of Israel.

Amos Oz[38]

Particularism is a bad idea whose time has come.

Diane Ravitch[39]

Isaac's Story

As an undergraduate, I attended Brooklyn College. At that time, the student body was overwhelmingly Jewish. One of my closest friends from those days, Ruthie, married into an Orthodox family. Today, her oldest daughter lives in Boston where she practices law and also teaches at a local law school. Needless to say, her parents are massively proud of her and want to see her and their grandchildren as often as possible. When they are in town, they sometimes stay with me.

One night, Ruthie and her husband Isaac and I sat around swapping stories from our family histories. Isaac remembers being a little boy in a Yeshiva elementary school during the Second World War. He describes himself as a good little boy, who worshipped his father, his Rabbi, and the teachers at the Yeshiva. He thought they were the giants of the universe – men who knew all, understood all, and could accomplish anything.

Gradually, Isaac became aware that the grown-ups in his world were doing a great deal of whispering behind closed doors. So, being a bright, curious, and energetic little boy, Isaac, of course, began lurking around those closed doors, trying to overhear as much as possible. What he heard made very little sense to him. He did not really understand what his elders were talking about. But he did understand the emotion that ran through their conversation: *fear*. Somewhere in the world something unimaginably terrible and senseless was happening to Jewish people. Watching Isaac's old man face as he tells the story, you can still see that little boy, listening furtively by the door, fearing above all his growing realization that the world was so big, so full of danger, that even the giants of his private universe trembled.

This memory could, of course, be the beginning of reconciliation – of realizing that today, there is a little Ishak somewhere in Gaza, or in a refugee camp, or even in a Palestinian community in Israel, listening at closed doors and learning that the world is so full of danger that the giants of his universe tremble before it. Sadly, the Isaac I know cannot "pay it forward," insisting, whenever Palestinians are mentioned, "They are all terrorists."

At least some people who reject Zionism do so less out of solidarity with Palestinian suffering than because they consider Zionism ill advised for Jews. Even had Palestine actually been a land without people, even had the establishment of a Jewish state not required ethnic cleansing, there are those who feel that Zionism is, at best, a project of Jewish self-ghettoization,[40] at odds with Judaism's own universalistic ethic.

Anthropology is the place to begin understanding the concern about self-ghettoization. Every society known to anthropologists is ethnocentric and develops a narrative that asserts that its own way of life is attuned to the nature of the universe and hence superior to all others.[41] Almost always, because it claims not only earthly but supernaturally sanctioned superiority, this narrative has a religious cast to it.

The particularism of this narrative can lend itself to many different political arrangements. Polytheistic societies can be very welcoming to outsider groups and alien gods, adding shrines, holidays, and sacrifices willy-nilly. Many indigenous tribes, when first encountering European explorers, simply adopted white men into specific families, thereby placing them within the web of known and shared obligations. So it is simply not true that the tribal organization of society is inherently thuggish and will always give rise to an ethos of competition, raiding, and warfare.

Nevertheless, particularism, ethnocentricity, and tribalism provide only a weak basis for universal human rights. Human beings from other, "inferior," groups can be accepted with greater or lesser generosity, but they are never really fully equal and, certainly, they are not fully equal as a matter of *right*.

Monotheism represents a radical break from ethnocentrism and tribalism. It posits that we are *all* the creation of a single omniscient, omnipotent deity, and hence we are all truly brothers and sisters, children of the same creative life force. Whether we are religious in the style of any of the monotheisms, Judaism, Christianity or Islam, or whether we prefer a more secular phrasing (substituting "evolution" for "god") monotheism is a philosophical breakthrough. It is a game-changer that presents us with intellectual and political challenges: to recognize all other human being and all other ways of life to be as valuable as our own and as entitled to rights as our own.[42]

The tension between the anthropological imperative of ethnocentricity, on the one hand, and the moral imperative of universalism, on the other, runs deep within Jewish history. Alan Wolfe, a scholar of religion, politics, and the arts, describes how the 12th century Jewish philosopher Maimonides stood at the intersection of the contradictory demands of theologically mandated universalism and anthropologically mandated particularism. Maimonides, Wolfe argues, believed that the superiority of Jews rested on Jewish law.[43] So, in fact, Maimonides rested his claims of Jewish superiority precisely on the fact that Jewish theology rejected the idea of tribal precedence in favor of a universal humanism. Had Maimonides needed a bumper sticker back in the 12th century, it might have read "I'm better than you because I believe we're equal."

In the contemporary world, Zionism continues to embody this tension between the universal and the particular. European Jews fled Christendom because of its abject failure to live up to universal values. Israelis congratulate themselves on being "the only democracy in the Middle East." And yet they violate their own professed ethical standards by denying the Palestinian claim to justice. And, increasingly, they turn their backs on the world in favor of a "Jews first, Jews only, Jews always" stance that permeates their political and cultural behavior. The admittedly imperfect institutions of the United Nations, the International Court of Justice, and the International Criminal Court, Amnesty International, Human Rights Watch, *B'Tselem* must all be repudiated because they do not always side with Israel; "universal jurisdiction" must be denounced because it might be used to prosecute Israeli war crimes as it has been used against Pinochet; the rules of war need to be revised to legitimate the kind of behavior Israel chose during Operation Cast Lead and Operation Protective Edge.

On the cultural side, one of Israel's leading, internationally acclaimed writers, A.B. Yehoshua, argues that one cannot be fully Jewish apart from Israel and apart from the Hebrew language; Israeli Jews, he says, are full Jews, whereas those living outside Israel are only partial Jews.[44] In this he echoes Theodor Herzl, Zionism's founder, who anticipated that, after the establishment of a Jewish state, all Jews who refused to move to Israel (which is well over half of the world's Jews) should simply be redefined as non-Jews.[45]

Nor is Yehoshua alone in his convictions about the link between Israel and Jewish identity. Some years ago the Israeli government paid for public service TV ads that ran in America, but were quickly withdrawn in the face of objections even by American Zionists. One ad showed a young American man in Israel coming home to the apartment he obviously shared with an Israeli girl. He sees that all the lights in the apartment have been dimmed and candles lit everywhere. He immediately begins to act amorous, only to be rebuffed by the girl who, we see, is watching a program for Holocaust Remembrance Day. The candles are to commemorate the dead, and the young American Jewish man is shown to be utterly clueless. Were he to commit to a life in Israel, we are supposed to conclude, he would not make such an oafish mistake again. In a similar ad, Jewish grandparents are Skyping with their young grandson, now living in America. The child innocently asks them whether they've put up their Christmas tree yet. The Jewish grandparents glance at each other, aghast. Only in Israel, these ads suggest, can Jews learn to perform their Jewishness appropriately.

In 2006, when Yehoshua first made his assertions, Tony Karon, a Jewish South African journalist and veteran of the anti-Apartheid struggle replied in a *Ha'aretz* column, entitled "How Jewish is Israel?"[46] Karon provides reassurance for those who worry less about the risks of annihilation and more about the temptations of assimilation. He is worth quoting at length because many others, such as theologian Marc Ellis[47] and former Knesset speaker Avraham Burg[48] echo his comments.

In his op. ed. piece, Karon argues:

[I]f..we define "Jewish" on the basis of the universal ethical challenges at the core of Judaism, then ... the Diaspora [is] an essential condition of Jewishness ... [M]ost of us choose freely to live, as Jews have for centuries, among the nations ... That choice is becoming increasingly popular among Israeli Jews, too ... hardly surprising in an age of accelerated globalization that feeds dozens of diasporas and scorns national boundaries ... I am not religious, but I share Burg's belief that Judaism is fundamentally an ethical challenge epitomized for me by the famous "on-one-leg" definition by Hillel: "That which is hateful unto yourself, do not do unto others; all the rest is commentary." ... I can't see anything Jewish about investing hills and piles of stones with a spiritual significance worth dying and killing for ... Judaism's universal ethical calling can't really be answered if we live only among ourselves ... All of the great Jewish intellectual, philosophical, moral and cultural contributions to humanity I can think of were products not of Jews living apart, but of our dispersal among the cultures of the world. Maimonides or Spinoza, Marx, Freud, Einstein or Derrida; Kafka, Proust or Primo Levi; Serge Gainsbourg or Daniel Barenboim; Lenny Bruce or Bob Dylan – I could go on *ad nauseum* – all are products of our interaction with diverse influences in the Diaspora ... Jewish identity is always in flux and contested. The Zionist moment is a comparatively brief one in the sweep of Jewish history, and I'd argue that Judaism's survival depends instead on its ability to offer a sustaining moral and ethical anchor in a world where the concepts of nation and nationality are in decline.

ZIONISM AND THE PROMISE OF SAFETY

Instead of seeing the [Israeli] state as a means of saving the world's Jews, they demanded that the world's Jews defend the community in Palestine.

Tom Segev[49]

Israel is today the most dangerous place in the world for Jews. Since its establishment, more Jews were hurt in wars and terror attacks that took place in Israel than anywhere else. The war in Gaza took this one step backward – it endangered world Jews as well, as no other war has before it.

Gideon Levy[50]

Israel has flipped the whole conversation about safety. We must all guarantee the safety of the Occupier. Why is no one asking about the safety of the Occupied, the Palestinians?

Diana Buttu[51]

Mira's Story

Mira, one of my graduate students in sociology, is the granddaughter of Holocaust survivors. Out of her own family's past she has become deeply committed to peace with justice and thus devoted her doctoral dissertation to studying peacemakers on both sides of various world conflicts, including the Palestinian-Israeli conflict.

One day we were discussing the ways in which most studies, especially early in one's career, are rooted in autobiography. Mira told me about growing up in an American suburb. Her family actually had the iconic white picket fence bordering their garden, which was lushly landscaped with flowering bushes carefully cultivated by Mira's mother.

When Mira began to attend the local public school, she had to walk only as far as the corner, two houses to the left of her home, to catch the school bus. But on the very first day she noticed that her grandfather, who had survived Auschwitz and now lived with the family, would follow her, darting from bush to bush to conceal himself, to watch over her until the bus arrived. Mira, of course, was embarrassed by this behavior. But, for all the years she attended that elementary school, she could never persuade her grandfather that he could keep her safe by watching her progress from his second-story bedroom window.

The tension between the requirements of a universalistic ethic and particularism, tribalism, a preference for the familiar, can never be resolved definitively. As circumstances change, the relative strength of particularistic and universalistic appeals will also fluctuate.

How safe a group feels at any particular moment in time is certainly one determinant, perhaps the most important one, of the balance between particularism and universalism. Zionism is deeply rooted in the persecution Jews suffered in Christian Europe. It was designed specifically to produce a place of safety for Jews. It is therefore entirely fair to ask whether it has, in fact, accomplished its first and most important mission: to provide safety. At the same time of course, human rights standards demand that we be equally concerned for the safety of the other inhabitants of the land, the Palestinians.

Safety can come in a variety of forms. Is the country safe from invasion? Is it safe from internal collapse? Is it safe from the enmity of its neighbors? Are individuals within the country safe from violence? Do people outside the country perceive it to be a safe place to visit and to invest? Is the country respected in international relations – is it safe from ridicule?

In the case of Israel, the answer to these questions is a resounding no.

From the beginning, Israel has insisted that it is in a continual state of existential threat: neighboring countries have repeatedly invaded; the Palestinians living under occupation have refused to fall in with Israel's plans for them; the Arab Spring has further undermined Palestinian docility; America is an insufficiently pliant ally (despite the fact that Trump moved the U.S. embassy to Jerusalem and re-imposed sanctions on Iran, he hasn't yet agreed to go to war against them); Israeli leaders have botched the strategic alliance with the United States[52]; significant numbers of Israeli citizens in the north and south live under actual or threatened rocket and missile fire; Israel is targeted by a global terror network; Iran is set to challenge Israel's nuclear monopoly in the Middle East; a growing Boycott, Sanctions, Divestment movement threatens business as usual with Europe; major international institutions are atavistically anti-Semitic. Even its own internal Palestinian citizens represent a "demographic threat" to Israel. And if all that isn't bad enough, there's a small and, so far, ineffective, but nevertheless newsworthy and photogenic dissent from within: Israeli professors who endorse the boycott movement against Israel,[53] youngsters who refuse military service because of the Occupation[54] or who speak out strongly against it after their period of compulsory military duty.[55]

As with most complex and difficult situations, there is enough blame to go around. Some of Israel's fears are well grounded – for example, rocket fire from Gaza, despite the low fatality rate, means that vast numbers of citizens in the south live in continuous fear.[56] Firing rockets at civilians, whether recklessly or deliberately, constitutes a war crime.[57]

Some of Israel's fears are exaggerated, probably for political purposes. For example, the evidence that Iran is capable of producing weapons grade atomic material is highly contested, although Israel talks about it as a *fait accompli*.[58]

Some of Israel's fears are seriously misguided. For example, the notion that their own Palestinian citizens represent a demographic threat makes sense only as pure racism.

And some of Israel's woes are entirely self-inflicted. Consider, for example, the *Knesset's* recent action in passing a law to redefine the ethnicity of Palestinian Christians in Israel. By legislative fiat, because the *Knesset* says so, Palestinian Christians are no longer Arabs.[59] Voila! Of course this arbitrary redefinition mirrors Herzl's contention that Jews who do not migrate to Israel should be reclassified out of Judaism. But, no matter which founding fathers are echoed, such bizarre legislation can only become fodder for a political satire. How could it be otherwise?

Whether the risks Israel perceives are real, exaggerated, or entirely imaginary, there is one thing glaringly missing from Israel's discourse on danger: *Israel never considers that its own behavior might be, in part, responsible for the difficulties it faces.* Recently, Ha'aretz columnist Eva Illuz wrote: "Open *Ha'aretz* on any given day. Half or three quarters of its news items will invariably revolve around the same two topics: people struggling to protect the good name of Israel, and people struggling against its violence and injustices."[60]

The problem is neither with the enumeration of Israeli offenses against human rights nor even with the idea of Israeli self-defense. The problem is Israel's complete blindness to the connection between the two. In the words of Henry Siegman, an Orthodox Rabbi and former head of the American Jewish Congress, "The seeming inability of most Israelis to engage in any self-examination blinds them to the injustices they have inflicted on a subject people."[61] It blinds them equally to the recognition that their Occupation is not sustainable indefinitely.

There are three especially important examples of this blindness.

First, while Israel is universally perceived to possess nuclear weapons, it refuses to admit the possibility that its own arsenal is fueling the arms race in the Middle East.

Second, Israel laments decisions by the International Court of Justice (declaring its separation wall illegal), votes in the U.N. General Assembly (recognizing Palestine as an observer state), boycotts from the European Union – but it never acknowledges that its illegal settlements, rather than *a priori* hatred of Jews, might be the source of the difficulties.

Third, Israel never considers that it is unsafe because it has made Palestinians unsafe.[62] Israel never acknowledges the legal and moral obligations of an occupier to the occupied population,[63] nor does it want to face the fact that there is no decent way to conduct a decades-long Occupation. Israel resolutely ignores all the historical precedents of decolonization struggles in which superior arms did not lead to victory. The French were better armed in Vietnam and Algeria. The British were better armed in India and in the American colonies. But the better-armed states were not able to defeat national liberation struggles in any of these instances.

Denial and self-pity is the pervasive theme in Israeli discourse; self-awareness is not much in evidence. For example, the protagonist in *Waltz with Bashir*, an award-winning Israeli film, discovers that he has lost all his memories of being at the Sabra and Shatila massacre as an Israeli soldier, although he knows he was there. The film depicts his quest to find his lost memories. At one point, he sees a psychologist, worried about his memory-loss of "what happened in the camps." Immediately the therapist advises him that his mind is not really grappling with what he saw at Sabra and Shatila; instead it is remembering "those other camps," i.e. the Holocaust. Israelis cannot hold on to a picture of themselves as victimizers; they must always take the role of the victim.[64] Similarly, in the midst of Operation Protective Edge, an Israeli cultural analyst explained in *Ha'aretz* that Britain's support for Palestinian rights is a marker of their desire to appear trendy, barely more than a fashion statement.[65] The possibility that British support for Gaza may be rooted in a commitment to human rights is just not thinkable.

In short, most Israelis have chosen not to listen to voices like that of Bassem Tamimi, the leader of the protests in Nabi Saleh (see Chapter 2) who addresses the military judge at one of his many hearings as follows: "The military prosecutor accuses me of inciting the protesters to throw stones at the soldiers. This is not true. What incites protesters to throw stones is the sound of bullets, the Occupation's bulldozers as they destroy the land, the smell of tear gas and the smoke coming from burnt houses."[66] Tamimi's voice is neither heard nor heeded.

The point here is not to deny that, as Israel's defenders like to say, "Israel lives in a very tough neighborhood." Nor is there any reason to temper our criticism of those who use Israel's unjust behavior as an excuse for renewed anti-Semitism, or as a justification for war crimes.

The point is that Israel's own rhetoric creates a dilemma. One the one hand we are implored to support Israel because Jews need a room of their own. But, at the same time, we are constantly being told that, no matter how much support we pour into Israel, it will continue to be steeped in existential threat, to teeter on the brink of annihilation. And then, in a further twist, Israel tries to claim our loyalties because their invincibility makes them an asset in the 'War on Terror.'"[67] This is, clearly, a worrisome and unreliable picture. Perhaps the bottom line here is: If the *raison d'être* for Zionism is Jewish safety, then 70 years of failure to achieve that goal might be reason enough to reevaluate the project.[68]

ZIONISM AND GLOBALIZATION

As peripheries, we are a part of a globalized process of "recolonization of the 'third world' by hegemonic western financial systems."

Khalil Nakhleh[69]

And even if Jews were to win the war ... [t]he 'victorious' Jews would live surrounded by an entirely hostile Arab population, secluded inside ever-threatened borders, absorbed with physical self-defense to a degree that would submerge all other interests and activities.

Hannah Arendt[70]

Maureen's Story

At a recent dinner party, conversation turned toward the idea put forward by Samuel Huntington that the West and Islam are engaged in a "clash of civilizations."[71] Maureen, an accountant, offered an anecdote in support of the idea. While in her MBA program she had heard the following story from a fellow student, a Jewish man of Moroccan heritage. He claimed that his best friend, also Jewish, also Moroccan by birth, had once been enrolled in a Muslim school in Morocco. By the end of the year, his friend had earned the highest grades in the class, especially in the study of the Qur'an. But he was not named the valedictorian, an honor he felt he deserved. In Maureen's telling of the story, her classmate and his friend understood this incident to be proof of atavistic anti-Semitism, disrespect for intellectual achievement, a mini clash of civilizations between Arabs and the West.

I argued that many other interpretations were possible. How many Yeshivas, I wondered, would allow Muslim boys (or Hindu or Buddhist or Christian ones) to enroll? How many non-Jews enrolled in a Yeshiva would flourish to the extent that Maureen's story suggested? Were a Muslim boy to earn the best grades studying Torah, would his teachers not argue that, for him, this was mere book learning, whereas for a Jewish boy it was a deeply felt blueprint for life?

Was the notion of a "clash of civilizations" really a necessary or helpful way to understand this anecdote, to think about our increasing interconnectedness?

Eve's Story

On one of my first visits to Jerusalem, the concierge at my hotel urged me to visit the Museum on the Seam. This Museum is dedicated to raising the difficult political questions of the area through international art. It is built into a Palestinian mansion that stands on the Green Line. In that spot, the Green Line functions as the seam line between Jewish West Jerusalem and Palestinian East Jerusalem. The site also abuts the old Mandelbaum Gate, the point of passage between Israeli Jerusalem and the parts of Jerusalem held by Jordan from 1948 to 1967. On the outside, the Museum on the Seam (designed by Arab architect Anton Barmki in 1932) embodies classical Palestinian architecture, with its stone walls and arched windows. Inside it has been gutted and fitted out as an art gallery with blank walls, covered over windows, a gift shop, and alcoves that can show film clips along with the art. The architecture inside the Museum on the Seam would be equally at home in an art gallery in Santa Fe, Hong Kong, Stockholm, or Buenos Aires. The Museum's very architecture represents an uneasy balance between the local and the global.

The previous three analyses take Zionism at it at its word, as a project rooted in European Jewish history. This Zionism is backward looking, not only in its preoccupation with the Holocaust, but also in its dedication to ideas of nationalism rooted in 19th century ideals of ethnic purity.[72] Intensely nationalistic as it is, Zionism utterly rejects modern notions of strength from diversity or interdependence, hewing to a kind of "first draft" nationalism that seemed antiquated until quite recently.

But what if Zionism was to be evaluated not on its depiction, accurate or distorted, of a bygone world, but for its capacity to lead to a better future for the people it aims to protect? What would Zionism contribute to our ability to navigate the biggest challenges we face: globalization and climate change? No nation-state today knows what to do about either. Perhaps this catastrophic unpreparedness accounts for the retreat to an earlier and more racist sense of national identity not only in America, but in much of Europe as well.

Globalization means different things in different disciplines, but most definitions emphasize the convergence of at least these elements:

- Economics – trade and capital flows,
- Technology – for example social media, the ability to create and use "big data," production technologies that allow for dramatic changes in industrial strength world-wide,
- Politics – including shifting regional defense alliances and the emergence of supra-national free trade zones and governance mechanisms,
- Organizational forms – from NGOs, international aid and humanitarian regimes, to governance structures like the WTO that are based entirely in the capitalist logic with no accountability to the public good,
- Culture – art, music, food diffusing globally while Western cultural practices, sometimes called "McDonaldization,"[73] transform the 3rd world,
- People – migration and refugee flows.

All the dimensions of globalization intertwine with one another and also with climate change. For Americans, climate change has been mostly about warming trends that lead to melting ice caps and concomitant sea level rise, exacerbating coastal storm surges. This definition is inadequate. Climate change is far more diverse. It includes, most significantly for the Middle East, changes in rainfall and inland water tables and the consequent advance of arid areas, called desertification. Such changes, in turn, interact with economic, social, political, cultural, and technological developments, to shape who has access to a sustainable food supply or adequate water, and, therefore, who remains in their ancestral homeland and who will be uprooted to become refugees. Thus the phenomena of climate refugees and political refugees become intertwined.

What climate change uniquely adds to the difficulties associated with globalization is a sense of urgency. As Thomas Friedman says of climate change: "We are going from 'later' to 'now' ... . Later is officially over. Later will be too late."[74]

Israeli author Eyal Weizman and his Palestinian co-author Fazal Sheikh argue that most of the conflicts in the Middle East today – Palestine/

Israel, Syria, Iraq, Bahrain, Yemen, Libya – are, in large part, fueled by desertification and its associated flow of climate refugees. About the Negev they write: "[T]he Negev has become one of the most contested frontiers in Palestine. ... [T]his one is not demarcated by fences and walls but rather by a seam between two climate conditions: the sub-tropical Mediterranean climate zone and the arid desert belt."[75]

Along with climate change, politics created this seam line and politics are trying to change it. Consider the case of the pine tree and the goat as a parable for the political drivers of climate change. From its inception, Zionism has labored to make the land of Palestine look more European, first by the removal of Palestinians and the destruction of their villages, and then by assiduously cultivating pine trees, planted over the remains of ethnically cleansed villages to obliterate even the memory of their existence, and also to make the land look more alpine. Having done so, Israel then makes claims for its care of the land. This tactic is an example of greenwashing.[76] The difficulty with this plan (in addition to its connection to ethnic cleansing) is that pine trees are not adapted to the climate, require excessive water to thrive, and create pine barrens in their shade (as we saw in Chapter 5).

To further expedite ethnic cleansing, Israelis simultaneously forbade Palestinians to own black goats, whose milk, meat, and hides were necessary for the Bedouin's way of life in the Negev and elsewhere. What went unnoticed was the goat's contribution of foraging ground cover plants, thus removing an accelerant for the forest fires likely to occur, particularly dry years and especially in pine groves. In the last few years, just such catastrophic forest fires have devastated Israel. The ferocity of the fires was fed by the pine needles and brush the absent goats had not eaten. And thus, the ban on Palestinian black goats is now being reconsidered,[77] though the decimation of Bedouin communities is on-going.[78]

Similar cases of the unhappy confluence between politics and climate change could, not doubt, be found in every corner of the globe; the possibility that a Trump-induced trade war with China will close off the market for America's recycled trash serves as but one example.

In the past, we hoped that the operation of markets and states would be sufficient tools to guarantee the common good. This has not proven to be the case.

Market systems have certainly produced a dazzling world of material plenty, albeit unequally distributed. But market systems are also built around the logic of growth that cannot be ecologically sustained. Market systems lend themselves to the commodification of public goods like rain water and the human genome[79]; to the creation of a world-wide system of production that situates manufacturing in the lowest wage, least regulated countries, thereby promoting global inequalities, exploitation, and pollution.[80] Many of these harms are done in small, almost invisible increments dispersed over the globe, and can be masked by the amazing increase in material productivity we see all around us.

There are, of course, also attempts to harness the power of the market to socially and environmentally just ends: projects focused on appropriate technologies, micro-lending, corporate social responsibility, ecologically sustainable supply chains, and fair labor practices. It is far beyond the scope of this work to assess the balance between productive and counterproductive forces within market economies. Suffice it here to say simply that the very existence of movements designed to "tame" markets, like the ones named above, attest to the struggle.

Similarly, states have also failed to live up to the hopes of Enlightenment philosophers. They have not produced a world of safety and orderliness where ordinary people can pursue their life goals without fear of violence. People who are suspicious of state power, usually conservatives, ask: "Who guards the guardians?" and the answer, they fear, is "No one." In the last one hundred years alone we have seen the horrors of state sponsored violence over and over again: the Armenian genocide, two world wars, the Holocaust, the *Nakba*, Apartheid, the Gulag, the Great Leap Forward and the Cultural Revolution, the killing fields of Cambodia, the Bosnian genocide, the Rwandan genocide, innumerable other small, dirty wars and the emergence of asymmetric warfare, that continue until this day. Moreover, the disasters produced by state-sponsored violence are not subtle and incremental; the stench of burning corpses can be found on every continent. Concern about murderous tyranny is every bit as well-founded as is the concern about corporate greed.

And now, the instruments we already know to be unsatisfactory – markets and states – are not at all ready to meet the main challenges of the 21st century. There are, of course, some positive instances of globalization, for example the use of social media by the brave men and women in Tahrir Square.[81] But, equally, globalization has brought us supra-national governing bodies like the World Trade Organization (WTO), which are simply not accountable to any version of the public good. Climate change, with its tight time-line is yet more ominous. It would be hard to find even a single positive example of climate change mitigating harm to traditional livelihoods or protecting refugee rights.

Given the profound uncertainties we face, I would argue that Zionism plays a particularly unhelpful role in building a better future, for two reasons.

First, because of Zionism's insistence on an every-expanding settlement project and Palestinian resistance to it, both parties remain locked into a backward facing struggle against each other's nationalist aims. Neither party is free to concentrate on a future that is anything more than an endless repetition of the past. Avraham Burg, a former Israeli Knesset leader and now an Israeli dissident, describes this as the victory of People of the Land (i.e. Zionists) over the People of the World (largely Diaspora Jews).[82]

Second, Zionism has built a stockade-like culture and society, in which Israel has lived by the sword since its inception. Not surprisingly, therefore, Israel is a pioneer in combat technologies, surveillance, and security protocols. Given the profound taproots that militarism has in Israeli circumstance, Zionism pushes Israel to situate itself at the most repressive end of the spectrum of responses to globalization and climate change.[83] Jeff Halper refers to this process as securitization,[84] noting that the Occupied Territories are the most monitored, controlled, and militarized place on earth.[85]

We know that Israeli arms merchants and security consultants advertise their products as "tested on human subjects."[86] Israeli film journalist Yotam Feldman summarizes his travels with Israeli arms dealers to international arms expos:

[T]he product [the Israelis] are selling is unique. Rather than rifles, rockets or bombs, Israeli companies sell their experience. The long-running conflict with the Palestinians has created a unique and unrivalled laboratory for testing technologies and ideas relating to 'asymmetric warfare' – a conflict between a state and civil or irregular resistance. *In this manner the Israeli conflict with the Palestinians may be seen as a national asset – rather than a burden* (italics mine). Following the 9/11 attacks, the Afghanistan war and the second Iraq war, countries all over the world have become increasingly interested in the way the Israeli army controls civilian populations, how it fights in urban areas, and how it deals with terror and guerrilla tactics.[87]

This process of securitization had multiple endpoints. First, Israel has no incentive to ever come to terms with the Palestinians since no settlement will make Palestinians more useful to Israelis than they are at present as guinea pigs. The second is that Israeli security protocols will come to redefine policing around the world. Already, in America, we see that 49 of our 50 states use Israeli police instructors to train local, state, and federal police agencies and, most recently, even campus police departments.[88]

Which brings us back to Maureen's story at the beginning of this section. She cannot imagine anything that transcends the Israeli version of the "clash of civilizations" narrative. But what if that clash is not between Islam and Christianity? What if that clash is between securitization and the Bill of Rights; between Israeli security training and Black Lives Matter?[89]

NOTES

[1] Richard Dawkins and Jeremy Coyne. (2005, September 1). One Side can be Wrong, *The Guardian,* retrieved from http://www.theguardian.com/science/2005/sep/01/schools.research

[2] Bassem Tamimi is quoted in David Shulman. (2014, May 22). Occupation: the Finest Israeli Documentary, *New York Review of Books*, p. 32.

[3] Anita Shapira, a left-leaning labor historian, traces the rising commitment to military "transfer" that eventuated in the *Nakba* in Anita Shapira (1992). *Land and Power, The Zionist Resort to Force, 1881–1948*, New York: Oxford University Press.

[4] The slogan "a land without people for a people without land" was the work of a British Protestant Zionist, the Earl of Shaftsbury, but it was quickly adopted by and became associated with an early Jewish Zionist, Israel Zangwill. For Shaftsbury, see Adam Garfinkle, On the Origin, Meaning, Use and Abuse of a Phrase, *Middle Eastern Studies* 27 (1991): 539 ff. For Zangwill and other Zionists, see Shapira, *op. cit.*, pp.41ff, and Zangwill's own work in *Speeches, Articles and Letters* (1937), 210.

[5] Zangwill, *Ibid.*

[6] Ghada Karmi. (2007). *Married to Another Man: Israel's Dilemma in Palestine* (London: Pluto Press) p. v. and Avi Shlaim. (2000) *The Iron Wall: Israel and the Arab World* (New York: W.W. Norton and Co.), p. 3.

Recently, Shai Afsai, a Zionist polemicist, has challenged the authenticity of the phrase without, however, being able to dispute that early Zionist leaders, whether they were given to poetic language or not, knew that Palestine was inhabited by Palestinians. See Shai Afsai. (2012, October 12). The "Married to Another Man" Story, *Jewish Ideas Daily*, retrieved from http://www.jewishideasdaily.com/5148/features/the-married-to-another-man-story/

[7] The imbalance arises largely because Jews are only 2% of the American population. Thus, although the percentage of Zionists in their ranks is probably much higher than in neighboring Christian communities, the sheer numerical weight of the Christian community is such that there are more Christian than Jewish Zionists in the U.S.

[8] Henri Laurens, quoted by Abdel Jawad, in Benvenisti, Gans, and Hanafi (eds.) (2007). *Israel and the Palestinian Refugees.* (Berlin: Springer Verlag) p. 76.

[9] Benjamin Beit-Hallahmi. (1993). *Original Sins: Reflections on the History of Zionism and Israel* New York: Olive Branch Press.

[10] Among those to arrive at this position more recently are psychologist Mark Braverman. (2010). *Fatal Embrace: Christians, Jews and the Search for Peace in the Holy Land*, Austin, Texas: Synergy Books.

Rabbi Brant Rosen. (2012). *Wrestling In the Daylight: A Rabbi's Path to Palestinian Solidarity,* New York: Just World Books.
philosopher Judith Butler (2012). *Parting Ways: Jewishness and the Critique of Zionism* New York: Columbia University Press, and the late historian Tony Judt. (2002, October 23). Israel: An Alternative Future, *New York Review of Books,* retrieved from http://www.nybooks.com/articles/archives/2003/oct/23/israel-the-alternative/
For earlier statements of skepticism about Zionism by prominent Jewish thinkers, including Freud, Buber, Einstein and Arendt, see, for example, Adam Schatz (ed.) (2004). *Prophets Outcast: A Century of Dissident Jewish Writing about Zionism and Israel* New York: the Nation Books, and Tony Kushner and Alisa Solomon (eds.) (2003). *Wrestling with Zion: Progressive Jewish-American Responses to the Israeli-Palestinian Conflict,* New York: Grove Press, 2003.

[11] Patricia Marks Greenfield. (2014, September 26). An Israel equal for all, Jewish or not, *Washington Post,* retrieved from http://www.washingtonpost.com/opinions/an-israel-equal-for-all-jewish-or-not/2014/09/26/83151758-3a05-11e4-9c9f-ebb47272e40e_story.html

[12] Gideon Levy. (2018, July 8). "One State, One Vote," *Ha'aretz,* retrieved from https://www.haaretz.com/opinion/.premium-one-state-one-vote-1.6246981

[13] Leon Uris. (1958). *Exodus* New York: Doubleday.

[14] Sara Roy, Living with the Holocaust: the Journey of a Child of Holocaust Survivors," in Adam Schatz (ed.) (2004). *Prophets Outcast: A Century of Dissident Jewish Writing about Zionism and Israel.* (New York: Nation Books), pp. 344–353. Peter Beinart. (2013). *The Crisis of Zionism.* New York: Picador Press.

[15] Data about population size is always a politically sensitive and contested topic in Palestine and Israel. The number of settlers is particularly controversial. Arutz Sheva, a settler source, acknowledges 389, 250 Jewish settlers in the West Bank and another 375,000 in East Jerusalem, whose "annexation" is universally recognized as illegal, totaling some 764,000 illegal settlers. These numbers date from 2014, and the same source claims that by now the number of settlers has risen to 800,000. *Arutz Sheva,* retrieved from http://www.israelnationalnews.com/Articles/Article.aspx/18210#.VpK885scTIU
The population growth rate in the settlements, though declining, is still approximately twice as high as that in Jerusalem, see Jacob Magid. (2018, January 21). Settler growth rate declines for sixth straight year, *The Times of Israel,* retrieved from https://www.timesofisrael.com/settler-growth-rate-declines-for-sixth-straight-year/

[16] Zena Tahhan. (2017, November 28). How Israeli leftists trivialize the Palestinian cause, *+972,* retrieved from https://972mag.com/how-israeli-leftists-trivialize-the-palestinian-cause/131031/

[17] Benny Morris. (2004, January 8). Survival of the Fittest interview in *Ha'aretz,* retrieved from http://www.haaretz.com/survival-of-the-fittest-1.61345

[18] Expert estimates of Holocaust tend to converge both in a range of numbers, and also in the inclusion of enormous populations of non-Jews. See, for example Donald L. Niewyk. (2000). *The Columbia Guide to the Holocaust* New York: Columbia University Press.
R. J. Rummel. (1992). *Democide Nazi Genocide and Mass Murder.* New York: Transaction Books.
Timothy Snyder. (2010). *Bloodlands,* New York: Basic Books.
Hellmuth Auerbach, Opfer der nationalsozialistischen Gewaltherrschaft in: Wolfgang Benz (ed.). (1992), *Legenden, Lügen, Vorurteile. Ein Wörterbuch zur Zeitgeschichte.* Dtv:

Neuauflag; Dieter Pohl. (2003), *Verfolgung und Massenmord in der NS-Zeit 1933–1945*, WBG Wissenschaftliche Buchgesellschaft.

[19] On any given day, a *New York Times* reader can find information on the expansion of settlements. For example, on the day this is being written, March 20, 2014, the *New York Times* reports that the Israeli state has announced an additional 2,000 housing units for the settlements and the city of Jerusalem granted building permits for an additional 200 housing units in occupied East Jerusalem. Jodi Rudoren. (2014, March 20). Israel: Settlement Plans Renew Palestinian Outrage, *New York Times*, retrieved from http://www.nytimes.com/2014/03/21/world/middleeast/israel-settlement-plans-renew-palestinian-outrage.html?_r=0. This kind of settlement expansion shows how even in the West Bank, Palestinians are allowed to live only in a small, crowded and constricted areas, usually in Areas A or B.

[20] Cf. Ahad H'am, Excerpt from 'Truth from Eretz Israel, in Adam Schatz (ed.) *op. cit.*, pp. 31–34. For Magnes see: Arthur A. Gored (ed.) (1982). *Dissenter from Zion: From the Writing of Judah L. Magnes* Cambridge: Harvard University Press.

[21] Paul Mendes-Flor (ed.) (1983). *A Land of Two Peoples: Martin Buber on Jews and Arabs* Chicago: University of Chicago Press.

[22] David Remnick. (2014, November 17). The One State Reality, *The New Yorker*, retrieved from http://www.newyorker.com/magazine/2014/11/17/one-state-reality

[23] Albert Einstein, Speech to the National Labor Committee for Palestine, New York, 17 April, 1938, in Schatz, *op. cit.*, pp 63–64.

[24] Hannah Arendt. (1948, May). To Save the Jewish Homeland: There is Still Time," *Commentary*, pp. 398–406.

[25] John Judis. (2014). *Genesis: Truman, American Jews, and the Origins of the Arab/Israeli Conflict*. New York: Farrar, Strauss and Giroux. Judis writes: "Labor rejected Herzl's *strategy* for creating a state ... but they accepted his elementary *commitment* to establishing a Jewish state...They also accepted Ahad Ha'am's emphasis on gradually building a Zionist culture that could undergird a Zionist state, but they defined "state" and "nation" in such a way as to exclude Palestine's Arabs." He is quoted (with reservations) by Bernard Avishai. (2014, April 14). Truman's Folly? *The Nation*, retrieved from http://www.thenation.com/article/179024/trumans-folly

[26] Akin Ajayi. (2014, January 28). Is Zionism Never Having to Say You're Sorry? *Ha'aretz*, retrieved from http://www.haaretz.com/culture/books/.premium-1.571045

[27] *Ibid.*

[28] *Ibid.*

[29] Lecture by Rabbi Arik Ascherman, President, Rabbis For Human Rights, to Boston College Students, Holy Land Hotel, Jerusalem, December 29, 2013.

[30] Anarchists Against the Wall, retrieved from http://awalls.org/

[31] Breaking the Silence, retrieved from http://www.breakingthesilence.org.il/

[32] Ben Ehrenreich. (March 15, 2013). Is this where the Third Intifada will start? *New York Times*, retrieved from http://nabisalehsolidarity.wordpress.com/2013/03/16/new-york-times-article-on-nabi-saleh-is-this-where-the-third-intifada-will-start/

[33] Sami Abou Shehadeh and Fadi Shbaytah. (2009, February 26). Jaffa: from eminence to ethnic cleansing, *The Electronic Intifada*, retrieved from http://electronicintifada.net/content/jaffa-eminence-ethnic-cleansing/8088, http://electronicintifada.net/content/jaffa-eminence-ethnic-cleansing/8088

[34] Avraham Burg. (2014, January 24). The Future of Yesterday, *Ha'aretz*, retrieved from http://www.haaretz.com/weekend/week-s-end/.premium-1.570166

[35] Philip Weiss. (2014, March 3). Poll: If two states collapse, American overwhelmingly favor 'democracy.' *Mondoweiss*. Retrieved from http://mondoweiss.net/2014/03/collapse-americans-democracy.html

[36] Peter Beinart. (2010, May 12). The Failure of the American Jewish Establishment, *The New York Review of Books*, retrieved from http://www.nybooks.com/articles/archives/2010/jun/24/failure-american-jewish-establishment-exchange/

[37] Isaac Asimov. (1993). *Asimov Laughs Again.* (New York: William Morrow) p. 92.

[38] Amoz Oz quoted in Roger Cohen. (2014, December 20). What Will Israel Become? *New York Times*, retrieved from http://www.nytimes.com/2014/12/21/opinion/sunday/roger-cohen-what-will-israel-become.html?_r=0

[39] Diane Ravitch. (1990, Summer). Multiculturalism: E Pluribus Plures, *American Scholar* 59(3): 337–354.

[40] See, for example, Gideon Levy. (2014, March 16). Israel's nation-state talk means the return of the yellow star, *Ha'aretz*, retrieved from http://www.haaretz.com/opinion/.premium-1.580021

[41] A. Irving Hallowell provides a fascinating account of what happens to tribal narratives when the tribe is and knows itself to be thoroughly defeated. Traditionally, young Ojibwa men were expected to embark on a vision quest and to meet spirits like the Great Bear who would direct them toward the right adult path in life. But, as humiliation, defeat and confinement to a reservation befell the Ojibwa, young men began encountering the spirit of the Mosquito, who told them that the spirits could no longer do anything for them. A. Irving Hallowell. (1964). *Culture and Experience.* New York: Shocken Books.

[42] Barrington Moore. (1967). *The Social Origins of Dictatorship and Democracy.* Boston, MA: Beacon Press.

[43] Alan Wolfe. (2014). *At Home in Exile: Why Diaspora is Good for the Jews* Boston, MA: Beacon Press.

[44] For a summary of this very controversial position, first articulated in 2006, see A.B. Yehoshua calls American Jews Partial Jews, *Tablet: A New Read on Jewish Life*, February 9, 2013, retrieved from http://www.tabletmag.com/scroll/124689/a-b-yehoshua-calls-american-jews-partial-jews

[45] Uri Avnery. (2013, September 11). The Judaization of Israel, *Gush Shalom*, retrieved from http://zope.gush-shalom.org/home/en/channels/avnery/1383915646/

[46] Karon is also a former editor of *Time* and now a journalist with *Al Jazeera*. Tony Karon. (2006, May 19). "How Jewish is Israel?" *Ha'aretz*, retrieved from http://www.haaretz.com/print-edition/opinion/how-jewish-is-israel-1.188095

[47] Marc Ellis, a theologian, makes a distinction between Constantinian and prophetic Judaism. The former occurs (as does its cousin, Constantinian Christianity, and, by extension, though Ellis never uses this term, Constantinian Islam) when a faith tradition allows itself to become a state religion, a servant to power. Prophetic faiths, by contrast, maintain their integrity as moral and ethical systems, suspicious of state machinations, and dedicated to speaking truth to power. For example: Marc H. Ellis. (2009). *Judaism Does Not Equal Israel: The Rebirth of the Jewish Prophetic.* New Press.

[48] Avraham Burg. (2009). *The Holocaust is Over and We Must Rise from the Ashes.* London: Palgrave.

[49] Tom Segev. (2002). *Elvis in Jerusalem* (New York: Picador) p. 280.

[50] Gideon Levy. (2014, August 14). Gevalt, anti-Semitism! *Ha'aretz*, retrieved from http://www.haaretz.com/opinion/.premium-1.610481

[51] Diana Buttu. (2014, March 19). What Happens After the Peace Process? talk at Boston College sponsors by Americans for Informed Democracy and Students for Justice in Palestine.

[52] In a *Ha'aretz* interview, former Israeli minister Ephraim Sneh says: "If we'd had responsible leadership in the past few years, it would have reached an understanding with the United States that Israel will be flexible on the Palestinian issue and America will be tough on the Iranian issue. Together we would have built a strong regional front versus Tehran and stood strong against the steady Islamization process that is shaking up the region. But Netanyahu and [Defense Minister Ehud] Barak did the exact opposite. They brought U.S.-Israel relations to an all-time low." In Ari Shavit. (2012, August 23). Countdown: Former Minister Ephraim Sneh fears another Hiroshima, *Ha'aretz*, retrieved from http://www.haaretz.com/weekend/magazine/ari-shavit-s-countdown-former-minister-ephraim-sneh-fears-another-hiroshima-1.460280

[53] Boycott from Within, retrieved from http://www.boycottisrael.info/
Who Profits, retrieved from http://whoprofits.org/

[54] Israeli Youth. (2014, March 10). We Refuse to Serve in the Occupation Army: Letter from the *Shministim*, retrieved from http://www.commondreams.org/news/2014/03/10/israeli-youth-we-refuse-serve-occupation-army and Israeli high school student leader calls youths' refuse to serve 'declaration of war,' *Mondoweiss*, March 17, 2014, retrieved from http://mondoweiss.net/2014/03/student-refusal-declaration.html
Moriel Rothman, "How Can You Tell that Israeli Refuseniks are Scaring the System?" *+972*, retrieved from http://972mag.com/how-can-you-tell-that-israeli-refuseniks-are-scaring-the-system/88360/

[55] Breaking the Silence, retrieved from http://www.breakingthesilence.org.il
Yesh Din retrieved from http://yesh-din.org/; Yesh G'vul retrieved from www.yeshgvul.org.il

[56] *B'Tselem*, "Statistics – Rocket and Mortar Fire into Israel" documents 44–46 fatalities, at least 10 of them Palestinian, retrieved from http://www.btselem.org/israeli_civilians/qassam_missiles#data

[57] *Ibid.*

[58] A colloquial but, nonetheless, adequate summing up of Iran's disputed nuclear capabilities is provided by Max Fisher. (2013, November 20). 9 questions about Iran's nuclear program you were too embarrassed to ask, *Washington Post*, retrieved from http://www.washingtonpost.com/blogs/worldviews/wp/2013/11/25/9-questions-about-irans-nuclear-program-you-were-too-embarrassed-to-ask/

[59] Jonathan Lis. (2014, February 25). Knesset Passes Bill Distinguishing Between Muslim and Christian Arabs, *Ha'aretz*, retrieved from http://www.haaretz.com/news/national/.premium-1.576247

[60] Eva Illuz. (2014, February 7). 47 Years a Slave: A New Perspective on the Occupation" *Ha'aretz*, retrieved from http://www.haaretz.com/news/features/.premium-1.572880

[61] Henry Siegman. (2014, November 26). Will Greater Israel Transform into Greater Palestine? *Huffington Post*, retrieved from https://www.huffingtonpost.com/henry-siegman/will-greater-israeli -tranform_b_6220806.html

[62] B'Tselem statistics show that since the end of Operation Cast Lead, i.e. in a period of relative calm, Israelis have killed 562 Palestinians while Palestinians have killed 37 Israelis.

Similarly, if we focus only on women and children in the same time period, 11 Israeli women and children were killed by Palestinians and 100 Palestinian women and children were killed by Israelis. This means that the approximate ratio of Israeli to Palestinian lethal violence is 10:1. Retrieved from http://www.btselem.org/statistics/fatalities/after-cast-lead/by-date-of-event

[63] Kristen Boon. (2009). The Obligations of the New Occupier: The Contours of Jus Post Bellum, *International and Comparative Law Review*, 31: 57–84.

[64] Nathalie Rothschild. (2008, November 19). *Waltz with Bashir*: Post-Zionist stress disorder, *Spiked*, retrieved from http://www.spiked-online.com/newsite/article/5944#.VAHhREikWdM

[65] Eyal Winter. (2014, August 30). Why are Brits who know little about Israel so active against it? *Ha'aretz*, retrieved from http://www.haaretz.com/.premium-why-are-brits-so-active-against-israel-1.5261855

[66] Bassem Tamimi is quoted in David Shulman, *op. cit.* p. 32.

[67] Ilan Pappe (2017). *The Biggest Prison on Earth: A History of the Occupied Territories*. London: One World Books, p. 62.

[68] Years ago, the sociologist, later Senator, Daniel Patrick Moynihan made a similar point to the American left. If a generation of "war on poverty," "the preferential option for the poor," "maximum feasible participation" by the formerly excluded – in short the entire Great Society project in all its permutations – had failed to achieve any positive results, then liberals could not go on indefinitely asking for more appropriations for programs they themselves described as ineffective. Daniel Patrick Moynihan. (1970m 2nd ed.). *Maximum Feasible Misunderstanding: Community Action in the War on Poverty*, New York: Free Press.

[69] Khalil Kankleh. (2012). *Globalized Palestine: A National Sell-Out of a Homeland* (Trenton: The Red Sea Press), p. 235.

[70] Hannah Arendt, *op. cit.* p. 403.

[71] Samuel Huntington. (2011). The clash of Civilizations and the Remaking of World Order. New York: Simon and Shuster.

[72] Tony Judt, Israel: The Alternative, *New York Review of Books*, October 23, 2003, retrieved from http://www.nybooks.com/articles/archives/2003/oct/23/israel-the-alternative/

[73] George Ritzer. (2003). *The McDonaldization of Society*. Los Angeles: Pine Forge Press.

[74] Thomas Friedman. (2017, August 2). Climate Shifts Aren't Limited to Weather, *New York Times*, retrieved from https://www.nytimes.com/2017/08/02/opinion/climate-change-technology-globalization-china.html

[75] Eyal Weizman and Fazal Sheikh. (2005). *The Conflict Shoreline: Colonization as Climate Change in the Negev Desert* (New York: Steidl/Cabinet Books), p. 9.

[76] Ben Lorber. (2018, June 15). Israel's Environmental Colonialism and Eco-Apartheid, *The Bullet* (a publication of the Canadian Socialist Party), retrieved from https://socialistproject.ca/2018/06/israels-environmental-colonialism-and-ecoapartheid/

[77] Jonathan Cook. (2017, December 1). In age of forest fires, Israel's law against Palestinian goats proves self-inflicted wound for Zionism, *Mondoweiss*, retrieved from http://mondoweiss.net/2017/12/israels-palestinian-inflicted/

[78] David Halbfinger and Rami Nazzal. (2018, June 24). As Israel Pushes to Build, Bedouin Homes and Schools Face Demolition, *New York Times*, retrieved from https://www.nytimes.com/2018/06/24/world/middleeast/israel-bedouins-demolition.html

79 Adrienne Wright. (2013, May 24). Patenting the Human Genome, *Medical Press*, retrieved from http://medicalxpress.com/news/2013-05-patenting-human-genome.html
    William Finnegan. (2002, June). Bolivia: Leasing the Rain. Public Broadcasting System, retrieved from http://www.pbs.org/frontlineworld/stories/bolivia/

80 Charles Derber. (2010). *Greed to Green: Solving Climate Change and Remaking the Economy*. New York: Paradigm Publishers.

81 But already, Israelis and others are mining the internet for oppressive political ends. See, Rebecca L. Stein. (2015). *Digital Militarism: Israel's Occupation in the Social Media Age*, Stanford, California: Stanford University Press.

82 Avraham Burg. (2017, September 21). Rosh Hashanah as the Battle of Netanyahu vs. Soros, *Ha'aretz*, retrieved from https://www.haaretz.com/opinion/.premium-rosh-hashanah-as-the-battle-of-netanyahu-vs-soros-1.5452542

83 For discussions of Israel as a routine part of global capitalist dynamics see, for example, Joshua Sperber (2015, Autumn). BDS, Israel, and the World System, *Journal of Palestine Studies* 45(1): 8–23, and Jonathan Nitzan and Shimshon Bichler (2002) *The Global Political Economy of Israel*, London: Pluto Press.

84 Jeff Halper. (2015). *War against the People: Israel, the Palestinians and Global Pacification*, New York: Pluto Press.

85 Halper, *ibid.* p. 143.

86 Yotam Feldman. (2013). "The Lab," Tel Aviv: Gum Film/Cinephil.
    See also Naomi Klein. (2007, June 15). Gaza: Not Just a Prison, a Laboratory, *Common Dreams*, retrieved from http://www.commondreams.org/archive/2007/06/15/gaza-not-just-prison-laboratory
    See also Coalition of Women for Peace (Israel). (2018, June). A Lab and A Showroom: The Israeli Military Industries and the Oppression of the Great March of Return in *Gaza Retrieved* from https://mail.google.com/mail/u/0/#inbox/164520af5a81ce09?projector=1&messagePartId=0.1
    see also: Meron Rapoport (2018, July 2) Thanks to Gaza protests, Israel has a new crop of 'battle tested' weapons for sale, +972, retrieved from https://972mag.com/thanks-to-gaza-protests-israel-has-a-new-crop-of-battle-tested-weapons-for-sale/136523/

87 The Lab (film review) *Al Jazeera* May 8, 2014, retrieved from https://www.aljazeera.com/programmes/witness/2014/05/lab-20145475423526313.html

88 Halper, op. cit.; With Whom are many U.S. Police Departments Training? With a Chronic Human Rights Violator – Israel, Amnesty International, n.d. Retrieved from https://www.amnestyusa.org/with-whom-are-many-u-s-police-departments-training-with-a-chronic-human-rights-violator-israel/
    Tufts SJP, TYPD brings 'Deadly Exchange' to Tufts, *The Tufts Daily*, February 14, 2018, retrieved from https://tuftsdaily.com/opinion/2018/02/14/op-ed-tupd-brings-deadly-exchange-tufts/

89 Kristian Davis Bailey. (2014, August 19). The Ferguson/Palestine Connection, *Ebony*, retrieved from https://www.ebony.com/news-views/the-fergusonpalestine-connection-403

CHAPTER 11

CONCLUSION

Hope and History

All people live in their country. But for Palestinians, our country lives in us.

Palestinian proverb

True peace is not merely the absence of tension, it is the presence of justice.

Martin Luther King[1]

Yuval's Story

Yuval is a member of *Combatants for Peace*, a group of Israel soldiers who meet with their Palestinian counterparts to create cross-border peace education projects. Some time ago Yuval came to Boston College as part on a panel discussion of the film *Little Town of Bethlehem*. In the film, three men, a Palestinian Christian, a Palestinian Muslim, and a Jewish Israeli, talk about how they chose to become part of the *Combatants for Peace*. Yonatan Shapira is the Israeli interviewed in the film, and he was scheduled to speak at BC but, at the last minute, he chose to join the Gaza flotilla. Yuval took his place.

In the film, Yonatan talks about how scared he was the first time he went to Bethlehem in order to meet with his Palestinian counterparts. He was out of uniform, with no bulletproof vest, no gun, and no armed comrades around him. He was not even sure if there really would be a meeting or if he would be kidnapped.

During the Q&A that followed the screening, Yuval was asked whether he, too, had been terribly frightened when he began working with *Combatants for Peace*. He replied that he was, but not for the same reasons as Yonatan. Because Yuval began his work years later, he

© KONINKLIJKE BRILL NV, LEIDEN, 2019 | DOI:10.1163/9789004394148_011

already knew that he was in no danger of being kidnapped or shot. But, he said, there were nevertheless dangers or an entirely different sort.

He grew up, as boys in happy homes do, loving his father and identifying with him. He knew his father to be a good man. And he also knew that his father had fought in the Yom Kippur (1973) War. When he thought about that at all, he simply told himself that his father, being a good man, would only have killed bad people.

But, in the course of his first meeting with the Palestinian members of *Combatants for Peace* Yuval met a man who had also fought in the 1973 war, in the very same battle as his father. Yuval's father might have killed or been killed by this very Palestinian, who, Yuval realized, was also a good man.

"Then," he confessed, "I got really scared. Because I realized that everything I'd based my life on was a lie, and I would have to rebuild it from the ground up."

Facebook Post

My dad received his U.S. passport in the mail, with place of birth stating 'Israel.' He placed the passport back in the envelope, returned it to the passport agency with a sticky note saying: 'I was born in the state of Palestine, the city of Jerusalem in 1941, there was no Israel then, the state of Israel occupied my homeland in 1948. Kindly reinstate my correct identity.' 2 weeks later, passport corrected, Palestine reinstated, no questions asked. My ultimate respect to the system and hats off to baba!!

The Israeli-Palestinian conflict is a human rights disaster. Because of it, more than 12 million people live in perpetual fear – fear of invasion, displacement, or expulsion; fear of bombs and rockets; fear of delegitimation; fear of assassination; fear of governments on both sides that use a constant state of emergency to entrench anti-democratic practices; fear of violence, whether from the "other side" or from rivalries between militias or political groups on their own side; and, most of all, fear of never having a normal life. For half of those people, the fear can be papered over by access to a relatively affluent western life style; for the other half, deprived of secure access to water,[2] homes,[3] and freedom of movement,[4] even that is not possible.

Part of this human rights disaster arises from the incompatible desires of the Zionist and Palestinian communities, each of which lay claim to all the land of historic Palestine. In the face of that conflict, the world has imposed upon them the necessity of separation on highly unequal terms. This is a violation of the human right to self-determination for both peoples.

But history is full of intractable conflicts that, in the end, got settled. *One of the reasons this particular conflict seems so intractable is that no one is insisting on human rights as the standard to which both sides should be held.*

Instead, from Balfour to Oslo, all attempts to settle the Palestinian-Israeli conflict have used a framework emphasizing Israel's self-defined and ever-expanding security needs, and not the human rights of all the people involved. Seventy-one years of enforcing Israel's "security needs" over Palestinian rights has brought no one peace or justice, a point ignored by the allegedly tough-minded proponents of *realpolitik,* especially among the U.S. negotiators who have been such significant arbiters of the course of events.

The whole thrust of this book has been to argue that human rights standards would create a more equitable and hence a more durable resolution.

Human rights standards are valuable but not easily enforced. Without the political will to enforce them, they are toothless. International bodies can be selective and racist in naming injustice[5]; many attempts to ensure rights ironically create dependency.[6] The continuing gap between the high flown rhetoric and the disappointing performance of international organizations, governments, NGOs, and social movements can lead to cynicism and despair.[7]

However, the fundamental premise is correct: all human beings, even those you fear, dislike, or compete with are as valuable as you are. This premise implies that the measure of any group (family, school, hospital, work place, political party, local or national community) is the degree to which it allows all its members to function as their best selves and contribute to the common good. Such a standard relieves the oppressed of life-draining struggles that should not be necessary. It also relieves oppressors of the costs of training themselves to control others who will, inevitably, resist such domination. Recognizing human rights must be at the foundation of any set of rules for organizing community life.

Human rights standards are practical as well as idealistic, because they create the basis for choosing among policies. For example, human rights doctrine reminds us that power imbalances between opposing sides in a conflict can subvert the valuing of each human life. Such practical recognition is the basis for protecting victims of domestic violence from their abusers and workers from their bosses. It applies equally to conflicts between groups and nations, as in the present case.

Human rights standards clearly state the obligations of an occupying force to the civilians of the occupied population. For example, they give refugees the right to return home. This is a right that has been accorded Jews wishing to "return home" to Israel after an absence of more than two thousand years. It has yet to be accorded to Palestinians, some who actually experienced expulsion in their own lifetimes. Human rights also uphold the right of citizens to live a normal existence, free from the violence of state and private actors.

And finally, a human rights point of view enlarges our framework – we can ask how other intractable conflicts, especially those between colonial settlers and indigenous populations, came to (or failed to) find a just and stable resolution over time.

In colonial projects, settlers always espouse some noble purpose but, inevitably, they fail to apply the values they claim to the people they are conquering or displacing. Our hearts go out to refugees from persecution and oppression, including Jews fleeing Nazism. But when persecuted refugees become colonizers who, in their turn, try to exploit, or expel, or destroy the indigenous population, the inconvenient others who stand in the way of their political dreams, human rights give us the leverage to object and to call for change. *At a bare minimum, it requires us to refrain from supporting the oppressors.*

Those looking for a model for settling entrenched and bitter conflicts often compare Palestine/Israel to South Africa. Not just because South Africans, like Israelis and Palestinians, struggled about whether armed resistance was legitimate and what price it might exact internally[8] as well as externally. Not only because boycotts were an essential part of the struggle for justice. But because, however long and winding the path, in South Africa both sides eventually accepted that neither could strike a knock-out blow, that the other was not going to be uprooted, and that, therefore, the choice came down to eternal warfare or sitting down to settle the mess.

The question for us, then, is: what do we think is impeding Israel and Palestine from arriving at the point where, confronted with a choice between eternal warfare and "settling the mess," they choose the latter.

LESSONS FROM THE PAST

We Know Something about the History of the Conflict

We know that the land of Palestine and Israel has been traversed, often conquered, by most of the empires of the past, European (Greek, Roman, Crusaders), Asian (Seljuks, Mamlukes, Ottomans) and North African (Egyptians) since time immemorial.

We know that in the late 19th century, given the emerging nationalist reorganization of Europe, a small subset of European Jews calling themselves Zionists developed the aspiration to found a nation of their own, far from the reach of Christendom.

We know that they were driven by an extraordinary singleness of purpose across a century and a half of efforts. We know that, at present, Zionism has succeeded in gaining control over all the land of historic Palestine, but has not succeeded in securing the consent of half the people who live under its authority or its regional neighbors.

Beginning in the 1890s, we know that Zionists were both strategic and imaginative in building organizations that furthered their purposes, gaining political legitimacy (WZO), funding their efforts (JNF), recruiting settlers for their cause (JA). We know that by 1947 their militias, later the IDF, were strong enough to accomplish a major expulsion of the Palestinian inhabitants of historic Palestine in conjunction with the founding of the Israeli state. We know that once established, the Israeli state was endlessly inventive in creating mechanisms to acquire more and more of historic Palestine. The Custodian of Absentee Property was the principal tool that enabled Israelis to take Palestinian land inside Israel. In the Occupied Territories, settlement building, military suppression, and a bogus peace process served to control Palestinians and to take their land.

The story of Zionism is actually a rare case in history: one where there is enough documentation, including oral history,[10] to understand the motives of the actors; and where there is an exceptional consistency between their words and their deeds, sustained over the entire period of their existence. Zionists have always said that they plan to take all the land and, day-by-day, they are doing so, exactly as promised. In the week that this passage was written for the first edition, Israelis expropriated another 1,000 acres of Palestinian land near Bethlehem[11] and gave the green light to hundreds more settlement units[12]; any other week since then would have been much the same. In so choosing, Israelis have ignored peace offers, risked alienating allies, and fed the hatred of Zionism in their immediate neighborhood. But still they keep going on the path they have set for themselves.

We know that the Palestinians have never been passive in the face of Zionist ambitions. They responded at first civilly with petitions, then non-violently, with a general strike, then with recurring armed struggle (the Arab Rebellion and the Second *Intifada*), with political programs such as secular pan-Arabism and today, perhaps, political Islam, with grassroots non-violent resistance (the first *Intifada*) and with an appeal, via the BDS campaign, for international solidarity.

We know something about the ideas (Zionism and nationalism) that drove the history. Zionism is a kind of Jewish nationalism. It developed in the context of a European political system being reorganized into the map of nation-states we know today. And like the "first draft" of many nationalist projects, it called for an ethno-religiously exclusive society, drawing on notions of a racially homogeneous community. But, where almost all European variants of nationalism, even those with established state churches, have become more egalitarian, multi-cultural, and multi-racial over time, Zionism continues to accept only Jews as legitimate participants in its national life.[13] Since fully half of the people living under the sway of the Israeli state are neither Jews nor Zionists, this is a recipe for catastrophe.

Palestinian nationalism is rooted in similar circumstances: an empire (in the Palestinian case, the Ottoman Empire) being transformed into modern nation-states. And like Israeli nationalists, Palestinians have maintained their aspirations with extraordinary consistency over generations. But Palestinian nationalism is distinctive in having persisted so long without the apparatus of a state to sustain it. Along with Kurdish nationalism, Palestinian national identity is produced from the bottom up, by grass roots activities of everyday people largely without the assistance of national institutions – schools, archives, and museums – to support it.[14]

We know that in response to the on-going turbulence in Palestine/Israel, the world has decided that Israelis and Palestinians should be separated into two states. The world, speaking through the United Nations, recommended that two nations be created in a land not much bigger than New Jersey. The original General Assembly Resolution 181 proposed two states, coming into existence simultaneously, linked by economic exchanges, and geographically entwined with one another. Today Resolution 181 has turned into hardened dogma that there exists a "universally agreed upon two-state solution," despite the fact that, on the ground, less than twelve percent of historic Palestine remains under even nominal Palestinian control. In short, the world has decided to affirm a rigid and distorted version of Resolution 181 without enforcing it, as Israel uses settlement growth to make the two-state solution daily more impossible.

The one thing the world has *not* done is to listen to either Palestinians or Israelis, to ask how the world looks through their eyes.

I remember the first time I went from Jerusalem to Ramallah via *Qalandiya*. In those days the *Qalandiya* checkpoint was still a series of Quonset huts in a muddy field, not the intimidating terminal it is today. I was in a yellow plate taxi and we drove through the checkpoint without my even having to show a passport – going into the Occupied Palestinian Territories is easy; getting out is not. The only reason we had to slow down was to drive around the long queue of Palestinian women crossing through the pedestrian section of the checkpoint, or rather, not crossing, but waiting patiently, bags of shopping in one arm and little children held by the hand. It was the children I noticed most … tiny, big-eyed three and four year olds, reaching w-a-a-y up to hold mommy's hand, and staring, staring, staring with an eerie silence at what was going on around them: their mothers, tired and resigned, stepping aside for the heavily armed soldiers circulating through the crowd, shoving at people or yelling at them. Next I noticed the vendors, usually people with some oranges or cigarettes spread on a blanket in the mud, or perhaps, among the more established, a tray with an urn and some teacups, using the interminable wait to do a little business. I do not believe that many Israelis are prepared to look through the eyes of those children.

On a recent trip, I spent the night of New Year's Eve in an Emergency Room at a Jerusalem hospital with two of my students. For a sociologist, the ability to go backstage and see people going about their business and paying no attention to outsiders is a real gift. I remember the Israeli woman, heavily pregnant and bleeding who was called into the ER first and the old Palestinian lady in a wheel chair and on an oxygen tank who was gasping for breath and who was called in last. I also remember the Palestinian boy, probably about 13 or 14 years of age, writhing in pain, leg shackled to a chair in the ER waiting room, handcuffed and surrounded by three IDF soldiers with machine guns. But most of all, I remember that not a single Israeli looked his way. *How did they learn where not to look?*

How have we, as Americans, learned not to look or listen? For example, whole books have been produced on the Israeli separation wall and its graffiti. But even when we *try* to listen, we listen mostly to each other: we read the English graffiti; we admire the artistry of Banksy. Typically we do not ask what the Arab writing on the wall is saying.[15] Typically, we love the image of the little girl in a pink dress being floated up and over the wall by a bouquet of balloons. We don't spend much time on the drawing of the angry young boy with the slingshot. We are not really listening to the people whose lives are on the line.

Perhaps the most telling example of western tone-deafness comes from the Russell Tribunal hearings on Palestine. The Russell Tribunal is a privately constituted body that works to overcome the crimes of silence. Eminent community members are invited to convene hearings focused on various trouble spots around the world: Argentina under the Generals, Chile after the overthrow of Allende, America's conduct in Vietnam, and, most recently, the fate of Palestinians under Occupation. At the fourth meeting of the Russell Tribunal on Palestine, British jurist Michael Mansfield, a proponent of the Apartheid analogy for understanding the Israeli Occupation, attacked a Palestinian witness who chose to name the Palestinian experience as sociocide. Mansfield's attempts at bullying the witness were, appropriately, met with hostility from the audience, but the incident remains as signature moment: a senior Western white man, a self-defined champion of justice, insisting that a Palestinian witness (at the time, the Dean of the Law School at Birzeit University) did not rightly understand his own experience and so was not fit to name it.[16]

Small wonder, then, that the world is not acting on the demands for justice as defined by a broad array of Palestinian civil society: (1) equal rights for Palestinian citizens of Israel, (2) a resolution of the refugee problem in accord with international law which recognizes the refugee's right of return, and (3) the end to Occupation.[17] Even the Israeli demand for security remains ever elusive as the Occupation expands and Palestinian creativity in resisting it does too.

Jewish tradition demands we remember that with freedom comes the responsibility to fight for a redeemed world.[18]

Naamah Kellman

Not everything that is faced can be changed, but nothing can be changed until it is faced.[19]

James Baldwin

TOOLS FOR CHANGE SIGNS OF HOPE

In this difficult situation, most of the changes we hear about in the international press are bad ones.

In Israel, a right-wing, intensely nationalistic legislature just voted to consolidate the supremacy of Zionist doctrine into the Basic Laws of the country. The fact that Israel is now *officially* a state of the Jewish people rather than a state of its citizens, and that this change is part of its *constitutional* framework, means that, henceforth, Israel's occasionally independent Supreme Court will be obliged to favor Jewish claims over all others.[20]

Among the Palestinians, the political leadership remains divided. The prime minister is in failing health and no succession plans have emerged – a situation that is very likely to exacerbate the chronic factionalism of Palestinian politics.

In the region, the intense struggle for pre-eminence between the Saudis and the Iranians is leading to an increasing rapprochement between Israel and Sunni states. Collateral damage from these developments includes the abandonment of the Palestinian cause by its Arab allies.

In the United States, the Trump administration's action in moving the U.S. Embassy to Jerusalem means that the arbiter of all formal or informal dealings between Israelis and Palestinians is now officially on the Israeli side.

Nevertheless, these headline-grabbing developments are not the only things happening on the ground. On the class trips we see that, beneath the intransigent surface of the conflict, individual resilience and creativity provide hope for a future in which the equal rights of all are respected.

For example, I have always been struck by how many of the Palestinian men we meet are named Moussa and Aisa, the Arabic for Moses and Jesus. Adults do not name their children after the prophets of groups they despise.

Also hopeful is the Palestinian sense of irony that allows villagers to subvert the very tools of their oppressors into life-affirming symbols. In *Nabi Saleh*, villagers make garlands of spent tear gas canisters to string between their houses, and in the *Bili'in*, women use spent tear gas canisters as bud vases, planting whole hillsides of them on land reclaimed from the Separations Wall.[21]

Among settlers in the Occupied Territories, there are vigilante groups that try to prevent Jewish girls from dating Arab men.[22] The presence of vigilantes is always horrifying, but there is also good news implied here: among younger women, even in settler communities, there is a willingness to socialize with Palestinians, even to date them. This, too, is reason to hope.

During the second *Intifada*, Israeli motorists who got lost in Ramallah were lynched,[23] but just recently, there have been three separate stories about stranded Israeli motorists who were rescued and helped by Palestinians.[24]

All three incidents occurred in places that official Israeli wisdom depicts as especially dangerous: opposite a refugee camp on the outskirts of Tulkarem, and in the Jordan Valley where whole Palestinian villages had just been demolished. After being helped to change a flat tire in the middle of an off-limits Area A village, Israeli writer Ilana Hammerman returned to the big red sign outside the village. It reads: "Entrance for Israeli citizens is forbidden, dangerous to your lives and against Israeli law." Across the sign she pasted another sign. It says: "Israelis, do not be afraid. Refuse to be enemies."[25]

Before Operation Protective Edge (and its overture, Operation Brothers' Keeper), Israel held over 5,000 Palestinian political prisoners.[26] Palestinian prisoners in Israel are uniformly denied conjugal visits. But, despite this ban, Palestinians have repeatedly succeeded in smuggling prisoner's sperm to their families. Fifteen babies have now been born to prisoners' wives by means of smuggled sperm.[27] It is infinitely sad to me that Israeli Jews, who constantly remind us of their close encounter with deliberate extinction, cannot recognize the life force in this story and respond to it with the traditional Jewish toast: *L'Chaim*, to life.

In addition to gallant personal efforts, there are also many examples of Palestinians and their Israeli allies mounting more organized efforts to achieve equality, justice, and human rights.

The principal tools, used alone or together are:

- education – getting people to understand the conflict from all sides;
- law – using international legal standards to secure rights for the dispossessed;
- service – helping those who need to recover from the conflict;
- resistance – mobilizing those who are brave enough to struggle against existing injustices or to prevent new ones from arising;
- economic tools – using market forces to secure social justice.

In this section, I will provide examples of each of those tools in use, showing also how all parties to the dispute (Palestinians in the West Bank, East Jerusalem, and Gaza, Palestinian citizens of Israel, Palestinian refugees, Diaspora Palestinians, Jewish Israelis, and internationals) are active in trying to craft a solution. These examples are meant only to be evocative – they are less than the tip of the iceberg of projects and efforts already under way in Israel and Palestine.

Educational efforts are generally focused on making the narrative more inclusive (or maintaining it as it is, tilted heavily in favor of one side or the other). Thus, an Israeli NGO, *Zochrot* (Remembrance) labors to insert the *Nakba* into the Israeli school curriculum and into public consciousness. Working against them, Israeli textbooks situate the Palestinians at the end of a long line of oppressors trying to destroy the Jews: first Pharaoh, then the Tsar, then the Nazis, and now the Arabs.[28]

Palestinians manifest a touching faith in learning, for example in the way they typically introduce themselves by bragging about their children's education: "Hello. My name is Mustafa/Tarek/Shadi/Omar. I have four/five/ six children. Two of them are lawyers, one is a teacher, one is a doctor, and one is an engineer." We never leave a Palestinian meeting without being exhorted to tell their story, because they believe (let us hope not naively) that if only Americans knew about them, everything would change for the better.

Just recently, Peter Beinart, who styles himself a liberal Zionist, suggested that education of a very particular, focused sort was the key to transforming this conflict. He proposes that young American Jews launch a Freedom Summer, parallel to the Freedom Summer of the civil rights movement, and go to Palestine to support Palestinian rights groups and Palestinian civil society projects. He argues that this massive and intensive exposure to the conflict, reaching older American Jews via trusted sources, their children and grandchildren, would be the most strategic way to change the American political climate decisively and quickly.[29] Changing Jewish opinion would then allow the American government much more freedom to hold Israel to human rights standards.

Beinart frames his project as calling upon young American Jews to save Israel from itself (i.e. to salvage the two-state solution). Undoubtedly some young American Jews could be recruited on that basis. But a Freedom Summer program potentially has much wider appeal as well, among non-Zionist Jews, but also among college students and church groups more broadly. The Freedom Summer project is particularly strategic because it recognizes that inconvenient facts by themselves seldom have the power to rearrange long-held, emotionally laden frameworks. Beinart's project would introduce new insights via trusted and emotionally compelling channels – that is its real genius.[30]

In a similar vein, a group of American rabbis has sought to educate the leaders of the American Jewish community about the Israeli-Palestinian issue by inviting them to meet with Palestinians. Through an NGO named Encounter,[31] American Jewish leaders are invited to travel to Palestine, and to experience Palestinian realities in order to become committed to finding a just resolution to the Occupation. Participants are taken to some of the most contentious spots, like Hebron and East Jerusalem, and are asked to bear witness to the human costs of Occupation.

Perhaps because of their educational achievements, Palestinians are deeply invested in using *legal and advocacy instruments* to pursue their rights. Groups like *Adalah, Hamoked,* and the Arab Association for Human Rights in Israel, and *Al Haq* and *Addameer* in the West Bank, all advocate and litigate on behalf of Palestinian rights to land, to due process, to prisoners' rights, etc.

The Palestinian Authority has applied for membership via the United Nations to the International Court of Justice and the International Criminal Court. Membership in these institutions might allow them to move their struggle with Israel into international forums. Even the United States, normally Israel's uncritical financial, military, and diplomatic patron, suspended air travel to Tel Aviv for 36 hours during Operation Protective Edge (ostensibly for security reasons) and delayed the delivery of hellfire missiles for longer than that,[32] signaling the possibility of invoking the Arms Export Control Act to restructure relations with Israel.

While legal remedies restructure the playing field, *service* work cares for people injured by the conflict. Normally service work is designed to achieve apolitical humanitarian ends, but in the Israeli-Palestinian context, even service work is profoundly politicized. Medical services, services to traumatized or under-served children, all are shaped by the conflict in which they are embedded. Thus, for example, the Lajee Center that serves refugees in Aida Camp in Bethlehem, teaches children media skills by showing them how to monitor Israeli military incursions into the camp, and the Gaza Community Mental Health Center devotes most of its time to helping war-traumatized individuals.

Resistance to Occupation exists in every imaginable form: village committees in places like Nabi Saleh, Bili'in, Budrus, and Nili'in that hold weekly protests; in Israeli Apartheid Weeks and Open Hillels spreading across American, Canadian, and European campuses; in the support by Diaspora Palestinians for projects like the summer camp Go Palestine that teaches children about their Palestinian heritage; and in the sentence that every Palestinian has spoken more than once: "To exist is to resist."

In some instances, Israeli partners enlarge the Palestinian capacity for resistance: Anarchists Against the Wall, Combatants for Peace, Family Circle of the Bereaved, One Democratic State, and Who Profits? are all Israeli organizations that work with Palestinians, on behalf of objectives set by Palestinian civil society.

Economic action is perhaps the single most promising tool of resistance, especially the Boycott, Sanctions, and Divestment movement.

The thinking behind the call for boycott, sanctions, and divestment has tap roots that go all the way back to the Enlightenment, which posited that human beings were rational and could therefore be trusted to organize and govern themselves without authoritarian leaders of church or state telling them what to do. Philosophers like Adam Smith, David Ricardo, Thomas Malthus, and Jeremy Bentham applied the premise of human rationality to economic activity. They saw the market as more than a merely technocratic achievement for producing and distributing goods. The market, they hoped, would be a realm of freedom in which people could work, consume, and invest as they wished; could seek to create a just society out of the sum total of labor, consumer, and investor decisions to reward responsible behavior and penalize oppressive or exploitative behavior.

The current BDS movement draws on this tradition, asking people to boycott Israeli, especially settlement goods in their individual lives as consumers, to avoid these same companies as investors, and to urge their local, state, and national governments to use economic tools to penalize the Israeli occupation of Palestine (for example, by cancelling tax exemptions for churches and synagogues that invest in settlement real estate, or by labeling or even banning settlement goods, or by refusing to invest public employee retirement funds in companies profiting from the Occupation). BDS is a nonviolent movement, rooted in international law. Imagination is the only limit to the projects that might be included in the BDS movement.

There is considerable precedent in America for BDS activities: the Abolitionists urged consumers to boycott sugar and cotton produced by slaves; Quakers, early on, urged consumers to avoid alcohol and tobacco products, Caesar Chavez and the farm workers union called for a boycott of fruits and vegetables produced by exploited non-union workers, and Nestle's became a boycott target, accused of using harmful sales techniques in third world countries in order to sell baby formula at the expense of breast feeding.

The Palestinian BDS movement was founded by a call from Palestinian civil society for an academic and cultural boycott of Israel in 2004 and for a more general economic boycott in 2005.[33] At first, this movement was effective primarily as an educational tool, to begin a conversation about Israeli behavior toward Palestinians. Its earliest successes were modest: calling for sanctions against such companies as Motorola (a supplier of military hardware for Israel) and Caterpillar (the manufacturer of the bulldozers used by Israelis to demolish Palestinian homes), the occasional wildcat dockers' refusal to unload an Israeli cargo ship, an occasional success in booing an Israeli team off an international playing field, random pickets signs and leaflets outside the international performance of an Israeli symphony or ballet company.

But, over the years, the boycott has been gathering steam in multiple arenas. With increasing frequency,

- Israeli companies are excluded from public (Norway, Holland) and private (TIAA-CREFF) pension fund portfolios, especially the social responsibility funds;
- Israeli products are de-shelved by supermarket chains: Agrexco is the first Israeli company to go into liquidation after numerous European chains refused to stock their agricultural products;
- Israeli companies or their international investors and affiliates are dropped as contract partners: the French transport company Veolia and the American company Leviev are particular targets; Veolia has lost billions of dollars in contracts and has announced withdrawal from some Israeli projects; recently Holland and Spain ended relations with the Israeli water company Mekorot;
- Israeli entries are excluded from international competitions: Spain refused to allow architects from the Ariel settlement to submit entries for an architecture prize;
- Churches and universities around the world endorse the boycott call.[34]

Until now, the BDS movement has been focused on what *not* to do, which products, speakers, investments to shun. A complementary movement telling us what *to* do to make positive investments in peace, prosperity, and sustainability in Israel/Palestine is also emerging. Such groups as Americans for a Vibrant Palestinian Economy seek to mobilize the Palestinian Diaspora community and others interested in long term, sustainable economic development in the area[35] without minimizing the difficulties they face.[36]

If it is such a good idea, why isn't it being done already?[37]

The [politicians] were not describing what was true, but what would have to be true to justify what they planned to do next.
Hannah Arendt, paraphrased by Elliot Lusztig[38]

Peacemaking doesn't mean passivity. It is the act of interrupting injustice without mirroring injustice, the act of disarming evil without destroying the evildoer, the act of finding a third way which is neither flight nor fight but the careful, arduous pursuit of reconciliation and justice.

A Liturgy for Ordinary Radicals[39]

CONCLUSION: FINDING THE TIPPING POINT

As this book draws to a close, it is natural to ask what comes next, what will the "day after" look like. If there is any truth to the idea that history repeats itself, then two developments, deeply rooted in the traditions of the Israeli and Palestinian communities respectively, are quite likely to occur sooner rather than later.

Given Zionism's mission to occupy the whole of historic Palestine, and given the present right-wing ruling coalition government, the state of Israel is very likely to formally annex all or part of the West Bank.[40] Is this clearly a violation of international law? Yes. Will there be a number of objections from the U.N. and the E.U.? Certainly. Will anyone actually do anything about it? Very unlikely.[41]

On the Palestinian side, the failing health of the leader who allows no successor to emerge, the traditional factional rivalry, and the desperate circumstances in which Gazans live, make it very possible that the whole machinery of the Palestinian Authority will implode. If that happens, Israel and the U.S. may well try to resuscitate it, since the PA serves to control its own people and also to receive international donor funds that relieve Israel of many of the financial costs of occupation. Will such attempts at resuscitation succeed? Possible, but not probable. Will there be a period of chaos and deep uncertainty that invites further repression? Almost certainly.

For the first time, public opinion polls in Palestine and Israel show that less than half of either community believe the two-state solution is still viable. The number of people on both sides who favor a non-violent solution to the conflict is about double the number who favor violence.[42] Yet the array of tools we have examined – education, law, service, resistance, market forces – have not yet been sufficient to lever the course of events onto a new and better track. Why not? And what should we be doing in the face of this failure?

As I hope this book has made clear, the fate of Israel and Palestine will be determined by the interactions among the Israelis, the Palestinians, and the great powers, especially the United States. Most Israelis are intensely Zionist; only a few are willing to acknowledge that Palestinians are human beings who have equal rights. Palestinians, to date, have no successful formula

317

for expressing their political will, despite their educational attainments and entrepreneurial spirit. But, I would argue, it is the behavior of the United States, legitimating and supporting Israel's most aggressive and expansionist plans, which turns an asymmetric conflict into a catastrophic cycle of oppression, resistance, and violence.

Despite the fact that Americans like to think that their culture supports the underdog, in this case, we have not only sided with, but actually done much to create the wildly disproportionate military, economic, and diplomatic power enjoyed by Israel. It is beyond the scope of this book to tease out how much of America's one-sidedness is created by the Israel lobby,[43] how much by the fact that, in the context of the cold war, we have never sided with national liberation struggles unless they presented themselves as anti-Communist,[44] and how much is due to corporate interests in military hardware and security protocols.[45] Suffice it to say that America's conduct in Israel and Palestine has profoundly changed the course of history and has done so with, at best, reckless disregard for human rights and international law.

If this analysis is correct, then it seems to me the path forward, at least for Americans, is pretty clear. The work for Americans is here at home.

When I wrote the first edition of this book, I used the Black American experience as a point of entry for American readers to understand the conflict between Palestine and Israel. I emphasized the similarities between the civil rights struggle and Zionism as historic examples, exploring the choices made by small minorities in both mistreated communities to exit and to build a new society elsewhere. In both cases, the émigrés became the new boss who acted much like the old boss and the story did not end well.

Today the comparison has shifted to focus on the similarities between the African American and Palestinian experience. Both illustrate the ways in which, unless we dedicate ourselves to making it otherwise, already oppressed communities will bear the brunt of the upheavals caused by globalization and climate change. There is a lot of political exhortation that reminds us that all struggles for human rights (and against racism, classism, misogyny, anti-Semitism, Islamophobia, homophobia, ageism, ableism, etc.) are variations of the same struggle. In the case of the Palestinian and the African American communities the similarity is not only moral but also practical – both communities deserve so much more than to be the test labs for new technologies and new tactics of repression. Perhaps this very concrete starting point is where Americans need to begin, remembering the exhortation of Rabbi Abraham Joshua Heschel, that "in a free society, some are guilty, but all are responsible."[46]

President John F. Kennedy liked to quote a Chinese proverb: "A journey of thousand miles begins with a single step." My hope is that reading this book has become that first step and that now, knowing what can no longer be ignored, you will wish to take further steps to building an just and lasting peace for all the people between the river and the sea.

NOTES

[1] Danny Glover. (2014, August 18). Stand with Keith Ellison and Barbara Lee to End the Blockade of Gaza, *Huffington Post,* retrieved from http://www.huffingtonpost.com/danny-glover/stand-with-keith-ellison-_b_5689392.html6

[2] "Not Enough Water in the West Bank?" *Visualizing Palestine,* retrieved from http://visualizingpalestine.org/visuals/west-bank-water. "Thirst," *Visualizing Occupation*: *Distribution of Water,* retrieved from http://972mag.com/visualizing-occupation-distribution-of-water/49925/

[3] Israeli Committee against House Demolitions (ICAHD), retrieved from http://icahd.org/

[4] B'Tselem – The Israeli Information Center for Human Rights in the Occupied Territories. Restriction of Movement: Checkpoints, Physical Obstructions and Forbidden Roads, retrieved from http://www.btselem.org/freedom_of_movement/checkpoints_and_forbidden_roads

[5] Mahmood Mamdani. (2004). *Good Muslim, Bad Muslim: America, The Cold War and the Roots of Terror.* New York: Pantheon Books.

[6] Sa'ed Atshan. (2013). Prolonged Humanitarianism: The Social Life of Aid in the Occupied Palestinian Territories, Doctoral Dissertation, Harvard University Department of Anthropology.

[7] Lori Allen. (2003). *The Rise and Fall of Human Rights: Cynicism and Politics in Occupied Palestine.* Stanford: Stanford University Press.
Jeremy Wildeman and Sandy Marshall. (2014, May 21). By Mis-diagnosing Israel-Palestine, donor aid harms Palestinians, *Open Democracy,* retrieved from https://www.opendemocracy.net/arab-awakening/jeremy-wildeman-sandy-marshall/by-misdiagnosing-israelpalestine-donor-aid-harms-pales

[8] Zoe Wicomb. (2000). You *Can't Get Lost in Capetown.* New York: City University of New York Feminist Press.

[9] George Santayana. (1905). *Reason in Common Sense: The Life of Reason.* (Dover Publications, Volume 1), p. 284.

[10] Saleh Abdel Jawad. (2009). The Credibility and Limits of Refugee Oral Testimonies, *The Nakba: 60 years of Dispossession, 60 years of Resistance.* Paper presented at a SOAS conference, London, February 21–22, 2009.

[11] Isabel Kershner. (2014, August 31). Israel Claims Nearly 1,000 Acres of West Bank Land Near Bethlehem, *New York Times,* retrieved from http://www.nytimes.com/2014/09/01/world/middleeast/israel-claims-nearly-1000-acres-of-west-bank-land-near-bethlehem.html?_r=0

[12] Israel publishes tender for 283 settlement homes. (2014, September 5) *The Times of Israel,* retrieved from http://www.timesofisrael.com/israel-publishes-tender-for-283-settlement-homes/

[13] European nation states are not the only ones to try to balance multi-cultural inclusiveness with nationalist zeal. In the Arab world, Morocco is notable for its attempt to redefine its national character in the direction of cultural diversity. See Einat Levi. (2018, August 10). What Israel can learn from Morocco's multiculturalism, *+972*, retrieved from https://972mag.com/what-israel-can-learn-from-moroccos-multiculturalism/137171/

[14] Benedict Anderson. (2006, Revised Edition). *Imagined Communities*. London: Verso Books.

[15] Amahl Bishara. (2012). *Back Stories: U.S. News Production and Palestinian Politics.* Stanford: Stanford University Press.

[16] Saleh Abdel Jawad. (2012, November 3). *Russell Tribunal On Palestine*, New York, retrieved from https://www.youtube.com/watch?v=fd_tx9-r25s, at minute 27.17.

[17] Palestinian Civil Society Call for BDS, retrieved from http://www.bdsmovement.net/call

[18] Naamah Kellman. (2012, April 24). The Necessity of Hope, *Jerusalem Post*, retrieved from http://www.jpost.com/Features/In-Thespotlight/The-necessity-of-hope

[19] https://kinfolk.com/confronting-history-james-baldwin/

[20] David Halbfinger and Isabel Kershner. (2018, July 19). Israeli law declares the Country the Nation-State of the Jewish People, *New York Times*, retrieved from https://www.nytimes.com/2018/07/19/world/middleeast/israel-law-jews-arabic.html

[21] Damien Gayle. (2013, October 2). Creative Palestinian gardener uses hundreds of spent tear gas canisters as plant pots, *Daily Mail*, retrieved from http://www.dailymail.co.uk/news/article-2441997/Palestinian-gardener-uses-spent-tear-gas-canisters-PLANT-POTS.html

[22] National Public Radio did a story on vigilantes trying to prevent Jewish-Arab dating as early as 2009, Sheera A. Frenkel. (2009, October 12). Vigilantes Patrol for Jewish Women Dating Arab Men *NPR Morning Edition*, retrieved from http://www.npr.org/templates/story/story.php?storyId=113724468
In 2013, Mairav Zonszein reports that the practice continues, this time with IDF involvement. She details the cooperation between Israeli checkpoint soldiers and a group, *Yad La'achim* whose announced purpose is to "save Jews from assimilation." Soldiers record and turn over to the group the names of every Jewish woman they see riding in a car or chatting with a Palestinian. Mairav Zonszein. (2013, September 25). IDF soldier passes IDs of Jewish girls who socialize with Arabs to anti-assimilation NGO, *+972*, retrieved from http://972mag.com/idf-soldier-passes-ids-of-jewish-girls-who-socialize-with-arabs-to-anti-assimilation-ngo/79349/

[23] Martin Asser. (2000, October 13). Lynch mob's brutal attack, *BBC News Online*, retrieved from http://news.bbc.co.uk/2/hi/middle_east/969778.stm

[24] Gideon Levy. (2014, April 10). Helpless Israelis on a West Bank Road, *Ha'aretz*, retrieved from http://www.haaretz.com/opinion/.premium-1.584868

[25] *Ibid.*

[26] PHOTOS: Palestinian prisoners, supporters struggle for freedom. (2014, April 17). *+972*, retrieved from http://972mag.com/photos-palestinian-prisoners-and-supporters-struggle-for-freedom/89783/

[27] *Ibid.* photo #8.

[28] Nurit Peled-Elhanan. (2012). *Palestine in Israeli School Books: Ideology and Propaganda in Education.* London: I. B. Tauris.

[29] Peter Beinart. (2014, August 18). The next steps for liberal Zionists after Gaza: a Freedom Summer with Palestinians, *Ha'aretz*, retrieved from http://www.haaretz.com/opinion/.premium-1.612998

[30] Brendan Nyhan. (2014, July 6). When Beliefs and Facts Collide, *The New York Times*, retrieved from http://www.nytimes.com/2014/07/06/upshot/when-beliefs-and-facts-collide.html?_r=0&abt=0002&abg=1

[31] http://www.encounterprograms.org/

[32] Amos Harel. (2014, August 29). The summer Israel's security bubble wrap burst, *Ha'aretz*, retrieved from http://www.haaretz.com/news/diplomacy-defense/1.613053/

[33] For a full history of the Palestinian boycott movement see "Timeline," *BDS Movement for Freedom, Justice, Equality*, retrieved from http://www.bdsmovement.net/timeline

[34] For information on the general Palestinian boycott movement see https://bdsmovement.net/what-is-bds. For information on the academic and cultural boycott see https://bdsmovement.net/pacbi/pacbi-call. For information on the 2005 call for an economic boycott, see https://bdsmovement.net/call

[35] http://www.a4vpe.org/pages/home_en.php

[36] Robert Wade. (2014, October 24). Organised Hypocrisy on a Monumental Scale, *London Review of Books*, retrieved from http://www.lrb.co.uk/2014/10/24/robert-wade/organised-hypocrisy-on-a-monumental-scale

[37] Comment to author at a Leadership for Change Workshop, Boston College.

[38] Elliot Lusztig, retrieved from https://twitter.com/search?q=Elliot+Lusztig
Hannah Arendt. (1973). *The Origins of Totalitarianism*. (New York: Harcourt, Brace, Jovanovich) pp. 348–350.

[39] https://www.goodreads.com/work/quotes/12689683-common-prayer-a-liturgy-for-ordinary-radicals

[40] Omri Boehm. (2018, July 26). Did Israel Just Stop Trying to be a Democracy? *New York Times*, retrieved from https://www.nytimes.com/2018/07/26/opinion/israel-law-jewish-democracy-apartheid-palestinian.html
Nadia Ben-Youssef. (2018, July 28). The Nation State Law Sets Legal Parameters for Complete Takeover of Historic Palestine, *Palestine Square*, retrieved from https://palestinesquare.com/2018/07/28/jewish-nation-state-law-sets-legal-parameters-for-complete-takeover-of-historic-palestine/

[41] Amir Tibon. (2015, July 26). Hurricane Season//American Jews Say Current Storm with Israel Will Pass, Just Like all the Others Did, *Ha'aretz*, retrieved from https://www.haaretz.com/us-news/.premium-american-jews-say-current-storm-with-israel-will-pass-1.6316559

[42] Henriette Chacar. (2018, August 13). Israeli, Palestinian support for two states hits record low, +972, retrieved from https://972mag.com/israeli-palestinian-support-for-two-states-hits-record-low/137227/

[43] John Mearsheimer and Stephen Walt. (2006). *The Israel Lobby and U.S. Foreign Policy*. New York: Farrar, Strauss, and Giroux.

[44] Joseph Massad. (2006, March 25). "Blaming the Israel Lobby," *Counterpunch*, retrieved from http://www.counterpunch.org/2006/03/25/blaming-the-israel-lobby/

[45] Naomi Klein. (2008). *Shock Doctrine: The Rise of Disaster Capitalism*. New York: Picador. Jeff Halper. (2015). *War Against the People: Israel, the Palestinians and Global Pacification*. London: Pluto Press.

[46] https://ubcgcu.org/2014/04/06/the-wisdom-of-abraham-heschel/

PART 4

SUPPLEMENTARY MATERIAL

APPENDIX A: TIME LINE

Year/Era	Israel/Palestine Events	World Events
750–1140	—	• Caliphate rules much of Middle East, North Africa, and the Iberian Peninsula.
1281	—	• Founding of the Ottoman Empire.
1290	—	• Expulsion of the Jews from England.
1490s	—	• Expulsion of the Jews from Iberia.
1529	—	• *Siege of Vienna.* The high-water mark for Ottoman penetration of Europe. The siege failed, and after two more European victories against the Ottomans in the Battle of Vienna (1683) and the subsequent Great Turkish War (1683–1699), the Ottoman hold on Europe was definitively ended.
1655	—	• Cromwell "readmits" Jews to England as part of the process of preparing for the return of the Messiah.

1800s	• Palestine occupied by Ottoman Turks.
	
	• 1831–1840: Egypt temporarily wrests control of Syria and Palestine from the Ottomans.
	  ○ May–June 1834: Palestinian revolt against Egyptian domination.
	  ○ 1840: Turkish dominion over Syria and Palestine restored until end of WWI.
	
	• 1839–1876: Turkish education and land reform laws (*Tanzimat* laws) create basis for land ownership in Palestine under Ottoman and all subsequent regimes.
	
	• 1878–1882: First successful Zionist colony in Palestine founded at Petah Tikvah.
		• Rise of European nationalism (France, Germany, Italy, etc.).
		
		• 1817: American Colonization Society (ACS) established by a group of white Americans interested in transporting free black Americans to Liberia, marking the beginning of the Back-to-Africa movement. Zionism, similarly, is a minority movement with an opportunistic destination (Liberia was the only land in West Africa under U.S. control; Palestine was seen by the British Empire as a better fit for the Zionist project than lands such as Argentina or Uganda).
		
		• 1880's: Zionist colonies established by Maurice de Hirsch and the Jewish Colonization Association in Argentina.

(*cont.*)

© KONINKLIJKE BRILL NV, LEIDEN, 2019 | DOI:10.1163/9789004394148_012

Year/Era	Israel/Palestine Events	World Events
	• 1897: Meeting of the first Zionist Congress in Basel, Switzerland, convened by Herzl. Two major achievements of the meeting: (1) creation of the Zionist Organization (later the WZO); (2) endorsement of the Basel Plan, which declared "the aim of Zionism is to create for the Jewish people a home in Palestine secured by law."	• 1894–1899: Jewish French army captain Alfred Dreyfus tried and convicted of espionage/treason in France (pardoned in 1899). Antisemitic political scandal covered closely by journalist Theodor Herzl, then a Paris correspondent for Viennese newspaper *Die Neue Freie Presse*.
PRE-WWI 1900s	• 1901: Jewish National Fund founded by the 5th Zionist Congress to buy and develop land in Palestine for Jewish settlement. • 1908: The Palestine Office, a branch of the Zionist Organization, founded in Jaffa to help early Zionist arrivals in their dealings with Ottoman functionaries. Retitled the Palestine Zionist Executive in 1921 as it shifted its focus towards working with the British Mandate to make good on the promises of the Balfour Declaration. Renamed again in 1929 to what it is known as today, the Jewish Agency—legally separate from but effectively associated with the Zionist Organization and JNF.	• 1907: *Imperial Conference*. British Prime Minister Henry Campbell-Bannerman convenes conference to systematize the nomenclature of the British Empire. Included in the deliberations—which took place before WWI, during the Ottoman period—is a definition of Western interest in the Middle East that includes the need to insert a foreign body into the Arab world to exhaust its powers in never-ending wars. • 1914: Black rights leader Marcus Garvey establishes the United Negro Improvement Association (UNIA), whose central mission was to instill pride in black people based on their common African roots. Garvey was a proponent of the Pan-African ideology that was popular amongst black people in early 20th century America, as "Jim Crow" laws at the time were violently oppressive towards black Americans.
WWI	• 1914–1916: *Hussein-McMahon Correspondence*. Exchange of diplomatic memos in which the British encouraged a nationalist Arab revolt against the Ottoman Empire and promised Arab political independence in return for their opening a second front against the Ottomans. • 1916: *Sykes-Picot Agreement*. Anglo-French agreement to divide up Turkish Empire, allocating Lebanon, Syria and N. Iraq to France; Palestine, Jordan and S. Iraq to England.	• Turks—deeply indebted to France and hostile to Russia, with whom they share a long common border—side with Austria-Hungary and Germany.

(cont.)

Year/Era	Israel/Palestine Events	World Events
	• 1917: *Balfour Declaration.* Pledge by the British government to create a "Jewish homeland" within Mandate Palestine (see Sykes-Picot, above). The Balfour Declaration was issued prior to the end of WWI, in the hopes of recruiting German Jews to defect from the Kaiser's realm. The language was precise in calling Palestine *"a"* Jewish homeland and not *"the"* Jewish homeland for fear of creating a pretext for expelling Jews from Europe.	
PRE-WWII	• 1921: *Jaffa Riots.* Triggered by rival Jewish militias, resulting in 47 Jewish and 48 Palestinian deaths. These riots are the first in which some Palestinians kill Jews but others shelter Jews. No known instance of Jews sheltering Palestinians.	• 1922: Egypt achieves "limited independence," final British withdrawal in 1956. First of many Arab states to gain independence during this time period.
	• 1929: *Wailing Wall Riots.* Palestinian opposition, primarily to the British (but also to expanding Jewish settlements), expressed in widespread riots, including the Hebron Massacre of 68 Jews who, ironically, were not Zionists.	• 1932: Iraq achieves independence from Great Britain, renegotiated in 1947. • 1933: Hitler comes to power in Germany.

	• 1936–1939: Great Arab Rebellion against the British in Palestine, in large part because of policies favoring expansion of Jewish settlements.
	  ○ 1936: 6-month general strike from April to October, when Palestinians refused to staff Jewish-owned workplaces or buy Jewish goods.
	
	  ○ 1937: Great Britain's Peel Commission Report recommends partition of Palestine into one Jewish and one Muslim State, over the objections of both the Muslim and Jewish communities. This is the first partition plan.	

(cont.)

Year/Era	Israel/Palestine Events	World Events
	○ 1939: Great Britain's White Paper of 1939 shelves the Peel Commission proposal in favor of a unified country with proportional Jewish/Palestinian representation supervised by the British. ○ The rebellion ends in 1939 with the defeat and disarmament of Palestinian forces by a heavily armed *Yishuv.*	
WWII, 1940s	• 1947: *U.N. Resolution 181.* Called for end of the British Mandate in Palestine, the creation of the state of Israel on 55% of the land of Mandate Palestine, the creation of a Palestinian state on 44% of the land; and the creation of a UN administered international zone around the holy sites: Jerusalem to Bethlehem. • December, 1947–July 1949: *Al-Nakba/Israeli War of Independence* ○ Began with Zionist militia violence (Haganah, IZL, Lehi), creating 350,000 Palestinian refugees. ○ Upon British withdrawal from Palestine, Israel unilaterally declared itself into existence on May 15, 1948. ■ On that same day, President Truman made America the first country to recognize Israel. Russia followed shortly after, giving Israel two strong allies in America and Russia. ○ Shortly thereafter, six Arab armies (Lebanese, Egyptian, Jordanian, Syrian, Iraqi, and combined Arab league forces) unsuccessfully invaded Israel, but were unable to secure the land the U.N. had designated for a Palestinian state.	• 1942: Wannsee Conference formalizes commitment by Nazis to the "final solution" to the "Jewish Question" (i.e., genocide). • 1943: Lebanon achieves independence from France. • 1946: Syria achieves independence from France. • 1946–1989: Cold War allows Israel and the Arab States to play off the West vs. the Soviet Union. • January 1948: Jordan achieves independence from Great Britain. • 1948–1951: Political upheaval in Arab front-line states in response to Arab humiliation of 1948: assassinations of prime minister of Egypt, prime minister of Lebanon, king of Jordan; overthrow of Syrian and Egyptian regimes by military coups.

(cont.)

Year/Era	Israel/Palestine Events	World Events
	○ The newly formed Israeli Defense Forces create an additional 300,000–400,000 Palestinian refugees; level 85% of Palestinian villages and towns; annex half of Resolution 181 Palestine into the Israeli state.	
	• 1948: Israel declares a State of Emergency aimed at controlling Palestinians (which persists to this day). Such an arrangement subjects Palestinians to the brutality of military law.	
	• 1948–1955: Mass emigration of Arab Jewish communities (Baghdad, Cairo, Damascus, Beirut, Tunisia, Morocco, etc.) to Israel—partly with Israeli incentives, collusion and dirty tricks (e.g. Mossad agent Yehuda Tagar's bombing of Jewish cafes in Baghdad to get Iraqi Jews to emigrate to Israel).	
	• July 1949: Armistice lines become the "Green Line" now generally accepted in all official Israel-Palestinian and multi-lateral negotiations as the appropriate borders for a two state solution (cf. UN Resolution 242). Jordan occupies the West Bank portion of what would be Palestine, and Egypt the Gaza/Sinai area.	
1950s	• 1950: Law of Return passed, which created an inalienable right for Jews anywhere in the world to move to Israel with the support of the state. This is a critical part of the Basic Laws that Israel began to develop in the early 1950s, which formally made the case that Israel is the state of the Jewish people rather than its citizens.	• 1955: *Bandung Conference*. Founding conference of the Non-Aligned Movement with which African and Asian states sought to position themselves apart from the Cold War.

(*cont.*)

Year/Era	Israel/Palestine Events	World Events
	• 1950: UN creates two organizations in response to the Palestinian plight: the UN Conciliation Commission on Palestine (UNCCP) and the UN Relief Works Agency (UNRWA). The UNCCP's advocacy was ineffective due to Israeli intransigence and exists today only as a repository for Palestinian land records. The UNRWA is tasked with humanitarian work in Palestinian refugee camps, leaving no agency in the UN that is responsible for Palestinian advocacy.	• 1955–1979: *Baghdad Pact.* An attempt by Middle East nations (Iran, Iraq, Pakistan, Turkey) to create a regional mutual defense treaty modeled on NATO. Direct British participation and indirect U.S. involvement. Regime changes destabilized the efforts—Iraq, for example, withdrew as early as 1958.
	• 1954: Nasser's peace overtures rebuffed by Israel, per Ben Gurion's diaries.	• 1958: Soviet Union agrees to fund the Aswan Dam project, which helped protect Egypt's cotton-filled farmlands from Nile floodwater. U.S. withdrew from funding partly due to American cotton growers' fears of competition with Egypt.
	• 1956: Israelis participate in Anglo-French invasion of Suez Canal (Egypt); but Israelis retreat instantly in response to Eisenhower's demands that they do so. ○ The United States disapproved of the Suez Canal invasion so as to not look hypocritical in their denunciation of the Soviet invasion of Hungary (a similarly powerful country invading foreign lands), which was happening around the same time.	• 1958–1961: Nasser (Egypt) and Shukri al-Kuwati (Syria) agree to join their national aspirations in the formation of the United Arab Republic (UAR); a short-lived effort, though the idea of a pan-Arab development (secular, rhetorically socialist, and opposed to Israel) persists in the form of "Nasserism."

1960s	• 1964: Palestine Liberation Organization (PLO) founded at Arab League summit in Cairo under Nasser's tutelage in the hope of keeping the Palestinian cause within the Pan-Arab movement.
	  ○ PLO initially eschewed violence, unlike the Fateh group, founded under Syrian auspices in 1958.
	
	  ○ 1969: PLO and Fatah merged under Fatah leader Yasir Arafat, marking the de facto end of the secular pan-Arab response to Zionism.
		—

(*cont.*)

Year/Era	Israel/Palestine Events	World Events

	• June 5–11, 1967: *The Six Day War*
	  ○ Israel occupies the remainder of the projected Palestinian state, holding East Jerusalem, Gaza, the West Bank and the Golan Heights, collectively known as the Occupied Territories. East Jerusalem has since been annexed (illegally) to Israel and is no longer acknowledged by them to be part of the OPT.
	
	  ○ In recent years Israel has taken to calling the OPT "disputed areas."
	
	• 1967: *Khartoum Resolution.* Establishes a pan-Arab boycott and non-recognition of Israel until it gives back the land occupied by the Six Day War. This signifies Arab acceptance of the two-state solution, which was reiterated in 1988, again in 1993, and annually since the Arab Peace Initiative in 2002.
	
	• 1967: *U.N. Security Council Resolution 242.* Censures Israeli occupation and calls for withdrawal from the occupied territories and the creation of a Palestinian state on the 1949 armistice green line—allocating to the Palestinian state 22% of historic Palestine.
	
	• 1968: *The Battle of Karameh.* PLO under Yasir Arafat defeat Israelis in one battle.
	
	• forces in Karameh, Jordan. The battle achieved mythic status in Palestinian lore and inspired thousands of Palestinians to join the PLO.	

1970s	• 1970: *Black September.* Fearful that the PLO would overthrow his monarchy, Jordan's King Hussein ordered the killing of an estimated 30,000 Palestinians. The PLO was expelled from Jordan to Lebanon.	• 1972: *Munich Olympics.* Palestinians capture Israeli wrestling team who are, ultimately, killed in a cross-fire during a German rescue attempt.

(cont.)

Year/Era	Israel/Palestine Events	World Events
	• 1973: *The Yom Kippur War.* Fought between Israel and most of the Arab states the 1948 war. The Nixon administration announces the Kissinger Doctrine, the decision to commit the U.S. to arming Israel to the level that would always enable it to withstand simultaneous attacks from all of its surrounding frontline states. • March 30, 1976: *Land Day.* An Israel-wide demonstration by its Palestinian citizens against land expropriations. Land Day marks the first appearance of Palestinian citizens of Israel as powerful political actors. 6 Palestinian citizens were killed, approximately 100 wounded, and hundreds arrested. Anniversaries of Land Day are commemorated by the Palestinian community in both Israel and the Occupied Palestinian Territories. For example, the March of Return of 2018 began as a weekly Friday event in Gaza on March 30, 2018 and continues to this day. • 1978: *Camp David Accords.* Israel (Begin)/Egypt (Sadat) agree to a bilateral peace treaty going into effect in 1979, and the establishment of a Palestinian Authority to have some say in the governance of the West Bank and Gaza. This neutralization of Egypt was key in the facilitation of further Israeli aggression.	• 1973: Arab OPEC oil embargo imposed on the U.S. as a response to the Kissinger Doctrine. • 1975: *UN General Assembly Resolution 3379.* Equates Zionism with racism. • 1975: *Israel-South Africa Agreement.* Outlines the two nations' cooperation on nuclear issues and is a sign of the close relationship between Israel and Apartheid South Africa. • 1975–1990: Lebanese Civil War • 1979: Egypt expelled from the Arab League after Sadat signed the bilateral peace treaty at the Camp David Accords. Sadat was assassinated by members of Islamic Jihad in 1981. • 1979: *Overthrow of the Shah in Iran.* The new Islamic government is adamantly opposed to Israel and the United States. Israel was previously on good terms with Iran under the Shah, as they sought to forge strong alliances with the Muslim states of Turkey and Iran in order to keep their front line Arab neighbors at bay.
1980s	• 1982: Expulsion of the PLO from Lebanon to Tunisia, as Lebanese Christian militias (supported by Israeli forces) slaughtered upwards of 2,750 Palestinians during the Sabra and Shatila massacres in September.	• 1980–1988: *Iran/Iraq War.* Tempted by the overthrow of the Shah, Iraq invades Iran in 1980. The two countries fight until 1988 in a war that preoccupied Arab diplomats, effectively distracting them from issues concerning Palestinian rights.

(cont.)

Year/Era	Israel/Palestine Events	World Events
	• 1987–1993: *First Intifada.* Palestinian non-violent resistance to Israeli occupation. *B'Tselem* estimates: 1224 Palestinians killed and 104 Israelis killed.	• 1982–2000: *Israeli occupation of Southern Lebanon* ○ 1982: Israelis sanction and support Phalangist massacre in Sabra and Shatila, Palestinian refugee camps in Beirut ○ Occupation becomes a quagmire for Israel.
	• 1988: Hamas, the Palestinian branch of the Muslim Brotherhood, is founded during the First Intifada.	• 1989: The fall of the Berlin Wall and the subsequent rapid unraveling of the Soviet Empire, deprive Palestinians of their most powerful foreign sponsor. Americans no longer accept Russians as political refugees, leading to an influx of Russian Jews into Israel (nearly one million from 1989–2006). Russian immigrants helped bolster the "white" Israeli population and entered Israel with a fuller set of rights than Palestinians born there.
1990s	• 1991–1993: *Madrid Conference.* Initiated by Bush '41 and continues in a series of secret Israeli and Palestinian meetings. • Seeds the Oslo Accords (Rabin, Arafat, Clinton) in 1993, which required Palestinians to end violence and (implicitly) and required Israelis to cease settlement expansion. Neither side complied, with Israeli settlements doubling in size between Oslo ('93) and Camp David summit (2000). ○ Negotiations included "multi-track" meetings to address questions of water, environment, arms control, refugees and economic development. ○ Madrid marks the first face-to-face meetings of Israel and front-line Arab states: Syria, Lebanon and Jordan.	• 1990–1991: *First Gulf War.* PLO, headed by chairman Yasser Arafat, sides with Iraq and is therefore excluded from the Madrid conference, where Palestinian interests are represented by the Jordanian delegation and by independent Palestinians (e.g. Hannan Ashrawi). • 1994: *Jordanian-Israeli Peace Treaty.* Makes Jordan the second Arab country (behind Egypt) to sign a peace accord with Israel

(cont.)

Year/Era	Israel/Palestine Events	World Events
	○ The biggest harvest, for Israel, was the breaking of the Arab diplomatic blockade begun in 1967, and recognition by Oman, Qatar, Tunisia, Morocco and Mauritania.	
	○ For Palestine, PLO leaders (like Yasir Arafat) were allowed to leave Tunisia and return to their community in Palestine.	
	• 1994: Palestinian Authority (foreseen in the '78 Camp David Accords) comes into being with administrative authority in some parts of the West Bank and Gaza.	
	• 1994: *Cave of the Patriarchs Massacre.* Dr. Baruch Goldstein (an American-born Israeli doctor) enters the Ibrahimi mosque in West Bank and shoots 29 Muslim worshippers and wounds an additional 150, before he was beaten to death. The response of Hebron settlers – turning his grave into a major shrine, is particularly hurtful to Palestinian trust in the "peace process."	
	• 1996: *Tunnel Riots.* Palestinians in Jerusalem protested the opening of the Western Wall Tunnel, believing that Israeli tunnel expansion impairs the integrity of the *al-Aqsa* Mosque in the *Haraam al Sharif.*	
	• 1998: *Wye River Accord.* Unimplemented peace agreement between Israel and Palestine, signed by Netanyahu and Arafat under Clinton's tutelage.	
2000s	• 2000–2005: *Second Intifada.* More militarized than the first, in part because the Palestinian Authority has received arms under the Oslo process. ○ B'Tselem estimates 3466 Palestinians killed, 998 Israelis killed.	• 2000: Israel withdraws from Lebanon, signaling their defeat in a war of attrition between the two countries. • 2001: September 11 bombing of the World Trade Center

(*cont.*)

Year/Era	Israel/Palestine Events	World Events

	• 2000: *Camp David Summit.* Clinton, Barak, and Arafat meet but fail to produce an agreement.
	
	• 2000: Israel begins construction of the Separation Barrier. If completed as planned, it would be twice the length of the Green Line and only 15% would lie on Israel's recognized border with Palestine.
	
	• 2001: *Taba Meetings.* Barak modified his proposal but was met with no counter-offer from Arafat.
	  ○ Israelis score a major public relations victory in claiming that Arafat rejected Barak's "generous proposal."
	
	  ○ Accounts of the Camp David Summit and Taba meetings by Aaron David Miller (assistant to Clinton's chief negotiator, Dennis Ross) show that the American position was based on Israeli "security needs" rather than Palestinian "rights" or international law.
	
	• 2003: *Geneva Initiative.* Draft of a peace treaty written by both Israelis and Palestinians.
	  ○ Led to the creation of Israeli and Palestinian NGOs (Heskem and the Palestine Peace Coalition, respectively) that work towards solving the conflict.
	
	• 2004: International Court of Justice rules that the Separation Wall is illegal.
	
	• 2004: Death of PLO Chairman Yasser Arafat.
	
	• 2005: Election of PLO leader Abbas. Mahmoud Abbas as Palestinian Authority President.
		• 2002: *Beirut Summit.* Initiated by Arab States, calling for a return to Green line borders, two state solution with the creation and recognition of a Palestinian state, normalization of Arab-Israeli relations. This offer is known as the Arab Peace Initiative. It has been reiterated at every subsequent Arab League summit.
		
		• 2002: *Road Map for Peace.* Proposed by the "quartet" (US, EU, UN, Russia) and called for the Palestinian Authority to leash Palestinian militias and for Israel to cease increasing settlements. Never implemented.
		
		• 2003: *Iraq War.* Initiated by the U.S. and the "coalition of the willing" (countries that supported the U.S. invasion). After 9/11, the U.S. went into a period of intense Islamophobia and made it clear that it could not function as an even-handed mediator in the Israel-Palestine conflict.
		
		• 2004: The International Court of Justice issues advisory opinion that Israel's Separation Barrier is a violation of international law.
		
		• 2006: The Baker-Hamilton Report (a bi-partisan analysis of US interests in Iraq) links the resolution of I/P issues to regional peace efforts, and to US ability to withdraw safely from Iraq.
		
		• 2007: *Annapolis Peace Conference.* Attended by President Bush '43 (U.S.), Prime Minister Olmert (Israel), and President Abbas (Palestine). Yields no new results.

(cont.)

335

Year/Era	Israel/Palestine Events	World Events
	• 2005: Unilateral withdrawal of Israeli settlers from Gaza. However, Israelis continue to control Gazan access to food, water, medical supplies, personal movement outside of Gaza, etc. • 2006: Election of Hamas to majority position in the Palestinian Authority Parliament. • 2006: Election of Kadima government in Israel. • 2006: Israeli Foreign Minister Tzipi Livni acknowledges that the separation wall is going to be the unilaterally Israeli defined international border. • Dec. 2008–January 2009: *Operation Cast Lead.* An Israeli massacre in response to rocket fire from Gaza. Over 1,400 Palestinians killed by Israel. Among Israeli casualties are 3 civilians and 10 soldiers (4 of whom were killed by friendly fire. Prior withdrawal of Israeli settlers in 2005 allows Israel to carpet bomb Gaza. ◦ Operation Cast Lead becomes the subject of the Goldstone Report.	
2010s	• 2011: Palestinians seek to internationalize the quest for a state by going to the U.N. and seeking full member status. They are upgraded from an observer entity to an observer state (i.e., non-voting) within the U.N. System. • 2012: *Operation Pillar of Defense.* Massacre carried out by Israel in an attempt to subdue Palestinian resistance in Gaza. 174 Palestinians killed, of whom 107 were civilians. Four Israelis killed: 2 soldiers and 2 civilians. • June 2014: *Operation Brother's Keeper.* Military operation carried out by the IDF after the kidnapping of three Israeli teenagers. 5 Palestinians killed and hundreds arrested.	• 2013: Shuttle diplomacy conducted by President Obama's Secretary of State, John Kerry, yields no new results. • 2016: U.S. foreign aid gives Israel $3.8 billion dollars and provides $2.5 million dollars to the Palestinian Authority

(cont.)

Year/Era	Israel/Palestine Events	World Events
	• July 2014: *Operation Protective Edge*. Israeli massacre in Gaza. On the Israeli side, 67 soldiers and 4 civilians died. 2310 Palestinians were killed.	
	• May 2018: Following Trump's move of the U.S. Embassy to Jerusalem, Palestinian and Israeli polls show that more than 50% of their respective constituents now feel that the two-state solution is no longer viable. Among those on both sides who hold this belief, about twice as many favor a non-violent political solution over a military solution.	• May 2018: Trump moves U.S. Embassy from Tel Aviv to Jerusalem.
	• July 2018: Israeli prime minister Netanyahu welcomes Hungarian prime minister Viktor Orbán as a "true friend of Israel," despite Orbán's praise of Nazi collaborators and antisemitic past.	
	• March 2018–present: *March of Return*. Palestinians in Gaza protest on behalf of the refugees' right of return (90% of Gazans hold refugee status). 1 Israeli soldier has been killed. On the Palestinian side, 168 people have been killed along with thousands injured.	

APPENDIX B: STUDY QUESTIONS

Preface
1. When did you first hear about the Palestine-Israel conflict? Who brought it to your attention? What was the context?
2. Consider some incidence in which you did volunteer work, joined a social movement, went to a demonstration, or wrote a letter to the editor. How did you come to be engaged with the issue that was the focus of your efforts? What mix of personal and public factors motivated you?
3. Did any teacher or class help you to focus your attention on matters of public concern? If so, what did that teacher do that captured your attention?

Chapter 1: Introduction: Tell Our Story
1. Try to remember images of Jews and Arabs in movies or television shows you have seen. What shows included identifiably Arab and Jewish character? How often do you see Jewish Americans portrayed in mainstream media? Are characters even identified as Jewish? How often do you see Arab Americans portrayed in mainstream media? How are they identified?
2. Close your eyes. Try to notice the pictures that come into your mind when someone says "(S)He's an Arab" or "(S)He's a Jew."
3. In this chapter, I make the argument that the great powers have always been self-serving in their interventions abroad. Think about some major American interventions abroad. Does that analysis seem to apply to the actions of our government?
4. Think of a struggle in American society – perhaps between whites and African Americans, or between men and women, between those who are pro-life vs. those who are pro-choice; those who are for or against the NRA, etc. Pick one such conflict. Who are the major parties? What position do they articulate? How do they articulate it – what images and metaphors do they use? How much time do they spend articulating their own position? How much effort do they make to disparage those who disagree with them?

Chapter 2: Encountering the Story
1. Have you ever been on a trip to a poor country (e.g. the Dominican Republic, Haiti, many of the Caribbean Islands)? Did you see poor people while you were a tourist? What was done to make them more or less visible?

© KONINKLIJKE BRILL NV, LEIDEN, 2019 | DOI:10.1163/9789004394148_013

2. In your own community, do you know where the poorest people live? Have you been to see their neighborhoods? Do you know any of them?

3. Does the architecture of your city make it harder to encounter people unlike yourself (in age, race, or class)? How do highways separate or link communities? How do schools help (or hinder) people in negotiating difference?

Chapter 3: Basic Ideas: Human Rights, Race, and Nation

1. Have you ever read the Universal Declaration of Human Rights? If you did so, did you find it convincing? Overly ambitious? Lacking in certain ways?

2. Are there any convincing arguments against human rights doctrine that you would consider?

3. Assuming you think that every society should help its members become the best possible version of themselves, how important are social and economic rights?

4. Nobody says they want to be a racist. Yet people of color point to many instances of racist behavior. Assuming that you do not wish to be a racist, what list of behaviors would you avoid in order to achieve your aim? How might you get information to add to that list?

5. Have you heard charges of racism that you found unconvincing? If so, what made you reject the claims? Do the distinctions among personal, cultural and structural racism help you to think this through?

6. Much of American conversation about race identifies only white people and African Americans. How many other racial groups can you name? What do you know about them and where/how do you find it out?

7. What are your earliest associations with being an American? Who taught you about being an American? What content did they identify as quintessentially American?

8. When you were learning American history in school, how was the American revolution against the British described? Was the British colonization of America ever described as "a colonial settler project?"

9. Have you ever travelled abroad? If so, what did you discover about your own identity as an American that came from interacting on a daily basis with many people who are not American?

Chapter 4: Zionism – the idea that changed everything

1. What are your images of the Holocaust, and where do they come from? Stories of relatives? School discussions? Movies or other art forms?

2. How was material about the Holocaust taught in your schools?
3. Were you taught about the Holocaust's non-Jewish victims?
4. Were you taught about any of the other cases of mass killings like the Armenian genocide, the Cambodian killing fields, the Soviet Gulag, the Bosnian or Rwandan genocides?
5. How as World War II explained in your school. How much of this history of World War II concerned battles? How much was focused on the Holocaust? How much was focused on other subjects (e.g. anti-Nazi resistance in various countries), economic factors in the war, etc.?

Chapters 5–8: History Section
Think of any social movement that has touched your life: civil rights, the anti-war movement, environmentalism, feminism.
1. Who first began to name the problem.
2. Who challenged them or denied the problem.
3. What tools or actions proved most useful in bringing about change?
4. What tools were most useful for mobilizing allies?
5. What tools were most useful for convincing the indifferent?
6. What tools were most useful for dealing with opponents?

Chapter 9: Four Frames
1. How was American history taught in your elementary and high school? Was it a triumphalist narrative, telling the story of European settlers bringing civilization to a wilderness? How were the rights of Native Americans addressed? How was the doctrine of manifest destiny evaluated?
2. When did you first encounter "hyphenated histories" like black history, women's history, Latino history? How much space did they have in the curriculum?
3. Were you taught critical reasoning skills in assessing historical data? Were you asked to list supporting and critical arguments for particular historical interpretations?

Chapter 10: Zionism Revisited
1. If you were to make the argument that Zionism is a toxic doctrine, how would you respond to the accusation that you are trying to destroy Israel?
2. How do other groups, i.e. not Jews, respond to their histories of being the victims of prejudice and discrimination? How is this experience narrated by African Americans? Latinos? American Indians/First Nations peoples?

341

3. How do African American, Latino, Amerindian narratives strike a balance between their histories of victimization and their history of achievements?
4. What other tools, besides Zionism, might be available to ensure the safety of Jews?
5. In your estimation, what are the major challenges to social justice characteristic of the 21st century?

Chapter 11: Hope and History
1. For purposes of a church talk or even a dinner table conversation, how would you summarize the balance of power between the forces of injustice and efforts at reform and resistance?
2. Is there any particular solution or process you would advocate for resolving the Israel/Palestine conflict? If so, what stories could you find that would make your position clear?
3. Which of the instruments of social change fits best into your life?
4. If you have ever participated in a social service project or a social change initiative, what have you learned from those experiences? What things worked or did not work for you personally? What things worked or did not work to accomplish the goal of the project?

REFERENCES

1 for 3. (n.d.). *Homepage*. Retrieved from http://1for3.org/

Abalimi Bezekhaya. (n.d.). *Homepage*. Retrieved from http://abalimi.org.za/

Abdel Jawad, S. (1998, January 8–14). War by other means. *Al Ahram Weekly*. Retrieved from http://weekly.ahram.org.eg/Archive/1998/1948/359_salh.htm

Abdel Jawad, S. (2001, April 16). Secret weaknesses. *Media Monitors Network*. Retrieved from http://www.mediamonitors.net/jawad2.html

Abdel Jawad, S. (2006). The Arab and Palestinian narratives of the 1948 war. In R. I. Rotberg (Ed.), *Israeli and Palestinian narratives of conflict: History's double helix* (pp. 72–114). Bloomington, IN: Indiana University Press.

Abdel Jawad, S. (2007). Zionist massacres: The creation of the Palestinian refugee problem in the 1948 war. In E. Benvenisti, C. Gans, & S. Hanafi (Eds.), *Israel and the Palestinian refugees* (pp. 59–127). Heidelberg: Spring Verlag.

Abdel Jawad, S. (2009, February 22). *The credibility and limits of refugee oral testimonies*. Paper presented at the Nakba, 60 years of Dispossession, 60 years of Resistance, London, UK. Retrieved from https://www.youtube.com/watch?v=vVNL2I-lggw

Abdel Jawad, S. (2012, November 3). *Russell tribunal on Palestine*. Retrieved from https://www.youtube.com/watch?v=fd_tx9-r25s, at minute 27.17

Abou Shehadeh, S., & Shbaytah, F. (2009, February 26). Jaffa: From eminence to ethnic cleansing. *The Electronic Intifada*. Retrieved from http://electronicintifada.net/content/jaffa-eminence-ethnic-cleansing/8088

Abo-Rkeek, M. (n.d.). *Desert daughter*. Retrieved from https://www.facebook.com/pages/Desert-Daughter/105407502848181

Abowd, T. P. (2014). *Colonial Jerusalem: The spatial construction of identity and difference in a city of myth, 1948–2012*. Syracuse, NY: Syracuse University Press.

Abu-Amr, Z. (1995). The significance of Jerusalem, A Moslem perspective. *Palestine-Israel Journal, 2*(2). Retrieved from http://www.pij.org/details.php?id=646

Abu Artena, A. (2018, August 17). One state: A view from Gaza. *Mondoweiss*. Retrieved from https://mondoweiss.net/2018/08/state-view-from/

Abu-Lughod, L. (2013). *Do Arab women need saving?* Cambridge, MA: Harvard University Press.

Abunimah, A. (2007). *One country: A bold proposal to end the Israeli-Palestinian impasse*. New York, NY: Picador Press.

Abunimah, A. (2008, September 9). A new Palestinian strategy or the same failed one? *The Electronic Intifada*. Retrieved from http://electronicintifada.net/content/new-palestinian-strategy-or-same-failed-one/7707

Abunimah, A. (2012, March). *Keynote*. Speech presented at Harvard One State Conference, Harvard University, Cambridge, MA. Retrieved from http://electronicintifada.net/blogs/ali-abunimah/audio-ali-abunimah-and-ilan-pappe-keynote-speeches-harvard-one-state-conference

Abunimah, A. (2012, May 13). Watch: The great book robbery: Israel's 1948 looting of Palestine's cultural heritage. *The Electronic Intifada*. Retrieved from http://electronicintifada.net/blogs/ali-abunimah/watch-great-book-robbery-israels-1948-looting-palestines-cultural-heritage

REFERENCES

Abunimah, A. (2012, November 11). When former CIA chief David Petraeus enraged the Israel lobby. *The Electronic Intifada.* Retrieved from http://electronicintifada.net/blogs/ali-abunimah/when-former-cia-chief-david-petraeus-enraged-israel-lobby

Abunimah, A. (2014, March 14). Does Israel have a right to exist as a Jewish state? *Mondoweiss.* Retrieved from http://mondoweiss.net/2014/03/abunimahs-justice-palestine.html

Abunimah, A. (2018, March 31). Israel admits, then deletes, responsibility for Gaza killings. *The Electronic Intifada.* Retrieved from https://electronicintifada.net/blogs/ali-abunimah/israel-admits-then-deletes-responsibility-gaza-killings

Abu Salem, H. (2017, June 22). Why is Netanyahu trying to disband the UNRWA? *Al Jazeera.* Retrieved from https://mail.google.com/mail/u/0/#label/localfolders%2Fpalestine%2FBOOK%2F2nd+edition+revisions%2F2Chap6/15cdfe18dc3bc04c

Abu Sitta, S. (2000). *The Palestinian Nakba 1948.* London: The Palestine Return Centre.

Abu Sitta, S. (2013, April 6–7). *Reconstructing Palestine: Reversing ethnic cleansing.* Paper presented at the Right of Return Conference, Boston University, Boston, MA. Retrieved from http://www.plands.org/en/article-speechs/2013/re-constructing-palestine

Acocella, J. (2002, June 17). A hard case: The life and death of Primo Levi. *The New Yorker.* Retrieved from http://www.newyorker.com/archive/2002/06/17/020617crbo_books?currentPage=all

Activestills. (2014, April 17). PHOTOS: Palestinian prisoners, supporters struggle for freedom. *+972.* Retrieved from http://972mag.com/photos-palestinian-prisoners-and-supporters-struggle-for-freedom/89783/

Activist Boats Reach Gaza Strip. (2008, August 23). *BBC News.* Retrieved from http://news.bbc.co.uk/2/hi/middle_east/7578880.stm

Adalah – The Legal Center for Arab Minority Rights in Israel. (n.d.). *Discriminatory laws in Israel.* Retrieved from https://www.adalah.org/en/content/view/7771

Adalah – The Legal Center for Arab Minority Rights in Israel. (n.d.). *Homepage.* Retrieved from http://adalah.org/eng/

Adalah – The Legal Center for Arab Minority Rights in Israel. (n.d.). *National priority areas – Economic efficiency law, 2009.* Retrieved from https://www.adalah.org/en/law/view/506

Addameer. (n.d.). *Homepage.* Retrieved from http://www.addameer.org/

Aderet, O. (2014, May 1). Israel at 66. *Ha'aretz.* Retrieved from http://www.haaretz.com/news/national/.premium-1.588482

Adva Center. (2014, September 9). Report: Settlements receive disproportionate state funding. *Ha'aretz.* Retrieved from http://www.haaretz.com/business/.premium-1.614765

Afsai, S. (2012, October 12). The "married to another man" story. *Jewish Ideas Daily.* Retrieved from http://www.jewishideasdaily.com/5148/features/the-married-to-another-man-story/

Ahren, R. (2014, July 31). PA to sign Rome statute of the ICC. *The Times of Israel.* Retrieved from http://www.timesofisrael.com/pa-to-sign-rome-statute-of-international-criminal-court/

Ajayi, A. (2014, January 28). Is Zionism never having to say you're sorry? *Ha'aretz.* Retrieved from http://www.haaretz.com/culture/books/.premium-1.571045

Akram, F., & Rudorem, J. (2014, August 22). Executions in Gaza are a warning to spies. *New York Times.* Retrieved from http://www.nytimes.com/2014/08/23/world/middleeast/israel-gaza.html?_r=0

Akram, S. (2001/2002). Palestinian refugees and their legal status. *Journal of Palestinian Studies, 31*(3), 36–51.

Al Bustan. Retrieved from https://www.bustan.org/on/default.asp

Al Jazeera. (2011, January 28). Thousands protest in Jordan. *Al Jazeera.* Retrieved from http://www.aljazeera.com/news/middleeast/2011/01/2011128125157509196.html

Al Jazeera. (2015, October 23). Rabbi attacked by alleged Jewish settler in West Bank. Retrieved from https://www.youtube.com/watch?v=FpecFERU9wQ

Al Jazeera English. (2009, November 8). *Israeli separation barrier cuts family from village* [Video file]. Retrieved from https://www.youtube.com/watch?v=c5uBA3F1Ghw

Al Jazeera English. (2013, July 6). *Al-Kurd family home takeover (Sheikh Jerrah)* [Vido file]. Retrieved from http://www.youtube.com/watch?feature=endscreen&NR=1&v=wlQf41CJjjc

Al Jazeera Staff. (2017, April). Palestinian Authority to stop funding Gaza electricity. *Al Jazeera News.* Retrieved from https://www.aljazeera.com/news/2017/04/palestinian-authority-stop-funding-gaza-electricity-170427105910755.html

Alexandrowicz, R. (Director). (2012). *The law in these parts* [Motion picture]. Israel: RO*CO Films International.

Alimi, E. (2007). *Israeli politics and the first Palestinian Intifada: Political opportunities, framing processes and contentious politics.* London: Routledge.

Allen, L. (2013). *The rise and fall of human rights: Cynicism and politics in occupied Palestine.* Stanford, CA: Stanford University Press.

Almalki, A., & Ashour, A. (2014, July 27). Shujayea: Massacre at dawn. *Al Jazeera.* Retrieved from http://www.aljazeera.com/programmes/specialseries/2014/07/shujayea-massacre-at-dawn-201472621348901563.html

Alper, L. et al. (2016). *The occupation of the American mind: Israel's public relations war in the United States.* Northampton, MA: Media Education Foundation.

Al-Qaws. (n.d.). *Homepage.* Retrieved from http://www.alqaws.org/siteEn/index/language/en

Alrowwad. (n.d.). *Homepage.* Retrieved from http://www.alrowwad-acts.ps/

Alsaafin, L. (2011, November 14). Palestinians clarify goal of "freedom rides" challenge to segregated Israeli buses. *The Electronic Intifada.* Retrieved from http://electronicintifada.net/blogs/linah-alsaafin/palestinians-clarify-goal-freedom-rides-challenge-segregated-israeli-buses

Al Sabawi, K. (2011, May 22). *TEDxRamallah – Khaled Al Sabawi: Keeping Palestine cool* [Video file]. Retrieved from http://www.youtube.com/watch?v=9fD2bMavK8Y

Amara, A., Abu-Saad, I., & Yiftachel, O. (Eds.). (2013). *Indigenous (in)justice: Human rights law and Bedouin Arabs in the Naqab/Negev.* Cambridge, MA: Harvard Law School Human Rights Program.

American Friends Service Committee. (n.d.). *Israel's settlement policy in the occupied Palestinian territory.* Retrieved from https://afsc.org/resource/israel%E2%80%99s-settlement-policy-occupied-palestinian-territory

Americans for a Vibrant Economy. (n.d.). *Promoting economic partnerships between Americans and Palestinians.* Retrieved from http://www.a4vpe.org/pages/home_en.php

Amichai, R. (2011, March 12). Jewish couple and three children killed in West Bank. *Reuters.* Retrieved from http://www.reuters.com/article/2011/03/12/us-palestinians-israel-violence-idUSTRE72B0B920110312

Amnesty International. (n.d.). *With whom are many U.S. police departments training? With a chronic human rights violator – Israel, amnesty international.* Retrieved from https://www.amnestyusa.org/with-whom-are-many-u-s-police-departments-training-with-a-chronic-human-rights-violator-israel/

Anarchists against the Wall. (n.d.). *Homepage.* Retrieved from http://www.awalls.org/

REFERENCES

Anderson, B. (1991). *Imagined communities*. London: Verso Press.

Ankori, G. (2006). *Palestinian art*. London: Reaktion.

An Open Letter to LGBTIQ Communities and Allies on the Israeli Occupation of Palestine. (2012, January 24). Retrieved from http://www.queersolidaritywithpalestine.com/

Applied Research Institute-Jerusalem. (n.d.). *Homepage*. Retrieved from http://www.arij.org/

Arafat, Y. (1988). *Arafat's speech to the UN general assembly* [Speech]. Retrieved from http://www.mideastweb.org/arafat1988.htm

Aren, R. (2017, July 20). Decrying "betrayal" Hungary Jews say Netanyahu ignoring them. *The Times of Israel*. Retrieved from https://www.timesofisrael.com/decrying-netanyahu-betrayal-hungary-jews-say-pm-ignoring-them/

Arendt, H. (1948, May). To save the Jewish homeland: There is still time. *Commentary*, pp. 398–406.

Arendt, H. (1973). *The origins of totalitarianism*. New York, NY: Harcourt Brace Jovanovich.

Arens, M. (2008, October 28). The fence, revisited: Do our politicians have the courage to admit they made a mistake by building the security barrier? *Ha'aretz*. Retrieved from http://www.haaretz.com/print-edition/opinion/the-fence-revisited-1.256157

Arnold, T. W. (1937). *The folklore of capitalism*. New Haven, CT: Yale University Press.

Arutz Sheva. Retrieved from http://www.israelnationalnews.com/Articles/Article. aspx/18210#.VpK885scTIU

Ascherman, A. (Presenter). (2013, December 29). *Rabbis for human rights*. Speech presented at Holy Land Hotel, Jerusalem, Israel.

Ashly, J. (2017, September 18). Drowning in the waste of Israeli settlers. *Al Jazeera*. Retrieved from https://www.aljazeera.com/indepth/features/2017/09/drowning-waste-israeli-settlers-170916120027885.html

Ashrawi, H. (2014, March 31). Talk presented at John F. Kennedy School of Government, Harvard University, Cambridge, MA.

Asimov, I. (1992). *Asimov laughs again: More than 700 favorite jokes, limericks and anecdotes*. New York, NY: William Morrow.

Asser, M. (2000, October 13). Lynch mob's brutal attack. *BBC News*. Retrieved from http://news.bbc.co.uk/2/hi/middle_east/969778.stm

Associated Press. (2011, February 12). Algerian protest draws thousands. *CBC News*. Retrieved from http://www.cbc.ca/news/world/algeria-protest-draws-thousands-1.1065078

Ateek, N. (2005, January 16). Suicide bombing from a Palestinian perspective. *Peace Palestine*. Retrieved from http://peacepalestine.blogspot.com/2005/01/naim-ateek-suicide-bombing-from.html

Atshan, S. (2013). *Prolonged humanitarianism: The social life of aid in the occupied Palestinian territories* (Unpublished doctoral dissertation). Harvard University, Cambridge, MA.

Atshan, S. (n.d.). *The empire of critique*. Stanford, CA: Stanford University Press.

Auerbach, H. (1992). Opfer der nationalsozialistischen Gewaltherrschaft. In W. Benz (Ed.), *Legenden, Lügen, Vorurteile. Ein Wörterbuch zur Zeitgeschichte*. Dtv: Neuauflage.

Avinieri, S. (1981). *The making of modern Zionism: The intellectual origins of the Jewish state*. New York, NY: Basic Books.

Avishai, B. (2005, January). Saving Israel from itself: A secular future for the Jewish State. *Harper's, 310*(1856), 37. Retrieved from https://harpers.org/archive/2005/01/saving-israel-from-itself/

Avishai, B. (2014, April 14). Truman's folly? *The Nation*. Retrieved from http://www.thenation.com/article/179024/trumans-folly

Avnery, U. (2004, December). The boss has gone crazy. *Counterpunch*. Retrieved from http://www.counterpunch.org/2004/12/11/the-boss-has-gone-crazy/

Avnery, U. (2009, January 19). The boss has gone mad. *Counterpunch*. Retrieved from http://www.counterpunch.org/2009/01/19/the-boss-has-gone-mad/

Avnery, U. (2010, April 9). Damage control. *Gush-Shalom*. Retrieved from http://zope.gush-shalom.org/home/en/channels/avnery/1283599151/

Avnery, U. (2013, September 11). The judaization of Israel. *Gush-Shalom*. Retrieved from http://zope.gush-shalom.org/home/en/channels/avnery/1383915646/

Ayturk, I. (2010). Revisiting the language factor in Zionism: The Hebrew language council form 1904–1914. *Bulletin of SOAS, 73*(1), 45–64.

Badil Resource Center. (2010–2012). *Survey of Palestinian refugees and internally displaced persons, VII*. Retrieved from http://reliefweb.int/sites/reliefweb.int/files/resources/Survey2012.pdf

Badil Resource Center. (n.d.). *Homepage*. Retrieved from http://www.badil.org/

Bahour, S. (2014, May 24). Israel declares war on Palestinian banks. *Talking Points Memo*. Retrieved from http://talkingpointsmemo.com/cafe/israel-declares-war-on-palestinian-banks

Bahour, S. (2014, November 5). *Flavors of end: Jung und Naiv in Israel & Palestine*. Retrieved from https://www.youtube.com/watch?v=L8RAZuqildE

Bakri, N., & Goodman, D. (2011, January 27). Thousands in Yemen protest against the government. *The New York Times*. Retrieved from http://www.nytimes.com/2011/01/28/world/middleeast/28yemen.html

Balbus, I. D. (1973). *The dialectics of legal repression: Black rebels before the American criminal courts*. New York, NY: Russell Sage Foundation.

Baldwin, J. Retrieved from https://kinfolk.com/confronting-history-james-baldwin/

Bannoura, S. (2014, August 27). Ministry of health: 2,145 Palestinians, including 578 children, killed by Israel's aggression. *International Middle East Media Center*. Retrieved from http://www.imemc.org/article/68969

Bar, Z. (2009, October 18). Comment/How do Turkey and Israel measure each other's love? *Ha'aretz*. Retrieved from http://www.haaretz.com/print-edition/opinion/comment-how-do-turkey-and-israel-measure-each-other-s-love-1.5928

Barkat, A. (2007, July 24). Ex-minister Rubinstein: State should reclaim land given to the JNF. *Ha'aretz*. Retrieved from http://www.haaretz.com/news/ex-minister-rubinstein-state-should-reclaim-land-given-to-jnf-1.226146

Barnes, K. C. (2004). *Journey of hope: The back-to-Africa movement in Arkansas*. Chapel Hill, NC: University of North Carolina Press.

Becker, H. (1953). Becoming a Marihuana user. *The American Journal of Sociology, 59*(3), 235–242.

Beddegenoodts, J. (2012, January 26). *We are Nabi Saleh (Trailer)* [Video file]. Retrieved from https://www.youtube.com/watch?v=DdyD8yZ68NA

Be'er, Y., & Abdel Jawad, S. (1994). *Collaborators in the occupied territories: Human rights abuses and violations*. Jerusalem: B'Tselem. Retrieved from http://www.google.com/url?sa=t&rct=j&q=&esrc=s&source=web&cd=1&ved=0CB4QFjAA&url=http%3A%2F%2Fwww.btselem.org%2Fdownload%2F199401_collaboration_suspects_eng.rtf&ei=SXg8VOnQA9SvyATK1IKQBw&usg=AFQjCNF4d4qcywLQ9KhxPMXDyndHMdvPDQ&sig2=MdroDnX799S8SBCkVXeKyg&bvm=bv.77161500,d.aWw

Beinart, P. (2010, May 12). The failure of the American Jewish establishment. *The New York Review of Books*. Retrieved from http://www.nybooks.com/articles/archives/2010/jun/24/failure-american-jewish-establishment-exchange/

REFERENCES

Beinart, P. (2012). *The crisis of Zionism*. New York, NY: Times Books.

Beinart, P. (2014, August 18). The next steps for liberal Zionists after Gaza: A freedom summer with Palestinians. *Ha'aretz*. Retrieved from http://www.haaretz.com/opinion/.premium-1.612998

Beinin, J. (1999, March 26). The demise of the Oslo process. *The Middle East Report*. Retrieved from http://www.merip.org/mero/mero032699

Beit-Hallahmi, B. (1993). *Original sins: Reflections on the history of Zionism and Israel*. New York, NY: Olive Branch Press.

Ben-Gurion, D. (1938 June 7). Address at the Mapai political committee. In S. Flapan (Ed.), *Zionism and the Palestinians*. New York, NY: Barnes and Noble.

Benmelecha, E., & Berrebi, C. (2007). Human capital and the productivity of suicide bombers. *Journal of Economic Perspectives, 21*(3), 223–238.

Benn, A. (2014, May 1). Netanyahu: Hero of the binational state? *Ha'aretz*. Retrieved from http://www.haaretz.com/opinion/.premium-1.588380

Bennett, N. (2014, November 5). For Israel, two-state is no solution. *The New York Times*. Retrieved from http://www.nytimes.com/2014/11/06/opinion/naftali-bennett-for-israel-two-state-is-no-solution.html

Ben-Youssef, N. (2018, July 28). The nation state law sets legal parameters for complete takeover of historic Palestine. *Palestine Square*. Retrieved from https://palestinesquare.com/2018/07/28/jewish-nation-state-law-sets-legal-parameters-for-complete-takeover-of-historic-palestine/

Berger, P. L., & Neuhaus, R. J. (1996). *To empower people: From state to civil society*. Washington, DC: American Enterprise Institute Press.

Bermant, A. (2018, July 4). Israel's long history of cooperation with ruthless, anti-semitic dictators. *Ha'aretz*. Retrieved from https://www.haaretz.com/israel-news/.premium-not-just-orban-israel-has-long-cooperated-with-anti-semitic-dictators-1.6243037

Bertelsen, J. S. (1997). *Nonstate nations in international politics: Comparative system analysis*. New York, NY: Praeger.

Bhabha, H. K. (1994). Narrating the nation. In J. Hutchinson & A. D. Smith (Eds.), *Nationalism* (pp. 306–312). New York, NY: Oxford University Press.

Bhaba, H. K. (1999). Liberalism's sacred cow. In S. M. Okin (Ed.), *Is multiculturalism bad for women?* (pp. 79–84). Princeton, NJ: Princeton University Press.

Birzeit University Right to Education Campaign. (n.d.). *The electronic Intifada*. Retrieved from http://electronicintifada.net/people/birzeit-university-right-education-campaign

Bishara, A. (2012). *Back stories*. Stanford, CA: Stanford University Press.

Bluestone, B., & Harrison, B. (1984). *The deindustrialization of America: Plant closings, community abandonment and the dismantling of basic industry*. New York, NY: Basic Books.

Blumenthal, M. (2013, August 20). How school privatization hawks teach for America promote Israel. *The electronic Intifada*. Retrieved from http://electronicintifada.net/content/how-school-privatization-hawks-teach-america-promote-israel/12700

Boehm, O. (2018, July 26). Did Israel just stop trying to be a democracy? *New York Times*. Retrieved from https://www.nytimes.com/2018/07/26/opinion/israel-law-jewish-democracy-apartheid-palestinian.html

Boon, K. (2009). The obligations of the new occupier: The contours of Jus Post Bellum. *Loyola L.A. International and Comparative Law Review, 31*, 57–84.

Botstein, L. President of Bard College. (2004, April). [Personal interview].

Boycott from Within. Retrieved from http://www.boycottisrael.info/

Boycott! Supporting the Palestinian BDS call from Within. (n.d.). *Palestinians, Jews, citizens of Israel, join the Palestinian call for a BDS campaign against Israel.* Retrieved from http://boycottisrael.info/node?page=1

Boyko, H. (2010, May 2). Likud MK says wants Jewish state... with the Palestinians. *News that Matters.* Retrieved from http://ivarfjeld.com/2010/05/02/likud-mk-says-wants-jewish-state%E2%80%A6-with-the-palestinians

Braverman, M. (2010). *Fatal embrace: Christians, Jews and the search for peace in the Holy Land.* Austin, TX: Synergy Books.

Breaking the Silence. (2012). *Our harsh logic: Israeli soldiers' testimonies from the occupied territories, 2000–2010.* New York, NY: Holt.

Breaking the Silence. (n.d.). *Homepage.* Retrieved from http://www.breakingthesilence.org.il/

B'Tselem. (2011, January 1). *Administrative detention.* Retrieved from http://www.btselem.org/administrative_detentionB'Tselem

B'Tselem. (2011, January 1). *The separation barrier.* Retrieved from http://www.btselem.org/separation_barrier

B'Tselem. (2013, March 6). *How to build a fence in Hebron.* Retrieved from https://www.youtube.com/watch?v=qC4EEPVRBsE

B'Tselem. (2014). *Checkpoints, physical obstructions, and forbidden roads.* Retrieved from http://www.btselem.org/freedom_of_movement/checkpoints_and_forbidden_roads

B'Tselem. (2014). *Settler violence: Lack of accountability.* Retrieved from http://www.btselem.org/topic/settler_violence

B'Tselem. (2014). *Water crisis.* Retrieved from http://www.btselem.org/water/discrimination_in_water_supply

B'Tsele. (2017, November 11). *East Jerusalem.* Retrieved from https://www.btselem.org/jerusalem

B'Tselem. (2017, November 11). *Water.* Retrieved from https://www.btselem.org/water

B'Tselem. (n.d.). *Homepage.* Retrieved from http://www.btselem.org/

B'Tselem. (n.d.). *Settlements: Background.* Retrieved from http://www.btselem.org/settlements

B'Tselem. (n.d.). *Statistics: Fatalities after operation cast lead.* Retrieved from http://www.btselem.org/statistics/fatalities/after-cast-lead/by-date-of-event

B'Tselem. (n.d.). *Statistics on settlements and settler population.* Retrieved from http://www.btselem.org/settlements/statistics

B'Tselem. (n.d.). *Statistics – Rocket and mortar fire into Israel.* Retrieved from http://www.btselem.org/israeli_civilians/qassam_missiles#data

Buffet, P. (2013, July 26). The charitable-industrial complex. *The New York Times.* Retrieved from http://www.nytimes.com/2013/07/27/opinion/the-charitable-industrial-complex.html?adxnnl=1&adxnnlx=1375102921-qUCOBf5k/L9yNj8QczeHjA

Bullard, R. D. (Ed.). (2005). *The quest for environmental justice: Human rights and the politics of pollution.* New York, NY: Counterpoint.

Burawoy, M. (2005). 2004 Presidential address to the American sociological association: For public sociology. *American Sociological Review, 70,* 4–28.

Burg, A. (2009). *The holocaust is over: We must rise from its ashes.* New York, NY: Palgrave Macmillan.

Burg, A. (2011, April 1). When the walls come tumbling down. *Ha'aretz.* Retrieved from http://www.haaretz.com/weekend/magazine/when-the-walls-come-tumbling-down-1.353501

REFERENCES

Burg, A. (2014, January 24). The future of yesterday. *Ha'aretz*. Retrieved from http://www.haaretz.com/weekend/week-s-end/.premium-1.570166

Burg, A. (2017, September 21). Rosh Hashanah as the battle of Netanyahu vs. Soros. *Ha'aretz*. Retrieved from https://www.haaretz.com/opinion/.premium-rosh-hashanah-as-the-battle-of-netanyahu-vs-soros-1.5452542

Burston, B. (2018, June 26). Zionism's terrorist heritage. *Ha'aretz*. Retrieved from https://www.haaretz.com/opinion/.premium-zionism-s-terrorist-heritage-1.6217633

Bush, G. H. W., & Scrowcroft, B. (1998). *A world transformed*. New York, NY: Knopf.

Butler, J. (2012). *Parting ways: Jewishness and the critique of Zionism*. New York, NY: Columbia University Press.

Butler, J. (2017, April 1). *Address to the Biennial Jewish voice for peace national members meeting*. Retrieved from https://www.facebook.com/JewishVoiceforPeace/videos/vb.186525784991/10156505121949992/?type=2&theater

Buttu, D. (2009, March 19). *What happens after the peace process?* Speech presented in Boston College, Chestnut Hill, MA.

Campbell, R., & Spangler, E. (2000). The curious history of the toxics use reduction planner. In H. Lopata & K. Henson (Eds.), *Unusual occupations: Current research in occupations and professions*. Stamford, CT: JAI Press.

Carsten, J. (Ed.). (2000). *Cultures and relatedness: New approaches to the study of kinship*. Cambridge: Cambridge University Press.

Carter, J. (2006). *Palestine: Peace not apartheid*. New York, NY: Simon and Shuster.

Carter, J. (2006, January). *Palestinian elections: Trip report by former U.S. president Jimmy Carter*. Retrieved from http://www.cartercenter.org/news/documents/doc2287.html

Casbari, C. D. (2014, June 15). So long and thanks for nothing. *Ha'aretz*. Retrieved from http://www.haaretz.com/opinion/.premium-1.598872

Cassidy, J. (2014, April 29). John Kerry and the A-word: Three takeaways. *The New Yorker*. Retrieved from http://www.newyorker.com/online/blogs/johncassidy/2014/04/john-kerry-and-the-a-word-three-takeaways.html?mbid=social_mobile_tweet

Center for Constitutional Rights. (n.d.). *Mamilla cemetery in Jerusalem*. Retrieved from http://ccrjustice.org/Mamilla

Center for Development in Central America. (n.d.). *Appropriate technology*. Retrieved from http://jhc-cdca.org/projects/appropriate-technology/

Central Intelligence Agency. (2014). Middle East: Gaza strip. *The World Factbook*. Retrieved from https://www.cia.gov/library/publications/the-world-factbook/geos/gz.html

Central Intelligence Agency. (2014). Middle East: Israel. *The World Factbook*. Retrieved from https://www.cia.gov/library/publications/the-world-factbook/geos/is.html

Central Intelligence Agency. (2014). Middle East: West Bank. *The World Factbook*. Retrieved from https://www.cia.gov/library/publications/the-world-factbook/geos/we.html

Chacar, H. (2018, August 13). Israeli, Palestinian support for two states hits record low. *+972*. Retrieved from https://972mag.com/israeli-palestinian-support-for-two-states-hits-record-low/137227/

Churchill, W. (1946 March 5). *The sinews of peace* [Speech]. Retrieved from http://history1900s.about.com/od/churchillwinston/a/Iron-Curtain.htm

Cited in Beirut's hidden Jewish Community. (2011, November 15). *Deutsche Welle*. Retrieved from http://www.dw.de/beiruts-hidden-jewish-community/a-6654644

Cloward, R., & Piven, F. F. (1993). *Regulating the poor*. New York, NY: Vintage Books.

CNN Staff. (2012, June 3). Syria-related clashes rage in Lebanon, leaving 13 dead. *CNN*. Retrieved from http://www.cnn.com/2012/06/03/world/meast/lebanon-syria-violence/index.html

Coalition of Women for Peace (Israel). (2018, June). *A lab and a showroom: The Israeli military industries and the oppression of the great march of return in Gaza*. Retrieved from https://mail.google.com/mail/u/0/#inbox/164520af5a81ce09?projector=1&message PartId=0.1

Coates, T. (2015). *Between the world and me*. New York, NY: Spiegel and Grau. Retrieved from https://www.goodreads.com/quotes/8236915-but-race-is-the-child-of-racism-not-the-father

Cohen, D. (2014, March 27). Repression and resistance in Bethlehem's Aida refugee camp. *Mondoweiss*. Retrieved from http://mondoweiss.net/2014/03/repression-resistance-bethlehems.html

Cohen, D. N. (2014, April 6). Who has the right to celebrate Israel? *Ha'aretz*. Retrieved from http://www.haaretz.com/jewish-world/jewish/.premium--who-has-the-right-to-celebrate-israel-1.5244129

Cohen, G. (2014, April 6). Senior IDF commander's jeep vandalized in West Bank settlement. *Ha'aretz*. Retrieved from http://www.haaretz.com/.premium-vandals-slash-jeep-tires-of-idf-commander-1.5244175

Cohen, M. (1994). *Under crescent and cross: The Jews in the middle ages*. Princeton, NJ: Princeton University Press.

Cohen, R. (2014, December 20). What will Israel become? *New York Times*. Retrieved from http://www.nytimes.com/2014/12/21/opinion/sunday/roger-cohen-what-will-israel-become.html?_r=0

Combatants for Peace. (n.d.). *Homepage*. Retrieved from http://cfpeace.org/

Convention on the Prevention and Punishment of the Crime of Genocide. (1948). *Audiovisual library of international law*. Retrieved from http://legal.un.org/avl/ha/cppcg/cppcg.html

Coogan, M. (2014, March 23). Is the U.S. quietly imposing travel sanctions on Israeli officials? *Mondoweiss*. Retrieved from http://mondoweiss.net/2014/03/imposing-sanctions-officials.html

Cook, J. (2017, May 11). *Israel's Jewish nation-state bill 'declaration of war.'* Retrieved from https://www.jonathan-cook.net/2017-05-11/israels-jewish-nation-state-bill-declaration-of-war/

Cook, J. (2017, December 1). In age of forest fires, Israel's law against Palestinian goats proves self-inflicted wound for Zionism. *Mondoweiss*. Retrieved from http://mondoweiss.net/2017/12/israels-palestinian-inflicted/

Cook, J. (2018, March 19). US smoothes Israel's path to annexing the West Bank. *Mondoweiss*. Retrieved from http://mondoweiss.net/2018/03/smooths-israels-annexing/

Dabashi, H. (2006). *Dreams of a nation: On Palestinian cinema*. New York, NY: Verso.

Dattel, L. (2017, August 15). More Israelis left Israel than moved back in six year period. *Ha'aretz*. Retrieved from https://www.haaretz.com/israel-news/.premium-more-israelis-left-israel-than-moved-back-data-reveals-1.5442809

Davis, U. (1977). *Israel: Utopia incorporated: A study of class, state and corporate kin control*. London: Zed Books.

Davis-Bailey, K. (2014, August 19). The Ferguson/Palestine connection. *Ebony*. Retrieved from https://www.ebony.com/news-views/the-fergusonpalestine-connection-403

REFERENCES

Dawkins, R., & Coyne, J. (2005, September 1). One side can be wrong. *The Guardian*. Retrieved from http://www.theguardian.com/science/2005/sep/01/schools.research

Deaths as Israeli Forces Storm Gaza Aid Ships. (2010, May 31). *BBC News*. Retrieved from http://www.bbc.co.uk/news/10195838

Degani, A. (2014, April 29). Guess who else fears that Israel will be labeled an apartheid state? *Mondoweiss*. Retrieved from http://mondoweiss.net/2014/04/israel-become-apartheid.html

Deger, A. (2014, March 21). Israel teens dressed as KKK and in 'Black face' for mock lynching at school Purim party. *Mondoweiss*. Retrieved from http://mondoweiss.net/2014/03/israeli-dressed-lynching.html

De Maio, M. (2011, November 23). Peace is a poisoned word. *Cognitive Liberty*. Retrieved from http://cognitiveliberty.net/2011/peace-is-a-poisoned-word/

Derber, C. (2010). *Greed to green: Solving climate change and remaking the economy*. New York, NY: Paradigm Publishers.

Derfner, L. (2012, November 26). Ehud Barak to step down: On his de-evolution and Israel's. *+972*. Retrieved from http://972mag.com/ehud-baraks-de-evolution-and-israels/60889/

Derfner, L. (2013, August 12). Israel's everyday racism: And how American Jews turn a blind eye to it. *The Jewish Daily Forward*. Retrieved from http://forward.com/articles/182171/israels-everyday-racism-and-how-american-jews-tu/

De Soto, H. (2000). *The mystery of capital: Why capitalism triumphs in the west and fails everywhere else*. New York, NY: Basic Books.

De Tocqueville, A. (2002). *Democracy in America*. Chicago, IL: University of Chicago Press.

Deutsch, K. (1969). *Nationality and its alternatives*. New York, NY: Knopf.

dfedwing. (2009, December 1). *Al-Kurd family home take-over (Sheikh Jarrah)* [Video file]. Retrieved from https://www.youtube.com/watch?feature=endscreen&NR=1&v=wlQf41CJjjc

Dias, E. (2014, September 12). Yale Chaplain explains resignation after Oped about Israel and anti-semitism. *Time*. Retrieved from http://time.com/3340634/yale-chaplain-bruce-shipman-israel-anti-semitism/

Doyle, A. C. (2001). *The sign of the four*. London: Penguin Classics.

Dugard, J. (n.d.). *Apartheid and occupation under international law*. Retrieved from http://www.auphr.org/index.php/news/4227-sp-9067

Ehrenreich, B. (2013, March 15). Is this where the third intifada will start? *The New York Times*. Retrieved from http://www.nytimes.com/2013/03/17/magazine/is-this-where-the-third-intifada-will-start.html?pagewanted=all

Ehrlich, G. (1992, May 6). Not only in Deir Yassin. *Ha'ir*.

Einstein, A. (2004). Speech to the national labor committee for Palestine, New York, 17th April, 1938. In A. Schatz (Ed.), *Prophets outcast: A century of dissident Jewish writing about Zionism and Israel* (pp. 63–64). New York, NY: The Nation Books.

Einstein, A. (n.d.). *Quotes about Zionism: It would be my greatest sadness to see Zionists (Jews) do to Palestinian Arabs much of what Nazis did to Jews*. Retrieved from http://www.goodreads.com/quotes/tag/zionism

Eisenstadt, S. (1992). *The Jewish historical experience in comparative perspective*. New York, NY: State University of New York Press.

Eldar, A. (2010, August 16). Citizens, but not equal. *Ha'aretz*. Retrieved from http://www.haaretz.com/print-edition/opinion/citizens-but-not-equal-1.308265

Ellis, M. H. (2009). *Judaism does not equal Israel: The rebirth of the Jewish prophetic.* Retrieved from http://www.encounterprograms.org/

Entous, A. (2018, July 9). The maps of Israeli settlements that shocked Barack Obama. *The New Yorker.* Retrieved from https://www.newyorker.com/news/news-desk/the-maof-israeli-settlements-that-shocked-barack-obama

Epstein, Y. (2013, June 19). The hidden question. In Gill, N. (Ed.), *The original 'no': Why the Arabs rejected Zionism, and why it matters.* Retrieved from http://www.mepc.org/articles-commentary/commentary/original-no-why-arabs-rejected-zionism-and-why-it-matters

Erikson, K. (2004). *The Wayward Puritans.* Upper Saddle River, NJ: Prentice Hall.

Essed, P. (1991). *Understanding everyday racism: An interdisciplinary theory.* Newbury Park, CA: Sage Publications.

EU Presidency Statement on Palestinian Legislative Council Elections. (2006, January 26). Retrieved from http://www.eu-un.europa.eu/articles/fr/article_5626_fr.htm

Falk, R. (2007, July 7). *Slouching toward a Palestinian Holocaust.* Retrieved from http://www.countercurrents.org/falk070707.htm

Farsakh, L. (2017). The 'right to have rights': Partition and Palestinian self-determination. *Journal of Palestine Studies, 47*(1), 62–63.

Feldman, Y. (2014). *The lab.* Retrieved from http://www.aljazeera.com/programmes/witness/2014/05/lab-20145475423526313.html

Filc, D. (2009). *Circles of exclusion: The politics of health care in Israel.* New York, NY: Cornell University Press.

Files KKKL1-7. Central Zionist archive, Jerusalem, Israel.

Finnegan, W. (2002). Leasing the rain. *Frontline World.* Retrieved from http://www.pbs.org/frontlineworld/stories/bolivia/leasing.html

Fisher, M. (2013, November 20). 9 questions about Iran's nuclear program you were too embarrassed to ask. *The Washington Post.* Retrieved from http://www.washingtonpost.com/blogs/worldviews/wp/2013/11/25/9-questions-about-irans-nuclear-program-you-were-too-embarrassed-to-ask/

Flapan, S. (1979). *Zionism and the Palestinians.* New York, NY: Barnes and Noble.

Foner, E. (2015). *Gateway to freedom: The hidden history of the underground railroad.* New York, NY: W.W. Norton and Co.

Ford, L. (n.d.). *Women at the back of the bus! Separate sex seating on buses for orthodox Jews* [Video file]. Retrieved from https://www.youtube.com/watch?v=DejnrvU4z9w

Foundation for Middle East Peace. (n.d.). *Israeli central bureau of statistics. Statistical abstract of Israel: Comprehensive settlement population, 1972–2010.* Retrieved from http://www.fmep.org/resource/comprehensive-settlement-population-1972-2010

Foxman, A. (2014, May 18). Israel cannot wait any longer to crush price tag attacks. *Ha'aretz.* Retrieved from https://www.haaretz.com/opinion/.premium-crush-price-tag-attacks-1.5248670

Frenkel, S. A. (2009, October 11). Vigilantes patrol for Jewish women dating Arab men. *NPR Morning Edition.* Retrieved from http://www.npr.org/templates/story/story.php?storyId=113724468

Friedberg, R. M. (2001). The impact of mass migration on the Israeli labor market. *The Quarterly Journal of Economics, 166*(4), 1371–1408.

Friedman, T. (1982, September 26). The Beirut massacre: The four days. *The New York Times.* Retrieved from http://www.nytimes.com/1982/09/26/world/the-beirut-massacre-the-four-

days.html?module=Search&mabReward=relbias:w,{%222=%22:=%22RI:17=%22}=&p
agewanted=6

Friedman, T. (2014, February 19). Breakfast before the MOOC. *The New York Times.* Retrieved from http://www.nytimes.com/2014/02/19/opinion/friedman-breakfast-before-the-mooc.html

Friedman, T. (2017, August 2). Climate shifts aren't limited to weather. *New York Times.* Retrieved from https://www.nytimes.com/2017/08/02/opinion/climate-change-technology-globalization-china.html

Galdos, G. (2014, July 31). Gaza war prompts Latin Americans to break ties with Israel. *Channel 4 News.* Retrieved from http://www.channel4.com/news/gaza-strip-latin-america-israel-diplomatic-brazil-argentina

Gareau, B. (2013). *From precaution to profit: Contemporary challenges to environmental protection in the Montreal protocol.* New Haven, CT: Yale University Press.

Garfinkle, A. (1991). On the origin, meaning, use and abuse of a phrase. *Middle Eastern Studies, 27,* 539.

Garroutte, E. (2003). *Real Indians: Identity and survival of Native America.* Berkeley, CA: University of California Press.

Gayle, D. (2013, October 2). Creative Palestinian gardener uses hundreds of spent tear gas canisters as plant pots. *Daily Mail.* Retrieved from http://www.dailymail.co.uk/news/article-2441997/Palestinian-gardener-uses-spent-tear-gas-canisters-PLANT-POTS.html

Gaza Activists Boat Docks. (2009, October 28). *JTA: The global Jewish news source.* Retrieved from http://www.jta.org/2008/10/28/news-opinion/gaza-activist-boat-docks

Gellner, E. (1994). Nationalism and modernisation. In J. Hutchinson & A. D. Smith (Eds.), *Nationalism* (p. 62). New York, NY: Oxford University Press.

Gelvin, J. (2005). *The Israel-Palestine conflict: One hundred years of war.* London: Cambridge University Press.

Gelvin, J. (2007). *The Israeli-Palestine conflict: On hundred years of war.* Cambridge: Cambridge University Press.

Gendzier, I. (2011, November). Why the U.S. recognized Israel. *Israeli Occupation Archive.* Retrieved from http://www.israeli-occupation.org/2011-11-09/irene-gendzier-why-the-us-recognised-israel/

Gendzier, I. (2015). *Dying to forget: Oil, power, Palestine and the origins of United States foreign policy in the Middle East.* New York, NY: Columbia University Press.

Geneva Convention Relative to the Treatment of Prisoners of War. (1949, August 12). *6 U.S.T. 3316, 75 U.N.T.S. 135.* Retrieved from https://www.icrc.org/customary-ihl/eng/docs/v2_rul_rule130

Genovese, E. (1976). *Roll Jordan, roll: The world the slaves made.* New York, NY: Vintage Press.

Gerlitz, R. (2014, March 28). The correlation between Arab economic power and attacks by the Right. *+972.* Retrieved from http://972mag.com/the-correlation-between-arab-economic-power-and-attacks-by-the-right/89045/

Gill, N. (2013, June 19). The original "no": Why the Arabs rejected Zionism, and why it matters. *Middle East Policy Council.* Retrieved from http://www.mepc.org/articles-commentary/commentary/original-no-why-arabs-rejected-zionism-and-why-it-matters

Gisha: Legal Center for Freedom of Movement. (2009, September 21). *Teaching Gaza a lesson.* Retrieved from http://gisha.org/en-blog/2009/09/21/teaching-gaza-a-lesson/

Gisha: Legal Center for Freedom of Movement. (2010, July 7). *Unraveling the closure of Gaza*. Retrieved from http://gisha.org/UserFiles/File/publications/UnravelingTheClosureEng.pdf

Glendon, M. A. (1998). Knowing the universal declaration of human rights. *Notre Dame Law Review, 73*(5), 1153–1176.

Glover, D. (2014, August 18). Stand with Keith Ellison and Barbara Lee to end the blockade of Gaza. *Huffington Post*. Retrieved from http://www.huffingtonpost.com/danny-glover/stand-with-keith-ellison-_b_5689392.html

Gold, S. (2014, August 22). Hamas executes 18 'collaborators' in Gaza. *Ha'aretz*. Retrieved from http://www.haaretz.com/news/middle-east/1.611989

Goldberg, J. J. (2014, July 26). Israel's latest fib: 'Gaza tunnels were surprise.' *The Jewish Daily Forward*. Retrieved from http://blogs.forward.com/jj-goldberg/202855/israels-latest-fib-gaza-tunnels-were-surprise/#.U9PmnChGIrA.facebook#ixzz38bZjJCjm

Golden, D. (2012, November 1). Why the professor went to prison. *Bloomberg Business Week*. Retrieved from http://www.businessweek.com/articles/2012-11-01/why-the-professor-went-to-prison

Goldstone, R. (2009, September). *Human rights in Palestine and other occupied Arab territories* (Report No. GE.09-15866). United Nations.

Goodkind, N. (2018, June 28). Alexandria Ocasio-Cortez is democrats' new rising star. Will the DSA's support for an Israel Boycott slow her down? *Newsweek*. Retrieved from http://www.newsweek.com/alexandria-ocasio-cortez-israel-palestine-bds-socialists-999888

Goodreads Website. Retrieved from https://www.goodreads.com/work/quotes/12689683-common-prayer-a-liturgy-for-ordinary-radicals

Gordon, N. (2018, January 4). The new anti-semitism. *London Review of Books, 40*(1), 18ff. Retrieved from https://www.lrb.co.uk/v40/n01/neve-gordon/the-new-anti-semitism

Gored, A. A. (Ed.). (1982). *Dissenter from Zion: From the writing of Judah L. Magnes*. Cambridge, MA: Harvard University Press.

Gorenberg, G. (2006). *The accidental empire, Israel and the birth of the settlements, 1967–1977*. New York, NY: Henry Holt.

Gouldner, A. (1970). *The coming crisis of western sociology*. New York, NY: Basic Books.

Greenberg, J. (1997, September 1). The babies from Yemen: An enduring mystery. *New York Times*. Retrieved from https://www.nytimes.com/1997/09/02/world/the-babies-from-yemen-an-enduring-mystery.html

Greenfield, P. A. (2014, September 26). An Israel equal for all, Jewish or not. *Washington Post*. Retrieved from http://www.washingtonpost.com/opinions/an-israel-equal-for-all-jewish-or-not/2014/09/26/83151758-3a05-11e4-9c9f-ebb47272e40e_story.html

Greenstein, T. (2017, September 8). Lessons from Finkelstein: A response to Seth Anderson. *Mondoweiss*. Retrieved from https://mondoweiss.net/2017/09/finkelstein-response-anderson/

Gurvitz, Y. (2014, May 11). It's the little things about occupation. *+972*. Retrieved from http://972mag.com/its-the-little-things-about-occupation/90744/

Haag, M. (2018, May 14). Pastor who said Jews are going to hell led prayer at Jerusalem embassy opening. *New York Times*. Retrieved from https://www.nytimes.com/2018/05/14/world/middleeast/robert-jeffress-embassy-jerusalem-us.html

Ha'am, A. (2004). Excerpt from 'truth from Eretz Israel.' In A. Schatz (Ed.), *Prophets outcast: A century of dissident Jewish writing about Zionism and Israel*. New York, NY: The Nation Books.

REFERENCES

Ha'aretz. (2003, September 25). Taxes/decades of tax breaks for the settler population. *Ha'aretz*. Retrieved from http://www.haaretz.com/print-edition/business/taxes-decades-of-tax-breaks-for-the-settler-population-1.101212

Ha'aretz. (2010, March 17). U.S. general: Israel-Palestinian conflict foments anti-U.S. sentiment. *Ha'aretz*. Retrieved from http://www.haaretz.com/news/u-s-general-israel-palestinian-conflict-foments-anti-u-s-sentiment-1.264910

Ha'aretz. (2012, January 13). Supreme court thrusts Israel down the slope of apartheid. *Ha'aretz*. Retrieved from http://www.haaretz.com/print-edition/opinion/supreme-court-thrusts-israel-down-the-slope-of-apartheid-1.407056

Ha'aretz. (2014, April 30). "Price tag" attacks spread into Israel, go unpunished. *Ha'aretz*. Retrieved from http://www.haaretz.com/news/diplomacy-defense/1.588285

Ha'aretz. (2017, May 1). This is how Israel inflates its Jewish majority. *Ha'aretz*. Retrieved from https://www.haaretz.com/opinion/editorial/this-is-how-israel-inflates-its-jewish-majority-1.5466549

Hajjar, L. (2005). *Courting conflict: The Israeli military court system in the West Bank and Gaza*. Berkeley, CA: University of California Press.

Halbfinger, D., & Nazzal, R. (2018, June 24). As Israel pushes to build, Bedouin homes and schools face demolition. *New York Times*. Retrieved from https://www.nytimes.com/2018/06/24/world/middleeast/israel-bedouins-demolition.html

Halbfinger, D., & Kershner, I. (2018, July 19). Israeli law declares the country the nation-state of the Jewish people. *New York Times*. Retrieved from https://www.nytimes.com/2018/07/19/world/middleeast/israel-law-jews-arabic.html

Hallowell, A. I. (1964). *Culture and experience*. New York, NY: Shocken Books.

Halper, J. (2010). *The global pacification industry: An Interview*. Retrieved from https://www.youtube.com/watch?v=SVa0QbH8YcA

Halper, J. (2010, February 26). The second battle of Gaza: Israel's undermining of international law. *The Monthly Review*. Retrieved from http://mrzine.monthlyreview.org/2010/halper260210.html

Halper, J. (2014, August 18). Globalizing Gaza. *Counterpunch*. Retrieved from http://www.counterpunch.org/2014/08/18/globalizing-gaza/print

Halper, J. (2015). *War against the people*. London: Pluto Press.

Halper, J. (2018, May 3). The one democratic state campaign' program for a multicultural democratic state in Palestine/Israel. *Mondoweiss*. Retrieved from http://mondoweiss.net/2018/05/democratic-multicultural-palestine/?utm_source=Mondoweiss+List&utm_campaign=f67fddf1a9-RSS_EMAIL_CAMPAIGN&utm_medium=email&utm_term=0_b86bace129-f67fddf1a9-332399817&mc_cid=f67fddf1a9&mc_eid=d3e0ecd0a6

Hamad, S. (2010). *Born Palestinian, born Black*. Brooklyn, NY: Upset Press.

Hamas Charter. (1988). Retrieved from http://www.hamascharter.com/

Hammami, R. (1995). NGOs: The professionalization of politics. *Race and Class, 37*, 51–63.

Hammond, D., & Jablow, A. (1992). *The Africa that never was*. New York, NY: Waveland Press. Also published as Dorothy Hammond and Alta Jablow. (2012). *The myth of Africa*. New York, NY: Library of the Social Sciences.

Hanafi, S. (2009). Spacio-cide: Colonial politics, invisibility and rezoning in Palestinian territory. *Contemporary Arab Affairs, 2*(1), 106–121.

Haokets. (2013, July 12). The Yemeni Baby affair: What if this was your child? *+972*. Retrieved from https://972mag.com/the-yemenite-baby-affair-what-if-this-was-your-child/75672/

Harel, A. (2006, January 2). Palestinian truce main cause for reduced terror. *Ha'aretz*. Retrieved from http://www.haaretz.com/print-edition/news/shin-bet-palestinian-truce-main-cause-for-reduced-terror-1.61607

Harel, A. (2014, August 29). The summer Israel's security bubble wrap burst. *Ha'aretz*. Retrieved from http://www.haaretz.com/news/diplomacy-defense/1.613053/

Harel, A. (2018, March 6). Israel finds new regional allies: Greece and the Sunni states. *Ha'aretz*. Retrieved from https://www.haaretz.com/israel-news/israeli-finds-new-regional-allies-greece-and-the-sunni-states-1.5866886

Harel, A. (2018, March 7). Mahmoud Abbas' health deteriorates and Israel prepares for a bloody succession fight. *Ha'aretz*. Retrieved from https://www.haaretz.com/israel-news/.premium-health-of-palestinian-leader-mahmoud-abbas-82-deteriorates-in-recent-1.5883942

Harris, G. (2014, March 28). Borrowed time on disappearing land. *The New York Times*. Retrieved from http://www.nytimes.com/2014/03/29/world/asia/facing-rising-seas-bangladesh-confronts-the-consequences-of-climate-change.html?_r=0

Hartman, B. (2011, July 30). Larger housing protests set to take place in 10 cities. *Jerusalem Post*. Retrieved from http://www.jpost.com/National-News/Larger-housing-protests-set-to-take-place-in-10-cities

Hartman, B. (2014, August 28). 50 days of Israel's Gaza operation protective edge—by the numbers. *Jerusalem Post*. Retrieved from http://www.jpost.com/Operation-Protective-Edge/50-days-of-Israels-Gaza-operation-Protective-Edge-by-the-numbers-372574

Harvard Kennedy School. (2012). *Israel/Palestine and the one state solution* [Conference]. Retrieved from http://www.onestateconference.com/

Harvey, D. (2007). *A brief history of neoliberalism*. New York, NY: Oxford University Press.

Hass, A. (2013, December 26). Israel: Palestinian farmers to blame for settler attacks on their Land. *Ha'aretz*. Retrieved from https://www.haaretz.com/.premium-price-tag-victims-to-blame-israel-says-1.5304165

Hass, A. (2014, May 29). A lawyer for every labor. *Ha'aretz*. Retrieved from http://www.haaretz.com/news/features/.premium-1.596134

Hass, A. (2014, October 12). A nightmare question highlights the importance of oral history. *Ha'aretz*. Retrieved from http://www.haaretz.com/news/national/.premium-1.620414

Hassan, Z. (2018, June 17). Palestine sets precedent with legal complaint. *Al Shabaka Policy Analysis*. Retrieved from https://al-shabaka.org/memos/palestine-sets-precedent-with-legal-complaint/

Hasson, N. (2017, June 3). How a small group of Israelis made the western wall Jewish again. *Ha'aretz*. Retrieved from https://www.haaretz.com/israel-news/.premium.MAGAZINE-how-israel-quietly-demolished-the-western-walls-muslim-neighborhood-1.5478700

Hatuqa, D. (2014, September 21). Israel in grave breach over Informants. *Al Jazeera*. Retrieved from http://www.aljazeera.com/news/middleeast/2014/09/spying-palestinians-war-crime-20149215553352273.html

Heller, A. (2013, August 17). Israeli Defy stereotypes Amid peace talks. *Associated Press*. Retrieved from http://aronheller.com/articles/israeli-settlements-peace-talks/

Herman-Peled, H., & Peled, Y. (2011). Post-post-Zionism: Confronting the death of the two-state solution. *New Left Review, 67*, 97–118.

Heruti-Sover, T. (2014, September 9). Report: Settlements receive disproportionate state funding. *Ha'aretz*. Retrieved from http://www.haaretz.com/business/.premium-1.614765

Herzel, T. (1896). *The Jewish state*. Retrieved from https://www.jewishvirtuallibrary.org/jsource/Zionism/herzl2.html

Herzel, T. (n.d.). *Old new land (Altneuland)*. New York, NY: Create Space Independent Publishing Platform.

Herzel, T. (n.d.). *Zionism quotes: Zionism demands a publicly recognized and legally secured homeland in Palestine for the Jewish people*. Retrieved from http://www.brainyquote.com/quotes/keywords/zionism.html#MtRltxmvCjtPP6vR.99

Heschel, A. J. Retrieved from https://ubcgcu.org/2014/04/06/the-wisdom-of-abraham-heschel/

Higgins, A. (2009, January 24). How Israel helped spawn Hamas. *Wall Street Journal*. Retrieved from https://www.wsj.com/articles/SB123275572295011847.html

Hirschman, A. (1970). *Exit, voice, and loyalty*. Cambridge, MA: Harvard University Press.

Hitchens, C. (2011). *Hitch-22: A memoir*. London: Twelve.

Hobsbawm, E. (1994). The nation as invented tradition. In J. Hutchinson & A. D. Smith (Eds.), *Nationalism* (pp. 76–82). New York, NY: Oxford University Press.

Hoffman, A. (2007). *Incantation*. New York, NY: Little Brown and Company.

hooks, b. (1994). *Teaching to transgress*. New York, NY: Routledge.

Horovitz, D. (2014, July 13). Netanyahu finally speaks his mind. *The Times of Israel*. Retrieved from http://www.timesofisrael.com/netanyahu-finally-speaks-his-mind/

Horowitz, A., Ratner, L., & Weiss, P. (2011). *The Goldstone report: The legacy of the landmark investigation of the Gaza conflict*. New York, NY: Nation Books.

Hovel, R. (2013, October 3). Supreme court rejects citizens' request to change nationality from 'Jewish' to 'Israeli.' *Ha'aretz*. Retrieved from http://www.haaretz.com/news/national/.premium-1.550241

Hroub, K. (2017). A newer Hamas? The revised charter. *Journal of Palestine Studies, 46*(4), 100–111.

Huber, P. (1990, July 9). The lawyers versus the homeless. *Forbes*, p. 92. Retrieved from http://overlawyered.com/articles/huber/clozaril.html

Humanists of Utah. (2002). *Why can't I own a Canadian?* Retrieved from http://www.humanistsofutah.org/2002/WhyCantIOwnACanadian_10-02.html

Human Rights Watch. (2010). *Israel/West Bank: Separate and unequal*. Retrieved from http://www.hrw.org/news/2010/12/18/israelwest-bank-separate-and-unequal

Huneidi, S. (2001). CO 733/18, Churchill to Samuel, telegram, private and personal, 25 February 1922. In S. Huneidi (Ed.), *A broken trust: Herbert Samuel, Zionism and the Palestinians* (p. 57). I.B. Tauris & Co Ltd.

Hunter, F. R. (1993). *The Palestinian uprising: A war by other means*. Berkeley, CA: University of California Press.

Huntington, S. (2011). *The clash of civilizations and the remaking of world order*. New York, NY: Simon and Shuster.

Hyde, W. (2006). The tortuous route of Black American history. In J. T. Campbell (Ed.), *Middle passage: African American journeys to Africa, 1787–2005*. New York, NY: Penguin Press.

Ibish, H. (2012, August 28). Bulldozing the special relationship. *Foreign Policy*. Retrieved from http://www.foreignpolicy.com/articles/2012/08/28/bulldozing_the_special_relationship

Ighbaria, M. (2018, June 8). I am a Palestinian woman in Israel: You don't get to define my labels. *Ha'aretz*. Retrieved from https://www.haaretz.com/opinion/i-am-a-palestinian-woman-in-israel-you-don-t-get-to-define-my-labels-1.6246707

Ignatieff, M. (1999). The stories we tell: Television and humanitarian aid. *The Social Contract,* *10*(1), 1–8.

Illouz, E. (2004). From the Lisbon disaster to Oprah Winfrey: Suffering as identity in the era of globalization. In U. Beck, N. Sznaider, & R. Winters (Eds.), *Global America? The cultural consequences of globalization.* Liverpool: Liverpool University Press.

Illuz, E. (2014, February 7). 47 years a slave: A new perspective on the occupation. *Ha'aretz.* Retrieved from http://www.haaretz.com/news/features/.premium-1.572880

Institute for Middle East Understanding. (2014). *50 days of death and destruction: Israel's "operation protective edge."* Retrieved from http://imeu.org/article/50-days-of-death-destruction-israels-operation-protective-edge

Institute for Sustainable Communities. (n.d.). *Homepage.* Retrieved from http://www.iscvt.org/

Israeli Central Bureau of Statistics. *Statistical abstract of Israel: Comprehensive settlement population, 1972–2010, quoted by the foundation for Middle East peace.* Retrieved from https://fmep.org/resource/comprehensive-settlement-population-1972-2010

Israeli Committee against House Demolitions. (n.d.). *Homepage.* Retrieved from http://icahd.org/

Israel Diplomatic Network. (2013, February 1). *Zagreb: Population of Israel on the eve of 2013: 8 million.* Retrieved from http://embassies.gov.il/zagreb/Pages/Population-of-Israel-on-the-eve-of-2013---8-Million.aspx

Israeli Knesset. (2011, July 12). *Law for the prevention of damage to State of Israel through boycott.* Retrieved from http://www.justice.gov.il/NR/rdonlyres/2210C972-7884-481B-805F-E486F5FBC1E9/29067/2304.pdf

Israeli Ministry of Foreign Affairs. (2000, August 22). The fruits of peace. Retrieved from http://www.mfa.gov.il/mfa/foreignpolicy/peace/guide/pages/the%20fruits%20of%20 peace.aspx

Israeli Ministry of Foreign Affairs (2001). PM Sharon Address the Knesset's Special Solidarity Session, 16, September 2001. Retrieved from http://mfa.gov.il/MFA/PressRoom/2001/ Pages/PM%20Sharon%20Addresses%20the%20Knesset-s%20Special%20Solidari.aspx

Israel/Palestine: Mapping Models of Statehood and Paths of Peace Conference. (2009, June). York University, Toronto, Ontario. Retrieved from http://www.yorku.ca/ipconf/ speakers.html

Israel Pocket Library. (1973). *Zionism.* Jerusalem: Keter Books.

Israel Publishes Tender for 283 Settlement Homes. (2014, September 5). *The times of Israel.* Retrieved from http://www.timesofisrael.com/israel-publishes-tender-for-283-settlement-homes/

Israeli Youth. (2014, March 10). *We refuse to serve in the occupation army.* Retrieved from https://www.commondreams.org/news/2014/03/10/israeli-youth-we-refuse-to-serve-occupation-army

Jad, I. (2004). *The NGO-isation of Arab women's movements.* Retrieved from http://www.ism.italia.org/wp-content/upoads/the-NGO-isation-of-Arab-women-s-movements-by-islah-jad-2004.pdf

Jad, I. (2009). *The demobilization of women's movements: The case of Palestine.* Retrieved from https://www.awid.org/sites/default/files/atoms/files/changing-their-world-demobilization-of-womens-movements-palestine.pdf

James, M. (2014, April 20). Female in Gaza. *The New York Times.* Retrieved from http://www.nytimes.com/2014/04/20/opinion/sunday/female-in-gaza.html?_r=0

Jenkins, D. (1975). *Black Zion: The return of Afro-Americans and West Indians to Africa*. London: Wildwood House.

Jewish Agency of Israel. (n.d.). *Live from Ukraine: In fast-paced operation, Jewish agency rescues group of immigrants from Donetsk*. Retrieved from http://www.jewishagency.org/blog/1/article/

Jewish Agency of Israel. (n.d.). *Project TEN: Global Tikkun Olam*. Retrieved from http://www.jewishagency.org/jewish-social-action/program/215

Jewish National Fund. (n.d.). *Homepage*. Retrieved from http://www.jnf.org/

Jewish National Fund. (n.d.). *Our history*. Retrieved from http://www.jnf.org/menu-3/ourhistory/

Jewish National Fund. (n.d.). Retrieved from http://www.jspace.com/org/jewish-national-fund-jnf/258

Jewish Settlers Receive Hundreds of Thousands in Compensation for Leaving Gaza While Palestinians Working for Them Get Nothing. (2005, August 16). *Democracy Now!* Retrieved from http://www.democracynow.org/2005/8/16/jewish_settlers_receive_hundreds_of_thousands

Jewish Telegraph Agency. (2014, May 28). ADL joins Native American groups calling for Redskins name change. *Ha'aretz*. Retrieved from http://www.haaretz.com/jewish-world/jewish-world-news/1.595800

Jewish Virtual Library. (n.d.). *Israel society & culture: Jewish Agency for Israel (JAFI)*. Retrieved from http://www.jewishvirtuallibrary.org/jsource/Orgs/jafi.html

Jewish Virtual Library. (n.d.). *Jewish population of the world*. Retrieved from http://www.jewishvirtuallibrary.org/jsource/Judaism/jewpop.html

Jewish Virtual Library. (n.d.). *Zionist congress*. Retrieved from https://www.jewishvirtuallibrary.org/jsource/Zionism/First_Cong_&_Basel_Program.html

Jewish Voice For Peace. (n.d.). *Deadly exchange: Ending US-Israel police partnerships, reclaiming safety, campaign within its BDS efforts*. Retrieved from http://www.deadlyexchange.org

Jhally, S. (Director). (2006). *Reel bad Arabs* [Motion picture]. Northampton, MA: Media Education Foundation.

Jhally, S., & Ratzkoff, B. (Directors). (2003). *Peace, propaganda and the promised land* [Motion picture]. Northampton, MA: Media Education Foundation.

John Snow Institute. (n.d.). *Homepage*. Retrieved from http://www.jsi.com/JSIInternet/

Johnson, S. M., & Campbell, R. R. (1981). *Black migration in America: A social demographic history*. Durham, NC: Duke University Press.

Jones, D., & Whitmarsh, I. (Eds.). (2010). *What's the use of race? Modern governance and the biology of difference*. Cambridge, MA: MIT Press.

Jordan, J. (1989). *Moving towards home*. London: Virago.

Judis, J. (2014). *Genesis: Truman, American Jews, and the origins of the Arab/Israeli conflict*. New York, NY: Farrar, Strauss and Giroux.

Judt, T. (2003, October 23). Israel: The alternative. *New York Review of Books*. Retrieved from http://www.nybooks.com/articles/archives/2003/oct/23/israel-the-alternative/

Kampfner, J. (2002, November 18). NS interview: Jack Straw. *The New Statesman*. Retrieved from http://www.newstatesman.com/node/156641

Kanaaneh, R. A. (2009). *Surrounded: Palestinian soldiers in the Israeli military*. Stanford, CA: Stanford University Press.

Kane, A. (2010, November 4). The real Yitzhak Rabin. *Mondoweiss*. Retrieved from http://mondoweiss.net/2010/11/the-real-yitzhak-rabin.html

Kane, A. (2014, March 21). The battle over Palestine is raging: And Israel is losing: An interview with Ali Abunimah. *Mondoweiss*. Retrieved from http://mondoweiss. net/2014/03/palestine-raging-abunimah.html

Kankleh, K. (2012). *Globalized Palestine: A national sell-out of a homeland*. Trenton, NJ: The Red Sea Press.

Karon, T. (2006, May 19). How Jewish is Israel? *Ha'aretz*. Retrieved from http://www.haaretz.com/print-edition/opinion/how-jewish-is-israel-1.188095

Kasrils, R. (2009, March 17). Who said nearly 50 years ago that Israel was an apartheid state? *Media Monitors: Commentary*. Retrieved from http://links.org.au/node/960

Kate. (2014, April 23). Israeli settlers release wild boars on Palestinian farmland to destroy crops. *Mondoweiss*. Retrieved from http://mondoweiss.net/2014/04/israeli-settlers-palestinian.html

Kate. (2014, April 30). Israel approved almost 14,000 new settler homes and demolished over 5,000 Palestinian structures during 9 months of peace talks. *Mondoweiss*. Retrieved from http://mondoweiss.net/2014/04/demolished-palestinian-structures.html

Katz, Y. (2012, March 10). Easy to start, hard to end. *The Jerusalem Post*. Retrieved from http://www.jpost.com/Defense/Analysis-Easy-to-start-hard-to-end

Kaufman, A. (2011, December 25). WATCH: Ultra-Orthodox spit on "immodest" 8-year-old girl in Beit Shemesh. *+972 Magazine*. Retrieved from http://972mag.com/watch-ultra-orthodox-spit-on-immodest-8-year-old-girl-in-bet-shemesh/31268/

Kaufman, A. (2014, August 25). Israelis on Facebook wish death for Holocaust survivors against protective edge. *+972 Magazine*. Retrieved from http://972mag.com/nstt_feeditem/israelis-on-facebook-wish-death-for-holocaust-survivors-against-protective-edge/

Kearney, M. (2014, August 20). What would happen if Palestine joined the international criminal court? *The Electronic Intifada*. Retrieved from http://electronicintifada.net/content/what-would-happen-if-palestine-joined-international-criminal-court/13783

Keller, A. (2014, February 14). *From Canaan to Spain* [Blog post]. Retrieved from http://adam-keller2.blogspot.co./2014/02/from-canaan-to-spain.html

Kelman, N. (2012, April 24). The necessity of hope. *The Jerusalem Post*. Retrieved from http://www.jpost.com/Features/In-Thespotlight/The-necessity-of-hope

Keret, E. (2014, July 25). Israel's other war. *The New Yorker*. Retrieved from http://www.newyorker.com/books/page-turner/israels-other-war?src=mp

Kershnar, S., Levy, M., Benjamin, J., Scandrett, E., Deutsch, J., Schwartzman, D., & Kovel, J. (2011). Greenwashing apartheid: The Jewish national fund's environmental cover-up. In *JNF: Colonizing Palestine since 1901, JNF eBook* (Vol. 4). Retrieved from http://stopthejnf.org/documents/JNFeBookVol4.pdf

Kershner, I. (2008, December 16). UN human rights investigator expelled by Israel. *The New York Times*. Retrieved from http://www.nytimes.com/2008/12/16/world/middleeast/16mideast.html?_r=0

Kershner, I. (2014, August 31). Israel claims nearly 1,000 acres of West Bank land near Bethlehem. *The New York Times*. Retrieved from http://www.nytimes.com/2014/09/01/world/middleeast/israel-claims-nearly-1000-acres-of-west-bank-land-near-bethlehem.html?_r=0

Khalidi, R. (1997). *Palestinian identity: The Construction of modern national consciousness*. New York, NY: Columbia University Press.

Khalidi, R. (2006). *The iron cage: The story of the Palestinian struggle for statehood*. Boston, MA: Beacon Press.

Khalidi, R. (2013). *Brokers of deceit: How the U.S. has undermined peace in the Middle East*. Boston, MA: Beacon Press.

REFERENCES

Khalidi, R. (2017). The hundred years' war on Palestine. *Journal of Palestine Studies, 47*(1), 6–17.

Khalidi, W. (Ed.). (1992). *All that remains: The Palestinian villages occupied and depopulated by Israeli in 1948*. Washington, DC: Institute for Palestine Studies.

Kharmi, G. (2007). *Married to another man: Israel's dilemma in Palestine*. London: Pluto Press.

Khoury, J. (2017, August 25). Israel revokes citizen of hundreds of Negev Bedouin, leaving them stateless. *Ha'aretz*. Retrieved from https://www.haaretz.com/israel-news/.premium-israel-revokes-citizenship-of-hundreds-of-bedouin-1.5445620

Kimmerling, B. (2006). *Politicide: The real legacy of Ariel Sharon*. London: Verso Press.

Kimmerling, B., & Migdal, J. S. (2003). The Revolt of 1834 and the making of modern Palestine. In *The Palestinian people*. Cambridge, MA: Harvard University Press.

King, M. L. Jr. (1963). *I have a dream* [Speech]. Retrieved from http://www.americanrhetoric.com/speeches/mlkihaveadream.htm

Klein, N. (2007). *The shock doctrine*. New York, NY: Henry Holt and Company.

Klein, N. (2007, June 15). Gaza: Not just a prison, a laboratory. *Common Dreams*. Retrieved from http://www.commondreams.org/archive/2007/06/15/gaza-not-just-prison-laboratory

Klingbail, S., & Shiloh, S. (2012, December 5). Bye, the beloved country: Why almost 40 percent of Israelis are thinking of emigrating. *Ha'aretz*. Retrieved from http://www.haaretz.com/news/features/bye-the-beloved-country-why-almost-40-percent-of-israelis-are-thinking-of-emigrating.premium-1.484945

Klingman, J. (2014, April 11). Blackonomics: Black capitalism – Fulfillment or failure? *Black Press USA*. Retrieved from http://www.blackpresusa.com/blackonomics-black-capitalism-fulfillment-or-failure

Koelbl, S. (2011, March 28). It will not stop: Syrian uprising continues despite crackdown. *Spiegel Online*. Retrieved from http://www.spiegel.de/international/world/it-will-not-stop-syrian-uprising-continues-despite-crackdown-a-753517.html

Kramer, M. (2010, February). Superfluous young men. *Sandbox*. Retrieved from http://www.martinkramer.org/sandbox/2010/02/superfluous-young-men/

Kramer, S. (Director). (1967). *Guess who's coming to dinner* [Motion picture].

Kra-Oz, T. (2013, February 9). A.B. Yehoshua calls American Jews Partial Jews. *Tablet: A New Read on Jewish Life*. Retrieved from http://www.tabletmag.com/scroll/124689/a-b-yehoshua-calls-american-jews-partial-jews

Kreisky Forum. (n.d.). *Alternatives to partition: Principles of Jewish Israeli-Palestinian partnerships*. Retrieved from http://www.kreisky-forum.org/non-public-1.html

Kubovich, Y. (2018, March 21). Who's hiding Israeli airforce participation in major exercise with UAE and US? *Ha'aretz*. Retrieved from https://www.haaretz.com/israel-news/who-s-hiding-iaf-participation-in-major-exercise-with-uae-1.5919421

Kucinich, D. (2009, January 6). Israel may be in violation of arms export control act. *The World Post*. Retrieved from http://www.huffingtonpost.com/rep-dennis-kucinich/israel-may-be-in-violatio_b_155709.html

Kuhn, T. (1996). *The structure of scientific revolutions* (3rd ed.). Chicago, IL: The University of Chicago Press.

Kuntsman, A., & Stein, R. (2015). *Digital militarism: Israel's occupation in the social media age*. Stanford, CA: Stanford University Press.

Kushner, T., & Solomon, A. (Eds.). (2003). *Wrestling with Zion: Progressive Jewish-American responses to the Israeli-Palestinian conflict*. New York, NY: Grove Press.

Kuwaiti Stateless Protest for Third Day. (2011, February 20). *Middle East online.* Retrieved from http://www.middle-east-online.com/english/?id=44476

Kweli, T. (n.d.). *Around my way* [Audio file]. Retrieved from http://rapgenius.com/Talib-kweli-around-my-way-lyrics

Kysia, A. (2014, April 7). A people's history of Muslims in the United States. *Zinn Educational Project.* Retrieved from http://www.juancole.com/2014/04/peoples-history-muslims.html?

Lach, E. (2014, January 2). Pamela Geller's anti-Muslim ad hits snag in Boston. *Talking Points Memo.* Retrieved from http://talkingpointsmemo.com/muckraker/geller-ad-boston

Lajee Center. (n.d.). *Homepage.* Retrieved from http://www.lajee.org/

Landsmann, C. (2018, August 18). How Israeli right-wing thinkers envision the annexation of the West Bank. *Ha'aretz.* Retrieved from https://www.haaretz.com/israel-news/.premium.magazine-how-israeli-right-wing-thinkers-envision-the-west-bank-s-annexation-1.6387108

Langstraat, J. (2006). *New Boston marriages: News representations, respectability and the politics of same sex marriages* (doctoral dissertation). Boston College, Chestnut Hill, MA.

Laqueur, W. (1972). *The history of Zionism.* London: Wiedenfeld and Nicholson.

Larcom, B. (2004, October). *"Nueva Vida" means new life!* Retrieved from https://www.globaljusticecenter.org/papers/%E2%80%9Cnueva-vida%E2%80%9D-mens-new-life

Larger Housing Protests Set to Take Place in 10 Cities. (2011, July 30). *Jerusalem post.* Retrieved from http://www.jpost.com/National-News/Larger-housing-protests-set-to-take-place-in-10-cities

Laron, G. (2017, June 6). Was Israel under existential threat in June 1967? *Counterpunch.* Retrieved from https://www.counterpunch.org/2017/06/06/was-israel-under-existential-threat-in-june-1967/

Lawrence of Cyberia. (2010, March 19). *Tell me again: Who made the desert bloom?* [Blog post]. Retrieved from http://lawrenceofcyberia.blogs.com/news/2010/03/palestinians-made-the-desert-bloom.html

Lazare, S. (2014, March 10). Israeli youth: 'We refuse to serve in the occupation army.' *Common Dreams.* Retrieved from http://www.commondreams.org/headline/2014/03/10-5

League of Arab States. (1967). *Khartoum resolution.* Retrieved from http://www.thejewishvirtuallibrary.org/the-khartoum-resolutions

Lehn, W., & Davis, U. (1988). *The Jewish national fund.* London: Kegan Paul International.

Lendman, S. (2009, February 27). 'Worse than apartheid': The movement to boycott Israel. *Pulse.* Retrieved from http://pulsemedia.org/2009/02/27/worse-than-apartheid-the-movement-to-boycott-israel/

Lerner, D., & Whitehouse, E. (2018, May 10). Not Muslim, not Jewish: Ancient community in the West Bank feels increasingly Israeli. *Ha'aretz.* Retrieved from https://www.haaretz.com/israel-news/.premium.magazine-for-ancient-samaritan-community-a-new-test-of-loyalty-1.6075509

Leunig, M. (2012, December 11). Just a cartoonist with a moral duty to speak. *The Sunday Morning Herald.* Retrieved from https://blackwar.org/art/

Leupp, G. (2014, November 26). A brief history of Jerusalem: Eternal, undivided Jewish capital? *Counterpunch.* Retrieved from http://www.counterpunch.org/2014/11/26/a-brief-history-of-jerusalem/

Levi, E. (2018, August 10). What Israel can learn from Morocco's multiculturalism. *+972.* Retrieved from https://972mag.com/what-israel-can-learn-from-moroccos-multiculturalism/137171/

Levin, A. (2002). The hidden history of Zionism. *International Socialist Review*, p. 24. Retrieved from http://www.isreview.org/issues/24/hidden_history.shtml

Levine, G. (2014, October 14). 40,000 unprocessed voter registrations go to court. *Al Jazeerz America*. Retrieved from http://america.aljazeera.com/blogs/scrutiner/2014/10/14/georgia-voter-registrationsgotocourt.html

Levy, G. (2010, July 15). Tricky Bibi. *Ha'aretz*. Retrieved from http://www.haaretz.com/print-edition/opinion/tricky-bibi-1.302053

Levy, G. (2012, February 19). Enemies, a hate story. *Ha'aretz*. Retrieved from http://www.haaretz.com/print-edition/opinion/enemies-a-hate-story-1.413424

Levy, G. (2014, March 16). Israel's nation-state talk means the return of the yellow star. *Ha'aretz*. Retrieved from http://www.haaretz.com/opinion/.premium-1.580021

Levy, G. (2014, April 10). Helpless Israelis on a West Bank road. *Ha'aretz*. Retrieved from http://www.haaretz.com/opinion/.premium-1.584868

Levy, G. (2014, May 7). Parental love, Israeli style. *Ha'aretz*. Retrieved from http://www.haaretz.com/opinion/.premium-1.589407

Levy, G. (2014, August 14). Gevalt, anti-semitism! *Ha'aretz*. Retrieved from http://www.haaretz.com/opinion/.premium-1.610481

Levy, G. (2018, July 8). One state, one vote. *Ha'aretz*. Retrieved from https://www.haaretz.com/opinion/.premium-one-state-one-vote-1.6246981

Levy, G., & Levac, A. (2014, March 30). The most surreal place in the occupied territories. *Ha'aretz*. Retrieved from http://www.haaretz.com/weekend/twilight-zone/.premium-1.582447

Lior, I. (2013, August 28). Israel readies for mass deportation of African migrants. *Ha'aretz*. Retrieved from http://www.haaretz.com/news/national/.premium-1.544032

Lis, J. (2014, February 25). Knesset passes bill distinguishng between Muslim and Christian Arabs. *Ha'aretz*. Retrieved from http://www.haaretz.com/news/national/.premium-1.576247

Lis, J. (2014, May 11). Israeli ministers approve bill aimed at blocking prisoner swaps. *Ha'aretz*. Retrieved from http://www.haaretz.com/news/diplomacy-defense/.premium-1.589987

Lis, J. (2014, May 11). Ministers debating bill to oblige Israeli firms to do business with settlements. *Ha'aretz*. Retrieved from http://www.haaretz.com/news/national/1.589985

Lis, J. (2018, June 4). Knesset council bans bill to define Israel as a state for all its citizens. *Ha'aretz*. Retrieved from https://www.haaretz.com/israel-news/.premium-knesset-council-bans-bill-to-define-israel-as-state-for-all-citizens-1.6145333

Liska, A. (1974). The attitude-behavior consistency controversy. *American Sociological Review, 39*, 261–272.

Lorber, B. (2018, June 15). Israel's environmental colonialism and eco-apartheid. *The Bullet*. Retrieved from https://socialistproject.ca/2018/06/israels-environmental-colonialism-and-ecoapartheid/

Lusztig, E. *Paraphrase of Arendt*. Retrieved from https://twitter.com/search?q=Elliot+Lusztig

MacAllister, K. (2008). Applicability of the crime of apartheid to Israel. *Badil Resource Center*. Retrieved from http://www.badil.org/en/al-majdal/item/72-applicability-of-the-crime-of-apartheid-to-israel

Mack, E. U.S. embassy celebrations: A who's who of the Israeli arms trade. *+972*. Retrieved from https://972mag.com/u-s-embassy-opening-a-whos-who-of-the-israeli-arms-trade/135681/

MacLeod, J. (1995). *Ain't no makin' it*. Boulder, CO: Westview Press.

Moynihan, D. P. (1970). *Maximum feasible misunderstanding: Community action in the war on poverty* (2nd ed.). New York, NY: Free Press.

Mozgovaya, N. (2011, March 23). Barak: Israel facing regional 'earthquake' and diplomatic 'tsunami.' *Ha'aretz*. Retrieved from http://www.haaretz.com/news/diplomacy-defense/barak-israel-facing-regional-earthquake-and-diplomatic-tsunami-1.351285

Myrdal, G. (1944). *An American dilemma*. New York, NY: Harper & Brothers.

Na'aman, O. (2012, November 13). The checkpoint. *Boston Review*. Retrieved from http://www.bostonreview.net/world/checkpoint-oded-naaman

Nabulsi, K. (2006, May 15). From generation to generation. *The Electronic Intifada*. Retrieved from http://electronicintifada.net/content/generation-generation/5966

Naimark, N. (1997). *The Russians in Germany: A history of the Soviet zone of occupation, 1945–1949*. Cambridge, MA: Harvard University Press.

Naor, M. (2002). *Zionism: The first 120 Years*. Jerusalem: Jewish Agency for Israel: Zionist Library.

Netanyahu, B. (2013). *Netanyahu's speech at Bar-Ilan* [Speech]. Retrieved from http://www.timesofisrael.com/full-text-of-netanyahus-speech-at-bar-ilan/

New Clashes in Occupied Western Sahara. (2011, February 27). *Afrol news*. Retrieved from http://afrol.com/articles/37450

Niewyk, D. L. (2000). *The Columbia guide to the Holocaust*. New York, NY: Columbia University Press.

Nimni, E. (Ed.). (2003). *The challenge of post-Zionism: Alternatives to Israeli fundamentalist politics*. London: Zed Books.

Nitzan, J., & Bichler, S. (2002). *The global political economy of Israel*. London: Pluto Press.

No Camels Team. (2013, January 20). Desert daughter: A Bedouin woman's success story. *No Camels*. Retrieved from http://nocamels.com/2013/01/desert-daughter-a-bedouin-womans-success-story/

Noy, O. (2017, September 15). Is Israel turning its Bedouin citizens into a stateless people? *+972*. Retrieved from https://972mag.com/is-israel-turning-its-bedouin-citizens-into-a-stateless-people/129775/

Nyhan, B. (2014, July 6). When beliefs and facts collide. *The New York Times*. Retrieved from http://www.nytimes.com/2014/07/06/upshot/when-beliefs-and-facts-collide.html?_r=0&abt=0002&abg=1

Ofir, J. (2017, December 23). We should "exact a price" from Ahed Tamimi "in the dark, Israeli journalist says. *Mondoweiss*. Retrieved from http://mondoweiss.net/2017/12/should-israeli-journalist/

Ofir, J. (2018, June 16). Israeli lawmaker: Jewish race is the greatest human capital, the smartest. *Mondoweiss*. Retrieved from http://mondoweiss.net/2018/06/lawmaker-greatest-smartest/

Omar-Man, M. (2014, May 28). Jerusalem by the numbers: Poverty, segregation and discrimination. *+972*. Retrieved from http://972mag.com/jerusalem-by-the-numbers-poverty-segregation-and-discrimination/91425/

Omni, M., & Winant, H. (1994). *Racial formation in the United States*. New York, NY: Routledge.

Palestine Seeking FIFA Sanctions against Israel. (2014, May 14). *Israel Hayom*. Retrieved from http://www.israelhayom.com/site/newsletter_article.php?id=17491

Palestinian Academic and Cultural Boycott of Israel. (2011). *Israel's anti-BDS law: Proving the effectiveness of the boycott*. Retrieved from http://www.pacbi.org/etemplate.php?id=1677

Palestinian Campaign for the Academic & Cultural Boycott of Israel. (n.d.). *Key documents.* Retrieved from http://pacbi.org/einside.php?id=69

Palestinian Fair Trade Association. (n.d.). *Homepage.* Retrieved from http://www.palestinefairtrade.org

Palestinian National Council. (1974). *Palestine liberation organization: Ten point plan.* Retrieved from http://www.jewishvirtuallibrary.org/jsource/Terrorism/PNCProgram1974.html

Palumbo, M. (1987). *The Palestinian catastrophe: The 1948 expulsion of a people from their homeland.* London: Faber and Faber.

Pappe, I. (2006). *The ethnic cleansing of Palestine.* Oxford: One World Press.

Pappe, I. (2012, March). *Keynote.* Speech presented at Harvard One State Conference, Harvard University, Cambridge, MA. Retrieved from http://electronicintifada.net/blogs/ali-abunimah/audio-ali-abunimah-and-ilan-pappe-keynote-speeches-harvard-one-state-conference

Pappe, I. (2014, July 13). Israel's incremental genocide in the Gaza ghetto. *The Electronic Intifada.* Retrieved from http://electronicintifada.net/content/israels-incremental-genocide-gaza-ghetto/13562

Pappe, I. (2017). *The biggest prison on earth: A history of the occupied territories.* London: One World Publications.

Peled, M. (2013). *The general's son.* Charlottesville, VA: Just World Books.

Peled, Y., & Rouhana, N. (2007). Traditional justice and the right of return of the Palestinian refugees. In E. Benvenisti, C. Gans, & S. Hanafi (Eds.), *Israel and the Palestinian refugees* (pp. 141–157). New York, NY: Springer.

Peled-Elhanan, N. (2007, January 29). Let our children live. *Counterpunch.* Retrieved from http://www.counterpunch.org/2007/01/29/let-our-children-live/

Peled-Elhanan, N. (2012). *Palestine in Israeli school books: Ideology and propaganda in education.* Tauris Academic Studies.

Peretz, D. (1958). *Israel and the Palestine Arabs.* Washington, DC: The Middle East Institute.

Peteet, J. (2016). Language matters: Talking about Palestine. *Journal of Palestine Studies, 45*(2), 24–40.

Pfeffer, A., & Stern, Y. (2007, December 29). High court delays ruling on JNF land sales to non-Jews. *Ha'aretz.* Retrieved from http://www.haaretz.com/news/high-court-delays-ruling-on-jnf-land-sales-to-non-jews-1.229946

Pike, S. W., McAdam, A., & Barbrow, B. (2011). *Christmas break in Palestine* [Video file]. Retrieved from https://vimeo.com/13478028

Piterberg, G. (2013). Eurozionism and its discontents. *New Left Review, 84*, 43–65.

Piven, F. F., & Cloward, R. (1993). *Regulating the poor: The functions of public welfare.* New York, NY: Vintage Books.

Pohl, D. (2003). *Verfolgung und Massenmord in der NS-Zeit 1933–1945.* Wissenschaftliche Buchgesellschaft.

Pollitt, K. (1999). Whose culture? In S. Muller Okin (Ed.), *Is multiculturalism bad for women?* (p. 27). Princeton, NJ: Princeton University Press.

Polya, G. (2013, December 8). Honor anti-apartheid hero Nelson Mandela's words: "Our freedom is incomplete without the freedom of the Palestinians." *Countercurrents.* Retrieved from http://www.countercurrents.org/polya081213.htm

Preminger, O. (Director). (1960). *Exodus* [Motion picture]. Washington, DC: Carlyle Productions.

Prince, S. (n.d.). The Rashomon effect. *The Criterion Collection*. Retrieved from http://www.criterion.com/current/posts/195-the-rashomon-effect

ProCon.org. (n.d.). *Israeli-Palestinian conflict: Population statistics*. Retrieved from http://israelipalestinian.procon.org/view.resource.php?resourceID=000636#chart10

Qumsiyeh, M. (2011). *Popular resistance in Palestine: A history of hope and empowerment*. London: Pluto Press.

Qumsiyeh, M. (2018, February 25). *Human rights newsletter* [blog]. Retrieved from http://lists.qumsiyeh.org/listinfo/humanrights

Rabie, K. (2014, March 1). *Housing: The production of the state, and the day after*. Reading presented at New Directions in Palestinian Studies Symposium, Brown University, Providence, RI.

Rapoport, R. (2018, July 2). Thanks to Gaza protests, Israel has a new crop of 'battle tested' weapons for sale. *+972*. Retrieved from https://972mag.com/thanks-to-gaza-protests-israel-has-a-new-crop-of-battle-tested-weapons-for-sale/136523/

Ravid, B. (2014, March 25). Israeli government doc: Population exchange legal under international law. *Ha'aretz*. Retrieved from http://www.haaretz.com/news/diplomacy-defense/.premium-1.581784

Ravid, B. (2014, April 19). U.S. Intelligence objects to visa waiver for Israelis. *Ha'aretz*. Retrieved from http://www.haaretz.com/news/diplomacy-defense/1.586303

Ravid, B. (2014, May 13). Britain grants Livni temporary immunity from arrest warrants during visit. *Ha'aretz*. Retrieved from http://www.haaretz.com/news/diplomacy-defense/.premium-1.590453

Ravitch, D. (1990). Multiculturalism: E pluribus plures. *American Scholar, 59*(3), 337–354.

Reinarman, C., & Levine, H. G. (1997). *Crack in America: Demon drugs and social justice*. Berkeley, CA: University of California Press.

Rejwan, N. (2004). *The last Jews in Baghdad*. Austin, TX: University of Texas Press.

Remnick, D. (2014, November 17). The one state reality. *The New Yorker*. Retrieved from http://www.newyorker.com/magazine/2014/11/17/one-state-reality

Richter, F. (2011, February 14). Protester killed in Bahrain 'day of rage': Witnesses. *Reuters*. Retrieved from http://uk.reuters.com/article/2011/02/14/uk-bahrain-protests-idUKTRE71D1G520110214

Ritzer, G. (1993). *The mcdonaldization of society*. Los Angeles, CA: Pine Forge Press.

Riwaq. (n.d.). *Homepage*. Retrieved from http://www.riwaq.org/home

Robbins, A. (2014, March 28). UN human rights council resolution warning companies to 'terminate business interests in the settlements' or face possible criminal liability gets watered down. *Mondoweiss*. Retrieved from http://mondoweiss.net/2014/03/resolution-companies-settlements.html

Rodinson, M. (1973). *Israel a colonial settler state?* New York, NY: Pathfinder Press.

Rogan, E. L., & Shlaim, A. (Eds.). (2001). *The war for Palestine: Rewriting the history of 1948*. Cambridge, MA: Cambridge University Press.

Rose, T. (1994). *Black noise: Rap music and Black culture in contemporary America*. Middletown, CT: Wesleyan.

Roseman, M. (2002). *The Wannsee conference and the 'final solution.'* New York, NY: Metropolitan Books.

Rosen, B. (2012). *Wrestling in the daylight: A Rabbi's path to Palestinian solidarity*. New York, NY: Just World Books.

Rothchild, A. (2010, January 5). Beautiful resistance in Bethlehem's Aida refugee camp. *Mondoweiss*. Retrieved from http://mondoweiss.net/2010/01/beautiful-resistance-in-bethlehems-aida-refugee-camp

Rothman, M. (2014, March 13). How can you tell that Israeli Refuseniks are scaring the system? *+972*. Retrieved from http://972mag.com/how-can-you-tell-that-israeli-refuseniks-are-scaring-the-system/88360/

Rothschild, N. (2008, November 19). Waltz with Bashir: Post-Zionist stress disorder. *Spiked*. Retrieved from http://www.spiked-online.com/newsite/article/5944#.VAHhREikWdM

Roy, S. (2004). Living with the Holocaust: The Journey of a child of Holocaust survivors. In A. Schatz (Ed.), *Prophets outcast: A century of dissident Jewish writing about Zionism and Israel* (pp. 344–353). New York, NY: The Nation Books.

Rozovsky, L. (2017, April 16). Why members of the 'Putin Aliyah' are abandoning Israel. *Ha'aretz*. Retrieved from https://www.haaretz.com/israel-news/members-of-the-putin-aliyah-are-abandoning-israel-1.5460939

Rubinger, D. (2008). *Israel through my lens: Sixty years as a photojournalist* [Book cover]. London: Abbeville Press.

Rudoren, J. (2013, August 4). In a West Bank culture of conflict, boys wield the weapon at hand. *The New York Times*. Retrieved from http://www.nytimes.com/2013/08/05/world/middleeast/rocks-in-hand-a-boy-fights-for-his-west-bank-village.html?_r=0

Rudoren, J. (2013, September 5). Israel backs limited strike against Syria. *The New York Times*, p. A1. Retrieved from https://www.nytimes.com/2013/09/06/world/middleeast/israel-backs-limited-strike-against-syria.html

Rudoren, J. (2014, March 18). A divide among Palestinians on a two-state solution. *The New York Times*. Retrieved from http://www.nytimes.com/2014/03/19/world/middleeast/a-divide-among-palestinians-on-a-two-state-solution.html?_r=0

Rudoren, J. (2014, March 20). Israel: Settlement plans renew Palestinian outrage. *The New York Times*. Retrieved from http://www.nytimes.com/2014/03/21/world/middleeast/israel-settlement-plans-renew-palestinian-outrage.html?_r=0

Rudoren, J. (2014, October 17). In exodus from Israel to Berlin, young nation's fissures show. *The New York Times*. Retrieved from http://www.nytimes.com/2014/10/17/world/middleeast/in-exodus-from-israel-to-berlin-young-nations-fissures-show.html

Ruebner, J. (2013). *Shattered hopes: Obama's failure to broker Israeli-Palestinian peace*. London: Verso Books.

Rummel, R. J. (1992). *Democide: Nazi genocide and mass murder*. New York, NY: Transaction Books.

Russell Tribunal on Palestine. (n.d.). *About*. Retrieved from http://www.russelltribunalonpalestine.com/en/about-rtop

Ryan, C. (1999). *Prime time activism*. Boston, MA: South End Press.

Sadeh, S. (2014, August 12). How Israel's arms manufacturers won the Gaza war. *Ha'aretz*. Retrieved from http://www.haaretz.com/business/.premium-1.610032

Said, E. (1979). *Orientalism*. New York, NY: Vintage Books.

Said, E. (1999, January 10). The one state solution. *The New York Times*. Retrieved from http://www.nytimes.com/1999/01/10/magazine/the-one-state-solution.html

Said, E. (2000). *Out of place: A memoir*. New York, NY: Vintage Books.

Said, E. (2000). Invention, memory, place. *Critical Inquiry, 26*(2), 175–192.

Said, E. (2004). *From Oslo to Iraq and the road map*. New York, NY: Pantheon.

Said-Foqahaa, N. (2012). The waiting room: Private communication with the author.

Salamanca, O. J. (2014, February 28). *Hooked on electricity: The charged political economy of electrification in the Palestinian West Bank.* Reading presented at New Directions in Palestinian Studies Symposium, Brown University, Providence, RI.

Salameh, F. (2006). Vous êtes Arabe, puisque je vous le dis! [You're an Arab if I say so!]. *Middle Eastern Review of International Affairs, 1*(1), 52–58.

Saleh, M. (2017, December 12). *Is the Campbell-Bannerman document real or fake? Al Zaytouna centre for studies and consultations.* Retrieved from https://eng.alzaytouna.net/2017/09/28/political-analysis-campbell-bannerman-document-real-fake/

Samuel, V. H. (1946). *Grooves of change.* New York, NY: Bobbs Merrill.

Sand, S. (2009). *The invention of the Jewish people.* New York, NY: Verso Books.

Santayana, G. (1905). *Reason in common sense: The life of reason.* New York, NY: Dover Publications.

Sarid, Y. (2014, November 21). Adelson, Netanyahu and our kingdom of priests and holiness. *Ha'aretz.* Retrieved from http://www.haaretz.com/opinion/.premium-1.627582

Sasson, S. (1999). Culture beyond gender. In S. Muller Okin (Ed.), *Is multiculturalism bad for women?* (p. 76). Princeton, NJ: Princeton University Press.

Saxe, L., Kadushin, C., Hecht, S., Rosen, M. I., Phillips, B., & Kelner, S. (2004). *Evaluating birthright Israel: Long term impact and recent findings.* Waltham, MA: The Cohen Center for Modern Jewish Studies, Brandeis University.

Saxe, L., Shain, M., Wright, G., Hecht, S., Fishman, S., & Sasson, T. (2012). *Jewish futures project: The impact of Taglit-Birthright Israel: 2012 update.* Retrieved from http://www.brandeis.edu/cmjs/pdfs/jewish%20futures/JFP2012Report.pdf

Schatz, A. (Ed.). (2004). *Prophets outcast: A century of dissident Jewish writing about Zionism and Israel.* New York, NY: The Nation Books.

Schneider, D. (1984). *A critique of the study of kinship.* Ann Arbor, MI: University of Michigan Press.

Schocken, R. (2013, August 27). Jewish and then democratic. *Ha'aretz.* Retrieved from http://www.haaretz.com/opinion/.premium-1.543070

Scholch, A. (1993). *Palestine in transformation, 1856–1882: Studies in social, economic and political development.* Washington, DC: Institute for Palestine Studies.

Schotten, H. (2014, August 30). Suppose Gaza were a woman. *Ma'an News Agency.* Retrieved from http://www.maannews.net/eng/ViewDetails.aspx?ID=723865

Schulenberg, E. (2012, January 24). Israel arrests Hamas lawmakers in Jerusalem. *The Jewish Press.* Retrieved from http://www.jewishpress.com/news/israel/israel-arrests-hamas-lawmakers-in-jerusalem/2012/01/24/

Schulman, S. (2011, November 22). Israel and 'pinkwashing.' *The New York Times.* Retrieved from http://www.nytimes.com/2011/11/23/opinion/pinkwashing-and-israels-use-of-gays-as-a-messaging-tool.html?_r=1

Schulze, K. (2009). *The Jews of Lebanon: Between coexistence and conflict* (2nd ed.). Sussex: Sussex Academic Press.

Schur, E. (1972). *Labeling deviant behavior: Its social implications.* New York, NY: Joanna Cottler Books.

Schwartz, Y. (2018, May 10). More Israelis are moving to the U.S.: and staying for good. *Newsweek.* Retrieved from http://www.newsweek.com/2018/05/18/israel-brain-drain-technology-startup-nation-religion-palestinians-economy-919477.html

Segev, T. (1998). *1949: The first Israelis.* New York, NY: Henry Holt.

Segev, T. (1999). *One Palestine, complete.* New York, NY: Metropolitan Books.

REFERENCES

Segev, T. (2000). *The seventh million: Israelis and the Holocaust.* New York, NY: Picador Press.

Segev, T. (2001). *Elvis in Jerusalem.* New York, NY: Henry Holt and Company.

Segev, T. (2005). *1967: Israel, the war, and the year that transformed the Middle East.* New York, NY: Henry Holt.

Selod, S. (2014). Citizenship denied: The racialization of Muslim American men and women post-9/11. *Critical Sociology.* Retrieved from http://crs.sagepub.com/content/early/2014/03/31/0896920513516022

Selod, S., & Embrick, D. G. (2013). Racialization and Muslims: Situating the Muslim experience in race scholarship. *Sociology Compass, 7*(8), 644–655.

Shabi, R. (2009, April 3). Israeli exports hit by European boycotts after attacks on Gaza. *The Guardian.* Retrieved from http://www.theguardian.com/world/2009/apr/03/israel-gaza-attacks-boycotts-food-industry

Shafir, G. (1996). *Land, labor and the origins of the Israeli-Palestinian conflict, 1882–1914, updated edition.* Berkeley, CA: University of California Press.

Shafir, G. (2017). *A half-century of occupation: Israel, Palestine, and the world's most intractable conflict.* Berkeley, CA: University of California Press.

Shafir, G. (2017, May 31). Why has the occupation lasted this long? *Mondoweiss.* Retrieved from https://mondoweiss.net/2017/05/occupation-lasted-this/

Shahian, A. E. A. (2000, May 30). *Quotes.* Retrieved from http://www.wildolive.co.uk/quotes.htm

Shakespeare, W. (2002). *The merchant of Venice.* Washington, DC: Folger Shakespeare Library.

Shalev, C. (2018, July 3). Menachem begin would be ashamed of Netanyahu's whitewash of Hungary's Anti-Semitism, Poland's Holocaust revisionism. *Ha'aretz.* Retrieved from https://www.haaretz.com/israel-news/premium-hungary-pm-orban-s-upcoming-visit-a-blot-on-netanyahu-s-record-and-a-stain-on-israel-s-history-1.6223675

Shamir, R. (2013). *Current flow: The electrification of Palestine.* Stanford, CA: Stanford University Press.

Shamir, Y. (Director). (2009). *Defamation.* Israel: First Run Features. Retrieved from https://archive.org/details/Defamation2010

Shams, A. (2014, February 11). Camp on the front line of struggle against occupation. *Ma'an News Agency.* Retrieved from http://www.maannews.net/eng/ViewDetails.aspx?ID=672795

Shapira, A. (1999). *Land and power: The Zionist resort to force, 1881–1948.* Stanford, CA: Stanford University Press.

Shapiro, T., & Oliver, M. (1995). *Black wealth, White wealth: A new perspective on racial inequality.* London: Routledge.

Sharp, J. (2008, January 2). *U.S. foreign aid to Israel: Congressional research service report to congress.* Retrieved from http://www.dtic.mil/dtic/tr/fulltext/u2/a484671pdf

Shavit, A. (2012, August 23). Countdown: Former Minister Ephraim Sneh fears another Hiroshima. *Ha'aretz.* Retrieved from http://www.haaretz.com/weekend/magazine/ari-shavit-s-countdown-former-minister-ephraim-sneh-fears-another-hiroshima-1.460280

Shavit, A. (2013). *My promised land: The triumph and tragedy of Israel.* New York, NY: Spiegel & Grau.

Sheizaf, N. (2012, March 25). One or two states? The status quo is Israel's rational choice. *+972.* Retrieved from http://972mag.com/one-or-two-states-the-status-quo-is-israels-rational-third-choice/39169/

Sheizaf, N. (2014, May 12). What is the Israeli right's one-state vision? *+972*. Retrieved from http://972mag.com/what-is-the-israeli-rights-one-state-vision/90755/

Sheizaf, N. (2014, August 16). Netanyahu is talking to Hamas: It's about time. *+972*. Retrieved from http://972mag.com/netanyahu-is-talking-to-hamas-its-about-time/95570/

Shenhav, Y. (2006). *The Arab Jews: A post-colonial reading of nationalism, religion and ethnicity*. Stanford, CA: Stanford University Press.

Sherwood, H. (2012, July 26). Population of Jewish settlements in West Bank up 15,000 in a year. *The Guardian*. Retrieved from http://www.theguardian.com/world/2012/jul/26/jewish-population-west-bank-up

Shlaim, A. (2001). *The Iron Wall, Israel and the Arab world*. New York, NY: Norton.

Shohat, E. (1999). The invention of the Mizrahim. *Journal for Palestine Studies, 29*(1), 5–20.

Shpurer, S. (2013, July 30). The Israeli bank that opens its doors to everyone—except Arabs. *Ha'aretz*. Retrieved from http://www.haaretz.com/business/.premium-1.538667

Shulman, D. (2014, May 22). Occupation: The finest Israeli documentary. *New York Review of Books*. Retrieved from http://www.nybooks.com/articles/archives/2014/may/22/occupation-finest-israeli-documentary/

Siegman, H. (2014, September 1). A slaughter of innocents. *Democracy Now!* Retrieved from http://www.democracynow.org/2014/9/1/a_slaughter_of_innocents_henry_siegman

Siegman, H. (2014, November 26). Will greater Israel transform into greater Palestine? *Huffington Post*. Retrieved from https://www.huffingtonpost.com/henry-siegman/will-greater-israel-transform_b_6220806.html

Skop, Y. (2014, April 24). 50,000 Holocaust survivors in Israel live in poverty. *Ha'aretz*. Retrieved from http://www.haaretz.com/news/national/.premium-1.586970/

Slyomovic, S. (2007). The rape of Qula, a destroyed Palestinian village. In A. Sa'di & L. Abu-Lughod (Eds.), *Nakba: Palestine, 1948 and the claims of memory*. New York, NY: Columbia University Press.

Smith, A. D. (1998). *Fires in the mirror*. New York, NY: Dramatists Play Service.

Smith, C. (2013). *Palestine and the Arab-Israeli conflict: A history with documents* (8th ed.). New York, NY: St. Martin's Press.

Snyder, T. (2010). *Bloodlands*. New York, NY: Basic Books.

Sommer, A. K. (2013, July 26). Symbol of struggle against Haredi coercion bids farewell to Beit Shemesh. *Ha'aretz*. Retrieved from http://www.haaretz.com/blogs/routine-emergencies/.premium-1.538039/

Spangler, E. (1981). Small winnings: Blue collar students in college and at work. In M. Lewis (Ed.), *Research in social problems and public policy* (Vol. I, pp. 15–41). Greenwich, CT: JAI Press.

Spangler, E. (1986). *Lawyers for hire: Salaried professionals at work*. New Haven, CT: Yale University Press.

Spangler, E. (2009). Sexual harassment: Labor relations by other means? In C. Levenstein (Ed.), *At the point of production: The social analysis of occupational and environmental health* (pp. 167–178). New York, NY: Baywood Publishing.

Spangler, E. (2010, June 14). Attacking humanitarian aid. *Counterpunch*. Retrieved from http://www.counterpunch.org/2010/06/14/attacking-humanitarian-aid/

Spangler, E. (2011, October 11). The "generous" offer. *Counterpunch*. Retrieved from http://www.counterpunch.org/2011/10/11/the-story-of-the-generous-offer/

Spangler, E. (2012). No exit: The shadow of the Nakba in Palestinian film. In J. Michalczyk & R. Helmick (Eds.), *Through a lens darkly: Films of genocide, ethnic cleansing, and atrocities* (pp. 205–216). New York, NY: Peter Lang.

Spangler, E. (2013). Book review: Women's NGOs in Pakistan by Afshan Jafar and transnationalism reversed: Women organizing against gendered violence in Bangladesh by Elora Halim Chowdhury. *Gender and Society, 27*(3), 435–438.

Spangler, E., Levenstein, C., Fuzesi, Z., & Tishtian, L. (1993). Occupational medicine and the state: Lessons from Hungary. *New Solutions, 4*(1), 52–57.

Sperber, J. (2015). BDS, Israel, and the world system. *Journal of Palestine Studies, 45*(1), 8–23.

Squires, G. D. (1994). *Capital and communities in Black and White: The Intersections of race, class and uneven development.* New York, NY: State University of New York (SUNY) Press.

Stamatopoulos-Robbins, S. (2014, February 28). *Infrastructure and materiality in Palestine studies.* Reading presented at New Directions in Palestinian Studies Symposium, Brown University, Providence, RI.

Stenger, C. (2008, December 30). What victimology does not account for. *The Guardian.* Retrieved from http://www.theguardian.com/commentisfree/2008/dec/30/gaza-hamas-palestinians-israel

Stenger, C. (2012). Israel missed its chance—again. *The Daily Beast.* Retrieved from http://www.americantaskforce.org/daily_news_article/2012/11/27/israel_missed_its_chance%E2%80%94again

Stephens, B. (2017, April 29). The climate of complete certainty. *The New York Times.* Retrieved from https://www.nytimes.com/2017/04/28/opinion/climate-of-complete-certainty.html

Stern, Y. (2007, March 28). Study: Arabs may be poorer, but Jews get more welfare funds. *Ha'aretz.* Retrieved from http://www.haaretz.com/news/study-arabs-may-be-poorer-but-jews-get-more-welfare-funds-1.216881

Stern, Y. Z., & Ruderman, J. (2014, March 3). Op-ed: Why 'Israeli' is not a nationality. *Jewish Telegraphic Agency.* Retrieved from http://www.jta.org/2014/03/03/news-opinion/israel-middle-east/op-ed-why-israeli-is-not-a-nationality

Stewart, C. (2012, October 23). The new Israeli apartheid: Poll reveals widespread Jewish support for policy of discrimination against Arab minority. *The Independent.* Retrieved from http://www.independent.co.uk/news/world/middle-east/the-new-israeli-apartheid-poll-reveals-widespread-jewish-support-for-policy-of-discrimination-against-arab-minority-8223548.html

Stiglitz, J. (2014, March 16). On the wrong side of globalization. *The New York Times.* Retrieved from http://opinionator.blogs.nytimes.com/2014/03/15/on-the-wrong-side-of-globalization/?_php=true&_type=blogs&_r=0

Such, R. (2018, June 24). Ending colonialism in Palestine. *The Electronic Intifada.* Retrieved from https://electronicintifada.net/content/ending-colonialism-palestine/24756

Sudan Police Clash with Protestors. (2011, January 30). *Al Jazeera.* Retrieved from http://www.aljazeera.com/news/africa/2011/01/2011130131451294670.html

Suez Crisis. (2003). *The concise Oxford dictionary of politics.* Oxford: Oxford University Press.

Supreme Court Petition: H.C. 9205/04. *Adalah v. The Israel lands administration, the minister of finance and the Jewish national fund and H.C. 9010/04.* The Arab Center for Alternative Planning, et al. v. The Israel Lands Administration, et al. Retrieved from http://www.adalah.org/en/content/view/6558

Supreme Court Thrusts Israel Down the Slope of Apartheid. (2012, January 13). *Ha'aretz.* Retrieved from http://www.haaretz.com/print-edition/opinion/supreme-court-thrusts-israel-down-the-slope-of-apartheid-1.407056

Suu Kyi, A. S. (n.d.). *Freedom from fear: Quotes about human rights.* Retrieved from http://www.goodreads.com/quotes/tag/human-rights

Tabar, L., & Desai, C. (2017). Decolonization is a global project: From Palestine to the Americas. *Decolonization: Indigeneity, Education & Society, 6*(1): i–ix.

Tahan, S. (2017, November 28). How Israeli leftists trivialize the Palestinian cause. *+972.* Retrieved from https://972mag.com/how-israeli-leftists-trivialize-the-palestinian-cause/131031/

Tamimi, B. (2014, February 17). *Nabi Saleh night raid 18 2 2014* [Video file]. Retrieved from https://www.youtube.com/watch?v=gNXgZdMta-k

Taub, G. (2017, October 19). The Israeli peace camps algorithms. *Ha'aretz.* Retrieved from https://www.haaretz.com/opinion/.premium-1.818260

Taxes/Decades of Tax Breaks for the Settler Population. (2003, September 25). *Ha'aretz.* Retrieved from http://www.haaretz.com/print-edition/business/taxes-decades-of-tax-breaks-for-the-settler-population-1.101212

Taylor, M. (2013, December 8). Israel apologists attempted to discredit Mandela with false Israel apartheid quote. *Mondoweiss.* Retrieved from http://mondoweiss.net/2013/12/apologists-discredit-apartheid.html

Tessler, M. (1994). *The history of the Israeli-Palestinian conflict.* Bloomington, IN: Indiana University Press.

Text: The Beirut Declaration. (2002, March 28). *BBC News.* Retrieved from http://news.bbc.co.uk/2/hi/world/monitoring/media_reports/1899395.stm

The Campbell-Bannerman Report. (1907). Retrieved from https://archive.org/stream/imperialconferen02jebbuoft/imperialconferen02jebbuoft_djvu.txt

The Carter Center. (2014, November 10). *Israel and the occupied Palestinian territory.* Retrieved from http://www.cartercenter.org/countries/israel_and_the_palestinian_territories.html

The Declaration of Independence. Retrieved from http://www.archives.gov/exhibits/charters/declaration_transcript.html

The East Jerusalem YMCA. (n.d.). *East Jerusalem YMCA rehabilitation program.* Retrieved from http://www.ej-ymca.org/index.php?option=com_content&view=article&id=68&Itemid=142

The Geneva Convention and the Rules of War. (1949). Retrieved from https://www.icrc.org/en/war-and-law/treaties-customary-law/geneva-conventions

The Global Religious Landscape: Muslims. (2012, December 18). *Pew research center.* Retrieved from http://www.pewforum.org/2012/12/18/global-religious-landscape-muslim/

The Guardian Staff. (2011, November 28). Israeli sanctions mean Palestinian Authority cannot pay employees' wages. *The Guardian.* Retrieved from https://www.theguardian.com/world/2011/nov/28/israel-sanctions-palestinian-authority-wages

The Guardian Staff. (2014, August 12). UK government to block arms export to Israel if military action resumes. *The Guardian.* Retrieved from http://www.theguardian.com/politics/2014/aug/12/british-arms-exports-israel-gaza-block-suspension?CMP=EMCNEWEML6619l2

The International Court of Justice. (2004, July 9). *Legal consequences of the construction of a wall in the occupied Palestinian territory: Advisory opinion* [Press release]. Retrieved from http://www.icccij.org/files/case-related/131/131-20040709-ADV-01-00-EN.pdf

REFERENCES

The Jerusalem Fund. (2009, March 3). *Hisham B. Sharabi memorial lecture: Apartheid and occupation under international law with John Dugard.* Retrieved from http://www.thejerusalemfund.org/ht/display/ContentDetails/i/5240/pid/897

The One State Declaration. (2007, November 29). *The Electronic Intifada.* Retrieved from http://electronicintifada.net/content/one-state-declaration/793

The Palestine Papers. (n.d.). *Meeting with president Clinton, White House, 23.12.2000.* Retrieved from http://transparency.aljazeera.net/files/48.PDF

The Parents Circle-Families Forum. (2014). *In Wikipedia.* Retrieved from http://en.wikipedia.org/wiki/The_Parents_Circle-Families_Forum

The White House. (1961, July 25). *The Berlin crisis: Radio and television address to the American people* [Radio program]. Retrieved from http://www.jfklibrary.org/Asset-Viewer/Archives/JFKWHA-045.aspx

Thrall, N. (2017). *The only language they understand: Forcing compromise in Israel and Palestine.* New York, NY: Holt.

Thucydides. (1960). The Athenian representative to Melos. In R. W. Livingstone & R. Crawley (Eds.), *The history of the Peloponnessian war.* New York, NY: Oxford University Press.

Tibon, A. (2015, July 26). Hurricane season/American Jews say current storm with Israel will pass, just like all the others did. *Ha'aretz.* Retrieved from https://www.haaretz.com/us-news/.premium-american-jews-say-current-storm-with-israel-will-pass-1.6316559

Tilley, V. (2010). *The one-state solution: A breakthrough for peace in the Israeli-Palestinian deadlock.* Ann Arbor, MI: University of Michigan Press.

Tolts, M. (2009). *Post-Soviet Aliyah and Jewish demographic transformation.* Paper presented at the 15th World Congress of Jewish Studies, Jerusalem, Israel. Retrieved from http://bjpa.org/search-results/publication/11924

Traubmann, T. (2007, March 21). Shimon Tzabar, 81, dies in London. *Ha'aretz.* Retrieved from http://www.haaretz.com/print-edition/news/shimon-tzabar-81-dies-in-london-1.216138

Tsurkov, E. (2014, May 8). Israel hasn't recognized one Sudanese refugee. *+972.* Retrieved from http://972mag.com/israel-hasnt-recognized-one-sudanese-refugee/90633

Tufts, S. J. P. (2018, February 14). TYPD brings 'deadly exchange' to Tufts. *The Tufts Daily.* Retrieved from https://tuftsdaily.com/opinion/2018/02/14/op-ed-tupd -brings-deadly-exchange-tufts/

Turkey to Send Another Freedom Flotilla to Gaza. (2014, July 26). *Middle East monitor.* Retrieved from https://www.middleeastmonitor.com/news/europe/13059-turkey-to-send-another-freedom-flotilla-to-gaza

Turkish Prime Minister Erdogan Has Pledged a Turkish Naval Escort to the Gaza Flotilla. (n.d.). *Al Jazeera.* Retrieved from http://www.aljazeera.com.tr/haber/erdogan-savas-gemileri-koruyacak

Tutu Foundation. Retrieved from https://www.traffickinginstitute.org/incontext-archbishop-desmond-tutu/

UK Government to Block Arms Export to Israel if Military Action Resumes. (2014, August 12). *The Guardian.* Retrieved from http://www.theguardian.com/politics/2014/aug/12/british-arms-exports-israel-gaza-block-suspension?CMP=EMCNEWEML6619I2

UNESCO. (n.d.). http://data.uis.unesco.org/

UNESCO Cuts Funding for Palestinian Youth Magazine Over Hitler Praise. (2011, December 23). *The Telegraph.* Retrieved from http://www.telegraph.co.uk/news/worldnews/middleeast/palestinianauthority/8975423/Unesco-cuts-funding-for-Palestinian-youth-magazine-over-Hitler-praise.html

United Nations Country Team. (2012). *Gaza in 2020: A livable place? Palestinian territory: United Nations relief and works agency for Palestine refugees.* Retrieved from http://www.unrwa.org/newsroom/press-releases/gaza-2020-liveable-place

United Nations Educational, Scientific, and Cultural Organization. (n.d.). *UIS.Stat. Statistics on college enrollment.* Retrieved from http://stats.uis.unesco.org/unesco/TableViewer/tableView.aspx?ReportId=168Statistics on college completion

United Nations General Assembly. (2012, November 29). *General Assembly votes overwhelmingly to accord Palestine 'Non-member observer state' status in United Nations.* Retrieved from http://www.un.org/News/Press/docs/2012/ga11317.doc.htm

United Nations General Assembly. (1973). *Convention on the suppression and punishment of the crime of Apartheid.* Retrieved from http://legal.un.org/avl/ha/cspca/cspca.htm

United Nations General Assembly Resolution 181. (1947, November 29). Retrieved from http://www.yale.edu/lawweb/avalon/un/res181.htm

United Nations Office for the Coordination of Humanitarian Affairs. (2013). *Fragmented lives: Humanitarian overview.* Retrieved from http://www.ochaopt.org/vontent/fragmented-lives-humanitarian-overview-2016

United Nations Office for the Coordination of Humanitarian Affairs. (2014, June–August). *Humanitarian bulletin monthly report.* Retrieved from http://www.ochaopt.org/documents/ocha_opt_the_humanitarian_monitor_2014_10_03_english.pdf

United Nations Office for the Coordination of Humanitarian Affairs. (2014). *Occupied Palestinian territories: Bedouin communities in area C at risk of forcible transfer.* Retrieved from http://reliefweb.int/map/occupied-palestinian-territory/occupied-palestinian-territory-bedouin-communites-area-c-risk

United Nations Office for the Coordination of Humanitarian Affairs. (2018). *Occupied Palestinian territories: West Bank access restrictions.* Retrieved from http://www.ochaopt.org/content/wesst-bank-access-restrictions-october 2017

United Nations Office for the Coordination of Humanitarian Affairs (UNOCHA). (2018, June 13). *Humanitarian snapshot: Casualties in the context of demonstrations and hostilities in Gaza.* Retrieved from https://www.ochaopt.org/content/humanitarian-snapshot-casualties-context-demonstrations-and-hostilities-gaza-30-march-12 2018

United Nations Office of the High Commissioner for Human Rights. (1948). *The universal declaration of human rights.* Retrieved from http://www.ohchr.org/EN/UDHR/Pages/Introduction.aspx

United Nations Office of the High Commissioner for Human Rights. (1965). *International convention on the elimination of all forms of racial discrimination.* Retrieved from http://www.ohchr.org/EN/ProfessionalInterest/Pages/CERD.aspx

United Nations Relief and Works Agency for Palestine Refugees in the Near East. (n.d.). *Homepage.* Retrieved from http://www.unrwa.org/palestine/refugees

United Nations Relief and Works Agency for Palestine Refugees in the Near East. (n.d.). Retrieved from https://www.unrwa.org/what-we-do/eligibility-registration

United Nations Relief and Works Agency for Palestine Refugees in the Near East. (n.d.). https://www.unrwa.org/where-we-work/gaza-strip

United Nations Relief and Works Agency for Palestine Refugees in the Near East. (n.d.). https://www.unrwa.org/where-we-work/west-bank

United Nations Security Council Resolution 242. (1967, November 22). Retrieved from http://unispal.un.org/DPA/DPR/7D35E1F729DF491C85256EE700686136

United States Department of State. (2013, July 26). *U.S. relations with Liberia.* Retrieved from http://www.state.gov/r/pa/ei/bgn/6618.htm

REFERENCES

Uris, L. (1958). *Exodus*. New York, NY: Doubleday.

Urquhart, C. (2006, April 15). Gaza on the brink of implosion as aid cut-off starts to bite. *The Observer*. Retrieved from http://www.theguardian.com/world/2006/apr/16/israel

US Loses UNESCO Voting Rights After Stopping Funds Over Palestine Decision. (2013, November 8). *The Guardian*. Retrieved from http://www.theguardian.com/world/2013/nov/08/us-unesco-voting-funds-palestine-decision

Vaidya, S. K. (2011, February 27). One dead, dozen injured as Oman protest turns ugly. *Gulf News*. Retrieved from http://gulfnews.com/news/gulf/oman/one-dead-dozen-injured-as-oman-protest-turns-ugly-1.768789

Velasquez-Manoff, M. (2017, December 10). Should doctors ignore race? Science, after all, has revealed how arbitrary those categories are. *The New York Times*. Retrieved from https://www.nytimes.com/2017/12/08/opinion/sunday/should-medicine-discard-race.html

Visualizing Occupation. (n.d.). Distribution of water. *+972*. Retrieved from http://972mag.com/visualizing-occupation-distribution-of-water/49925/

Visualizing Palestine. (n.d.). *Not enough water in the West Bank?* Retrieved from http://visualizingpalestine.org/visuals/west-bank-water

Wade, R. (2014, October 24). Organised hypocrisy on a monumental scale. *London Review of Books*. Retrieved from http://www.lrb.co.uk/2014/10/24/robert-wade/organised-hypocrisy-on-a-monumental-scale

Waging Peace: Boston Conference on One-State Settlement Draws Large Crowd. (2009, November). *Washington report on Middle East affairs*. Retrieved from http://www.wrmea.org/2009-july/waging-peace-boston-conference-on-one-state-settlement-draws-large-crowd.html

Weber, M. (1946). Class, status, and party. In H. Gerth & C. W. Mills (Eds.), *From Max Weber: Essays in sociology* (pp. 180–195). New York, NY: Oxford University Press.

Weber, M. (1946). Politics as a vocation. In H Gerth & C. W. Mills (Eds.), *From Max Weber: Essays in sociology* (pp. 77–129). New York, NY: Oxford University Press.

Weber, M. (1946). Science as a vocation. In H. Gerth & C. W. Mills (Eds.), *From Max Weber: Essays in sociology* (pp. 129–159). New York, NY: Oxford University Press.

Weber, M. (1946). The social psychology of the world religions. In H. Gerth & C. W. Mills (Eds.), *From Max Weber: Essays in sociology* (pp. 267–301). New York, NY: Oxford University Press.

Wedoud, Y. (2011, February 26). "Facebook Generation" continues Mauritania protests. *CNN*. Retrieved from http://www.cnn.com/2011/WORLD/africa/02/26/mauritania.protest/index.html

Weiss, P. (2014, March 3). Poll: If two states collapse, American overwhelmingly favor 'democracy.' *Mondoweiss*. Retrieved from http://mondoweiss.net/2014/03/collapse-americans-democracy.html

Weiss, P. (2014, March 17). Israeli high school student leader calls youths' refuse to serve 'declaration of war.' *Mondoweiss*. Retrieved from http://mondoweiss.net/2014/03/student-refusal-declaration.html

Weiss, P. (2014, April 5). No thanks for Zionist 'chaperones': Wesleyan declares itself an Open Hillel. *Mondoweiss*. Retrieved from http://mondoweiss.net/2014/04/chaperones-wesleyan-declares.html

Weiss, P. (2017, June 27). Yakov Rabkin's devastating critique of Zionism: It is opposed to jewishtradition and liberalism. *Mondoweiss*. Retrieved from https://mondoweiss.net/2017/06/devastating-tradition-liberalism/?utm_source=Mondoweiss+List

Weiss, P. (2017, August 24). As many as 1 million Israelis have left for the U.S. *Mondweiss*. Retrieved from https://mondoweiss.net/2017/08/many-million-israelis/

Weizman, E., & Sheikh, F. (2015). *The conflict shoreline, colonialism as climate change in the Negev Desert*. Gottingen: Steidl Verlag.

We Killed Jesus, We're Proud of it. Retrieved from http://www.youtube.com/watch?v=M539PgDjbas

Wesley, D. A. (2009). *State practices and Zionist images: Shaping economic development in Arab towns in Israel*. Oxford: Berghahn Books.

White, B. (2012). *Palestinians in Israel: Segregation, discrimination and democracy*. London: Pluto Books.

White, B. (2012, January 12). Israel's high court upholds racist 'citizenship law' to avoid 'national suicide. *The Electronic Intifada*. Retrieved from http://electronicintifada.net/blogs/ben-white/israels-high-court-upholds-racist-citizenship-law-avoid-national-suicide

White, B. (2014, January 10). Did Israeli apartheid wall really stop suicide bombings? *The Electronic Intifada*. Retrieved from http://electronicintifada.net/blogs/ben-white/did-israeli-apartheid-wall-really-stop-suicide-bombings

Whitelam, K. (1996). *The invention of ancient Israel: The silencing of Palestinian history*. New York, NY: Routledge.

Whitmarsh, I., & Jones, D. (Eds.). (2010). What's the use of race? Modern governance and the biology of difference. Cambridge, MA: MIT Press.

Who Profits. (n.d.). *Homepage*. Retrieved from http://www.whoprofits.org/

Why Can't I Own a Canadian? (2002). Retrieved from http://www.humanistsofutah.org/archivalsample/archive-2001-2010/2002-2

Wicomb, Z. (2000). *You can't get lost in Capetown*. New York, NY: City University of New York Feminist Press.

Wildeman, J., & Marshall, S. (2014, May 21). By mis-diagnosing Israel-Palestine, donor aid harms Palestinians. *Open Democracy*. Retrieved from https://www.opendemocracy.net/arab-awakening/jeremy-wildeman-sandy-marshall/by-misdiagnosing-israelpalestine-donor-aid-harms-pales

Wilkins, B. (2014, March 10). Desmond Tutu urges boycott of 'apartheid' Israel. *Digital Journal*. Retrieved from http://digitaljournal.com/news/world/desmond-tutu-urges-boycott-of-apartheid-israel/article/375545

Wilson, S. (2006, March 22). Russian Bloc in Israel looks to a strongman. *The Washington Post*. Retrieved from http://www.washingtonpost.com/wp-dyn/content/article/2006/03/21/AR2006032101721.html

Winstanley, A. (2013, August 11). 'The old will die and the young will forget'-Did Ben-Gurion say it? *The Electronic Intifada*. Retrieved from http://electronicintifada.net/blogs/asa-winstanley/old-will-die-and-young-will-forget-did-ben-gurion-say-it

Winter, E. (2014, August 30). Why are Brits who know little about Israel so active against it? *Ha'aretz*. Retrieved from http://www.haaretz.com/.premium-why-are-brits-so-active-against-israel-1.5261855

Wolfe, A. (2014). *At home in exile: Why diaspora is good for the Jews*. Boston, MA: Beacon Press.

Wolfe, P. (2006). Settler colonialism and the elimination of the native. *Journal of Genocide Research, 8*(4), 387.

Wong, E. (2014, May 31). China moves to calm restive Xinjiang region. *The New York Times*. Retrieved from http://www.nytimes.com/2014/05/31/world/asia/chinas-leader-lays-out-plan-to-pacify-restive-region.html?_r=0

Wright, A. (2013, May 24). Patenting the human genome. *Medical Press*. Retrieved from http://medicalxpress.com/news/2013-05-patenting-human-genome.html

Yapp, M. E. (1987). *The making of the modern near East, 1792–1923*. London: Longman.

Yesh Din. (n.d.). *Homepage*. Retrieved from http://yesh-din.org/

Yesh G'vul. (n.d.). *Homepage*. Retrieved from http://www.yeshgvul.org.il/en/about-2/

Yeshua-Lyth, O. (2014, June 3). Discrimination is legal, there are no Israelis: Reading the Supreme Court's decisions on Israeli nationality. *Mondoweiss*. Retrieved from http://mondoweiss.net/2014/06/discrimination-decisions-nationality.html

Yoaz, Y. (2005, January 28). JNF, treasury seeks formula for continued Jews-only land sales. *Ha'aretz*. Retrieved from http://www.haaretz.com/print-edition/news/jnf-treasury-seek-formula-for-continued-jews-only-land-sales-1.148521

Young, C. (2014). Black ops: Black masculinity and the War on Terror. *The American Quarterly, 66*(1), 35–67.

Yousef, D. (2009, April 30). Palestine's Holocaust museum. *Al Jazeera*. Retrieved from http://www.aljazeera.com/focus/2009/04/2009429133130101883.html

Zangwill, I. (1937). *Speeches, articles and letters*. Unknown: Soncino Press.

Zarchin, T., Khoury, J., & Lis, J. (2012, January 12). Supreme court upholds ban on Palestinians living with Israeli spouses. *Ha'aretz*. Retrieved from http://www.haaretz.com/print-edition/news/supreme-court-upholds-ban-on-palestinians-living-with-israeli-spouses-1.406812

Zemlinskaya, Y. (2010). Between militarism and pacifism: Conscientious objections and draft resistance in Israel. *Central European Journal of International and Security Studies*. Retrieved from http://www.academia.edu/179941/Between_Militarism_and_Pacifism_Conscientious_Objection_and_Draft_Resistance_in_Israel

Zerubavel, Y. (1995). *Recovered roots: Collective memory and the making of Israeli national tradition*. Chicago, IL: University of Chicago Press.

Zirin, D. (2014, March 3). After latest incident, Israel's future in FIFA is uncertain. *The Nation*. Retrieved from http://www.thenation.com/blog/178642/after-latest-incident-israels-future-fifa-uncertain#

Zochrot. (n.d.). *Homepage*. Retrieved from http://zochrot.org/en

Zogby, J. (2017, November 12). The danger of ignoring Arab opinion: 100 years since Balfour. *+972*. Retrieved from https://972mag.com/the-danger-of-ignoring-arab-opinion-100-years-since-balfour/130658/

Zonszein, M. (2013, September 25). IDF soldier passes IDs of Jewish girls who socialize with Arabs to anti-assimilation NGO. *+972*. Retrieved from http://972mag.com/idf-soldier-passes-ids-of-jewish-girls-who-socialize-with-arabs-to-anti-assimilation-ngo/79349/

Zunes, S. (2002, May 1). Why the US supports Israel. *Foreign Policy in Focus*. Retrieved from http://www.fpif.org/articles/why_the_us_supports_israel

ABOUT THE AUTHOR

Eve Spangler has always positioned her work within public sociology, using scholarly methods to contribute to the struggle for social justice. Class inequality has been the focus of much of her early work. She has investigated the career patterns of blue collar college graduates (they rarely catch up to their more privileged classmates); the experiences of professionals as their work is reorganized from independent to salaried forms (they lose autonomy); and the safety and health of workplaces (generally better served by labor militancy than by managerial enlightenment). Through these studies, she has also become interested in gender, e.g. around issues of sexual harassment at work, and in issues of race, especially as Islamophobia, an emerging form of racism, complicates American participation in a just resolution to the Israeli-Palestinian conflict. Her recent work over the last decade is focused on human rights and social justice struggles in Palestine and Israel.

INDEX

Made in the USA
Middletown, DE
29 July 2021